# A Companion to Romanticism

*Blackwell Companions to Literature and Culture*

This new series offers comprehensive, newly written surveys of key periods and movements, and certain major authors, in English literary culture and history. Extensive volumes provide new perspectives and positions on contexts and on canonical and post-canonical texts, orientating the beginning student in new fields of study and providing the experienced undergraduate and new graduate with current and new directions, as pioneered and developed by leading scholars in the field.

1  A Companion to Romanticism                    *Edited by Duncan Wu*

# A COMPANION TO
# ROMANTICISM

## EDITED BY **DUNCAN WU**

BLACKWELL
*Publishers*

Copyright © Blackwell Publishers Ltd 1998
Introduction and arrangement copyright © Duncan Wu 1998

First published 1998

2 4 6 8 10 9 7 5 3 1

Blackwell Publishers Ltd
108 Cowley Road
Oxford OX4 1JF
UK

Blackwell Publishers Inc.
350 Main Street
Malden, Massachusetts 02148
USA

*British Library Cataloguing in Publication Data*

A CIP catalogue record for this book is available from the British Library.

*Library of Congress Cataloging in Publication Data*

A companion to Romanticism / edited by Duncan Wu.
p.     cm. — (Blackwell companions to literature and culture; 1)
Includes bibliographical references and index.
ISBN 0–631–19852–0 (hbk. : alk. paper)
1. English literature—19th century—History and criticism—Outlines, syllabi, etc.
2. English literature—18th century—History and criticism—Outlines, syllabi, etc.
3. Romanticism—Great Britain—Outlines, syllabi, etc. I. Wu, Duncan. II. Series
PR457.C58   1997
820.9 145–dc21          97–928          CIP

Typeset in 10.5/12.5 pt Garamond 3
by
Pure Tech India Ltd, Pondicherry
Printed in Great Britain by T. J. International, Cornwall
This book is printed on acid-free paper

# Contents

## Part I Contexts and Perspectives 1790–1830

## Part II Readings

# Part III Genres and Modes

# Part IV Issues and Debates

# Introduction

It is one of the more delicious ironies of modern criticism that the renewal of interest in Romantic studies over the last decade or so has comprised a drastic questioning of the concept of Romanticism itself. For those who can remember, life in the early 1980s was more sedate; the choice then, broadly speaking, was between the orthodoxy represented by such critics as M. H. Abrams, and deconstruction. Two developments have changed that. First, a multiplicity of fresh critical methodologies has reinvigorated analysis of literary texts – those with most impact being, probably, new historicism and feminism. New historicism has been particularly fruitful as a source of provocation, stimulating much valuable work in various schools either opposed or deriving from it.

Feminism has inspired the second major development: reform of the canon, the biggest shake-up of all. The blinkers that seemed to preclude critics from reading much besides the 'big six' (Blake, Wordsworth, Coleridge, Keats, Shelley and Byron) have given way to the rediscovery of Charlotte Smith, Helen Maria Williams, Mary Tighe, Anna Laetitia Barbauld, Felicia Hemans, and many other women writers. Anthologies devoted solely to them began to appear in 1992; two are now in print, and there are at least four others in the pipeline. When in recent times can there have been no less than six collections either in print or preparation featuring the work of exactly the same group of writers – and women writers at that? The test of scholarly acceptance is the appearance of critical editions: the first to present the complete poetical works of a female Romantic poet (Charlotte Smith) appeared in 1993; more are promised. Besides this, Woodstock Books has published a series of facsimile editions of important volumes by Romantic women, with introductions by Jonathan Wordsworth.

Given such hectic activity in the publishing world, it is doubly odd that Romanticism has come to seem so compromised as a literary concept. It was slippery enough when those writers associated with it were comparatively few in number; the expansion of the canon has made it seem more elusive than ever. Hardly a year passes without the publication of a new volume the title of which reflects this creeping agnosticism: *At the Limits of Romanticism*, *Re-Visioning Romanticism*, *Questioning Romanticism*, and so on. Such sustained anxiety reflects an unease, not just about the way the subject has been conceived, but about how it is evolving. On one level, we should be reassured; it is proof, were any needed, of the ability of the literature to renew itself. But none of these developments have made it any easier to teach – in fact, its problematizing serves only to underline the difficulties entailed in doing so. It may still be possible to offer some sort of plausible definition of the Augustan and Victorian periods – but what do teachers say about Romanticism? Which authors and works do they place on the syllabus? Do they espouse a methodology, and, if so, which one and on what basis? Each teacher has to find their own answers to these questions, and it is no one's business to prescribe what those may be. But in the midst of the debate, there is a desperate need for a book that draws some of the threads together, takes stock of the situation, and presents readers with the materials with which to formulate their own answers. This is what *A Companion to Romanticism* aims to provide.

This book is a pedagogical tool devised to meet the needs of teacher and student, and contributors were asked to write with that constituency in mind. It is structured in four parts. The first, 'Contexts and Perspectives 1790–1830', provides essential background information in the form of essays on the historical, intellectual, and literary context, including specific studies of reading patterns of the period, literature and religion, and Romantic precursors. 'Readings', the second section, offers critical introductions to both canonical and non-canonical works in all genres – *Lyrical Ballads*, Keats's *Odes*, *Prometheus Unbound*, as well as *Beachy Head*, *Psyche*, *Records of Woman*, *A Series of Plays*, *The Old Manor House* and so forth. The third section, 'Genres and Modes', examines the fields of the drama, the novel, literary criticism, the Gothic, parody and travel writing.

The final section introduces the reader to 'Issues and Debates'. It may not be possible to cover all theoretical stances in a book of this kind, but the most important are dealt with here: feminism, gender criticism, new historicism, eco-criticism, dialogic approaches and many others. It also includes essays on a number of important topics such as imagination, the German influence, scientific developments and apocalypse.

Carol Shiner Wilson and Joel Haefner, the editors of *Re-Visioning Romanticism*, speculate on the future of the discipline: 'Late Georgian, Regency, and early Victorian culture will be reinvented and critiqued through the agency of old texts reread and new texts found. In particular, the untold stories of British culture – its social history and its marginalized subjects – will affect the way we look at canonized and uncanonized texts.'[1] This prospect is eerily familiar: it is a description of what new historicism has been up to for the last decade. The future they envisage is the present writ large. But it would be a mistake to think that new historicism, or any single theoretical perspective, holds The Answer. Assuredly, new historicism has been instrumental in reviving the subject, but while it may usefully determine the parameters of such multi-volume projects as the Cambridge Studies in Romanticism, edited by Marilyn Butler and James Chandler, it would be regrettable were it simply to replace old orthodoxies with new. A reference work capable only of confirming the prejudices of a single perspective is useless; what contemporary readers need is an accessible source that embodies the range of critical thought. *A Companion to Romanticism* is designed to do precisely that. Contributors are drawn from all sides of the spectrum, and, although given titles, they were free to pursue their own preoccupations. The 'Readings' section alone contains work by authorities as diverse as

1 *Re-Visioning Romanticism: British Women Writers 1776–1837* ed. Carol Shiner Wilson and Joel Haefner (Philadelphia, 1994), p. 11.

Nelson Hilton, David Bromwich, Jonathan Wordsworth and John Lucas. In the 'Issues and Debates' section there are articles by Susan Wolfson, David Simpson, Morton D. Paley, Douglas B. Wilson, Angela Esterhammer and Alan Richardson, among others. The result is a volume intended both to juxtapose varying approaches and to reflect the catholicity of opinion and preoccupation in the field.

Like Romanticism itself, present-day criticism of the subject is neither cohesive nor unified. And that remains the source of its enduring strength. The fact is, modern critics comprise a community defined by its plurality. Aware of each other's work, they influence each other, disagree, and write vastly different kinds of criticism. By bringing together some of the finest of these talents, this book provides the reader with a means, if not of reconstituting Romanticism, at least of gathering together some of its component parts.

Duncan Wu
*Glasgow*

# Acknowledgements

First and foremost, I have been exceedingly fortunate in my choice of contributors, whom I wish to thank for meeting the requirements of this volume so efficiently, to an exemplary standard. Production of this volume has been a lengthy business, and I have benefited from the advice of a number of people along the way; I thank them all.

The Master and Fellows of St Catherine's College, Oxford, kindly elected me to a Visiting Fellowship that made work on this volume far less arduous than it would otherwise have been. My greatest debt must be to my colleagues at the University of Glasgow for granting me the study leave without which this book could not have been completed, and particularly to Pat Reilly and Richard Cronin who as Heads of Department sanctioned it. I thank all my colleagues for tolerating my absence from the Department of English Literature with good grace.

As always, I am grateful to Andrew McNeillie at Blackwell for his patient support and encouragement during work on this book.

The editor and publishers gratefully acknowledge the copyright holder for permission to reproduce material from John Clare: *Cottage Tales* edited by Eric Robinson, David Powell, and P. M. S. Dawson (The Mid Northumberland Arts Group and Carcanet Press, 1993). Copyright © Eric Robinson 1993, reproduced by permission of Curtis Brown Group Ltd, London. Also from John Clare: *The Shepherd's Calendar* edited by Eric Robinson and David Powell (Oxford University Press, 1993). Copyright © Eric Robinson 1993, reproduced by permission of Curtis Brown Group Ltd, London.

# Abbreviations

| | |
|---|---|
| Abrams *ML* | M. H. Abrams, *The Mirror and the Lamp* (New York, 1953) |
| Beer | *Samuel Taylor Coleridge: Complete Poems* ed. John Beer (London, 1993) |
| CC | *Collected Coleridge Series*, Bollingen Series 75 |
| CC *Biographia* | *Biographia Literaria* ed. James Engell and Walter Jackson Bate (2 vols, Princeton, 1983) |
| CC *Lay Sermons* | *Lay Sermons* ed. R. J. White (Princeton, 1972) |
| CC *Lectures 1795* | *Lectures 1795 On Politics and Religion* ed. Lewis Patton and Peter Mann (Princeton, 1971) |
| CC *Lectures on Literature* | *Lectures 1808–1819 On Literature* ed. R. A. Foakes (2 vols, Princeton, 1987) |
| CC *Marginalia* | *Marginalia* ed. George Whalley and Heather Jackson (5 vols, Princeton, 1982–) |
| CC *Table Talk* | *Table Talk* ed. Carl Woodring (2 vols, Princeton, 1990) |
| CC *Watchman* | *The Watchman* ed. Lewis Patton (Princeton, 1970) |
| *DWJ* | *Journals of Dorothy Wordsworth* ed. Ernest de Selincourt (2 vols, London, 1951) |
| EHC | *The Poetical Works of Samuel Taylor Coleridge* ed. E. H. Coleridge (2 vols, Oxford, 1912) |
| *EY* | *Letters of William and Dorothy Wordsworth: The Early Years, 1787–1805* ed. Ernest de Selincourt, revd Chester L. Shaver (Oxford, 1967) |
| *Grasmere Journals* | *Dorothy Wordsworth: The Grasmere Journals* ed. Pamela Woof (Oxford, 1991) |
| Griggs | *The Collected Letters of Samuel Taylor Coleridge* ed. E. L. Griggs (6 vols, Oxford, 1956–71) |
| Howe | *The Complete Works of William Hazlitt* ed. P. P. Howe (21 vols, London, 1930–4) |
| Jones | *The Letters of Percy Bysshe Shelley* ed. Frederick L. Jones (2 vols, Oxford, 1964) |

| | |
|---|---|
| *LY* | *The Letters of William and Dorothy Wordsworth: The Later Years*, ed. Ernest de Selincourt, *i: 1821–8*, revd Alan G. Hill (Oxford, 1978); *ii: 1829–34*, revd Alan G. Hill (Oxford, 1982); *iii: 1835–9*, revd Alan G. Hill (Oxford, 1982); *iv: 1840–53*, revd Alan G. Hill (Oxford, 1988) |
| McGann | George Gordon, 6th Baron Byron, *The Complete Poetical Works* ed. Jerome J. McGann and Barry Weller (7 vols, Oxford, 1980–93) |
| Marchand | *Byron's Letters and Journals* ed. Leslie A. Marchand (12 vols, London, 1973–82) |
| Masson | *The Collected Writings of Thomas De Quincey* ed. David Masson (14 vols, Edinburgh, 1889–90) |
| *MY* | *The Letters of William and Dorothy Wordsworth: The Middle Years*, ed. Ernest de Selincourt, *i: 1806–11*, revd Mary Moorman (Oxford, 1969); *ii: 1812–20*, revd Mary Moorman and Alan G. Hill (Oxford, 1970) |
| *Notebooks* | *The Notebooks of Samuel Taylor Coleridge* ed. Kathleen Coburn (6 vols, Princeton and London, 1957– ) |
| Rollins | *The Letters of John Keats 1814–1821* ed. Hyder E. Rollins (2 vols, Cambridge, Mass., 1958) |
| *Romanticism* | *Romanticism: An Anthology* ed. Duncan Wu (Oxford, 1994) |
| *Romanticism: A Critical Reader* | *Romanticism: A Critical Reader* ed. Duncan Wu (Oxford, 1995) |
| Woof | Dorothy Wordsworth, *The Grasmere Journals* ed. Pamela Woof (Oxford, 1991) |
| *W: Prose Works* | *The Prose Works of William Wordsworth* ed. W. J. B. Owen and Jane Worthington Smyser (3 vols, Oxford, 1974) |
| *WPW* | *The Poetical Works of William Wordsworth* ed. Ernest de Selincourt and Helen Darbishire (5 vols, Oxford, 1940–9) |

# PART ONE
# Contexts and Perspectives
# 1790–1830

# 1

# Romanticism: The Brief History of a Concept

*Seamus Perry*

## Romanticism as a Problem

Of course, *romantic* is used in several senses; but it is important to us as it appears with a capital 'R', or as an '-ism' – a literary–historical classification which labels certain writers and writings of the later eighteenth and early nineteenth century, and the ideas character-istically found in those works (and often in later works, too). It is a troublesome concept, and there is a good case for not worrying at it too much, or at least for not insisting on it doing work it won't readily do. But currently, as Paul Hamilton has observed, 'Definitions of romanticism appear to be back in favour with critics and theorists', and his qualification to this – 'provided they focus on questions of ideology' – doesn't really affect the intrinsic troubles of definition;[1] so going over the old problem at the moment feels timely.

The difficulty is not just knowing what it really means, but knowing even *how to go about deciding* what it really means. One way is to return to the authors we have always known to be Romantic, and then generalize a concept out from what we find: following this route, Thomas McFarland identifies more than fifteen 'hallmarks' of Romanticism.[2] The method is circular, obviously, because you must presuppose what is 'Romantic' to make the selection of works you need from which to deduce an idea of 'Romanticism'; but this circularity is intrinsic to the pursuit. 'A literary taxonomy,' writes David Perkins, 'includes a name . . . , a concept, and a canon of works subsumed under that concept. Reasoning goes from the concept to the canon, from the canon to the concept': in other words, you can't help 'reasoning in a hermeneutic circle from a concept to a set of texts and from the set of texts to the concept'.[3] The only alternative to beginning with a canon that already anticipates your concept, is to begin with a pure concept of 'Romanticism', a Platonic Idea, quite free of any empirical basis, and then let that concept determine your choice of canonical texts: this sounds like something only an angel would do, though there are in fact a few cases. However, for anyone less than willing to resign the claims of history, like a literary historian, that way out of the hermeneutic circle is unlikely to be very attractive.

Still, the empirical alternative has its shortcomings too: all of McFarland's criteria, for example, may indeed be seen in many authors well known as being 'Romantic', though not all of them in any single writer; and this leaves open a permanent, frustrating appeal to exception. Whatever generalization I make from the canon of 'Romantics' I have in mind, you can always reply, 'But now, what about Byron? He's very well known to be a great Romantic, known across Europe for it; and he doesn't fit your definition at all'. (There have been ingenious attempts to solve this sort of problem by distinguishing between 'positive' and 'negative' Romanticisms;[4] but I think René Wellek is right to see such resolutions as merely verbal.)[5] Furthermore, many of the criteria McFarland finds seem actually contradictory: 'a love of the particular' and 'a longing for the infinite', say, or 'external nature' and 'a preoccupation with dreams';[6] and clearly, once a concept-label comes to cover several contradictory things, it risks losing its usefulness altogether, a point made in an important essay by A. O. Lovejoy.[7]

Both canon and concept enter the critical vocabulary as the gifts of tradition; but neither is fixed. The canon of works may always be changed, with new works added, or emphases changed, for all kinds of reasons (we should not expect a general rule there); and the new evidence offered by the reformed canon will, in turn, alter the concept subsuming that canon; and vice versa. In this way, the fluctuating canon of 'Romantic' texts and the concept of 'Romanticism' work one against the other, nudging themselves round an endless circle of redefinition; and this is how the concept comes to have a history of its own: it is a history of revision.

Returning to the history of the term 'Romantic' is especially illuminating because it shows how what are otherwise very contradictory elements all come to have the one label. It is, I think, misconceived to pore over all the things we know, somehow instinctively, to *be* 'Romantic', trying to tease out the unifying element they have in common: that leaves us with an array of incompatibles which we struggle to work into some encompassing pattern, or forces us into a covert prescriptiveness in our initial selection of a canon. But if we look instead at the history of the word's use, then we will see that, for instance, to hold that Scott and Blake are both 'Romantic' may be a perfectly good use of language; but that to understand from this the existence of some underlying sameness ('Romanticism'), is to fall victim to something very like a pun, or an optical illusion. With some luck, we shall begin to see a profound theoretical mystery ('What is the nature of Romanticism?') gracefully resolve itself into the accumulation of historical contingencies ('What work has "Romantic" been made to do?').

## The Making of 'Romanticism'[8]

The single most important fact about the word, as it applies to the literary history of the British Isles, is that it is a posthumous invention: the Romantics did not know that was what they were. Writers of the time were certainly classified by contemporary critics, but as the 'Lake School' (Wordsworth, Coleridge and Southey), the 'Demonic School' (most notoriously, Byron), the 'Cockney School' (Leigh Hunt and Keats), and so forth – often to the disgruntlement of the writers concerned, predictably. To be sure, the *word* 'romantic' is found, and it describes a sort of literature, but it does not feature as the name of a literary grouping;[9] and most of the writers concerned would not have chosen it, had they been given the chance: as Ian Jack says, 'Wordsworth, Byron, Shelley, and Keats did not regard themselves as writing "romantic" poems and would not – in fact – have been particularly flattered if they had been told that that was what they were doing'.[10]

They would not have been flattered because the word meant something different then. 'Romantic' is current from the early seventeenth century, according to *OED*; and it means, unsurprisingly, 'resembling the tales of romances', as the first definition in Johnson's dictionary puts it: either strictly, as a point of artistic classification, or more loosely, having the kind of qualities normally thought to characterize romance – 'Improbable; false', 'Fanciful; full of wild scenery' (Johnson's second and third definitions). *OED* has an engaging seventeenth-century example of simple outrage in 'The romantic and visionary scheme of building a bridge over the river at Putney'; but it goes on to quote from the mid-nineteenth century, 'A romantic scheme is one which is wild, impracticable, and yet contains something which captivates the fancy'. Such a softening of rational disapproval to a kind of charmed indulgence seems to characterize the word in the later eighteenth century; and this is the sense of 'romantic' as it features in the writers whom we now think of as themselves 'Romantic'.

Coleridge, for example, obviously knew the word in its more simply derogatory sense; but, as one who, in defiance of rationalist educational theory, positively approved of children reading 'Romances, & Relations of Giants & Magicians, & Genii' (to Poole, 16 October, 1797; *Romanticism*, 514), he also uses the term with great indulgence, and often positive rapture. In *Kubla Khan*, for example, 'that deep romantic chasm' is 'A savage place, as holy and enchanted / As e'er beneath a waning moon was haunted / By woman wailing for her demon-lover' (ll. 12; 14–16; *Romanticism*, 514–15): a choice example of the link between 'romantic' and the sort of things you might find in an old romance. Coleridge's connection of the 'romantic' with the 'Gothic mind' in his *Philosophical Lectures* is similarly influenced by its connotations of the wonders of medieval romance.[11] In this sense, he considered *himself* a romantic poet, at least in some of his poems: the division of labours he recalls making with Wordsworth for the *Lyrical Ballads* project is one between a poetry devoted to 'things of every day' (Wordsworth's) and a different sort (his own) 'directed to persons and characters supernatural, or at least romantic' (*Biographia Literaria*, chapter 14; *Romanticism*, 575): *The Ancyent Marinere* (as it was spelt in 1798) and *Christabel* are the poems he probably has in mind. It is not surprising, then, that Coleridge's poems were often described by nineteenth-century critics too as 'romantic', though not uniquely so. 'By *romantic* poems,' wrote Thomas Arnold in 1862, 'we mean, poems in which heroic subjects are epically treated, after the manner of the old romances of chivalry';[12] and for him the exemplary figure is Scott, with Byron's Oriental tales coming next. Pater, writing in 1865, still restricts the word: '*The Ancient Mariner*, as also, in its measure, *Christabel*, is a "romantic" poem, impressing us by bold invention, and appealing to that taste for the supernatural'.[13] This is very like the sense in which Coleridge himself would have used the word, and it is used by other critics to describe poems like *The Eve of St Agnes*. (Incidentally, 'romantic' meaning 'to do with a love affair', is surprisingly recent: *OED* says late twentieth century.)

The first person, according to David Perkins, who describes the English poets of the early nineteenth century, especially the 'Lake School', forming a 'Romantic School', is Hippolyte Taine in 1863:[14] this is done by an analogy with the French 'Romantics' of the early nineteenth century; and the German historian Brandl does a similar trick, simply re-christening the Lakers 'Romantic' by analogy with the German 'Romantics'. The analogy is not very tight: on the model of the Romantic School in Germany, as defined by Heine, Brandl must assert that not only Coleridge and Scott, but also, most improbably, Wordsworth, 'drew endless inspiration from the Middle Ages'.[15] This is still the sense of 'Romantic' at work in two excellent books on the subject by Henry Beers, written at the end of the nineteenth century.

When Beers defends his definition, it is by asking rhetorically, 'what Englishman will be satisfied with a definition of *romantic* which excludes Scott?': the answer to which, in the university departments anyway, must now be 'almost everyone'. On the other hand, if you were to have asked, 'who would be satisfied with a definition of *romantic* which excludes Wordsworth?', the nineteenth-century answer would similarly be, 'almost everyone'. Wordsworth, as Beers had recognized, is by his criterion 'absolutely unromantic in contrast with Scott and Coleridge', for Coleridge, 'at his best' – that is to say, in *Christabel* and *The Ancient Mariner* – 'was a romantic poet'.[16] Wordsworth's anti-romanticism is often remarked by nineteenth-century observers: when Hopkins surveys his literary ancestors in 1881, for example, he divides them into 'the Romantic school (Romantic is a bad word) of Keats, Leigh Hunt, Hood, indeed of Scott', the 'Lake poets', and the 'sentimental school, of Byron, Moore, Mrs. Hemans, and Haynes Bailey':[17] Wordsworth's 'Lake school' is defined *against* the 'Romantic'.

In the later nineteenth and early twentieth century, a change in the canon of works gathered together under the name 'Romantic' caused a shaking-up of the concept. This happened, I suppose, for many reasons: some figures, like Wordsworth, came to seem more relevant or central than others, like Southey. The writers of the day are always a prominent influence on a period's conception of the past (Dante feels more central to things after T. S. Eliot); and the literary culture of the later nineteenth century was probably responsible for a large part of this redefinition of the canon, though other factors must have been at work too, including ideological ones. Whatever the causes, it is at this time that the label comes to cover most of the authors whom we instinctively put under it. That 'Romantic' was the name to hand for the new general sense of what was important in late-eighteenth- and early-nineteenth-century literature is simply a contingency of the story.[18] Three related events seem of especial importance in the redefinition of the canon: the marginalization of Byron and Scott, both of whom were once the very central exempla; the growing centrality of Wordsworth; and, a little later, the rise and rise of Blake. These changes in the canon were obviously not due to the poetry in question somehow changing: it is the *use of the label* which has changed. By the time of Leavis's *New Bearings in English Poetry* (1932), the identification of 'the great Romantics, Wordsworth, Coleridge, Byron, Shelley and Keats' could be passed off with casual confidence:[19] Scott has simply disappeared, and, as we read further in Leavis, we find that Byron's position is actually equivocal too, not exactly a Romantic at all, but a late-comer Augustan, whose weaknesses are evidence of 'how completely the Augustan order has disintegrated'.[20] The revision of the canon is certainly striking: where Wordsworth had once represented an intractable case for historians seeking a generally pervasive revival of romance in poetry, he now becomes the dominant figure ('The Age of Wordsworth'); and where Beers had once rejected a definition because it would not fit the romance-like qualities of Scott, the criterion of medievalism is rejected by Grierson in 1923 because it will not fit the new test-case, Wordsworth.[21] 'Romantic' is getting out of hand, W. P. Ker complained in one of his lectures as Oxford Professor of Poetry, insisting that 'romantic does mean something', namely '"the fairy way of writing . . . a world of fine fabling"': Ker is battling bravely for the nineteenth-century use;[22] but the battle was already lost.

A modern romanticist would probably not choose medievalism or romance or wondrous mystery as the central criteria for Romanticism, but rather, idealism and egotism, or perhaps primitivism and a turn to nature. It is not hard to see a likely conflict between these definitions; and it lies at the heart of the 'genuine impasse' in Romanticism diagnosed by Paul de Man: 'Is romanticism a subjective idealism. . . . Or is it instead a return to a certain form of naturalism after the forced abstraction of the Enlightenment?'[23] In fact, both these rival senses emerge in the modern history of the classification. Wordsworth comes to exemplify in an especially intense way this kind of naturalism: Walter Raleigh wrote in 1903, 'There was for him no question of the return to Nature', but this was only because 'he had never deserted her'.[24] Raleigh relates this to Rousseau, 'the father of the literary Romantics', an attribution of paternity which Babbitt would later take up in his *Rousseau and Romanticism* and pass on to T. S. Eliot. Elsewhere, the 'naturalness' returned to is more a kind of literary primitivism, seen in the poets' decision to model their art on folk ballad literature, as collected by Bishop Percy, rather than, say, the neo-classicist 'artifice' of Pope: Percy's *Reliques* were 'the germ of the great romantic revolution in literature', said the historian Shaw.[25] (The point is intricate because an important part of the neo-classical aesthetic is also an appeal to 'nature': 'Romantic' nature seems the creature of a very broad shift of attitudes, the 'counter-enlightenment', which reconceptualizes nature as particular, local, and concrete, rather than general, abstract and ideal; but that is a rather different story.)

If the naturalism of Romanticism began to be an important new criterion, thanks to the growing predominance of Wordsworth in the Romantic canon, so, increasingly, was de Man's alternative theme: 'subjective idealism'. A certain archetype of the poet, living in the dreamily introverted remoteness of his own consciousness, had been current throughout the nineteenth century, Coleridge and Shelley being especially important exempla of the type: the mind is its own place for such figures, and their sense of the reality of inwardness comes to displace the vulgar claims of the external world, the theme of a poem like Tennyson's *The Poet's Mind*. This stress on the 'interior' also grew more important as a specific characteristic of the 'Romantic', especially as Romanticism came to be placed in a kind of parallel with the anti-empiricist philosophy of German idealism. In an elegant little book published in 1926, Lascelles Abercrombie marks the shifting ground on this point especially clearly (though without pursuing the German line). Abercrombie says that the 'true antithesis' is not romanticism and classicism, as Schlegel had said, but 'romanticism and realism'; and that, consequently, Romanticism is marked by *a tendency away from actuality*: 'We see the spirit of the mind withdrawing more and more from commerce with the outer world, and endeavouring, or at least desiring, to rely more and more on the things it finds within itself,' he writes, adding later that romanticism 'takes its most obvious form in *egoism*'.[26]

The rise of Blake is a part of this growing conception of idealism as fundamental to a definition of the Romantic. In the course of distinguishing the romantic from the realist, Abercrombie had referred to 'Blake, Coleridge, Shelley, Byron and the rest': he is not the first to put Blake so prominently, though it does not yet seem unquestionable to do so. For Leavis in 1932, as we have seen, Blake did not automatically suggest himself as one of the 'great Romantics' at all; but by the time of Harold Bloom's significantly titled *The Visionary Company* (1961), Blake has become the exemplary Romantic. *The Visionary Company* is greatly influenced by the work of Northrop Frye, who had himself earlier promoted the claims of Blake in *Fearful Symmetry* (1947), in the course of which book he had remarked with casual authority that 'idealism is a doctrine congenial to poets':[27] a dubious rule of thumb; but it points to a rough equation between 'Romanticism' and 'idealism', which in turn affects the working Romantic canon. Shelley ('All things exist as they are perceived': 'Defence of Poetry': *Romanticism*, 967) and Blake ('Mental Things are alone Real')[28] fit well enough and parts of Wordsworth too ('the mind / Is lord and master'; *The Prelude*, XI.271–2; *Romanticism*, 452); the bulk of Byron less obviously so, and most of Clare, say, even less.

This, I think, is probably the dominant definition of 'Romanticism' at the time of writing, for critics who try to define it at all; and the most emphatic of them are those who deplore such idealism, and so take up a basically anti-Romantic stance: this is the 'ideological' definition of Romanticism that I began by mentioning. Jerome McGann's *The Romantic Ideology* (1983) launched a genre of books, 'critiqueing' Romantic idealism from a Marxist, 'materialist' viewpoint. 'Ideology' here means 'false consciousness', that is to say, error; and for a philosophical materialist, idealism is false consciousness *par excellence*, as Lenin for one argued. 'The subject matter and . . . style' of a poem like *Kubla Khan*, says McGann, are '"ideal"', and the romantic poet seeks to 'escape' the historical world 'through imagination and poetry'.[29] The charge of escapism has always been made against the proponents of subjective idealism and the 'world within': it is at the heart of Arnold's famous portrait of Shelley; and here it returns, with a political charge and philosophical credentials, as a general position of anti-'Romanticism'.

Broadly speaking, then, McGann and the ideological school take as their target the idealist concept of Romanticism; and the generality of McGann's critique ('the Romantic ideology') depends upon his view that this conception is fairly consensual: 'informed persons *do* generally agree on what is comprised under the terms Romantic and Romantic Movement'. The difficulties in his book come when he sets against this a sense of 'Romantic' for which he claims deep *historical* sanction: against the Romantic ideologues, he introduces the countering figure of Byron, but not merely as a virtuous alternative to their bad Romanticism (though he is that), but as someone *really historically* 'Romantic' – 'the single most important figure in the history of European Romanticism'[30] – who has been left out of the scheme (for ideological reasons, I suppose). Byron was indeed edged out of the Romantic canon, as we have seen; but we cannot therefore say that he is somehow undoubtedly, historically 'Romantic'. That seems to misunderstand the kind of term 'Romantic' is: oddly for a 'historicist', it is to ignore its history, and to take it for a piece of evidence of the wrong sort.

## Some Conclusions

There is a general case against literary classifications, which echoes the bias towards 'minute particulars' you find, say, in Blake: 'Romantic is a bad name for the poetry of the nineteenth century because it sets you looking for a common quality when you ought to be reading or remembering individual poems'.[31] That the human mind enjoys rival apprehensions, is awake to diverse particulars (like poems) as well as to unifying similarities (like literary classifications), is itself a subject of great interest to many 'Romantic' writers as well as Blake: 'Reason respects the differences, and imagination the similitudes of things,' as Shelley wrote ('Defence of Poetry'; *Romanticism*, 956). Someone working with a concept like 'Romanticism' experiences a similar tussle of impulses: it is, as M. H. Abrams once remarked, 'one of those terms historians can neither do with nor make do without'.[32] Shelley implies that both views are necessary; and this is a good lesson: for while 'individual poems' are indeed the subject matter of literary history, we still need organizing concepts that subsume them, like 'Romanticism', to *do* literary history, or to think historically about literary works, at all.

Degree courses, academic specialisms, and anthologies have to be called *something* of course; but the issue is more profound than that. Perkins says: 'A literary history cannot have only one text for its subject, and it cannot describe a great many texts individually';[33] and classifications like 'Romantic' help us to deal with masses of data that would otherwise be unmanageable. The concept of 'Romanticism' does not catch the specifics of what actually happened, and so the charge of historical misrepresentation is always open. But then it would be no use if it *did* somehow reproduce those specifics: the whole point of such organizing concepts is to save us from the endless complication of the truth, at least for the time being. No doubt, the end of criticism is to see the truth and see it whole; but the whole truth is a good deal, and concepts like 'Romantic' are a way of bracketing-out vast complexities while we concentrate on a small corner of reality, or a way of getting a wide picture, more or less, before we begin to discover empirical details challenging the general theory that led us to them in the first place. The corollary of this is that we cannot learn anything about 'Romanticism', in the way that we can learn about Wordsworth's politics or the impact of Taylor's translations of Plotinus or responses to the war against France; but we *can* use it as a way of learning about those other things, and we can also learn about the ways in which it has been used, so long as we keep in mind that we are learning about the history of literary reception, and not about a fixed historical object called 'Romanticism'.

## NOTES

1  Hamilton, 'A shadow of a magnitude', p. 11.
2  McFarland, *Romantic Cruxes*, p. 13.
3  Perkins, *Is Literary History Possible?* pp. 73, 85.
4  Peckham, 'Toward a theory of Romanticism, p. 15.
5  Wellek, 'Romanticism re-examined', pp. 200–1.
6  McFarland, *Romantic Cruxes*, p. 13.
7  Lovejoy, 'On the discrimination of Romanticisms', p. 232.
8  I draw here especially on Perkins, *Is Literary History Possible?* pp. 85–119; and Wellek, 'The concept of Romanticism in literary history'.

9  'Romantic' does designate one literary classification in Coleridge's own lifetime, the opposite of 'classic'. This distinction first appears in the lectures of Schlegel, delivered in 1808–9 and published in German in 1809–11, and widely popularized by Mme De Staël's *De l'Allemagne* (1813); and Coleridge echoes it in his lectures. But the distinction separated out late medieval and Renaissance art from that of antiquity: Coleridge's use, for example, is clearly not distinguishing between his own poetry or his generation's and the poetry of the eighteenth

century, which would be the modern usage I
have in mind.

10    Jack, *English Literature*, p. 410.

11    Coleridge, *Philosophical Lectures*, p. 291.

12    Arnold, *A Manual of English Literature*, pp. 285,
      286.

13    Pater, 'Coleridge', p. 96.

14    See Perkins, *Is Literary History Possible?* pp. 96–7.

15    Brandl, *Samuel Taylor Coleridge*, pp. 220, 222.

16    Beers, *Romanticism in the Nineteenth Century*, pp.
      vi, 50, 51, 54.

17    To R. W. Dixon, 1 December, 1881; in Hopkins,
      *Correspondence*, p. 98.

18    On the contingencies of literary history, see Per-
      kins, *Is Literary History Possible?* p. 109.

19    Leavis, *New Bearings in English Poetry*, p. 7.

20    Leavis, *Revaluation*, p. 153.

21    Grierson, *Classical and Romantic*, p. 8.

22    Ker, 'Romantic fallacies', p. 79.

23    De Man, 'The rhetoric of temporality', p. 198.

24    Raleigh, *Wordsworth*, p. 45.

25    Shaw, *Outlines of English Literature*, p. 390.

26    Abercrombie, *Romanticism*, pp. 7, 33, 49, 135.

27    Frye, *Fearful Symmetry*, p. 14.

28    Blake, 'A vision of the last judgment', p. 617.

29    McGann, *The Romantic Ideology*, pp. 101, 131.

30    Ibid. pp. 18, 27.

31    Ker, 'Romantic fallacies', p. 78.

32    Abrams, 'Rationality and imagination', p. 117.

33    Perkins, *Is Literary History Possible?* p. 61.

## REFERENCES AND FURTHER READING

Abercrombie, Lascelles, *Romanticism*, Secker, London,
     1926.

Abrams, M. H. 'Rationality and imagination in cul-
     tural history', in *Doing Things With Texts: Essays in
     Criticism and Critical Theory*, ed. Michael Fischer,
     1989; repr. Norton, New York, 1991.

Arnold, Thomas, *A Manual of English Literature, His-
     torical and Critical, with an appendix of English
     metres*, Longman, London, 1862.

Beers, Henry A., *A History of English Romanticism in
     the Eighteenth Century*, Kegan Paul, Trench, Trüb-
     ner, London, 1899.

—— *A History of English Romanticism in the Nineteenth
     Century*, Kegan Paul, Trench, Trübner, London,
     1902.

Blake, William, 'A Vision of the Last Judgment'
     (1810), in *The Complete Writings of William Blake*,
     ed. Geoffrey Keynes, Oxford University Press, Lon-
     don, 1966.

Brandl, Alois, *Samuel Taylor Coleridge and the English
     Romantic School*, 1886, tr. Lady Eastlake, John Mur-
     ray, London, 1887.

Coleridge, S. T., *The Philosophical Lectures of Samuel
     Taylor Coleridge, Hitherto Unpublished*, ed. Kathleen
     Coburn, Pilot Publishers, London, 1949.

de Man, Paul, 'The rhetoric of temporality', in *Blind-
     ness and Insight: Essays in the Rhetoric of Contemporary
     Criticism*, 2nd edn, 1983; repr. Routledge, London,
     1989.

Frye, Northrop, *Fearful Symmetry: A Study of William
     Blake*, 1947; repr. Princeton University Press,
     Princeton, 1990.

Grierson, H. J. C., *Classical and Romantic*, Cambridge
     University Press, Cambridge, 1923.

Hamilton, Paul, '"A shadow of a magnitude": The
     dialectic of Romantic aesthetics', in *Beyond Roman-
     ticism: New Approaches to Texts and Contexts*, ed.
     Stephen Copley and John Whale, Routledge, Lon-
     don, 1992.

Hopkins, Gerard Manley, *The Correspondence of Gerard
     Manley Hopkins and Richard Watson Dixon*, ed.
     Claude Colleer Abbott, Oxford University Press,
     London, 1935.

Jack, Ian, *English Literature 1815–1832*, 1963; corr.
     repr. Clarendon Press, Oxford, 1970.

Ker, W. P., 'Romantic fallacies' in *The Art of Poetry:
     Seven Lectures 1920–1922*, Clarendon Press, Oxford,
     1923.

Leavis, F. R., *New Bearings in English Poetry: A Study of
     the Contemporary Situation*, 1932; revd edn. 1950;
     repr. Chatto and Windus, London, 1971.

—— *Revaluation: Tradition and Development in English
     Poetry*, 1936; repr. Chatto and Windus, London,
     1969.

Lovejoy, A. O., 'On the discrimination of Romanti-
     cisms', 1924, in *Essays in the History of Ideas*, Johns
     Hopkins University Press, Baltimore, 1948.

McFarland, Thomas, *Romantic Cruxes: The English
     Essayists and the Spirit of the Age*, Clarendon Press,
     Oxford, 1987.

McGann, Jerome J., *The Romantic Ideology: A Critical
     Investigation*, University of Chicago Press, Chicago,
     1983.

Pater, Walter, 'Coleridge', in *Appreciations: With an
     Essay on Style*, 1889; repr. Macmillan, London,
     1910.

Peckham, Morse, 'Toward a theory of Romanticism',
     *PMLA* 61 (1951), 5–23.

Perkins, David, *Is Literary History Possible?* Johns Hopkins University Press, Baltimore, 1992.

Raleigh, Walter, *Wordsworth*, Arnold, London, 1903.

Shaw, T. B., *Outlines of English Literature*, John Murray, London, 1849.

Wellek, René, 'The concept of Romanticism in literary history', in *Concepts of Criticism*, ed. Stephen G. Nichols, Jr, 1963; repr. Yale University Press, New Haven, 1964.

—— 'Romanticism re-examined', in *Concepts of Criticism*, ed. Stephen G. Nichols, Jr, 1963: repr. Yale University Press, New Haven, 1964.

Whalley, George, 'England / Romantic – Romanticism', in *'Romantic' and its Cognates / The European History of a Word*, ed. Hans Eichner, Manchester University Press, Manchester, 1972.

# 2

# Preromanticism

## *Michael J. Tolley*

The idea of preromanticism is common enough, but it is not always easy to find out what it means. For instance, Alastair Fowler's recent *A History of English Literature* does not mention preromanticism in the relevant chapter entitled 'Later Classicism and the Enlightenment'; and two recent books on Sensibility have appeared in which preromanticism is absent. These books, G. J. Barker-Benfield's *The Culture of Sensibility* (1992) and Ann Jessie Van Sant's *Eighteenth-Century Sensibility and the Novel* (1993), seem to have been determined by a theory that the novel is to be divorced from Romanticism as such. However, I tend to agree with Stuart Atkins in his article in the *Princeton Encyclopedia of Poetry and Poetics* (1965, 1974) that the novels of sensibility are amongst other works that 'reveal a turning away from neoclassicism' or, in England, Augustanism, and so are to be called preromantic. Such novels, especially, are those of Samuel Richardson: *Pamela*, *Clarissa* and *Sir Charles Grandison*. Sterne encouraged sentimentalists but was not a preromantic writer, whatever his disciple Henry Mackenzie may have thought in such novels as *The Man of Feeling*. However, in this essay I shall deal more with poetry than with drama, painting, essays, and fiction.

Fowler begins weightily by stating that what characterized the Enlightenment 'everywhere was a commitment to clarity'. I shall argue that preromanticism is more preoccupied with what cannot be clarified. I look for signs of a retreat from reason and a delight in vagueness or mystery. Liberty could be invoked by both sides, radically as a retreat from analysis or enthusiastically as a discovery of the divine.

Preromanticism itself has been found earliest in sentimental comedy and the philosophy of Anthony Ashley Cooper, third Earl of Shaftesbury, who exposed an idea of sensibility within human beings that was not merely developed there by reason or disciplined education. One work of his, *The Moralists* (1711), was subtitled 'A Rhapsody' and encouraged an association between the goodness in humanity and that in nature, which was called 'romantic'. Sentimental comedy also based itself in the good-natured human heart and was a sign of optimism of a kind found also in Steele's the *Tatler* and, with Addison's help, the *Spectator*. Dramatic tragedies were also found after the Restoration period but in fewer numbers. Poets wrote nature poetry in quest of locations for contemplation and some discovered more than a release from urbane life in their preference. Lady Winchelsea's *Nocturnal Reverie* and Dyer's *Grongar Hill* remained in the anthologies. James Thomson developed a similar sensitive feeling for nature in *The Seasons* and even one of awe, beyond delight.

Such titles as *The Enthusiast; or, the Lover of Nature* (Joseph Warton, 1744), *The Pleasures of Melancholy* (Thomas Warton, 1747), or *The Pleasures of the Imagination* (Mark Akenside, 1774) make it clear that a love of reason is not the prime desire of the authors. Thomas Warton finds, however, in 'Verses on Sir Joshua Reynolds's Painted Window at New College, Oxford' (1782), enlightened art to 'reconcile / The willing Graces to the Gothic pile', though at first he had resented such a modern intrusion on his wish to 'muse on the magnificence of yore' by exploring 'With Gothic manners Gothic arts'. In *The Pleasures of Melancholy*, Thomas Warton is content to be post-Miltonic rather than preromantic, and becomes more open in his fourth sonnet, 'Written at Stonehenge' (1777), when he can allow his fancy to enjoy several alternative sources of origin for 'the mighty pile'. William Collins wrote *Persian Eclogues* (1742), enjoying Eastern 'elegancy and wildness of thought' and the unfinished *Ode on the Popular Superstitions of the Highlands of Scotland, Considered as the Subject of Poetry* (1749–50), not to mock them but rather hoping to walk through Scotland's 'lowly glens' or 'stretching heaths by Fancy led'. The British countryside was already seen to be under threat in Oliver Goldsmith's *The Deserted Village* (1770) and the mood of sensibility was tinged with nostalgia. Goldsmith's novel *The Vicar of Wakefield* (1776) has been praised *ad nauseam* for its idyllic charm but (taking aside its providential scheme) it portrays life as a struggle against various confining forces of justice that deter domestic and individual quests for liberty.

Some of the poets were capable of making critical attacks on the Augustan values, notably Joseph Warton, who in his *Essay on the Genius and Writings of Pope* (1756) decided that satire and didactic moral writing belonged to a second-rate class of poetry. Joseph Warton preferred sublime and pathetic writing. Edward Young also criticized Pope, in his *Conjectures on Original Composition* (1759), for using heroic couplets to translate Homer, not blank verse – his own major verse form, as in the *Night Thoughts* of 1742–5, which Pope called bombastic in places. Most recent readers have been disappointed by *Night Thoughts*, but Blake thought very highly of Young and illustrated the whole poem, page by page. Blake thought highly, too, of Ossian, whose poetry, 'translated or edited' by James Macpherson, did not convince Edward Gibbon in chapter six of *Decline and Fall of the Roman Empire* (1776). Gibbon did not really see the 'untutored Caledonians' as 'glowing with the warm virtues of nature' when they were opposed to 'the degenerate Romans, polluted with the mean vices of wealth and slavery', during the third century AD. The Ossianic discovery seems almost to have been prompted by Thomas Gray's discovery of sublimity in *The Bard* (1757). A need to find values better than those of neo-classical England was maintained by Aphra Behn in *Oroonoko, or The Royal Slave* (1688), and much later in the eighteenth century, in Lord Monboddo's idea that the South Seas nourished ideal conditions of existence; an anonymous poem of 1774, *Otaheite*, found in the Tahitians freedom from toil, anxiety, false modesty and sexual constraint (Bernbaum, *Guide Through the Romantic Movement*, 1930, p. 21). Londoners could even admire a real noble savage in Omai (see E.H. McCormick's book, 1977) or, less convincingly, in travelling Australian Aborigines.

One way of finding out what a group of writers shared is in a check of their typical reading. Romantics read some writers whom we call preromantics; such people as Gray,

Collins, Ossian and Chatterton, the older authors in Bishop Percy's collection of ballads –
and the writers behind the newer ones. The preromantics are sometimes to be thought of as
Post-Augustan writers, who not only anticipated the Romantic flowering but showed
ways of leaving the strictly classical values of the British Augustan age behind them. The
new openness in their period to Gothicism or to Orientalism suggested a preference for
what Edward Gibbon in the 1770s would highlight as signs of a decline and fall in strictly
classical values. The alternative writers embraced sentiment and tenderness of feeling.
Samuel Johnson sometimes indicates by his disapproval which writers are no longer
Augustan. The 'Graveyard school' of poets, amongst them Thomas Gray and Edward
Young, preferred to embrace sensibility and to travel from tomb to tomb; others would
move from mountain to sublime mountain. Nature and the past were allowed to contribute to human feelings, rather than merely (as in Swift) to good, sensible behaviour. The
preromantic movement ran with such Renaissance figures as Spenser, Shakespeare and
Milton and would in turn encourage Blake, Wordsworth (both Miltonians), Keats and
radical writers such as Shelley and Byron. Other preromantic writers were more limited in
the excitement they provoked in the next half-century, such as Smart or Burns; others were
better known then than they are now, such as Akenside and the Wartons.

Several of those who wrote in the middle or later eighteenth century, turning outwards
from urbane values, preferring loneliness to sociability, were not by any means all the same
kind of writer. The same may be said of those known to be Romantics, and those known to
be Augustans. Dryden and Pope could write emotionally; Byron, Keats and Shelley were
excited by science, Wordsworth by technology. Some preromantic writers were both
rational and radical, some more interested in Longinian rhetoric and feelings. Often,
what one is looking for in the so-called age of Sensibility is a kind of threshold awareness
of classicism and emotive passion, combined with a preference for local and even individual
values.

This turn can be seen in the work of William Collins, whose *Ode to Simplicity* is full of
classical longings, somewhat Apollonian in mood, fused from Renaissance speculation.
Simplicity herself is allowed only a hazy background, and her babe Fancy might alternatively be the daughter of Pleasure. In *The Golden Ass* by Apuleius, the post-Augustan
story of Cupid and Psyche ends with the notion that their child was Pleasure – and Collins
would have found this idea reiterated in Spenser's retelling of the tale in his account of the
Garden of Adonis, in *The Faerie Queene*, III. vi.50–1, but offering as the child-figure
Amoret, though still with Psyche as her nurse. In the preromantic period esoteric
vagueness might be better than stark clarity. Relevantly, Fowler has noted, when writing
of James Beattie's *The Minstrel* (1771–4), Kant's suggestive idea that aesthetic experience
might show a 'deliberate purposelessness'. Collins's *Ode to Simplicity* is a brilliant exercise in
scholastic evasion provoked by semantic complexity. He generates poetry out of a confessed
need to invoke simple powers of song inside himself, while professing that he lacks these
powers. Thus, in the first stanza, Collins evokes mixed values in a lightly varied metric
scheme:

> O thou by Nature taught
> To breathe her genuine thought,
> In numbers warmly pure and sweetly strong:

> Who first on mountains wild
> In Fancy, loveliest child,
> Thy babe or Pleasure's, nursed the powers of song!

Simplicity acts, not to be banal, but to discipline or educate complex functions so that purity acquires warmth and strength sweetness.

> Though taste, though genius bless
> To some divine excess,
> Faints the cold work till thou inspire the whole;
> What each, what all supply
> May court, may charm our eye,
> Thou, only thou can'st raise the meeting soul!

The idea of the 'meeting soul', an idea found in Milton's *L'Allegro*, has been freshly considered by Collins, and expresses a powerful insight into the work performable by the poetic text.

Only abundant illustration can show a reader just what a strong preromantic writer might find in older poets. For instance, there are country sounds in the pastoral poetry of Gray and Collins, which derive from those harsh dissonant noises in Milton's *Lycidas* and Shakespeare's *Macbeth* – and in other writers, as editors remark. Milton seems determined to enounce the throaty sounds of the rustic piper, to catch the tone of his archaic elegies – and encharm them in his seventeenth-century English voice, using sounds stronger than they appear to modern readers; he talks about 'berries harsh and crude' and, when evening comes, he hears that 'the grey-fly winds her sultry horn'. To Shakespeare the sound came more languorously: 'The shard-borne beetle with his drowsy hums / Hath rung night's yawning peal' (*Macbeth*, III.ii.42–3). To Dryden, in his play, *Indian Emperor*, I.i.119, the ideas are repeated: 'Which drowsily like humming beetles rise'. For Gray, in the second stanza of the *Elegy*, 'all the world a solemn stillness holds, / Save where the beetle wheels his droning flight, / And drowsy tinklings lull the distant folds'. For Collins (*Ode to Evening* 9–16), these sounds should be quietened by the muse:

> Now air is hushed, save where the weak-eyed bat
> With short shrill shriek flits by on leathern wing,
>     Or where the beetle winds
>     His small but sullen horn,
> As oft he rises midst the twilight path,
> Against the pilgrim borne in heedless hum:
>     Now teach me, maid composed,
>     To breathe some softened strain....

Roger Lonsdale adds yet more instances of usage for Collins: John Albert Cooper's *The Power of Harmony* (Nov. 1745), 43–4: 'the stillness of the grey-ey'd Eve, / Broke only by the beetle's drowsy hum' (in which 'Broke' is, I think, too powerful a word, not because of the alliterative initial, but because of the 'oak' sound); and Thomas Warton's *Song Imitated from A Midsummer Night's Dream* II: 'the beetle's sullen hum' (we need to know for Collins that one of the meanings of 'sullen' was 'solemn'). In Robert Burns, we get a Scottish version of the same material, in the last stanza of *The Twa Dogs. A Tale*, where he recalls Gray's *Elegy*, I suppose somewhat mockingly, but also authentically from his northern point of view:

> By this, the sun was out o' sight,
> An' darker gloamin brought the night:
> The *bum-clock* humm'd wi' lazy drone,
> The kye stood rowtan i' the loan. . . .

A similar effect is found in Burns's better-known *The Cotter's Saturday Night*, which has an epigraph from Thomas Gray's *Elegy*, and begins with the kine as 'miry beasts retreating frae the pleugh', but uses a Spenserian stanza, much as Thomson, another Scottish poet, did in *Liberty* (Burns uses Thomsonian or Gray-like personifications). Through *The Seasons*, Thomson influenced such English pastoral writers as William Collins and William Cowper, but the debt was returned back when Burns (and Robert Fergusson earlier) wished to exaggerate the Scottish values of what had become an English pastoral mode. Burns's emphasis is pointedly nationalistic; he evokes Wallace in his final stanza. Burns also emphasizes the authenticity of Scottish education (established even on Saturday night, spent at home with the psalms and Bible stories, where new lovers might meet with due licence and parental approval), perhaps simply in the spirit that things are done better north of the border, even ale-making. Burns was a notable panegyrist of national drinks. Although he is sometimes labelled as a sentimentalist rather than a preromantic (in *Robert Burns and the Sentimental Era*, Carol McGuirk attacks those critics who diminish Burns's importance as a Scottish writer), he may be considered within the range of our subject because his work, often one of translation from southern British modes or from other Scottish modes into a version which suited himself, was often meant as a work in progress rather than as one which meant a fully finished pattern had been achieved. Burns's linguistic differences were not formulaic but authorial.

Although the preromantic period is often confused with the Age of Enlightenment, we can distinguish enlightened poetry, which typically includes that of the Augustan writers, as well as of writers of sensibility, many essayists and picturesque or neo-classical painters, from the stricter group of preromantics. Akenside, for instance, who appears conveniently by a showing of three poems in *Enlightened England*, a 1947 anthology edited by Wylie Sypher and long out of print, seems to show three kinds of poetry. In an excerpt of 242 lines from the third book of *The Pleasures of Imagination*, which is in almost unreadable Miltonic blank verse, Akenside invokes an inane figure of Nature ('searchless Nature') in a deistic way using generalized poetic diction, and gives a conventionalized account of the nightingale:

> When, joined at eve,
> Soft murmuring streams and gales of gentlest breath,
> Melodious Philomela's wakeful strain
> Attemper, could not man's discerning ear
> Through all its tones the symphony pursue;
> Nor yet this breath divine of nameless joy
> Steal through his veins, and fan the awakened heart;
> Mild as the breeze, yet rapturous as the song?

Elsewhere, Akenside decides it is time to put in a passage about stormy weather, in an account of taste:

> Hence, when lightning fires
> The arch of heaven, and thunders rock the ground,
> When furious whirlwinds rend the howling air,
> And ocean, groaning from his lowest bed,
> Heaves his tempestuous billows to the sky;
> Amid the mighty uproar, while below
> The nations tremble, Shakespeare looks abroad
> From some high cliff superior, and enjoys
> The elemental war. But Waller longs
> All on the margin of some flowery stream
> To spread his careless limbs amid the cool
> Of plantane shades, and to the listening deer
> The tale of slighted vows and love's disdain
> Resound soft-warbling all the livelong day:
> Consenting Zephyr sighs, the weeping rill
> Joins in his plaint melodious, mute the groves,
> And hill and dale with all their echoes mourn.
> Such and so various are the tastes of men!

This is all very well, but it is material for an essay and its main themes should be the differences between various poets. What have Shakespeare and Waller to do with an abstract storm? *The Tempest* is not the only place Shakespeare associated with bad weather. Waller is not even writing about storms at all. Thus, the connoisseur may think that in Akenside we have an anticipation of Beethoven's Sixth Symphony, and others may think that Shelley thought about similar ideas in *Ode to the West Wind*, but what we actually get is vague Hartleyan associative verse.

Akenside's *Inscription for a Grotto* is a neo-classical poem in blank verse which is all composed in Latinate, that is, periodic sentences. The flowers were placed by Glycon:

> He with cowslips pale,
> Primrose, and purple lychnis, deck'd the green
> Before my threshold, and my shelving walls
> With honeysuckle cover'd. Here at noon,
> Lull'd by the murmur of my rising fount,
> I slumber: here my clustering fruits I tend;

This is peaceful in a way that would attract Reynolds when painting in the mode of Poussin, but although it may have influenced Coleridge, it is not highly imaginative.

The nightingale returns in *Ode to the Evening Star* (1772), which is a poem I should label preromantic. The evening star itself, of course, stirred Blake's fancy, but the evening bird is the main subject, and Akenside provides a plot in which to hear its song, superior I suppose to that of Keats in *Ode to a Nightingale* – Keats is simply present there, responding, and seeking initiation. The speaker of the Horatian ode in 13 stanzas arrives at a favourite wood as a psychologically necessary retreat from his graveyard musings over the tomb of a beloved virgin, 'fair Olympia', because they had both loved to visit 'Olympia's haunt' and enjoy the sound of Philomela. The mood is close to Thomas Gray's in the *Elegy* and also to that of Wordsworth and his sister in *Tintern Abbey*. There is a false note when 'She now prolongs her lays' is met by a rhyming line, 'The wakeful heifers gaze', but the poem's Gray-like conclusion is noble:

> Whoe'er thou art, whom chance may bring
>     To this sequester'd spot,
> If then the plaintive Syren sing,
> Oh softly tread beneath her bower,
> And think of heaven's disposing power,
>     Of man's uncertain lot.
>
> Oh think, o'er all this mortal stage,
>     What mournful scenes arise:
> What ruin waits on kingly rage:
> How often virtue dwells with woe:
> How many griefs from knowledge flow:
>     How swiftly pleasure flies.
>
> O sacred bird, let me at eve,
>     Thus wandering all alone,
> Thy tender counsel oft receive,
> Bear witness to thy pensive airs,
> And pity nature's common cares
>     Till I forget my own.

Another preromantic poem which seems to look forward to later writers is *Ode to Spring* by Anna Laetitia Barbauld (1743–1825), a Horatian poem using 13 unrhymed stanzas of four lines, two pentameters and two trimeters. The mood is like Blake's, evoking a feeling of calm tenderness, enjoyed with melancholy eyes:

> Sweet is thy reign, but short: the red dog-star
> Shall scorch thy tresses, and the mower's scythe
>     Thy greens, thy flowerets all,
>     Remorseless shall destroy.
>
> Reluctant shall I bid thee then farewell;
> For O! not all that Autumn's lap contains,
>     Nor Summer's ruddiest fruits,
>     Can aught for thee atone,
>
> Fair Spring! whose simplest promise more delights,
> Then all their largest wealth, and through the heart
>     Each joy and new-born hope
>     With softest influence breathes.

James Macpherson, that notable preromantic figure from Scotland, needs further mention; his pretended translations from Celtic oral poets under the pseudonym of one of their own heroes, Ossian, aroused the wrath of Samuel Johnson but the delight of more credulous Londoners, Blake amongst them, in later years. The prose-poetry of Ossian was a model for Blake in the lines of his own prophetic verses. Ossian could be admired by the lovers of Britain as a northern inventor of biblical or classical epic, and the same trick was tried by Chatterton in his medieval poems under the pseudonym Rowley. Such works might have fitted better with the Welsh *Mabinogion*, if that had been sufficiently available. Nowadays, that group of texts is linked with the equally fictional post-Romantic Arthurian legends.

Northern myths, associated with bards, druids and fates, but not much with the tiny clans of elves and fairies adopted by nineteenth-century taste, were exploited notably by Thomas Gray, a skilled linguist, whether in a Pindaric ode, *The Bard*, or in more balladic odes, such as *The Fatal Sisters* or *The Descent of Odin*. These translations were aided by studies of the Norse sagas, which were augmented by archeological speculations from such writers as Thomas Stukely, bent on arousing a Saxon rule in Britain that was opposed to the Roman Empire somewhat earlier than it need have been. Fascination with early language led also to a new discovery of the prosody within biblical, as well as Welsh, prophetic texts, such as were proposed by Robert Lowth and others. These innovations hardened into a new, if wildly over-speculative, historical scheme of post-diluvian racial travels from Palestine throughout the globe. Scientific discoveries, including those popularized by Erasmus Darwin, weakened theological traditions about physics, botany, chemistry and chronology. They advanced the development of deism, a rational religion without divine revelation or, indeed, any 'religion' at all.

In protest against the social approval of rationalism which fostered Calvinism, the Methodists tried to awaken a more worshipful religion amongst the people. Some writers, such as the Anglican Christopher Smart, would be accounted mad, only to write magnificent secular and religious poetry in their refuges from reason. William Cowper came to embody the movement most strikingly, in being so over-inflicted by Calvinism and a kind of despair about his own future life, as to prefer suicide to public activity in London. In his country retreat, Olney, Cowper wrote superb hymns but also moved to an activity of writing, whether poetry or personal prose epistles, as a means of keeping himself sane enough to enjoy a small society, helped by patrons, and to celebrate his domestic pursuits, whether found in gardening or local birds and animals, or the finest details of country life, especially through his late Miltonic blank-verse poem, *The Task*. This poem influenced Coleridge most obviously, as is seen in the 'conversational poems'. Cowper's own poetry of despair marks one preromantic pole or nadir. This is a long way from Burns's celebration of *John Barleycorn*, just as Cowper's cup that cheers is alien to that in the Scottish tavern. Samuel Johnson, on the other hand, would drink or be teetotal at different times of life, yet even he had fears about death not unlike those of Cowper.

Cowper's fears about death appear strikingly in *The Castaway* (1799, published 1803), in which 'such a destin'd wretch as' himself is washed off his boat and fights 'with death a lasting strife, / Supported by despair of life'. His comrades on ship cannot directly help him in the storm; they hear his cries until he sinks after 'he drank the stifling wave'. Unlike the Lycidas figure, 'No poet wept him', though he was mentioned in the work of

the historian, Anson. Cowper chose to write about this anonymous castaway in order to
trace his own misery in the plight of another:

> No voice divine the storm allay'd,
>     No light propitious shone;
> When, snatch'd from all effectual aid,
>     We perish'd, each alone:
> But I beneath a rougher sea,
> And whelm'd in deeper gulphs than he.

The sadness of this late poem overwhelms the joy of Cowper's *Olney Hymns* of the 1770s
(published 1779), amongst them *Walking with God* and *Light Shining out of Darkness*, which
we are told preceded an attempt to commit suicide, with its remarkable and still-quoted
lines,

> God moves in a mysterious way,
>     His wonders to perform;
> He plants his footsteps in the sea,
>     And rides upon the storm.

In this poem, as it were, Cowper explained his own paralysis of will:

> Judge not the LORD by feeble sense,
>     But trust him for his grace;
> Behind a frowning providence,
>     He hides a smiling face.

The bitter-sweet nature of Cowper's life and the good humour of his conversational verse
rendered him delightful to his more sentimental readers in the preromantic and Romantic
period.

Madness or insanity as such, however, is in itself no mark of a preromantic writer, and
Donald Davie has rightly protested against this idea. As he points out in his Introduction
to *The Late Augustans* (p. xxvi), there 'is no evidence that' *A Song to David*, Smart's best-
known poem, 'was written in insanity', and that even *Jubilate Agno*, first published in
1939, was wrongly arranged in that printing and is much more regular in its structure
than it then appeared to be. I agree with Davie that madness or some other absence of
reason is not enough to qualify a poet to be hailed a preromantic.

The principal qualities of preromantic poetry are still easily to be found in Blake's early
printed verse and prose poetry, whether in *Poetical Sketches* or, more radically, *The French
Revolution*. In *Poetical Sketches* (1783) Blake attempted the range of preromantic styles, in
order to criticize the Augustan values he rejected and to embrace the sources of originality.
He made the mistake in these writings of imitation, to write Shakespeare, radical poet of
nature, in a Shakespearian style; to write in a Spenserian mode, but getting each stanza
prosodically 'wrong'; to imitate the northern ballad, but inventing only an unhistorical
subject; to imitate Percy's collection with a *Mad Song*; to write an unconvincing balladic
Gothic poem, *Fair Elenor*. Blake's seasonal and diurnal lyrics, however, follow Milton,

Thomson and Collins but add intense personal and patriotic feelings, including those from the biblical orient, which enlarge the allegorical personifications of his subjects into human figures of joy or terror. His love poems are not merely conventional; in places they anticipate the strength of *Songs of Experience*, especially *How sweet I roam'd*. His control of tone in *To the Muses* moves well beyond mockery, nevertheless, to the grace of Keats or Shelley:

> Whether on Ida's shady brow,
>   Or in the chambers of the East,
> The chambers of the sun, that now
>   From antient melody have ceas'd;
>
> Whether in Heav'n ye wander fair,
>   Or the green corners of the earth,
> Or the blue regions of the air,
>   Where the melodious winds have birth;
>
> Whether on chrystal rocks ye rove,
>   Beneath the bosom of the sea
> Wand'ring in many a coral grove,
>   Fair Nine, forsaking Poetry!
>
> How have you left the antient love
>   That bards of old enjoy'd in you!
> The languid strings do scarcely move!
>   The sound is forc'd, the notes are few!

Before we all became cynical, the War for Freedom in America and especially the French Revolution encouraged idealistic poets as well as politicians and theorists. However, it may be a good thing that Blake's poem about the matters in France, which was apparently meant to be an epic account of the events on the Continent, was so speedily overwhelmed by historical events that it was quenched after a partial printing. Few readers now gain much pleasure from Blake's refined allegories and apocalyptic action. The poem appears remarkably distinct in its action from known history and what its action would be in later books is as nebulous as the chaotic democratic forces that whirled through that once hierarchical vortex to spout later in the more terrifying Cromwellian form of Napoleon. Such major English writers as Blake, Coleridge, Wordsworth and Southey, to encourage Marxist historians, loved what they should rather have loathed in revolutions; yet their own Utopian schemes of pantisocracy would have been equally destructive to the English poets involved with that idea, had they, too, been tried to success.

If Kant's idea of 'deliberate purposelessness', which, I take it, comes from his discussion of gardens in the second book of his *Critique of Aesthetic Judgement*, is to be our guide to preromanticism, then it is served well by picturesque landscape, a delight in sketching and 'unfinished' pictures and the work of Sterne, and it continues to offer a great pleasure to readers and viewers, as a change from regular neo-classicism or Augustanism. However, it falls into the fault of gardens which work deliberately against regular patterns, only in certain preconceived ways, so that such gardens become in themselves tiresome. One wishes to dismiss writers who wish to see only Spenser, Milton and Shakespeare in their unregulated views: one would rather see something truly fanciful or imaginative. By the same token, one finds something wrong with those poets who specialize in seeing themselves, or their art, by surprise. In Collins one can admire recognition of the problem, but in Coleridge's *Kubla Khan* one would rather see a full visionary description of the damsel than a speculation supposedly interrupted by a person from Porlock. This aporia entangles known Romantics, perhaps especially those of the first generation, and known preromantics. It is not the business of a mere critic to evade this entanglement. The American and French Revolutions also were beginnings, not endings. The moment of choice between radicalism and revision is, not surprisingly, inevitable in major early Romantic writers.

## REFERENCES AND FURTHER READING

Barker-Benfield, G. J. *The Culture of Sensibility: Sex and Society in Eighteenth-Century Britain*, Chicago, University of Chicago Press, 1992.

Bernbaum, Ernest, *Guide Through the Romantic Movement*, New York, Ronald Press, 1949.

Calder, Angus and Donnelly, William (eds) *Robert Burns: Selected Poetry*, London, Penguin Books, 1991.

Davie, Donald (ed.) *The Late Augustans*, London, Heinemann, 1963.

Fowler, Alastair, *A History of English Literature*, Oxford, Basil Blackwell, 1987.

Lonsdale, Roger (ed.) *The Poems of Thomas Gray: William Collins: Oliver Goldsmith*, London, Longmans, 1969.

McCormick, E. H. *Omai: Pacific Envoy*, Auckland, Auckland University Press / Oxford University Press, 1977.

McGuirk, Carol, *Robert Burns and the Sentimental Era*, Athens, University of Georgia Press, 1985.

Milford, H.S. (ed.) *The Poetical Works of William Cowper*, London, Oxford University Press 1947.

Preminger, Alex (ed.) *Princeton Encyclopedia of Poetry and Poetics*, London, Macmillan, 1975.

Sypher, Wylie (ed.) *Enlightened England*, New York, Norton, 1962.

Van Sant, Ann Jessie, *Eighteenth-century Sensibility and the Novel: The Senses in Social Context*, Cambridge, Cambridge University Press, 1993.

# 3

# From Revolution to Romanticism: The Historical Context to 1800

## David Duff

All literature bears traces of the historical moment which gives rise to it, but at certain moments the relationship between history and literature becomes formative in more fundamental ways. The literature of the Romantic period is a powerful example of this, but the evidence is partially obscured by the fact that Romantic texts often seek to transcend their historical circumstances, and to project their readers onto an imaginative plane where the particularities of time and place are forgotten. Such impulses, most obviously associated with certain types of lyric and with the narrative genre which gives Romanticism its name, romance, have opened Romantic texts to the charge of escapism – or, in more recent criticism,[1] to the claim that Romantic writing frequently contrives to deny or 'displace' history by talking of other things (imagination, creativity, nature, the self) when it is really concerned with historical or political matters. These are arguments that have to be considered carefully, since they alert us to important tensions in Romantic poetics and in the word 'Romantic' itself (a retrospective label, carrying an obvious ahistorical bias). But they need to be set against the large number of Romantic texts – across all the literary genres – in which the engagement with history is direct and explicit. What these reveal is that history is a pervasive, even obsessive concern of Romantic writers, reflected not only in their fascination with the past but also in their equally intense, if often troubled perception of their own historical moment. The era which saw the revival of 'old romance' and the ascendancy of the subjective lyric also witnessed the birth of the historical novel, and produced numerous other works which openly address the social and political realities of their own time. In contemporary criticism too, the reciprocal influence of literature and history was a developed topic of discussion, often focused on the distinctly Romantic concept of the 'spirit of the age', or what the Germans called the *Zeitgeist*.

In exploring the historical context of English Romanticism, it therefore makes sense to begin with the Romantics' own impressions about the historical forces that shaped their writings. For William Hazlitt, author of a collection of essays actually entitled *The Spirit of the Age* (1825), there was no doubt that the central historical experience of his generation was the French Revolution. The revolution, with all its repercussions, was for Hazlitt not only the major political event of the period but also formed the model ultimately for its most characteristic literary achievements, notably the 'poetical experiments' of its greatest poet, William Wordsworth.[2] This view was echoed some years later by his fellow essayist Thomas De Quincey who, again commenting on the impact of the French Revolution on Wordsworth, spoke of the 'transformation which it wrought in the whole economy of his thoughts', and of the almost 'miraculous expansion which it gave to his human sympathies'.[3] For Percy Bysshe Shelley, born three years after the fall of the Bastille, the memory alone appears to have had a similar effect, since a substantial portion of his work is devoted, directly or indirectly, to what he once termed 'the master theme of the epoch – the French Revolution'.[4] Recognizing this, a contemporary reviewer of Shelley's work reaffirmed how in the 'wild burst of the French Revolution . . . no department of civil and military life, no branch of science, or region of taste and literature, was untouched by this general concussion.'[5] Even at a distance of 20 years or more, recalled another observer, 'everything was connected with the Revolution in France . . . not this thing or that thing, but literally everything was soaked in this one event'.[6]

These are arresting claims but they are not untypical. The notion that in the last years of the eighteenth century and the early years of the nineteenth, Britain experienced a 'revolution in literature' analogous to and partly inspired by the political revolution in France was already commonplace by 1816, and remains central to current explanations of the development of Romanticism.[7] To understand why political events in a neighbouring country should have had such a transformative effect on the literary life of Britain, we must first reflect on the phenomenon of the French Revolution itself, and examine the political and cultural conditions in which English writers responded to and interpreted that phenomenon. For it is a striking fact that though the literary culture of France, like every other aspect of French life, was profoundly affected by and indeed implicated in the political upheavals of the Revolutionary years, the aesthetic revolution that we call Romanticism, which enters its major phase in England in the 1790s, does not occur in France until the 1830s. The dominant aesthetic of Revolutionary France was essentially the same as that of the *ancien régime*: neo-classicism. It has been said that the French poet in that period does not write, he fights; but there may be a more general paradox involved. The cultural history of the last two centuries has repeatedly shown that art and literature that are revolutionary in their political content are often conservative in their form, just as literature that is revolutionary in an aesthetic sense may well be reactionary ideologically – a consideration that has some bearing on the politics of English Romanticism.

Why, then, was the imaginative impact of the French Revolution so great across the Channel, and why, at this crucial remove, did the revolutionary experience prove so seminal to the development of English Romantic literature? These are complex questions, not least because events in France provoked such a wide spectrum of response, with attitudes shifting markedly during successive phases of the Revolution, and as the domestic political situation altered. Almost from the start, English reactions to the French Revolution became bound up with the cause of political reform at home, the prospect or threat of which led to a dramatic alteration of the political climate, including a realignment of parliamentary groupings, a polarization of public opinion, and a far-reaching debate on the meaning of events in France and the desirability or otherwise of political change in Britain. The intellectual focus of this debate was the 'pamphlet war' of the 1790s, an aggressive but astonishingly fertile set of exchanges which produced not only some highly effective polemic but also several major works of political theory. This conflict of ideas, images and political discourses, which embraced fundamental questions about the nature of society, the basis of government, the doctrine of 'rights', the notion of political justice, the relation between the sexes, even the very concept of 'reason', was, for many British intellectuals, the principal medium through which the whole revolutionary phenomenon was registered and analysed, and political attitudes formed. As such, it forms a key part of the intellectual background to English Romanticism. Of the major 'first-generation' poets, only Wordsworth experienced Revolutionary France at first hand, but all actively participated in the Revolution debate, either by writing political pamphlets themselves or other forms of political journalism, or through the (equally politicized) medium of poetry, fiction and drama. Though some lived to regret their involvement in the ideological controversy of the early 1790s, or at least to reject the radical positions they had adopted within that conflict, the modes of thought and expression which characterize the Revolution debate continued to influence their later, less overtly political work, just as the French Revolution itself remained central to their whole sense of history.

Even today, the sequence of events that began in Versailles and Paris in the summer of 1789 with the meeting of the Estates General and the Third Estate's decision to declare itself the National Assembly, retains an almost hypnotic charge. The Tennis Court Oath on 20 June; the revolutionary call to arms on 12 July; the capture and subsequent demolition of the Bastille; the all-night sitting of the National Assembly on 4 August which effectively abolished feudalism; the issuing of the Declaration of the Rights of Man and of the Citizen on 27 August; the Festival of Federation on the first anniversary of the fall of the Bastille; and then, on 10 August, 1792, the deposing of the king followed on 22 September by the declaration that France was now a Republic: these momentous actions and gestures have acquired a quasi-mythical quality, making it difficult even for analytical historians to make an entirely rational assessment of why things happened the way they did.

To those who actually lived through those years, it seemed, in the words of Robert Southey, as though 'a visionary world' was opening before them: 'Old things seemed passing away, and nothing was dreamt of but the regeneration of the human race'.[8] Like Wordsworth's famous description of how it was 'Bliss ... in that dawn to be alive' (from Book X of *The Prelude*),[9] Southey's retrospective comment captures perfectly the exhilaration and optimism with which the revolution was initially greeted by those of liberal or radical disposition. One modern commentator has spoken of the 'dizzying sense of total possibility'[10] experienced during the early years of the revolution, the political faith that made 'perfectibility' a household word, and turned 'regeneration' from a vague theological promise into a concrete political programme. In what Southey elsewhere refers to as this 'mania of man-mending',[11] it was believed that not only governments but whole societies as well as individual people could be 'perfected' by an act of secular will. This was the new, revolutionary faith (based largely on the teachings of Jean-Jacques Rousseau) that was to be institutionalized in Robespierre's so-called 'Republic of Virtue', and that led to the renaming of the Cathedral of Notre-Dame as the Temple of Reason and the adoption by the National Convention of a revolutionary calendar that renamed and renumbered the days, weeks and months, and proclaimed the first year of the Republic as Year One, 'L'An Un'. Its most sustained philosophical expression was Volney's *Ruins of Empire* (1791), Condorcet's *Outline of the Progress of the Human Spirit* (1794) and, in England, William

Godwin's *Enquiry Concerning Political Justice* (1793), all three of which interpret the French Revolution as the prelude to a great age of Utopian fulfilment.

If such writings and actions lend credence to de Toqueville's claim that the French Revolution 'created the politics of the impossible' and 'turned blind audacity into a cult',[12] they confirm, too, De Quincey's perception that the central dynamic of revolution was that of *transformation* – of unexpected, rapid and total change. What Edmund Burke and other opponents of the revolution found so abhorrent and disturbing, that the French revolutionists 'left nothing, no, nothing at all *unchanged*',[13] was for sympathizers or 'enthusiasts' precisely what made revolution such an enabling, liberating force – its demonstration that even the most settled habits and features of a society or an individual *could* be altered and amended. Before 1789, this idea hardly existed, certainly outside a religious context. The word 'revolution' itself, although sometimes used as a term of political description, had until then generally carried a sense almost opposite to the modern one: designating motion backwards, or a return to the point at which something began (from the root verb 'to revolve'). Now it meant motion forwards: the abolition of the past, of the *ancien régime* (a concept that is also invented at this time) and the inauguration of a totally new order of things.[14] This is the promise, the secular messianic myth of revolution.

According to the Mexican poet Octavio Paz, the whole history of modern poetry, from this time onwards 'has been nothing but the history of its relations to that myth', relations that have varied 'from seduction to revulsion, from loyalty to anathema, from idolatry to abjuration'.[15] But for the Romantic poet, the idea of revolution has a special interest, and a special affinity. For Romanticism seeks to effect in poetry what revolution aspires to achieve in politics: innovation, transformation, defamilarization. The French revolutionists' project of creating a revolutionary culture in which all traces of the corrupt, aristocratic past were removed, even to the point of replacing the kings, queens and knaves on playing cards with the 'génies', 'libertés' and 'égalités' of the Revolution has a precise analogy with Blake's attempt to 'cleanse the doors of perception'[16] through a radically innovative use of language, art and literary form; or with Shelley's formulation of the goal of poetry as being to 'strip the veil of familiarity from the world' and 'make us the inhabitants of a world to which the familiar world is chaos'.[17] Southey, too, hints at the correspondence between Romantic poetics and revolutionary politics, the implication of his comment being that the 'visionary world', previously the domain of poets, of apocalyptic prophecy or Utopian speculation, was now taking shape across the Channel. The realm of fantasy was now the realm of fact, and the language of speculation had become a language of description, an *exact* language. That extreme development of a visionary poetics which we call Romanticism thus seems to absorb and to organize itself around the transformational energies released by revolution.

In a more general sense, too, the French Revolution enhanced the role of the writer by revealing the power of ideas and of words. In the magnificent closing paragraph of his *Defence of Poetry* (1821), Shelley remarks how, in periods of 'beneficial change', 'there is an accumulation of the power of communicating and receiving intense and impassioned conceptions respecting man and nature', a power which Shelley believed to reside preeminently, if often unconsciously, among poets (the 'unacknowledged legislators of the world').[18] Underlying this claim – which articulates exactly the expansion of ambition to which so much Romantic literature bears witness – is an assumption that few at the time would have disputed: namely, that the French Revolution was actually the result of ideas ('conceptions') and the circulation of ideas. Coleridge makes this assumption explicit when he refers, in the prospectus to a series of lectures of 1795, to the 'revolutionary Powers' of Literature[19] – meaning here literature in its broadest sense, or the printed word in general. So, too, does Hazlitt in his *Memoirs of the Late Thomas Holcroft* (1816), when he describes the French Revolution as 'the only match that ever took place between philosophy and experience'.[20] Historians nowadays regard this as merely one of the factors contributing to the outbreak of the French Revolution (the 'intellectual origins' as opposed to other possible causes), but this was the explanation that dominated contemporary accounts, and the fact that 'Literature' was widely believed to have demonstrated its 'revolutionary Powers' – to be, in the words of another contemporary commentator, 'the great engine by which . . . all civilized states must ultimately be supported or overthrown'[21] (a perception enshrined in the coining, in the 1790s, of the word 'ideology') – acted as a tremendous stimulus to writers of all kinds – though it carried, too, a dangerous burden of responsibility, especially in a society, like Britain, that was resisting revolution.

This improbable marriage between philosophy and experience had also brought home the power of language, not just as the vehicle for ideas but as a potent historical force in its own right. In the extensive symbolism of the French Revolution, few symbols were more important than individual words such as virtue, sovereignty, liberty, citizen, nation – terms that acquired a political function almost independent of their meaning. Modern historians and literary analysts have made intensive study of the language of revolutionary oratory and writing,[22] but this is a topic of enquiry which had already attracted the attention of contemporary observers, both in France and Britain. The French literary critic and author Jean-François La Harpe, for instance, wrote a treatise after the Terror arguing that the key to the aberrations of the revolution lay in its fanatical language.[23] Responding to similar evidence – the transcripts of speeches delivered in the National Convention during the Reign of Terror – Coleridge, in the Preface to his and Southey's 'historical drama' *The Fall of Robespierre* (1794), had also commented on the 'empassioned and highly figurative language of the French orators',[24] and was to analyse elsewhere the fondness for abstraction which was another conspicuous feature of revolutionary discourse.[25] Notwithstanding obvious differences of linguistic function and context, there are again suggestive affinities here with Romantic literary discourse, which also frequently combines emotional intensity and rhetorical amplification with metaphorical extravagance and a relish for abstraction. Needless to say, the power of language is also a very common theme of Romantic writing.

Having noted all these analogies, however, we should be cautious about pressing them too far. If English Romanticism can be said to partake of the transformational energy, ideological self-consciousness and verbal momentum of the French Revolution, it is also the case that some of English Romanticism's most impressive achievements are made by writers who are either openly opposed to the revolution from the start, or who have already renounced their revolutionary allegiances. Moreover, the origins of the Romantic aesthetic, if we trace it back earlier in the eighteenth century, lie partly in a reaction against the Enlightenment philosophy in whose name the French Revolution was conducted. Romanticism, in other words, was a *contested* aesthetic, and a politically ambivalent one. Against the revolutionary Romanticism of Blake and Shelley, whose radical politics seem consistent with their aesthetic radicalism, we must set the more problematic cases of Coleridge and Wordsworth, whose experimentation with Romantic poetics increases as their political radicalism appears to decline; or the even more paradoxical case of Edmund Burke, the great counter-revolutionary who was also a theorist of the sublime, an exponent of the cult of sensibility, an advocate of chivalry and romance against Enlightenment rationalism, and a major influence on almost all the English Romantics. The German Romantic poet Novalis pinpointed the paradox when he remarked that there have been many anti-revolutionary books written for revolution, but 'Burke wrote a revolutionary book against revolution'.

The book to which Novalis refers, Burke's *Reflections on the Revolution in France*, was published in November 1790, at a point when British public opinion was still broadly supportive of the French Revolution, sentiments ranging from mild indifference to rapturous enthusiasm. Charles James Fox, leader of the Parliamentary Whig opposition, had declared it the best event that the world had ever known, and even the Tory Prime Minister, William Pitt, while not specifically welcoming it, had not condemned it. In the weeks after the fall of the Bastille, the *Morning Post* had marvelled at the 'sublime manner' in which the revolution was being conducted,[26] and the House of Lords itself had debated whether to hold a day of thanksgiving (the motion was defeated). For some, it was simply a case of France catching up with Britain, which had had its own 'Glorious Revolution' in 1688, and already enjoyed the liberties for which the French were now struggling. Others saw it as a step beyond. Particularly vocal among these were the various groups of religious Non-conformists or Dissenters who had made up the backbone of English radicalism since the time of the Civil War, and who – unlike the predominantly secular French intellectuals – interpreted this new turn in contemporary politics through the lens of biblical prophecy. The 'visionary world' inaugurated by the French Revolution was, according to this interpretation, none other than the restored paradise or 'new heaven and new earth' prophesied in the *Book of Isaiah* and the *Book of Revelation*. These apocalyptic hopes or expectations contributed greatly to the emotional and intellectual atmosphere of the 1790s, and, transmuted and internalized, helped to define the imaginative scope of English Romantic poetry.[27]

Burke's intervention shattered this consensus of approval or at least tolerance of the revolution. Rejecting the spiritual interpretation put forward by English Dissenters like Richard Price (whose unqualified praise of the French 'ardour for liberty' in his *Discourse on the Love of Our Country* is partly what provoked Burke's antithetical *Reflections*), Burke attacked the revolution at every level, declaring its political achievements to be illusory, its philosophical foundations specious, its perpetrators cruel and fanatical, and its English sympathizers wholly deceived.

Through an artful rhetoric of concealment and selective emphasis, and in brilliantly eloquent prose, Burke transfers attention from the political revolution itself to the 'revolution in sentiments, manners, and moral opinions' manifest in the behaviour of the revolutionists. Instead of dwelling on the storming of the Bastille, an irrepressible symbol of the overthrow of despotism, Burke requires his readers to visualize the rough-handling of Marie-Antoinette by the revolutionary crowd at Versailles during the events of 5–6 October 1789, presenting this as an act of indelicacy and insubordination which symbolized the death of the 'age of chivalry' and the beginning of a new, morally impoverished age of 'sophisters, oeconomists and calculators'.[28] Fashionable nostalgia for the Middle Ages – already a stock piece of eighteenth-century romanticism – is thus reworked into an ideological defence of the *ancien régime*, just as, in other parts of the book, the traditional metaphor of the body politic is extended into a complex organic vision of the nature of society. By contrast, the revolutionists are portrayed not as the forces of enlightenment but rather as sorcerers, enchanters and necromancers attempting, with their political 'incantations', to perform 'unnatural' deeds such as devouring their parent – in other words, drafting a new constitution.

Burke's 'Manifesto of a Counter Revolution', as James Mackintosh shrewdly described the *Reflections*,[29] had an instantaneous effect in mobilizing opposition to the French Revolution and to the whole idea of revolutionary politics, now perceived as a direct threat to British freedom and security. Public opinion rapidly polarized, and the Parliamentary Whigs – the party to which Burke nominally belonged, as a former champion of libertarian causes – split into two factions, those sympathetic to the revolution (led by Fox) and those opposed to it (led by the Duke of Portland). Outside Parliament, resistance to revolution became a popular political cause in its own right, fuelled by 'loyalist' organizations like John Reeves's Association for the Preservation of Liberty and Property against Republicans and Levellers (formed in November 1792), which produced a steady stream of populist, conservative propaganda. Though Burke himself often felt isolated and undervalued, as later tracts such as his almost hysterical *Letter to a Noble Lord* (1796) show, his writings served as an inspiration for the whole 'anti-jacobin' onslaught of the 1790s and beyond, supplying much of its imagery as well as of its emotional force and intellectual rationale. Burke's prestige only increased as the increasingly violent turn of events in France – the September Massacres of 1792, the execution of Louis XVI in January 1793, the outbreak of war with Britain and Holland in February 1793, and the onset of the Jacobin Terror later in the same year – appeared to confirm his original analysis of the character and tendency of the revolution; a warning which Burke repeated in ever more ferocious language up to his death in 1797. Analysing the history of the period 30 years later, Hazlitt scarcely exaggerates when he credits Burke, in a suitably Burkean metaphor, with having 'stood at the prow of the vessel of the state, and with his glittering, pointed spear harpooned the Leviathan of the French Revolution, which darted into its wild career, tinging its onward track with purple gore.'[30]

Paradoxically, however, the *Reflections* also gave a tremendous boost to the radical movement, and Burke was often ironically toasted to that effect at radical meetings of the 1790s. By depicting the French Revolution in such lurid colours, and presenting such an obviously romanticized vision of the traditional order, Burke roused others into an equally determined defence of the revolution, and of the political principles that lay behind it. In the pamphlet war that followed the publication of the *Reflections*, 'friends of liberty' of every complexion took issue with Burke's tendentious arguments and emotive prose, countering these, more often than not, with an Enlightenment rhetoric of demystification and an appeal to the newly radicalized doctrine of political rights. These are certainly the dominant idiom of Mary Wollstonecraft's *Vindication of the Rights of Men* (1790) and its famous sequel, her pioneering feminist tract *A Vindication of the Rights of Woman* (1792). Philosophically the most impressive response to Burke was Godwin's *Enquiry Concerning Political Justice* (1793), which rejected revolution and other forms of political action as means of change while simultaneously envisaging a future state of society which exceeded even the most optimistic forecasts of the French philosophers. Other notable responses were Catherine Graham's *Observations on the Reflections* (1790), James Mackintosh's *Vindiciae Gallicae* (1791), Joseph Priestley's *Letters to the Right Hon. Edmund Burke* (1791), John Thelwall's *Sober Reflections* (1796), Coleridge's *Conciones ad Populum* (1795) and Wordsworth's (unpublished) *Letter to the Bishop of Llandaff* (1793).[31]

By far the most important and influential reply to the *Reflections*, however, was Thomas Paine's *Rights of Man*, published in two parts in 1791 and 1792. Characterizing himself a 'citizen of the world', and adopting the same incisive, plain-speaking style he had perfected in his American revolutionary tract *Common Sense* (1776), Paine makes a devastating attack on both the substance and style of Burke's polemic, offering his own assessment of the political gains of the French Revolution together with a radical critique of the British parliamentary system and detailed proposals for political and social change. Alternately parodying and quarrelling with Burke, Paine seeks to ridicule Burke's submission to the authority of the past, to expose the sentimentality of his portrayal of the French royal family and of hierarchy in general, and to reveal his concomitant disregard for the sufferings and needs of ordinary people ('He pities the plumage, but forgets the dying bird').[32] Though a skilled rhetorician himself, Paine makes a point of deconstructing Burke's rhetorical strategies, implying throughout that Burke is under the spell of his own eloquence and over-stocked imagination – but that Paine's own reasoning is based entirely on the evidence of facts and the dictates of common sense ('I scarcely ever quote; the reason is, I always think'). Quite apart from its effectiveness as polemic, however, *Rights of Man* is also a brilliant exposition of the radical case: never before had the doctrine of rights, the cornerstone of Enlightenment political philosophy, been presented in such a lucid and accessible form, and such simple, persuasive arguments made for the basic principles of political and social equality.

Just how accessible Paine's political prose was to prove is suggested by the sales of *Rights of Man*, the two parts of which are estimated to have sold as many as 200,000 copies between 1791 and 1793 (Burke's *Reflections*, by comparison, sold approximately 30,000 copies, itself a remarkable figure for the time). Many of these were cheap reprints sold by radical booksellers and publishers like Joseph Johnson, Daniel Isaac Eaton and Thomas Spence, who in addition printed extracts from this and other 'levelling' works from the past and present in weekly journals or miscellanies with titles like *Pig's Meat*, *Politics for the People or Hog's Wash*, and *Twopence Worth of Pig's Bristles* (all of which allude to Burke's notorious reference to the common people as a 'swinish multitude'). Also involved in the distribution of Paine's writings and other radical literature was the newly revived Society for Constitutional Information, originally founded in the 1780s to promote the cause of parliamentary reform and then relaunched, with a more radical agenda, by John Horne Tooke in November 1790. More radical still were the newly formed 'corresponding societies', the most important of which was the London Corresponding Society created in January 1792 by the shoemaker Thomas Hardy. With a membership mainly of working men, and activities that included political discussions, mass meetings, and the mainten-ance of links with the French National Convention, the London Corresponding Society was the popular vanguard of the radical movement, and, especially in the years 1792–4, marked the ascendancy of the Painite agenda in the campaign for parliamentary reform.

The response of the British government to the extraordinary upsurge of political radicalism at all levels of society was a series of increasingly draconian measures intended to curtail the activities of the corresponding societies and prevent the free circulation of ideas. In May 1792, the same month in which the guillotine was used in Paris for the first time, George III issued a Proclamation against Seditious Writings, which resulted seven months later in Paine, who had meanwhile fled to Paris, being tried *in absentia* and convicted of seditious libel – the first of many such prosecutions, throughout the 1790s, of booksellers, writers and other radical activists. The anti-radical campaign increased in intensity following the declaration of war between Britain and France in February 1793, after which time democratic sympathies of any kind were liable to be interpreted as traitorous as well as seditious. With the suspension of Habeas Corpus in May 1794, the scene was set for the infamous Treason Trials, in which 12 leading London radicals including Hardy, Horne Tooke, John Thelwall and Thomas Holcroft were arrested and charged with High Treason – an offence which carried the death penalty.

Of the three who were actually brought to trial, all were acquitted, a verdict which some have seen as a vindication of the English legal system (others tried under Scottish law were not so fortunate, a number of prominent radicals having recently been sentenced to transportation to Botany Bay). Yet the fact that the trials took place at all is a measure of the severity of Pitt's counter-revolutionary 'Terror', as Godwin – a friend of the defendants and another potential victim of Pitt's anti-sedition legislation – describes it in the preface to his highly successful political novel *Caleb Williams* (1794). In such conditions, Godwin writes, 'even the humble novelist might be shown to be constructively a traitor'.[33] Charles Pigott makes a similar point in his mock-serious *Political Dictionary* (1795) when he records that the very word '*Enquiry* – according to the modern construction, signifies Sedition . . . and they who are *audacious* enough to claim this *obsolete* privilege, expose themselves to the penalties of fine, pillory, or imprisonment'.

Despite the verdict of the Treason Trials, there was to be no relaxation of Pitt's Terror. Habeas Corpus was again suspended in 1798, and further restrictions on the right of assembly and the freedom of speech were imposed by the Two Acts of 1795 and the Six Acts of 1799, the latter of which banned outright the London Corresponding Society and outlawed the emergent trades unions. Although radical politics played some part in the British naval mutinies at Spithead and the Nore in April 1797 and in the abortive rebellion by the United Irishmen under Wolfe Tone in May–August 1798 (which failed despite French military backing), the radicals became steadily more isolated as government repression continued and the war with Revolutionary France turned more and more people away from politics towards the patriotic defence of the realm. By the end of the decade, most of the leading radicals of the early 1790s were either in exile or in retreat, and the revolution debate had degenerated into the indiscriminate satire of the *The Antijacobin, or Weekly Examiner*, a Tory journal (partly written by government ministers) launched in 1797 with the express purpose of stamping out 'JACOBINISM in all its shapes, and in all its degrees, political and moral, public and private'.[34]

Romantic writers were directly involved in the ideological struggles of the 1790s, and the experience of political reaction and repression was arguably as important to their imaginative development as the original stimulus of the French Revolution. According to Shelley and other second-generation Romantics, writers of Wordsworth's generation had been 'morally ruined' by what appeared to be 'the melancholy desolation of all their cherished hopes',[35] and had betrayed the cause of liberty by succumbing to reactionary pressures and turning apostate. That a startling shift of political opinion had occurred is undeniable if we compare, say, the overt republicanism of Wordsworth's *Letter to the Bishop of Llandaff* (1793) with the political quietism and religious orthodoxy of *The Excursion* (1814), or the young Coleridge of the inflammatory *Conciones ad Populum* (1795) and the pantisocracy project with the middle-aged Coleridge of *The Statesman's Manual* (1816), or, the most notorious apostate of all, the Jacobinical Robert Southey, who wrote a drama about the Peasants' Revolt, *Wat Tyler*, in 1794, and Southey the poet laureate of 1821, who wrote the grossly sycophantic elegy for George III, *A Vision of Judgment* (1821).

To define exactly how and when this shift occurred is not easy, however, and scholars still disagree about the political trajectories of the so-called 'Lake poets', not least because their own autobiographical testimony in this regard is fragmentary and misleading. What is interesting is that the language of Utopian idealism and apocalyptic vision, indeed the whole transformational texture of revolutionary discourse, remains a central feature of Romantic writing long after the political ambition of realizing such goals in the external world has been renounced. But this is now shadowed by a language of disillusion and despair, and it is in moods of alienation or depression that Romantic writing often yields its most powerful insights, or achieves greatest intensity of expression. Moving between the emotional extremes of joy and dejection, hope and despair, certainty and fear, Romantic poetry thus appears to mirror the psychological patterns of the French Revolution, and, at its most complex, to internalize also the ideological conflict of the revolution debate. Though Romantic writing sometimes seeks to displace or transcend its historical determinants, the very idea of what it is to write poetry – the Romantic aesthetic of inspiration and collapse, of energy and imagination – becomes informed by and subject to the same unstable dynamic as that of revolution. It is the co-existence of these elements – the enormous expansion of imaginative scope and the obsessive turning of the mind back upon itself, the heightened awareness of literature's ideological function along with a deepened sense of the autonomy of the aesthetic (or what Blake calls poetry's 'own proper sphere of conception and visionary execution')[36] – that makes the whole phenomenon of Romanticism such a fascinating paradigm of the relationship between literature and history.

## NOTES

1   See, for example, Alan Liu, 'The History in "Imagination"', *Romanticism: A Critical Reader*, pp. 84–119.

2   Howe, XI, 86–7.

3   De Quincey, 'William Wordsworth' (1839), Masson, II, 273–4.

4   Jones, I, 504.

5   *The Monthly Review*, March, 1819.

6   A Cockburn, *Memorials of his Time* (1856), p. 80, quoted in Briggs, *The Age of Improvement* p. 129.

7   Modern investigation of this topic begins with M. H. Abrams's influential essay 'English Romanticism: The spirit of the age' (1963) and his book *Natural Supernaturalism* (1971), which both document contemporary perceptions of the influence of the French Revolution, including Hazlitt's and De Quincey's comments on Wordsworth, reproduced here, and Francis Jeffrey's remarks in 1816 on the causes of 'the revolution in our literature' ('Spirit of the age', p. 92). More recent scholarship is cited in the bibliography below.

8   *The Correspondence of Robert Southey with Caroline Bowles*, ed. Edward Dowden (Dublin: 1881), p. 52, quoted by Abrams, 'Spirit of the Age', p. 94.

9   Book X, line 692, in *Romanticism* p. 438. One of the few passages of *The Prelude* to be published in Wordsworth's lifetime, lines 689–726 of Book X (in the 1804 text) were first published in 1809, and reprinted under the title 'French Revolution, As It Appeared to Enthusiasts at Its Commencement' in Wordsworth's *Poems of 1815*.

10  Steiner, *In Bluebeard's Castle*, p. 20.

11  Letter to John May, 26 June 1797, in Cobban, *The Debate on the French Revolution*, p. 376.

12  MS fragment from the 1850s, quoted by Palmer, *The Age of Democratic Revolution*, II, p. 130.

13  Burke, *A Letter to a Noble Lord* (1796), in Butler, *Revolution Controversy*, p. 51.

14  See Robert Darnton, 'What was revolutionary about the French Revolution?' in Jones, pp. 18–29.

15  Paz, 'Poetry, myth, revolution', pp. 65–6.

16  *The Marriage of Heaven and Hell* (1790), in *Romanticism*, p. 84.

17  *A Defence of Poetry* (written 1821), in *Romanticism*, p. 967.

18  *Romanticism*, p. 969.

19  CC *Lectures 1795*, pp. 255–6.

20  Howe, III, pp. 155–6.

21  Thomas J. Mathias, *The Pursuits of Literature: A Satirical Poem* (7th edn, London: 1798), quoted by Kelley, *Women, Writing and Revolution*, p. 9.

22  See, for instance, Hunt, *Politics, Culture and Class*, ch. 1: 'The Rhetoric of Revolution'.

23  *Du Fanatisme dans la langue révolutionnaire* (3rd edn, Paris: 1797), cited by Hunt, *Politics, Culture and Class*, p. 19.

24  EHC, II, p. 495.

25  See CC *Lay Sermons*, pp. 15–16.

26  *Morning Post*, 21 July 1789, quoted by Hobsbawm, *The Age of Revolution*, p. 73.

27  See Abrams, 'Spirit of the Age', pp. 95–8, and *Natural Supernaturalism*, *passim*.

28  Burke, *Reflections*, pp. 175, 169–70.

29  *Vindiciae Gallicae* (1791), in Butler, *Revolution Controversy*, p. 92.

30  Howe, XIII, 51–2.

31  Some of these are extracted in Butler, *Revolution Controversy*, and Cobban, *The Debate on the French Revolution*. Full texts of over a hundred key pamphlets of the revolution debate are reproduced in Claeys, *Political Writings of the 1790s*. For a rhetorical analysis of the pamphlet war, see Boulton, *The Language of Politics*.

32  Paine, *Rights of Man*, p. 73.

33  Godwin, *Caleb Williams*, Preface of 1795. The original preface was suppressed.

34  Prospectus to *The Antijacobin*, in Butler, *Revolution Controversy*, p. 216.

35  Preface to *Laon and Cythna; or, The Revolution of the Golden City* (London: 1817), in Shelley, *Poems and Prose*, p. 55.

36  *A Descriptive Catalogue* (1809), in Blake, *Complete Writings*, p. 576.

## WRITINGS

Burke, Edmund, *Reflections on the Revolution in France* (London: 1790), ed. Conor Cruise O'Brien, Penguin, Harmondsworth, 1969.

Godwin, William, *Caleb Williams* (London: 1794), ed. David McCracken, Oxford University Press, Oxford, 1982.

——*Enquiry Concerning Political Justice* (3rd. edn, London: 1798), ed. Isaac Kramnick, Penguin, Harmondsworth, 1976.

Hazlitt, William, *The Spirit of the Age* (London: 1825), Howe, XI.

Paine, Thomas, *Rights of Man* (London: 1791–2), ed. Henry Collins, Penguin, Harmondsworth, 1969.

## REFERENCES AND FURTHER READING

Abrams, M. H., 'English Romanticism: the spirit of the age', in *Romanticism and Consciousness: Essays in Criticism*, ed. Harold Bloom, Norton, New York, 1970, pp. 91–119.

——*Natural Supernaturalism: Tradition and Revolution in Romantic Literature*, Norton, New York, 1971.

Bindman, David, *The Shadow of the Guillotine: Britain and the French Revolution*, exhibition catalogue, British Museum, London, 1989.

Blake, William, *Complete Writings*, ed. Geoffrey Keynes, Oxford University Press, London, 1966.

Boulton, James T., *The Language of Politics in the Age of Burke and Paine*, Routledge & Kegan Paul, London, 1963.

Briggs, Asa, *The Age of Improvement 1783–1867*, Longman, London, 1959.

Butler, Marilyn, *Romantics, Rebels and Reactionaries: English Literature and Its Background 1760–1830*, Oxford University Press, Oxford, 1981.

—— (ed.) *Burke, Paine, Godwin and the Revolution Controversy*, Cambridge University Press, Cambridge, 1984.

Christie, Ian, *Wars and Revolutions: Britain 1760–1815*, Edward Arnold, London, 1982.

Claeys, Gregory (ed.) *Political Writings of the 1790s: French Revolution Debate in Britain*, 8 vols, Pickering and Chatto, London, 1995.

Cobban, Alfred (ed.) *The Debate on the French Revolution 1789–1800*, 2nd edn, A. & C. Black, London, 1960.

Coleridge, Samuel Taylor, *The Collected Works of Samuel Taylor Coleridge*, Gen. ed. Kathleen Coburn, Princeton University Press, Princeton, 1961–.

—— *The Complete Poetical Works of Samuel Taylor Coleridge*, ed. E. H. Coleridge, 2 vols, Clarendon Press, Oxford, 1962.

Colley, Linda, *Britons: Forging the Nation 1707–1837*, Pimlico, London, 1992.

Cranston, Maurice, *Philosophers and Pamphleteers: Political Theorists of the Enlightenment*, Oxford University Press, Oxford, 1986.

Crossley, Ceri and Small, Ian (eds) *The French Revolution and British Culture*, Oxford University Press, Oxford, 1989.

Dickinson, H. T., *British Radicalism and the French Revolution 1789–1815*, Blackwell, Oxford, 1985.

Duff, David, *Romance and Revolution: Shelley and the Politics of a Genre*, Cambridge University Press, Cambridge, 1994.

Everest, Kelvin (ed.) *Revolution in Writing: British Literary Responses to the French Revolution*, Open University Press, Milton Keynes, 1991.

Hanley, Keith and Selden, Raman (eds) *Revolution and English Romanticism: Politics and Rhetoric*, Harvester Wheatsheaf, Hemel Hempstead, 1990.

Hobsbawm, E. J., *The Age of Revolution: Europe 1789–1848*, Sphere, London, 1980.

Hunt, Lynn, *Politics, Culture and Class in the French Revolution*, Methuen, London, 1986.

Jones, Howard Mumford, *Revolution and Romanticism*, Harvard University Press, Cambridge, Mass. 1974.

Jones, Peter (ed.) *The French Revolution in Social and Political Perspective*, Arnold, London, 1996.

Kelley, Gary, *Women, Writing, and Revolution 1790–1827*, Clarendon Press, Oxford, 1993.

Kennedy, Emmet, *A Cultural History of the French Revolution*, Yale University Press, New Haven, 1989.

Palmer, R. R., *The Age of Democratic Revolution: A Political History of Europe and America, 1760–1800*, 2 vols, Princeton University Press, Princeton, 1959, 1964.

Paulson, Ronald, *Representations of Revolution (1789–1820)*, Yale University Press, New Haven, 1983.

Paz, Octavio, 'Poetry, myth, revolution', *The Other Voice: Essays on Modern Poetry*, trans. Helen Lane, Harcourt Brace Jovanovich, New York, 1991, pp. 59–74.

Pigott, Charles, *A Political Dictionary*, London, 1795.

Prickett, Stephen, *England and the French Revolution*, Macmillan, London, 1989.

Shelley, Percy Bysshe, *Poems and Prose*, ed. Timothy Webb, Everyman, London, 1995.

Steiner, George, *In Bluebeard's Castle: Some Notes Towards the De-definition of Culture*, Faber & Faber, London, 1989.

Williams, Gwyn, *Artisans and Sans-Culottes: Popular Movements in France and Britain during the French Revolution*, 2nd edn, Libris, London, 1989.

# 4

# Beyond the Enlightenment: The Philosophical, Scientific and Religious Inheritance

*Peter J. Kitson*

The term 'Romanticism' is usually used to describe a literary and philosophical movement that occurred in the late eighteenth and the early nineteenth centuries. The term is often used to distinguish the thought and literature of the period from that of the late seventeenth and eighteenth centuries, or of the 'Enlightenment', and the expressions 'Enlightenment' and 'Romanticism' are frequently used to suggest contrasting ways of looking at the world.[1] Simply put, such a contrast might be expressed in terms of binary oppositions, such as reason *versus* emotion; objectivity *versus* subjectivity; spontaneity *versus* control; limitation *versus* aspiration; empiricism *versus* transcendentalism; society *versus* the individual; public *versus* private; order *versus* rebellion; the cosmopolitan *versus* the national, and so on. Recent writing, however, has tended to problematize this opposition, arguing that there is not so clean a break between the ideas of the eighteenth century and those of the Age of Romanticism as might at first be apparent.[2] Nevertheless, it can be argued that the canonical Romantic poets were both building upon and reacting against the thought of their predecessors, sometimes breaking with the major trends (as in the case of Coleridge's rejection of Enlightenment empiricism) or alternatively pushing that body of thought into more extreme positions than were usual in the Enlightenment (as with Blake's, Shelley's and Byron's radical scepticism concerning established institutions and their suspicion of the higher claims of idealist thought).

The writers and thinkers of the Enlightenment imagined themselves as emerging from centuries of darkness and ignorance into a new age enlightened by reason, science and a respect for humanity. For Immanuel Kant, who wrote an essay entitled *Was ist Aufklarung?* (What is Enlightenment?), it was a time of humanity's coming of age, a process of mental liberation from the bondage of error and oppression. More than a set of shared beliefs or dogma, the Enlightenment stood for an attitude and a sceptical method of thought. For Kant, the motto of the time was Horace's *Sapere aude* or 'Dare to know'. All received ideas and opinions were to be subject to the light of 'reason'. Enlightenment thought took to extremes the systematic doubt championed by René Descartes in his *Discourse sur la methode* (1637). The great Enlightenment endeavour to collect and systematize all knowledge is best demonstrated in the project of the *Encyclopédie* (1751–72), on which numerous *philosophes* collaborated. Generally, there was an attempt to systematize and codify nature and society. Isaac Newton described the laws of motion and John Locke attempted to delineate the faculties of the mind. In the field of natural philosophy the Swedish naturalist Carl von Linné or Linnaeus designed a system to classify all the plants of the earth according to their reproductive parts in 24 (later 26) basic configurations in his *Systema natura* (1735) and *Philsophica botanica* (1761).[3] J. F. Blumenbach did the same for humanity with his five-fold classification of human types as Caucasian, Mongolian, Ethiopian, American and Malayan in his *De Generis Humani Varietae Nativa* (1775). The first naturalistic account of the earth, including its mineralogical, botanical and zoological productions appeared in Buffon's *Histoire naturelle*, the first three volumes of which appeared in 1749. Buffon's history paid no attention to biblical accounts of creation but, instead, applied Newtonian principles to the natural world. Montesquieu's *De L'esprit des Lois* (1748) revolutionized the way people looked at government and society by showing how it was shaped by outside forces, such as geography, politics, religion and climate, and Adam Smith's *The Wealth of Nations* (1776) applied the scientific method to outline the ways in which a modern economy functioned. Although primarily associated with the French *philosophes*, such as Voltaire, Diderot, Montesquieu and Rousseau, the Scottish philosopher David Hume, and the American thinkers, Benjamin Franklin and Thomas Jefferson, it was from the work of the English thinkers, Thomas Hobbes, John Locke and Isaac Newton, that the Enlightenment took its origins.

# I

For the thinkers of the Enlightenment, knowledge was limited to those things that could be known from the senses. Their thought was predominantly empirical, that is, they believed that knowledge was derived from experience. In this they adopted the scientific method advocated by Francis Bacon, who argued in his *The Advancement of Learning* (1620) that all knowledge must be based on careful observation. Bacon was also sceptical of received opinion, arguing that 'If a man begin in certainties he will end in doubts, but if he begin with doubts he shall end in certainties'. The most celebrated exponent of this doctrine in the late seventeenth century was the British physician and philosopher John Locke. Locke's *Essay Concerning Human Understanding* (1690) laid the foundations of an Enlightenment theory of mind. Locke, following the lead of the seventeenth-century materialist philosopher Thomas Hobbes, dismissed the notion of both neo-Platonists and Rationalists that there existed in the human mind certain innate or *a priori* ideas. For Locke, accepting the knowledge of our own existence (which we have by intuition) and the knowledge of God (which we deduce by the application of reason), all ideas derive from sensation. Locke compared the human mind to a blank sheet of paper upon which experience writes, or to an empty cabinet which experience fills. The human mind is thus originally passive, and knowledge is arrived at by relating the ideas left in the mind by sensation. He distinguished two types of experience: sensation, the mind's perception of the world, and reflection, the mind's perception of its own operation. By reflecting upon simple ideas the mind is able to generate ideas. To account for this process, Locke developed the theory of the 'association of ideas', by which knowledge of an object is built up from the simple ideas of perception. Thus we develop an idea of a snowball from a complex cluster of simple ideas, such as coldness, colour, shape, texture and so forth, which we experience together. As the ideas in the mind were mere representations of the world rather than direct manifestations, Locke denied that we could have knowledge of anything that lacked perceptible qualities, thus strictly limiting the realm of the knowable to things which gave rise to sense impressions.

Locke's empiricism did not go unchallenged, yet the acceptance and popularization of his psychological theories by the *philosophe* and propagandist of the French Enlightenment, Voltaire, assured its success. Voltaire, in a series of publications, combined Descartes's and Bacon's sense of doubt with the empiricism of Locke and Newton. For Wordsworth and Coleridge, however, it was rather the variety of empiricism developed by Locke's admirer David Hartley, in his *Observations on Man* (1749), which most decisively influenced their ideas. Hartley proposed a materialist physiological basis for the working of the association of ideas, by which external objects created vibrations in the mind, thus forming the basis of ideas. Through the process of association we arrive at complex knowledge. For Hartley, we are led by the association of ideas to a sense of morality and of divinity, or, in Hartley's terminology, 'Theopathy'. Hartley's notion is that God has so arranged the world that if we subject ourselves to the right environments we are inevitably led to benevolence and a love of God.

Such ideas were profoundly influential on the work Wordsworth and the early Coleridge, who employed associationist aesthetics as a way of understanding the mind's interaction with nature. In his poem *The Tables Turned* Wordsworth argues that

> One impulse from a vernal wood
> May teach you more of man,
> Of moral evil and of good,
> Than all the sages can.
> (*Romanticism*, p. 236)

In the Preface to *Lyrical Ballads* (1800) he argued that the poems in the collection were written to illustrate the 'primary laws of our nature: chiefly as far as regards the manner in which we associate ideas in a state of excitement'. The *Ballads* took 'low and rustic life' as their subject because in that situation 'the passions of men are incorporated with the beautiful and permanent forms of nature' (*Romanticism*, p. 252). It has frequently been remarked that Wordsworth's psychological and aesthetic theories are deeply rooted in the associationist epistemology of the Enlightenment.[4] Nevertheless, there is something new, perhaps, in Wordsworth's obsessive exploration of the psychology of his own self in his autobiographical poem *The Prelude* (1805). Although one could perhaps reconcile the thought of *Tintern Abbey* with Lockeian psychology where 'the mighty world' of sense impression is perceived and 'half-created', it is not so easy to dove-tail the poem's hesitant transcendentalism with Locke's stricter limitations of knowledge:

> a sense sublime
> Of something far more deeply interfused,
> Whose dwelling is the light of setting suns,
> And the round ocean, and the living air,
> And the blue sky, and in the mind of man –

A motion and a spirit, that impels
All thinking things, all objects of all thought,
And rolls through all things.

(*Romanticism*, pp. 242–3)

William Blake's rejection of the empiricist tradition, or 'the philosophy of the five senses', was more extreme. In *There is no natural religion* Blake claimed, in contradistinction to Locke and Hartley, that 'Man's perceptions are not bounded by organs of perception. He perceives more than sense (though ever so acute) can discover' (*Romanticism*, p. 50). For Blake, empiricism was a shallow and arid philosophy, and his writings are replete with attacks upon the 'mind forg'd manacles' ('London', *Romanticism*, p. 73) it imposed. The most sustained, philosophical attack upon empiricism by a Romantic poet, however, was carried out by Coleridge. He began his intellectual life as an admiring disciple of the psychology of Hartley. Never an adherent of the materialism of the French Enlightenment, Coleridge found Hartley's blend of Christian moralism with associationist epistemology very congenial, so much so that he named his first-born son Hartley Coleridge. Much of Coleridge's poetry of the 1790s presents a situation where the subject is passive, receptive to sense impressions, especially the poems *Frost at Midnight*, *The Ancient Mariner* and *The Eolian Harp*. Coleridge, however, had always had an interest in other models of the human mind. He found the work of the Anglo-Irish cleric George Berkeley fascinating. Berkeley questioned Locke's distinction between primary and secondary qualities, arguing that both were contingent on the workings of the human mind: thus, he concluded that there was no reality independent of the mind, *esse est percipi*. Coleridge fused such idealist notions with older Platonic suggestions, which he found in his reading of such seventeenth-century divines and mystics as Ralph Cudworth and Jacob Boehme, in poems such as *The Destiny of Nations* (1796) and *Frost at Midnight*. As the end of the century loomed, Coleridge began to feel uneasy about a philosophy which stressed the passivity of the mind in perception. It was, however, the work of the German philosopher Immanuel Kant which finally allowed him to break with the empiricist model of the mind. Prior to Kant, the British philosopher David Hume had taken the scepticism of the Enlightenment to its logical conclusion. In his *Treatise of Human Nature* (1739–40) Hume argued that the notions that we have of cause and effect are simply linked to the way in which we experience the events in space and time and that such notions of causation have no objective existence. Thus, one's knowledge of causation is a matter of habit or custom, not a logical certainty. Hume expressed radical scepticism about the nature of the human self, concluding that what one called the self was merely an ever-changing 'bundle of sensations'. It was this position that Kant inherited when he effected his 'Copernican revolution' in European thought and laid the foundations for the 'Romantic' Idealism of Schelling, Kante, Fichte and Hegel in Germany and for that of Coleridge, De Quincey and Carlyle in Britain.

In his *Critique of Pure Reason* (1781) Kant attempted to reconcile the claims of empiricism with those of rationalism and Platonism, or the idea that there existed in the mind certain innate or *a priori* ideas. He argued by an exhaustive process of deduction that all knowledge derives from experience yet it is dependant on *a priori* or, in his terms, 'transcendental' structures in the mind, such as the concepts of space and time. For Kant, such concepts were present in the mind and not absolutes of experience. Kant was thus led to distinguish between that which is knowable, the representation of the object in the human mind, and that which is unknowable, the pure object or the 'thing-in-itself' (*ding in sich*). As well as the concepts of space and time, Kant argued that notions of God, freedom and eternity were likewise part of the transcendent realm, unknowable in themselves, but necessary for us to make sense of reality. The attraction of Kant's philosophy to Coleridge and the Romantics was that it assigned an active and creative role to the mind in the formation of human knowledge. Furthermore, Kant allowed an important role for the artistic imagination which had been somewhat restrained in the empiricist writings of Hobbes, Locke, Hartley and Hume. In the *Critique of Judgement* (1790) Kant distinguished between three kinds or powers of imagination. The first is the *reproductive imagination*, which is close to the Lockeian mode of the association of ideas. The second is the *productive imagination*, which operates between sense perception and allows us to carry on the work of discursive reasoning. The third is the *aesthetic imagination*, which is free of the laws which govern the understanding and which works through symbols. Kant's three-fold distinction corresponds to Coleridge's famous division of the powers of the mind in chapter XIII of *Biographia Literaria* into the *fancy*, the *primary imagination* and the *secondary imagination*. The fancy receives all its materials 'ready made from the law of association' and corresponds to the empiricist explanation of the mind. The primary imagination is the faculty which mediates between sensation and perception, actively ordering these faculties into a body of knowledge. Without this principle they would simply be a mere 'chaos of sense impressions'. For Coleridge, imagination is 'the living power and prime agent of all human perception', it is a creative power analogous to the divine, 'a repetition in the finite mind of the eternal act of creation in the infinite I AM'. The secondary imagination, which corresponds to Kant's aesthetic imagination, is that which deals with artistic creation:

> The secondary imagination I consider as an echo of the former, co-existing with the conscious will, yet still as identical with the primary in the *kind* of its agency, and differing only in *degree*, and in the *mode* of its operation. It dissolves, diffuses, dissipates, in order to recreate; or, where this process is rendered impossible, yet still at all events it struggles to idealize and to unify. It is essentially *vital*, even as all objects (*as* objects) are essentially fixed and dead. (*Romanticism*, p. 574).

The workings of the primary imagination are involuntary and it belongs to all, but the secondary imagination is the artistic imagination, under the conscious control of the will struggling to unify the patterns of experience into an artistic whole.

Coleridge's sophisticated philosophisings were not common among the Romantic poets. Byron, the most empiricist of the Romantics, wished, in *Don Juan*, that Coleridge 'would explain his explanation' (*Romanticism*, p. 770). Nevertheless, most of them accepted the high valuation placed on the creative imagination. Wordsworth makes the creative imagination the hero of spiritual autobiography in *The Prelude*. It is akin to the creative powers of nature and is 'reason in her most exalted mood' (*Romanticism*, pp. 465–7). Shelley, who did not share Coleridge's notion of the transcendent, nevertheless complained of the limitations of empiricism. In *The Sensitive Plant* he expresses this dissatisfaction in terms derived from neo-Platonic thought:

> But in this life
> Of error, ignorance and strife,
> Where nothing is, but all things seem
> And we are shadows of the dream
>
> For love, and beauty, and delight,
> There is no death or change: their might
> Exceeds our organs, which endure
> No light, being themselves obscure.[5]

Shelley's absolutes are, of course, not Kant's and Coleridge's God, freedom and immortality, but the human ideals of love, beauty and delight. In *The Defence of Poetry* Shelley clearly distinguishes the empirical reason from the higher imaginative powers of the mind: 'Reason is the enumeration of quantities already known; imagination is the perception of the value of those qualities . . . Reason is to Imagination as the instrument to the agent, as the body to the spirit, as the shadow to the substance' (*Romanticism*, p. 956). Thus, we see how the Romantics adopted and developed trends in Enlightenment philosophy. Even Coleridge never rejected associationism completely, but found it to be an accurate way of describing the operations of the fancy and the understanding as powers of the mind. He came to believe, however, that it only described half the story and left undiscovered the workings of the higher intuitive faculty of the mind which he named, following Kant, as the 'Reason' (*Vernunft*).

## II

It is in the field of scientific thought that the Romantic reaction against Enlightenment ideas is most clearly visible, although this is only the case if we take Enlightenment science as synonymous with Newtonian science. Certainly, Newtonian thought dominated the early Enlightenment, although other theories of matter were current and available.

Newton laid the foundations for the progress in science of the time. He was one of the principal discoverers of the calculus in mathematics, he solved some of the mysteries of light and optics and, most importantly, he formulated the three laws of motion and derived from them the law of universal gravitation. His great work *Principia* (1687) demonstrated that gravity was a property of matter in motion and that it was the same force for all bodies. The planets were kept in motion by the attractive power of the sun. Thus, the universe is filled with space (or alternatively Newton speculated with the existence of an omnipresent medium called 'ether'). What Newton effectively did was, like Locke, to banish God (or the first cause) from the realm of the physical world, which became solely the arena of physical forces (or second causes). Although Newton hypothesized the universe to be a great machine, his system also had strong religious overtones. He demonstrated that motion is always decaying and that the earth's axis was slipping from its proper place. Such defects could be remedied only by the direct intervention of God. Newton believed that rather than establishing a belief in materialism, he had, instead, given a scientific demonstration of the necessity for the existence of a Supreme Being, if not necessarily the God of Christianity. Indeed, Newton devoted much critical energy in explicating the prophetical books of the Bible in manuscripts posthumously published as *Observations upon the Prophecies of Daniel and the Apocalypse of St John*. It was Voltaire's popularization of Newton's work, *Les Elémens de la philosophie de Newton* (1738), which introduced his ideas to a wider audience and established them as the cornerstone of Enlightenment science.

It was not science but Newtonian science that the Romantics reacted against. It was as though the banishing of the divine from nature had emptied the world of its mystery. It was this demystification of nature that they resented. Although the vehemence of Blake's denunciations of Newtonianism is not typical, its general drift is. Blake showed a constant and total opposition to Newton and his works. This can be seen in his famous depiction of Newton sitting on a rock, examining on the floor in front of him a geometrical figure of a triangle within a circle and measuring the base of the triangle with a pair of compasses, thus ignoring the wonders of the stars and the heavens to concentrate on abstract reasoning. In *The Song of Los* (c.1795), Blake mythologizes the institution of Enlightenment thought, whereby 'a philosophy of five senses' is given 'into the hands of Newton and Locke' by a weeping Urizen, while 'Clouds roll heavy upon the Alps round Rousseau and Voltaire'.[6] In *Jerusalem* Blake writes of the 'Loom of Locke' being washed by 'the Water-wheels of Newton'.[7] Almost as hostile is Keats's dismissal of Newton's science of optics in *Lamia* (1817):

> Do not all charms fly
> At the mere touch of cold philosophy?
> There was an awful rainbow once in heaven:
> We know her woof, her texture; she is given
> In the dull catalogue of common things.
> Philosophy will clip an Angel's wings,
> Conquer all mysteries by rule and line,
> Empty the haunted air, and gnomèd mine –
> Unweave a rainbow.[8]

Keats's criticism of contemporary science's tendency to demystify the world may have echoed Wordsworth's warning against an overweening analytical faculty in *The Tables Turned*, whereby 'Our meddling intellect / Misshapes the beauteous form of things – / We murder to dissect' (*Romanticism*, p. 236). Yet Wordsworth also had a high regard for 'great Newton's own etherial self' (*Prelude*, II. 270; *Romanticism*, p. 316) and for his achievements in science. His main anxiety was that such scientific triumphs might obscure the higher truth of poetry. In Book Five of *The Prelude*, he describes an apocalyptic dream of Coleridge's where the dreamer encounters a Bedouin Arab who carries a stone and a shell, respectively symbols of science and of poetry. Both are precious and are to be saved from the oncoming deluge. The stone represents 'the adamantine holds of truth / By reason built', but the shell the Arab tells 'Is something of more worth . . . A god – yea, many gods' (lines 38–9, 71–114; *Romanticism*, pp. 337–8).

Although Newton's work dominated the scientific thought of the Enlightenment it did not go unchallenged. The late eighteenth-century reaction against the mechanistic conception of nature and its growing preference for an organic model to describe the world, which many have seen as the important discriminator between Enlightenment and Romantic attitudes, had its origins in the Enlightenment itself.[9] Newton's great rival, the German philosopher Gottfried Wilhelm von Leibniz, provided an alternative hypothesis to explain the natural world. Against Newton's explanation of matter as composed of solid particles acted upon by external forces, Leibniz argued in his *Monadology* (1714) that the universe is composed of countless centres of spiritual force or energy, programmed by God at the beginning of time, known as monads. Each monad represents an individual microcosm, mirroring the universe in varying degrees of perfection. Leibniz maintained that such a harmonious arrangement was a part of the divine plan and that any apparent evil in the universe could be explained away as subservient to a higher good. This Leibnizian order was ruthlessly satirized in Voltaire's *Candide* (1759) in the character of Dr Pangloss, who believes all is for the best in 'the best of all possible worlds'. This notion that matter is active, made up from forces of energy, was then also available in the Enlightenment. It seems to have attracted the young Coleridge.[10] Although intensely admiring of Newton, he was critical of those trends in Newtonian thought which banished the first cause to the realm of the unknowable and thus provided an encouragement for materialism and atheism. In *The Destiny of Nations* (1796) Newton is among the 'modern sages' who cheat themselves 'With noisy emptiness of learnèd phrase' of second causes, thus 'Untenanting creation of its God'.[11] For Coleridge, Newton gave us a conception of God as 'alternately operose and indolent'.[12] It seems that Coleridge, although fascinated by Newton's discoveries, never accepted his materialist assumptions about matter upon which they were premised, preferring instead a vitalistic theory closer to that of Leibniz's monadology. Later on in *The Destiny of Nations* Coleridge raises the possibility that matter is composed of 'Infinite myriads of self-conscious minds' making up 'one all-conscious Spirit' who directs 'his component Monads'.[13] In coming to his belief in a vitalistic universe Coleridge may have had the work of the British theologian and natural philosopher Joseph Priestley in mind. Priestley's *Disquisitions concerning Matter and Spirit* (1777) argued that every atom was a point of force acting by means of attraction and repulsion on its neighbours. These *foci* of energy were organized by the Deity, and the physical world was made up of his energy.[14] Like Priestley, the young Coleridge denied that matter and spirit were distinct properties. A similar view of matter was held by Coleridge's friend, the chemist Sir Humphry Davy, who strongly supported the dynamic view of nature in several publications from 1799 onwards. It is also possible that Coleridge was reverting to an older pre-Newtonian, neo-Platonic view of nature. This sense of nature as vital leads in the direction of pantheism, where God is immanent in nature and not transcendent. In *The Eolian Harp* Coleridge asks

> And what if all of animated nature
> Be but organic harps diversely fram'd,
> That tremble into thought, as o'er them sweeps,
> Plastic and vast, one intellectual breeze,
> At once the soul of each and God of all?
>
> (*Romanticism*, p. 506)

For Coleridge, pantheism was always a tempting option but one which he struggled to resist all his life.[15] So, too, Shelley, who was fascinated by contemporary scientific theories, hypothesized the activity of matter. His character Eusebes in the dialogue *A Refutation of Deism* (1814) perhaps speaks for the poet when he argues that 'Matter is not inert. It is infinitely active and subtile'.[16] The speculations of the Shelley circle concerning the origins and nature of the vital force were reflected in Mary Shelley's Gothic novel *Frankenstein* (1818, revised 1831) which, many have argued, functions as a critique of Enlightenment scientific aspiration. The novel is informed by debates in contemporary science and Victor Frankenstein combines the pre-Newtonian obsession with the first cause with an awareness of the achievements of the eighteenth century. Victor's tutor Waldman tells him how

> The ancient teachers of this science . . . promised impossibilities, and performed nothing. The modern masters promise very little; they know that metals cannot be transmuted, and that the elixir of life is a chimera. But these philosophers, whose hands seem only made to dabble in dirt, and their eyes to pore over the microscope or crucible, have indeed performed miracles. They penetrate into the recesses of nature, and show how she works in her hiding places. They ascend into the heavens: they have discovered how the blood circulates, and the nature of the air we breathe. They have acquired new and almost unlimited powers; they can command the thunders of heaven, mimic the earthquake, and even mock the invisible world with its own shadows.[17]

It is important to stress that such intellectual enquiries as those of Coleridge and Percy and Mary Shelley represent as much an engagement with the substantial body of scientific thought that had arisen from debates within the Enlightenment as a rejection of it.

## III

It was in the area of religion that mainstream Enlightenment thought most obviously showed itself as advocating an 'Age of Reason'. The eighteenth century developed a new sense of historical time. Up to the middle of the eighteenth century it was commonly accepted that the universe was the special creation of the God of Christianity. The seventeenth-century divine, Archbishop Usher, painstakingly working through Old Testament chronology, found that the creation occurred around 4,004 BC. Buffon's *Natural History* (1749–) showed that the earth must be much older than this. Work in the geological sciences (especially that of James Hutton later in the century) challenged the biblical account of the age of the earth and the accuracy of stories of the flood.[18] The *philosophes* used the insights of natural philosophy to challenge the beliefs and institutions of the Catholic Church in France and established religion elsewhere. Although very few Enlightenment thinkers were actually atheists, preferring a form of belief known as Deism which accepted the existence of a Supreme Being in accordance with Newtonian science but which denied any dogma associated with belief, they vehemently attacked the super-stition and corruption they believed to exist in the eighteenth-century Church; their object was, in Voltaire's famous phrase, to *Écrasez l'infame* of organized religion.[19]

John Locke's *The Reasonableness of Christianity* (1694) had maintained that Christianity was compatible with reason, but this meant removing those irrational elements from belief and establishing a kind of minimum programme where a belief in obscurities and mysteries was not regarded as essential to salvation. David Hume took Locke's scepticism much further. Hume employed his sceptical philosophy to demolish the argument from design (that the existence of God could be demonstrated from the creation). Hume further argued in his *Natural History of Religion* (1757) that no reasonable man could believe in miracles. The great eighteenth-century historian Edward Gibbon in his *Decline and Fall of the Roman Empire* (1776–) postulated that it was a barbaric Christianity that was responsible for the destruction of the civilized Roman Empire and that Christianity was merely another form of paganism. Thomas Paine's *The Age of Reason* (Part I, Paris, 1794; Part II, London, 1795) further demystified Christian orthodoxy seeking to establish a pure Deism. Paine regarded the Bible as a mixture of poetry and 'trash'. The natural philosopher and theologian Joseph Priestley, in numerous works, attempted to purge Christianity of its 'corruptions' and re-establish a pure Christianity which was fully compatible with the dictates of reason. Priestley became a Unitarian Christian who believed in the full humanity of Christ. His work was profoundly influential on the early Coleridge who, in the 1790s, professed himself to be a Unitarian Christian and preached at Unitarian meetings. Although in Britain the Enlightenment may have conducted its debates primarily in terms of piety, and in France in terms of natural religion, it did have its atheistic and materialistic wing, including such figures as Diderot, Baron d'Holbach, Maupertuis, and later in the century Constantin Volney, Charles Dupuis, William Godwin and Erasmus Darwin. Generally, such writers proposed a materialist and deterministic account of nature and of the mind and they regarded religion as the response of primitive societies to the forms of a nature whose workings they could not comprehend.

Towards the end of the eighteenth century biblical scholarship itself entered a new and more sophisticated phase with the 'higher criticism' originating from the scholarship of J. G. Eichhorn. Eichhorn's *Introduction to the Old Testament* (1780–3) argued that the Bible was analogous to a work of art and thus it should be analysed in terms which reflect its status as a conscious artefact rather than as the literal truth of God's word.[20] This was not an influential theory in British intellectual circles until later in the nineteenth century, when it was reflected in the essays of Matthew Arnold (such as *Literature and Dogma*, 1873) and the novels of George Eliot. Coleridge, however, did know Eichhorn's work. He attended his lectures at the University of Göttingen while in Germany in 1798, and, although he disagreed with Eichhorn as to the purely aesthetic nature of scripture, his comments on the symbolism of the Bible in works such as *The Statesman's Manual* (1817) show his assimilation of higher critical thought. For Coleridge, the truths of the Bible were primarily spiritual and symbolic rather than literal: 'the living *educts* of the Imagination'.[21] Although often opposed to institutional forms of religion, all the Romantics (including Byron) held a high view of the Bible as a repository of deep spiritual and artistic truths.

The modernist writer T. E. Hulme memorably described the Romantic poets as the 'proponents of spilt religion' and it is true that Blake, Wordsworth and Coleridge, in their different ways, attempted to restore a sense of spirituality to man and nature in the wake of the Enlightenment assault on the traditional forms of Christianity. It was generally perceived that the Church of England had become inert and remote from people's lives, staffed by absentee clerics who accepted generous stipends and spent their times in leisure pursuits. In many ways the Romantics responded to the new currents of feeling that arose in the last quarter of the eighteenth century as a reaction to the aridity of much enlightened rationalist thought and which manifested themselves in such diverse ways as Rousseau's cult of sensibility in France, the *Sturm und Drang* movement in Germany, and in the Methodist movement begun by John Wesley and the Evangelical Revival of Christianity in Britain. The fervid emotionalism of the brand of Christianity practised by John and Charles Wesley has often been likened to the stress on feeling and passion to be found in all the canonical Romantic poets.[22] In religious thought there was a renewed stress on the individual's personal relation to God. Indeed, M. H. Abrams argued influentially that what the Romantic poets did in essence was to secularize and naturalize the founding myths of the Judaeo-Christian religion, internalizing Eden, the Fall and the New Jerusalem into states of the human mind: innocence, experience and restoration.[23]

The late eighteenth century was also a time when religious sects usually organized around charismatic individuals and espousing apocalyptic brands of mystical thought multiplied. William Blake was, for a time, attracted to the writings of the Swedish mystic Emmanuel Swedenborg and attended the New Jerusalem Church of his disciples in Eastcheap before repudiating Swedenborgian teachings in *The Marriage of Heaven and Hell* (1790). Various millenarian prophets and sects arose in the 1790s identifying the French Revolution with the prophecies of Daniel and Revelation. Most notable were the popular prophets Richard Brothers and Joanna Southcott, but they were only two of many.[24] This reading of political events in terms of biblical prophecy attracted both plebeian and polite audiences. Joseph Priestley accepted that the French Revolution had been foretold in Revelation and Coleridge's philosophical and religious poem *Religious Musings* versified a similarly political interpretation of prophecy. The whole notion of the poet as prophet which is so dear to Blake, Wordsworth, Coleridge and Shelley can be seen as, in part, a response to this upsurge in the apocalyptic expectations raised by the French Revolution. In the context of the popular millenarian prophets, the working-class visionary William Blake no longer appears as an idiosyncratic and isolated individual. Fuelling this equation of the poet with the prophet was Robert Lowth's rediscovery earlier in the century of the principles which lay behind Hebrew poetry and which informed the prophecies of Holy Writ. Lowth's *Lectures on the Sacred Poetry of the Hebrews* (Latin 1753; translated 1787) established the Romantic claim that the highest form of poetry was prophecy which mediated divine truth and which also enhanced the status of the poet in an age of material and scientific progress.[25]

All the canonical Romantic poets worked within the contexts established by Christianity and, although they may have been at times hostile to the established institutions of Church and State, they can all be called Christians in some sense. Coleridge travelled the intellectual path from Priestley's Unitarianism to the Trinitarianism and Anglicanism of his later years. His Christianity was always, however, a sophisticated blend of theological, philosophical and political speculation. In his late treatise *On the Constitution of the Church and State* (1830) he argued for a revival of the Anglican Church according to the theory of a National Church which would provide a cultural and spiritual balance reconciling the forces of permanence (the landed gentry) and progression (the mercantile spirit) which were at work in the land. This National Church would educate the nation through the means of a 'clerisy', a body of men who would act as a repository for the cultural and spiritual inheritance of the nation. Wordsworth, despite his strong pantheistic beliefs, conformed to Anglicanism in later life.

Blake's religious sense was always singular but he accepted the ideals of 'mercy, pity, peace and love' which he believed to be the message preached by Christ ('The Divine Image', *Romanticism*, p. 60). In *The Marriage of Heaven and Hell* he presents a demonic reading of Christianity, criticizing its oppressive institutional forms which ossify the creative and prophetic energies into restrictive dogma and imprisoning codes of belief: 'Thus men forgot that all deities reside in the human breast' (*Romanticism*, p. 82). It was Shelley, however, who was the closest of all the Romantics to the Enlightenment scepticism rejected by Coleridge and Wordsworth. In a series of prose treatises, *The Necessity of Atheism* (1811), *A Refutation of Deism* (1814), *On Christianity* (1817) and *On the Doctrines of Christ* (1817), he argued in clear Enlightenment terms, informed by the work of Hume, d'Holbach, Godwin and Volney, against the superstitions and irrationalities of orthodox Christianity. For Shelley, Christ was the pattern of a benevolent reformer who preached equality and pacifism, but whose message was distorted and perverted by vested interests. Like Blake, Shelley had a tendency to equate the God of the Old Testament with restriction and restraint and to view the Satanic as positive energy. Shelley identified what others called 'God' with a mysterious creative power at work in the universe, although in poems such as *Mont Blanc* he depicted this power as remote, destructive and unknowable. Like Coleridge, Shelley was also very interested in esoteric philosophies and religions and he often used ideas and images from the philosophies of Gnosticism, Manichaeism, Zoroasterianism and Platonism in his poetry.[26] Even Byron, usually regarded as the least religious of the Romantics, was drawn to religious subjects. His work, especially *Cain* (1821), also shows a revisionary engagement with scripture. Generally, Byron's poetry presents a sceptical and non-conformist voice in religious matters, yet most critics now agree that his work also contains an underlying religious sense.[27] The Romantics therefore can be seen to respond to the challenging intellectual debates that had begun with the Enlightenment project and to respond to its implications in matters of science, philosophy and religion.

## NOTES

1 Abrams *ML*; Wellek, 'The Concept of Romanticism', pp. 113–17.
2 Butler, *Romantics, Rebels and Reactionaries*; Bewell, *Wordsworth and the Enlightenment*.
3 Larson, *Interpreting Nature*.
4 Abrams *ML*, pp. 103–4; Butler, *Romantics, Rebels and Reactionaries*, p. 57.
5 *Shelley: Selected Poems*, pp. 100–1.
6 *Blake: The Complete Poems*, pp. 244–5.
7 Ibid., p. 259.
8 *Keats: The Complete Poems*, pp. 645–6.
9 For this, see Abrams *ML*, pp. 156–217.
10 Wylie, *Young Coleridge*.
11 Beer, p. 112.
12 EHC, II, p. 1113.
13 Beer, pp. 112–13.
14 Piper, *The Active Universe*, pp. 33–7; see also Wylie, *Young Coleridge*.
15 McFarland, *Coleridge and the Pantheist Tradition*.
16 *The Prose Works of Percy Bysshe Shelley*, I, p. 116.
17 Shelley, *Frankenstein*, pp. 47–8.
18 Hampson, *The Enlightenment*, pp. 218–50.
19 Manuel, *The Eighteenth Century Confronts the Gods*.
20 Prickett, 'The religious context', pp. 115–63, pp. 153–6; Shaffer, '*Kubla Khan*'.
21 CC *Lay Sermons*.

22  Prickett, 'The religious context', pp. 125–9.
23  Abrams, *Natural Supernaturalism*.
24  Harrison, *The Second Coming*; McCalman, *Radical Underworld*; Mee, *Dangerous Enthusiasm*.

25  Prickett, 'The religious context', pp. 144–51.
26  Shelley, *Shelley and Scripture*, pp. 1–14.
27  Hirst, *Byron, the Bible and Religion*, pp. 9–24.

## WRITINGS

Allott, Miriam (ed.) *Keats: The Complete Poems*, Longman, Harlow, 1970.

Murray, E. B. (ed.) *The Prose Works of Percy Bysshe Shelley*, vol. I, Clarendon Press, Oxford, 1993.

Shelley, Mary, *Frankenstein*, ed. M. K. Joseph, Oxford University Press, Oxford, 1980.

Stevenson, W. H. (ed.) *Blake: The Complete Poems*, 2nd edn, Longman, Harlow, 1989.

Webb, Timothy (ed.) *Shelley: Selected Poems*, Dent, London, 1977.

## REFERENCES AND FURTHER READING

Abrams, M. H., *Natural Supernaturalism: Tradition and Revolution in Romantic Literature*, W. W. Norton, New York and London, 1971.

Bewell, A., *Wordsworth and the Enlightenment: Nature, Man, and Society in the Experimental Poetry*, Yale University Press, New Haven and London, 1989.

Butler, M. *Romantics, Rebels and Reactionaries: English Literature and its Background 1760–1830*, Oxford University Press, Oxford, 1982.

Cunningham, A. and Jardine, Nicholas, *Romanticism and the Sciences*, Cambridge University Press, Cambridge, 1990.

Engel, J., *The Creative Imagination: Enlightenment to Romanticism*, Harvard University Press, Cambridge, Mass., 1981.

Gaull, M., *English Romanticism: The Human Context*, W. W. Norton, New York, 1988.

Gay, P., *The Enlightenment: An Interpretation*, 2 vols, Weidenfeld and Nicolson, London, 1970.

Hampson, N., *The Enlightenment: An Evaluation of its Assumptions, Attitudes and Values*, Penguin, Harmondsworth, 1968.

Harrison, J. C. F., *The Second Coming: Popular Millenarianism 1780–1850*, Routledge & Kegan Paul, London, 1979.

Hirst, W. Z. (ed.) *Byron, the Bible and Religion: Essays from the Twelfth International Byron Seminar*, University of Delaware Press, Newark, 1991.

Larson, J. L., *Interpreting Nature: The Science of Living Form from Linnaeus to Kant*, Johns Hopkins University Press, Baltimore and London, 1994.

McCalman, I., *Radical Underworld: Prophets, Revolutionaries and Pornographers in London 1795–1840*, Clarendon Press, Oxford, 1988.

McFarland, T., *Coleridge and the Pantheist Tradition*, Oxford University Press, Oxford, 1969.

Manuel, F. E., *The Eighteenth Century Confronts the Gods*, Atheneum, New York, 1967.

Mee, J., *Dangerous Enthusiasm: William Blake and the Culture of Radicalism in the 1790s*, Clarendon Press, Oxford, 1992.

Piper, H. W., *The Active Universe: Pantheist and the Concept of Imagination in the English Romantic Poets*, Athlone Press, London, 1962.

Prickett, S., 'The religious context', in *The Romantics: The Context of English Literature*, Methuen, London, 1981.

—— *Words and the Word: Language, Poetics, and Biblical Interpretation*, Cambridge University Press, Cambridge, 1986.

Shaffer, E. S., *'Kubla Khan' and 'The Fall of Jerusalem': The Mythological School in Biblical Criticism and Secular Literature 1770–1880*, Cambridge University Press, Cambridge, 1975.

Shelley, B., *Shelley and Scripture: The Interpreting Angel*, Clarendon Press, Oxford, 1994.

Wellek, R., 'The concept of Romanticism in literary history', in *Concepts of Criticism*, Yale University Press, New Haven and London, 1963.

Wylie, I., *Young Coleridge and the Philosophers of Nature*, Clarendon Press, Oxford, 1989.

# 5

# Britain at War: The Historical Context

*Philip Shaw*

Oh, bloody and most bootless Waterloo,
Which proves how fools may have their fortune too
Won, half by blunder, half by treachery;
Oh, dull Saint Helen! with thy jailer nigh –
Hear! hear! Prometheus from his rock appeal
To earth, air, ocean, all that felt or feel
His power and glory, all who yet shall hear
A name eternal as the rolling year;

        . . .

A single step into the wrong has given
His name a doubt to all the winds of heaven;
The reed of Fortune, and of thrones the rod,
Of Fame the Moloch or the demigod;
His country's Caesar, Europe's Hannibal,
Without their decent dignity of fall.[1]

## I

On 18 June 1815, Napoleon Bonaparte, the so-called 'scourge of Europe', was finally defeated at the Battle of Waterloo. Initial reactions to the Allied victory were divided. As Tory bards prepared to eulogise the heroic Wellington, younger liberal writers were openly unsure about their feelings. Whether Napoleon was seen as the betrayer of revolutionary ideals or as the apotheosis of high Romantic identity, his commanding presence had made a difference. The tragically inclined Lord Byron received the loss as a personal blow. The radicals Hazlitt, Thelwall and Godwin were reportedly stunned. Even the unsympathetic Shelley, who had described the Emperor as a 'tyrant', a 'slave' who 'danc[ed] and revel[ed] on the grave / Of Liberty',[2] could yet admit that with his defeat, that 'master theme of the epoch in which we live – the French Revolution',[3] had come to a close.

What then were the political consequences of this event? For working-class radicals the wars of 1793–1815 'had been a deliberate attempt by the British aristocracy to crush revolution and support despotism and tyranny on the continent because they feared the triumph of liberalism and democracy at home'.[4] To the more moderate Whig opposition the conflict had been both unjust and unnecessary. Whilst its conclusion was generally welcomed its settlement seemed less than satisfactory: with power back in the hands of the *ancien régime*, the cause of liberty and reform seemed like a distant dream.[5] Conservatives, meanwhile, basked in the warmth of reflected glory. To the Liverpool administration, Waterloo marked the culmination of a long and bitter struggle between warring principles: on the one hand the cause of King, Church and Constitution; on the other the forces of mob-rule, atheism and anarchy. With the fall of Napoleon, so the argument ran, the peace and stability of Europe had been secured. By 1851, the argument had become orthodoxy, allowing Sir Edmund Creasy to proclaim, in a striking anticipation of current 'end-of-history' debates, that the age of global conflict was at an end. The waste and ruin of war had given way to the bloodless conflicts of economic competition: 'in the arts that minister to our race's support and happiness, and not to its suffering and destruction'. Moreover, its passing had allowed Britain to expand its dominion overseas. With 17 new colonies, the nation was more than ever the leading power in the world:

> No battle-field ever witnessed a victory more noble, than that, which England, under her Sovereign Lady [Queen Victoria] and Royal Prince [Albert], is now teaching the peoples of the earth to achieve over selfish prejudices and international feuds, in the great cause of the general promotion of the industry and welfare of mankind.[6]

With hindsight this is, of course, an extraordinarily fatuous claim. When Creasy adopted Byron's comment, 'Thou first and last of fields, king-making victory!',[7] as an epigram for Waterloo he seems unaware of the characteristic irony with which the poet imbued his sense of the event. In this respect the *Fifteen Decisive Battles* reads like a typical product of its times: confident, optimistic and bullish. It is possible, however, to detect beneath the surface rhetoric a self-subversive undertow, at odds with the prevailing tone of triumph and elation. For whilst Creasy may have wished to regard Waterloo as the closing chapter on a history of violence and destruction, there is a compelling sense in which the new era of peaceful expansion falls short of the passions evoked in a clash of arms. In common with a number of contemporary documents – one thinks especially of Arnold's 1853 Preface to *Poems* or of Carlyle's *Heroes and Hero Worship* (1843) – the modern age lacked the essential ingredient of heroism. As 'dark and dreadful' as it was, the master theme of the Romantic period retained a tremendous emotional potency. To understand the full significance of the age of conflict in British culture we must return to the events that gave it its birth.

## II

The French Revolution began life as a political *coup de théâtre*. Its effects were immediate and lasting. On 9 August 1789, shortly after the fall of the Bastille, the Whig politician Edmund Burke wrote in a letter to Lord Charlemont:

> Our thoughts of everything at home are suspended, by our astonishment at the wonderful Spectacle which is exhibited in a Neighbouring and rival Country – what Spectator and what

actors. England gazing with astonishment at the French struggle for Liberty and not knowing whether to blame or applaud![8]

Burke's astonishment at the sublime spectacle unfolding before him was tempered swiftly by the belief that 'the [French] people are not fit for Liberty, and must have a Strong hand like that of their former masters to coerce them'. The letter set the pattern, not only for the chauvinistic characterizations of Burke's *Reflections on the Revolution in France* (1790) but also for a long line of similarly prejudicial pamphlets, articles and reviews. To establishment observers, the French were an ill-disciplined, unruly and unconstrained people. Unlike the English, who in the previous year had celebrated the centenary of their own constitutional revolution, the French lacked the civilizing qualities of tolerance, good sense and moderation: 'Those who have made the exhibition of the 14th of July are capable of every evil. They do not commit crimes for their designs; but they form designs that they may commit crimes. It is not their necessity, but their nature that impels them'. By 1791, following the flight of the monarchy and their subsequent imprisonment, Burke was predicting a long and total war:

> The mode of civilized war will not be practised; nor are the French who act on the present system entitled to expect it. They, whose known policy is to assassinate every citizen whom they suspect of tyranny . . . must look for no modified hostility. . . . The hell-hounds of war, on all sides, will be uncoupled and unmuzzled. The new school of murder and barbarism, set up in Paris, having destroyed (so far as it lies) all the other manners and principles which have hitherto civilized Europe, will destroy also the mode of civilized war, which more than anything else, has distinguished the christian world.[9]

The energies aroused in Burke by the revolution led to his adoption of an increasingly apocalyptic tone. In his *Remarks on the Policy of the Allies* (1793) he describes the struggle against France as a 'religious war'; in the second of the *Letters on a Regicide Peace* (1796) it is a 'new crusade'.[10] It is important to remember that prior to the revolution wars were not regarded as ideological; they were certainly not the result of a clash of 'systems'. For the most part, conflicts were provoked by territorial disputes fuelled by economic considerations. As Clive Emsley has written, 'the governing classes of the *ancien régime* had more in common with each other than with many of those whom they ruled, and in war they did not seek unconditional surrender or the total destruction of their enemies'.[11] Military campaigns were limited affairs, conducted by small armies under the command of the governing classes; often their troops had little or no emotional attachment to their country or its cause. The concepts of nationality and patriotism were, as we shall see, largely the product of the Napoleonic era. Burke recognized that the 'armed doctrine' of the revolutionary government represented an entirely new force in world politics. It would take more than an army of paid hirelings to defeat it.

From the outset, however, it was evident that the patriotic resistance Burke wished for would not be immediately forthcoming. Many Britons, inspired by memories of the Glorious Revolution, regarded the events in France as an echo of their own struggle against monarchical tyranny. The nation was divided between conservatives and reformists; between those calling for an extension of the popular rights won during the English Revolution and those who feared a descent into anarchy. Support for the French cause came from a range of quarters: from the Foxite Whigs – the liberal wing of the party opposed to the conservatives Burke, Windham and the Duke of Portland – to the popular reformist groups headed by the London Corresponding Society and the Society for Constitutional Information. Official tolerance of revolutionary sympathizers was, however, to be short-lived. By 1792, enraged by the Revolutionary government's confrontation with the Dutch (whose security Britain had sworn to defend), and fearful of the effects of 'French principles' on the general public, the government of Pitt the younger sought to mobilize opinion against the French. It found overt support for this aim in the form of the Association for Preserving Liberty and Property against Republicans and Levellers. Set up to check the spread of liberal ideas amongst the propertied classes as much as to counter the influence of the radical societies, the Association Movement achieved a great deal in the way of marshalling loyalist sentiment – so much so that by the close of 1792 there was a detectable swing in favour of war against France.

The militarization of society, the Alien Act (which authorized the deportation of undesirable foreigners) and the halting of grain exports did much to heighten the tension between the British government and France. At the same time, a power struggle within the National Convention led to a situation where, to maintain its patriotic front, the ruling Girondist party were forced to make hostile speeches against Pitt. The French Republic refused to moderate its proclamations or to resolve the situation in Holland. Unable to back down, the Convention stole a lead over Britain by declaring war on 1 February 1793. To British reformers the effect of this declaration was devastating. When Britain returned the declaration of war ten days later, the link between republican politics and patriotic ideals had been irrevocably severed. Henceforth, as radicals throughout the land were to discover, one could no longer call for reform without, at the same time, being branded a traitor.

Wordsworth, writing in *The Prelude* (1799–1806), offers a vivid description of this dilemma:

> And now the strength of Britain was put forth
> In league with the confederated host;
> Not in my single self alone I found,
> But in the minds of all ingenuous youth,
> Change and subversion from this hour. No shock
> Given to my moral nature had I known
> Down to that very moment – neither lapse
> Nor turn of sentiment – that might be named
> A revolution, save at this one time.
> All else was progress on the self-same path
> On which, with a diversity of pace,
> I had been travelling: this, a stride at once
> Into another region.
>
> . . .
>
>               I felt
> The ravage of this most unnatural strife
> In my own heart; there lay it like a weight
> At enmity with all the tenderest springs

> Of my enjoyments. I who with the breeze
> Had played, a green leaf on the blessed tree
> Of my beloved country (nor had wished
> For happier fortune than to wither there),
> Now from my pleasant station was cut off
> And tossed about in whirlwinds.   (X, 231–58)

In this passage the poet looks back on his involvement in the revolutionary cause with a mixture of disdain, embarrassment and regret. It was, after all, the fall of the Bastille that had supplied his earlier self with a sense of the transformative power of collective action. Writing over ten years later, Wordsworth transforms the historical sense of 'revolution' (line 239) rendering it as mental or internal change. Having privatized history the poet is in a position to disperse his guilt: support for France, he tells us, was high in the minds of '*all ingenuous youth*'. In the lines that follow (249–58), Wordsworth uses the figure of nature to represent political disagreement as 'unnatural strife'. The effect of this is once more to minimize active political engagement, for while radicalism has strong ideological claims, it is the Burkean image of the 'blessed tree' of the nation that has the greatest emotional force.[12] Patriotic feeling, therefore, returns the poet to a sense of personal and public responsibility. Yet it would be wrong to assume patriotism is inherently repressive. As Linda Colley has argued, the roots of patriotism can be traced to the popular radicalism of the English Revolution. By 1804, however, it had become a key element in the discourse of conservative reaction, enabling former republicans, such as Wordsworth, to resituate themselves in favour of the establishment. Within the poetry, the trope of natural disruption is used to diffuse the charge of political apostasy. As a 'green leaf on the blessed tree' of his country, the native Wordsworth has cast himself as an innocent victim of his times, subject to tempests of contention over which he has no control.[13]

But to what extent was Wordsworth's a common experience? Contrary to Pitt's expectations the French declaration of war did not result in immediate political unanimity. For a time, opinion continued to be divided between radicals and reformers critical of the government's support for monarchical absolutism and Burkean conservatives who believed that the war was just and necessary since it was conducted against a new type of enemy, 'one who fights not merely to subdue states, but to dissolve society – not to extend empire, but to subvert government – not to introduce a particular religion, but to extirpate all religion'.[14] Yet, by 1792, it would seem that the collective front of the peace and reform movement had crumbled with the rise of popular nationalism. Within the Whig party, the split between Fox and Portland led to the formation of a 'third party' and, by 1794, to a complete division. For most of the remainder of the war years, the government was made up of a coalition united in their hatred of France and their distrust of popular reform. It was to be some time before an effective opposition would once again operate in Britain.

It would be inaccurate to suggest, however, that the antiwar pro-reform movement simply disappeared as, throughout the war, the reform societies continued to play an important role in agitating against the state. Although their numbers fell toward the end of 1793, a combination of economic disruption, food shortages, antipathy towards military service and military losses gave renewed impetus to the societies. The repressive measures that followed, including the suspension of Habeas Corpus (1794), the Seditious Meetings and Treasonable Practices acts (1795), have been described by Emsley as an attempt on the part of the establishment to defend itself against native forces openly supporting the ideology of the enemy. Whilst the government may have overestimated the extent to which the popular societies posed a genuine threat to the state, it is fair to say that by the close of 1796 a majority of the country, oppressed by provision shortages, angered by the inequities of the recruiting system and aware of the failure of British forces to win a significant victory, was moving in favour of peace.

What, then, were the effects of war on ordinary family life? The recruitment of men into the regular forces and the militia meant that labourers were scarce and their wages high.[15] In some areas the deficiency in labour was supplemented by the employment of women. Fluctuations in the war-time economy, however, ensured that work could no longer be considered a guarantee of family security. As a consequence, many women were forced to rely on their parishes for poor relief. Throughout the 1790s the female vagrant and the destitute widow were to become recurrent figures in anti-war verse.[16] Wordsworth, in particular, seems to have been haunted by this image. Although his career as a political campaigner was short-lived, as a poet he continued to point out the debilitating effects of war. By far the most telling of Wordsworth's early productions is the nightmarish vision of *Salisbury Plain* (1793–4). During the summer of 1793 the poet had spent a month on the Isle of Wight 'in view of the fleet which was then preparing for sea off Portsmouth at the commencement of the war'. He then journeyed across Salisbury Plain. His experiences on this trip, real and imagined, were to prove decisive in formulating the poet's attitude to war, culture and the development of the self. As he writes in the *Advertisement*:

> The monuments and traces of antiquity, scattered in abundance over that region, led me unavoidably to compare what we know or guess of those remote times with certain aspects of modern society, and with calamities, principally those consequent upon war, to which, more than other classes of men, the poor are subject.[17]

In the poem (a text that Wordsworth was to continue to revise right up until 1842) we are thus invited to make an explicit link between the sufferings of the poor during war and their treatment in peacetime. This is conveyed through the tale of the press-ganged sailor and the female vagrant, both of whom have suffered as a direct result of government policy. Beyond this, the poet suggests through the references to druid sacrifices at Stonehenge, that violence is ingrained in the very notion of human society. According to David Collings, *Salisbury Plain* is an illustration of the idea that a culture divided by class is a culture inherently at war with itself; the struggle against France is merely an outward projection of this condition.[18]

## III

So far the conflict had been conducted overseas; its social consequences were measured by economic hardship and loss of manpower. Between October 1797 and May 1798, however, it was possible to observe Napoleon's vast 'Army of England' encamped on the Normandy coasts. The proximity of the invasion force, together with the collapse of peace negotiations, the success of pro-government journals such as the *Anti-Jacobin* and the wide circulation of patriotic prints and papers was to prove decisive in uniting the country against the French.

Not all patriots were entirely happy with the new national mood. Coleridge's *France: an Ode* (February 1798) and *Fears in Solitude* (April 1798) were written in the very period when the alarm was at its strongest.[19] Although both works offer resounding support for the nation in its struggle against Napoleon, the poet is not averse to criticizing the vulgarity of patriotic sentiment. In *Fears in Solitude* the invasion is described as an act of Providence, brought about as a punishment for the hypocrisy of British society. Coleridge identifies several targets, including the newspapers that put 'dainty terms for fratricide' into the mouths of 'boys and girls / And women' (101–10; *passim*):

> As if the soldier died without a wound;
> . . . as if the wretch,
> Who fell in battle, doing bloody deeds,
> Passed off to Heaven, *translated* and not killed (114–18)

a government that neglects its own people:

> Contemptuous of all honourable rule,
> Yet bartering freedom, and the poor man's life
> For gold, as at a market! (58–60)

and that oppresses people overseas. These factors, along with the rise of atheism and an attendant decline in the domestic affections, have combined to make a people

> clamorous
> For war and bloodshed, animating sports,
> The which we pay for, as a thing to talk of,
> Spectators and not combatants! (90–3)

The sense in which war was consumed by the public as a form of spectacle, 'as if the soldier died without a wound', was certainly true for the majority of the population. To the geographically isolated British, bombarded by propaganda and bowed by social repression, words, like specular wounds, have become detached from their meanings. Coleridge's purpose in this poem is to reconnect the abstract consumption of war with its material consequences:

> all-avenging Providence,
> Strong and retributive, should make us know
> The meaning of our words, force us to feel
> The desolation and the agony
> Of our fierce doings (122–6)

For all its power and passion, however, the poem cannot help but register the sense of Coleridge's alienation from his 'brethren' (151). In refusing to worship the images of idolatry that beguile his fellows, Coleridge is unavoidably set apart as an 'enemy': 'Such have I been deemed' (172). While on a public level the poet seeks to reinforce a sense of national responsibility and religious zeal in his readers, on a personal level he is haunted by the realization that such thoughts exist only in the realm of fiction.

With the exception of the brief respite known as the Peace of Amiens (March 1802 to May 1803),[20] the anticipated French invasion continued to haunt the minds of men. Centralization of the self was a vital tenet of Napoleon's commanding philosophy. He claimed that in war 'men are nothing; one man is everything'.[21] This egotism extended to the treatment of allies and the governing of defeated states, including, if all went to plan, a subjugated Britain. When Napoleon was proclaimed First Consul for life in 1802 and then hereditary Emperor in 1804, many radicals who had opposed the war with Revolutionary France now supported the struggle against dictatorship.[22] The champion of liberty, defender of the republic and scourge of the *ancien régime*, could now be recast, by patriots of all shades, as an enemy of national independence. By 1803, loyal sentiments were detectable at every level of society: from the former anti-war poet and preacher William Frend to the women of Neath who proposed setting up as an armed militia. In popular cartoons and prints, the figurehead for the rise in pro-war feeling was not a heroic Pitt or Addington but the national archetype of John Bull or Jolly Jack Tar; Napoleon was no longer at war with the Crown, Church and Constitution, but with the 'people'. If we overlook the extent to which the establishment sought to manufacture consent – through propaganda and the Combination Acts[23] – then it would seem that the upsurge in patriotic sentiment was spontaneous. Coleridge's plea for national unanimity had at last been answered. It is such a feeling that encouraged Wordsworth to write in his *Lines on the Expected Invasion, 1803* that republicans and monarchists alike could unite in response to 'your Country's call' and to claim in his sonnet *To the Men of Kent* that 'In Britain is *one* breath'.[24]

A stern test of this newly forged sense of nationhood was offered in the long period of discontent between 1808 and 1812. Following Lord Nelson's destruction of the French fleet at the Battle of Trafalgar in 1805, the invasion threat receded and with it the fervent patriotism that had sustained the war effort. In the years that followed, the lethal combination of trade blockades, economic depression and food shortages led to renewed calls for peace. With the exception of the distraction afforded by Wellesley's victories in the Peninsular campaign,[25] popular reactions to the war had reached an all-time low, so much so that when, in the summer of 1812, Luddites rose up against their employers, over 12,000 soldiers were deployed to control the uprising – more than had been sent to Portugal in 1808.

Events like this suggest that, in many respects, Britain was a nation at war with itself. That a full-scale revolution never took place is due partly to the residual influence of propaganda and patriotism but also to a complex psychological investment in the spectacle of war. One has only to consult the pages of Jane Austen to realize how inured the public had become to the sight of troops, installations and military manouvres. In Austen, especially, it is not so much the effective significance of war that comes across as its glamorous facade. As Mary Robinson writes in her poem *The Camp* (1802):

> Tents, *marquees*, and baggage-waggons;
> Suttling-houses, beer in flagons;

Drums and trumpets, singing, firing;
Girls seducing, beaux admiring;
Country lasses gay and smiling,
City lads their hearts beguiling;
Dusty roads, and horses frisky,
Many an *Eton boy* in whiskey;

. . .

Lordly gen'rals fiercely staring,
Weary soldiers, sighing, swearing!
*Petit-maitres* always dressing,
In the glass themselves caressing;
Perfum'd, painted, patch'd, and blooming
Ladies – manly airs assuming!

. . .

Tradesmen, leaving shops, and seeming
More of *war* than profit dreaming;
Martial sounds and braying asses,
Noise, that ev'ry noise surpasses!
All confusion, din, and riot,
Nothing clean – and nothing quiet.[26]

With its swirling, incantatory rhythm, the poem conveys a vivid sense of the extent to which war had levelled, accelerated and intensified the relations between class and gender, work and play. In *The Camp* military life takes the form of a carnival; its giddy pleasures carried along on a tide of sexual enticement, masquerade and narcissistic abandon. Thus, for all the hardship war entailed, many people were attracted to the armed forces 'not just by apprehension [of Napoleon and invasion] but by the excitement of it all, by a pleasurable sense of risk and imminent drama, by the lure of a free, brightly coloured uniform and by the powerful seduction exerted by martial music'.[27]

But such pleasures were fleeting as, for the most part, economic and social pressures militated against the grand illusion of heroic endeavour. When at last peace did arrive, following the successes of the Allied campaigns in Europe and the abdication of the Emperor in April 1814, it was greeted with welcome relief. A correspondent for the *Tyne Mercury* wrote that the victory festivals were proof of a truly 'united kingdom'. Yet, within a few weeks, industrialists and politicians were bemoaning the resulting economic slump: 'This peace makes all very slack'.[28] It took a final act of history to revitalize the Burkean war spirit. Napoleon's escape from Elba, his march to Paris and his subsequent reinstatement as Emperor of France had all the trappings of an apocalyptic romance. Indeed, it is this feeling that recurs throughout the accounts of this period, from the poetry of Lord Byron to the pages of Leigh Hunt's *Examiner*. As I claimed at the beginning of this essay, Bonaparte's ignoble defeat at the Battle of Waterloo and his subsequent exile on the remote island of St Helena set the seal on a romantic career defined by self-sufficiency, genius and intense egotism. In 1800, the poet Robert Southey described him as 'the greatest man that events have called into action since Alexander of Macedon'.[29] By 1815, an older, more sober man would denounce him as an evil tyrant. Yet, whether he was to be detested or revered, Napoleon had come to embody a certain ideal of cultural virility.[30]

But more significant than Napoleon is the influence of war itself, not only as a theme of Romantic writing but also as a principle of style. The violent passions that had permeated the writings of Burke were taken up in the tropes and cadences of both prose and poetry. One powerful sense in which war affected the literary imagination is conveyed in the writings of Goethe. The poet had accompanied the Allied advance into France in 1792:

> I had now arrived quite in the region where the balls were playing across me: the sound of them is curious enough, as if it were composed of the humming of tops, the gurgling of water, and the whistling of birds. . . . In the midst of these circumstances, I was soon able to remark that something unusual was taking place within me. I paid close attention to it, and the sensation can be described only by similitude . . . so that you feel yourself, as it were, quite one with the element in which you are.[31]

This is an example of the poeticization of war. In order to achieve his condition of aesthetic detachment the poet creates verbal correspondences between the sound of musket fire and the sounds of nature. By rendering his experience as poetic, Goethe is able to master history, to claim that he has become at one with it. In the writings of Wordsworth, Coleridge and Byron, however, it is war that attains the state of mastery, casting, in the case of *The Prelude*, the poet into another region, separating the preacher, in the case of Coleridge, from his congregation, and condemning the Napoleonic hero, in the shape of Byron, to eternal exile. The war would resurface, in one form or another, in the hyperbolic conflicts of Shelley and Keats, in Anna Laetitia Barbauld's inventive poem of social protest, *Eighteen Hundred and Eleven* (1812), in the domestic and political poetry of Mary Robinson and Felicia Hemans, but also in the veiled textures of Jane Austen and the Brontes. In the world of society it was to emerge in the bloody conflicts of Spa and Spitalfield in 1816 and 1817, and at St Peter's Square in Manchester in 1819 (the Peterloo massacre).

Perhaps, then, the war against revolutionary and imperial France is justly described as a Romantic war. In the movement away from the eighteenth-century conception of war as a limited, self-contained activity, to the Napoleonic notion of total war, we seem to shift, as it were, from an Enlightenment worldview to a recognizably Romantic one. With its emphasis on 'the place of the incalculable and imaginative',[32] the struggle against France exceeded the expectations of rational thought. Above all it confirmed Burke as the first thinker to realize that there are experiences that go beyond the realm of the concept. As the military theorist Carl von Clausewitz wrote in 1832:

> We must, therefore, decide to construe War as it is to be, and not from pure conception, but by allowing room for everything of a foreign nature which mixes up with it and fastens itself upon it – all the natural inertia and friction of its parts, the whole of the inconsistency, the vagueness and hesitation (or timidity) of the human mind: we shall have to grasp the idea that War, and the form which we give it, proceeds from ideas, feelings, and circumstances which dominate for the moment; indeed, if we would be perfectly candid we must admit that this has even been the case where it has taken its absolute character, that is, under Buonaparte.[33]

All of which is not to say that war is simply irrational or incoherent. Rather, what Clausewitz reminds us of is the irreconcilable opposition between theoretical ideals and historical events. Like Romanticism itself, the Napoleonic wars reflected this opposition in a variety of forms: in the figure of the genius rising above rules to command the field of circumstances; in the ambivalent relation between foreign foe and significant 'other'; in the sense of unceasing strife, manifested at every level: from the nation to the subject; from the family to the battle-ground; from working class to ruling class.

## NOTES

1   Byron, *The Age of Bronze*, pp. 223–40; in McGann, VII, p. 8. The war against France provides the context and inspiration for a number of Byron's poems. See especially *Childe Harold's Pilgrimage*, III, xvii–xlv; *Ode to Napoleon Bonaparte*; *Don Juan*, IX, i–x.
2   Shelley, *Feelings of a Republican on the Fall of Bonaparte* (1817), in *The Complete Poetical Works*, p. 527.
3   Jones, I, p. 504.
4   Gash, 'After Waterloo', p. 153.
5   The age of French imperialism was succeeded by the formation of the 'Holy Alliance', the league of Russia, Prussia and Austria. Opponents of the Alliance, such as Byron and Shelley, maintained that Napoleon had been defeated only in order to restore despotic monarchies and to deprive countries of their right to self-determination.
6   Creasy, *The Fifteen Decisive Battles of the World*, p. 352.
7   From *Childe Harold's Pilgrimage*, III, xvii in McGann, II, p. 82.
8   Burke quoted by Conor Cruise O'Brien in Burke, *Reflections*, pp. 13–14.
9   Burke, 'Letter to a member of the National Assembly' (1791). Cited in Burke, *Reflections*, pp. 60–2.
10  Ibid., p. 61.
11  Emsley, *British Society and the French Wars*, p. 2.
12  See Manning, *Reading Romantics*, pp. 175–6. Wordsworth's investment in local patriotism may be compared with William Blake's internationalism. See Butler, *Romantics, Rebels, and Reactionaries*, p. 44.
13  Drawing on historical documents and biographical evidence Nicholas Roe has argued that Wordsworth was an active participant in the pro-reform antiwar movement. See Roe, *Wordsworth and Coleridge*.
14  A statement from a pro-war 'Friend to Peace', cited in Emsley, *British Society and the French Wars*, p. 19.
15  For a detailed assessment of the militarization and its effects on the male populace see Colley,

*Britons*, pp. 283–319. Colley argues that patriotism 'transcended the divisions between the social classes' and helped to contain domestic agitation as well as supplying a ready source of manpower for the armed forces.' For a reading that places more emphasis on the strength of working-class resistance to the war see Thompson, *The Making of the English Working Class* and Emsley, *British Society and the French Wars*.
16  See the introduction to Bennett, *British War Poetry*.
17  Wordsworth, *Guilt and Sorrow or Incidents Upon Salisbury Plain*, originally published in *Poems, Chiefly of Early and Late Years* (1842). This reference is taken from Gill, *The Salisbury Plain Poems*, p. 217.
18  See Collings, *Wordsworthian Errancies*, chapter 1.
19  Reprinted in *Romanticism*, pp. 518–26.
20  Prompted by French losses in Syria and Egypt.
21  For an informed and lively account of Napoleon's career see Chandler, *Napoleon*.
22  The French invasion of Italy in 1796 and the domination of Switzerland in 1798 helped to turn moderate republican opinion against Napoleon.
23  In 1799 the London Corresponding Society and other radical groups were once again suspended.
24  Wordsworth, *Lines on the Expected Invasion, 1803* and *To the Men of Kent* in *WPW*, III, pp. 120–1.
25  Napoleon encountered fierce partisan resistance in Portugal and Spain. Britain's involvement in the Iberian Peninsula from 1808 helped to unite conservatives and liberals alike in the defence of national independence. See, for example, Wordsworth's pamphlet on *The Convention of Cintra* (1809) and related poems 'Dedicated to National Independence and Liberty', Coleridge's essays for *The Courier* and canto 1 of Byron's *Childe Harold's Pilgrimage* (1812). P. M. S. Dawson offers an interesting and lucid account of the relation between national liberty and first- and second-generation Romantic writing in his essay 'Poetry in an age of revolution', pp. 48–73.

26  First published in the *Morning Post* under Robinson's pseudonym Oberon; text here from the
*Spirit of the Public Journals*, 5 (1802), p. 234,
reprinted in McGann, *The New Oxford Book of
Romantic Period Verse*, p. 228.

27  See Colley, *Britons*, pp. 306–9. In this context
one recalls the reactions of Mrs Bennet and her
more gullible daughters in Jane Austen's *Pride
and Prejudice* (1813) when a militia regiment is
stationed close to their home.

28  For a fuller account of the reception of Waterloo
see Emsley, *British Society and the French Wars*,
pp. 161–82.

29  Southey in a letter to Thomas Southey, 2 February
1800 in *New Letters of Robert Southey*, I, pp. 221–2.

30  There are a number of interesting readings of the
influence of Napoleonism on British Romanticism. See, in particular, Lean, *The Napoleonists*
and Simon Bainbridge's penetrating study,
*Napoleon and British Romanticism*.

31  This account is quoted by Creasy, *The Fifteen
Decisive Battles of the World*, pp. 346–8.

32  The theoretical background to this closing statement can be found in Rose, 'Why war?', pp. 21–
4, 27–8.

33  Clausewitz, *Vom Kriege*, pp. 368–70.

## WRITINGS

Bennett, B. (ed.) *British War Poetry in the Age of
Romanticism: 1793–1815*, Garland, New York and
London, 1976. A generous selection of pro-and
anti-war poetry.

Burke, E., *Reflections on the Revolution in France*, ed.
Conor Cruise O'Brien, Penguin, Harmondsworth,
1969. O'Brien's introduction, though strongly
biased against left-wing radicalism, remains one
of the best general essays on Burke's life and work.

Clausewitz, C. von, *Vom Kriege* (1832); *On War*, trans.
Col. J. J. Graham, ed. Anatol Rapoport, Penguin,
Harmondsworth, 1982.

Creasy, E., *The Fifteen Decisive Battles of the World*,
London, 1851; reprinted in the *Everyman's History
Library*, J. M. Dent, London, 1952.

Curry, Kenneth (ed.) *New Letters of Robert Southey*, 2
vols, Columbia University Press, New York and
London, 1965.

Emsley, C., *British Society and the French Wars, 1793–
1815*, Macmillan, London, 1979. An invaluable
source book for all aspects of the war.

Jones, Frederick L. (ed.) *The Letters of Percy Bysshe
Shelley*, 2 vols, Clarendon Press, Oxford, 1964.

Hutchinson, Thomas (ed.) *Poetical Works*, Oxford
University Press, Oxford, 1970.

McGann, J. J. (ed.) *The New Oxford Book of Romantic
Period Verse*, Oxford University Press, Oxford,
1993.

## REFERENCES AND FURTHER READING

Bainbridge, S., *Napoleon and British Romanticism*,
Cambridge University Press, Cambridge, 1995.

Butler, M., *Romantics, Rebels, and Reactionaries: English
Literature and its Background, 1760–1830*, Oxford
University Press, Oxford, 1982. One of the first
critical books to stress the importance of historical
contexts.

——(ed.) *Burke, Paine, Godwin, and the Revolution
Controversy*, Cambridge University Press, Cambridge, 1984. A selection of key documents written
during the revolutionary and war years.

Chandler, D., *Napoleon*, Purnell, London, 1973. A
fully illustrated introductory guide.

Christie, I., *Wars and Revolutions: Britain, 1760–1815*,
Edward Arnold, London, 1982.

Colley, L., *Britons: Forging the Nation, 1707–1837*,
Yale University Press, New Haven, 1992. Contains
important work on the significance of local patriotism during the Napoleonic wars.

Collings, D., *Wordsworthian Errancies: The Poetics of
Cultural Dismemberment*, Johns Hopkins University
Press, Baltimore, 1994. A theoretically informed
reading of the relationship between war, culture
and Wordsworth's poetry.

Cookson, J. E., *The Friends of Peace: Anti-war Liberalism in England, 1793–1815*, Cambridge University
Press, Cambridge, 1982.

Crossley, C. and Small, I. (eds) *The French Revolution
and British Culture*, Oxford University Press,
Oxford, 1989.

Dawson, P. M. S., 'Poetry in an age of revolution', in *The Cambridge Companion to British Romanticism*, ed. S. Curran, Cambridge University Press, Cambridge, 1993, pp. 48–73.

Favret, M. A., 'Coming home: the public spaces of romantic war', *Studies in Romanticism* 33 (1994), 539–48. An illuminating and original reading of the symbolic appropriation of femininity in wartime poetry.

Gash, N., 'After Waterloo: British society and the legacy of the Napoleonic wars', *Transactions of the Royal Historical Society* 28 (1978), 145–57.

Gill, S. C., *The Salisbury Plain Poems of William Wordsworth*, Cornell University Press, Ithaca NY, 1975.

Harvey, M. D., *English Literature and the Great War with France: An Anthology and Commentary*, Croom Helm, London, 1986.

Lean, E. T., *The Napoleonists: A Study in Political Disaffection, 1760–1960*, Oxford University Press, London, 1970.

Manning, P. J., *Reading Romantics: Text and Context*, Oxford University Press, Oxford, 1990.

Roe, N., *Wordsworth and Coleridge: The Radical Years*, Oxford University Press, Oxford, 1988.

Rose, J., 'Why war?' in *Why War? Psychoanalysis, Politics, and the Return to Melanie Klein*, ed. Jacqueline Rose, Blackwell, Oxford, 1993, pp. 15–40. A sophisticated theoretical perspective on the links between war and culture.

Thompson, E. P., *The Making of the English Working Class*, Penguin, Harmondsworth, 1968. A classic study of the rise of British radicalism.

# 6

# Literature and Religion

*Mary Wedd*

From the earliest civilizations to the present time people have looked at creation and found it, despite its wonders, an apparently purposeless exercise. If Tennyson's 'Nature, red in tooth and claw' and, for too many, Hobbes's description of the life of man as 'solitary, poor, nasty, brutish and short' are confirmed even in some degree by their personal observation, no wonder people have always asked, 'Can this be all?' Religions are imaginative ways of dealing with this question. In Britain, the answer for many centuries seemed to be found in some form of Christianity.

This attempt throughout the ages to make sense of what may be a senseless universe may seem to many now to be mere escapism, but it is not the only source of religious belief. There also seems to be built into human nature a sense, perhaps illusory but obstinate too, of something greater than humankind or the material world, with which mystics believe direct contact may be possible. Both these impulses appear to be particularly strong in poets, even when overtly they are anti-religious. Writers of the Romantic period were familiar with the concept of a spiritual world and the immortality of the soul in the work of Greek philosophers, particularly Plato and the neo-Platonists, whom Lamb reported to have heard Coleridge expounding in the cloisters of Christ's Hospital when they were schoolboys and whom Shelley translated when he was at Eton.

We tend to see history in 'movements', as though at some point in the seventeenth or eighteenth century (but when?) a curtain came down on medieval superstition and the taking of every word of the Bible literally; such a view of history would see the Enlightenment in its turn as superseded by the revolution of Romanticism, whereas really the ways of thought represented by these labels co-existed over a very long period. Intolerance and bigotry arising from the regarding of scriptures as sacrosanct, without taking any account of historical change or the function of symbolism, did not disappear. Neither did the eighteenth-century Deist approach, which saw the world as God's creation and the laws of nature, therefore, as the laws of God; while man had within him as guide God-given reason, so that the revelation brought by the scriptures, which caused such controversy and strife, was not really needed.

Meanwhile, in Britain, a homogeneity of culture difficult to imagine today continued regardless. There were many important movements and counter-movements and there were varying influences and regional differences, but writers could all assume in their educated readers a knowledge of the Classics and of the Bible. Divisions then were not, as now, between different religions but between denominational allegiances in Christian belief or, as always, between believers and non-believers, and Greek philosophy remained an important influence.

The basis for this common knowledge in the reading public was, of course, the system of education. Boys at public or grammar schools learnt Greek and Latin and attended church or chapel. At Christ's Hospital, where Coleridge, Lamb and Leigh Hunt were pupils, the Bible was read before every meal and at bedtime, in addition to church morning and evening on Sundays. Wordsworth, at Hawkshead Grammar School, went to church on all Sundays and Holy Days and as a small child at a Dame School at Penrith learnt passages from the Bible by heart. Byron at Harrow and Shelley at Eton were similarly trained. Shelley became a fine classical scholar and if he was put off the idea of conventional religion by the hypocrisy of such an institution as Eton then was, where institutionalized cruelty to children was meted out alongside a gospel of love, it was hardly surprising. Nevertheless, we know from Mary's journal that Shelley regularly read and studied the Bible. Keats learnt Latin but no Greek but, as many did, acquired a knowledge of the classical myths from reference books such as Lemprière's *Biblioteca Classica* and read Homer in translation: 'Oft have I travelled in the realms of gold'. For the 'educated class', which provided the core of the readership of literature, the twin forms of thought of Greece and of the Bible provided the basis of culture. Coleridge wrote in 1802, 'If there be any two subjects which have in the very depth of my nature interested me, it has been the Hebrew and Christian Theology and the Theology of Plato'.[1]

The 'educated class' did not include the working class or women and until the second half of the nineteenth century Catholics and Dissenters were excluded from Oxford and Cambridge. However, the Dissenting Academies provided an excellent education and Mrs Barbauld's father, Dr Aiken, was Principal of one of the most famous, the Warrington Academy. For the frustration of clever girls denied equality with their brothers, regardless of their respective intelligences, see George Eliot's autobiographical account in *The Mill on the Floss* (Book II, chapter I). Some girls were lucky in having an indulgent father or brother to teach them. A number, as George Eliot did, overcame their disadvantages – but note her *nom de plume*. Mary Lamb learnt Latin in her middle age and was soon teaching others. Coleridge's daughter Sara was a very learned woman, as she needed to be to work on her father's writings. In the same way, numerous working men aspired to education and did what they could to acquire it, though very many remained illiterate. In *The Excursion* Book IX (published in 1814) Wordsworth pleaded passionately for basic universal education, which did not come about until 1870. The main providers of the teaching of reading were the churches, particularly the Sunday schools, which used the Bible as their chief text.

Possession of the Bible, unlike the Classics, was not confined to the upper classes and it was widely read and studied in the home. Those who could not read relied on hearing it. Burns, who delighted to mock the 'holier-than-thou' in *To a Louse*, *Holy Willie's Prayer*, etc., also gave us *The Cotter's Saturday Night*. Blake, who did not go to school, grew up in a dissenting household where the Bible was central to family life and it is ubiquitous in his work. Walter Scott had known the Bible almost by heart from childhood. When he wanted to depict a foolish peasant-woman Covenanter of the seventeenth century in *Old Mortality*, he filled Mause Headrigg's mouth with a jumble of absurdly uncomprehending biblical quotations, which are entirely authentic.

The first thing, then, for a student of Romantic literature is to recognize the influence of the King James Bible on the art of writers, whether believers or not, both as to style and allusion. It was second nature to them. To the religious message they varied in their response from outright rejection, through modification and remaking, to a persisting struggle to come to terms with it; but, unlike many today, none was untouched by the text itself. Though he was by no means an orthodox Christian at the time, when Wordsworth wrote of 'these pastoral farms / Green to the very door' it would not have occurred to him that anyone would fail to be reminded, most appropriately, of the 'green pastures' of Psalm 23, particularly when associated with 'These waters, rolling from their mountain-springs / With a soft inland murmur' like 'still waters' or, in the Book of Common Prayer always used in church services, 'the waters of comfort'. When in *Michael* he wishes to 'shew that men who do not wear fine cloaths can feel deeply',[2] he gives the old shepherd a particular dignity by the use of biblical language; for example, 'he kissèd him and wept'. This, like the echo of 'The Lord is my Shepherd', both here and in *Tintern Abbey*, is an almost subliminal recognition for the reader, but more overt allusion is also present with the parallels with the Prodigal Son and with Abraham and Isaac. Failure to pick up these deeply integral references greatly impoverishes one's reading of the poetry.

The Old Testament stories and the Greek myths are more than just primitive tales, for they can often embody universal truths. In general, the atmosphere of ancient myth brings with it a sense of the sacred and of dissolving boundaries between two worlds. More specifically, it was not for nothing that Freud found a vehicle for one of his psychological theories ready-made in the myth of Oedipus. Shelley's remaking of Aeschylus's use of the story of Prometheus, so that the one suffering for the many could even forgive his persecutor, gave him scope for expression of the idealism and sense of the spiritual, as well as the rebellion against authority, which were ingrained in him but which he could not channel into conventional Christianity. Despite his vaunted atheism and the trail of destruction left by his private life, in its broadest sense religion is clearly recognizable in Shelley's poetry, including at least some of the ethical values that follow from it. For philosophy and religion are not merely concerned with transcendental reality, but also with the behaviour that is desirable in human beings as a consequence. What lay behind the concern for the poor, the underprivileged and the enslaved that led to the hope and enthusiasm for the French Revolution or for the cause of freedom? Why should those who were not personally involved care about the sufferings of others?

It seemed to some that the churches had imposed 'mind-forged manacles', tyrannical and repressive restrictions and punishments in the name of Christianity which were not at all in the spirit of the forgiving Jesus, who said 'Judge not, that ye be not judged', and 'I am come that they might have life, and that they might have it more abundantly'. Blake's *Garden of Love* expresses his feeling about this. To those who felt oppressed or repelled by the institutional tyranny of the churches, Shelley's revolt and the irreverence of Byron came as a welcome relief. In the course of time Blake's indignation at social evils and his creation of his own version of religion also provided for many an inspiring liberation. The clutter of man-made rituals and prohibitions, as well as the hypocrisy associated with organized religion, had come to hide the gospel message. In order to rediscover it, it was necessary to get back to the essential personality at the heart of the New Testament. How could this be reconciled, for example, with the monstrous Calvinist doctrine that the elect were chosen by God before birth for salvation, the others not? Imagine the effect on a sensitive child like Alfred Tennyson of his aunt's assurance that she was saved and he damned to eternal hell-fire.

By contrast, some were able to concentrate on the true core of the gospel. William Hazlitt was the son of a Unitarian minister, which was how he met Coleridge, and Joseph Priestley had been one of his teachers at Hackney College. Not believing in the Trinity or the divinity of Christ, he could, upon occasion, focus on the man. In his lecture on *The Age of Elizabeth I* he praises the translation of the Bible and then its description of Jesus. Despite the familiarity of his theme, Hazlitt gives the impression of coming almost with a shock of delighted surprise upon the personality of Jesus, stripped of all irrelevant institutional trappings, as though seeing him for the first time.

> There is something in the character of Christ too (leaving religious faith quite out of the question) of more sweetness and majesty, and more likely to work a change in the mind of man, by the contemplation of its idea alone, than any to be found in history, whether actual or feigned. This character is that of a sublime humanity, such as was never seen on earth before, or since.

He illustrates this with examples and concludes that

> He taught the love of good for the sake of good, without regard to personal or sinister views, and made the affections of the heart the sole seat of morality, instead of the pride of the understanding or the sternness of the will.

He emphasizes that 'The gospel was first preached to the poor, for it consulted their wants and interests, not its own pride and arrogance'.

This was hardly the practice of Mr Collins, Dr Grant or Mr Elton. Jane Austen's clergy are on the whole hardly a credit to their profession. She cannot resist an absurdity. 'Can he be a sensible man, sir?' asks Elizabeth of her father. 'No, my dear; I think not. I have great hopes of finding him quite the reverse.' Far from consulting the wants and interests of the poor, the livings which were often in the gift of local landowners were a useful way of providing for younger sons or other protégés of the rich, who could thus indulge their 'pride and arrogance'. No wonder the Established Church was associated with the tyranny of the upper classes. John Wesley, by contrast, though he himself never left the Church of England, differed from it in going out into the fields and preaching to crowds of the unlettered poor, assuring them that God's grace was open to all. Ideally, it was the task of the clergy to integrate all walks of life within the parish church. Where they fell short in entertaining ways one may enjoy the incongruity, as Jane Austen did. But in *Mansfield Park*, which she said was about ordination, where she is allowing herself to be openly in earnest, her real opinion of what a parson should be is made clear. The worldly Miss Crawford asserts that 'A clergyman is nothing' (chapter nine). Surely Edmund is speaking for his narrator when he says,

> I cannot call that situation nothing, which has the charge of all that is of first importance to mankind, individually and collectively considered, temporarily and eternally – which has the

guardianship of religion and morals, and consequently of the manners that result from their influence. No one here can call the *office* nothing. If the man who holds it is so, it is by neglect of his duty.

By 'manners', he says, he means 'conduct'. Jane Austen makes it clear, too, that care for the poor is of first importance to her.

When poor Sir Thomas was blaming himself for failing to educate his daughters in important things, 'He feared that principle, active principle, had been wanting.... They had been instructed theoretically in their religion, but never required to bring it into daily practice'.

This discrepancy between theory and practice was the biggest factor in bringing religion into disrepute. At the heart of the gospel is the Sermon on the Mount (*Matthew*, 5, 6, 7), given 'by Christ himself, for whose beneficent intentions', Leigh Hunt said Shelley 'entertained the greatest reverence'.[3] It is literally a counsel of perfection – 'Be ye therefore perfect' – and it would be surprising if human beings could entirely live up to it, but to claim to believe in Christ's teachings and to do the exact opposite is a noticeable failure. Byron did notice it and got much fun out of it:

> The Missal too (it was the family Missal)
> Was ornamented in a sort of way
> Which ancient mass-books often are, and this all
> Kinds of grotesques illumined; and how they
> Who saw those figures on the margin kiss all,
> Could turn their optics to the text and pray,
> Is more than I know – but Don Juan's mother
> Kept this herself, and gave her son another.

In the Sermon on the Mount the laws of the Hebrew religion which were current in the society in which Jesus lived are accepted but the spirit transcends them. It is not simply adherence to the Ten Commandments that is required, but a complete inner change of heart. Right actions stem from right emotions and thoughts and should be done without any parade of virtue, but as the quiet and natural outcome of an individual's love, compassion and concern for the life of the spirit. The Sermon turns ordinary human values on their head. Contrary to the common assumption, concentration on making money beyond the necessities of life, delighting in getting the better of competitors by clever 'dirty tricks', screwing the maximum out of employees or opponents even to their destruction, making a great show of wealth and success, these things are neither right nor do they bring lasting satisfaction. Instead of selfish blindness to the feelings of others, the Sermon tells us always to treat people as we would wish them to treat us. Beneath the trappings of contemporary social custom, this is Jane Austen's criterion. A settled habit of selfishness is her main aversion.

In *Songs of Innocence* Blake draws a picture of man in God's image, or God as man can understand him.

> To Mercy, Pity, Peace, and Love
> All pray in their distress;

> And to these virtues of delight
> Return their thankfulness.

But 'Ye shall know them by their fruits' and the face often seen is quite different, ruthless, envious, deceitful and full of hate. In *Songs of Experience*

> Cruelty has a human heart,
> And Jealousy a human face;
> Terror the human form divine,
> And Secrecy the human dress.

When a whole society seemed geared to callous indifference to the underprivileged, even including children, and to the suppression of those who wished to remedy this, disillusioned writers turned from conventional religion and looked for a new kind of faith. Like the deists earlier, some felt they *had* to believe that God had everything in hand and that an inevitable progress would automatically occur whereby we should 'see the abuses gradually corrected, and Christianity recovering its primitive beauty and glory', as Priestley put it. Coleridge called his first child David Hartley after Priestley's admired predecessor, who found that his theory of Association led to a belief in Necessity. Though brought up in the Church of England, Coleridge as a young man was a Unitarian. So was his friend Charles Lamb. When at the age of 21 he was faced with what he later called 'the day of horrors', on which his sister Mary in a fit of madness killed their mother, Lamb turned to Coleridge: 'Write – as religious a letter as possible'. Coleridge immediately wrote a remarkable letter in which he faced the crux of belief or non-belief: 'in storms like these, that shake the dwelling and make the heart tremble, there is no middle way between despair and the yielding up of the whole spirit unto the guidance of faith'.[4] A little later Lamb asks 'Are you yet a Berkleyan?' and associates this with being a Necessitarian.[5] Confronted in his own life with the inexplicable phenomenon of cruel and unmerited suffering, Lamb found help in the conviction of the coming of a New Heaven and a New Earth when, as Hartley put it, God 'the source of all good' will 'himself become, according to the Language of the Scriptures, All in All'. Before that millennial day, as the Book of Revelation makes clear, there must be violence and suffering, but in the end 'God shall wipe away all tears from their eyes; and there shall be no more death, neither sorrow nor crying, neither shall there be any more pain: for the former things are passed away' (*Revelation*, 21.4).

Berkeley's contribution for Coleridge at this time was his spiritual view of the universe, as opposed to the materialists. In sending *This Lime-tree Bower* to Southey, Coleridge wrote a note against the following lines, 'You remember I am a Berkeleian'. He imagines Lamb sharing an experience he has had in the Somerset countryside:

> So my Friend
> Struck with deep joy may stand, as I have stood,
> Silent with swimming sense; yea, gazing round
> On the wide landscape, gaze till all doth seem
> Less gross than bodily; and of such hues
> As veil the Almighty Spirit, when yet he makes
> Spirits perceive his presence.

Everything round us and we ourselves exist only as perceived by the Spirit that is God, which is the cause of everything and is in everything. The human mind, too, far from being a blank slate, has a creative part to play. Through it we can recognize God speaking to us in the world of nature. The concepts of mind and spirit melt into each other, so that 'all doth seem / Less gross than bodily'. If we ourselves are spirits, then it is reasonable to suppose that there are other spirits, just as God is the overall Spirit and that there can be communication between all of them. In *Frost at Midnight* the Hartleian Associationism which guides the oscillating movement of the poem leads into the Berkeleian wish for the baby, that he will

> see and hear
> The lovely shapes and sounds intelligible
> Of that eternal language, which thy God
> Utters, who from eternity doth teach
> Himself in all, and all things in himself.

Coleridge's preoccupation with these ideas at this time is also apparent in *The Ancient Mariner*, where they are combined with the superstitions of medieval Christianity appropriate to the period in which the poem is set. It appears at first sight to be about sin, expiation and redemption, but it does not fit any theological framework. It does, however, prepare the reader for Coleridge's later rejection of the mechanistic Necessitarianism he had accepted and his eventual return to Trinitarianism and the essential doctrines of the Church. His sense of guilt and isolation, so vividly embodied in *The Ancient Mariner*, demanded the comfort of God's forgiveness through the willing sacrifice of his Son, Jesus. Coleridge wrote in July 1802,

> My Faith is simply this – that there is an original corruption in our nature, from which and from the consequences of which, we may be redeemed by Christ – not as the Socinians say, by his pure morals or excellent Example merely – but in a mysterious manner as an effect of his Crucifixion – and this I believe – not because I *understand* it; but because I *feel*, that it is not only suitable to, but needful for, my nature and because I find it clearly revealed.[6]

But the doctrine of Original Sin and subsequent redemption does not solve the problem either of unmerited suffering or of why God ever permitted the Fall of his creation. As early as February 1797 Lamb was reminding Coleridge that he had projected a poem on the origin of evil, and encouraging him to work on it. But, as Coleridge was later to write, we have to take account of 'the nature and necessary limits of human consciousness. . . . What we cannot imagine we cannot, in the proper sense of the word, conceive'.[7] Coleridge understood in his heart that 'The life we seek after is a mystery; but so both in itself and in its origin is the life we have'.[8] Nevertheless, Keats was right about Coleridge being 'incapable of remaining content with half knowledge'.[9] Coleridge continued to wrestle with philosophic questions all his life and, unlike poor Mr Casaubon, he did 'read the Germans'. His later work had a considerable influence on certain major figures in the Victorian Church.

What, though, of the third person of the Trinity, the Holy Spirit? In a letter of September 1802, Coleridge contrasts the Greeks and the Hebrews. The former

in their religious poems address always the Numina Loci . . . All natural Objects were *dead* –
were hollow Statues – but there was a Godkin or Goddessling *included* in each. – In the
Hebrew Poetry you find nothing of this poor Stuff – . . . At best, it is but Fancy, or the
aggregating Faculty of the mind – not *Imagination*, or the *modifying*, and *co-adunating* Faculty.
This the Hebrew Poets appear to me to have possessed beyond all others – & next to them the
English. In the Hebrew Poets each Thing has a Life of it's own, & yet they are all one Life. In
God they move & live & *have* their Being – not *had*, as the cold System of Newtonian
Theology represents / but *have*.[10]

Berkeley, who was a bishop, would have thought of 'the one life within us and abroad' not
as pantheism but as the in-dwelling presence which is the Spirit of God.

Wordsworth, too, had 'felt / A presence . . . / A motion and a spirit, that impels / All
thinking things, all objects of all thought, / And rolls through all things'. The transcendental experience for him came through nature. Blake thought Wordsworth 'the greatest
poet of the age', but 'I fear Wordsworth loves nature, and nature is the work of the devil'.
To Crabb Robinson's very sensible objections to this Blake had no answer and 'did not
seem to understand me'. Both poets were visionaries but in very different ways. Perhaps
the Londoner Blake's Swedenborgian belief in direct conversing with angels and spirits
made it difficult for him to see that for Wordsworth nature was not a barrier but a window.
For him, as for Blake, it was his own experience that mattered. He could for a time
contentedly accept that Coleridge's theory of 'the One Life' fitted his case, but he did not
share Coleridge's rather cerebral taste for 'abstruser musings'. A deeply thoughtful man,
Wordsworth found that his picture of the world developed with his changing experience of
it. His enthusiasm for the French Revolution and his hopes that 'poverty, / At least like
this, would in a little time / Be found no more' were dashed, and he turned to Godwin's
belief that the hope for the future lay in denying the emotions and depending on 'the light
of circumstances, flashed / Upon an independent intellect'. It did not take him long to see
through this and to realize that it is emotion that motivates human beings and to pretend
otherwise is self-deception: 'Where passions have the privilege to work / And never hear
the sound of their own names'. All his hopes for a millennium shattered, he said, 'I lost /
All feeling of conviction, and, in fine, / Sick, wearied out with contrarieties, / Yielded up
moral questions in despair'. It was at this point that Dorothy 'preserved me still / A poet'.

Most of the poets of the Romantic period believed in the concept of the poet as prophet. If
revolutions do not work, perhaps the dissemination of the word will. Perhaps the pen *is*
mightier than the sword. Coleridge at the end of *Kubla Khan* draws a highly coloured picture:

> Beware! Beware!
> His flashing eyes, his floating hair!
> Weave a circle round him thrice,
> And close your eyes in holy dread,
> For he on honey-dew hath fed,
> And drunk the milk of Paradise.

The poet is a seer with a sacred and fearful vision. Wordsworth at the end of *The Prelude*
hopes that he and Coleridge may yet, by their writings, be useful to the nations, at present
sunk in 'ignominy and shame':

> Prophets of Nature, we to them will speak
> A lasting inspiration, sanctified
> By reason and by truth.

Shelley affirmed that poetry 'is as it were the interpenetration of a diviner nature through our own' and spoke of 'the poetry in the doctrines of Jesus Christ'. In the famous last sentence of *A Defence of Poetry* Shelley sums up the important influence that poetry was thought capable of exerting: 'Poets are the unacknowledged legislators of the world'.

So, when Dorothy 'made me seek beneath that name / My office upon earth and nowhere else', Wordsworth felt it a worthy calling. He felt that he had, through nature, been directly in touch with a spiritual world and that, in sharing this experience, he was fulfilling a useful mission. Sometimes he uses the word 'God' in relation to it, but he was not greatly concerned with the Church's teachings about redemption or immortality in his youth. 'On one subject we are habitually silent' writes Coleridge in May 1798, 'he loves and venerates Christianity – I wish he did more.'[11] However, the death of his brother John in 1805 had a profound effect on Wordsworth's thinking. 'A deep distress hath humanised my soul', he wrote in *Elegiac Stanzas*. Interestingly, in the *Ode to Duty*, basically composed the year before, he was already saying, 'Me this unchartered freedom tires;' and 'I long for a repose that ever is the same'. One is reminded of Newman in the next generation writing, 'I was not ever thus, nor prayed that Thou / Shouldst lead me on / I loved to choose and see my path; but now / Lead Thou me on'. It is as though they are both protesting that living independently of a higher power is unbearably wearisome, but whether it is an abdication of responsibility to give in to this remains a moot point.

The death of John Wordsworth was devastating, particularly as nature – in the form of the sea – had killed him. Writing to Sir George Beaumont on 12 March 1805, Wordsworth said,

> a thousand times have I asked myself, as your tender sympathy led me to do, 'why was he taken away' and I have answered the question as you have done. In fact, there is no other answer which can satisfy and lay the mind at rest. Why have we a choice and a will, and a notion of justice and injustice, enabling us to be moral agents? Why have we sympathies that make the best of us so afraid of inflicting pain and sorrow, which yet we see dealt about so lavishly by the supreme governor? Why should our notions of right towards each other, and to all sentient beings within our influence differ so widely from what appears to be his notion and rule, if everything were to end here? Would it be blasphemy to say that upon the supposition of the thinking principle being destroyed by death, however inferior we may be to the great Cause and ruler of things, we have *more of love* in our Nature than he has? The thought is monstrous; and yet how to get rid of it except upon the supposition of *another* and a *better world* I do not see.[12]

Experience taught Wordsworth to rethink his assumptions. 'So once it would have been, – 'tis so no more: / I have submitted to a new control'. Keats did not have time to perfect his philosophy of life but he was working on it. He could not accept Christianity or any rigid system that threatened 'negative capability', yet he wanted to make sense of things. His short life held more than its share of 'pains and troubles'. When he wrote of

> The weariness, the fever and the fret
> Here, where men sit and hear each other groan;
> Where palsy shakes a few, sad, last gray hairs,
> Where youth grows pale and spectre-thin and dies;
> Where but to think is to be full of sorrow
> And leaden-eyed despairs,
> Where Beauty cannot keep her lustrous eyes,
> Or new Love pine at them beyond tomorrow

he spoke from first-hand experience. Writing to George and Georgiana with the news of Tom's death, Keats says, 'I have scarce a doubt of immortality of some nature or other – neither had Tom'. But in a later letter he repudiates the conventional view of earth and heaven.

> The common cognomen of the world among the misguided and superstitious is 'a vale of tears' from which we are to be redeemed by a certain arbitrary interposition of God and taken to heaven – What a little circumscribed straightened notion! Call the world if you Please 'The vale of Soul-making'.

Adapting an idea of Bishop Joseph Butler, Keats sees human beings in the world as comparable to children in school.

> How then are souls to be made? How then are these sparks within which are God to have identity given them – so as ever to possess a bliss peculiar to each one's individual existence? How, but by the medium of a world like this? . . . Do you not see how necessary a World of Pains and troubles is to school an Intelligence and make it a Soul?[13]

In February of 1820 Keats recognized the drop of arterial blood as his death-warrant and began his year of 'posthumous existence', his last letter ending, 'I always made an awkward bow'.[14] In his final weeks, though among the books he asked for were *Pilgrim's Progress* and Jeremy Taylor's *Holy Living* and *Holy Dying*, Keats inveighed against the religious faith of Severn, who surely at this time was demonstrating Christian behaviour, attending his friend day and night. It was as though Keats was angrily envious of 'this cheap comfort' which he did not have, 'yet you know Severn I cannot believe in your book – the Bible'. He was not himself at this period, but all the same was expressing the integrity of honest disbelief, as he pleaded for euthanasia. Later, he became calm and was concerned for what the experience was doing to Severn. In saying 'I think a malignant being must have power over us – over whom the Almighty has little or no influence', he was protesting *in extremis* as many of us do, but throughout his poetry two strands intertwine, that of hope, aspiration and love of beauty and that of transience, suffering and loss. He was still learning and seeking to reconcile them when his life was cut short.[15]

There can be no doubt that concern with religious questions was of very deep import-ance to writers of the Romantic period and it is impossible to read their work adequately without taking it into account. They confronted in their own lives and expressed in their writing the basic spiritual experiences and theoretical problems of a religious view of the world. Whether they felt closely in touch with a higher presence, or whether they were aware only of an obligation to defend the freedom of others, there was a sense of aspiration among them. Equally, they came face to face with the insoluble problem of evil and tried to assimilate it into their philosophy. From a preoccupation with myth and an inheritance of the inspired language of Greek poetry and of the King James Bible, they forged an art that was concerned with the deepest and most important elements of human life: the relationship of men and women to one another in society, and the consciousness of a deeper reality than that of everyday material and mundane existence.

## NOTES

1  Griggs, II, p. 866.
2  *EY*, p. 315.
3  Leigh Hunt, *The Autobiography of Leigh Hunt*, p. 269.
4  Griggs, I, pp. 238–9.
5  Marrs, *The Letters of Charles and Mary Anne Lamb*, I, pp. 44, 89.
6  Griggs, II, p. 807.
7  Coleridge, *Aids to Reflection*, p. 79.

8  Ibid., p. 204.
9  Rollins, I, p. 194.
10  Griggs, II, pp. 865–6.
11  Griggs, I, p. 410.
12  *EY*, p. 556.
13  Rollins, II, p. 102.
14  Ibid., II, p. 360.
15  Gittings, *John Keats*, p. 615.

## REFERENCES AND FURTHER READING

Barth, J. Robert, SJ, *The Symbolic Imagination: Coleridge and the Romantic Tradition*, Princeton University Press, Princeton, 1977.

Beer, John, *Coleridge the Visionary*, Chatto and Windus, London, 1959.

Fuller, David, 'Shelley and Jesus', *Durham University Journal* LXXV, 2, July 1993, 211–23.

Harding, Anthony John, *Coleridge and the Inspired Word*, McGill-Queen's University Press, Kingston and Montreal, 1985.

Leigh Hunt, J. H., *The Autobiography of Leigh Hunt*, ed. J. E. Morpurgo, London, 1949.

Marrs, Edwin W. (ed.) *The Letters of Charles and Mary Anne Lamb*, 3 vols, Ithaca, NY, 1975–8.

Prickett, Stephen, *Words and the Word: Language, Poetics and Biblical Interpretation*, Cambridge University Press, Cambridge, 1986. Especially section 3.

Watson, J. R., *Wordsworth's Vital Soul: The Sacred and Profane in Wordsworth's Poetry*, Macmillan Press,

London and Basingstoke, 1982. Especially chapters 7, 8 and 12.

—— 'Romantic poetry and the Wholly Spirit', in *The Discerning Reader: Christian Perspectives on Literature and Theory*, ed. David Barratt, Roger Pooley and Leland Ryken, Leicester and Grand Rapids, Apollos, Baker Books, Inter-Varsity Press, 1995, pp. 195–217.

Willey, Basil, *The Seventeenth Century Background* and *The Eighteenth Century Background*, Chatto and Windus, London, 1934 and 1940. Reprinted in Ark Paperbacks. Essential reading for the thought of the periods.

Wordsworth, Jonathan, *William Wordsworth: The Borders of Vision*, Clarendon Press, Oxford 1982.

—— 'Lamb and Coleridge as One-Goddites', *The Charles Lamb Bulletin* 58, April 1987, 37–47.

# 7

# The Picturesque, the Beautiful and the Sublime

## *Nicola Trott*

Historically, the three terms of this essay's title have hoped to make an appeal to distinct categories of aesthetic experience: Joseph Addison set the stage, in his *Spectator* essay of 23 June 1712 (no. 412), by dividing those 'Pleasures of the Imagination' that are to be gained from looking at objects, into the '*Great, Uncommon*, or *Beautiful*'. Nowadays, such divisions are largely redundant, but for much of the eighteenth and nineteenth centuries they were the subject of heated debate, and, occasionally, rigorous definition.[1] One problem for the would-be definers was that the key terms were in common and often casual use. Take, for instance, Dorothy Wordsworth's account of Coleridge's farcical encounter at the Falls of the Clyde:

> C., who is always good-natured enough to enter into conversation with anybody whom he meets in his way, began to talk with [a] gentleman, who observed that it was a '*majestic* waterfall'. Coleridge was delighted with the accuracy of the epithet, particularly as he had been settling in his own mind the precise meaning of the words grand, majestic, sublime, etc., and had discussed the subject with Wm. at some length the day before. 'Yes, sir,' says Coleridge, 'it *is* a majestic waterfall.' 'Sublime and beautiful', replied his friend. Poor C. could make no answer.[2]

The categories will keep merging into one another, gathering synonyms as they go. Nevertheless, one essential, if not stable, opposition does develop, between the 'sublime' on the one hand and the 'beautiful' on the other. (The 'picturesque' is a kind of hybrid, which we shall come to presently.) And here the most influential figure is Edmund Burke, who in 1757 published anonymously *A Philosophical Enquiry into the Origin of our Ideas of the Sublime and Beautiful*. This work dominated thinking on aesthetics into the next century, even where its claims to be 'philosophical' were subjected to ridicule.

The *Enquiry* locates 'the Origin of Our Ideas of the Sublime and Beautiful' in the passions, and, specifically, in what for Burke are the 'leading passions' of 'self-preservation' and 'society' (p. 38). The beautiful concerns social or sexual relations, and turns upon feelings of pleasure; the sublime concerns the solitary individual, and turns upon the still more powerful feelings of terror or pain. As the associate of 'power' and the producer of the 'strongest emotion' (p. 39), the sublime is a privileged term – and this superior attraction recurs again and again in subsequent discussion. But the oppositional duality of beauty-and-sublimity, or 'Society and Solitude' (p. 43), is omnipresent in the later eighteenth and early nineteenth centuries. Their pairing or oscillation becomes a governing artistic structure: *Frankenstein* features the 'sublime' Mer de Glace versus the 'beautiful' Rhine; Wordsworth, a boy who is 'Fostered alike by beauty and by fear' (*The Prelude*, I, 307), and a poet who conceives himself as a sublime solitary in a dialectical relationship with the socializing influences of the beautiful (e.g. *The Prelude*, XIII, 216–36). De Quincey gives us the 'pleasures' and the 'pains' of opium, Coleridge a 'pleasure-dome' and 'savage place'; and Blake's oddball homocentrism stipulates 'The head sublime . . . the genitals beauty' (*Proverbs of Hell*).

After Burke, the next definitive landmark in the debate is the publication in 1790 of a work by the German philosopher Immanuel Kant. In *The Critique of Judgment*, Kant analyses the beautiful and the sublime in these terms (terms derived from his existing system of thought):[3]

> The beautiful in nature is a question of the form of the object, and this consists in limitation, whereas the sublime is to be found in an object even devoid of form, so far as it immediately involves, or else by its presence provokes, a representation of *limitlessness*, yet with a super-added thought of its totality. Accordingly the beautiful seems to be regarded as a presentation of an indeterminate concept of understanding, the sublime as a presentation of an indeterminate concept of reason.

You will notice that Kant polarizes the aesthetic categories according to the faculties to which they are said to refer: the beautiful is assigned to the understanding (*Verstand*), the sublime to the reason (*Vernunft*). I shall return to these rather complex matters later: for the moment, it is enough to recognize that the sublime is without the 'form' or 'limitation' of the beautiful, and instead involves the (apparently contradictory) apprehensions of 'limitlessness' and 'totality'.

In what follows, I have adopted a loosely hierarchical arrangement, starting with the cult of the 'picturesque' and ending with the interpreting of the 'sublime', together with a taxonomy of its leading varieties. The order is not, and cannot be, chronological, but reflects my understanding that the Romantic period itself demonstrates some such movement away from the visual and pictorial as the appropriate models for art.

## The Picturesque

Early users of the word are conscious of its French or Italian roots;[4] by 1767 the 'picturesque' has been naturalized, and is itself applied to nature, as a term designating 'that peculiar kind of beauty, which is agreeable in a picture'.[5] In essence, it becomes a way of looking at landscape by criteria drawn from painting.

The picturesque, then, serves the often rivalrous mistresses of art and nature. On the one hand it requires the application of artistic rules, on the other it appeals to the (heavily contested) ground of 'nature', whose appearances it claims both to imitate,[6] and to correct.[7]

The motives of the picturesque can be traced to three main sources. First, a recognition that a third term is needed for aesthetic experiences fitting into neither of the rather rigidly segregated categories of the sublime and the beautiful. The 'picturesque' sits, somewhat uneasily, between the two: 'parasitical sublimity' is Ruskin's judgement,[8] while Hazlitt, hovering between insult and explication, observes that the picturesque 'stands out' and so 'may be considered as...an excrescence on the face of nature'.[9]

Second, a greatly increased awareness of visual art, impelled by foreign travel, or the Grand Tour, which typically ended up in Italy, and yielded costly souvenirs;[10] the establishment of the Royal Academy and the *Discourses* of its first president, the painter Sir Joshua Reynolds; and the collections of Angerstein (on which the National Gallery is founded) and Sir George Beaumont (a patron and friend of Coleridge and Wordsworth).[11] The fashion in foreign art is summed up in three often-cited names: Claude Lorrain, Gaspar (or Nicolo) Poussin and Salvator Rosa[12] – a triumvirate whose membership is fixed as early as 1748 (by James Thomson, in his poem *The Castle of Indolence*, I, 38), and which rapidly becomes a way of indicating the beautiful and sublime qualities of British scenery.[13] Native artists, meanwhile – who include Constable and Turner, of course, but also a host of lesser knowns[14] – respond to a new demand for images of landscape (as opposed to portrait, history or genre painting), and pioneer the visual discovery of the English Lakes, the Alps and the Rhine.

Third, and last, a burgeoning interest in landscape itself. This is an offshoot of eighteenth-century gardening: 'English landscape', says a character in Tom Stoppard's *Arcadia*, 'was invented by gardeners imitating foreign painters who were evoking classical authors. The whole thing was brought home in the luggage from the grand tour'. Indeed, Pope was heard to say that 'all gardening is landscape painting'. Two important components were Thomson's long georgic poem *The Seasons* and the carefully cultivated naturalness of the country house – the invention of the ha-ha, for instance, which had the effect of suppressing the boundaries between 'park' and 'garden'.[15] Great surviving examples of such cultivated naturalness, by William Kent and Lancelot 'Capability' Brown, are at Blenheim, Stowe, and Rousham (all near Oxford), while Humphry Repton's exquisite *Sketches and Hints on Landscape Gardening* (1794) reproduces the designs by which he hoped to 'establish Fixed Principles in the Art of Laying Out Ground'. Brown replaces the formal geometry of avenue and terrace with the asymmetrical forms and sinuous curves of Burke's definition of beauty; his comparatively monotonous 'sweeps' and 'belts' of lawn and wood in their turn give way to picturesque discontinuities of line, in rock or chasm or broken tree.

Towards the end of the eighteenth century, the 'domestic tour', as it is known, becomes almost as chic as the 'grand'. This penchant for going native is greatly encouraged by the outbreak of war with France in 1793, and promoted by a glut of publications, one of the most important being *A Guide to the Lakes* by Thomas West.[16] West's *Guide* establishes the convention of viewing a given scene from an optimum position or 'station' (a formality Romanticism claims to do without)[17] and includes a classic early account of touring the Lakes, by the poet Thomas Gray.[18] Apart from his terror at the sublimities of Borrowdale, Gray's most indicative record is of rounding Helm Crag and coming upon a paradisal view of Grasmere (later the home of the Wordsworths):

Just beyond it, opens one of the sweetest landscapes that art ever attempted to imitate.... Not a single red tile, no gentleman's flaring house, or garden walls, break in upon the repose of this little unsuspected paradise. (West, *Guide*, p. 209)

The opening of Britain to 'picturesque' observation takes in caves, quarries and mines[19] as well as lochs, pikes and gills. Apart from the English Lake District (the playground of newly rich industrialists), there are three further regions of special importance: North Wales (especially Snowdonia), the border valley of the River Wye (site of Tintern Abbey) and the Scottish Highlands.

The chief guardians of things picturesque were William Gilpin, Uvedale Price and Richard Payne Knight. Price and Knight were county squires (at Foxley and Downton Castle, Herefordshire) and spilt a good deal of ink squabbling over terms. Wordsworth corresponded with Price on the subject of the sublime (Price was good enough to praise the poet's efforts in a letter of 3 June 1806), while both he and Coleridge read Price's *Essay on the Picturesque* (revised 1796) and annotated Knight's *Analytical Inquiry into the Principles of Taste* (3rd edn, 1806).[20] But it was Gilpin, a Cumbrian-born vicar, schoolmaster and amateur painter, who was in many ways the inventor of the picturesque tour. Seven journeys to different parts of the British Isles, conducted 'relative chiefly to Picturesque Beauty' and illustrated by Gilpin himself, were initially circulated in manuscript among high society, and then published in the form with which the young Wordsworth was familiar (from copies of the Wye, Lakes and Highland tours).

The main desideratum of the picturesque is contrast (as against the smoothness of the beautiful or vastness of the sublime), whether by irregularity or roughness, variety or novelty.[21] Although the consequences are often slightly ludicrous – as when Gilpin offers to roughen up a contour or give an appropriately 'shaggy' look to cattle – it is a rhetoric eminently suited to the English countryside. There are also many innovative elements, the most significant being the application of Burkean aesthetics to landscape.[22] The obscurity central to Burke's sense of the sublime (see 'The sublime', below) is naturalized in gulfs or abysses, the conditions of twilight or moonlight, and the atmospheric effects of mist or cloud – all of which, as Gilpin puts it, 'leave room for the imagination'.[23] Needless to say, the British climate perfectly upholds this uncertainty principle. And there is a direct lineage between the kinds of observation taught by the picturesque and the symbolic ventures of Romantic landscape, beginning in Beattie or Radcliffe, and culminating in Wordsworth or Keats.[24] In the 'Climbing of Snowdon' in Book XIII of *The Prelude* – an episode that carries numerous echoes of picturesque tours and poetry – the action of the mist in transforming the scene images the power that Wordsworth claims for the imagination.

Another picturesque import to Romanticism is *chiaroscuro*, the Italian term[25] for the painterly handling of light and shade (though to Constable it is nothing less than 'the soul and medium of art').[26] Once again, the picturesque makes the transference to landscape; and the perception of such contrasts in the natural world is extended, by Romantic writers, to the making of metaphors for their own creativity: for Hazlitt, himself an accomplished painter, *chiaroscuro* is the 'medium of imagination' (Howe, XVIII, 122–3); for Coleridge, it describes the 'poetry of nature' in its use of the 'modifying colours of the imagination' (CC *Biographia*, chapter 14).

A further influence on the Romantics is the liking for ruins: Gilpin acclaims the sacking of the monasteries as a national work of art, and memorably suggests taking an improving mallet to Tintern Abbey. Such an aesthetic of the ruinous, or incomplete, contributes to the Romantic fascination with fragmentation and the fragmentary. Lastly, the picturesque is literary as well as pictorial: Gilpin applies Virgil, Shakespeare, Milton and a raft of eighteenth-century poets to the evocation of landscape; and, although in general hostile to the textualizing of nature, the Romantics have a considerable interest in the arts of its representation and inscription.

Wordsworth's first major publication, *An Evening Walk* (1793), 'does' the Lake District, where he grew up, according to the best models of the picturesque tour. Already, though, there is a greater specificity than in the often rather generalized observations of the guides. Such attentiveness is especially apparent in the remarkable writings of the poet's sister, Dorothy Wordsworth – most famously and impressionistically the journals she kept at Alfoxden in 1798 and Grasmere in 1800–2, but also, for instance, her extremely fine *Recollections of a Tour made in Scotland, 1803*. The Wordsworths were passionate walkers and tour-takers (the routes have been reproduced by Donald E. Hayden), Coleridge an obsessional nature-noter and fell-climber (indeed, the very first, according to Molly Lefebure). Wordsworth also produced his own much reprinted *Guide through the District of the Lakes* and tried his hand at landscape-gardening, at Dove Cottage in Grasmere, at Coleorton, the Nottinghamshire home of the Beaumonts, and in the grounds of Rydal Mount, his last Lake District home.

The picturesque was a passing fad: a 'strong infection of the age' is Wordsworth's summary verdict, in *Prelude* XI. Not surprisingly, its jargon and conventions produced some lively satire. In *The Lakers* (1798), a 'Comic Opera' by the Revd James Plumptre, the irrepressible heroine, Beccabunga Veronica, halts at 'Crow Park, Mr West's second station', to admire Derwentwater, which she (incorrectly) compares to 'Claude and Poussin',[27] before turning to use her 'Claude-Lorrain' glass:[28]

> I must throw a Gilpin tint over these magic scenes of beauty. . . . What illusions of vision! The effect is inexpressibly interesting. The amphitheatrical perspective . . . the picturesque luxuriance of the bowery foliage . . . the horrific mountains, such scenes of ruin and privation! the turfy hillocks, the umbrageous and reposing hue of the copsy lawns, so touchingly beautiful (I, iii)

William Combe's poetical *Tour of Doctor Syntax, In Search of the Picturesque*[29] takes off Gilpin, while Thomas Love Peacock, in *Headlong Hall* (1816), features an encounter between Marmaduke Milestone, alias Humphry Repton, and one Mr Gall:

> 'Allow me,' said Mr Gall. 'I distinguish the picturesque and the beautiful, and I add to them, in the laying out of grounds, a third and distinct character, which I call *unexpectedness*.'
> 'Pray, sir,' said Mr Milestone, 'by what name do you distinguish this character, when a person walks round the grounds for the second time?' (ch. 4)

Last but not least, there is Austen. In *Northanger Abbey*, Catherine Morland's happy ignorance of the picturesque gives Henry Tilney the still happier opportunity of delivering 'a lecture' on the subject, in which his instructions were so clear that she soon began to see beauty in every thing admired by him, and her attention was so earnest, that he became perfectly satisfied of her having a great deal of natural taste. He talked of foregrounds, distances, and second distances – side-screens and perspectives – lights and shades; – and Catherine was so hopeful a scholar, that when they gained the top of Beechen Cliff, she voluntarily rejected the whole city of Bath, as unworthy to make part of a landscape. (ch. 14)

Austen points the way to the Victorian critique of the picturesque on moral grounds – a critique seen at its best in John Ruskin's *Modern Painters*, Elizabeth Gaskell's *North and South* (chapter three) and chapter 39 of George Eliot's *Middlemarch*, where it is charged with a basic antipathy to humanity, and a preference for tumble-down hovels and blasted heaths over neat homes and cultivated soil. (This question of the politics of the picturesque has again been taken up, mostly from a 'new historical' perspective, in much of the recent criticism.)[30]

In the main, the sticking-point for the Romantics is rather different. Wordsworth and Coleridge's eventual repudiation of the picturesque is underwritten, in part by a claim (however disingenuous) to unmediated experience, in part by a quite different, emotional and spiritual, philosophy of nature. The picturesque becomes stigmatized for trying to apply the 'rules of mimic art. . . . To things above all art',[31] as though it were at once a copyist and a mocker of nature. The shift from 'imitation' to 'originality' necessarily brings the Romantic and the painterly aesthetic into conflict. With its visual criteria, its correction of nature's 'faults' and its use of the 'framing' device of the lens, the picturesque is seen to impose unacceptable limits. What is more, Romanticism is most powerfully drawn to the much stronger aesthetic category of the sublime.


## The Sublime

'Sublime' conveys a sense of height or loftiness (it probably derives from the Latin *sub* 'up to' and *limen* 'lintel', and is akin to *altitudo, elatio*). By attribution, it comes to signify the highest in a particular category: accordingly, we get such modifiers as the 'sublime style', the 'sublime of war', the 'moral sublime'. But although the sublime invariably comes 'top' in any aesthetic hierarchy, the application of the term is notoriously loose. Its popular manifestations can be especially surprising: Cole Porter's *You're the Top*, for instance, offers the charming endearment, 'You're sublime. You're a turkey dinner. . .'

'Sublime' as an adjective, meaning 'raised aloft', 'high up', is found in Beattie and early Wordsworth, and in both is associated with the thrill of mountain summits. As Marjorie Hope Nicolson has shown, the notion that mountains – the topographical core of the Romantic sublime – are anything other than 'hideous . . . Warts' is of relatively recent date: in 1688, John Dennis was one of the first English travellers to express positive enjoyment of the Alps. A succession of more or less willing Alpine tourists (from Addison in 1699, to Gray and Walpole in 1739, and Wordsworth in 1790) brought familiarity; and, with Napoleon, improved roads bred, if not contempt, then at least a kind of confidence.

The Alps seemed to demand a new aesthetic scale: in *Descriptive Sketches* (1793), the poem of his 1790 tour, Wordsworth noted that 'their sublime features' would have been 'insulted' by his working 'title of Picturesque', since their confinement to 'the cold rules of painting' would have given his reader

> but a very imperfect idea of those emotions which they have the irresistible power of communicating to the most impassive imaginations. The fact is, that controuling influence, which distinguishes the Alps from all other scenery, is derived from images which disdain the pencil [paintbrush].

Ironically enough, Wordsworth's note depends upon a passage in Gilpin (*Observations of Cumberland*, I, 121–2): the fact that, as Christopher Hussey in *The Picturesque* observes, the picturesque 'had to decide repeatedly at what point it ceased to be possible to delineate' was often an excuse for trespassing into 'sublime' territory.

Like the picturesque, the sublime had essential sites. The Grande Chartreuse was one, Mont Blanc and Chamonix another. In 1744, William Windham's record of a visit to Mont Blanc was most unusual. By the time Byron and the Shelleys got there, in 1816, the scene was almost *de rigueur*, though in their case it had unprecedented results: this is the landscape which enters Byron's journal and Shelley's letters; which becomes the explicit subject of both *Childe Harold's Pilgrimage* canto 3 (stanza 62, 'All that expands the spirit, yet appals') and *Mont Blanc*; and which provides the settings for Byron's *Manfred*, located 'amongst the Higher Alps', Shelley's *Prometheus Unbound*, and Mary Shelley's *Frankenstein*.

From the experience of the sublime, we turn to treatises 'On the Sublime' (a rather different thing). There is a long history of serious-minded commentary on the subject, beginning with *Peri Hypsous*, thought to be by Longinus, in the first century, and gaining in density from the mid eighteenth (about the time that the concept of '*the* sublime' becomes established in English): to the name of Burke, may be added those of Baillie,[32] Beattie, and Payne Knight; to Kant, Schiller, Herder, and John Paul Richter.

*Peri Hypsous* is the foundation of what is often called the 'rhetorical sublime'. Although the Greek original is concerned with excellence of expression rather more than with exaltation of composition, it is translated as a work 'On the Sublime', and was available in English from 1652, and in Boileau's influential *Traité du Sublime*, from 1674. Romantic writers focus on the notion that certain aspects of the sublime style – namely, grandeur of thought or conception, together with vehemence or intensity of passion – are dependent upon a nobility of soul or character. This is an analogy made by Hazlitt and Keats in particular,[33] and by the Wordsworth who writes of the soul's 'obscure sense / Of possible sublimity, to which / With growing faculties she doth aspire' (*The Prelude*, II, 336–8). The moral qualities of the rhetorical sublime come into play especially in reference to *Paradise Lost*, the Romantics' 'pre-eminent' example: Coleridge contrasts the bogus 'arithmetical sublime' of Klopstock (a German epicist), who 'mistakes bigness for greatness', with the true sublimity of Milton, whose greatness arises 'from images of effort and daring, and also from those of moral endurance'.[34]

The Longinian tradition (which has been exhaustively treated by Samuel H. Monk and Theodore Wood) is both long and specifically literary. Another leading tradition is that of the 'natural sublime' – or, to use Keats's coinage of 1818 – the 'material sublime'. This seems to have developed earliest in Britain, and is crucial to Romanticism. According to Nicolson, 'The discovery that makes the most profound difference between older and "modern" landscape was of what we now call the "Sublime" in Nature'. The discovery involves a shift away from the classical aesthetic requirements of regularity and harmony. In the older, orderly sense, the 'Sublime of Nature' is already becoming a cliché by 1727, when Pope's *Peri Bathous: or The Art of Sinking in Poetry* (a parody of Longinus) catalogues its elements as 'the Sky, the Sun, the Moon, Stars, &c.' But the modern sublime sought to encompass irregular, even chaotic, forces. An important work here is Thomas Burnet's *Telluris Theoria Sacra* (1681) – translated as *The Sacred Theory of the Earth* (1684), and known to both Wordsworth and Coleridge – which explained the disorderly appearance of mountains as the ruins left by the Deluge, or second Chaos.

Despite evident continuities, the history of the sublime is also one of schism. One of the principal divisions, as we have seen, is between the 'rhetorical' and 'natural'. Another, which I shall come to shortly, is between the 'empiricist' and 'idealist'. The sublime, then, has been conceived in various and often contradictory ways: as God-dependent (Coleridge) and God-denying (Shelley); as physiological (Burke) and transcendental (Kant). It has been seen as invoking unity or refusing closure; as inhering in the object or the mind; as involving the senses or referring to reason; and as diminishing or magnifying the human subject (or both in succession, as in Kant and Schiller and some British Romantics). One thing most commentators agree on is that the sublime escapes the limits of representation (the limits observed, of course, by the picturesque). As a result, the sublime presumes an aesthetic of excess or non-representability (and on this basis has lately been taken up by Derrida and Lyotard as exemplary of the critical philosophy). The Romantic period has proved fertile ground for modern interpretations of the Kantian sublime, from the psychoanalytic (Thomas Weiskel and Neil Hertz) to the formalist (Frances Ferguson). In addition, a number of full-length studies have been devoted to individual writers and artists, as well as genres: Blake (Vincent Arthur de Luca), Wordsworth (Albert O. Wlecke), Shelley (Angela Leighton), Keats (Stuart A. Ende), Turner (Andrew Wilton), Macpherson (Fiona Stafford), the Gothic (Vijay Mishra) and visual art (James B. Twitchell and Morton D. Paley).

## Burke and the Romantics

In Burke, the beautiful arouses 'love'; the sublime, more surprisingly, 'delight' (*Enquiry*, pp. 35–7). By connecting powerful enjoyment with situations of risk or danger, the *Enquiry* gives positive value to the ostensibly negative responses they produce. Burke popularizes, though he does not originate, the kinds of perception that are summarized in John Brown's contemporary catchphrase of 'beauty in the lap of horror'. His emotive psychologizing organizes a newly extreme or oxymoronic sense of the conflicts involved in aesthetic experience, encouraging writers to think in terms of a 'pleasing terror'[35] or 'severe delight', even of being 'fostered' by fear.

The Burkean sublime is defined by its ability to pre-empt the efforts of rational analysis – a manoeuvre which corresponds to the disdain in which the mere understanding is held in much Romantic thought:

> Hence arises the great power of the sublime, that far from being produced by them, it anticipates our reasonings, and hurries us on by an irresistible force. (*Enquiry*, p. 57)

In a similar vein, Burke ends his 'Introduction on Taste' (which was prefixed to the second edition of 1759) by undoing its careful argument for the development of the powers of 'judgment':

> the judgment is for the greater part employed in throwing stumbling blocks in the way of the imagination, in dissipating the scenes of its enchantment, and in tying us down to the disagreeable yoke of our reason. (Ibid. p. 25)

This kind of ambivalence – once it is tied to a biographical story, of the 'growth'-and-yet-'impairment' of the poet's mind – becomes one of the major characteristics of Wordsworthian Romanticism.

Most influential of all, perhaps, is Burke's aesthetic of 'obscurity'. This stems from a rejection of (Enlightenment) clarity for a darkness that is 'more productive of sublime ideas than light' (*Enquiry*, p. 80). In a conviction that nothing 'can strike the mind with its greatness ... whilst we are able to perceive its bounds', Burke famously declares that 'A clear idea is therefore another name for a little idea' (ibid., p. 63). Sublime response is induced by conditions of 'darkness', 'privation' and 'solitude'. A preference for suggestion over definition, for the limitless over the lucid, is repeatedly expressed in the Romantic period – as, for instance, in the evocative negations of Wordsworth's 'dim and undetermined sense / Of unknown modes of being', and the explicitly Burkean murk within which he casts his early experience of mountain-forms: 'In my thoughts / There was a darkness – call it solitude / Or blank desertion' (*The Prelude*, I, 420ff.). Keats, similarly, conceives of 'a shadow of a magnitude' (*On Seeing the Elgin Marbles*, p. 14) and Coleridge defines as beautiful a 'mountain in a cloudless sky', but as sublime 'the same with its Summit hidden by Clouds, & seemingly blended with the Sky'.[36]

A vital element in the cult of obscurity is Burke's advocacy of poetry, on the assumption that, being more obscure than the visual image, language, poetic language especially, is also more emotive, and hence more efficient at raising the all-important passion of the sublime. This textual sublime bears witness to a weakening of the classical aesthetic, summed up in Horace's motto *ut pictura poesis* ('as in a painting, so also in a poem'). The most significant aspect of Burke's case is that it rests very largely on the example of *Paradise Lost*. In casting Milton as the pre-eminent poet of the sublime, the *Enquiry* plays a crucial role in how his work is mediated to a 'Romantic' consciousness. The exemplary episode is Milton's description of Death (II, 666ff., 'The other shape, / If shape it might be called that shape had none ...'), which fulfils all the Burkean criteria, being 'dark, uncertain, confused, terrible, and sublime to the last degree' (*Enquiry*, p. 59). Among the Romantics' many reimaginings of this shapeless shape, are Wordsworth's Discharged Soldier (*The Prelude*, IV, 360ff.) and Shelley's Demogorgon (*Prometheus Unbound*, II, iv, 2–7). The most impressive critical application of Milton's lines is made by Coleridge, in a lecture of 9 December 1811:

> The grandest efforts of poetry are where the imagination is called forth, not to produce a distinct form, but a strong working of the mind, still offering what is still repelled, and again creating what is again rejected; the result being what the poet wishes to express, namely, the substitution of a sublime feeling of the unimaginable for a mere image.

Unlike the definite image, the indefinite word leaves an empowering residue of the unexpressed and inexpressible. Like Burke before him (*Enquiry*, pp. 61–4), Coleridge draws the moral that Milton's lines '[exhibit] the narrow limit of painting, as compared with the boundless power of poetry'. In point of fact, Coleridge is a connoisseur of visual art (as was Burke in the *Enquiry*, pp. xli–xliv), but, for the purposes of argument, tends to equate the pictorial in poetry with minuteness of detail and lack of vision. This estrangement of the once 'sisterly' arts of poetry and painting is one context in which to see the Romantic repudiation of the picturesque. (The grand exception to the Burkean rule is Blake. His opposition might be expected given that he is a painter, but stems from a wholesale rejection of the art establishment. Against mainstream aesthetics, he insists upon 'determinate and bounding form', and a sublimity of 'Minute Discrimination'.)[37]

The 'strong working of the mind' to which poetry summons the imagination, whether of writer or reader, suggests the subjective labour to which Romanticism is drawn, and which has been well expressed by Albert O. Wlecke:

> Reflexive consciousness discovers the 'shapelessness' of the sublime in its own structure of awareness – a structure unable to 'close itself off' with respect to any clear and distinct object of consciousness. (Wlecke, *Wordsworth and the Sublime*, pp. 81–2)

In its quest after the non-finite and the unconditioned, the Romantic seeks an eternally receding horizon: Wordsworth's apostrophe to imagination climaxes with 'something evermore about to be';[38] Blake's proverbial wisdom holds that 'The most sublime act is to set another before you' (*Marriage of Heaven and Hell*).

Burke's description of the sublime involves a number of ideological issues. One is its naturalizing of the divine: God-like attributes of power, infinity and so forth are located in impressive natural phenomena (stormy seas, mountain ranges, etc.). The ideology of mountain-landscape, running all the way from Burnet to Coleridge, is dramatically exposed when Shelley attempts to engage with – and to dismantle – the entire structure. In *Mont Blanc*, Shelley seeks to imagine a sublime without the underpinning supernatural origin from which the discourse has gained its authority; and, at the same time, 'to repeal / Large codes of fraud and woe' (in religion and politics) to which the sublime has traditionally lent a legitimacy. Another point at issue concerns sexual politics. Briefly, the sublime is associated with 'masculine' qualities of strength and size (those capable of invoking admiration, awe or terror); the beautiful with 'feminine' qualities of smallness, smoothness and delicacy. This more or less explicit gendering of aesthetics is pervasive but mostly goes unscrutinized. One important exception is Mary Wollstonecraft, who questions both the gender alignment and its hierarchical basis, by twitting those 'libertines' who 'assume that woman would be unsexed by acquiring strength of body and mind, and that beauty, soft bewitching beauty! would no longer adorn the daughters of men' (*A Vindication of the Rights of Woman*, ch. 12). Finally, there is the question of the sublime's entanglement in history. In 1789, the French Revolution was popularly inaugurated with the sacking of the Bastille. In 1790, Burke turned decisively against the French and their supporters among his own party in the Commons (the Whig Opposition), by publishing his damning *Reflections on the Revolution in France*. This work not only began the whole conservative backlash against the revolution; it also lead to an overt politicizing of the sublime, as defined by the much earlier *Enquiry*, on both the 'left' and 'right' of the debate. This process gained a grisly credibility when, from 1792–4, the danger of the Burkean sublime became associated with actual revolutionary violence, its terror with *the* Terror. The sublime was suddenly available to (post-)revolutionary interpretation; and, by the same token, the rhetoric of revolution became merged with that of the sublime.[39] Such a convergence of discourses had many effects (amongst the most innovative being seen in the vogueish genre of the Gothic novel).

## Empiricism and Idealism

'Who', asks Kant in the *Critique of Judgment*, 'would apply the term "sublime" even to shapeless mountain masses towering one above the other in wild disorder... or to the dark tempestuous ocean, or such like things?' The answer, as Kant himself is well aware, is almost everyone, and Burke in particular:

> A level plain of a vast extent on land, is certainly no mean idea; the prospect of such a plain may be as extensive as a prospect of the ocean; but can it ever fill the mind with any thing so great as the ocean itself? (*Enquiry*, pp. 57–8)

The explanation Burke offers for the difference between sea and land is that 'to things of great dimensions, if we annex an adventitious idea of terror, they become without comparison greater'. And, being risky, the ocean is necessarily more productive of terror than the plain. But, in either case, notice, it is the 'idea' of the thing – or the 'idea of terror' attached to it – which produces the sublimity. So, although the *Enquiry* does indeed find certain objects 'sublime', it is strictly speaking only the *ideas* of these objects that have this quality.[40]

Burke's rhetoric betrays the rich confusions of empiricist thinking. His sublime is an object so great as to 'fill' the mind; 'Our imagination loves to be filled with an object', as Addison had remarked in the *Spectator* (no. 412). Burke describes in some detail how this fullness comes about: in the 'astonishment' caused by 'the great and sublime in *nature*', 'the mind is so entirely filled with its object, that it cannot entertain any other, nor by consequence reason on that object which employs it' (*Enquiry*, p. 57).

A 'Romantic' version of this 'empiricist' moment occurs in Byron's account, in canto 4 of *Childe Harold*, of entering St Peter's in Rome (for Kant on St Peter's, see the *Critique of Judgment*, p. 100). The hugeness of the man-made object gives it the status of a natural phenomenon: at first, the experience is 'Like climbing some great Alp, which still doth rise'. At last, however, 'The fountain of sublimity displays / Its depth'. In between is the unfolding drama of the mind's relations to the building:

> Thou seest not all; but piecemeal thou must break,
> To separate contemplation, the great whole...

Where Burke's sublime is immediate and irrational, Byron's is achieved by stages and by analysis, as the 'eloquent proportions' – the proportions that make St Peter's a work of art, not an Alp of nature – emerge into consciousness:

> Till, growing with its growth, we thus dilate
> Our spirits to the size of that they contemplate.

A sublime, not of objects or the ideas of objects, but of the mind, is first given decisive and coherent form by Immanuel Kant. *The Critique of Judgment* presents the 'transcendental counterpart to Burke's merely "physiological" or psychological treatment of sublimity' (Körner, *Kant*, p. 190). And it does so by appealing over the head, as it were, of sense-experience, to the 'supersensible':

> *The sublime is that, the mere capacity of thinking which evidences a faculty of mind transcending every standard of sense. (Critique of Judgment, p. 98)*

This faculty is the reason. Neither nature nor, it follows, the faculty by which nature is apprehended (imagination) are sublime. An immediate difficulty arises here, in that British Romanticism typically accords the highest status (often including transcendental powers) to the imagination.[41] From a Romanticist perspective, Kant has a somewhat anomalous position. He notably preferred Milton and Pope to the German Romantic poets; and, although by far the most important philosopher of aesthetics in the period, he was at the time practically unknown in Britain – with the important exception of Coleridge (from about 1801) and also Thomas Beddoes, Henry Crabb Robinson and Thomas De Quincey.[42] Nevertheless, Kant's is the paradigmatic analysis of what has been called the 'sublime of crisis'. This analysis is one context in which to examine the mind–nature split that lies at the divided heart of Romanticism. And the analogy with Kant justly reflects the complexities of the Romantic sublime, wherever a sense of power and triumph is produced out of quite opposite feelings, of inadequacy or bafflement.

It happens this way. Faced with an object of overwhelming size (the unending series of sense-data), the imagination recoils, but is rescued by the reason, whose ideas 'demand that unlimited sequences be thought as completed' (Körner, *Kant*, p. 191). The apparent failure of the imagination is merely a necessary prelude to a recognition of illimitable capacity:

> The point of excess for the imagination . . . is like an abyss in which it fears to lose itself; yet again for the rational idea of the supersensible it is not excessive, but conformable to law, and directed to drawing out such an effort on the part of the imagination: and so in turn as much a source of attraction as it was repellent to mere sensibility. (*Critique of Judgment*, p. 107)

(Like Burke's psychology of the emotions, Kant's epistemology testifies to those affiliations of gender by which the sublime is recognized as 'an experience of masculine struggle and empowerment'.)[43]

In addition, Kant distinguishes between the 'mathematically'[44] and the 'dynamically' sublime. In the first, that which is great in nature is small in comparison with mind, which proposes its own ideas as *'beyond all comparison great'* (*Critique of Judgment*, p. 94). In the second, nature *is* considered as a might and 'looked upon as an object of fear' (so far, so Burkean); but our own 'power of resistance' ensures that, in truth, it 'has no dominion over us' (ibid., pp. 109–11).

Traces of the *Critique* are discernible in Wordsworth's own incomplete essay on 'The Sublime and the Beautiful' of 1811/12 (see *W: Prose Works*, II, pp. 349–60) – a piece that leads Raimonda Modiano to speculate that Coleridge 'managed to turn Wordsworth into a far more faithful disciple of Kant than he was himself' (Modiano, *Coleridge and the Concept of Nature*, p. 129). Just how much Wordsworth picked up from Coleridge is uncertain; but something of the Kantian conflict (of attraction-and-repulsion) and transition (from limitation to limitlessness) is continuously present in Wordsworth. Prime examples would be the apostrophe to imagination, in the account of 'Crossing the Alps', *The Prelude* VI (ll. 525–48), and the Book XI version of the 'spots of time' (ll. 258–73). And yet, to Keats at least, Wordsworth's poetry 'is a thing *per se* and stands alone', demanding the invention of a separate category, which he famously denominates the 'Wordsworthian or egotistical sublime' (letter of 27 October 1818).

The apparent self-sufficiency assumed by Keats's label may still seem to underplay the peculiar ambivalencies of Wordsworth – on the one hand repudiating the external for its deficiency, on the other being 'reconciled' to its 'realities' (e.g. *The Prelude*, VI, 452–61). In the more philosophical concerns of Coleridge, reservations about Kant produce equally creative results. Neither so transcendentalist as to deny the sublime to any sensuous form, nor so anti-transcendentalist as to seek it in the phenomenal, Coleridge devises a third way of encountering sublimity, through the symbol:

> No object of Sense is sublime in itself; but only so far as I make it a symbol of some Idea. The circle is a beautiful figure in itself; it becomes sublime, when I contemplate eternity under that figure.[45]

For the out-and-out Romantic idealist, we must turn, instead, to Blake, in whom reality is constituted by the mind, and 'Mental Things are alone Real' (*A Vision of the Last Judgement*). Given a Blakean imagination, 'One thought fills immensity' and there is nothing that is not sublime: rightly – that is, imaginatively – seen, 'everything would appear to man as it is: infinite' (*The Marriage of Heaven and Hell*).

## Coda

Blake and Coleridge remind us that the sublime has its roots in religion. In the former, the imagination is divinity itself; in the latter, the symbol is founded in the idea of the absolute unity of God as the ground of being, and, it follows, of the oneness of object and subject, world and mind. 'Unity' being the overriding ideal in Coleridge's thought, he naturally designates it 'sublime'. And the origins of this equation emerge, first in Coleridge's early Unitarianism (' 'Tis the sublime of man . . . to know ourselves / Parts and proportions of one wondrous whole', *Religious Musings*, 140–3) and then in Wordsworth's Coleridge-inspired pantheist equivocations, from *Lines Written a Few Miles above Tintern Abbey*, where the poet's reflections upon nature are said to bring

> a sense sublime
> Of something far more deeply interfused . . .
> A motion and a spirit that impels
> All thinking things, all objects of all thought,
> And rolls through all things. (ll. 96–103)

As Weiskel has shown, the oblivious or mystical experience (of 'being spread' through all that is, as part of the 'one life': see *The Prelude*, II, 418–30) is an important counterweight to the 'egotistical' and self-absorbing sublime.

Towards the end of his career, the sacred is once again the dominant note in Wordsworth's conception of sublimity: writing to Landor on 21 January 1824, he expresses a preference for religious works, and confesses that, even in poetry,

> it is the imaginative only, viz., that which is conversant [with], or turns upon infinity, that powerfully affects me . . . unless in those passages where things are lost in each other, and limits vanish, and aspirations are raised, I read with something too much like indifference – but all great poets are in this view powerful Religionists.

To the extent that it expresses the aspirant's reverence before an object of exemplary loftiness and power, much of the Romantic sublime is 'religionist' in temperament, if not in theme or content. This kind of attitude is a consistent feature of Keats's rendering of his own aesthetic ambitions, from the sonnets *On First Looking into Chapman's Homer* and *On Seeing the Elgin Marbles* ('each imagined pinnacle and steep / Of godlike hardship tells me I must die / Like a sick eagle looking at the sky'), to the opening of *The Fall of Hyperion*.

I shall give the last word to Coleridge, not because he is in any way 'definitive' (no one is), but because he returns us rather neatly to each of the three terms that have been under consideration here. He does so in a conversation of May 1821, and in the shape of his own controlling interest in the relationship of the parts to the whole – a totality which, as we have seen, is for him ultimately conceivable only by reference to the Godhead:

> When the whole and the parts are seen at once, as mutually producing and explaining each other, as unity in multeity, there results shapeliness, *forma formosa*. Where the perfection of *form* is combined with pleasurableness in the sensations, excited by the matters or substances so formed, there results the beautiful. . . .
>
> Where the parts by their harmony produce an effect of the whole, but there is no seen form of a whole producing or explaining the parts, i.e. when the parts only are seen and distinguished, but the whole is felt – the picturesque.
>
> Where neither whole nor parts, but unity, as boundless or endless *allness* – the Sublime. (Wittreich, pp. 252–3)

## NOTES

1   The eighteenth century produced a great many treatises on aesthetics and 'taste', among them works by Shaftesbury (1711), Francis Hutcheson (1725), William Hogarth (1753), David Hume (1757), Alexander Gerard (1774), Archibald Alison (1790), Henry Home, Lord Kames (1796), not to mention Voltaire and his fellow encyclopediasts in France.

2  *DWJ*, I, pp. 223–4.

3  Like Kant's two previous Critiques, of the Pure and Practical Reason, *The Critique of Judgment* seeks an *a priori* principle – here, of the reflective judgement: a principle which is related to feeling, and 'demands the fittedness of nature to the purpose of our understanding' (S. Körner, *Kant*, p. 182).

4  Pope, who uses the adjectival form in 1712, ascribes it to the French (see Quennell, *Romantic England*, p. 13); Uvedale Price claims to coin the term 'picturesqueness', and goes into its root in the Italian *'pittoresco'* (*An Essay on the Picturesque*, pp. 51, 54–5).

5  Gilpin, *An Essay upon Prints*, 'Explanation of Terms', p. 2; cf. Repton, *Sketches and Hints on Landscape Gardening* (1794), p. 57: 'By LANDSCAPE I mean a view capable of being represented in painting. It consists of two, three, or more, well marked distances, each separated from the other by an unseen space, which the imagination delights to fill up with fancied beauties, that may not perhaps exist in reality.' And Wordsworth's letter of January 1825: 'Many objects are fit for the pencil [paintbrush] which are not picturesque – but I have been in the habit of applying the word to such objects only as are so'.

6  Price asks 'that instead of the narrow, mechanical practice of a few English gardeners – the noble and varied works of the eminent painters of every age, and of every country, and those of their supreme mistress, Nature, should be the great models of imitation' (*Essay*, p. 375). William Mason translates Du Fresnoy's *De Arte Graphica* as *The Art of Painting* (1783), 'some leading rules to draw / From sovereign Nature's universal law' (ll. 92–3), while in his own poem, *The English Garden* (1781, corrected 1783), 'Art's unerring rule is only drawn / From Nature's sacred source' (II, 70–1): 'we see the picturesque principle exemplified and applied to the living scenery of Nature; but we are not for this reason to conceive that Nature is thus rendered subservient to an Art over which she has not herself previously presided' (*ibid.*, p. 138).

7  Gilpin, *Observations . . . of Scotland*, II, 'Account of the Prints', i: 'I have heretofore made confession to the public, that when I have seen a line out of place, I have a great propensity to correct it by one that is more picturesque.' His *Observations . . . of Cumberland, and Westmoreland* defines such action as letting 'the imagination loose': 'By the force of this creative power an intervening hill may be turned aside; and a distance introduced. . . . Thus the imagination . . . corrects one part of nature by another; and composes a landscape, as the artist composed his celebrated Venus, by selecting accordant beauties from different originals' (i, 119–21).

8  That is, 'a sublimity dependent on the accidents, or on the least essential characters, of the objects to which it belongs' ('The Lamp of Memory', sect. 12, *The Seven Lamps of Architecture*, 1849).

9  Howe, VIII, p. 317.

10  By the early nineteenth century, Britons possessed 80 Claudes, 100 Rosas; engravings of paintings were still more common.

11  Wordsworth first expressed interest in studying these collections in a letter to Beaumont, 25 December 1804. Beaumont's house in Grosvenor Square boasted Claude, Ruysdael and Richard Wilson.

12  Artists unmentioned by Pope and Addison, but examples of whose landscapes were owned by William Kent (according to Watkin, *The English Vision*, p. 14).

13  The Lake District tourist would proceed from 'the delicate touches of Claude, verified on *Coniston* lake, to the noble scenes of *Poussin*, exhibited on *Windermere-water* . . . to the stupendous romantic ideas of *Salvator Rosa*, realized on the lake of *Derwent*' (West's *Guide to the Lakes*, p. 10).

14  To name a few: Paul Sandby, Thomas Hearne, Joseph Farington, John Robert Cozens, William Coxe, Thomas Rowlandson, John 'Warwick' Smith, Joseph Wright of Derby, Philip de Loutherbourg, Julius Caesar Ibbetson, John Sell Cotman, Richard Wilson.

15  'At that moment appeared Kent, painter enough to taste the charms of landscape . . . and born with a genius to strike out a great system from the twilight of imperfect essays. He leaped the fence, and saw that all nature was a garden . . . he realized the compositions of the greatest masters in painting' (Horace Walpole, *Anecdotes of Painting in England*, 4 vols, 1765–71, IV, pp. 137–8). Cf. Wordsworth's lines on his own garden design (influenced by Addison's *Spectator* no. 477), *A Flower Garden at Coleorton Hall*, pp. 27–30 (and Rusell Noyes, *Wordsworth and the Art of Landscape*, Indiana University Press Bloomington, pp. 113, 120):

> We see not nor suspect a bound,
> No more than in some forest wild;
> The sight is free as air – or crost
> Only by art in nature lost . . .

16   First published 1778. Other set texts include William Hutchinson's *Excursion to the Lakes* (1774), John Brown's *Letter, Describing the Vale and Lake of Keswick* (printed in the Addenda to West's *Guide*), James Clarke's *Survey of the Lakes* (1787), Ann Radcliffe's 'Observations during a Tour of the Lakes' (1795), Joseph Wilkinson's *Select Views*, text by Wordsworth (1810).

17   Disguised touches remain, though, as in the view from Red Bank at the beginning of Wordsworth's *Home at Grasmere* (identified by Bicknell and Woof, *Discovery of the Lake District*, pp. 9–11).

18   'Gray's Journal', 1769, originally a series of letters to Dr Thomas Wharton; reprinted in Mason's edition of Gray (1775), and then in West's *Guide*.

19   The largest of ten articles in the Addenda to the third edition of West's *Guide* (1784) was an 'Extract from a Tour to the Caves in the West-Riding of Yorkshire'. See also James Plumptre, 'A journal of a Pedestrian Tour by the Caves in the West Riding of Yorkshire...in the Year 1797' (*James Plumptre's Britain*, ed. Ian Ousby, London, 1992); and Copley, 'William Gilpin and the Black-lead Mine'. Quarrying features in Wordsworth's *Evening Walk*, 139–50, and 'Unpublished Tour' (*W: Prose Works*, II, pp. 315–17).

20   See Edna Aston Shearer, 'Wordsworth and Coleridge Marginalia in a Copy of Richard Payne Knight's *Analytical Inquiry into the Principles of Taste*', *Huntington Library Quarterly* 1 (1937–8), pp. 71–94; and Dorothy Wordsworth to Lady Beaumont, 19 January 1806: 'My Brother thinks that Mr Price has been of great service in correcting the false taste of the Layers out of Parks and Pleasure-grounds' (*MY*, I, p. 3).

21   E.g. Price, *Essay*, 61: 'the two opposite qualities of roughness, and of sudden variation . . . are the most efficient causes of the picturesque'; Gilpin, *Remarks on Forest Scenery... Illustrated by the Scenes of New-Forest in Hampshire*, 2 vols (1791), I, p. 212: 'the wild and rough parts of nature produce the strongest effects on the imagination; and we may add, they are the only objects in landscape, which please the picturesque eye'; and *Observations of Scotland*, II, pp. 121–2: '*Simplicity*, and *variety* are the acknowledged foundations of all picturesque effect.... When the landscape approaches nearer *simplicity*, it approaches nearer the *sublime*; and when *variety* prevails, it tends more to the *beautiful*'.

22   Gilpin cites Burke frequently; for Price, see *Enquiry*, pp. xxxix–xli; see also Repton (*Sketches*, Introduction, p. xvi n. 35), Knight (*Analytical Inquiry*, pp. 74–93), and Hugh Blair, who adapts Burke to 'all the paraphernalia of Ossianic poetry, the cult of nature that was rapidly increasing in popularity' (Monk, *The Sublime*, p. 122).

23   Gilpin, *Observations of Cumberland*, I, p. 49; cf. John Brown's *Letter, Describing the Vale and Lake of Keswick*, where darkness means 'the eye is lost', and 'active fancy travels beyond sense, / And pictures things unseen' (West, *Guide*, p. 192); and Ann Radcliffe, *The Mysteries of Udolpho*, vol. IV, ch. 12, which alludes to Brown's *Letter*, quotes Beattie's *Minstrel* (the 'waste of vapour', also recalled by Wordsworth in *Descriptive Sketches*) and states that, 'To a warm imagination, the dubious forms, that float, half veiled in darkness, afford a higher delight, than the most distinct scenery, that the sun can shew', as 'the fancy...wanders over landscapes partly of its own creation'.

24   Heffernan, *Re-creation of Landscape*, p. 169: 'the transformations wrought by atmosphere in the natural world provided poets and painters alike with a model for the transformations they sought to achieve in their respective arts'. See Gilpin, *Observations of Cumberland*, I, p. 11, *Scotland*, I, p. 15, and *on the Western Parts of England* (1798), p. 166 ('the grand effects which may often be produced by, what may be called, *the scenery of vapour*. Nothing offers so extensive a field to the fancy in *invented* scenes; nothing subjects even the *compositions of nature* so much to the control and improvement of art. It admits the painter to a participation with the poet in the use of the machinery of *uncertain forms*; to which both are indebted for their *sublimest images*').

25   In 1721, the English translator of Leonardo Da Vinci's apocryphal *Treatise of Painting* notes that '*Clair-obscure*, by the *Italians* called, *Chiaro oscuro*, is the art of managing Lights and Shadows' (p. 44 n).

26   *John Constable's Discourses*, quoted in Heffernan, *Re-creation of Landscape*, p. 155.

27   The wrong pictorial analogy, since Derwentwater is associated with the 'sublime' style of Rosa.

28   Named after the French painter, habitually used by Gray, and described by Mason as 'a plano-convex mirror of about four inches diameter on a black foil, and bound up like a pocket-book' (West, *Guide*, p. 198 n). For illustrations and

discussion, see Andrews, *Search for the Picturesque*, pp. 67–73.

29  Illustrated by Thomas Rowlandson (1812); the series began in *Poetical Magazine* (1809).

30  See Copley and Garside, *The Politics of the Picturesque*: Robinson, *Inquiry into the Picturesque*, chapters 3–4; Bermingham, *Landscape and Ideology*; and Liu, *Wordsworth*, pp. 61–90.

31  *The Prelude*, XI, 154–5. As Heffernan, *Recreation of Landscape*, p. 12, points out, Wordsworth's diction echoes Thomson's *Spring*, 505–6, which acclaims 'nature...undisguised by mimic art'; the phrase also occurs in the specifically picturesque context of Payne Knight's *The Landscape* (1794), III, 305, a three-book didactic poem, 'Addressed to Uvedale Price', and read by Dorothy Wordsworth on 27 June 1800 (*DWJ*, I, p. 52).

32  John Baillie, *An Essay on the Sublime* (1747).

33  See Abrams *ML*, ch. 4 ii, ch. 6 ii.

34  Lecture, 4 March 1819: Wittreich, *The Romantics on Milton*, p. 244.

35  See especially the Burkean opening of chapter nine of Johnson's *Rasselas* (Dennis was expressing 'a delightful Horrour, a terrible Joy' as early as 1688: Andrews, *The Picturesque*, I, p. 92).

36  CC *Marginalia*, II, p. 1,070 (on Herder).

37  *A Descriptive Catalogue*; 'Annotations to Reynolds', Wittreich, *The Romantics on Milton*, p. 98 n. 9.

38  *The Prelude*, VI, 542; cf. Burke's theory of infinity in objects, where 'the imagination is entertained with the promise of something more, and does not acquiesce in the present object of the sense' (*Enquiry*, p. 77) and Gilpin's revision: the imagination refuses to be satisfied, 'not because it is entertained with a *promise of something more*; but because it has the power, of *creating something more itself*' (*Observations of Cumberland*, II, pp. 15–16).

39  E.g. Burke's ironizing of the revolutionary ideologues who 'find, on all sides, bounds to their unprincipled ambition in any fixed order of things. But in the fog and haze of confusion all is enlarged, and appears without any limit' (*Reflections*, p. 136).

40  Cf. *Critique of Judgment*, p. 92: 'the broad ocean agitated by storms cannot be called sublime. Its aspect is horrible, and one must have stored one's mind in advance with a rich stock of ideas, if such an intuition is to raise it to the pitch of a feeling which is itself sublime'.

41  Wordsworth and Coleridge do think of imagination in post-Kantian terms as 'reason in her most exalted mood' (*The Prelude*, XIII, 170) – *most* exalted, because 'reason' in a low-grade analytical sense is generally regarded as *opposed* to 'imagination'.

42  Dr Beddoes (the physician father of the poet) was a friend of Coleridge at Bristol and, aided by a large German library, was a pioneer Kantian. *The Monthly Magazine* for 1796 (which Wordsworth received in March 1797) offered his 'translated specimen from the Kritik des Urtheilskrafts' (corresponding to Kant's *Critique of Judgment*, pp. 199–201). Another early translator, Nitzsch, gave lectures in London.

43  Mellor, *Romanticism and Gender*, p. 87.

44  For Wordsworth's use of maths to convey sublimity, see *The Prelude*, XII, 145–52 and *W: Prose Works*, II, p. 357.

45  CC *Marginalia* II, p. 1,069 n. Coleridge's conclusion, that 'The Beautiful is the perfection, the Sublime the suspension, of the Comparing Power', is straight out of Kant: see *Critique of Judgment*, pp. 94–5, 98–9; and cf. Wordsworth's Kantian–Coleridgean definition in 'The Sublime and the Beautiful': 'whatever suspends the comparing power of the mind & possesses it with a feeling or image of intense unity, without a conscious contemplation of parts, has produced that state of the mind which is the consummation of the sublime' (*W: Prose Works*, II, pp. 353–4).

## Writings

Andrews, M. (ed.), *The Picturesque: Literary Sources & Documents*, 3 vols, Helm Information: Mountfield, East Sussex, 1994. Invaluable collection of primary material with commentary

Ashfield, Andrew and de Bolla, Peter (eds), *The Sublime: A Reader in British Eighteenth-century Aesthetic Theory*, Cambridge, Cambridge University Press, 1996. Useful anthology.

Burke, Edmund, *A Philosophical Enquiry into the Origin of our Ideas of the Sublime and Beautiful*, ed. James T. Boulton, Oxford, Basil Blackwell, 1987. Helpful Introduction

——*Reflections on the Revolution in France*, Harmondsworth, Penguin, 1969.

Gilpin, William, *Observations on the River Wye, and several parts of South Wales, &c. relative chiefly to*

*Picturesque Beauty; made in the Summer of the Year 1770*, Woodstock Books Facsimile, intro. J. Wordsworth, Oxford and New York, 1991.

—— *Observations, relative chiefly to Picturesque Beauty, Made in the Year 1772, on Several Parts of England; particularly the Mountains, and Lakes of Cumberland, and Westmoreland*, 2 vols, Woodstock Books Facsimile, intro. J. Wordsworth, Oxford and New York, 1996.

—— *Observations, relative chiefly to Picturesque Beauty, Made in the Year 1776, on several Parts of Great Britain; particularly the High-Lands of Scotland*, 2 vols, 1789.

Kant, Immanuel, *Critique of Judgment*, tr. J. C. Meredith, Oxford, Clarendon Press, 1952.

Longinus, *On the Sublime*, in *Classical Literary Criticism*, trans. T. S. Dorsch, Harmondsworth, Penguin, 1965.

Price, Sir Uvedale, *An Essay on the Picturesque, as compared with the Sublime and the Beautiful; and, on the Use Of Studying Pictures, for the purpose of Improving Real Landscape*, 2nd edn, enlarged, 1796.

West, Thomas, *A Guide to the Lakes, in Cumberland, Westmorland, and Lancashire*, 3rd edn, Woodstock Books Facsimile, intro. J. Wordsworth, Oxford, 1989.

## REFERENCES AND FURTHER READING

Andrews, Malcolm, *The Search for the Picturesque: Landscape Aesthetics and Tourism in Britain, 1760–1800*, Aldershot, Scolar Press, 1990. Excellent for early tours.

Barbier, Carl Paul, *William Gilpin: His Drawings, Teaching, and Theory of the Picturesque*, Oxford, Oxford University Press, 1963.

Bermingham, Ann, *Landscape and Ideology: The English Rustic Tradition, 1740–1860*, London, Thames & Hudson, 1987.

Bicknell, Peter and Woof, Robert, *The Discovery of the Lake District 1750–1810: A Context for Wordsworth*, Grasmere: The Trustees of Dove Cottage, 1982.

Brennan, Matthew, *Wordsworth, Turner, and Romantic Landscape: A Study in the Traditions of the Picturesque and the Sublime*, Columbia, SC, Camden, 1987.

Clarke, Michael, and Penny, Nicholas (eds) *The Arrogant Connoisseur: Richard Payne Knight, 1754–1824*, Manchester, Manchester University Press, 1982.

Copley, S., 'William Gilpin and the black-lead mine', in *The Politics of the Picturesque: Literature, Landscape, and Aesthetics since 1770*, ed. Stephen Copley and Peter Garside, Cambridge, Cambridge University Press, 1994.

Ferguson, Frances, *Solitude and the Sublime: Romanticism and the Aesthetics of Individuation*, New York and London, Routledge, 1992.

Heffernan, James A. W., *The Re-creation of Landscape: A Study of Wordsworth, Coleridge, Constable, and Turner*, Hanover and London, University Press of New England, 1984.

Hertz, Neil, *The End of the Line: Essays on Psychoanalysis and the Sublime*, New York, Columbia University Press, 1987.

Hipple, Walter John, *The Beautiful, the Sublime, and the Picturesque in Eighteenth-century British Aesthetic Theory*, Carbondale, Southern Illinois University Press, 1957.

Hussey, Christopher, *The Picturesque: Studies in a Point of View*, London: F. Cass, 1927).

Liu, Alan, *Wordsworth: The Sense of History*, Stanford, Stanford University Press, 1989.

Manwaring, Elizabeth, *Italian Landscape in Eighteenth Century England: A Study Chiefly of the Influence of Claude Lorrain and Salvator Rosa on English Taste 1700–1800*, New York and Oxford, Oxford University Press, 1925.

Mellor, Anne K., *Romanticism and Gender*, New York and London, Routledge, 1993.

Modiano, Raimonda, *Coleridge and the Concept of Nature*, London and Basingstoke, Macmillan, 1985.

Monk, Samuel H., *The Sublime: A Study of Critical Theories in XVIII-century England*, New York, Modern Language Association of America, 1935. Good on eighteenth-century theory.

Morris, David B., *The Religious Sublime: Christian Poetry and Critical Tradition in Eighteenth-century England*, Lexington, University Press of Kentucky, 1972. Chapter five includes Blake, Wordsworth, Coleridge.

Murdoch, John, *The Discovery of the Lake District: A Northern Arcadia and its Uses*, London, Victoria and Albert Museum, 1984.

Nicolson, Marjorie, *Mountain Gloom and Mountain Glory: The Development of the Aesthetics of the Infinite*, Ithaca, Cornell University Press, 1959.

Price, Martin, 'The picturesque moment', in *From Sensibility to Romanticism*, ed. F. W. Hilles and Harold Bloom, Oxford, Oxford University Press, 1965, 259–92.

Thorpe, Clarence DeWitt, 'Coleridge on the Sublime', in *Wordsworth and Coleridge: Studies in the*

*Honor of George McLean Harper*, ed. E. L. Griggs, Princeton, Princeton University Press, 1939, 193–219.

Quennell, Peter, *Romantic England: Writing and Painting 1717–1851*, London, Weidenfeld & Nicolson, 1970.

Watkin, David, *The English Vision: The Picturesque in Architecture, Landscape and Garden Design*, London, John Murray, 1982.

Watson, J. R., *Picturesque Landscape and English Romantic Poetry*, London, Hutchinson Educational, 1970.

Weiskel, Thomas, *The Romantic Sublime: Studies in the Structure and Psychology of Transcendence*, Baltimore and London, Johns Hopkins University Press, 1976. Difficult but rewarding psychoanalytic study.

Wilton, Andrew, *Turner and the Sublime*, London, British Museum Publications, 1980.

Wittreich, J. A., *The Romantics on Milton*, Cleveland and London, Case Western Reserve University Press, 1970.

Wlecke, Albert O., *Wordsworth and the Sublime*, Berkeley, Los Angeles and London: University of California Press, 1973.

Wood, Theodore E. B., *The Word 'Sublime' and its Context 1650–1760*, The Hague: Mouton, 1972.

# 8

# The Romantic Reader

*Stephen C. Behrendt*

To imagine 'the Romantic *reader*' (singular) is to imagine what never was. The problem is not that we lack sufficient historical facts and figures – adequate demographics – even though the evidence available after nearly two centuries is necessarily incomplete. Rather, our imaginary creature would inevitably end up like that most famous of Romantic Creatures, the poor outsized misfit whose terrible history Mary Shelley recorded in *Frankenstein* (1818). Like Frankenstein's Creature, our hypothetical Romantic reader would be at once too large and too unwieldy – and in any case too messily stitched together from ill-matched parts – to have either a real identity of its own or a proper resemblance to anything else. For 'the Romantic reader' was in truth not *a* reader but rather a dynamic array of highly diverse readers who comprised identifiable but flexible audiences that sometimes overlapped but more often did not. And while the reasons for which these readerships turned to printed materials in the first place varied widely, those reasons changed in a number of ways as the period progressed, so that readers of 1830 were very different from their predecessors of a half-century earlier. This essay explores some of the factors that affected who read, and what they read, during the roughly fifty years (1780–1830, give or take some few years at either end) that we usually think of as the Romantic period in England. In the process, it also considers what it might have meant to read in a Romantic fashion and thus to have been not just a reader during the Romantic period but also a 'Romantic reader'.

The eighteenth-century reading public, at least until the 1780s, was remarkably homogeneous despite the emergence of the artisanal and commercial middle class and the increasingly self-sufficient literature (and means of production) that evolved to satisfy the reading demands of this new audience. The typical eighteenth-century reader was comparatively well-educated, socially cultivated, and imbued with a sense of belonging to a cultural (if not specifically a national) community, and by the 1780s that reader was more and more likely to be a woman. The eighteenth century witnessed the rise of the novel, which catered especially to the tastes and experience of the emerging middle class, and the development of a steadily expanding range of print materials extending from the natural and physical sciences, philosophy (including aesthetics) and philology (including grammar and linguistics), to agriculture and husbandry, to works of a specifically religious (and especially evangelical) nature. It also saw the beginning of a large industry in works written for children or for adults charged with their education.

But books were expensive to produce: paper was expensive, and setting type by hand and printing on slow presses meant that producing 10,000 copies of a large book of 300 pages might tie up a press for as long as nine months. Such print runs were exceedingly rare, though; typically, far fewer than the thousand copies of Wordsworth's *Poems, in Two Volumes* (1807) were prepared for any single edition. Nevertheless, the price of books made their ownership difficult for any but the relatively well-to-do, since the average octavo volume of 1800 cost some ten shillings, which might make up the better part of a week's wages for a member of the working class. Major publishers often kept the prices of books artificially inflated by printing them in expensive editions as prestige goods, which meant that the actual *ownership* of books remained part of the privilege enjoyed by the upper classes, a point that is directly related to the vehemence with which both the privileged classes and the publishers who served them reacted against the spread in the 1790s and thereafter of mass-produced books and the cheap editions they permitted. Moreover, literacy was regarded among the privileged classes as an insulator against the supposed vulgarity of the lower classes that was understood to disqualify them (and their concerns) from serious consideration. Throughout the Romantic period the failure to employ 'polite' (i.e. 'correct') language in documents of all sorts (e.g. petitions to parliament) so stigmatized their authors that the documents were often disregarded entirely, no matter what the merits of their actual contents (see Smith, *The Politics of Language*). To use 'vulgar' language was then, as now, to advertise one's failure to rise to the linguistic – and therefore the social – standards of the dominant class or party. After Wordsworth claimed in his preface to the second edition of *Lyrical Ballads* (1800) to have avoided artificially inflated diction and employed 'the language really spoken by men', even his friend Coleridge observed in his *Biographia Literaria* (1817) that Wordsworth's idiom bore virtually no relation to the actual spoken language of the average English citizen but had been significantly modified and 'improved' to conform to the expectations for printed discourse.

The nature and size of readerships changed dramatically in the 1790s, as was made alarmingly apparent to the political and cultural establishment when the first part of Thomas Paine's *Rights of Man* (1791) generated such an enormous popular readership that both restrictive government legislation and a flood of reactionary counter-arguments in print were unleashed against it and its author. Nor was this sort of response confined only to the early period. When in 1818 the Radical publisher Richard Carlile republished Paine's *The Age of Reason* he was arrested and imprisoned as part of the crackdown on dissent. As it had done 25 years earlier, the government responded with repressive measures, including in 1819 the notorious 'six acts', which levied heavy new taxes on the sort of opposition periodicals whose cheap prices (and rousing rhetoric) had made them favourites among working-class readers. Still, the public appetite for oppositional materials remained as strong at the time as it had been in the 1790s; 1819–22 saw some 100,000 copies (in an astonishing 47 editions) of *The Political House that Jack Built*, written and published by the Radical publisher William Hone with wonderfully irreverent illustrations by George Cruikshank.

By the end of the eighteenth century Lord Stanhope's new iron printing press had made it possible to produce books much more rapidly (though not necessarily more cheaply), and the adoption in 1814 of steam-driven presses by the London *Times* made larger print runs of the daily papers possible. The numbers of books being produced had by 1800 already become staggering. In 1798, when *Lyrical Ballads* first appeared, for instance, it was but one of nearly 150 books *of poetry alone* published in England in that year. Indeed, between 1770 and 1830, more than 10,000 separate volumes *just of poetry* were published, while in 1792 alone some 6,000 printed items appeared in England. The cost of 'fine' books continued to rise as the new century began, in part because some publishers attempted to perpetuate the illusion that high price related directly to literary merit. But enterprising publishers like John Bell, James Lackington and John Cooke had already discovered that an enormous market existed for cheap books among newly literate and curious readers. Bell, for example, made huge profits from large series of reprinted works (his English poets series appeared already in 1777) which could be produced cheaply and marketed by shrewd appeals to nationalism, economy and pride of ownership. And already in 1791, in his memoirs, Lackington could justifiably claim credit for contributing significantly to literacy by his practices of cheaply remaindering recent unsold books rather than destroying them (as was usually done) and selling both used books and new ones. Moreover, as more and more books entered the market, second-hand bookstalls proliferated, providing at large discounts (and in less intimidating surroundings than those of the polite booksellers) books for which the established publishers charged their patrons premium prices.

The eighteenth century had also witnessed the first great flowering of periodical literature. Along with essays on a variety of topics these periodicals typically included numerous letters addressed to the editor (and readers), often written by the editors themselves when genuine readers did not write in sufficient numbers. The editorial exchanges that ensued often took on the conversational tone of a largely urban and typically urbane community of readers who approached their reading as active participants in a dialogue. By 1800 this, too, was changing, as periodicals proliferated (more than 80 literary journals alone appeared – albeit some only briefly – during the Romantic period) and became increasingly specialized as they sought to address the particular social, political, religious *and occupational* profiles of their intended audiences. Romantic periodicals became less conversational, too: readers were no longer invited to participate in dialogue but were, rather, harangued, cajoled, instructed, occasionally berated, and ultimately silenced, as may be seen from the diminishing space allotted to private contributors and the increasing prominence given to professional, paid 'correspondents' whose status would eventually be indicated by by-lines.

In *The Making of English Reading Audiences*, the best study to date of the Romantic literary periodical, Jon Klancher argues that the Romantic periodical effectively shaped the reading public (or, more accurately, publics) by drawing the attention of readers to the very activities of reading by which they were coming to define themselves and their social and political status. Discovering themselves as readers, these citizens also discovered from their reading shared social and political values, aspirations and resentments that forged group identities among them and distinguished them from the otherwise undifferentiated masses. William Godwin, the Utopian anarchist philosopher of the 1790s (and husband of the early feminist Mary Wollstonecraft, father of Mary Shelley, and father-in-law of Percy Bysshe Shelley), had declared in 1793 in his *Enquiry Concerning Political Justice* that the ideal community was one in which *conversation* held a special place. In order to move ever nearer an ideal society, according to Godwin, citizens needed to gather to discuss ideas formulated from their reading. Hence, he was particularly worried by the increasing tendency toward specialization, both in periodical literature and among society as a whole, which he correctly predicted would steadily decrease the common ground upon which this healthy conversation might take place. Ironically, 200 years later technological advances like the Internet have further isolated readers and undermined community by encouraging wholly private reading activities tied to one's computer, while at the same time, paradoxically, they are fostering a new sort of community through the potential for instantaneous discussion provided by the World Wide Web. The more things change in the modern world, it seems, the more they stay the same.

Unlike the market in fine books, the periodical market in the Romantic period was characterized by low prices and by very high numbers of copies. By 1810, major periodicals like the staunchly Tory *Quarterly Review* often printed as many as 5,000 copies. Nor was this all. The circulation of the *Quarterly Review* had risen to 14,000 in 1818 while that of *The Edinburgh Review*, the principal Whig journal, had reached 12,000 by 1818. Perhaps more startling, religious periodicals like *The Methodist Magazine* and *The Evangelical Magazine* had in 1807 already reached 18,000 to 20,000 copies each, capitalizing on the carefully cultivated appetite for morally uplifting reading fostered both by the fundamentalist and evangelical movements and by the increase in literacy that had resulted from the proliferation of 'Sunday schools' and other educational institutions associated with religious denominations. That these were often distributed without charge, of course, played no small part in these numbers and in the overall reading experiences of the comparatively large numbers who read (or had read to them) their earnest contents.

Not surprisingly, numerous journals like the ubiquitous John Bell's *La Belle Assemblée* (1806–32) addressed themselves specifically to female readers. However, journals like *The Lady's Magazine* (1770–1819) or *The British Lady's Magazine* (1815–19) offered more than society and fashion, including as they did sophisticated contributions (often written by women) on arts and letters, political matters and history (including in the latter journal an ongoing 'department' called 'Memoirs of Eminent Women'). Women readers, already numerous at the beginning of the period, became ever more so, and the expansion of reading matter both for and by women did much to effect significant social change by increasing both the sense of community among women and the sociopolitical activism that – for them scarcely less than for the men – grew in proportion to the increasing wealth of information available to them in print.

At the other end of the spectrum, one of the most famous radical journals of the Regency, Thomas Wooler's *Black Dwarf*, appeared in some 12,000 copies in 1819. Perhaps most remarkable of all was William Cobbett's *Political Register*, which he had begun in 1802 as a Tory journal but which by 1815 reflected Cobbett's strong radical populism. Published originally at prices as high as a shilling halfpenny, the journal by the middle of the Regency was still beyond the reach of most and the actual number of copies printed seldom reached 2,000. When in 1816 and afterward the Tory government attempted to quash resistance to its policies by clamping down on opposition publications, prosecuting opposition publishers, and eliminating the practice of reading-out of periodicals in public houses, Cobbett issued a pamphlet version of the *Political Register* priced at two pence.

Within a few months the circulation leapt to 40,000 or more – and perhaps to as high as 70,000 – far outstripping any other periodical of the time.

In fact, the actual figures for copies of periodicals printed during the Romantic period are misleading. For coffee-houses and pubs alike regularly subscribed to periodicals so that customers who might be unable to afford them on their own could find them in these public locations. Not only did the readership thus far exceed the number of copies; the number of 'readers' swells still further when we consider the many illiterate or only moderately literate citizens who heard the contents of these periodicals read out at the pubs, coffee-houses, clubs and trades centres in which both London and the provinces abounded.

Publication numbers for books are often equally misleading, for if the audiences for periodicals were expanded exponentially by public reading, so, too, were the numbers of book readers comparably augmented by the circulating libraries that sprang up throughout England in the Romantic period. Richard Altick, in what is arguably still the finest study of nineteenth-century British reading habits, explains that these circulating libraries (and the semi-private book clubs, or 'book societies', that enjoyed a parallel success) were designed to assist not just a middle-class audience of artisans, tradesmen and apprentices of limited, though growing, financial resources, but also strapped upper-middle-class and upper-class families who were finding it increasingly hard (and, ultimately, unnecessary) to afford new books when commonly held ones could be borrowed (see Altick, *The English Common Reader*, pp. 217–19). Driven by obvious self-interest, the literary elite and their publishers for the most part ridiculed both the works that made up the circulating libraries and the patrons that read them. Coleridge, for instance, in a well-known passage from chapter three of his *Biographia Literaria*, said of 'the devotees of the circulating libraries' that 'I dare not compliment their *pass-time*, or rather *kill-time*, with the name of *reading*. Call it rather a sort of beggarly day-dreaming, during which the mind of the dreamer furnishes for itself nothing but laziness, and a little mawkish sensibility'. And yet in 1821 it was claimed in the *Monthly Magazine* that there were at least 6,500 circulating libraries (or 'book societies') in England, serving more than 30,000 families.

In the most recent study of canonical British Romantic poets, their audiences and the literary market-place, William Rowland, Jr. writes that most were from the start 'ambivalent about the new reading audiences, and particularly about signs of the developing mass audience' (Rowland, *Literature and the Marketplace*, p. 18). Given the democratic impulses with which we often associate canonical authors like Wordsworth, Coleridge, Blake and Shelley, it is interesting to discover the extent to which they shared with the privileged classes the strong distaste for what we would call the average reader and the average citizen. In the preface to the 1800 edition of *Lyrical Ballads* Wordsworth excoriated the readers of 'frantic novels, sickly and stupid German tragedies, and deluges of idle and extravagant stories in verse'. The novels to which Wordsworth objected undoubtedly included the 'bestsellers' of his day, which were being published by the Minerva Press. These novels were for the most part romantic thrillers, the late eighteenth-century equivalent of the Harlequin romances of the later twentieth century, populated by a remarkable cast of young women in distress and dashing young men eager to save them from a perennial assortment of dastardly men (old or young), cruel parents, spiteful siblings and unfeeling institutions that can frequently be read as surrogates for the rigid patriarchal institutions of a reactionary English cultural establishment in the wake of the French Revolution. Of course, such fiction was intended to entertain, to titillate and to bring on paroxysms of sentimental indulgence; literature's old familiar duty to educate was largely irrelevant in this formula. This is precisely why authorities from religious sects to political parties and from critical reviewers to writers who styled themselves 'legitimate authors' inveighed mightily against the 'light literature' represented by the likes of the Minerva Press offerings, which they accused of undermining moral character.

In reality, the hidden motive for many among the privileged classes was the worry that access to pleasurable reading matter would further stimulate what they regarded as the dangerous growth of literacy among lower-class citizens devoid of reliable political, social and moral allegiances, for 'every new reader in the lower ranks of society meant another potential victim of radical contagion' (Altick, *The English Common Reader*, p. 76). Upper and middle classes agreed that 'the supreme threat came from below' and that 'the growth of the reading habit was to blame' for jeopardizing the familiar order of rank and privilege (Cranfield, *The Press and Society*, p. 120). Hence, the shrewdness of the plan devised by Hannah More and other reactionaries to combat the spread of 'seditious' or 'anti-Christian' works by creating the Cheap Repository Tracts (1795–8), a series of works of various lengths, in verse and in prose, retailing for a half-penny to one-and-a-half pence, which mimicked in physical appearance and in writing style the inexpensive and popular anti-establishment tracts and pamphlets but which instead inculcated sociopolitical conformity and moral convention. The lesson of the Cheap Repository Tracts for the mass production and consumption of reading matter was not wasted on the enterprising publishers who would attempt to duplicate their success by replicating their methods. Gradually, many of the intended readers came to recognize works like these, and like those distributed by the Christian Knowledge Society preaching stoic acceptance of social injustice, for what they were. As often as not, they came to reject them out of hand, just as they began by the middle of the Regency to regard with contempt whole balefuls of earnest moral, religious and sociopolitical writings being distributed free of charge. In other words once literacy was acquired and once occasional and initially difficult exercises in reading had evolved into a reading *habit*, readers became both more sophisticated and more selective.

This is precisely what the nominal custodians of culture feared. Coleridge, for instance, like so many of his contemporaries, altered his initial republican enthusiasm for 'the people' when it became clear that the 'people' would not submit obligingly to being tutored as the cultural elite desired. Often they disguised their criticism as a defence of tradition and 'quality'. Coleridge wrote in the *Biographia* that 'the multitude of books and the general diffusion of literature, have produced . . . lamentable effects in the world of letters', including the fact that 'literature at present demands the least talent or information' of any variety of published writing. Ironically, like Wordsworth, who had written in the 1800 preface to *Lyrical Ballads* that the poet 'is a man speaking to men' (which statement implies that all men are therefore at least potentially poets), Coleridge complains that the democratization of the arts has permitted everyone to feel a measure of equality and of artistry that compromises the privileged position of the writer-sage. Only the year before, in the 'Essay, Supplementary to the Preface' of his 1815 *Poems*, Wordsworth had likewise drawn an unflattering distinction between 'the people', which he idealized as sensible, thoughtful, even philosophical patriots, and 'the public', which he largely equated with what Carlyle would in *The French Revolution* derisively call 'the Mob'. Rowland stresses the irony of this situation when he notes that the parochialism of comments by writers like Wordsworth and Coleridge reveals their failure to grasp the true democratizing potential posed by the expansion of literacy and of the reading habit among all classes of society (Rowland, *Literature and the Marketplace*, p. 28). Shelley's 1819 observation in the preface to his *Prometheus Unbound* that he had addressed his works to the 'more select classes of poetical readers' merely underscores the self-isolating nature of the struggle faced by many Romantic writers in conceptualizing and 'conversing' with readers who were no longer familiar faces, nor even part of a community of shared interest or motivation. Under such circumstances, some literary figures increasingly styled themselves (as Blake and Shelley did) as spurned prophets or 'unacknowledged legislators' whose true merits would only be appreciated after the generations of contemporary readers for whom they professed contempt had passed away.

Unlike so many of the men, women writers tended to voice a better opinion of their readers and to trust more fully to their inherent good sense. Perhaps this was because so many women had turned successfully to writing as a means of supporting themselves and their families, either because they had been victims of disastrous marriages (like Mary Darby Robinson or Charlotte Turner Smith) or because the constraints of poverty or physical debility closed other options. The rise in the eighteenth century of the self-supporting writer – the novelist in particular – made it possible in the Romantic period for women to succeed financially at writing by providing what their audiences were eager to purchase, a lesson that Felicia Hemans learned particularly well. No longer regarded universally as oddities or monstrosities, as they were savagely styled in misogynist works like Richard Polwhele's *The Unsex'd Females* (1798), women authors were in fact among the period's most highly regarded *and financially successful*. Maria Edgeworth, for instance, earned the extraordinary sum of £11,000 from her writings, while there is little question that in the years following Byron's premature death in 1824 the two most popular poets in England were Felicia Hemans and Letitia Elizabeth Landon ('L. E. L.', who was also a prolific writer of fiction and criticism, as well as a successful editor with literary annuals like *Fisher's Drawing-Room Scrapbook*). Little matter that we can trace in the works of both the beginnings of the Victorian rewriting of woman as 'the angel of the house'; Hemans' works sold phenomenally well and Landon's were so eagerly anticipated that new issues of periodicals in which her works appeared before the identity of the mysterious 'L. E. L.' was known were certain to sell out in short order to readers eager for her latest offering. Indeed, the stunning sales of poetry and imaginative prose by women, which rivalled and often surpassed the numbers generated by all but the two male literary 'superstars' of the time – Byron and Scott – has in our own time prompted a re-evaluation of Romantic writing that acknowledges that any proper assessment of 'the Romantic reader' must take account of what was being *produced* by women, who made up a very substantial share of the authorial pool, and of what was being *consumed* by women, who made up an equally large portion of *that* pool.

The defining event of the early Romantic period was unquestionably the French Revolution, not just because of the impetus it lent to republican aspirations in England (and to reactionary repudiations of such aspirations), but also because its physical consequences for British citizens were so profound. The war that ensued, and that dragged on for roughly half the Romantic period, until Napoleon's final defeat at Waterloo in 1815, disrupted all aspects of daily life. While commerce and the economy were naturally impacted, no disruption was more profound than that which resulted from the continual consumption of British men in the armed forces, for their departure devastated many families for whom they had been principal if not exclusive providers. Their deaths or maiming in battle (or from disease, a still more common killer) further ruined those families, who were often thrown into inescapable poverty. Countless poems, plays, stories and other fictional works – not to mention ostensibly 'factual' reports in the periodicals – recounted the sufferings of all parties in this tragic drama, and the increasingly prevalent sense of personal, societal and psychological alienation brought on both by these events and by their continual reiteration in printed matter gradually became a hallmark of the second half of the Romantic period.

The second half of the Romantic period was governed less by any single defining event than by a pervasive volatility and instability, both on the 'macro' scale of national society, politics and economics and on the 'micro', quotidian level of the individual family unit and its circumstances. As the world moved uneasily but ever more rapidly (and irreversibly) into the modern urban, industrial, technological age of anxiety, reading matter reflected the disorientation, doubt and frustration of readers who were either newly disenfranchised by these changes or who were just now learning to recognize from their reading the extent of their longstanding disenfranchisement for other reasons. Both the book and periodical markets divided still further as they sought to satisfy the demands of readers searching, variously, for sensation, escape, personal self-help, professional improvement, cultural enrichment, and moral and spiritual sustenance. If the reading matter of the earlier half of the period abounded in sentimentalized accounts of disrupted families who were the domestic victims of war, the later period saw these victims replaced by stylized 'outsiders' like racially or ethnically ostracized figures (Blacks and Indians in particular) upon whom the conditions of marginality and victimization could be displaced. The later period saw, too, the rise of paradoxically charismatic outsiders like Byron's anti-social protagonists whose combined inability and refusal to accommodate their personal values to the increasingly valueless modern society struck a responsive chord with count-less readers.

That the most popular fictional vehicle of the earlier period, the Gothic romance, waned in popularity and was replaced by the historical novel for which Scott supplied the immensely successful prototype, suggests that later Romantic readers were attempting to discover in history rather than in fantasy some explanation for the present human condition, and that they were beginning to look more closely at their own national traditions for these explanations. This was natural enough, given that the progress of the French Revolution and the war that followed, and their implications for England, were matters of obvious urgency to all. The periodical press was filled with accounts of international events, which fostered among readers an increasing interest in geography and especially history. Readers turned more and more to print materials to satisfy their curiosity, as is evident from the growing number of publications on historical subjects generally and on recent history in particular.

At the same time, expanded reading of both scientific and 'practical' professional materials reveals the turn toward a personal and collective pragmatism that parallels the rise of Utilitarian thinking and foreshadows the 'work ethic' that would figure largely in Victorian ideology. The growth in what we would today call 'trades literature' – that is, materials specific to particular professions and their interests – reflects the recognition that reading offered a viable and individualized avenue for self-improvement. It also parallels the spread of 'mechanics institutes' designed 'to impart the elements of scientific knowledge to workingmen through classes, lectures, and libraries' (Altick, *The English Common Reader*, p. 188). These institutes, which are generally traced back to Dr George Birkbeck (who organized them in Glasgow at the beginning of the century) and J. Robertson and Thomas Hodgkin (who formed a comparable institution in London in 1824), proved of greatest value not in offering lectures and classes to exhausted workers, but rather in providing extensive libraries that promoted book-reading among the laboring classes, even when the books in these libraries varied widely in subject matter and quality. For if many of the books went unread, others were read over and over. Again, reading became a *habit*.

The bottom line, then, is that Romantic readers were increasingly *engaged* readers of texts of all sorts, readers whose exposure to print materials was growing at an astonishing rate, even in rural areas, and whose sophistication as readers and critics of what they read was likewise growing daily. These readers continued nevertheless to respond strongly to the perennial appeal of sentiment, whether in sensational fiction or in polemical (including propagandist) prose, in part in reaction to what already seemed to many to be an ever more alien and depersonalized world at large. The amount and type of poetry and fiction read, not surprisingly, reflected the relative readability of the texts, their availability for purchase or loan, and the extent to which they satisfied their readers' appetite for entertainment or escape, and as often happens the most popular works were not necessarily those which cultural history has subsequently branded as 'great'. Self-improvement texts were popular, from professional books and journals to spiritual guides, while predictably conventional conduct books of one sort or another continued to be perennial gifts to young debutantes and to new wives and mothers. Reading matter was understood by publishers and readers alike, no less than by politicians, to be an important vehicle for social control, and publishers and those who backed them (including political factions) invested increasing amounts of capital in the dissemination of their particular messages.

The reading public grew unabated, expanding and diversifying, so that by the end of the Romantic period it is fair to say that the reader as *consumer* had arrived. This was a reader who shopped and selected, whose sensibilities had been sharpened by exposure to an increasingly wide range of materials, for which she or he had slowly begun to have more time because of advances in working conditions, domestic conditions and print technology. Just as British society was slowly being democratized politically (as the First Reform Act of 1832 would demonstrate), so, too, was the democratization of the literate reading public advancing. And if the 'general reader', whose tastes the cultural elite continued to decry while its spokespersons strove to reform and reshape them, continued to prefer sensation to sense and entertainment to moral and intellectual instruction, that reader already prefigured the dominant profile of reading publics at the end of the twentieth century. Indeed, in virtually every important respect, the 'Romantic reader' was the parent of the contemporary reader.

REFERENCES AND FURTHER READING

Adburgham, Alison, *Women in Print: Writing Women and Women's Magazines from the Restoration to the Accession of Victoria*, London, George Allen and Unwin, 1972.

Altick, Richard D., *The English Common Reader: A Social History of the Mass Reading Public 1800–1900*, Chicago, University of Chicago Press, 1957.

Butler, Marilyn, *Romantics, Rebels, and Reactionaries: English Literature and its Background, 1760–1830*, New York, Oxford University Press, 1981.

Collins, A. S., *The Profession of Letters: A Study of the Relation of Author to Patron, Publisher, and Public, 1780–1832*, London, Routledge, 1928.

Cranfield, G. A., *The Press and Society: From Caxton to Northcliffe*, London, Longman, 1978.

Curran, Stuart, 'Women Readers, Women Writers', in *The Cambridge Companion to British Romanticism*, ed. Stuart Curran, Cambridge, Cambridge University Press, 1993, pp. 177–95.

Erickson, Lee, *The Economy of Literary Form: English Literature and the Industrialization of Publishing, 1800–1850*, Baltimore, Johns Hopkins University Press, 1996.

Harris, R. W., *Romanticism and the Social Order*, London, Blandford Press, 1969.

Jack, Ian, *The Poet and His Audience*, Cambridge, Cambridge University Press, 1987.

Klancher, Jon P., *The Making of English Reading Audiences, 1790–1832*, Madison, University of Wisconsin Press, 1987.

Lovell, Terry, *Consuming Fiction*, London, Verso, 1987.

Mellor, Anne K., *Romanticism and Gender*, New York, Routledge, 1993.

Nabholtz, John R., *My Reader, My Fellow-Labourer: A Study of English Romantic Prose*. Columbia, University of Missouri Press, 1986.

Raven, James, Small, Helen and Tadmor, Naomi (eds) *The Practice and Representations of Reading in England*, Cambridge, Cambridge University Press, 1996.

Richardson, Alan, *Literature, Education, and Romanticism: Reading as Social Practice, 1780–1832*, Cambridge, Cambridge University Press, 1994.

Rowland, William G., Jr, *Literature and the Marketplace: Romantic Writers and Their Audiences in Great Britain and the United States*, Lincoln, University of Nebraska Press, 1996.

Smith, Olivia, *The Politics of Language, 1791–1819*, Oxford: Clarendon Press, 1984.

Turner, Cheryl, *Living by the Pen: Women Writers in the Eighteenth Century*, London, Routledge, 1992.

Tyson, Gerald P., *Joseph Johnson: A Liberal Publisher*, Iowa City, University of Iowa Press, 1979.

Webb, R. K., *The British Working Class Reader, 1790–1848: Literacy and Social Tension*, London, Allen and Unwin, 1955.

# PART TWO
# Readings

# 9

# William Blake, *Songs of Innocence and of Experience*

### Nelson Hilton

'Read patiently take not up this Book in an idle hour the consideration of these things is the whole duty of man & the affairs of life & death trifles sports of time these considerations business of Eternity.' Blake's annotations to a volume he studied in 1798 (see Blake, ed. Erdman, p. 611, cited hereafter as E) can serve today to characterize the attention deserved and significance offered by the most familiar work of England's 'last great religious poet' (Ackroyd, *Blake*, p. 18) and 'greatest revolutionary artist' (Eagleton, in Larrissy's *William Blake*, p. ix).

What we know as his *Songs of Innocence and of Experience* begins in the publication, over the space of 35 years, of 50 copies of *Songs of Innocence* and 28 of *Songs of Experience*, from which were constituted the two dozen actual sets of the combined *Songs*, variously ordered and with a joint title page. The work in its full form consists of 54 designs and poems which only in the last few copies follow the sequence adopted by almost every modern edition. These Blake etched in relief on relatively small (7 × 11 cm) copper plates, printed, often coloured, and bound: his title page gives equal weight to his labours as 'Author & Printer', and expects no less of his readers.[1] Composition also was protracted – while the poems and designs of *Innocence* are dated 1789, three early drafts surface in a 1785 manuscript which also reveals the 28-year-old artist's predilection for 'making a fool' of the reader (E 453); *Songs of Experience* and the joint title page are dated 1794, and one poem (*To Tirzah*) appears a few years after that. The five epochal years between the title-page dates of *Innocence* and *Experience* bracket the bulk of Blake's so-called 'Bible of Hell', including remarkable works such as *The Marriage of Heaven and Hell* (*MHH*), *Visions of the Daughters of Albion*, and, also dated 1794, *The Book of Urizen*.

As part of the 'discovery' or 'invention' of childhood in the eighteenth century associated with the interest in early education shown by Locke, Rousseau and the Sunday school movement, the decades before the *Songs* saw the genre of short collections of devotional and moral poems for children emerge as a 'most prolific and controversial literary form' (Shrimpton, 'Hell's hymnbook', p. 22). The genre's mainstay was Isaac Watts's *Divine and Moral Songs Attempted in easy Language, for the Use of Children* (1715), influential enough to be parodied not only by Blake (in *A Cradle Song*), but still later in *Alice in Wonderland*; other titles could be cited, however, including Charles Wesley's *Hymns for Children* (1763); Christopher Smart's *Hymns for the Amusement of Children* (1770); and Anna Laetitia Barbauld's *Hymns in Prose for Children* (1781). These works make a small subset of eighteenth-century hymnody, itself arguably the most pervasively influential innovation of cultural discourse in Blake's time. While it has long been recognized that in terms of metrical and stanzaic variety, Blake's songs 'make as clear a parallel with eighteenth-century hymns, as they make a contrast with eighteenth-century lyric' (Holloway, *Blake*, p. 37), their contrast with the ideological burden of hymns has yet to be explored fully. If John Wesley could preface his brother's hymns with the hope that once children 'understand them they will be children no longer, only in years and stature', then Blake might counter that if adults could understand *his* songs, their 'doors of perception' might be cleansed (*MHH* 14). Following his own interpretation of the gospel, Blake thinks 'every Thing to be Evident to the Child' (E 664), and writes that 'the innocence of a child' can reproach the reader 'with the errors of acquired folly' (E 600). His songs 'about' or 'from the perspective of' a guiltless point of view offer parables to test what such pure perception might be, and how our sense might be folly.

The girl and boy learning to read at the lap of their nurse or mother who appear on the *Innocence* title page announce the 'scene of instruction' to be found in or behind almost every song. The quintessential object of instruction is, in one form or another, language and the concomitant ability to play with the symbolic order, and *Songs* might be taken as evoking stations along a gradient beginning with total ignorance of that realm of symbol and culture and ending with original artistic contribution. These various stations can be shuffled in the various sequences of different copies of *Songs* – there is no one developmental path, no single authorized reading. From a social perspective, the poems represent minute particulars from the spectrum of discourses across the social field. These different, often 'contrary', stations or moments are rooted in the individual poems and designs themselves, making lack of single meaning a crucial point about each of the *Songs*. Given inescapable divisions in self and society, a Wordsworthian 'common language of men' is impossible for Blake (Glen, *Vision and Disenchantment*, p. 106). There are no lyric effusions of emotion recollected, but rather dramatic stagings of language in action (see Gillham, *Blake's Contrary States*) – as the few readings which follow hope to suggest.

Many readers have found the ballad-like Introduction to *Innocence* a commentary on individual and cultural artistic development, which moves from ('pipes down') preverbal, pure sound inspiration to sung words to written text – and, simultaneously, from a state of presence and mutual participation to one of absence and emphatic separateness (the penultimate four lines which begin 'And I'). This process also foregrounds Blake's ongoing concern with identity (repetition, sameness) and difference, as elsewhere in the focus on 'echoing': in what sense is a song 'the same again' if it is rendered in words rather than sound? In Blake's time, especially with the popular 'Glee Club' movement, 'glee' was familiar as a song scored for three or more voices to make up a series of interwoven melodies – a meaning applicable throughout to these 'songs of pleasant glee'. The poem's closing sets up the paradoxical realization that the only way 'every child may joy to hear' the song is through its being sung by one who has learned to read. So we return to the issue of inspiration and transmission, of the 'pipe', the conduit, the *I* (to represent it typographically). The engendering spring of the song-stream comes to readers via the 'hollow reed' of the pipe and the pen, but for hearers requires that readers reinspire (literally, blow into again) the otherwise 'hollow read' of the text.

The child asks the piper to pipe, then to sing about 'a Lamb', and while *The Lamb* follows in one copy, *The Shepherd* comes next in most. These pastoral references, as well as the term 'innocence' itself, indicate the Christian imagery and themes which saturate *Songs*. The complex and idiosyncratic nature of Blake's Christianity has yet to receive full consideration, but any account must reckon with his apparent childhood in a private, radical Protestant sect, the Muggletonians (see Thompson, *Witness Against the Beast*), his later involvement with Swedenborg and the 'New Church', his professional connections to the Dissenters, and his own various pronouncements – those on the equivalence of Christ and imagination not least. In annotations written around the time of *Innocence*, Blake argues that 'our Lord is the word of God' (E 599), but also that 'the Poetic Genius . . . is the Lord' (E 603). The 'acquired folly' which innocence challenges concerns especially religious ceremony, tedious hymns and conventional theology, and their want of perception for that energetic, spiritual and intellectual vision which exists *in no sense*.

Orthodox Blake criticism takes *The Shepherd* as an evocation of familiar themes, with apparent parallels in traditional and contemporary devotional verse. But for Blake, always ready to read 'white' where we read 'black' (E 524), the poem may also invite us to reconsider what the sheep herd heard. To begin with, the cloying repetition in 'How sweet is the Shepherd's sweet lot' seems, literally, too sweet; and with the odd image that not the sheep, but the shepherd 'strays', brings up nagging associations of error, deviation, lack of guidance. 'For he hears the lambs' innocent call' offers a lame rationale for praise, and the curious logic culminates in the awkward grammar of the conclusion:

> He is watchful while they are in peace,
> For they know when their Shepherd is nigh.

*Songs* is filled with such worrying verbal and graphic minute particulars (the stance and expression of the illustrated shepherd make for another) which, if we let them work, tease us into thought – in this case all the more if we consider the dissonance with the biblical allusion, 'He shall feed his flock like a shepherd: he shall gather the lambs with his arm, and carry them in his bosom, and shall gently lead those that are with young' (Isaiah 40:11). It seems likely that one part of this glee reflects Blake's already longstanding meditation on the indictment penned by a similarly aged Milton of earlier faithless 'pastors' with their 'lean and flashy songs' (*Lycidas* 123).

If one wishes to locate the poems on some ideal gradient of language-acquisition, *Infant Joy* offers an obvious place to begin – and indeed it follows next in the same number of copies (11) as the common order. The poem appears to involve two voices, and many editors have felt compelled to 'improve' the text with quotation marks. A moment's reflection may suggest that we are overhearing the play of a mother and baby in an initial enactment of how, especially for the infant, language comes to us already articulated in forms we must learn to comprehend. The text foregrounds the role of name and calling, yet seems to associate 'joy' with a preverbal, unnamed state – indeed, 'infant' derives from the Latin *infans* or 'not speaking'. Unspeakable joy, perhaps. With an age of two days, the infant is on the eve of the traditional occasion for baptism and official recording of name

(Shakespeare's birthday, for instance, is hypothesized by subtracting three from the known baptismal date). This fall into language, into the symbolic machinery of society, is gain, in the eventual acquisition of skill with symbols, but also loss of the glory in undifferentiated potential. At the moment, for a moment, this latter joy assimilates the ineffable 'I AM' of Exodus and Coleridge's later 'primary imagination' – but 'The I am' cannot go unnamed for long.

*The Lamb* moves further along the language-acquisition gradient and into a paradigmatic scene of instruction. This evident response to the inspiring child's request for 'a song about a lamb' offers at the least a three-part glee: one for the Lamb as child, the 'bonnie lamb' of nursery rhymes and endearment; another for the young sheep also illustrated in the design; and another for the Agnus Dei. But by beginning with a question out of catechism ('Canst thou tell who made thee?' also begins a lesson in *The Pilgrim's Progress*, Part two) *The Lamb* tells any who have ears to hear that it has been to Sunday school and encoded one of the most popular of Wesley's *Hymns for Children*, 'Gentle Jesus, meek and mild':

> Lamb of God, I look to thee
> Thou shalt my example be;
> Thou are gentle, meek, and mild,
> Thou wast once a little child.

This source suggests how the child's naming or calling, based on the symbolic identifications which ground perception, unselfconsciously reflects her or his indoctrination. Such scenes of instruction show how we cannot talk about naming without entering into the context of power and the imposition of form, whether under the aegis of Louis Althusser's 'interpellation', Jacques Lacan's 'Name-of-the-Father', or whatever other theory one uses to situate the never-innocent discourse instruction which is 'education'. Blake knows as well as Lewis Carroll's Humpty-Dumpty that the question in naming is 'who is to be master', and the fact of the matter here is that Jesus never calls himself a Lamb.

Too young to formulate distinctions of logic and Logos, the child, like a lamb led to language, gets lost in figural possibilities and in differences between calling oneself and being called. The alteration the 'Author & Printer' makes between capitals and lower-case ('He'/'he', 'Lamb'/'lamb') further evokes the fusion or confusion in the child's inability to comprehend metaphor, even as the text conveys the child's joy in the exercise of his or her developing semiotic mastery: 'I'll tell thee, /. . . I'll tell thee!' Fresh from instruction, the child tries to pipe on 'the same again', but even as she or he delights gleefully in such empowerment, the insinuated discourses configure that energy for the maintenance of their own forms.

The repeated unpunctuated closing refrain, 'Little Lamb God bless thee', again problematizes identity – here of blessing and blessed, of subject and object – and modulates into the poem which follows more often than any other, *The Little Black Boy*. Among the most intimate of scenes of instruction, it challenges our sense of innocence as it shows the child take in 'slave religion' for comfort against an oppressive system which has made everything black and white. One of Watts's songs for children has God shining 'with beams of love' (*Praise for Creation and Providence*), but Blake deftly turns the tables to suggest these beams and their ideological freight as a cross the blacks 'learn to bear' with the great white father's other 'gifts'. The boy's pathetic conclusion, 'love me', reveals that however much his mother's pious lessons may, as he suggests, 'bore' him, the suffering they seek to buffer and alleviate is real.

Trauma also occupies *The Chimney Sweeper,* where children abandoned by their parents are to 'do their duty' despite the daily harm in their unimaginable working conditions. Critics often cite its last line, 'So if all do their duty, they need not fear harm', as an instance of irony in *Songs,* but if one thinks of irony as 'saying one thing while meaning another', the term is too limited. The glees of *Songs* say several things while meaning them all – and 'innocence' entails the accepting of them all. On the one hand, little Tom Dacre has a dream which evidently recycles the consoling scene of instruction offered by the frame narrator, and believes it to such extent that 'Though the morning was cold, Tom was happy & warm'. Ideology and the imaginary combine for this real power. On the other hand, the poem's slightly older speaker's detachment and unselfconsciousness (as in his transitions 'so', 'And so') heighten our sense of his pain and the force of the actuality he relates: 'So *your* chimneys I sweep' (emphasis added). The last line then tests your response-ability, which will decide its inflection and with that, your position *vis-à-vis* an 'all' who have not, by some reckonings, given due to the sweeps and who should perhaps fear possible harm at the hands of mobilized 'thousands of sweepers'. Imagine, for instance, the tone of Blake's contemporary Mrs Sarah Trimmer, a popular educator and pioneer in the Sunday school movement, who wrote in 1792 concerning the establishment of 'schools of industry' for the 'inferior sorts' of children:

> it cannot be right to train them *all* in a way which will most probably raise their ideas above the very lowest occupations of life, and disqualify them for those servile offices which must be filled by some of the members of the community, and in which they may be equally happy with the highest, if they will do their duty. (See Gardner, *Blake's Innocence,* p. 83)

*The Little Girl Lost* and *The Little Girl Found* are clearly to be taken together, as their shared middle plate insists. Like two other poems, *The School Boy* and *The Voice of the Ancient Bard,* they appear first in *Songs of Innocence,* but often move to *Experience* in the joint collection, suggesting again that the experience of changing perspective is crucial to *Songs.* The two poems seem obviously allegorical, but of what? The absence of compelling interpretations – invocations of the soul's journey, the myth of Persephone, and female adolescence notwithstanding – suggests that the text may be a failure of obscurity. But if one sees *Songs* as concerned with the learning of language, which means, inevitably, wrestling with figurative language and the symbolic transferences which permit allegory, metaphor and complex verbal meaning, then one might pause again over the protagonist's name, 'Lyca'. By way of context, consider Blake's treatment of another virginal figure in *The Book of Thel,* published the same year as *Songs of Innocence:*

> Ah! Thel is *like a* watry bow. And *like a* parting cloud.
> *Like a* reflection in a glass. Like shadows in the water.
> Like dreams of infants. *Like a* smile upon an infant's face (1.8–10)

Here again, as with *Infant Joy,* we circle around what has no name, and what in being named becomes defined and finite, subject to the limitations of our vocabulary. Lyca is like a figure for figuration – a literalization of what happens when, in her poem, we try to grasp or impose our 'fancied image' for all that might be meant by 'sleep', 'tree', 'lion', 'ruby tears'. Imagine *the poem itself*, that emanation of the artist's mind, as *The Little Girl Lost* (just like Wordsworth's *Lucy Gray*) and perhaps being found forever still the little girl is a distressing experience of innocence.

Point of view and desire for certainty are also at stake in the poem which often closes *Innocence*, 'On Anothers Sorrow'. Here every reader at least considers the possibility of another answer to the excessive rhetoric:

> Can a mother sit and hear,
> An infant groan an infant fear –
> No no never can it be.
> Never never can it be.

Even William Cowper, in a hymn Blake would have known, answers the analogous question 'Can a woman's tender care / Cease towards the child she bare' with an honest 'Yes, she may forgetful be'. In Blake's poem the reiterated 'Think not' collides with the concluding reality of 'our grief' (not 'another's' after all!) to end the poem, and *Innocence*, with 'moan'. So we confront at once our distance from such naive denial and the powerful (dare one say 'innocent'?) longing such fantasy exerts for at least some part of us. It is the chimney sweeper's consolation for Tom Dacre writ large, and sometimes as effective.

'Language is the house of Being', according to Heidegger's famous figure (see Steiner, *Martin Heidegger*, p. 127), but for Blake, as for Wordsworth, that structure becomes a prison-house maintained by 'pre-established codes', by cliché and convention. The warden of the prison-house, the fashioner of 'mind-forg'd manacles', the force that has barred us from the play of Being in language, as from the stunning energy of true poetry, can be seen as 'the bard'. The fallacy in crediting such assumed authority looms in the Introduction to *Songs of Experience*, where, by the eighth line, three distinct subjects 'might controll / The starry pole'. With its echoes of Jeremiah ('O earth, earth, earth, hear the word of the LORD') and the God of *Paradise Lost* ('past, present, future he beholds'), the bard seems to command reverence – but as in other cases, on inspection, the compelling language breaks into mumbo-jumbo, etched on a plate whose vista of stars is graphically barred by the cloud of words. Students of the Bible, and of Wesley's great hymn, *Wrestling Jacob*, will recognize that it is the opportunity to struggle for blessing or interpretation from a sacred messenger which is given 'till the break of day'. The religious references resonate with the particularly eighteenth-century, evangelical sense of 'experience' as the inner history of one's religious emotion (see *OED*, s.v., 4b) – indeed, 'hymn of experience' appears throughout accounts of Methodism.

The scene of instruction accosts the reader directly in *London*, whose speaker's repeated self-reference makes him or her emphatically 'here' and demanding dialogue. For 'I hear' asks implicitly, 'do you hear?' – which is to say, 'are you here?' 'He that hath ears to hear, let him hear', is one inspired teacher's reiterated elliptical comment, but the general lack of comprehension for the parables, says Jesus, fulfils the prophecy of Isaiah that 'hearing ye shall hear, and shall not understand; and seeing ye shall see, and shall not perceive' (Matthew 13:14). So what do we hear, here in this poem? 'Mine' or 'mind'? 'Forg'd' or 'fraudulent'? 'Man' in manacles? Whatever it is, however it works, it is everywhere mined and forged in the hearth of the heard and seen in the here and now of everyday Babelondon. Amidst the din of official 'chartered' ideologies and unexamined lives, the speaker strives to unlock the reader by the multiplication of significance, breaking chains of thought and speech at their weakest link, the idea of a single meaning, univocal sign. This deconstruction involves asserting a new synaesthetic logic for eye and ear. Thus, we are urged to hear *how* a sigh runs in blood, *how* the sweepers' cry makes pale a blackening St Paul's – in short, we must learn to see, hear in a new way:

> The mind-forg'd manacles *I hear*

> *H*ow the Chimney-sweepers cry
> *E*very blackning Church appalls,
> *A*nd the hapless Soldiers sigh
> *R*uns in blood down Palace walls

> But most thro' midnight streets *I hear*

The small shock of perceptual expansion occasioned by the acrostic can stand for the larger reconfiguring necessary if we are to attend truly to the voice of the barred.

In the final stanza, what is heard is not the 'curse' ending the second line but, again, *how* it blasts the 'tear' which ends the third and rhymes back to 'hear'. These rhymes, '. . . hear/ . . . curse/ . . . tear', bring to bear the contrary dictions of sight and sound as we hear, see them coalesce in the final sight and sound rhyme, 'hearse'. The oxymoronic image of the 'marriage hearse' points to the impossibility of imagining that sight and sound, sign and meaning can be eternally linked or chartered, and in its unexpected juxtaposition of 'hearse' for 'bed' asserts an intelligence and point of view which calls our own to account. That everyone who has stopped us with a claim to hear voices and see invisible marks can be dismissed as crazy does not mean that we are never to imagine the evidence of things unseen.

According to a recent collection of 'the top 500 poems' as determined by computer analysis of hundreds of anthologies, the now most published poem in the language is *The Tyger.* Or should we write, to follow the renaming in that anthology (Harmon, *The Top 500 Poems,* p. 1,077) and by some other editors, *The Tiger?* Would it make any difference to an artist who writes 'tiger' when he wishes, and who asserts elsewhere that 'Every word and every letter is studied and put into its fit place'? (E 146) What of the asymmetrical rhyme, in the beat of the poem's dread feet, of the word 'symmetry'? Shall we pronounce it to match with 'eye'? And what of the notoriously toy-like, even bemused feline whose illustration seems so incongruous with the celebrated words?

The poem's insistent rhetorical and figural emphasis – beginning with the opening hurdle of metaphor, 'Tyger Tyger, burning bright' – announces a text which will test the language sensitivity *Songs* explores. Either we are not concerned with a conventional 'tiger', or with usual 'burning', *or both.* Before the poem beguiles us to the self-congratulation of some imaginary theodicy by the answering of its questions, consider, with Jean-Jacques Lecercle, the implications:

> A question's purpose is not, as is commonly thought, to solicit information, but to elicit an
> answer, to establish a relation of power between questioner and questioned. It is a striking

feature of questions that he who asks them establishes, by the very act of asking them, his right to question, his expectation of an answer, and his power to elicit one. (Lecercle, *The Violence of Language*, p. 46).

In *The Tyger*, if we answer, we become like God – a temptation which has proved alluring enough, it would appear, to make the language's top poem. Well might the illustrated Tyger smile over this ultimate fooling of readers.

The decades of answers which make up 'Tyger studies' must be passed over for a few observations. Given the cost of copper, Blake etched both sides of the plates for *Songs* (using small dikes of wax around each side) and exact measurements indicate that the question 'Did he who made the Lamb make thee?' refers, in part, to the poem of that name only millimetres away on the flip side and a few years older. On the one hand, it is the 'Author & Printer' himself who dares seize the 'brightness of fancy; power of genius... poetic inspiration' which his contemporaries characterized as 'fire' (*OED*, s.v.). Part of that genius seems to concern the author's appropriation of Milton, who writes in *Paradise Lost* that the Creator 'of Celestial Bodies first the sun / A mighty Sphear he fram'd' (7.354–5). In a work dated the year after *Experience*, Blake's creator figure Los similarly makes a celestial body: he beats 'Roaring... bright sparks' with a 'vast Hammer' on 'the Anvil' until 'An immense Orb of fire he fram'd', at which he 'smiled with joy' (E 98) – momentarily regaining the flow, the peak experience of the artist's unspeakable 'infant joy'.

The very latest of the *Songs*, appearing only after the collection had been published initially, and linked through its curious name to Blake's later work, *To Tirzah* deserves special attention as a kind of coda. Using a dictionary to the Bible (Authorized Version) one can identify Tirzah as the one-time capital of the Northern Kingdom, memorable for a comparison to Jerusalem in the erotic lushness of Song of Songs (6:4), and Tirzah as the fifth of five daughters whose collective petition for inheritance decided women's rights in property for their culture. Given Blake's other emphases on 'five', one could associate the daughters with the senses, so that seeing only the sense of smell, sight, audition, and taste named in the poem, Tirzah might be associated with the remaining sense of touch. In fact, the AV's mistaking of 'Tirzah' for a form of the Hebrew verb *tirseh*, allows one to imagine the title translated as 'To Sensual Enjoyment'.

The obsession of the speaker in *To Tirzah* 'To rise from Generation free', must in part be referenced to the word's sexual sense as exemplified by Hume's argument that 'there is in all men, both male and female, a desire and power of generation more active than is ever universally exerted' (*OED*, s.v. 'generation'). The speaker's preoccupation strengthens through the second stanza's concern with 'The Sexes' and the story of how they generated or 'sprung from Shame & Pride', then 'blow'd' or blossomed (literally, exposed organs of generation) and died – at which point one might want to invoke Original Sin, but if 'Shame & Pride' preceded and engendered 'The Sexes', then that familiar story has been made strange. The mortality established with that sin weighs heavy on a speaker obsessed – in hymnal long measure – with 'Mortal Birth', 'my Mortal part' and 'Mortal Life', and while such concern is ostensibly obviated by the poem's penultimate line, the very existence of the text undercuts dramatically assurance that 'The Death of Jesus set me free'. Many hymns voice this idea, though few so bluntly; and *sin*, the hymns agree, is that from which the death of Jesus frees us, so that a disjunction opens between 'Generation', from which the speaker still wishes to rise free, and the implied condition of sin, from which he or she claims to be set free. Similarly, the sincerity of the speaker's attribution of 'false self-deceiving tears' is compromised dramatically by our understanding that such accusation comes from personal experience – that in calling Tirzah false, the speaker indicates his or her own weepy-eyed self-deception.

The question the speaker twice addresses to the mother, 'Then what have I to do with thee?' might evoke Jesus's apparently rude words to his mother at Cana: 'Woman, what have I to do with thee?' (John 2:4). Here again, as elsewhere in the poem and throughout the *Songs*, desire for simple meaning, a direct lock of words and meaning, begins to slide under the surfacing contradictions of a speaker who doesn't know what he or she is saying, another subject who hasn't learned to read aright. In fact the repeated question appears a number of times in the Bible, and for an author learned with the best in that 'great code of art' (E 274), the cumulative effect of these contexts subverts what might seem at first an obvious significant allusion. A review of its instances shows that to ask 'What have I to do with thee?' places one in the company of those who address some form of power while already deeply involved in events which will show that they have very much to do with what they question. Perhaps, indeed, only one possessed, like Legion, and not 'in his right mind' (Mark 5: 15; Luke 8:35–6) would treat with such dismissive rhetoric the crucial question of existence. In one contemporary hymn, Legion recalls how, 'Fill'd with madness, sin and woe', he was found by Jesus,

> Yet in this forlorn condition,
> When he came to set me free,
> I reply'd to my Physician,
> 'What have I to do with thee?' (Cowper and Newton, *Olney Hymns*, p. 407)

There is no space to enter the still greater scandal of the poem's illustration, which would further the sense that *To Tirzah* enacts the strained psychology of a hymn-singing 'Moral Christian' (E 877) and sexist upholder of the 'patriarchial religion' (E 171) who cannot imagine 'the improvement of sensual enjoyment' (*MHH* 15) or celebrate 'holy Generation! [*Image*] of regeneration!' (*Jerusalem* 7.65). But given the argument of *The Everlasting Gospel* that 'The Vision of Christ that thou dost see / Is my Visions Greatest Enemy' (E 524), and the context of hymns, *To Tirzah* serves to confirm that Blake's *Songs* are psalms and parables for the Bible of Hell.

NOTE

1   The best generally available facsimile of *Songs of Innocence and of Experience* is that edited by Lincoln. A hypertext version, which facilitates experience of the various sequences and includes annotated bibliographies, can be accessed at http://www.english.uga.edu/wblake; colour reproductions will be found at the web site for The Blake Archive.

WRITINGS

Blake, William, *Songs of Innocence and of Experience*, ed. Andrew Lincoln, London and Princeton, Blake Trust and Princeton University Press, 1991. This is the student's text of choice; includes useful notes and commentary.

Erdman, David V. (ed.) *The Complete Poetry and Prose of*

*William Blake*, New York, Doubleday, 1988. An electronic version is freely available on the Internet.

## REFERENCES AND FURTHER READING

Ackroyd, Peter, *Blake* London, Sinclair-Stevenson, 1995.

Bentley, G. E., *Blake Books: Annotated Catalogues of William Blake's Writings in Illuminated Printing, in Conventional Typography and in Manuscript, and Reprints thereof; Reproductions of his designs, Books with his Engravings, Catalogues, Books he owned, and Scholarly and Critical Works about him*, Oxford, Clarendon Press, 1977. Includes detailed descriptions of the various copies of *Songs*, and an extensive bibliography of criticism.

——*Blake Books Supplement: A Bibliography of Publications and Discoveries about William Blake 1971–1992, being a Continuation of Blake Books*, Oxford, Clarendon Press, 1995. Again, use the index to access criticism on particular poems.

Cowper, William and Newton, John, *Olney Hymns* (1779), vol. 3 of *The Works of John Newton*, Edinburgh, The Banner of Truth Trust, 1988.

Gardner, Stanley, *Blake's 'Innocence' and 'Experience' Retraced*, London and New York, Athlone Press and St Martin's, 1986. Good on London background.

Gillham, D. G., *Blake's Contrary States: The Songs of Innocence and of Experience as Dramatic Poems*, Cambridge, Cambridge University Press, 1966.

Gleckner, Robert F. and Greenberg, Mark L. (ed.) *Approaches to Teaching Blake's Songs of Innocence and of Experience*, New York, Modern Language Association, 1989. Highly useful collection of materials and approaches.

Glen, Heather, *Vision and Disenchantment: Blake's Songs and Wordsworth's Lyrical Ballads*, Cambridge, Cambridge University Press, 1983. Good on the context of eighteenth-century children's verse.

Harmon, William, *The Top 500 Poems*, New York, Columbia University Press, 1992.

Holloway, John, *Blake: The Lyric Poetry*, London, Edward Arnold, 1968.

Leader, Zachery, *Reading Blake's Songs*, Boston, Routledge & Kegan Paul, 1981.

Lecercle, Jean-Jacques, *The Violence of Language*, London, Routledge, Chapman and Hall, 1990.

Larrissy, Edward, *William Blake*, preface by Terry Eagleton, Oxford, Blackwell, 1985.

Lindsay, David W., *Blake: Songs of Innocence and Experience*, Atlantic Highlands, Humanities Press, 1989. One of the series 'the Critics Debate' – will they take up the dropped preposition?

Shrimpton, Nick, 'Hell's hymnbook: Blake's *Songs of Innocence and of Experience* and their models', in *Literature of the Romantic Period, 1750–1850*, ed. R. T. Davies and B. G. Beatty, New York, Barnes & Noble, 1976, pp. 19–35.

Steiner, George, *Martin Heidegger*, Harmondsworth and New York, Penguin Books, 1980.

Thompson, E. P., *Witness Against the Beast: William Blake and the Moral Law*, New York, The New Press, 1993.

Viscomi, Joseph, *Blake and the Idea of the Book*, Princeton, Princeton University Press, 1993. Exhaustive treatment of Blake's actual etching process and its consequences for his work.

Watts, Isaac, *Divine and Moral Songs for Children* (1715), London, The Religious Tract Society, 1837.

Wesley, Charles, *Hymns for Children, and Persons of Riper Years*, 4th edn, London, 1784. Preface by John Wesley.

# 10

# Edmund Burke, *Reflections on the Revolution in France*

## David Bromwich

Edmund Burke was already a famous politician and moral philosopher when his *Reflections on the Revolution in France* was published in 1790. He had served as a member of the House of Commons since 1765, where he was known for his leadership of the opposition to the American war, his plan for the reform of the king's budget, his committee reports on the conduct of the East India Company, and his substantial share in managing the impeachment of Warren Hastings, the Governor-General of Bengal. From 1765, Burke had also served as private secretary to Lord Rockingham, and after his patron's death in 1782 he remained a chief strategist of the Rockingham party, whose command was inherited by Charles James Fox. A description of him by Richard Pares as 'a high and dry anti-monarchist' is the fairest short characterization that has been offered by a historian. His *Philosophical Enquiry into the Origin of our Ideas of the Sublime and Beautiful*, published in 1757 and with added materials in 1759, did more than any other book to initiate the broad discussion of taste in relation to morals which preoccupied the philosophical literature of Europe in the later eighteenth century, and it led his admirers to hope for a literary fulfilment that his career, so impressive in other ways, could never supply in a traditional sense. This may explain Goldsmith's half-jocular criticism in *Retaliation*, that Burke was one 'Who, born for the universe, narrowed his mind, / And to party gave up what was meant for mankind'. Against this background the *Reflections* was read by contemporaries as a summing-up of his practical wisdom about statesmanship, but also as the climatic literary achievement his earlier and occasional writings had seemed to defer.

It has become customary to associate the *Reflections* with the *Sublime and Beautiful* by pointing out the antitheses they employ to advance their arguments. Fear and love, grandeur and delicacy, male gallantry and female vulnerability – these pairings are central to both books. But the early enquiry had judged our feelings on a non-moral basis: they were planted in us, we could not imagine human life without them, and to call them good or bad would be superfluous. By the time he writes the *Reflections*, Burke's praise of aristocratic delicacy, and his wish to guard the survival of lovely things just because they are lovely, have been thoroughly moralized. Beauty now is a quality of society and not of its women alone; and a good society will provide a shelter for beauty. It remains unclear how far the idea of sublimity can be applied in the context of revolution. A fallen aristocracy like that of France may evoke sublime admiration because of its ancient grandeur, its mysterious claim to divine and natural sanction. Yet the violence of the revolutionary crowd suggests a more immediate sublime idea. The physical threat brings *fear* – the elementary attribute of sublimity. The truth seems to be that for Burke, the sublime and beautiful belonged to a realm of uncontrollable feelings for which he saw no common use in political thought. He looked at politics as a field of deliberate action. Though its momentum verges on the theatrical and it lends itself to a narrative structure, he believed its performances should be kept as cool as possible. The only exception occurs at moments of crisis or necessity when the emotions of spectators must be worked up to a pitch of impassioned response. The revolutionists of 1789 had begun to recreate their society as a scene of perpetual necessity; and Burke's *Reflections* may be understood in some degree as a deliberately dramatized counter-response.

The form of government, Burke believed, which modern Europe had been tending to promote until 1789, was the most enlightened yet imaginable for humankind. It was a mixed constitutional system, in which a republican part (the assembly) took the dominant role of making and modifying policy, while its aggrandizement was held in check by a democratic part (the people) and by a monarchical part (the king). To assure the stability of such a system, the leading virtues of the statesman must be prudence, moderation and humility – the last defined as a gregarious seeking for qualified advice and assistance. Persons who embody such virtues can best be unified by the artifice of a political party: a group, bound by common loyalties, whose members agree to act together even in rare cases of disagreement. By its consistency of principle, and by the 'character' brought into view by an ideally representative leader, a party adds to the available stock of public wisdom and virtue. From this emphasis of his pre-revolutionary writings, any observer might have predicted Burke's reaction against the volatile shifts of opinion and loyalty in France, the apparent abundance and actual dearth of leadership, and the headlong alternations by which the assembly and the people seemed to repel any possible effort of constitutional balance. And yet the tenor of his speeches on reform in the 1770s and 1780s, where he often appeared to side with 'the people' against ministerial abuse or monarchical encroachment, made many expect he would somehow justify the French Revolution.

Most of those who had sympathized with the American War of Independence regarded the events of 1789 as similar in kind: a subject people was making the passage from despotism to republican rule, under a stronger impulse of democratic uniformity than had been possible in America. To Burke the event bore a far different complexion. When, for example, the Declaration of the Rights of Man asserted that 'the nation is essentially the source of all sovereignty, nor can any *individual*, or *any body of men*, be entitled to any authority which is not expressly derived from it'; and when it backed this assurance with the axiom that 'the law is an expression of the will of the community', it appeared that a social majority was constituting itself as a machine for governing which no power on earth could resist, and against which no plea for exemption or pity would be heard. A total revolution in the name of the people was gathering to itself the authority of a total state. Reform of society on this pattern, without the preservation of all that could be retained of its habits and customs, was an experiment Burke had always warned against:

A man full of warm speculative benevolence may wish his society otherwise constituted than he finds it; but a good patriot, and a true politician, always considers how he shall make the most of the existing materials of his country. A disposition to preserve, and an ability to improve, taken together, would be my standard of a statesman. Every thing else is vulgar in the conception, perilous in the execution. (*Reflections*, pp. 266–7)

'A disposition to preserve, and an ability to improve': these words of the *Reflections* might be matched in any of his earlier writings. But one element of the warning is new. Burke had never before enforced so severe a disjunction between patriotism and general benevolence.

His full title alludes not only to the revolution in France but 'the proceedings in certain societies in London relative to that event', and part of his aim was to satirize the cosmopolitan ideas of the Revolution Society and other radical associations for reform. The decorum of a letter 'intended to have been sent to a gentleman in Paris' allows Burke to comment on French developments from what he presents as a proper understanding of the English constitutional model. A wrong understanding of that model by English radicals can be shown to run exactly parallel to the errors of the revolutionists, who have lost too much in translation; while the disaster the French are making reflects a double discredit upon 'certain societies', whose enthusiasm now threatens two countries with anarchy. Burke's stimulus for writing was the sermon 'On the Love of our Country' by the Dissenting preacher and philosopher Dr Richard Price. This eloquent pamphlet by a venerable reformer embraced the French Revolution on the grounds that enlightened men and women owed their largest loyalty to the cause of human freedom. *Thou shalt love thy neighbour as thyself*, Price reminded his audience, and our neighbour may be a man or a woman anywhere. Our loyalty is not to a given plot of ground, or to the nation in which we are bred, but to the whole of humankind. It was the glory of the French Revolution, Price thought, to have blazoned this truth irresistibly, and as its rights and doctrines spread, its hopes ought to command the allegiance of every citizen of the world.

Burke's opening response to Price is dry and memorable. Our loyalties and affections, he says, are not acquired in the way that the 'spiritual doctor of politics' imagines they are, from the outside in. They can never be transplanted without being changed for the worse. 'To be attached to the subdivision, to love the little platoon we belong to in society, is the first principle (the germ as it were) of public affections. It is the first link in the series, by which we proceed towards a love to our country and to mankind' (p. 135). Burke adds to this moral analysis a disturbing psychological intuition. He suspects that many of those most drawn to a speculative sympathy are unlikely to be possessed of kindness or even practical decency. The agents of the Revolution and its theoretical advocates are so far gone in innovation that they have given up all ordinary habits of thought and conduct alike.

Much of the *Reflections* turns out to be a defence of habit, sometimes under the name of precedent (in law) or prescription (in custom). The defence is pressed to the length of paradox in Burke's largely ameliorative treatment of prejudice. The word had a strong pejorative sense in his day as in ours, but prejudice, says Burke, is really nothing but predisposition, and it works far better than abstract theory as an incitement to action:

Prejudice is of ready application in the emergency; it previously engages the mind in a steady course of wisdom and virtue and does not leave the man hesitating in the moment of decision, sceptical, puzzled, and unresolved. Prejudice renders a man's virtue his habit; and not a series of unconnected acts. Through just prejudice, his duty becomes a part of his nature. (Ibid., p. 183)

We conventionally suppose that action from habit or from previous knowledge is merely routine and therefore cold. Burke turns the analysis upside down.

He says that action from previous feeling is also action of the most spontaneous kind. This truth about feeling he traces to the 'mixed system of opinion and sentiment' that 'had its origin in the antient chivalry'; and, as the argument proceeds, a chivalric code of honour will be set against the revolutionary morality that deduces a given course of action from estimates of sheer utility. By evoking an ancient ethic of pride tamed by beauty, of masculine courage rendered unselfish, Burke is able to suggest the presence of a virtue in the old regime which its usurpers have heartlessly uprooted. He says of the moment in the October days when the queen's chamber at Versailles was invested by a mob and the queen herself assaulted: 'I thought ten thousand swords must have leaped from their scabbards to avenge even a look that threatened her with insult' (p. 170). Men of such valour, who can act from 'untaught feelings', will vanish from the scene forever with the triumph of the Revolution.

What can it mean to defend a *political* system in this miraculous style? Some such question was asked by supporters of the Revolution in the 1790s, and radical reformers in later years would ask it again and again. Burke was using rhapsody and elegy in the place of analysis and judgement. Yet, tactically, he had exchanged their discourse of the social contract for something entirely different, and by putting the defence of an old order on this thrilling basis, laid a rhetorical trap of enormous intricacy for the defenders of systematic change. If they should ask in return, What good is your chivalry? they would show themselves to be what Burke had called them, 'sophisters, oeconomists, and calculators', not men one could trust in an emergency. At the moment when one needed their help, they would wonder 'How much is it worth to us? And how much to me?' If the new order is generous, why can it not breed political foot-soldiers capable of stirring our blood? This crush of insinuation, *ad hominem* and none the less effective for that, prepares for an intuitive stroke of genius in Burke's treatment of the zealous theorists of the Revolution. He makes his readers believe that they are in fact cold men. By contrast, the moderation and 'sluggishness' of the English national temper may be felt to conceal unsuspected reserves of fellow-feeling.

Burke was the first to see that the French Revolution could be described as the work of ideologists — the word is not his, but the idea is there in his description of 'the political men of letters'. If the changes were undertaken on behalf of the people, that should not distract us from seeing that their energy comes from elsewhere. In the field all along, as patrons, have been 'turbulent, discontented men of quality', men like the Duc D'Orleans, who arranged for the bread shortage that prompted the march on Versailles. But just as important are idealists of political action, pamphleteers and coffee-house politicians from a middle station in society, whose mechanical learning and scientific enthusiasm make them suppose a country can be governed on a simplified geometrical plan. Their impatience springs from resentment — 'Something they must destroy, or they seem to themselves to exist for no purpose' (p. 147) — and that is another reason the Revolution has gone wrong.

Their self-trust is mixed with self-contempt, and, satisfied with 'the dust and powder of individuality', they disdain the helps from the past that might yield them a source of practical wisdom. 'You began ill, because you began by despising every thing that belonged to you' (p. 122). Having ventured a premature reduction of politics to a science, of the sort common among the whole-length adepts of enlightenment, they speak freely of 'the rights of men'. But since when have those rights been uniform?

> These metaphysic rights entering into common life, like rays of light which pierce into a dense medium, are, by the laws of nature, refracted from their straight line. Indeed in the gross and complicated mass of human passions and concerns, the primitive rights of men undergo such a variety of refractions and reflections, that it becomes absurd to talk of them as if they continued in the simplicity of their original direction. The nature of man is intricate; the objects of society are of the greatest possible complexity; and therefore no simple disposition or direction of power can be suitable either to man's nature, or to the quality of his affairs. (Ibid., pp. 152–3)

Burke here takes on himself to speak for nature in all its complexity. When, later, he says 'I do not like to see any thing destroyed; any void produced in society; any ruin on the face of the land' (p. 245), he comes close to affirming a principle of natural piety.

Apart from directing us to 'the method of nature' in society, Burke works out his case for gradual reform by interpreting the English habits of assimilation that made even the revolution of 1688 look gentler than it was. The leaders of the Lords and Commons, in the settlement of 1689, performed an act of usurpation, but by eulogistic redescription they treated the event as an act of continuity. James was forced to abdicate and his successors pulled out of the line of succession, not, it was insisted, to overthrow the system but in order to preserve it. Burke thinks that this difference, though it may seem verbal, matters greatly for the way reformers look at their actions and at themselves. If they stand in a continuity with the past, their very deference confirms the reality of a familiar human tribunal, to which their acts are answerable. By contrast, the French, boasting of their departures from precedent, have shown that they want their scheme to be admired as a thing absolutely new in the world. This break from the past, says Burke, involves the peril of setting up as the judge in one's own cause. The people are no more fit to be such a judge than a person would be. The makers of the Glorious Revolution were right to claim their fidelity to a time-honoured pattern and to conceal whatever might be disruptive in the character of their actions. 'They threw a politic, well-wrought veil over every circumstance tending to weaken the rights, which in the meliorated order of succession they meant to perpetuate' (p. 103). It is as important to assert the good of stability as it is to maintain a stable government.

In his discussion of 1689, Burke treats the working out of a historic reform on an analogy with the making of a work of art. The slow modifications of custom are received by the mind, so that they join its common stock, and the work of art is finally approved as if it were a work of nature. In this way, the usual Burkean metaphor for the artifice of governing – the building up and altering of a house – imperceptibly comes to be displaced by the organic metaphor of a plant that develops yet stays the same:

> The very idea of the fabrication of a new government, is enough to fill us with disgust and horror. We wished at the period of the Revolution, and do now wish, to derive all we possess

as *an inheritance from our forefathers*. Upon that body and stock of inheritance we have taken care not to inoculate any cyon alien to the nature of the original plant. (Ibid., p. 117)

Burke will say two years later, in the *Appeal from the New to the Old Whigs*, that 'art is man's nature'. The germ of all his political thinking may be the thought that habit enhances rather than opposes the natural character of human beings.

The feeling Burke hopes to summon against the French Revolution needs an object of reverence as well as one of shared antipathy. He finds this in the Queen of France – or rather, in the feelings he sees he is capable of having when he thinks of the Queen. The 20 pages that the *Reflections* devotes to a description of her fall and a meditation on the thoughts it inspires certainly look like a digression. But they have generally been treated as the heart of the book, and the tradition seems justified when one considers how much the sustained passage brings into view. It offers Burke's strongest case for the irreducibility of natural feelings; it draws a contrast once and for all between the honourable code of chivalry and the moral arithmetic of utility; it suggests the potency of the theatre as a school of moral sentiments; it gives reasons for rejecting a social contract positively recorded, in favour of a human 'partnership' spread out over generations; finally, it issues a warning on the dangers of democratic despotism. These pages are an extraordinary piece of moral psychology, but a paradoxical operation was required for Burke to enter into his eulogy; for Marie Antoinette was the Queen of France, not England: the focus of the affective loyalties of a rival nation, with whom England had been at war several times in the past century. France was a model sometimes despised, sometimes envied, almost never recommended as a model. In any case, she was a Catholic, and Burke was addressing readers in a Protestant country, who would be mostly immune to that particular source of appeal.

He gets past the difficulties by invoking the authority of a personal memory – a glimpse of the queen at Versailles in the early 1770s, a moment whose pathos and power now overwhelm him looking back. This reliance on personal testimony, on the force of anomalous details to clinch a public debate, was one of the things people had in mind when, in his own time, they spoke of Burke as 'Romantic'. The word called to mind the quixotic image of someone bound on far-reaching missions with utterly inappropriate means. Yet Burke's cry at his memory of the queen in her youth – 'Oh! What a revolution! And what an heart must I have to behold without emotion that elevation and that fall!' (p. 169) – is Romantic in a sense that will become vivid in the poetry of Wordsworth and Coleridge and Shelley. So is the contrast he draws between his excess of feeling and Dr Price's matter-of-fact approval of the taking of the king and queen from Versailles to Paris. 'Why do I feel so differently from the Reverend Dr Price? . . . For this plain reason – because it is *natural* I should' (p. 175). He offers personal sentiment as the sincere test of public conscience, appealing, as he does so, to an intimate self-inquest as his guide in moral questions. Burke pictures himself in this encounter as a man in a trance: he saw the queen 'just above the horizon' as if she were the morning star. He writes of her fallen state as if she were dead (though she is not), and suggests that her death when it comes will be a Roman suicide, 'the sharp antidote against distress' already 'concealed in her bosom'. With every plotted gesture, he assures that her fall will be read as a proper tragedy.

Several details in his praise of chivalry heighten the tragic effect. By a figurative cunning, Burke keeps in view the poignant irretrievability of the heroic mode of action he recalls. 'Dignified obedience', 'proud submission', 'sensibility of principle': unlike qualities, as our modern sense is apt to hear them, are yoked together almost routinely. The chevaliers who stand by the queen are endowed with a compliance, and a sensibility to distress, we might think characteristically feminine, to fit them for the rescue of a woman of majesty. Burke lays stress on the literally priceless nature of the good that has been sacrificed: the preservation of a creature like the queen signifies 'the unbought grace of life, the cheap defense of nations'. He concludes with a paradox, initially baffling, that aims to astonish. In the chivalric morality, we are told, 'vice itself lost half its evil, by losing all its grossness'.

The implied metaphor is *clothes make the man*. A system of naked vice is more evil than a system of vice that has refined away its grossness. One might translate the phrase as saying that modesty aids the cause of morality; but Burke has gone much further than that: his proposition means to aestheticize morality. So long as beauty prevails, all is not lost. The sentiment is scandalous, and this can obscure its practical force. Burke is saying that people who try to hide their vicious acts, because they pretend to a higher standard than their conduct actually satisfies, will, in the nature of things, commit less evil than those who make no effort to hide their wickedness. To be sure of not being seen to do evil, you will probably have to limit the amount that you do. The worst crimes are committed not by hypocrites but by tyrants who are perfectly shameless. And in this sense hypocrisy – the successful concealment of vice to preserve a standard of virtue – is half of morality. The makers of the French Revolution have created a morality that is levelling and anti-hypocritical but also illimitable in its wickedness. They have given up a decency that marked the civilization of Europe, in which 'the different shades of life' from high to low respected 'ideas, furnished from the wardrobe of a moral imagination, which the heart owns, and the understanding ratifies' (p. 171) So the moral standard was partly aesthetic from the first. The surface of beauty touches the depth of justice, for there is no life of principle without sensibility.

An element in Burke's analysis that is of permanent interest to political thought occurs at the climax of this passage. The majority in a democracy, he says, can never be made to share a feeling of shame. Their preponderance in numbers gives them an unembarrassable self-satisfaction, and their anonymity rules out even the possibility of individual regret. 'A perfect democracy is therefore the most shameless thing in the world. As it is the most shameless, it is also the most fearless' (p. 191). This warning will carry reverberations in the writings of Tocqueville and Mill, among others. Together with his view of the role of theory in reconstituting social life, it is a feature of his work that has made it seem an uncanny prophecy against totalitarianism.[1] But Burke's attack on the 'swinish multitude' that he fears will come to power in a revolution is also an attack on popular sovereignty in any form; his thoughts on democratic tyranny, well founded as they have proved, are linked to a contempt for the very idea of democracy.

Thomas Paine saw this and made it the motive of his reply to Burke in *The Rights of Man*. He addressed directly an audience of persons who would realize the largest practical gain from the coming of democratic rights. Burke's threat, that the debate about the revolution was really a debate about democracy itself, Paine asked his readers to accept as a promise, and from that point on his strategy was clear. Grant that politics is as theatrical an affair as Burke had made it, and suppose that 'a vast mass of mankind are degradedly thrown into the background of the human picture, to bring forward with greater glare, the puppet-show of state and aristocracy', and it will be at once a terrible and a banal consequence that they should exact a brutal revenge. But from whom do they learn such monstrous violence as that of capital punishments and the carrying of heads on pikes? 'They learn it from the governments they live under. . . . Lay then the axe to the root, and teach governments humanity'.[2] Whereas Burke's *Reflections* sold 19,000 copies in the six months after publication, a startling number for a work of its kind, Paine's reply sold 250,000 in the two years after the full text appeared, and many people learned to read in order to be able to read his book. It was with this effect in view that Albert Goodwin, a historian of the radical movements of the 1790s, summed up the unintended consequences of Burke's call to order: 'the publication [of the *Reflections*] did much to facilitate the advent of popular radicalism in Britain, by the controversy it provoked on the first principles of government'.[3] Burke did what all the revolution societies could never have done alone. He created the French Revolution for the English mind as a world-historical event.

The anti-democratic strain in the *Reflections* was well calculated to fix the attention of educated radicals of the 1790s. Wordsworth, for example, who declared in 1794 that 'I am of that odious class of men called democrats, and of that class I shall for ever continue',[4] left a record of his revulsion from Burke's sentiments in the unpublished text of his pro-regicidal *Letter to the Bishop of Llandaff*. But to see Burke in this light, as mainly a negative stimulus, is to frame the matter too narrowly. The *Reflections* brings to the discussion of society and of imagination certain emphases so original that no one, including Burke himself, could have foreseen all of their distant bearings. He had constructed politics and morality as a scene of imaginative sympathy with two characters, a sufferer and a spectator, and asked us to recognize, in the way we answer a cry of help or an appeal for loyalty, that in the response we give every ounce of our humanity is at stake. We can lose our hold of human nature itself by a failure here, and by a success we can not only confirm but strengthen the bonds of nature that make us what we are. It may have made a difference to Burke, but need not for his successors, whether the object of sympathy was the Queen of France or an idiot boy. Sympathy is the work partly of habit, but though it feels like 'wisdom without reflection', its claim on us is unconditional. A further emphasis salient in Burke is his belief that the means by which our habits of response are achieved must be imaginative and adaptive. He had thought long about this when he wrote his phrase about 'the wardrobe of a moral imagination'. In the theatre of human action, we come to understand ourselves as spectators, and the burden remains on each of us to continue to humanize ourselves. It is possible, Burke speculates, by a long train of corrupt responses for a human to become a monstrous being.

This way of looking at politics as a theatre of action in which the spectators come to know themselves gives tremendous shaping power to the dramatist, that is, the artist, and potentially marks out for art itself an unparalleled field of moral influence. Poets and novelists had long been understood as inspired witnesses, makers of a unique kind of ideal object. Burke seems to say that, to the extent that artists help to revive and create the feelings that make us what we are, they are themselves the prophets of human nature. Such a possibility seems utterly at odds with the prudential design of the writer of the *Reflections*; but, as one traces its impact on the next several generations, on writers working in genres far outside political theory, the conclusion becomes inescapable. Burke's fear of what can happen to men of theory when they separate themselves from family and neighbourhood and give a power above human feeling to an abstract projection of the mind can be traced to the last psychological detail in the story of *Frankenstein*. In a romance of altogether different character, Scott's *Redgauntlet*, the narrative appears so to have assimilated a Burkean irony regarding the mind's need of spectacle – 'a grand spectacle to rouze the imagination, grown torpid with the lazy enjoyment of sixty years security' – that the hero's participation in a failed rebellion is treated as an ideal rite of passage for coming to accept a historic inheritance. Blake in *The Marriage of Heaven and Hell* and elsewhere conducts a continuous allusive argument against Burke's defence of habit and apology for shame – never more buoyantly than in the proverb of hell, 'Drive your cart and your plow over the bones of the dead'.

Novalis, the German romantic aphorist, told the whole truth with éclat about the nature of Burke's contemporary influence: 'There are many anti-revolutionary books being written in favour of the revolution. Burke has written against the revolution a revolutionary book'. Much the same was said in a humbler style by Henry Wisemore, a member of the Unitarian Society, when he invited Burke to join the festivities with which some reformers would commemorate Bastille Day in 1791:

> If you had not written we should not have been blessed with Paynes Magnificent answer to you, which is a book that must tend to open the eyes of the People of England. Fourteen thousand are already sold and a society of staunch Patriots have subscribed a considerable sum to disperse a cheap edition throughout the Kingdom in order to undermine, *aristocracy, Church Power* and national prejudices, which will fall some years the sooner for your Romantic attempt to support them.[5]

Burke for some reason held on to this letter. Whatever a writer may think, and whatever readers may judge in a moment of acceptance or dismissal, the fate of a book like *Reflections on the Revolution in France* is never quite a finished fact.

## NOTES

1  See Arendt, *The Origins of Totalitarianism*, and Talmon, *The Origins of Totalitarian Democracy*.
2  Paine, *The Rights of Man*, pp. 59, 57–8.
3  Goodwin, *The Friends of Liberty*, p. 135.
4  *EY*, p. 119.
5  Letter of 16 April 1791 in Copeland, *Correspondence*, vol. 6, p. 247.

## REFERENCES AND FURTHER READING

Arendt, Hannah, *The Origins of Totalitarianism*, New York, 1951. Talmon, J. L. *The Origins of Totalitarian Democracy*, New York, Harcourt, Brace & Co., 1960.

Burke, Edmund, *Reflections on the Revolution in France*, ed. Conor Cruise O'Brien, Harmondsworth, Penguin, 1970.

Goodwin, Albert *The Friends of Liberty*, Cambridge, Mass., Harvard University Press, 1979.

Paine, Thomas *The Rights of Man*, Harmondsworth, Penguin, 1984.

Pares, Richard, *King George III and the Politicians*, London, Clarendon Press, 1953.

# 11

# Charlotte Smith, *The Old Manor House*

## *Miranda J. Burgess*

Published in 1793 soon after the French revolutionary execution of Louis XVI, but set during the War of American Independence (1776–83), *The Old Manor House* is the only historical novel by the liberal poet and novelist Charlotte Smith. Smith builds her narrative around a conventional romance plot – a love affair between Orlando Somerive, heir to the prosperous Rayland estate, and Monimia, the orphan niece of Mrs Lennard, the Rayland housekeeper. Had Smith's plot ended there, it would be indistinct from the Gothic romances of Ann Radcliffe, or from Smith's own early *Emmeline* (1788), *Ethelinde* (1789) or *Celestina* (1791). But *The Old Manor House* also examines the intersections of romance with economic and political life: Monimia's abusive charity upbringing, Orlando's disinheritance by a coalition of landed and moneyed interests, Orlando's military service against rebel colonists in New York, and Monimia's narrow escape from forced prostitution and debtor's prison in London complicate the progress of romance. The novel's American historical plot allows Smith to uphold the potential justice of revolution even during the onset of 'the Terror', the war between Britain and France, and the resulting anti-revolutionary fervour in Britain. At the same time, her glance at an earlier, Anglo-American revolution frees her to establish a logical connection between English political oppression and rebellion without attracting the charges of seditious libel that several of her contemporaries would face. Finally, by intertwining sentiment with public affairs, Smith can comment on the resemblance of domestic and political suffering – and the degree to which a political rebel, no less than an aristocrat, may be a domestic tyrant.

More than Smith's sympathetic account of revolutionary history, it was this double plotting of private sentiments and public events that irked contemporary reviewers. The *Anti-Jacobin Review* compared Smith unfavourably with Frances Burney, remarking that Smith 'may still produce entertainment, and even advantage to society, if she will abstain from politics, concerning which, her views are narrow and partial, her conclusions unjust, and her inculcations hurtful. The best of our female novelists interferes not with church or state. There are no politics in Evelina or Cecilia'. Although the reviewer's accuracy about Burney's novels is debatable, he usefully discriminates Smith's various complex relations with the separate spheres of late eighteenth-century social life in Britain. Like other 'female novelists', he suggests, Smith belongs in the 'narrow and partial' domestic realm of family life and personal relations. Custom and the *Anti-Jacobin* alike expect her to 'abstain from' the public sphere of Church, State, and political debate, implicitly reserved for males, and to confine herself to such private, sentimental matters as Orlando's court-ship of Monimia. It is because Smith does not respect the border between public and private life that the *Anti-Jacobin* declares her novels 'hurtful'. As the reviewer notes and *The Old Manor House* illustrates, Smith 'interferes' with public affairs – her plots and narrators venture beyond the domestic sphere that marks their expected limit.

Two centuries later, writers about the 1790s no longer believe that forays into politics by female novelists, even in that revolutionary decade, are necessarily tantamount to protest. Although Smith's readers continue to acknowledge the dissidence she conveys (e.g. Ty, *Unsex'd Revolutionaries*, p. 130), they also note that political critique gives way in her work to the formation of communities based on sentiment, especially after *Desmond* (1792), an account of revolutionary France and her final novel before the Terror (see Cole, '(Anti)feminist sympathies'; Watson, *Revolution*, pp. 36–9). These readers explain Smith's curtailment of protest by pointing out the increasing conservatism of late-century British response to the French Revolution, and the attacks on female self-assertion that accompanied it. That Smith wrote for money, some argue, made her attend especially cautiously to the trends of public debate (cf. Rogers, 'Romantic aspirations'). Thus, in *The Old Manor House* Monimia responds to economic deprivation, servitude and emotional tyranny not with defiance, but with tears: she is 'the weeping, trembling Monimia' throughout the first two volumes, and her emotion demands sympathy from those around her as well as from the reader. Monimia is frequently 'unable to speak' for emotion (p. 204), or 'terror . . . deprives her of the power of shedding tears' (p. 94). Her silence confirms that her tearful, trembling, sentimental body is not a protest, but a highly personal appeal for rescue or community.

In the final volumes of *The Old Manor House*, Monimia's friendship with Selina Somerive perfects the sentimental community that supersedes dissent. When Monimia's aunt and her husband, the corrupt attorney Roker, use a forged will to usurp the Rayland estate, to which the Somerives are heirs-at-law, and apprentice Monimia to a milliner by whom she is 'absolutely sold' to a rakish baronet (p. 479), neither Selina nor Monimia protests this economic injustice. Instead, they meet to weep and dream of rescue by Orlando – Selina's brother and Monimia's lover – who is fighting in America. 'I had still some sweeteners of my melancholy existence', Monimia later tells Orlando, 'for I sometimes met Selina, and wept with her' (p. 472), while Selina comments that 'though these short intervals were passed . . . in tears on both sides, they were the only pleasure we either of us tasted; and we have often said, that the consolation of the rest of the week was, that Monday would return at the beginning of the next!' (p. 431). Orlando himself regains the estate by means of boyhood friendship with a lawyer and married kinship with Mrs Roker rather than political reform. Once again, community compensates for oppression – and Smith, too, subsumes protest in sentimental romance, not only fortuitously restoring Orlando's inheritance, but also magically rewarding Selina's sentimental friendship with an unher-alded husband and inheritance on the last page of the novel. The conditions that produce poverty and sorrow – a socio-economic system that disallows women from supporting or protecting themselves; inheritance laws that whim and primogeniture can sway; the sexual predations of landed, moneyed men – remain unprotested, as well as unallayed.

Nevertheless, Smith is arguably more self-conscious in her substitution of sentiment for protest than her readers acknowledge or the weeping and trembling of Monimia seem to suggest. Smith's writing for money is indeed intimately connected with the themes and structure of *The Old Manor House*, but her financial troubles radicalize rather than chasten her narrative. For one thing, Smith could not see fiction as an art, and women as a gender, on a separate plane from political and economic events. That Monimia's emotions cannot be dissociated from her economic dependency, or her economic dependency from 'tyranny', is a lesson that Monimia teaches Orlando early in their courtship, declaring that protest against her employer 'would not be heard . . . but I should be immediately turned out of the house with disgrace; and I have no friend, no relation in the world but my aunt, and must beg my bread . . . and I shall never – never see you any more!' (p. 19). Smith's lack of money, like Monimia's and the Somerives's, was a product of specific legal and financial structures – primogeniture, inheritance, probate court and gender-biased marriage laws that mandated informal separation rather than divorce from a husband who continued to sign her book contracts but paid no support (Stanton, 'Charlotte Smith', pp. 376–7). The damage wrought by these institutions pervades her novel: even Lennard, having helped usurp Orlando's estate, is imprisoned by her husband to prevent her revealing the plot (p. 521). Because her own socio-economic woes resulted directly from marriage and motherhood, Smith was uniquely equipped to discuss the blurring of private and public spheres of concern, and her novel suggests that the separation of politics and economics from home and hearth is no more than ideology: a widespread, deeply felt belief promoted, among other ways, in romance. Smith's narrator names as her subject 'the politics of Rayland Hall' (p. 230). In most novels of the 1790s, this claim would be a contradiction in terms.

The line between politics and privacy is not the only boundary subjected to ideological scrutiny in *The Old Manor House*. In recent analyses of the French Revolution, theorists have tended to argue that the revolution's character as a discourse – that is, a series of rituals, texts and other forms of representation and theatre – outweighed any changes it produced in economic or social structures. Theorists of gender have applied similar analyses to sexual difference, so that sex, too, appears as a performance, albeit one that is usually unconscious (see Butler, *Gender Trouble*). Evidence for both analyses may be found in such late-eighteenth-century writers as Edmund Burke and Helen Maria Williams, whose texts lay both gender and history open to charges of fictionality. For Burke, the French Revolution was in large part a battle between the 'gothic ignorance' and 'tyranny' of the revolutionaries, symbolized by masculine women and abused heroines, and the 'chivalry' and sentiment of monarchical France and England, personified by domestic wives and pedestalled beauties; in her liberal account of revolutionary France, Williams inverted Burke's valuation of *ancien régime* and revolution. Smith's experience of injustice, which enabled her to take on public topics in an otherwise domestic novel, made *The Old Manor House* very much of its moment. It is, in other words, an intertextual work, alluding by parody or imitation to current pamphlets, histories and narratives of revolution. It reflects the literary forms, or genres, used by Burke and Williams, subtypes of the moral, often allegorical, highly conventional narrative genre called romance: the love plot of sentiment and chivalry, and the horrific scenes of Gothic. The slippage revealed between 'chivalric' sentiment and 'Gothic' terror, as well as between home and government, suggests that there is little difference between liberal and conservative accounts of revolution – or between revolution and the power revolutionaries claimed to replace.

By including the sentimental romance of Orlando and Monimia in *The Old Manor House*, Smith complicates what for most contemporaries was the simple opposition or resemblance of revolution and oppression. She demonstrates that revolution oppresses domestic lives, not because it differs from traditional socio-economic practices, but because it resembles them. Like Burke and Williams, Smith characterizes tyranny and rebellion as variants of Gothic and chivalric romance, but beneath both is a consistent level of violence. The violence that accompanies the smudging of genre boundaries in the novel suggests that it is the underlying reliance on romance that keeps both England and revolution from achieving genuine change. Both sides employ the powerful metaphor of romance – and, whether Gothic or sentimental, romance as Smith examines it demands masculine violence and feminine silence. Her novel reflexively acknowledges that, in the 1790s, sex, text and politics are bound up together.

In *The Old Manor House* Smith extends a critique begun in Elizabeth Inchbald's *Simple Story* (1791) and Mary Wollstonecraft's two *Vindications* (1790, 1792). Like Inchbald and Wollstonecraft, Smith links romance metaphors for revolution and history to women's silence in the British and French political arenas. But she also imports 'terror' into England, bringing home the Gothic narratives of Burke, Williams and Radcliffe to link the situations of women in Britain and revolutionary Europe. In Smith's novel of injustice and corruption, tyranny begins at home.

Smith's representatives of tyranny are the arch-Tory landholder, Grace Rayland, and Mrs Lennard, her housekeeper, the daughter of a merchant whose fortune was lost in the 'South Sea Bubble' of 1720. Together, these representatives of land and commerce confine and terrorize Monimia – Lennard in the hope that her niece's cowed obedience will help win 'the favour of her . . . affluent patroness' (p. 12) and Rayland from contempt for Lennard's family (pp. 10, 55). Forced into poverty and servitude, living in a mouldering turret above a possibly haunted vault, Monimia is a typical Gothic heroine. Smith's terms for the authority of Rayland and Lennard, however, are Gothic, chivalric and sentimental by turns: their basically chivalric attitudes to government and sentimental view of courtship easily give way to Gothic treatment of Monimia when masculine admiration is at stake. In contrast, Orlando, though a cousin to Rayland, represents a new kind of authority, and his ultimate inheritance of the Rayland estate and assumption of the Rayland name and baronetcy may suggest that the corrupt old order has been replaced. His virtue is emphasized by a plot that sets his 'romantic quixotism' (p. 152) in favourable contrast to a range of other men, all of whom are corrupt (Archdeacon Hollybourn and his attorney, Darby), or selfish (Orlando's brother Philip and uncle Woodford), or sexually profligate and violent (Sir John Belgrave, Stockton, General Tracy and Roker). Yet although these men are foils to Orlando, the novel finally demonstrates that Orlando's virtue differs too slightly from the 'Gothic' code it replaces or the mercantile selfishness to which it offers an alternative.

In particular, Orlando's attitude to Monimia, which wins him the derisive title 'Sir Roland, . . . most valorous chevalier' (p. 207) from Philip, shares much with that of Lennard, who, fond 'of odd romantic whim' (p. 12), is responsible for the 'romantic impropriety' of Monimia's name (p. 13). As though to highlight this resemblance,

Orlando's complicity in the chivalric ideals of Rayland and Lennard increases Monimia's Gothic torments. To be a Gothic heroine is to register on one's body the effects of tyranny, and it is this sensibility that attracts the romantic Orlando to Monimia. His first act on falling in love with her is to throw a ball through the window of Rayland Hall, where she sits sewing with Lennard and Rayland. Caught concealing the ball, Monimia is beaten and reduced to a sentimental tableau of tears: 'on the lovely neck of [Lennard's] victim . . . the marks of her fingers were to be traced many days afterwards' (p. 18). Yet far from avoiding Monimia in order to prevent further punishment, Orlando invades her rooms. When she flees 'in terror', he uses his 'superior strength and agility' to prevent her, trapping her as Lennard does: 'setting his back against the door, he insisted upon knowing the cause of her tears before he suffered her to stir'. His 'generous spirit revolted from every kind of injustice', Orlando threatens to 'appeal against the tyranny and cruelty' she suffers, but to Monimia revolt is a tyranny worse than oppression:

> she threw herself half frantic on her knees before him, and besought him rather to kill her, than to expose her to the terrors and distress such a step would inevitably plunge her into. (p. 19)

By the end of the novel Orlando will have learned 'that the romantic theory, of sacrificing every consideration to love, produced, in the practice, only the painful consciousness of having injured its object' (p. 517).

Nor is the household the only place where Smith associates Orlando's romantic nature with the Gothic tyranny of wealth and landed power. Rayland expects 'glory' from Orlando's American combat:

> accustomed . . . to high ideas of the military glory of her ancestors, and considering the Americans as rebels and round heads, to conquer them seemed to her to be not only a national cause, but one in which her family were particularly bound to engage. She had contemplated only the honours, and thought little of the dangers of war. (p. 329)

Orlando's political views encourage Rayland's, much as his treatment of Monimia upholds Lennard's, for his own ethics are similarly founded on 'chivalry' (pp. 249–50). He has 'been taught to love glory – What so sacred as the glory of his country? To purchase it no exertion could be too great [and]. . . no sacrifice should be regretted' (p. 348). Yet once he begins fighting on the English side in America, Orlando's 'good sense' rises 'in despite of this prejudice', and he finds himself losing faith in the cause. Although he 'quieted these doubts by referring to history', the narrator has already undermined him by defining history's warlike kings as 'the crowned murderers of antiquity' (p. 348), and English history as 'the dates of the most execrable actions of the most execrable of human beings' (p. 186). Although Orlando tells Rayland that the army is a profession 'honourable . . . to any name' (p. 222), he notes early in the novel that 'not one of our kings or heroes could have slept in their beds' if 'sanguinary monsters who are stained with crimes' were plagued by conscience (p. 49). In Smith's sceptical view, which she passes on even to the naive Orlando, the English state is propped up by acts of tyranny and Gothic violence, including war against its American colonies. She supports this claim in a footnote defending the

French Revolution – not by justifying revolutionary violence, but by insisting instead that England's own government has been guilty of worse:

> Those who have so loudly exclaimed against a whole nation struggling for its freedom, on account of the events of the past summer (events terrible enough, God knows!), are entreated to recollect how much the exploits of this [British American] expedition . . . exceed any thing that happened on the 10th of August, the 2nd of September, or at any one period of the execrated Revolution in France – and own, that there are savages of all countries – even of our own! (p. 360n.)

It is for 'savagery' that Orlando fights, even as he detects a gulf between chivalry and justice.

Above all, Smith emphasizes that British colonial 'savagery', though political in aim, is domestic in its methods. Supported by historical footnotes, she describes burned villages and forced marches of colonists, who are 'often driven' from their 'wretched temporary abodes . . . to make way for the English soldiers; and their women and children exposed to the tempest of the night, or . . . infinitely more dreadful, to the brutality of the military' (p. 356). She objects, in particular, to the use of 'native American auxiliaries', one of whom serves as the foremost emblem of British 'savagery':

> when Orlando saw in the hands of the Bloody Captain eleven scalps, some of them evidently those of women and children, others of very old, and consequently defenceless men; many of them fresh, which he said, with an air of triumph, he had taken from the enemies of the King of England within three weeks – the young unhardened Englishman shuddered with horror, and blushed for his country! (pp. 360–1)

In illustrating English 'tyranny', in government as in households, Smith highlights the ill treatment of those whose conventional place is within the protecting walls of the home: women, children and old men. Genres blur once more as she details the Gothic violence of the avowedly chivalrous British soldiers. Even Orlando's friend Lieutenant Fleming, a gentle career officer whom poverty has kept from rising through the ranks, repeats the government's defence of 'arming the Indians': 'this dreadful sort of warfare . . . can sooner conquer the rebels and reduce them to obedience, [which] . . . is in fact best for them' (p. 361). Paternal protection and Gothic violence unite in Smith's text; the 'cruelty' of the war is for the colonists' own good. Orlando himself objects only tacitly to Fleming's words and the Bloody Captain's scalps. His 'honour' prohibits him from 'living under the stigma of cowardice', and he fights on (p. 323).

Both government and household, as Smith represents them, slip easily from sentiment and chivalry into Gothic terror and tyranny. Orlando is the pivot on which the chivalric/ Gothic opposition turns, and the point at which the two genres fade into one another. Consequently, his place in the novel must be simultaneously political and domestic. It is appropriate, therefore, that Monimia bears the marks, not just of domestic, but also of political tyranny, and that she serves as the bridge between Orlando's chivalric and Gothic roles. Woven into the psychological language of 'terror' that surrounds Monimia is a self-conscious series of references to the narrative framework of revolution. When Lennard spins supernatural tales to frighten her niece into keeping her room at night, Orlando condemns her in the rationalist tones of the French Revolution: 'like all other usurped authority, the power of your aunt is maintained by unjust means, and supported by prejudices, which if once looked at by the eye of reason would fall. So slender is the hold of tyranny' (p. 44). Though he privately offers Monimia the 'reason' she lacks, however, Orlando publicly fights on the side of anti-revolutionary forces, and employs the language of chivalric romance to influence Monimia, accusing her, for example, of 'cruelty' (pp. 32, 39). At the same time, he uses terror against her when he desires. Like Lennard, he frightens to control her: ' "If you insist upon going . . . I shall be half tempted to let you travel through the chapel alone . . . and, to revenge myself for your desertion, expose you to meet the tall man in the white dress." . . . [A]fter insisting upon her promise to meet him the next night, he consented that she should return to her turret' (p. 49). Orlando's rhetoric links youthful liberalism with old money, sentiment with Gothic horror. As long as he consents to govern Monimia with the oppressive fictions he criticizes, he merely reproduces tyranny as terror. Revolutionary ideas, it seems, are in need of revolutionary change – as Orlando's final transformation into Sir Orlando Rayland of Rayland Hall confirms.

The novel's most distinctive feature is the stylized terror that attaches itself to Monimia, wielded equally by the new order and the old, and by Orlando, the link between them. A repetitive vocabulary gives Monimia's responses a circumscribed and choric quality: 'if I were to die', she repeats, 'I cannot conquer my terrors' (p. 39). Smith associates the experience of terror with loss of voice and of physical power, which Orlando's demands intensify: 'Monimia did not speak; she was not able' because of the 'additional terror' of his words (p. 41). Returning late to her room because he has detained her, Monimia begs for company: 'I am in such terror already, that if my aunt is very violent against me, I really believe I shall die on the spot' (p. 90). Her 'trembling companion' is the housemaid Betsy, who mirrors and magnifies her terror.[1] Creeping through the vault by candlelight, Monimia sees her own face in Betsy's:

'Do I tremble as much as you do, and do I look as pale?'
'Oh! hush . . . hush! I shall drop if I hear a voice – it sounds so among these hollow doors.'
(p. 47)

The scene ends as the women faint side by side.

The shared experience of Gothic helplessness unites women with each other, cutting across class lines, yet Smith does not uphold the community of fear as a substitute for rebellious solidarity. She imitates Monimia's own voicelessness, refusing to go beyond the limits that Monimia's faints and silences set for her narrative, and there are many moments at which fear prevents Monimia from telling the stories she needs to defend herself – and Smith from conveying necessary information to the reader. The events of the journey through the vault, for example, are related to the reader in Monimia's tremulous, inter-rupted telling. This narrative technique identifies the novelist as a member of the community whose subdued voices hold back her novel. If Monimia's terror silences her, Smith seems to suggest, contemporary insistence on Gothic portraits of revolution and Terror confine the female novelist to echoing the tremblings of heroines. As Orlando gains power by borrowing the *ancien régime* fictions of Lennard and Rayland, so the novelist gains a voice and audience by employing the Gothic, chivalric and sentimental conventions she critiques. Indeed, Monimia becomes 'infinitely more lovely than ever' to Orlando for being 'on his account a prisoner' (p. 26); Orlando finds pleasure in Monimia's visible terror and grief, kissing 'as marks of tender sensibility' the 'blistered' paper on which she records fears that he himself has caused, and his motives for contributing to her fears appear more than a little mixed (p. 261). Smith sardonically parallels Orlando's pleasure in Monimia's voiceless sensibility to her own relationship with the literary market.

If Smith has been subdued by poverty and the conservatization of the British press, Monimia is herself silenced by economic power held up by domestic authority, and by Smith's – and Orlando's – demands that she serve as a romance heroine. Smith writes the pressures on female writers *and* citizens into her double plot of public and domestic oppression. *The Old Manor House* is about the broad and debilitating effects of romance – on writing, politics and domestic life – as much as it is about revolution.

NOTE

1 'Betsy' is named 'Betty' throughout Smith's text, with the exception of pp. 46–8.

WRITINGS

Burke, Edmund, *Reflections on the Revolution in France*, ed. J. G. A. Pocock, Indianapolis, Hackett, 1987.

Inchbald, Elizabeth, *A Simple Story*, ed. J. M. S. Tompkins, Oxford, Oxford University Press, 1988.

Smith, Charlotte, *The Old Manor House*, ed. Anne Henry Ehrenpreis, Oxford, Oxford University Press, 1969; ed. Anne Henry Ehrenpreis, intro.

Judith Phillips Stanton, Oxford, Oxford University Press, 1989.

Williams, Helen Maria, *Letters Written in France, 1790*, facsimile ed. Jonathan Wordsworth, Oxford, Woodstock Books, 1989.

Wollstonecraft, Mary, *A Vindication of the Rights of Woman*, ed. Carol H. Poston, New York, W. W. Norton, 1975.

REFERENCES AND FURTHER READING

Anon., *Anti-Jacobin Review*, 'Charlotte Smith, *The Young Philosopher*, 1 (1798) 187–90.

Bartolomeo, Joseph F. 'Subversion of romance in *The Old Manor House*', *SEL* 33 (1993) 645–57.

Bowstead, Diana, 'Charlotte Smith's *Desmond*: the epistolary novel as ideological argument', in *Fetter'd or Free? British Women Novelists, 1670–1815*, ed. Mary Anne Schofield and Cecilia Macheski, Athens, Ohio, Ohio University Press, 1986, pp. 237–63.

Butler, Judith, *Gender Trouble: Feminism and the Subversion of Identity*, New York, Routledge, 1990.

Cole, Lucinda, '(Anti)feminist sympathies: the politics of relationship in Smith, Wollstonecraft, and More', *ELH* 58 (1991) 107–40.

Ellison, Julie, 'Redoubled feeling: politics, sentiment, and the sublime in Williams and Wollstonecraft', *Studies in Eighteenth-Century Culture* 20 (1990) 197–215.

Hunt, Lynn, *Politics, Culture, and Class in the French Revolution*, Berkeley and Los Angeles, University of California Press, 1984.

Johnson, Claudia L., *Equivocal Beings: Politics, Gender, and Sentimentality in the 1790s*, Chicago, University of Chicago Press, 1995.

Kelly, Gary, *English Fiction of the Romantic Period, 1789–1830*, London, Longman, 1989.

Outram, Dorinda, *The Body and the French Revolution: Sex, Class and Political Culture*, New Haven, Yale University Press, 1989.

Ozouf, Mona, *Festivals and the French Revolution*, Paris, Gallimard, 1976; trans. Alan Sheridan, Cambridge, Mass., Harvard University Press, 1988.

Rogers, Katharine M., 'Inhibitions on eighteenth-century women novelists: Elizabeth Inchbald and Charlotte Smith', *Eighteenth-century Studies* 11 (1977) 63–78.

——'Romantic aspirations, restricted possibilities: the novels of Charlotte Smith', in *Re-Visioning Romanticism: British Women Writers, 1776–1837*, ed. Carol Shiner Wilson and Joel Haefner, Philadelphia, University of Pennsylvania Press, 1994, pp. 72–88.

Stanton, Judith Phillips, 'Charlotte Smith's "literary business": income, patronage, and indigence', *The Age of Johnson* 1 (1987) 375–401.

Ty, Eleanor, *Unsex'd Revolutionaries: Five Women Novelists of the 1790s*, Toronto, University of Toronto Press, 1993.

Watson, Nicola J., *Revolution and the Form of the British Novel, 1790–1825: Intercepted Letters, Interrupted Seductions*, Oxford, Clarendon Press, 1994.

# 12

# Samuel Taylor Coleridge, *Kubla Khan*, *The Ancient Mariner* and *Christabel*

*Seamus Perry*

### Coleridge and Unity

The three great poems come several years before Coleridge's attempts to define the imagination theoretically, and they can seem the work of an entirely different kind of intelligence. But in fact there is a strong continuity: the predominant concerns of the later philosophical works can already be seen, and I shall try to root some out in this essay, concentrating especially on the central, twin Coleridgean concepts of imagination and unity.

Unity, he writes in his notebook, is the 'ultimate end of human Thought, and human Feeling' (*Notebooks*, III: 3,247); as he transcribed into the notebook from Jeremy Taylor, 'He to whom all things are one, who draweth all things to one, and seeth all things in one, may enjoy true peace & rest of spirit' (ibid., I: 876). There is, he writes in the *Biographia Literaria*, a 'high spiritual instinct of the human being impelling us to seek unity' (CC *Biographia*, II: 72), and one expression of this fundamental instinct is 'that gift of true Imagination, that capability of reducing a multitude into a unity of effect', as Coleridge told his lecture audience in 1811 (CC *Lectures on Literature*, I: 249). In philosophy, this gift would produce Coleridge's perfect 'system', 'the only attempt that I know of ever made', as he modestly put it, 'to reduce all knowledges into harmony . . . to unite the insulated fragments of truth' (CC *Table Talk*, I: 248); while in art, the unifying instinct would create beauty, which he succinctly defined as 'the many seen as one' (CC *Lectures on Literature*, II: 220).

It is an obvious paradox that so devoted an apostle of unity should have produced so many spectacularly disunified works himself. 'It is one of the ironies of his life,' says Humphry House, 'that he who saw so clearly, and expounded more fully than any English critic before him, the principle of the organic unity of a work of art, should have achieved that unity so rarely'.[1] The very least that you can expect of a poem aspiring to be a unified whole is that it is complete: our three poems are either evidently unfinished, explicitly left up in the air (*Christabel*); or announce themselves as fragmentary and include a preface to explain the circumstances of disappointment (*Kubla Khan*); or go through the motions of concluding, but actually leave off in an almost parodically irresolved way (*The Ancient Mariner*).

'Paradox' may seem rather a polite way of describing so huge and farcical a form of failure; but it was Coleridge's vocation to make failure a source of success: the three supernatural poems, hardly unified and whole themselves, instead put to the test notions of unity and wholeness. For all the many failings of his personality, Coleridge's inability to pull off the unity of a completed poem was not really the result of indolence or dissipation (look at the size of the collected works), but rather the result of his aptitude for entertaining at once perfectly incompatible positions: it is what Thomas McFarland has called his 'including temperament', his unsystematic capacity to be 'on all sides of a question at once'.[2] Because of this cast of mind, Coleridgean concepts normally come in pairs, and when you find an important term, you soon find that its vitality in his thought stems from the tense, antithetical relationship it has with a partnering term: 'Shakespeare is in all things, the divine Opposite or antithetic correspondent of the divine Milton' (*Notebooks*, IV: 4,714), for example. This antithetical habit holds true even of the apparently uncontestable Coleridgean attribute of unity, for so emphatic a regard for unity's excellence stems from an intense experience of its opposite: disunity and chaos (to be rude), diversity and individuality (to be more appreciative); and it is this unresolved state that the three great poems explore.

## The Mind and Nature in *Kubla Khan*

A letter Coleridge writes to John Thelwall, around the time of writing *Kubla Khan*, puts very clearly the antithesis between unity and the '*little things*' of sense perception:[3]

> I can *at times* feel strongly the beauties you describe, in themselves, & for themselves – but more frequently *all things* appear little – all the knowledge, that can be acquired, child's play – the universe itself – what but an immense heap of *little things*? – I can contemplate nothing but parts, & parts are all *little* – ! – My mind feels as if it ached to behold & know something *great* – something *one & indivisible* and it is only in the faith of this that rocks or waterfalls, mountains or caverns give me the sense of sublimity or majesty! (14 October, 1797; Griggs, I: 349)

A geography of caverns and water feels rather like Xanadu already; and the issues at stake in the letter are also those of the poem. We know he thought the problem a promising subject for poetry because of a later notebook entry which begins to plan an epic (never written, like many of Coleridge's most grandly conceived works): 'I would make a pilgrimage to the burning sands of Arabia . . . to find the Man who could explain to me there can be *oneness*, there being infinite Perceptions – yet there must be a *oneness*, not an intense Union but an Absolute Unity' (*Notebooks*, I: 556).

To speak of 'Absolute Unity' is to make unity an attribute of deity: 'divine unity' is one of the 'sublime truths' (CC *Biographia*, I: 226). In God, idea and reality are 'absolutely identical' (ibid., I: 275); as at the Creation, for example, when the ordered reality of the universe springs into being at God's word: 'the earth was without form, and void . . . God said, Let there be light: and there was light' (Genesis 1: 2, 3). Poets possess a small-scale version of God's innate creativity: 'Idly talk they who speak of Poets as mere Indulgers of Fancy, Imagination, Superstition, etc. They are the Bridlers by Delight, the Purifiers, they that combine them with reason and order, the true Protoplasts, Gods of Love who tame the Chaos' (*Notebooks,* II: 2,355).

The terrific creative act announced in the opening lines of *Kubla Khan* is an attempt at just such a divine taming of a natural multiplicity that, to the Khan, seems chaotic: establishing the tamed formality of the pleasure-dome gardens is making a kind of art; but the attempt is flawed, which is what *Kubla Khan* is about. The first lines are derived from an account of the Mongol emperor in *Purchas His Pilgrimage, or Relations of the World and the Religions Observed in All Ages* (1613): 'In *Xamdu* did *Cublai Can* build a stately Palace'. Coleridge adds a stress on the 'decree': the business of building and planting is entirely bypassed, as if its realization is taken for granted, just as we should take for granted the realization of God's decree. As is only appropriate for the work of God-like creativity, Kubla's gardens of art are a kind of paradise, rather like the fertile garden created by Milton's God, in which a 'fresh fountain . . . with many a rill / Watered the garden' (*Paradise Lost,* IV: 229–30): 'paradise' means an enclosed park or orchard.

They are planted in an elemental geography, implying a cosmic scale: 'Alph' recalls 'Alpha', the first of things, and the 'sunless sea' to which it runs, the last, a kind of 'Omega'. Alph's presumably subterranean (and so sunless and lifeless) destination subtly implies a grave undermining of the 'gardens bright'; and the suggestion of natural forces which the Khan's artistry cannot control or contain is intensified in the second verse paragraph, which announces its antithetical relationship with the first in its opening word: 'But'. Where the first verse exemplifies the harmonious criteria of beauty and orderliness, the second is full of the mountainous and discordant paraphernalia of the sublime: the sensory delights of the garden are suitably mild, tinkling 'rills' that are soon drowned out in the surrounding cacophony of 'wailing' and 'breathing' (though the wailing only happens in a metaphor). The river rises from the mighty fountain (24), then flows for five miles (25) before reaching the measureless caverns (27) where Khan has planted his gardens (3–4), and then plunges (presumably, since there is an enormous 'tumult') into the lifeless sea. One of the effects of juxtaposing the antithetical landscapes is a very startling shift of perspective, by which the pleasure dome, so impressive in the first stanza, is 'placed' in the second, over-shadowed by the enormity of its natural surroundings, the threatening power of which is finally symbolized in the Khan's hearing, amidst this wild tumult, disembodied prophecies of war, as if foretelling the fulfilment of a family curse. 'Whatever the Khan does', writes John Beer, subtlest analyst of the poem, 'he cannot escape the fact that his paradise must inevitably be lost';[4] as paradises are, after all. True, there is no explicit snake in his garden; but the rills *are* 'sinuous', which craftily insinuates 'sin' into the garden in serpentine shape ('the sinuous and over-varied lapses of a serpent, writhing in every direction': CC *Lectures on Literature,* II: 278), as if the rills are subtler versions of the Alph's 'meandering with a mazy motion' (which has a clear demonic echo: the fallen angels discuss theology 'in wandering mazes lost' in *Paradise Lost,* II: 561). Unbridled, 'demonic' nature is only imperfectly tamed by Kubla's ambitiously 'divine' creative act.

The civilizing perfection the Khan strives to create works by exclusion, attempting to shut out what is 'savage' with its 'walls and towers'. The small third verse, by contrast, represents an alternative kind of vision, an altogether more inclusive or comprehensive kind of unity, 'mingling' the artistry of the pleasure dome with the 'given' natural world of the chasm. A fulfilling fitting-together of extremes is implied in the adeptly antithetical correspondence the poem contrives between 'sunny pleasure dome' (illuminated, warm, convex) with 'caves of ice' (dark, cold, concave). ('Extremes meet' was Coleridge's favourite motto.) This reconciliation of the diverse worlds of verses one and two is what you would perceive were you to stand half-way down the length of the Alph, where the 'shadow' (that is, reflection) of the dome is seen to the audible accompaniment of the 'tumult' resounding from the caves of ice (the caverns measureless) at one end of the river's course, and the racket of the fountain at the other. It is a synaesthetic reconciliation of worlds that is virtual or ideal: it occurs within the consciousness of a notional percipient, left very general thanks to the passive voice ('Where was heard'). This synthesizing perceptual act is itself a kind of imagination; and although of a different kind to the absolute decree of the Khan, it, too, has a ring of divinity, its fortuitous splicing of sensuous realities constituting nothing less than a 'miracle'.

The miracle, however, is precarious, a fact underlined by Coleridge's choice of the dome's *reflection* as the element of human creativity present within the complete imaginative synthesis; and the precariousness of the vision is further emphasized in the last 18 lines of the poem. These lines work as a kind of doubting self-commentary on the apparent dialectical success of the first three verses: a very Coleridgean piece of ruinous integrity, snatching failure from the very jaws of aesthetic victory. The Abyssinian maid is evidently some kind of muse, and very intricate explanations have been offered of her origins, but I shall not go into them here.[5] She sings of 'Mount Abora', or 'Mount Amara' in the Crewe manuscript, an important clue because it takes us directly to *Paradise Lost*: 'Mount Amara, . . . by some supposed / True Paradise' (IV. 281–2). Her inspiration gives rise to a kind of paradisal recreation: it is a draught of 'the milk of Paradise' (54), and 'could' the poet 'revive' her song within himself, he would find himself able to 'build that dome in air, / That sunny dome! those caves of ice!' (42; 46–7). But the conditional mood is important, because, at the least, it allows for the possibility of failure, and, more perhaps, admits the wishfulness of the whole ambition. It seems to be the ingredients of the mingled vision described in the third stanza that the poet seeks to recreate: 'That sunny dome! those caves of ice!' But in fact the separated visionary which he conceives himself set to be, were inspiration to come, seems much nearer to the solitary, self-fulfilling creativity of the Khan, and his shutting-out of nature, than it is to the inclusive, though fleeting, imaginative act of the third verse, a parallel emphasized by their both being dome-builders. The poetic figure of Kubla Khan does not have a creativity involving the receptive senses; on the contrary, his is a recognisably Platonic portrait of the possessed poet (see, for example, *Ion*, 533e–34e), characterized specifically by *not* being 'in his senses', the connotations of which are extremely ambivalent. To speak of building domes in air is bravely close to speaking of building castles in the air, an unrespectably unworldly form of creation; and the reception the visionary poet seems likely to receive from bystanders ('Beware! Beware!': 49) does not, to say the least of it, obviously betoken a mentality at ease in the external world of human society.

So the poem describes a kind of authoritative, autonomous and deity-emulating creativity, but subjects it to an implicit criticism by contrasting it with an alternative kind of imaginative activity, one which also seeks to achieve unity but by the reconciliatory path of mingling opposites. Kubla certainly has a kind of genius, but, as Beer says, not of 'the highest type';[6] and the limitations to his genius are pointed by his ethical dubiety. Beer has very plausibly suggested that the Khan was connected in Coleridge's mind with

Adam's cursed fratricidal son Cain, subject of an abandoned prose poem, *The Wanderings of Cain,* also written about this time:[7] obviously a negative parallel; and even if we don't think of Cain, we can hardly separate the Khan from his dastardly reputation as a tyrant.

The inadequacy of the Khan's genius is later theorized by Coleridge as the syndrome of 'commanding genius': men of commanding genius 'must impress their preconceptions on the world without', which makes them despotic and cruel in times of war (impending in *Kubla Khan*), while, interestingly, 'in tranquil times [they] are formed to exhibit a perfect poem in palace or temple or landscape garden' (CC *Biographia,* I: 32). It is hard not to believe that Kubla was especially in Coleridge's mind describing a despotic landscape gardener; and we can now see the significance of the qualifying phrase 'Gods *of Love* who tame the Chaos' (my italics). The failing in commanding genius is a failure of love, the effect of an imposing, projective egotism; and the Khan's excluding hostility toward nature is a type of this. As he aged, Coleridge came to regard the 'demonic' energies of nature with the same mistrust as the Khan, even calling her 'the devil in a straight waistcoat' at one late stage.[8] But during the 1790s and for a good time thereafter, his natural sensibility was intense, as witnessed in poems of the same period, like *This Lime-Tree Bower my Prison* and *Frost at Midnight,* and in the extraordinarily rapt observation of the notebooks; and the entire direction of his religious thought (of which more in a moment) was towards embracing a more reconciling relationship between the 'Absolute Unity' of the deity and the diverse natural world. This the Khan rejects, showing, in an early and symbolic form, that 'crude egoismus', that 'boastful and hyperstoic hostility to NATURE' that Coleridge later found in the idealism of Fichte (CC *Biographia,* I: 158, 159): this is his imaginative failure.

The Coleridgean antithesis to commanding genius is 'absolute genius', possessors of which do not trouble the world without at all: they 'rest content between thought and reality', blessed with a God-like 'creative, and self-sufficing power' (ibid., 1: 32, 31). This avoids Khan-like tyranny, to be sure; but it may also turn into the introspective morbidity of a Hamlet. The poised, precarious centre of *Kubla Khan,* the contingent miracle of perceptual synthesis, tentatively offers an alternative to the failures of solipsism and egotistic despotism. It is a rich case of having-it-both-ways, which exemplifies the principle of imagination later formulated as 'the balance or reconciliation of opposite or discordant qualities' (CC *Biographia,* II: 16): the 'source of our pleasures in the fine Arts,' Coleridge told Humphry Davy, lies 'in the *antithetical* balance-loving nature of man' (Griggs, III: 30). Coleridge took very literally the notion that man was 'indeed made in God's Image, & that too in the sublimest sense – the Image of the *Creator*' (II: ibid., 709); but man has a 'double nature...as Man & God' (*Notebooks,* I: 1,710), himself an antithesis, his imagination properly 'at once both active and passive' (CC *Biographia,* I: 124). 'That gift of true Imagination' may indeed be a 'capability of reducing a multitude into a unity of effect'; but it admits the 'multitude' in the first place, in a way the Khan cannot bring himself to do.


## Coleridge and the Unitarian Vision: *The Ancient Mariner*

Coleridge's aesthetic vision of comprehensive unity, briefly glimpsed in the third verse of *Kubla Khan,* has its theological version during the 1790s in his Unitarian Christianity. The antitheses balanced in his religious vision are the same as in his conception of the reconciling imagination – which, indeed, is a development of it: the 'little things' of perception and the sublime unity of 'something *one & indivisible*'; and these extremes meet in a definition of God, not as the solitary and authoritarian Creator upon which the Khan modelled his own fiat, but as a pervasive and unifying energy.

This is not God as king and lord, but God as a diffused and ubiquitous life, not monarchical but communitarian: 'a religion for Democrats', as he told Thelwall (Griggs, I: 282); and Unitarianism was especially associated with radical politics in the 1790s. The 'unity' of Unitarianism is opposed to the orthodox doctrine of the Trinity: asserting the unity of God involves denying divinity to Jesus, who is a man of exemplary goodness, but only a man (his father was Joseph). If God is not present in the world in the Incarnation, this is not to say he is the remote clock-maker of Deism; on the contrary, he is immanently present in every aspect of nature, 'an omnipresent creativeness' in Coleridge's phrase (used of Shakespeare: CC *Table Talk*, I: 125), 'All-conscious Presence of the Universe! / Nature's vast ever-acting Energy! / In will, in deed, Impulse of All to All!' (*Destiny of Nations*, 460–2). This theology presents the faithful with a vision of the universe as 'something *great* – something *one & indivisible*': ' 'Tis the sublime of man, / Our noontide Majesty, to know ourselves / Parts and proportions of one wond'rous whole', and that whole unity is divine, for ' 'tis God / Diffused through all, that doth make all one whole' (*Religious Musings*, 134–6, 139–40). This new conception of God, and humanizing of Christ, involves a new conception of redemption: the atonement mysteriously (to Coleridge, deplorably) effected by the torture and murder of Jesus is now achieved in a sublime imaginative act of 'atonement' which 'draweth all things to one, and seeth all things in one': 'must I not be mad if I do not seek, and miserable if I do not discover and embrace, the means of at-one-ment?' (CC *Lay Sermons*, p. 55). Mad and miserable indeed, for without the animating presence of God, 'The moral world's cohesion, we become / An Anarchy of Spirits!', a mass of isolated and disunited individuals, each '[a] sordid solitary thing' (*Religious Musings*, 159, 163).

But this sublime and inclusive vision – that 'each Thing has a Life of it's own, & yet they are all one Life' (Griggs, II: 866) – has a troubling corollary. 'Impulse of All to All' puts it squarely: individual free will and action dissolve into the ubiquitous, one life of God. Coleridge did not fight shy of this conclusion, roundly declaring himself 'a Unitarian Christian and an Advocate for the Automatism of Man' (Griggs, I: 147), though, since God is famously good, that makes an odd theology for a radical, since it asserts that everything is Godly, and so by definition for the best. Still, believing everything to be for the best is not an oddity of Coleridge's: it is a major trend in eighteenth-century thought. Pope's *Essay on Man*, for instance, declares 'All Discord, Harmony, not understood; / All partial Evil, universal Good'.[9] It is hard not to see this as a basically obtuse response to the universe, the noble point of Voltaire's *Candide* (1759). The Optimist Pangloss fills Candide's head with a 'metaphysico-theologico-cosmo-codology' vulgarized from Leibniz, which Candide tries to keep a firm hold on; but, unsurprisingly, reality puts his faith under great strain, and finally, faced with the real-life miseries of slavery, it collapses into a more humane concern. Asked the meaning of Optimism, Candide forlornly replies, 'I'm afraid to say … that it's a mania for insisting that all is well when things are going badly.'[10]

As it happens, the slave trade is also a testing point for Coleridge's Optimism, since it is the focus for radical activity in his Bristol circles during the 1790s, a vivid and terrible example of the evil for which his sanguine theology could not decently account. 'Reasoning strictly and with logical Accuracy I should deny the existence of any Evil', he explained to his lecture audience, adding, 'I have been able to discover nothing of which the end is not good' (CC *Lectures 1795*, p. 105); and this is entirely logical, since 'that Being, who is "in will, in deed, Impulse of all to all" whichever be your determination, will make it ultimately the best' (Griggs, I: 159). Accordingly, '*Guilt* is out of the question', as he tells Thelwall, 'I am a Necessarian, and of course deny the possibility of it' (ibid., p. 213). 'I am as much a Pangloss as ever', he was still announcing to Southey in July 1797 (ibid., p. 334), which is defiant but also self-mocking, the sign of a kind of self-criticism. But the problem of evil was hardly to be dismissed as easily as that; and, like the puzzle of infinite perceptions co-existing with absolute unity, it looked a likely subject for a masterpiece, *The Origin of Evil, an Epic Poem* (*Notebooks*, I: 161). This was never written either, but Coleridge found himself apparently bound to 'return to the Question of Evil – woe to the man, to whom it is an uninteresting Question' (ibid., p. 1,622); and *The Rime of the Ancyent Marinere* is the greatest result.[11]

Readings of the poem have traditionally divided between those that see it as an exemplification of the Unitarian theology of the One Life, and those who see it as an absurdist 'nightmare' counter-vision of the 'Anarchy of Spirits' that would come in its absence. The first reading would see the shape of the poem as one of an act of wickedness (the shooting of the albatross), punishment (the Mariner's horrific experiences), repentance (blessing the watersnakes) and atonement (coming back to land once again). The second reading would stress instead the emphatic arbitrariness of the suffering (after all, the only man on the ship not to die is the man who committed the 'crime', and his judgement is decided by the roll of dice), the apparent randomness of the narrative (things don't get that much better for some time after the 'redemptive' blessing of the snakes), and the incompleteness or illusoriness of any 'atonement' (the Mariner is never freed of the neurotic compulsion to reconfess his crime, and cannot be part of the wedding celebrations). This division of responses is closely related to the great interpretative crux of the poem: what are we to make of the marginal comments added by Coleridge, in what sounds like a pastiche of seventeenth-century English, when the poem was republished in *Sibylline Leaves* in 1817? The marginal notes clearly gloss the poem as an account of sin and restoration: 'The ancient Mariner inhospitably killeth the pious bird of good omen', 'He blesseth them in his heart', 'The spell begins to break', 'The curse is finally expiated'. This is the first of our two readings, the proponents of which see the gloss as spelling out in clearer detail the moral that was always there. But critics in our second tradition point to the manifest inaccuracies and illogicalities of the gloss (*Who says* the bird is 'pious'? *Is* the curse ever 'finally expiated'?) and interpret it as the words of a definitely dramatized character, a wrong-headed antiquarian: the irrelevance of the hopeful tale told by the man in the margin only points up the cruel meaninglessness that characterized the story in the first place. (A third variant: that an older, more orthodox Coleridge returns to the poem, adding the marginal comments to try and tidy the story into something more pious.)[12]

We might ask how much of what we are told goes on, *did* go on, really? Our only witness is the Mariner himself; and he was hardly in his right state of mind for most of the period in question. Like *Heart of Darkness*, the poem is not about a disastrous journey, but about someone recounting their disastrous journey, not for the first time, which adds the important ingredient of possible fallibility. The likelihood of fallibility is increased by the Mariner being a medieval Catholic, as far from Coleridge in cast of mind as can be: his anti-Catholicism was very pronounced. This has led some critics to see the poem as a dramatic monologue, like Wordsworth's contemporaneous *The Thorn*, a poem narrated by a super-stitious seafarer with a disturbingly creative, over-active brain:[13] this fulfils the announce-ment in Wordsworth's preface to *Lyrical Ballads* that one business of the poems was to explore 'the manner in which we associate ideas in a state of excitement'.[14] In the Mariner's case it is not so much a case of immediate duress, as the excitement of repeated and obsessional re-creation: he has told his story 'ten thousand time since the voyage which was in early youth and fifty years before' Coleridge later said (*CC Table Talk*, I: 274). In the course of doing so, he has instinctively sought to refine a string of events into a patterned narrative, one determined by his ('Catholic') mentality; and, as in *The Thorn*, the interest of the poem as a whole may be as much in the way the story is told as it is in the story itself.

After all, it is the Mariner who discerns a plot of crime and punishment in his own experiences: Coleridge is careful to ensure that the turning points of the story fail perfectly to fit his interpretation. Immediately after the 'crime', the shooting of the albatross, the weather actually improves, and the crew, after initially abusing him, are soon congratulating him on killing 'the bird / That brought the fog and mist' (99–100). Then, after the obscure redemptive moment with the water snakes, during which his 'kind saint took pity' (286), he is still made to endure the horror of the 'ghastly crew' (340), and is evidently unreformed enough to make the pilot's boy think he's the devil when he gets back to shore (568–9). The crisis moments of the poem feel oddly empty or unacted, as if importance is being retro-spectively attributed to moments beyond recall on the grounds that momentous signifi-cance just simply *must* reside in them: the shooting is over before it is described (81–2), while the blessing may possibly be only a rationalization (as it were, '*surely*') from hindsight: 'Sure my kind saint took pity on me, / And I blessed them unaware' (286–7). (What is it to bless something 'unaware'?) Then again, it is the superstitious crew – whom we know to be erratic interpreters of signs – who single out the albatross as the cause of their becalming, hanging the bird round his neck; and the Mariner's mind revolves around the event as the explanation of his subsequent troubles with the tenacity of an *idée fixe*, interpreting it as a Cain-like crime ('wash away / The Albatross' blood': 512–13), and returning compulsively to the albatross or the cross-bow at the end of five of the seven sections. This is one way we 'associate ideas in a state of excitement': 'that state of madness which is not frenzy or delirium, but which models all things to the one reigning idea' (*CC Lectures on Literature*, I: 380) – an example of the mind's drive to unity in its more neurotically deplorable form.

*The Ancient Mariner* is certainly about the psychology of physical and emotional extremity; but Coleridge's poetic interest in superstition was not simply, like Words-worth's in *The Thorn*, the invitation it offered to rationalist demystification: indeed, he lamented to Hazlitt, who visited the poets in the spring of 1798, 'that Wordsworth was not prone enough to belief in the traditional superstitions of the place'.[15] Being 'prone' in this case licenses Coleridge to explore particular kinds of superstition, like a belief in evil, or in a 'Catholic' scheme of confession and atonement, which his own, enlightened Unitarianism officially disallowed him to indulge; and in this way it acts rather in the way he was later to identify as 'poetic faith', 'that willing suspension of disbelief for the moment' (CC *Biographia,* II: 6). It is not a question of his simply assenting to the crime-guilt-and-punishment scheme of the poem that the Mariner's remorseful conscience tries to impose upon the story, nor a matter of his seeing through the Mariner's unenlightened delusions to some naturalistic explanation: it is something hovering in between. Being a 'sordid solitary thing' exists in the Unitarian scheme only as a notional state of affairs, what things *would* be like *if* the diffused One Life of God did not bind everything into totality as He does, just as guilt and evil cannot *really* exist, except as part of the more general goodness of complete Providence. But Coleridge's antithetical temper comes into play, and in *The Ancient Mariner* these things are all felt to exist very vividly, in a fearfully unquestioned way, while, at the same time, being notionally contained by their dramatic attribution to a fallible narrator.

So, an important kind of doubleness is at work in the poem: an 'all-half believing Doubtfulness of all' (Griggs, I: 530).[16] The Mariner's own interpretation, largely followed by the man in the margin, seems only loosely attached at crucial moments to the story it is meant to explain; but the poem cannot entirely explain away as Catholic error the craving for atonement which so strongly haunts it. Parallels with other poems are suggestive: blessing the water snakes, for example, is anticipated by Coleridge's blessing of the (only slightly less winning) rook in *This Lime-Tree Bower,* a poem addressed to fellow Unitarian Charles Lamb, 'to whom / No sound is dissonant which tells of Life' (75–6). And the Mariner inadvertently implies a similar kind of redemptive natural harmony fleetingly and beautifully when he thinks up a metaphor for the noise made by sails: 'A noise like of a hidden brook / In the leafy month of June, / That to the sleeping woods all night / Singeth a quiet tune' (369–72). This doubleness extends to the end of the poem: Coleridge recalled telling Mrs Barbauld that, far from having 'no moral' (her complaint), it had 'too much' (CC *Table Talk,* I: 272), a comment which seems likely to refer, at least in part, to the obtrusiveness of the Mariner's closing moral ('He prayeth well, who loveth well / Both man and bird and beast': 612–13). The remark seems singularly inadequate as a response to his experiences: it doesn't seem to console the would-be Wedding Guest very much; and it has been interpreted as merely the deluded Mariner's sentiment, rather than Coleridge's. On the other hand, it is obviously a sentiment related to the great vision of unity that lies at the heart of Coleridge's Unitarian enthusiasm; and while, strictly, there is no point in praying to a One Life God ('Of whose omniscience and all-spreading Love / Aught to *implore* were impotence of mind'),[17] Coleridge came quickly to defend the value of prayer very strongly. The poem's double method extends to the last, then, ending with its dramatic method as unresolved as the Mariner's redemption, and the existence of evil an abiding question, the obscurity Lucky memorably enunciates in *Waiting for Godot:* that God 'loves us dearly with some exceptions for reasons unknown'.[18]

## Innocence and Atonement: *Christabel*

Coleridge returns to the problem of evil in *Christabel,* where the contradiction between the felt need for redemptive unity and the reluctance to accept orthodox notions of atonement becomes quite interminable.[19]

The poem has strong connections with both *Kubla Khan* and *The Ancient Mariner*. It shares the same medieval Catholic universe as *The Ancient Mariner* ('Jesu, Maria, shield her well!': i.54) and explores the same themes of transgression and corruption ('"Sure I have sinn'd!" said Christabel': ii.381). The portrayal of Geraldine has some likeness to the Mariner's, in the emphasis on her eyes, for example (i.246; ii.583). Yet she seems a representative, too, of the same 'demonic' nature the effects of which the Khan vainly struggled to keep outside the dome's precincts; like the earlier poem, the natural powers are associated with erotic love (as in the 'woman wailing for her demon lover'); and the sensational corruption of Sir Leoline's family that Geraldine works is analogous to the ruin prophesied for Kubla's precarious civilization. Unlike the Khan, however, Christabel is herself responsible for bringing these destructive energies into the safe enclave of the castle, inviting Geraldine back from 'the huge oak tree' where Christabel has gone to pray for her lover, who fills her dreams (i.27): like Pope's Belinda, Christabel has 'An Earthly Lover lurking at her Heart'.[20]

Like *The Ancient Mariner*, *Christabel* evades our attempts precisely to make out the author's own position. Undecidability in *Christabel* is an effect of the act of its telling being dramatized, not as a tale within a tale like the Mariner's, but by Coleridge's use of a story-teller who is manifestly unsure of what is going on: 'And what can ail the mastiff bitch?' (i.153), 'Alas! what ails poor Geraldine?' (i.207), and so forth. Some of his speculations seem ludicrously off the mark; he is determined never to think badly of his girl – 'And, if she moves unquietly, / Perchance, 'tis but the blood so free / Comes back and tingles in her feet. / No doubt, she hath a vision sweet' (i.323–6); and, when she is most under Geraldine's influence, the narrator gallantly insists that she assumes so terrible an expression only 'As far as such a look could be, / In eyes so innocent and blue!' (ii.611–12). His hopes throughout are rather pathetically sanguine, reminiscent of the Mariner's concluding motto: 'saints will aid if men will call / For the blue sky bends over all' (i.330–1).

The room for uncertainty created by this uncertain and partial narrator is filled by the ambiguous figure of Geraldine. Hazlitt was annoyed that Coleridge suppressed the line 'Are lean and old and foul of hue' that followed in manuscript after 'Behold! her bosom and half her side –' (i.252):[21] the line he thought necessary 'to make common sense of the first and second part', because it makes clear beyond doubt Geraldine's repellent witchery;[22] but the deletion is right precisely because it allows Geraldine's nature to remain obscure. Her influence is certainly baleful, and the narrator frets over Christabel's sleeping in the same bed with her, as if she is simply wicked; 'O shield her! shield sweet Christabel!' (i.254), 'ah woe is me!' (i.292). But in fact Geraldine's behaviour is also oddly inconsistent, especially in the first part, as if she is forced to an evil which she is not born to: as Beer remarks, both times she drinks the cordial made by Christabel's mother, she is suddenly sympathetic, wishing Christabel's mother were there after a first drink (i.203), and declaring '"All they who live in the upper sky, / Do love you, holy Christabel!"' (i.227–8) after the second.[23] That Geraldine is good corrupted, rather than intrinsically wicked, is not at all certain, but it fits the opening of the poem, in which there is light but it is somehow obscured: 'The thin gray cloud is spread on high, / It covers but not hides the sky' (i.16–17); and this would also be more fitting to a Unitarian scheme, in which 'all apparent Discord is but Harmony not understood' (CC *Lectures 1795*, p. 151). The question worried over in the poem is what the outcome will be when this obfuscation of innate goodness meets genuine innocence.

Uniquely amongst the supernatural poems, *Christabel* dwells upon the redemptive possibility of human relationship, though it is mostly frustrated – Christabel and her separated lover, Sir Leoline and his dead wife, Sir Leoline and Lord Roland de Vaux – and the ambience of the 'crime' that parallels the shooting in *The Ancient Mariner* is manifestly erotic, although we are denied a full view: 'A sight to dream of, not to tell!' (i.253). The prospect of relationship, of 'mingling identities' as Coleridge once put it in a letter (*Letters* I: 249), introduces us once again to the inclusive kind of Coleridgean unity we saw in the third verse of *Kubla Khan*: the unity of perfect marriage, 'a union of opposites, a giving and receiving mutually of the permanent in either, a completion of each in the other' (CC *Lectures on Literature*, II: 428). However, *Christabel*, like its partner poems, explores the theme of unity antithetically, by imagining its perversion; and it is a terrible parody of marriage, a vision of the quite unreciprocal *appropriation* of individuality, which constitutes the work's culminating horror: 'So deeply had she drunken in / That look, those shrunken serpent eyes, / That all her features were resigned / To this sole image in her mind: / And passively did imitate / That look of dull and treacherous hate!' (ii.601–6). This is certainly achieving a kind of unity, but it is a unity of confiscation, annihilating difference: Christabel is forced into becoming Geraldine. At which point, Sir Leoline leads Geraldine out, over the prostrate body of his daughter; and the poem ends, or rather doesn't end but is abandoned unresolved, unable to conceive how a redemption to the healthful unity of mingled but discrete differences could possibly occur, nor able to bear the prospect of evil's simple victory.

Coleridge gave several accounts of how the poem was going to finish: his first biographer Gillman records him saying that the story is 'founded on the notion, that the virtuous of this world save the wicked', and that by praying for her absent lover, Christabel 'defeats the power of evil in the person of Geraldine'.[24] Christabel's sufferings were 'vicarious', his son Derwent recalled him saying, 'endured for her "lover far away"'; but this time, he declared Geraldine 'no witch or goblin, or malignant being of any kind, but a spirit, executing her appointed task with the best good will'.[25] And in a notebook entry of 1823 he wrote, 'Were I free to do so, I feel as if I could compose the third part of Christabel, or the song of her desolation' (*Notebooks*, IV: 5,032), implying not Christabel's redemptive success, but her defeat. These very various accounts depend upon emphasizing different aspects of the ambiguity of Geraldine, her genuine wickedness or her obscure kind of goodness; added to that, they hinge on an ambiguity buried in the heroine's (and the poem's) unusual name. As critics have often pointed out, the word 'Christabel' amounts to an oxymoron, a semantic indecision between 'Christ', whose sufferings are traditionally held to have possessed atoning power, and 'Abel', whose innocence led him only to be slaughtered by Cain. It seems as though Coleridge hovered undecided between these two fates for Christabel, the second unbearable, the first emulating that theory of redemption by vicarious suffering which his Unitarianism rejected as 'perhaps the most irrational and gloomy Superstition that ever degraded the human mind' (CC *Lectures 1795*, p. 204).

'Perhaps 'tis pretty to force together / Thoughts so all unlike each other', Coleridge wrote in the oblique 'Conclusion' he added to part two of *Christabel* (ii.666–7); and he means to be self-deprecating. 'Force' is the pejorative term; but the description is close to one he later gave of the imagination successfully working 'by a sort of *fusion to force many into one*' (CC *Lectures on Literature*, I: 81). The three supernatural poems are early and implicit explorations of this paradox: they celebrate the ideal of unity in its aesthetic, theological and human forms; yet they are aware of the possibility of failure, and aware, too, of the dangers of the wrong kind of success.

## NOTES

1   House, *Coleridge*, p. 16.
2   McFarland, *Romanticism and the Heritage of Rousseau*, pp. 243, 82.
3   The poem was probably written in October or November, 1797: see Griggs's note (Griggs, I: 348–9) (for October) and Reed, *Wordsworth*, p. 208 n.33 (for November), which is supported by Shaffer, '*Kubla Khan*', pp. 106, 327 n.24. The connection between the letter to Thelwall and *Kubla Khan* is noted by Griggs.
4   Beer, 'Coleridge and poetry', pp. 45–90, 62.
5   See Beer, *Coleridge the Visionary*, pp. 251–5.
6   Ibid., p. 226.
7   Ibid., p. 222. The parallel is made more explicitly in Orson Welles's cinematic treatment of the poem, *Citizen Kane*.
8   Quoted from J. C. Hare, *The Mission of the Comforter* in CC *Lay Sermons*, 71 n.6.
9   Pope, *An Essay on Man*, i. 289–92.
10   Chapter 19; in Voltaire, *Candide and Other Stories*, p. 54.
11   *The Ancyent Marinere* was written between November 1797 and March 1798 (see Reed, *Wordsworth*, pp. 210, 228) and published, anonymously, in *Lyrical Ballads* (1798). A revised version, with modified spelling, appeared in the second edition of *Lyrical Ballads* (1800). I am taking my quotations from the 1817 text (*Romanticism*, pp. 578–95).
12   The first approach might be exemplified by Abrams; the second by Bostetter; the third by Empson. See 'Further reading'.
13   See Wordsworth's Note to *The Thorn* in *Romanticism*, pp. 248–9.
14   Preface (1802) to *Lyrical Ballads*; in *Romanticism*, p. 252.
15   'My First Acquaintance with Poets' (1823); in *Romanticism*, p. 652.
16   Coleridge uses the phrase of William Taylor; its suitability for Coleridge himself is pointed out by Shaffer, '*Kubla Khan*', p. 35.
17   *To a Friend* [Charles Lamb]; *Poems*, p. 44.
18   Beckett, *The Complete Dramatic Works*, p. 40.
19   Part One of *Christabel* was written in the spring and summer of 1798, after the completion of *The Ancient Mariner*. The second part was written in 1800; he reads it to the Wordsworths in August and again in early October: see Reed, *Wordsworth*, pp. 83, 92, 96. Its brief 'Conclusion' first appears in a letter of May, 1801 (*Letters*, II: 728) as a description of Coleridge's son, Hartley.
20   Pope, *The Rape of the Lock*, 144.
21   The ms. reading (misquoted by Hazlitt) is recorded in EHC I: 224.
22   De J. Jackson, *Coleridge*, p. 207.
23   Beer, *Coleridge the Visionary*, p. 186.
24   Gillman, *The Life of Samuel Taylor Coleridge*, p. 283.
25   Quoted in Beer, *Coleridge the Visionary*, pp. 176–7.

## REFERENCES AND FURTHER READING

Abrams, M. H. on 'The Ancient Mariner', *Natural Supernaturalism*, London, Oxford University Press, 1971, pp. 272–5.

Beckett, Samuel, *The Complete Dramatic Works*, London, Faber, 1986.

Beer, John, *Coleridge the Visionary*, London, Chatto and Windus, 1959.

—— 'Coleridge and poetry: I. Poems of the supernatural', in *Writers and Their Background: Coleridge*, ed. R. L. Brett, London, Bell, 1971.

Bostetter, Edward E., 'The nightmare world of "The Ancient Mariner"', *Studies in Romanticism* I (1962), 241–54.

Brisman, Leslie, 'Coleridge and the supernatural', in *Studies in Romanticism* XXI (1982) 123–59.

Empson, William 'The Ancient Mariner', in *Argufying: Essays on Literature and Culture*, ed. John Haffenden London, Chatto and Windus, 1987, pp. 297–319.

Gillman, James, *The Life of Samuel Taylor Coleridge,* London, Pickering, 1838.

Harding, Anthony John, 'Mythopoesis: the unity of *Christabel'*, in *Coleridge's Imagination,* ed. Richard Gravil, Lucy Newlyn and Nicholas Roe, Cambridge, Cambridge University Press, 1985, pp. 207–17.

House, Humphry, on 'Kubla Khan', *Coleridge: The Clark Lectures,* London, Hart-Davis, 1962, pp. 114–22.

Jackson, J. R., de J. (ed.) *Coleridge: The Critical Heritage,* London, Routledge and Kegan Paul, 1970.

McFarland, Thomas, *Romanticism and the Heritage of Rousseau,* Oxford, Clarendon Press, 1995.

McGann, Jerome J. 'The Ancient Mariner: The meaning of the meanings', in *The Beauty of Inflexions: Literary Investigations in Historical Method and Theory,* Oxford, Clarendon Press, 1985, pp. 135–72.

Paglia, Camille, on 'Christabel', *Sexual Personae: Art and Decadence from Nefertiti to Emily Dickinson,* New Haven, Yale University Press, 1990, pp. 317–46.

Reed, Mark L., *Wordsworth: The Chronology of the Early Years 1770–1799,* Cambridge, Mass, Harvard University Press, 1967.

Shaffer, E. S., *'Kubla Khan' and The Fall of Jerusalem: The Mythological School in Biblical Criticism and Secular Literature 1770–1880,* Cambridge, Cambridge University Press, 1975, pp. 17–144.

Tomlinson, Charles, 'Christabel', in *Interpretations: Essays on Twelve English Poems* ed. John Wain, London, Routledge and Kegan Paul, 1955, pp. 86–112.

Voltaire, *Candide and Other Stories,* trans. Roger Pearson, Oxford, Oxford University Press, 1990.

Wheeler, K. M. *The Creative Mind in Coleridge's Poetry,* London, Heinemann, 1981, pp. 17–41.

# 13

# Wordsworth and Coleridge, *Lyrical Ballads*

## *Scott McEathron*

Perhaps more vividly than any other poetical work of the period, the *Lyrical Ballads* of William Wordsworth and Samuel Taylor Coleridge documents Romanticism's impulse to merge artistic and social change. Featuring subjects from 'ordinary life', such as could be found 'in every village and its vicinity',[1] the collection expresses Wordsworth's conviction, phrased years later in a letter, that 'men who do not wear fine clothes can feel deeply'.[2] For Wordsworth and Coleridge, this egalitarian depiction of emotion was part of a larger model of literary reform – even of revolution – that required the repudiation of eighteenth-century modes of feeling and expression. *Lyrical Ballads* views English poetry as an effete, exhausted institution desperately needing to be regrounded in 'natural . . . human passions, human characters, and human incidents'.[3] First published anonymously in 1798, the volume rejects alike the manipulative emotionalism of Sensibility and the studied aestheticism of neo-classical diction, instead aspiring to convey authentic human feeling by way of simple ballads and the ordinary 'language of conversation in the middle and lower classes of society'.[4] Further, it asserts that such 'lower' forms of diction, which generally had been shunned by university-educated poets, are in fact a valid medium for philosophical poetry. And while its most famous works, Coleridge's *The Rime of the Ancient Mariner* and Wordsworth's *Tintern Abbey*, do not participate directly in the rustic-subjects experiment, their narrators' emotional autobiographies fix the horizon line for future Romantic explorations of individualism and subjectivity.

There are, of course, moments – indeed, whole aspects – in which *Lyrical Ballads* can be said to fall short of its vaunted ambitions. Like any self-consciously radicalizing artistic project, it opens itself up to charges of inconsistency and self-contradiction. Chiefly, the question of 'authenticity', which *Lyrical Ballads* uses to cross-examine the literary establishment, has inevitably and often rightly been used to cross-examine *Lyrical Ballads* itself. This line of criticism has descended, in fact, from Coleridge's own *Biographia Literaria* (1817), which questioned Wordsworth's representation of 'the real language of men' as well as the usefulness of his generalized notion of rustic life.[5] Still, and to a degree that is striking in the context of often-changing critical fashions, the reputation of *Lyrical Ballads* remains powerfully anchored in the language of its own claims, of what it set out to do. Its galvanizing influence on the Romantic era is unquestionable, and while its declarations of originality have been challenged,[6] their underlying excitement continues to be infectious for readers.

If *Lyrical Ballads* has come to be monumentalized as a turning point in literary history, however, its own history as a volume is fraught with complicated – though crucial – twists and turns. The volume was published in four different editions (1798, 1800, 1802, 1805), and was so altered by 1800 that, in the words of one critical study, 'The second edition . . . is altogether different in character from the original 1798 publication'.[7] The 1798 volume contained 19 poems by Wordsworth and 23 altogether, most of which were written in at least quasi-balladic form. The two-volume second edition was more than double the length of the first, and virtually all of its 38 new poems were Wordsworth's. His name now appeared, singly, on the title-page. The poems were preceded by a massive new critical 'Preface', which, though written at Coleridge's urging, was largely shaped by Wordsworth's concerns. In this Preface appeared the definitions, terms and explanatory passages that now tend to dominate critical analysis of the *Lyrical Ballads* project. The new poems themselves showed a shift in style; Wordsworth gave less attention to rustic speech *per se* and began to experiment with blank verse as a means of expressing the broader dignity and pathos of rustic life.

It is sometimes difficult to know to what extent these items dating from 1800 and after – that is, the Preface, the new poems, Wordsworth's increasing control of the project, Coleridge's critique in the *Biographia* – can be legitimately applied to discussions of the famous 1798 volume. None the less, these post-1798 developments have become integral to the reputation and scholarly understanding of *Lyrical Ballads*, so that even as this essay turns 'back' to the poems and circumstances of the first edition, it inevitably draws on these later works, terms and ideas. Obviously *Lyrical Ballads'* status as a collaboration is also a highly vexed issue, but it should be made clear from the outset that while the project eventually and decisively became Wordsworth's, there simply would never have been a *Lyrical Ballads* without Coleridge.[8]

William Wordsworth and Samuel Taylor Coleridge first met in the autumn of 1795, but it was June 1797, when Coleridge tramped 40 miles to see Wordsworth and his sister Dorothy at Racedown Lodge in Dorset, that saw the blossoming of the friendship. 'We both have a distinct remembrance of his arrival', the Wordsworths later recalled, 'He did not keep to the high road, but leaped over a gate and bounded down the pathless field by which he cut off an angle.'[9] Almost instantaneously, the men's acquaintance burst into ecstatic friendship. They read to one another their most recent works,[10] and took long walks filled with laughter and good feeling, political talk and literary planning. Coleridge once described himself as a figure of *'indolence capable of energies'*;[11] this friendship produced energies. His visit lasted only three weeks, but prompted a remarkable transformation of circumstance: in early July, William and Dorothy abandoned the isolation they had so consciously sought at Racedown Lodge and moved north to Alfoxden House, four miles from Coleridge and his wife Sara at Nether Stowey.

In the months that followed the men were together constantly. As Wordsworth put it later, with words that capture the suddenness, exuberance and excess of it all, they 'Together wantoned in wild poesy' (*The Prelude*, XIII. 414). Coleridge thought Words-worth 'capable of producing . . . the FIRST GENUINE PHILOSOPHICAL POEM', and described him as 'a very great man – the only man, to whom *at all times* & in *all modes of excellence* I feel myself inferior . . . for the London Literati appear to me to be very much like little Potatoes – i.e. *no great Things*! – a compost of Nullity & Dullity'.[12] The Wordsworths saw in Coleridge a dazzling type of the inspired poet, something like a benevolent version of the oracular bard who later appeared in Coleridge's own *Kubla Khan*. The men's early attempts to collaborate on individual poems proved comically frustrating,[13] but they talked so continually about poetry, Coleridge later recalled, that they could hardly be sure which one of them 'started any particular Thought'.[14] Thriving on each other's company, they grew in creativity and confidence, and soon began producing the great poetry for which they are now remembered.[15]

The men's shared political sympathies helped in the rapid evolution of their intimacy. Both had been enthusiastic supporters of the French Revolution, and though disenchanted by its betrayal of its origins, maintained strong democratic beliefs.[16] Temperamentally they were quite different. Coleridge was the more effusive personality, animated by an assortment of intellectual desires. An avid reader (a 'library-cormorant', he called himself), an aspiring philosopher and a vigorously believing Christian, his taste ran to 'Accounts of all the strange phantasms that ever possessed your philosophy-dreamers'.[17] 'From my early reading of Faery Tales, & Genii &c &c', he wrote, 'my mind had been habituated *to the Vast*'.[18] Coleridge was also notoriously talkative: 'In digressing, in dilating, in passing from subject to subject, he appeared . . . to float in air, to slide on ice'.[19] His charisma was legendary – though those who heard his sprawling disquisitions often professed not to know exactly what he was talking about.

Wordsworth was far more reserved, had little interest in systematic philosophy, and was, according to Coleridge, 'at least a *Semi*-atheist'.[20] But beneath his quiet exterior lurked powerful ambition and a mind equally habituated to the Vast. In his later autobiographical poem *The Prelude* Wordsworth would describe his psychic education not as a Coleridgean fascination with books and tales of the supernatural, but as a full-scale immersion in the sometimes frightening infinitude of the natural world: 'Fair seed-time had my soul, and I grew up / Fostered alike by beauty and by fear' (*The Prelude*, 1. 306–7). In nature Wordsworth sensed elemental connections to the human spirit and imagination. It was once said of his poetry that 'It is as if there were nothing but himself and the universe',[21] and in his most magnificent passages of blank verse Wordsworth seems to encounter directly the power behind nature's visible forms. Such passages (found for example in *The Ruined Cottage* and later in *The Prelude*) employ an elevated voice and stately metre reminiscent of Milton.[22] Yet Wordsworth was ever mindful of the potential of humbler poetic forms. *Lyrical Ballads* records several of his efforts to evoke deep human feeling, and our intuitive affinity for nature, through simple tales told in simple rhyming verse.

Amidst the myriad schemes for joint and individual publication which Wordsworth and Coleridge were contemplating, *Lyrical Ballads* emerged almost randomly, an outgrowth of Coleridge's *Ancient Mariner* (a poem originally planned with the hope of five pounds from a literary magazine).[23] That the *Ancient Mariner* served to kindle the entire project may initially seem odd, since its length, archaic spellings and relentless supernaturalism make it arguably the most anomalous poem of the finished collection.[24] Wordsworth later worried about the poem's apparent strangeness, but it seems that at first he and Coleridge had planned more verse of this sort,[25] their idea being to balance works based upon supernatural 'incidents and agents' with works reflecting 'the loveliness and the wonders of the world before us'.[26] Both sorts of poems would portray heightened states of consciousness, and trace the way the mind 'associates ideas in a state of excitement'.[27]

In practice the volume didn't maintain this balance. While Coleridge struggled unsuccessfully to complete several long supernatural pieces,[28] Wordsworth in a three-month span – March to May 1798 – produced a dozen ballad-like poems on 'natural subjects taken from common life'.[29] The volume opens with the mesmerizing *Ancient Mariner* and closes with *Tintern Abbey*, Wordsworth's superb blank-verse reflection on his growth through nature. The poems in between, despite many clear resemblances, display varieties of tone, subject, form and diction that defy a single concise formulation. Coleridge thought the poems functioned best when considered collectively: *Lyrical Ballads* is '*one work*', he said, 'as an Ode is one work', and the 'different poems are as stanzas, good relatively rather than absolutely'.[30] Still, it is perhaps easier to think of the poems not as a single entity, but as a set of related (sometimes overlapping) groups.

Several thematic and topical groupings are immediately visible within *Lyrical Ballads* 1798: poems of the supernatural (e.g. *The Ancient Mariner*, *Goody Blake and Harry Gill*); poems on human suffering (*The Thorn*, *The Dungeon*, *The Female Vagrant*, *Simon Lee*); poems on children's psychology (*We Are Seven*, *Anecdote for Fathers*); poems suspicious of books and intellectualism (*The Nightingale*, *The Tables Turned*); and poems that exalt nature (*Tintern Abbey*, *Lines Written at a Small Distance from my House*).[31] But it is equally useful to group the poems along formalist and tonal lines, and doing so brings different affiliations unexpectedly to light. If we focus on *Lyrical Ballads'* dramatic dialogues, for example, we find repeated instances of questioning, even badgering narrators in poems otherwise dissimilar: *Expostulation and Reply*, *We Are Seven*, *Anecdote for Fathers*, *Old Man Travelling*, *The Last of the Flock*. Dramatic differences of tone distinguish the various poems on human suffering. While *The Mad Mother* and the *Complaint of the Forsaken Indian Woman* generate compassion, for example, they could also be said to veer toward voyeurism. Meanwhile, *The Idiot Boy*, *Old Man Travelling*, *Simon Lee* and *The Thorn* intermix empathy and ironic detachment.[32]

In the 'Advertisement' to *Lyrical Ballads*, Wordsworth and Coleridge asserted that they intended their 'strange and awkward' experimental poetry to militate against literary convention. So it comes as no surprise that at least some of the poems take up the subject of poetry itself. Wordsworth's *Lines left upon a Seat in a Yew-Tree* and Coleridge's *The Nightingale* feature men of poetic temperament whose sensitivity has gone bad. The doomed young man of the *Yew-Tree* lines begins life with 'lofty views', only to be disappointed by the world's callousness and indifference. Taking this neglect as evidence of his superiority, he finds 'morbid pleasure' (28) in his isolation:

> his spirit damped
> At once, with rash disdain he turned away,
> And with the food of pride sustained his soul
> In solitude (18–21)

But, as the poem warns, 'pride, / Howe'er disguised in its own majesty, / Is littleness' (46–8)[33] and his wilful sequestration leads to melancholy, decay and eventual death. Similarly,

*The Nightingale* tells the lamentable tale of a poet who 'filled all things with himself / And made all gentle sounds tell back the tale / Of his own sorrows' (19–21). Poetic tradition is part of the problem here – specifically, the practice of depicting the Nightingale's song as one of grief. This arbitrary convention too easily infects the mind, promoting in the poetically inclined a fanciful, self-induced and unnecessary misery. As an antidote the poem offers 'A different lore', in which 'Nature's sweet voices [are] always full of love / And joyance!' (41–3):

> [The poet] had better far have stretched his limbs
> Beside a brook in mossy forest-dell
> By sun or moonlight, to the influxes
> Of shapes and sounds and shifting elements
> Surrendering his whole spirit, of his song
> And his fame forgetful! So his fame
> Should share in nature's immortality (25–31)

In highlighting the almost subjective qualities of nature – its active powers of 'joyance' and replenishment for those willing to 'surrender' – Coleridge implicitly rejects a melancholic strain of eighteenth-century verse[34] in which nature exists as a mere backdrop for the morose 'higher' emotions of an isolated poetic consciousness. He also looks askance at a related phenomenon, the so-called 'cult of Sensibility', which influenced artistic expression and identity formation over the last half of the century. 'Sensibility', basically a capacity for acute emotional response to scenes of distress, was theoretically a vehicle for virtue and benevolence, but often promoted a self-regard that precluded social action. As Coleridge had noted elsewhere, 'Sensibility is not Benevolence. Nay, by making us tremblingly alive to trifling misfortunes, it frequently prevents it, and induces effeminate and cowardly selfishness'.[35]

In the 1800 Preface Wordsworth pursues his own critique of misdirected feeling in slightly different terms. 'The human mind is capable of being excited without the application of gross and violent stimulants', he implores with palpable desperation.

> The invaluable works of our elder writers, I had almost said the works of Shakespear [sic] and Milton, are driven into neglect by frantic novels, sickly and stupid German Tragedies, and deluges of idle and extravagant stories in verse.[36]

Ranging freely across genres, but doubtless thinking of novels like Lewis's *The Monk*, Beckford's *Vathek* and Goethe's *The Sorrows of Young Werther*, Wordsworth is denouncing both the 'degrading thirst after outrageous stimulation' and the sensational plot elements that provoke it: abductions, torture, hauntings, tragic love affairs, suicide, murder, incest, rape. His lyrical ballads demote the status of narrative incident: 'the feeling therein developed gives importance to the action and situation and not the action and situation to the feeling'.[37]

While perfectly coherent on its own terms, Wordsworth's intention of reordering the relative importance of plot and feeling may not be clearly apparent in poems like *The Mad Mother*, *The Thorn* and *The Last of the Flock*, which themselves revel in tragic and pathetic 'situations'. But Wordsworth's tableaux of woe are never simply devices for linking together strings of sensational events. 'Incidents are among the lowest allurements of poetry', he wrote to Coleridge in 1798, 'in poems descriptive of human nature, however short they may be, character is absolutely necessary'.[38] The attempt is to construct psychological portraits which take time to develop, and occasionally suspend the action. Even when fixated upon distress, these poems reject the formulaic impulse of Sensibility in favour of an analytical approach to 'the history or science of feelings'.[39]

It is nature that anchors and 'frames the measure' of human feeling: such is the didactic claim that motivates several of the ballads written by Wordsworth in the spring of 1798. In *Lines Written at a Small Distance from my House* Wordsworth tries to coax Dorothy away from their usual routine of reading and study with the promise of nature's 'blessing in the air' (5):

> One moment now may give us more
> Than fifty years of reason;
> Our minds shall drink at every pore
> The spirit of the season. (25–8)

The companion poems *Expostulation and Reply* and *The Tables Turned*, inspired by a 'conversation with a friend who was somewhat unreasonably attached to modern books of moral philosophy',[40] sketch a day-long discussion over the relative merits of, on one hand, academic knowledge and, on the other, the 'Spontaneous wisdom' (19) to be found in the natural world. In this exchange it is the narrator of *The Tables Turned* who speaks for Wordsworth:

> One impulse from a vernal wood
> May teach you more of man,
> Of moral evil and of good
> Than all the sages can. (21–4)

These poems employ a plainness of diction intended to reflect truths so intuitively central to human existence as to make elaboration unnecessary and even inappropriate. And yet they also contain images that resonate with unexpected power:

> Sweet is the lore which nature brings,
> Our meddling intellect
> Misshapes the beauteous forms of things –
> We murder to dissect.

> Enough of science and of art,
> Close up these barren leaves;
> Comes forth, and bring with you a heart
> That watches and receives.
> (*The Tables Turned*, 25–32)
> To her fair works did nature link
> The human soul that through me ran,
> And much it grieved my heart to think
> What man has made of man.
> (*Lines Written in Early Spring*, 5–8)

By incorporating richly suggestive phrasings ('We murder to dissect', 'What man has made of man') into rapid, declarative metres, Wordsworth's ballads achieve a lingering complexity – as if to suggest that while nature's truths may be instinctively felt, their full comprehension requires a lifetime of devoted 'watching and receiving'.

Perhaps the more famous – or notorious – of the volume's ballads are those featuring the weak and vulnerable: children, beggars, deserted mothers, old men, many of them infirm, destitute, or even deranged. These poems frequently depict the wrenching pain of loss, often fixing upon a single moment that embodies a long process of dissolution and decline. *Simon Lee* recounts an old huntsman's physical decay through his difficulty in wielding an axe; in *The Last of the Flock* a shepherd's herd (and his happiness) have dwindled down almost to nothing. In *The Mad Mother* and *The Complaint of a Forsaken Indian Woman* abandoned women cling desperately to their infants; maternity – even tormented maternity – represents for each the last link to sanity and human hope.

Some readers may find the intense emotionalism of these poems deeply affecting; some may find them maudlin, overwrought, or even silly. But Wordsworth was convinced that the emotional lives of humble persons had a special clarity that demanded prolonged attention. In perhaps the best-known passage from the extended Preface to the second edition (1800), he argued that

> Low and rustic life was generally chosen because in that situation the essential passions of the heart find a better soil in which they can attain their maturity... because in that situation our elementary feelings... may be more accurately contemplated and more forcibly communicated.[41]

Wordsworth would try to bring to his poetry the 'plainer and more emphatic language' of these feelings, which, he argued, was 'a more permanent and a far more philosophical language than that which is frequently substituted for it by Poets'.[42] The notion that educated people could learn something about themselves from reading tales of the peasantry repelled some critics; in the words of Francis Jeffrey (a writer for the *Edinburgh Review* and Wordsworth's long-time nemesis), 'the love, or grief, or anger of a clown, a tradesman, or a market-wench' is 'itself a different emotion' than the 'love, or grief, or indignation of an enlightened and refined character'.[43] Jeffrey's protest helps crystallize the radicalism of these poems. To locate in humble and rustic life the revelation of *universal* human feeling – 'the primary laws of our nature' – was to overturn a prevailing social psychology which had denied significance, complexity and nuance to the 'feelings' of the uneducated. Wordsworth did more than bring these feelings into the literary arena; as he wrote in the 1800 Preface, he 'endeavoured to look steadily'[44] at them. Poems like *We Are Seven* and *The Last of the Flock* force our participation far past the point of comfort, appropriating the pointed refrains of the ballad form to convey psychic fixation ('"O Master! we are seven"') and anguish ('"For me it was a woeful day"'). In the attempt 'to communicate impassioned feelings', Wordsworth noted, 'there will be a craving in the mind' to 'cling to the same words, or words of the same character';[45] and he extends his use of repetition to show – through careful alterations of key phrases – the high-speed cycles and reversals of impassioned feelings, what he called the 'fluxes and refluxes' of the active imagination. Thus, the shepherd's continual reference to a 'woeful day' in *The Last of the Flock* gives history – and intrinsic worth – to his agony and derangement.

Wordsworth's sympathy with the poor, weak and disenfranchised is, then, one of the primary legacies of *Lyrical Ballads*. Yet this sympathy is rarely simple or straightforward. Once we begin taking serious account of the narrators, the poems' attitude towards suffering becomes difficult to summarize. Consider the divided speaker of *Simon Lee*. For the first 80 lines he appears to be telling old Simon's story mainly for sport, using Simon's advancing age and frailty as an occasion for demonstrating his belief in his talent as a balladeer:

> Of years he has upon his back,
> No doubt, a burthen weighty;
> He says he is three score and ten,
> But others say he's eighty. (5–8)

The narrator so enjoys the constraints of the form, which demands frequent, pithy rhymes, that he is willing to denigrate the story he's attempting to tell.

> What more I have to say is short,
> I hope you'll kindly take it;
> It is no tale, but, should you think,
> Perhaps a tale you'll make it. (77–80)

When he finally reaches the narrative, it is over and done with in a moment: after watching Simon struggling to remove a rotten stump, the speaker takes the axe and, with 'a single blow', severs the root. Recounting Simon's tears of thanks, however, the speaker becomes earnest and reverent, and the poem closes with quiet but complicated wisdom:

> I've heard of hearts unkind, kind deeds
> With coldness still returning,
> Alas, the gratitude of men
> Has oft'ner left me mourning. (101–4)

The painful sympathy in these lines may seem at odds with the speaker's earlier self-indulgence, but perhaps Wordsworth relies upon the ballad form to make the turn plausible. The long introduction, with its jokes, detours and evasions, may allow the speaker the time he needs to face the pathos looming at the end of his tale.

Possibly, then, in *Simon Lee* Wordsworth manipulates tone so as to surprise us into compassion. But in other poems the marked separation between narrator and rustic figure makes the tone harder to assess. *Old Man Travelling*, for example, seems to break into two parts. In the first the narrator admiringly describes the old man as 'insensibly subdued / To settled quiet' (7–8), led by nature to a 'perfect' peace. He then discovers, however, that the man is actually journeying to see his dying son – at which point the poem abruptly ends, with no attempt whatever to reconcile these disparate images. We may decide that the narrator's sudden silence shows his embarrassment over having presumed the old man to have been at peace. Or it may equally reveal the narrator's baffled acceptance of the old man's composure in the face of a personal tragedy. Any such judgement, however, must remain conjectural.

If we know too little about the narrator of *Old Man Travelling*, we know too much about the narrator of *The Thorn*. Wordsworth included with the 1800 edition a remarkably detailed note describing the narrator as a retired man with a 'small independent income' who is 'talkative' and 'prone to superstition'. Readers may find him a little dull, Wordsworth confesses, but he is trying to show how such men 'communicate impassioned feelings'.[46] Under these circumstances, with the poem filtered through the consciousness of an explicitly superstitious, impassioned (and tedious?) old man, it is difficult to evaluate his obsessive rehearsal of Martha Ray's sad story, or even to say with certainty that the poem's larger point lies in offering her compassion. *The Idiot Boy* presents other difficulties. Wordsworth says he 'never wrote anything with so much glee',[47] but we must wonder about the poem's supposed humour. Certainly, it offers a sort of extended sight gag in the vision of Johnny, and then Betty Foy, and finally Susan successively trooping into town, each out to rescue the one who has gone before. But if this is pleasure, it seems to be the pleasure of superiority, as we are invited to participate in the narrator's apparent mocking of poor, irrational Betty.

Why is Wordsworth's attitude so difficult to divine in some of these poems? Part of the answer may be found in chapter 14 of *Biographia Literaria*, where Coleridge notes that Wordsworth hoped 'to give the charm of novelty to things of every day . . . by awakening the mind's attention from the lethargy of custom'.[48] Poems like *Old Man Travelling*, *The Idiot Boy* and *The Thorn* approach us obliquely, presenting situations whose drama lies in our own decision to assert meanings never made explicit in the verse itself. Similarly, the dramatic dialogues *Anecdote for Fathers* and *We Are Seven* depend upon our willingness to be agents of discovery, since we must work against Wordsworth's narrators, as well as with them, to gain the poems' insights into human psychology. We also must remember, as both the 1798 Advertisement and the 1800 Preface make clear, that Wordsworth had other interests as a poet beyond the sympathetic depiction of human misery. These poems were, first and last, 'experiments', written 'with a view to ascertain how far the language of conversation in the middle and lower classes of society is adapted to the purposes of poetic pleasure'.[49] If they were to be of any value as experiments, they had to involve real artistic risk. So although we may ultimately feel bewildered rather than illuminated by the idiosyncratic narrators of *The Thorn* and *The Idiot Boy*, their presence testifies to the artistic daring of Wordsworth's scheme.

For most readers the collection's two most successful poems are the ones that frame it: Coleridge's *Ancient Mariner* and Wordsworth's *Tintern Abbey*, works central to the achievement of each poet and which openly reveal their different artistic strengths and preoccupations. The blank-verse meditation of *Tintern Abbey*, spoken in what Coleridge called Wordsworth's 'own character, in the impassioned, lofty, and sustained diction, which is characteristic of his genius',[50] is utterly dissimilar to the *Mariner's* surreal, galloping and indeed frightening narrative. Yet the poems have important, surprising affinities.

The 'bright-eyed marinere' (44) and the Wordsworthian narrator who gazes over the Wye Valley recount personal histories that, while ostensibly addressed to others (the Wedding-Guest and Dorothy, respectively), are fundamentally internal. Each is trying to assimilate, and make sense of, his movement from a past period of innocent happiness into the perilous world of self-knowledge and self-consciousness. Each poem imagines – though in radically different terms – a restorative, elemental link between the human spirit and natural creation. Each, however, derives its ultimate power not from its clearest statement of faith and affirmation, but from its particular qualities of narrative voice.

The Mariner's tale is the darker. His earlier exploration of the land of 'Mist and snow' (49) has also been a bewildering confrontation with himself – that is, with his weakness, wilfulness, humanity. Though recovered from the immediate crisis of the journey, he has by no means transcended its awful revelations, and is compelled to revisit them as he tells his story over and again. Thus, his blithe concluding moral of natural harmony ('He prayeth best who loveth best, / All things both great and small': 647–8) is never allowed to fully neutralize the haunted self-loathing that seems ultimately to govern the poem: 'And a million million slimy things / Lived on – and so did I' (230–1).

The speaker of *Tintern Abbey,* on the other hand, cannot miss his way, certain that his disappointments and sufferings shall be turned to the good. Even so, the poem is remarkable for the subtlety of the emotional states it evokes. Things have been lost in Wordsworth's life, and though he insists he has found 'Abundant recompense' (89) for them, the fact of loss is allowed to remain a palpable, unextinguished presence in the poem. Throughout *Tintern Abbey* exhilarating emotional heights are attained through an embrace of stillness and quietude. Thus, the poem's first great crescendo – its blissful revelation of a visionary link between nature and humanity – is realized as a slow, lingering hush:

> And even the motion of our human blood
> Almost suspended, we are laid asleep
> In body, and become a living soul;
> While with an eye made quiet by the power
> Of harmony, and the deep power of joy,
> We see into the life of things. (45–50)

Similarly, while the poem's most decisive statement of belief may be found in the soaring declaration that Wordsworth has found 'In nature and the language of the sense' the 'guide, the guardian of my heart, and soul / Of all my moral being' (109–12), it is perhaps even more masterful in the lines preceding, as Wordsworth gives voice to the powers of loss and quiet reflection:

> For I have learned
> To look on nature not as in the hour
> Of thoughtless youth, but hearing oftentimes
> The still, sad music of humanity,
> Nor harsh nor grating, though of ample power
> To chasten and subdue. And I have felt
> A presence that disturbs me with the joy
> Of elevated thoughts, a sense sublime
> Of something far more deeply interfused,
> Whose dwelling is the light of setting suns,
> And the round ocean and the living air,
> And the blue sky, and in the mind of man (89–100)

In another defining romantic text, Shelley's *Prometheus Unbound*, the 'deep truth is image-less', but at this moment in *Tintern Abbey* Wordsworth seems, at least momentarily, to have glimpsed that deep truth, and to have shown us the outlines of its huge, shadowy forms. He is, in this sense, a seer and a prophet of 'all of the mighty world / Of eye and ear' (107–8), just as surely as the lonely Mariner is the prophet of some awful inner truths about human conduct and alienation. Wordsworth finds, through and within nature, an ele-mental power that both awakens the human mind and follows from it:

> A motion and a spirit that impels
> All thinking things, all objects of all thought,
> And rolls through all things. (101–3)

The speakers in *The Ancient Mariner* and *Tintern Abbey* are two clear prototypes of what we now call the Romantic artist. The Mariner's power derives from his isolation, indeed from his sin; the darkness of his tale is the very source of its attraction. He is our conduit to the unconscious, to a whole complex of fears about our capacity for violence and corruption. In *Tintern Abbey*, Wordsworth speaks in a different voice: patiently confident and self-commanding. Doubts are swept up in hope, and Wordsworth's tenacious belief in nature's restorative power is revealed as an expression of his abiding faith in the human mind. Thus, while *Lyrical Ballads* gives us the instabilities that come with experimentation – uncertain parody, competing narrative voices, ambiguities of tone and judgement – it begins and ends with the authority of the spoken word and the surety of the visionary imagination.

## NOTES

1   CC *Biographia*, II, 6.
2   *EY*, p. 315 Wordsworth's remark, made specific-ally in regard to the poems *Michael* and *The Brothers* from the 1800 edition, is broadly applic-able to the poems of the 1798 first edition.
3   *W: Prose Works*, I, 116.
4   Ibid.
5   See especially *Biographia Literaria* chapters 14, 17 and 18.
6   Ever since Robert Mayo's 1954 essay, which sees striking topical similarities between the magazine poetry of the 1790s and the poems of the *Lyrical Ballads*, the question of the volume's 'originality' is one scholars have approached cautiously. See espe-cially Ryskamp, 'Wordsworth's *Lyrical Ballads*', Jacobus, *Tradition and Experiment*, Parrish, *The Art of the Lyrical Ballads*, and Averill, *Wordsworth*.
7   Jones and Tydeman, *Wordsworth*, p. 14.
8   See especially Jacobus, *Tradition and Experiment*, pp. 59–82, and Parrish, *The Art of the Lyrical Ballads*, pp. 34–79.
9   *LY*, IV, 719.

10  Wordsworth's drama *The Borderers* and *The Ruined Cottage*; Coleridge's drama *Osorio*.
11  Griggs, I, 260.
12  Ibid., p. 334.
13  Wordsworth recalled that they abandoned their attempt to work together on *The Ancient Mar-iner*, because 'our respective manners proved so widely different that . . . I could only have been a clog' (*WPW*, I 361). On another occasion they attempted a three-canto poem on the death of Abel. Coleridge recalled, 'Methinks I see his grand and noble countenance as at the moment when having dispatched my own portion of the task at full finger-speed, I hastened to him with my manuscript – that look of humorous despon-dency fixed on his almost blank sheet of paper, and then its silent mock-piteous admission of failure struggling with the sense of the exceed-ing ridiculousness of the whole scheme – which broke up in a laugh' (EHC, I, 287).
14  Griggs, II, 830. Questions about how ideas evolved and modulated as they passed back and

forth between the men have continued to fascinate scholars. Among excellent recent discussions, see McFarland, *Romanticism and the Forms of Ruin* (especially pp. 56–103 and 137–215), Magnuson, *Coleridge and Wordsworth* and Ruoff, *Wordsworth and Coleridge*. These discussions make it clear, however, that neither the men's friendship nor their literary relationship was free from significant pain and conflict.

15 In the years between 1797 and 1804, the time of his greatest intimacy with Wordsworth, Coleridge produced virtually all of his finest poetry. Wordsworth's 'great period' extended somewhat longer, but the chronological parallels are none the less striking.

16 Both Wordsworth and Coleridge were associated with radical circles, especially in the first half of the 1790s, and had friends who were tried for treason late in the decade. Coleridge's published political writings, however, made him the far more visible figure. For a comprehensive account, see Roe, *Wordsworth and Coleridge*.

17 Griggs, I, 260.

18 Ibid., p. 354.

19 Howe, XVII, 113.

20 Griggs, I, 216.

21 Howe, XIX, 11.

22 See, for example, in the 13-book *Prelude*, Bk 1, lines 1–54, 306–452; Bk 6, lines 453–572; Bk 13, lines 1–143.

23 For a thorough account of the complex issues surrounding the printing and publication of the 1798 edition, see Foxon, 'The printing of *Lyrical Ballads*'.

24 See Fraistat, *The Poem and the Book*, especially pp. 57–78 and 93–4, for an extended discussion of the importance of the *Ancient Mariner* for the coherence and unity of the entire 1798 volume.

25 See Reed, 'Wordsworth, Coleridge'.

26 CC *Biographia*, II, 6–7. Wordsworth's ability to offer revitalized impressions of the natural world may, in fact, be more readily visible in later lyric poems like *The Rainbow* and *Stepping Westward* (as well as in the epic *Prelude*), than in the poems of the 1798 *Lyrical Ballads*.

27 *W: Prose Works*, I, 122–4.

28 Coleridge later said that he was 'preparing among other poems, 'The Dark Ladie', and the 'Christabel', in which I should have more nearly realized my ideal. . . . But Mr. Wordsworth's industry had proved so much more successful, and the number of his poems so much greater, that my compositions, instead of forming a bal-

ance, appeared rather an interpolation of heterogeneous matter' (CC *Biographia*, II, 7–8.).

29 *WPW*, I, 361. Technically, the English ballad-stanza is defined as a quatrain, rhyming a b c b, with alternating lines of iambic tetrameter and trimeter. There are also many common variations. For excellent discussions of the literary ballad and its relationship to Wordsworth and Coleridge's experimental 'lyrical ballads', see Jacobus, *Tradition and Experiment*, especially pp. 209–61, and Parrish, *The Art of the Lyrical Ballads*, especially pp. 80–148, both of which offer comprehensive, clearly written accounts of the literary milieu from which *Lyrical Ballads* emerged, as well as numerous perceptive readings of individual poems.

30 Griggs, I, 412.

31 Wordsworth himself, ever sensitive to the shifting boundaries by which a given work can change its appearance, placed and replaced his poems over a period of years within an evolving series of conceptual categories. Wordsworth's 'relational' habit of thinking is best seen in the architectural metaphor he used in 1814 to describe his poetry. His great (and unfinished) philosophical work *The Recluse* was 'the body of a gothic church', while his autobiographical poem *The Prelude* served as its 'ante-chapel'. The rest of his poems, he continued, 'when they shall be properly arranged, will be found by the attentive Reader to have such connection with the main Work as may give them claim to be likened to the little cells, oratories, and sepulchral recesses, ordinarily included in those edifices' (*W: Prose Works*, III, 5–6).

32 See Bialostosky, *Making Tales* for a detailed account of Wordsworth's narrators.

33 All citations of poems from the 1798 *Lyrical Ballads* are from *Romanticism*.

34 This includes poetry by Joseph and Thomas Warton, Thomas Gray, Edward Young and William Collins, among others. See 'Preromanticism', pp. 12–22, above.

35 CC *Watchman*, p. 139.

36 *W: Prose Works*, I, 128.

37 Ibid., I, 128–30.

38 *EY*, p. 234.

39 *WPW*, II, 513. See Averill, *Wordsworth*, for an admirable account of Wordsworth's complex dilineations of pathos and misery.

40 *W: Prose Works*, I, 117.

41 Ibid., 124.

42 Ibid.

43  Madden, *Southey*, p. 72.
44  *W: Prose Works*, I, 132.
45  *WPW*, II, 513.
46  Ibid., 512–13.

47  Ibid., 478.
48  CC *Biographia*, II, 7.
49  *W: Prose Works*, I, 116.
50  CC *Biographia*, II, 8.

## WRITINGS

Wordsworth, William, *Lyrical Ballads, and Other Poems, 1797–1800*, ed. James Butler and Karen Green, Ithaca, Cornell University Press, 1992.

## REFERENCES AND FURTHER READING

Averill, James H., *Wordsworth and the Poetry of Human Suffering*, Ithaca, Cornell University Press, 1980.

Bialostosky, Don H., *Making Tales: The Poetics of Wordsworth's Narrative Experiments*, Chicago, University of Chicago Press, 1984.

Campbell, Patrick, *Wordsworth and Coleridge: Lyrical Ballads*, London, Macmillan, 1991.

Danby, John F., *The Simple Wordsworth: Studies in the Poems 1797–1807*, London, Routledge, 1960.

Foxon, D. F., 'The printing of *Lyrical Ballads*, 1798', *Library* 5th series, 9 (1954) 221–41.

Fraistat, Neil, *The Poem and the Book: Interpreting Collections of Romantic Poetry*, Chapel Hill, University of North Carolina Press, 1985.

Gill, Stephen, *William Wordsworth: A Life*, Oxford, Oxford University Press, 1989.

Jacobus, Mary, *Tradition and Experiment in Wordsworth's Lyrical Ballads 1798*, Oxford, Clarendon Press, 1976.

Jones, Alun R. and Tydeman, William (eds) *Wordsworth: Lyrical Ballads*, London, Macmillan, 1972. Casebook.

McFarland, Thomas, *Romanticism and the Forms of Ruin: Wordsworth, Coleridge, and Modalities of Fragmentation*, Princeton, Princeton University Press, 1981.

Madden, Lionel, (ed.) *Southey: The Critical Heritage*, London, Routledge, 1972.

Magnuson, Paul, *Coleridge and Wordsworth: A Lyrical Dialogue*, Princeton, Princeton University Press, 1988.

Mayo, Robert, 'The contemporaneity of the *Lyrical Ballads*', *PMLA* 69 (1954) 486–522.

Parrish, Stephen Maxfield, *The Art of the Lyrical Ballads*, Cambridge, Mass., Harvard University Press, 1973.

Reed, Mark L., 'Wordsworth, Coleridge and the "Plan" of the *Lyrical Ballads*', *University of Texas Quarterly* 34 (1964–5) 238–53.

Roe, Nicholas, *Wordsworth and Coleridge: The Radical Years*, Oxford, Oxford University Press, 1988.

Ruoff, Gene, *Wordsworth and Coleridge: The Making of the Major Lyrics 1802–1804*, New Brunswick, Rutgers University Press, 1989.

Ryskamp, Charles, 'Wordsworth's *Lyrical Ballads* in their time', in *From Sensibility to Romanticism* ed. Frederick W. Hilles and Harold Bloom, New York, Oxford University Press, 1965, pp. 357–72.

Wordsworth, William, *Lyrical Ballads*, ed. Michael Mason, London, Longman, 1992. Critical introduction and 1805 edition of poems.

Wordsworth William, and Coleridge, Samuel Taylor, *Lyrical Ballads 1798*, ed. W. J. B. Owen, Oxford, Oxford University Press, 1969.

——*Lyrical Ballads*, ed. R. L. Brett and A. R. Jones, London, Routledge, 1991, Includes texts of poems from 1798 and 1800 editions.

# 14

# Dorothy Wordsworth, *Journals*

## Pamela Woof

The only portrait in oils of Dorothy Wordsworth declares her a writer. Crosthwaite in 1833 paints her, elderly and frail-looking, seated with ink and pen at her side and an open writing book on her knee. It is a true portrait. Certainly, her Scottish and Continental journals of 1803 and 1820 were copied out for friends, and there was a short-lived idea of publishing the former in 1822–3; her account of the deaths of the Greens in sudden snow and mist was circulated in 1808 and succeeded in raising money for the orphan children; a few verses and descriptive passages appeared in print discreetly from 1810 in Words-worth's volumes. But contemporaries generally could not know her as a writer and she herself refused the title: 'I should detest the idea of setting myself up as an Author'.[1] Crosthwaite's portrait has become truer with time, as her private journals have come to be valued, not only as commentary on Wordsworth's poetry (the emphasis of William Knight, her first editor in 1897), but as essential literature in themselves. She was no fiction writer plotting other worlds, but her own world is brought before us, satisfyingly historical and satisfyingly imagined.

How did she come to write? From the age of six, on her mother's death in 1778, she lived in Halifax, separated totally from father, brothers, and the house and garden in Cockermouth where she had been born. She was 'put out of the way of many recollections in common with my Brothers'.[2] The father died, Dorothy still absent, in 1783, and on her moving to live with grandparents above their draper's shop in Penrith in 1787 she met her brothers again. She was 15, irked by the necessary sewing of shirts for them, but never-theless delighted. She wrote to her friend Jane Pollard in Halifax:

> My Grandmother is now gone to bed and I am quite alone. Imagine me sitting in my bed-gown, my hair out of curl and hanging about my face, with a small candle beside me. . . . You know not how forlorn and dull I find myself now that my Brs are gone neither can you imagine how I enjoyed their company when I could contrive to be alone with them which I did as often as possible. Ah! Jane if the partial affection of a Sister does not greatly magnify all their merits, they are charming boys.[3]

Properly dutiful as brothers, the 'charming boys' took her reading in hand, and Dorothy by 'working' (sewing) intensively, set out on her lifelong serious reading:

I ha[ve] a very pretty little collection of Books from my Brothers . . . the Iliad, the Odyssey, [?] works, Fielding's works, Hayley's poems, Gil Blas (in French), Gregory's Legacy to his Daughters, and my Brother Ric[hard] intends sending me Shakespeare's Plays and the Spec[tator.] I have also Milton's Works, Dr. Goldsmith's poems, [and] other trifling things, I think I hear you say 'how will [you] have time to read all these?' I am determined to re[ad a] great deal now both in French and English. My Grandmr sits in the shop in the afternoons and by working par[ticularly] hard for one hour I think I may read the next, withou[t be]ing discovered, and I rise pretty early in a morning so [I hope] in time to have perused them all. I am at present [reading] the Iliad and like it very much, My Br Wm read [a part] of it.[4]

Debarred the discipline of the Classics in Greek or Latin, Dorothy Wordsworth acquired the freedom of English literature from Chaucer to Burns, and literature becomes a presence in her writing. Cowper, Goldsmith, Wordsworth, Beattie, Gray, Burns and Shakespeare appear in the early letters. Twice, Dorothy exclaims to Jane Pollard, 'How we are squandered abroad!'[5] thus converting Shylock's dismissive phrase for Antonio's rich argosies into a lament for the scattered riches of her own family, her brothers, far-flung from each other and from her. Dorothy's returning to a phrase here is the first of many returns: to a phrase, a rhythm, a word, a poet, an idea, a place, even a path.

From late 1788, Dorothy, almost 17, lived with her newly married Uncle William Cookson at Forncett Rectory in Norfolk, Jane Pollard still her correspondent:

. . . prayers at nine oclock (you will observe it is winter) after breakfast is over we are to read, write, and I am to improve myself in French till twelve oclock when we are to walk and visit our sick and poor . . . after tea my Uncle will sit with us and either read to us or not.[6]

But the babies came and the orderly young lady became 'superintendent of the nursery . . . a very busy woman'.[7]

In space, time and in experience Dorothy Wordsworth was again isolated from her brothers. For instance, on a visit to Windsor she could not see the king and his family 'without loving them'; to her, the 'Doctrine of Liberty and Equality' was 'new-fangled' and she was 'too much of an aristocrate'.[8] Wordsworth, meanwhile, in violent Paris, was willing to take up the service of democracy 'however dangerous' (*The Prelude*, X. 137–9). Dorothy's isolation was countered by one sustaining hope, a dream of keeping house for Wordsworth and having Jane stay 'for at least a year':

I have laid the particular scheme of happiness for each Season. When I think of Winter I hasten to furnish our little Parlour, I close the Shutters, set out the Tea-table, brighten the Fire. When our Refreshment is ended I produce our Work, and William brings his book to our Table and contributes at once to our Instruction and amusement, and at Intervals we lay aside the Book and each hazard our observations upon what has been read without the fear of Ridicule or Censure. We talk over past days, we do not sigh for any Pleasures beyond our humble Habitation "The central point of all our joys" oh Jane![9]

Dorothy's quoted line, a reference to Wordsworth's alpine herdsman and his joy in returning to his hut (*Descriptive Sketches*, 571), adds force to her feeling, as does her larger allusion to an eighteenth-century poetic ideal: an evening of tea, books, reading aloud and embroidery – plain sewing in Dorothy's case (see Cowper's 'Winter Evening': 'Now stir the fire, and close the shutters fast', *The Task*, IV, 36ff.). Her dream soon recurs: she, her brother, and Jane will inhabit a 'little cottage' and in fancy

> our parlour is in a moment furnished; our garden is adorned by magic; the roses and honeysuckles spring at our command, the wood behind the house lifts at once its head and furnishes us with a winter's shelter, and a summer's noon-day shade. My dear friend...[10]

This was to become reality in Grasmere, with Mary Hutchinson, not Jane (then married), completing that fervent eighteenth-century dream idyll that had included 'moonlight walks', 'morning rambles', 'all the sweets of female friendship' and mornings when 'we will work, William shall read to us' (*ibid.*). The garden of roses and honeysuckles was realized and Wordsworth, for example, on 24 November 1801, did read to the women: 'After tea Wm read Spenser now & then a little aloud to us. We were making his waistcoat.'[11] Yet the real place differed from fantasy: a goose had to be cooked; there was a cold wind, a shower; a single tree was intensely noticed, and the plight, in their own dialect, of their poor neighbours the Ashburners was evoked. And Dorothy more often than Wordsworth read the poetry aloud.

The eighteenth-century sensibility became modified. We see it develop: in August 1793, Dorothy had written to Jane:

> the melancholy Pleasure of walking in a Grove or Wood while the yellow leaves are showering around me, is grateful to my mind beyond even the exhilarating charms of the budding trees, while Music echoes through the Grove.[12]

Such language, worthy of Marianne Dashwood with her passion for dead leaves, and such indulgence in feeling is tempered. On 23 October 1802 Dorothy could write: 'It is a breathless grey day that leaves the golden woods of Autumn quiet in their own tranquillity, stately & beautiful in their decaying'.[13] At first she had described these golden woods of autumn as 'tranquil & silent & stately in their decay'. Her revised balancing phrases catch the rhythmic movement towards dissolution, while the continuous 'decaying' rather than the completed 'decay' prolongs nature's participation in decline. The 'melancholy Pleasure' and the explicit 'Music' of 1793 are unnecessary, for the harmonies are in the polished sentence itself.

The company of writers helped Dorothy. After more absence she got to know her brother William as an adult: at Halifax and Keswick in 1794, at Racedown in 1795–7, and at Alfoxden in 1797–8, where Coleridge walked, talked and wrote alongside Dorothy and Wordsworth. Both poets noticed things, and Coleridge often wrote them down. Dorothy began to keep a journal; her eye, Coleridge had noted, was 'watchful in minutest observations of nature'. Here is a night sky:

> Went to Poole's after tea. The sky spread over with one continuous cloud, whitened by the light of the moon, which, though her dim shape was seen, did not throw forth so strong a light as to chequer the earth with shadows. At once the clouds seemed to cleave asunder, and left her in the centre of a black-blue vault. She sailed along, followed by multitudes of stars, small, and bright, and sharp. Their brightness seemed concentrated, (half-moon).[14]

This has been observed, and human reaction is absent save in sentence movements. The sky's initial inactivity is conveyed by the passive, verbally incomplete 'spread', the passive 'was seen' and the negative 'did not throw forth'; like the continuous cloud, the phrases and clauses wrap around each other. But with the dramatic 'At once' sentences become simpler, verbs stronger, until, with the fourth sentence, the moon's free activity announces itself in the immediate strong verb, 'She sailed along'.

Wordsworth's *A Night-Piece* raises the subject of the connection between the journal and the poetry: the poem has words and phrases identical with Dorothy's but it is none the less uncertain which account precedes the other. Dorothy wrote presumably on 25 January 1798; and Wordsworth said positively, but many years later, that he composed the poem 'on the road . . . extempore'.[15] Of course, he revised before publication in 1815 and he may well have refreshed his memory from the journal; while that same journal account could itself have behind it both the shared conversation of the two writers on that night road and the extempore draft composition of the poet. Dorothy and Wordsworth – and Coleridge, too – shared talk as well as writing. The conversations are lost but their effects are seen in the common phrases and perceptions, while the reader has a sharpened sense of difference in approach of poet and prose writer. *A Night-Piece* can illustrate this. Wordsworth introduces a 'musing man' who is startled into awareness of the sky's drama and whose glimpse of the immensity of heavenly movements leaves him 'not undisturbed' by a 'deep joy'. Wordsworth follows in bold abstractions the mind's reaction to the scene; Dorothy presents it. For her, only the drama of cloud, moon and stars exists and from the way she expresses, that we approach obliquely her mind's reaction. Here, as in other instances, are two accounts, beginning probably in conversation,[16] that emerge from different creative imaginations.

Journals, though they can have no intentional structure, do grow, as life does, towards pattern. In the Grasmere Journals, May 1800–January 1803 (with a ten-month gap in 1801), one might follow several narrative lines: the story of the making of the garden, the impassioned farewell to it in July 1802 and the joyful return in October; the story of Wordsworth's courtship and his marriage to Mary Hutchinson, Dorothy's high emotion, and then the practical job of making cakes for the social return to Town End – 'We had 13 of our neighbours to Tea' (17 October 1802);[17] the story of Wordsworth's compositions, revisions, physical sicknesses as a result, Dorothy's sympathetic talking, copying and writing – spontaneously, as when she recalled her butterfly-chasing as a child (14 February 1802) and Wordsworth's quick composition of 'Stay near me' – or deliberately, as when she described her meeting with the beggar mother and children, an occurrence of 27 May 1800 but not written down until 10 June after walking and presumably talking with Wordsworth; or, deliberately again, when she described so precisely the leech gatherer, a man they had both met on 26 September 1800, but who was not mentioned in the journal until 3 October, when Dorothy had been walking with Wordsworth as he 'talked much about the object of his Essay for the 2nd volume of LB'.[18] There is the story of Coleridge, his excited coming to the Lake District, a stranger to it, and then his depression, his inability to finish *Christabel*, his sense of failure with the writing of the 'Letter to Sara' that became 'Dejection'. Or the stories of people: those who lived in the valley, the story of community; and those who passed through, the homeless and poor. The quick-changing weather and light, the recurrent seasons, offer another pattern. Dorothy's own story is there, both written and unconsciously present, her intense happiness in balance with her apprehension that domestic change will bring loss, a return of separation. There is the story of the writing of the journal: the hasty jottings on the day; the summaries of days, even weeks; the expansive writing when Wordsworth might be sleeping, away, out, working; the emendations and insertions; the writing of the moment, in the present tense.

Such narratives are historical, and interesting as they are as they mingle together, they do not explain the ultimate fineness of the journal. The Alfoxden Journal, though brief and incomplete (the manuscript has disappeared and we cannot know how much Knight excised), demonstrates Dorothy's new confidence in depicting visual change. Her night-sky of 25 January is one instance. Here, her concern is aural:

> The sun shone bright and clear. A deep stillness in the thickest part of the wood, undisturbed except by the occasional dropping of the snow from the holly boughs; no other sound but that of the water, and the slender notes of a redbreast, which sang at intervals on the outskirts.[19]

The stillness suggests silence, a silence emphasized by low sound, the occasional dropping of snow. Beyond, the sun and the redbreast's slender notes make the same contrast with shade and silence, and remind us of Dorothy Wordsworth's being so at home with what she has read. Cowper had written:

> No noise is here, or none that hinders thought.
> The redbreast warbles still, but is content
> With slender notes, and more than half suppressed.
> (*The Task*, VI, 76–8)

Years later 'slender' returns, attached to the robin: ill, in February 1835, Dorothy wrote, 'my own companion Robin cheared my bed-room with its slender subdued piping'. The allusion is probably unconscious by now, and, alongside 'slender', Cowper's 'more than half suppressed' is compressed into 'subdued'.

Another feature of Dorothy Wordsworth's prose is the hanging participle that floats outside sentences and outside time. Alongside the strong verbs, 'The trees almost *roared*' (1 February 1798), phrases exist unattached: 'The turf fading into the mountain road' (23 January 1798), 'The unseen birds singing in the mist' (1 March 1798). Because they have no full verb to anchor them into particular time, such phrases imply actions continuously in process, extraordinary, in seeming to have no beginning or ending. At times, even the participle is omitted and the cluster of nouns soars free:

> W & S[toddart] did not rise till 1 o clock. W very sick & very ill. S & I drank tea at Lloyds & came home immediately after, a very fine moonlight night – The moonshine like herrings in the water.[20]

The quick play of that moonshine moves so swiftly that, as we read, the whole walk home, not just the passing by water, seems to be shifting in moonlight. We can imagine it, even perhaps, some real moonlight night, see it. Time is collapsed, and with the domestic herrings making strange moonshine familiar, space also contracts. The words that reach this timelessness have only the length of a phrase and are embedded amongst particular completed actions. The real poet in Dorothy is here, in that, amidst crowded happenings in space and time, she can perceive and express something that is timeless. This is something that poetry does.

> We should have gone to Mr Simpson's to tea but we walked up after tea. Lloyds called. The hawthorns on the mountain sides like orchards in blossom. Brought rhubarb down. It rained hard.[21]

Amongst these bald completed actions, hawthorns take on suddenly all the sweetness and short-lived beauty of fruit trees in valleys. And every year in the middle of ordinary goings-on such transformation may be seen, or may be imagined as we read the journal.

And in a week, on 16 June, Dorothy reports: 'The lower hawthorn blossoms passed away, those on the hills are a faint white'. Co-existing with her more transcendent writing is plain observation:

> We were stopped at once, at the distance perhaps of 50 yards from our favorite Birch tree it was yielding to the gusty wind with all its tender twigs, the sun shone upon it & it glanced in the wind like a flying sunshiny shower – it was a tree in shape with stem & branches but it was like a Spirit of water – The sun went in & it resumed its purplish appearance.[22]

Dorothy uses simile here with the freedom of metaphor. This birch, a known, repeatedly seen tree, a wooden rooted plant, for a moment changes its nature; it becomes water under two guises, first a flying sunshiny shower, where 'flying' gives it all the liberty that trees cannot have, and second, a Spirit of water, having something of divinity about it; then, in the next moment, it falls back to the ordinary 'purplish appearance' of a rooted autumnal tree. Dorothy Wordsworth can move freely in and about material substances. Water can turn to air and then to a voice: 'There was no one waterfall above another – it was a sound of waters in the air – the voice of the air' (29 April 1802). She sees a vital world in metamorphosis:

> We watched the Crows at a little distance from us become white as silver as they flew in the sunshine, & when they went still further they looked like shapes of water passing over the green fields.[23]

Black crows become not only white with something of a metallic sheen, but that very firmness melts to water, not running water, but impossible shapes of water in movement over the green fields.

There is contrast here. On a larger scale, clear opposites set off the account of a pauper funeral on 3 September 1800. Dorothy had time to write because Wordsworth and John had gone on to Helvellyn and were not back until ten at night. After the matter-of-fact bread, cheese and ale for some ten men and four women, there is a deepening catalogue into darkness: the black painted coffin, the respectful singing for the woman, dead and with no forward life in kindred or children, the house dark within, the tears. A brilliant contrast follows: the sun shining outside, the beauty of the prospect, the vivid green of fields and a sense of holiness common to the natural world and to human life; Dorothy weeps. The transition from life to death is commonplace and quick; she says it all in writing that the 'green fields' are 'neighbours of the churchyard'. There is no formulation in abstract terms, nor any need to point the contrast in sacredness with the not-eminently holy parson. The latter, worsened by drink from the previous day's Fair, returns the account to the communal life, and Dorothy's taking up the morning's ironing again until seven o'clock and then writing her journal while waiting for her brothers gives shape to the day's entry and brings us back to domestic life.

Domestic events, everyday images, steady the transcendent in Dorothy's writing, and the momentary escapes from time give buoyancy to the domestic. Before she could see the birch tree's numinousness, she had to return for her fur tippet and warm spenser, it was so cold. The practical fact is not subordinated; the language does not rank experience.

In the midst of that celebration where wild daffodils dance and almost laugh with the wind, there is a contrasting quiet domestic image; not all the daffodils among the mossy stones join in nature's dance: 'some rested their heads upon these stones as on a pillow for weariness'[24] and there are, as in any human company, 'a little knot & a few stragglers'. They are real plants too, the last in a list of spring flowers; Dorothy has meticulously added the scentless violets and strawberries that she had forgotten. Then she and Wordsworth speculate, with a touch of the naturalist's spirit of scientific enquiry, as to whether the lake had floated the seeds ashore.[25] This walk of 15 and 16 April 1802 is carefully described, probably on 17 April: apart from the insertion of the two flowers, Dorothy has gone back twice to emphasize the power of the wind: she has added the clause modifying the wind, 'that blew upon them over the Lake' and the sentence, 'This wind blew directly over the Lake to them'. Clearly, she wanted to stress the wonder of the partnership of that elemental force in dance with fragile passing flowers, subject, like humans, to weariness, time and mortality. In a letter to Mary Hutchinson of 16 April, begun before the journal entry, the wind is 'furious' and 'almost took our breath away', but it has no special relationship with daffodils – indeed, there are no daffodils.

The journal, not the letter, is the place for the more exploratory writing, and certainly for the most private. Writing to Jane Pollard, now Jane Marshall, a few days before Wordsworth's wedding, Dorothy speaks in general terms of her love for Mary Hutchinson as a Sister and her entire approval of

> this Connection between us, but, happy as I am, I half dread that concentration of all tender feelings, past, present, and future which will come upon me on the wedding morning ... I seem to myself to have scarcely any thing left to wish for but that the wedding was over, and we had reached our home once again.[26]

She knew that she dreaded the wedding rather than the marriage, but still that concentration of all tender feelings – which must have included some fear of change for her in her brother's heart and home – did indeed provide Dorothy with an ordeal. She did not attend the wedding, but she wrote up the events of 4 October 1802 in detail, along with a summary of the July journey to London and Dover, the August stay in Calais to see Annette and daughter Caroline, and the return, with Mary, to Grasmere. She wrote this retrospective account probably during the last week of October and her formal tone dissolves as she recalls her own part as a player in that rite of passage. Her private blessing of the marriage by wearing the ring and giving it to Wordsworth, and his reassurance to her of continued love by momentarily restoring it, was too important a symbolic gesture not to be recorded. (It was, of course, later crossed out, probably by Dorothy, and perhaps, one might speculate, as seeming, with hindsight, too dramatic, or too personal, were other eyes to read.)

At some three weeks' distance Dorothy narrates her actions of that morning almost as of another person, factually. Her unusual drama of motion from trance-like stillness to compulsive movement conveys, without analysing, the turmoil of feeling. And she is precise: at first she saw 'the two men running up the walk that came to tell us it was over', and then the faster participle is substituted for the clause and verb, 'coming to tell us'. The drama needs that speed, and it is drama: 'I could stand it no longer'; but after the fast semi-conscious movement towards Wordsworth she needs to savour the meeting, and in the act of writing she changes from one verb to two: 'faster than my strength could carry me till I fell [upon his bosom]'; but 'fell' is crossed out and the sentence continues, 'till I met my beloved William & fell upon his bosom'. With its contrasts, its drama and its deliberation, this is sophisticated, controlled writing.

The wedding leads to the journey home, and for Dorothy revisitings on the way and 'dear recollections' of the journey to Grasmere of December 1799, when she and Words-worth 'first began our pilgrimage together'. Mary is soon incorporated into Dorothy's pattern of returns. On 31 October 1802,

> Mary & I walked to the top of the hill & looked at Rydale. I was much affected when I stood upon the 2nd bar of Sara's Gate. The lake was perfectly still, the Sun shone on Hill & vale, the distant Birch trees looked like large golden Flowers.[27]

With precision, Dorothy inserts the word 'distant' to make possible the 'large golden Flowers' of birch trees; but more, she is repeating a walk and a contemplative time with Mary of the previous autumn: 'Mary & I walked as far as Saras Gate before Supper – we stood there a long time' (18 November 1801)[28] and the scene then developed is one of contrasts: they see a lake both calm and partly ruffled; there is the sound of water, yet the lake into which it falls is quiet, while a storm gathers. The village is in full moonlight but Helm Crag is in shade, while the mountains, in light and shade, 'Dappled like a sky', become momentarily as insubstantial and as full of change and excitement as the air above them.

Returnings and revisitings form one of the patterns in Dorothy's writing, and time can almost stand still at such moments. On 29 November 1805 Dorothy evokes for Lady Beaumont the quiet atmosphere of a winter night in Dove Cottage:

> The Children are now in bed. The evening is very still, and there are no indoor sounds but the ticking of our Family watch which hangs over the chimney-piece under the drawing of the Applethwaite Cottage, and a breathing or a beating of one single irregular Flame in my fire.[29]

Lady Beaumont could well have found pleasure in the allusion to Coleridge's *Frost at Midnight*, while the modern reader who knows the Grasmere Journals will recall also an evening of peace at Dove Cottage:

> It is about 10 o clock, a quiet night. The fire flutters & the watch ticks I hear nothing else save the Breathings of my Beloved & he now & then pushes his book forward & turns over a leaf.[30]

The small specific noises, as in the Alfoxden Journal, are the sounds of silence.

Such patternings can exist happily within writing that does not seek for form. And there are pleasing shapes in the vignettes that bring to life strangers and vagrants of the road. There is a compressed powerful shape when the writing is composed under pressure: a half-day's activity can be crammed into a few words: 'I working & reading Amelia. The Michaelmas daisy droops' (7 November 1800). In that juxtaposition such different rhythms are suggested: Dorothy's busy sewing and the long pace of reading Fielding, while out of doors, in the animation of 'droops', the extended progress of autumn begins to be felt. Nothing is abstract; all is concrete. Coleridge one day walked into Dove Cottage 'with a sack-ful of Books &c & a Branch of mountain ash he had been attacked by a Cow – he came over by Grisdale – a furious wind. Mr Simpson drank tea' (10 June 1802).[31] We are given in compressed form here an entire character of Coleridge: he brings a sackful of books up and along Helvellyn – in a letter of 16 June Dorothy says she would not have carried those books to Ambleside for five shillings – and he brings a branch of mountain ash. Coleridge with these emblems is a man who shoulders a vast heritage, and a man responsive to life's growth and decay. Along with the accuracy of reporting there is a suggestion here of Matthew with his bough of wilding and the aura of time and death from Wordsworth's *Two April Mornings*.

Dorothy Wordsworth is not a tentative writer; there is hardly a subjunctive mood or an 'if' in the whole journal. We believe in what she says. There are no two ways about 'I broiled Coleridge a mutton chop which he ate in bed' (1 September 1800).[32] There is no justifying of the days, there are no apologies. She does not detail the reasons for what Wordsworth called her 'nervous blubbering' for Coleridge; we have the fact, 'at last I eased my heart by weeping'. We have the fact of her calm, staggering assumption, and we almost believe it: 'The beauty of the Moon was startling as it rose to us over Loughrigg Fell' (30 August 1800).[33] 'As it rose to us' comes naturally to Dorothy Wordsworth at the end of an ordinary day of 'baking Bread pies & dinner', walking, reading Boswell, having a headache, visitors, walking again and rowing, going to George Mackereth's to hire a horse, having supper and Thomas Ashburner's bringing their '8th Cart of coals since May 17th'.

The problems that could face an early nineteenth-century woman writer with a brilliant professional writing brother have not been central in my discussion. Nor have I advanced hypotheses of suppression. I have concentrated on the prose of her journals rather than on her relatively late verse. It is in her prose that I find her a poet, as the journals' everyday histories and perceptions of timelessness jostle along together, keeping the mind on the stretch for surprise. The reader finds the shapes and patterns. Few moralizing abstractions diffuse the feeling; rhythms, generally colloquial, can suddenly be lyrical or, for a moment, in a metrical balance. The prose is full of actions, none too small, recounted reassuringly in sequence and in main verbs, as a child might tell: 'In the evening we walked to the Top of the hill, then to the bridge, we hung over the wall, & looked at the deep stream below' (22 February 1802).[34] Wordsworth, that same night, tired with reading *Peter Bell* and talking, 'went to bed in bad spirits'. There is no commentary. The poems, of course, are deliberate compositions, and they have in consequence more unity of tone, more abstraction, more contemplation, more retrospective movement. They fascinate, for they tell us a good deal about Dorothy as she thought about her life and grew older. The journals do not tell us about life; they evoke it as it was lived in the felt wind, rain and sun of recurring seasons.

They have both multiplicity and a sense of oneness, for the single persona who writes has an open heart and mind: no sardonic attitude, no ironic superior stance destroys the people or the place. We need have no defensive guard; we can celebrate and welcome the constant liftings out of time into timelessness. Our eye for historical truth and our imaginations are satisfied.

'The Skobby sate quietly in its nest rocked by the winds & beaten by the rain' (17 May 1800).[35] This chaffinch in its nest anticipates the swallows whose story Dorothy follows in June and July 1802, when their nest is built, ruined, rebuilt. We have one of Dorothy's evocative rhythmical repetitions, 'rocked by the winds & beaten by the rain'. This wind and something of this language Dorothy returns to in her last coherent letter to her niece Dora in spring 1838. And she returns to lifelong concerns: there is the need for news, events belonging to time, facts – as we have them in the journal – about the people amongst whom she lived; there is the lasting vitality of the poetry she had read as a young woman – here, Wordsworth's bleak adjective 'naked', that had described so many crags, pools, walls and bare places, is applied devastatingly to seeds of life, the 'naked seed-pods' of laburnum, and here, too, wonderfully remembered in the quotation (despite a preposition change), is Spenser's dark wood from *The Faerie Queene*, and behind his wood, Dante's; in all this there is that combination of the things of time – news, deaths – with the things that transcend time: Spenser's and Wordsworth's art, and recurrent nature; there is that old sense of loss and abandonment and a sense that her own life has not been an easy pilgrimage; and then, even in the confinements of pain and an upstairs room, there is a soaring into true observation of birds, the life of trees and a wind which has that elemental force that years before rocked a skobby's nest and galvanized daffodils into dance, a wind here that makes the laburnum shiver and the pine trees rock from their base:

> My dearest Dora
> They say I must write a letter – and what shall it be? News – news I must seek for news. My own thoughts are a wilderness – 'not pierceable by power of any star' – News then is my resting-place – News! news!
>     Poor Peggy Benson lies in Grasmere Church-yard beside her once beautiful Mother. Fanny Haigh is gone to a better world. My Friend Mrs Rawson has ended her ninety and two years pilgrimage – and *I* have fought and fretted and striven – and am here beside the fire. The Doves behind me at the small window – the laburnum with its naked seed-pods shivers before my window and the pine-trees rock from their base. – More I cannot write so farewell![36]

The persistent patterns of a great writer.

## Notes

| | | | |
|---|---|---|---|
| 1 | *MY*, I, 454. | 6 | Ibid., p. 19. |
| 2 | *EY*, p. 663. | 7 | Ibid., p. 99. |
| 3 | Ibid., pp. 6–7. | 8 | Ibid., p. 83. |
| 4 | Ibid., p. 8. | 9 | Ibid., p. 88. |
| 5 | Ibid., pp. 16, 25. | 10 | Ibid., p. 97. |

11  Woof, p. 41.
12  *EY*, pp. 110–11.
13  Woof, p. 133.
14  *DWJ*, I, 14.
15  *WPW*, II, 503.
16  For instances of Dorothy's specific recording of Wordsworth's observations, see entries for 4 November 1800, 22, 24, 29 April 1802, 12 May, 13 June 1802; and for more extended stories told by Wordsworth to Dorothy and recorded by her, see the account of Alice Fell, 16 February 1802 and Wordsworth's retelling to Dorothy of Aggy Fisher's account to him of a woman in the vale and her dead children, 3 June 1802.
17  Woof, p. 133.
18  Ibid., p. 23.
19  *DWJ*, I, 9.
20  Woof, p. 30.
21  Ibid., pp. 107–8.
22  Ibid., p. 40.
23  Ibid., p. 87.
24  Compare the snowdrops that 'put forth their white heads' (20 January 1798) and the still trees that 'only gently bowed their heads, as if listening to the wind' (2 April 1798): returnings to an image.
25  The pseudo-narcissus, or wild daffodil, unlike the garden daffodil, is indigenous and propagates by seed rather than bulb.
26  *EY*, pp. 377–8.
27  Woof, p. 133.
28  Ibid., p. 39.
29  *EY*, p. 648.
30  Woof, p. 82.
31  Ibid., p. 108.
32  Ibid., pp. 19–20.
33  Ibid., p. 19.
34  Ibid., p. 71.
35  Ibid., p. 3.
36  *LY*, III, 528.

## WRITINGS

Levin, S. (ed.), 'The collected poems of Dorothy Wordsworth', in *Dorothy Wordsworth and Romanticism*, New Brunswick and London, Rutgers University Press, 1987.

Wordsworth, D., *George and Sarah Green – A Narrative*, ed. E. de Selincourt, Oxford, Clarendon Press, 1936.

——*Journals of Dorothy Wordsworth*, ed. M. Moorman, London, Oxford University Press, 1971.

——*Letters of Dorothy Wordsworth: A Selection*, ed. A. G. Hill, Oxford, Clarendon Press, 1985.

——*The Continental Journals*, reprint of *Hamburgh Journal* and *Journal of a Tour on the Continent*, ed. E. de Selincourt, new introduction by H. Boden, Bristol, Thoemmes Press, 1995.

Wordsworth, W., *Descriptive Sketches*, ed. Eric Birdsall, Ithaca, NY, Cornell University Press, 1984.

——*Oxford Authors: William Wordsworth*, ed. S. Gill, Oxford and New York, Oxford University Press, 1984.

——*The Fenwick Notes of William Wordsworth*, ed. J. Curtis, London, Bristol Classical Press, 1993.

## REFERENCES AND FURTHER READING

Alexander, M., 'Dorothy Wordsworth: the grounds of writing', *Women's Studies* 14 (1988) 195–210.

de Selincourt, E., *Dorothy Wordsworth: A Biography*, Oxford, Clarendon Press, 1933.

Gill, S., *William Wordsworth: A Life*, Oxford, Clarendon Press, 1989.

Gittings, R. and Manton, Jo, *Dorothy Wordsworth*, Oxford, Clarendon Press, 1985.

Heinzelman, K., 'The cult of domesticity – Dorothy and William Wordsworth at Grasmere', in *Romanticism and Feminism*, ed. A. K. Mellor, Bloomington, Indiana University Press, 1988, pp. 52–78.

Levin, S. M., *Dorothy Wordsworth and Romanticism*, New Brunswick, Rutgers University Press, 1987.

McCormick, A. H., '"I shall be beloved – I want no more": Dorothy Wordsworth's rhetoric and the appeal to feeling in *The Grasmere Journals*', *Philological Quarterly* (1990) 471–93.

McGavran, J. H., Jr, 'Dorothy Wordsworth's Journals – putting herself down', in *The Private Self: Theory and Practice of Women's Autobiographical Writings*, ed. S. Benstock, Chapel Hill, North Carolina Press, 1988, pp. 230–53.

Mellor, A. K. (ed.) *Romanticism and Feminism*, Bloomington, Indiana University Press, 1988.

—— *Romanticism and Gender*, New York and London, Routledge, 1993.

Wolfson, S., 'Individual in community: Dorothy Wordsworth in conversation with William', in *Romanticism and Feminism*, ed. A. K. Mellor, Bloomington, Indiana University Press, 1988, pp. 139–66.

Woof, P., 'Dorothy Wordsworth's Grasmere journals: the patterns and pressures of composition', in *Romantic Revisions*, ed. R. Brinkley and Keith Hanley, Cambridge, Cambridge University Press, 1992, pp. 169–90.

—— 'Dorothy Wordsworth's journals and the engendering of poetry', in *Wordsworth in Context*, ed. P. Fletcher and John Murphy, Lewisburg, Penn., Bucknell University Press, 1992, pp. 125–55.

—— *Dorothy Wordsworth, Writer*, The Wordsworth Trust, Grasmere, 1994.

—— 'The Alfoxden Journal and its mysteries', *The Wordsworth Circle* 26, 3 (1995), 125–33.

# 15

# Joanna Baillie, *A Series of Plays*

## *Janice Patten*

> *It is hate! black, lasting, deadly hate!*
> *Which thus hath driven me forth from kindred peace,*
> *From social pleasure, from my native home,*
> *To be a sullen wand'rer on the earth,*
> *Avoiding all men, cursing and accurs'd.*
> [*De Monfort*, 2.2]

First published anonymously in 1798, these lines allude to the basic polarities inherent in the period we call Romanticism. At first glance, we might think that they had been written by William Wordsworth, Samuel Taylor Coleridge or Lord Byron, but they were in fact lines written by a quiet, soft-spoken woman of Hampstead. Bluestocking poet and dramatist, Joanna Baillie's works were lauded from 1798 to 1851 in England, Germany, Scotland, Sri Lanka, the United States and were translated into German and Sinhalese. She was hailed as 'our great new poet' by literary communities, was visited by aspiring writers on pilgrimage and was at the centre of a medical, social and literary so-called *salon* or *conversazioni*. In addition to her contributions in the field of drama, she sponsored new legislation on copyright laws; fought for anti-slavery legislation; supported new and deserving younger writers; sponsored the publication of England's first slave narrative, *Olaudah Equiano or Gustavus Vassa*; wrote lyrics which were put into songs and ballads by George Thomson; composed songs for which music was provided by Haydn, Kozeluch and Beethoven; produced *The Beacon* and *The Election*, which were performed as light operas; wrote theological doctrines; corresponded with United States clergyman Sir William Ellery Channing on religious matters; and wrote the first and only ballad about Sir William Wallace, whose bravery was honoured in the 1995 film *Braveheart*. When Baillie's anonymous collection containing her first important plays appeared, reviewers and fellow poets/dramatists/writers alike assumed that the 72-page Introductory Discourse to *A Series of Plays on the Passions: in which it is Attempted to Delineate the Stronger Passions of the Mind, Each Passion Being the Subject of a Tragedy and a Comedy* was so 'revolutionary' in its own way that 'a learned man' must be the author of the volume. Her Introductory Discourse to the three plays contained in that first volume appeared in the same year as another anonymous publication, Wordsworth and Coleridge's *Lyrical Ballads*, yet it is significant to note that

Baillie's prose explanation of her new poetics supersedes that contained in Wordsworth's now more famous 1800 edition. Besides the Discourse, the volume contains three plays: *Basil*, a tragedy on love; *De Monfort*, a tragedy on hate; and *The Tryal*, a comedy on love.[1] In these works, she inaugurates a new poetics which raises the importance of imagination to new heights, and dramatizes in beautiful natural language persons of 'humble and lowly class' as they respond to 'beauty', or labour under self-doubt, haunted by memories, often wandering alone in nature. Her reputation grew steadily among her contemporaries, and she became so well known that she claimed many leading artists and writers as her intimate friends and admirers: William Wordsworth, Robert Southey, William Sotheby, Mary Berry, Sarah Siddons, Samuel Rogers, Sir George Beaumont, Lucy Aikin, Anna Laetitia Barbauld, Maria Edgeworth and Felicia Hemans. Lord Byron hailed Baillie as 'our only dramatist since Otway', while Sir Walter Scott championed her even more enthusiastically as 'the best dramatic writer since the days of Shakespeare and Massinger'. Mary Berry, a woman who was to become one of Baillie's many lifelong friends and supporters, writes in her journal on 19 March 1799 that 'all the great guns of taste', Sir George Beaumont, Charles Fox, Uvedale Price and Richard Payne Knight, communicated with one another about the excellent qualities of these wonderful new plays (II, 88–9). While only seven of her plays were staged during her lifetime, in England, Scotland, and the United States, they each attracted much attention.

In the Introductory Discourse Baillie argues part of the task particularly belonging to tragedy is that of 'unveiling the human mind under the dominion of those strong and fixed passions', which can only be expressed in solitude. Baillie's particular strengths are in her characterizations of the visionary spirit, alienated sensibility, the fragmented self, the romantic sublime and poetic madness. In the *Series of Plays* she depicts, as she expresses it in remarkably Wordsworthian phrases, 'a passion that is permanent in its nature' yet 'varied in its progress' (p. 50). She dramatizes passion in her tragic heroes, saying of them, 'the chief antagonists they contend with must be the other passions and propensities of the heart, not outward circumstances and events' (p. 59). Simply speaking, in her *Series of Plays* Baillie gives priority to character and imagination over plot and circumstance. She worked on these ideas for over 60 years, supporting herself, her sister and her mother with the profits from her sales. In addition to the immensely popular first volume of *A Series of Plays*, she published another volume in 1802 (containing *The Election*, a comedy; *Ethwald*, a tragedy on ambition; and *The Second Marriage*, another comedy); a third in 1812 (containing *Orra*, a tragedy on fear; *The Dream*, a tragedy on fear of death; *The Siege*, a comedy on fear; and *The Beacon*, a musical on hope), and volumes containing what she terms miscellaneous plays, but which nevertheless carry out her main emphasis on the passions. In what follows, I shall discuss the important aspects of *De Monfort* (1798) and briefly mention important themes and methods of dramatization in *Basil: A Tragedy, The Family Legend: A Tragedy* (1810), *Constantine Paleologus: The Last of the Caesars* (1805) and *Orra* (1812), a few of the plays which represent the range of her dramatic contributions from 1798 to 1836. In these plays particularly, her dynamic portrayals of inner fears, of fantasies, of visions, of hauntings, reveal her preoccupation with psychological motives and desires as the basis of tragic character. Her depiction of character – which, for reasons I shall explain presently, is grounded in her awareness of scientific (particularly medical and psychological) information – probes the inner workings of memory, imagination, perception and passions, as men and women form their comprehension of reality. The inner eye's vision, she knew, often conflicts with the physical eye's sight; the dream is often shown to be superior to common rational observations. That Baillie's dramas portray a vitality emanating from a scientific perspective calls for more intense study today if we are to accord her work the attention and significance that has been denied to it since her own time.

As Frederick Burwick explains in his essay in this volume (see pp. 323–32) the Romantic drama, both that which was performed and that which was read, directs our attention to its theoretical regard for matters aesthetic and dramatic. The play between illusion and delusion informs Baillie's dramas, yet we ask how did her dramatic representations fit with other Romantics' sense of the drama, with Coleridge's experimentations, Shelley's visual panoramas and Byron's mental theatre? In her systematized, almost analytical approach, she articulates a sublime and often unconscious fear of death and disintegration of self; specifically, she examines with almost scientific precision the play of illusion in human consciousness. Drama becomes for Baillie the expressive, projective dialogue and visualization of internal realities, symptoms of internal conflicts and fantasies.[2] John Philip Kemble once referred to her as the 'metaphysical' dramatist, suggesting that she dealt with conceptions about the passions which seemed to be beyond the physical world (Boaden, p. 186). Her approach is founded on the realization that all cognition is based on passion, that knowing is essentially a matter of inner perception. While her uncles and brother explored the unknown world of internal physical properties in their pioneering attempts to map surgery and medicine in new directions, Baillie's plays uncover a symbiosis of mind and body which proleptically reflects modern psychology and medicine.

What follows is a very brief sketch of her family background, which I include only because this family's unique professional interests influenced her work. The daughter of a university professor (her father was a Lecturer at Glasgow University), Baillie learned geometry, philosophy and Latin in her teens; she blossomed in the intellectual community which surrounded her father. Her work also shows the influence of her first readings at seven years of age: those of James Macpherson's *Ossian* and of Shakespeare's dramas. She was a self-educated woman, as many women of this period were; but beyond that her development received particular stimulus from the interests of her two uncles, William and John Hunter, the famous physicians and anatomists, and from the medical career of her brother, Matthew, with whom she was very close for most of her life. Author of *Morbid Anatomy*, the first scientific discussions to relate the morbidity of an organ with its symptoms, Matthew Baillie and his uncle William were the first physicians to study the problems involved with women's anatomy, particularly obstetrics. Her *Series of Plays* illustrates how a hero's actions are symptoms caused by an excessive or over-powerful passion of the mind. Her use of illusion, of imagination, of epistemology, of actions as symptoms of pathological mental conditions, all fall within this vitalist–Romantic tradition, linking her works through the power of the sign and symptom to those of her brother. Of the three medical men in Baillie's family, perhaps the best known was John Hunter, who had a strong theoretical perspective that complemented his clinical experiments and gave his thoughts significance and application beyond the laboratory, reflecting fundamental principles about life and consciousness that influenced the literary creations of his niece. Hunter's work could be defined as explications of various phases of life exhibited in organized structures, both animal and vegetable, from the simplest to the most highly differentiated; he studied the human body 'in cases of sudden death to compare the normal state of the organs with those of diseased bodies' (Allen, *Hunterian*, p. 19); and his comparative analysis led to his insight into what he called *an animating principle in all nature*. This theoretical work put Hunter at the centre of the vitalist–mechanist debate that involved the whole intellectual community during the early nineteenth century, including literary figures like Coleridge; and Hunter's authority was cited by both sides until after his death. Baillie also found herself at the centre of this debate as it occurred in the literary world. For the last 50 years of her life, she lived in Hampstead near her uncles' and her brother's laboratory, and it was in this highly charged climate that she became the centre of a literary *salon*.

A sister and niece in this family of anatomists and royal physicians, Baillie found rich physiological and psychological material for her dramas. Her brother's and her uncles' professional connections with the royal family also inspired dramatic themes of intrigue, madness and disease.[3] Both of her uncles and her brother were physicians to the royal family at one time or another, and her brother attended the deranged George III. King George III's mental condition paints the dramatic background to her plays. On a broader scale, dramatic themes of turmoil and change explain some of the violence of Georgian times. Baillie lived for almost a century, witnessing the prevalent malice and corruption, the revolutionary mentality, the rise of the industrial nation, the end of the Napoleonic era and of the Regency in England, the Peterloo massacre, and the rise of the influence of science, mechanization and materialism. In her plays, we see men and women driven to murderous acts; but her stronger themes involve the consequential secrecy and guilt associated with them. She dramatizes human struggles with consciousness, relative to public perceptions, and inner battles between action and suffering.

Baillie portrays the psychological dilemma of heroes who project all painful and unpleasant sensations or feelings in their mind onto others; her heroes attribute these malignant thoughts and desires to someone else, as we will see in *De Monfort*. In De Monfort's deep self-hatred, in ambition's tenacious hold on Ethwald (*Ethwald*, 1802) and in Basil's divided loyalties (*Basil*, 1798), the weaker the identity, the more likely the figure to go mad. Delusion in the extreme clothes the madman, but illusion fits the imaginative poet. Basil, De Monfort, Constantine Paleologus, Orra and Ethwald deny their own delusion, the destructive nature of the unconscious or subconscious fears, and their own psychological responsibility. However, in a moment of keen dramatic awareness, they realize that destructive forces do not lie elsewhere; they realize that they have become progressively deceived by their own mental fixations. Their sense of external reality has been gradually transformed by their inner vision, their vital core, their passions of the mind. Baillie's *Series of Plays* provides the key to much of the literature of the period because she anticipates the male Romantics both generally and specifically. Here, I wish to refer to a few of the plays to suggest just how her work is psychologically innovative, how it limns the dilemma of the vitalist–mechanist debate, evokes the Burkean sublime, and is, at the core, highly Romantic.

Of the three plays contained in the first volume of *A Series of Plays on the Passions*, the best known is *De Monfort*. Baillie's first stage success came with the 1800 production at

Drury Lane, featuring Sarah Siddons and John Philip Kemble in the leading roles of Jane De Monfort and her brother, De Monfort. James Boaden, in his memoirs of Kemble, recounts how the play came to be produced: Mr Kemble 'had been struck with *De Montfort* [sic] 'and explained his intention to 'make some alterations' so as to make it a better 'stage representation' and play the lead himself, 'consigning' Jane 'to the care of Mrs Siddons' (255).

The production of the play, including actors, directing and stage scenery, of course all derived from the unique conceptual content and story of the play. The setting of Baillie's five-act tragedy is Germany in the late Middle Ages. Its plot is simple: De Monfort, plagued by hatred for Rezenvelt ever since they were boys, finally kills him. It is here that Baillie sets forth her hero 'whose secret soul, / With all its motley treasure of dark thoughts, / Foul fantasies, vain musing, and wild dreams' (1.2) curses his existence. Echoing Gothic literature of the eighteenth century, but, more importantly, anticipating the Byronic hero (Byron, we remember, was attracted to Baillie's work) and the theme of androgyny in the work of both Byron and Shelley, Baillie presents a hero consciously driven by ignoble motives of pride and humiliation which he himself despises, yet possibly motivated (subconsciously) by a far more powerful drive – incestuous desire. From a modern psychoanalytical perspective, perhaps this might explain De Monfort's suffering as arising from unacknowledged attraction to his sister. Another view might be that De Monfort sees Rezenvelt as his negative double, containing all the negative emotions he himself had felt toward his mother, and Jane, De Monfort's sister, might represent the idealized mother; a personification of the union which existed once between his mother and him, but which can no longer be maintained. The object of De Monfort's hatred, Rezenvelt, is not only his rival since boyhood, the person who saved his life and made him feel utterly weak, inferior and demeaned, but also the man who, De Monfort is told, has attracted his sister's love. From the tension between conscious ignoble motivations, somehow too powerful to resist, and subconscious attraction between two noble souls of the same parentage, Baillie develops her tragedy. The action deals with the internal struggle of De Monfort to resist his hatred of Rezenvelt and forbear the impulse to murder. The play opens with his old landlord and servant narrating and explaining a change in De Monfort's appearance since last they saw him. The servant Jerome's comment, 'All this is strange – something disturbs his mind' (1.1.), sets the tone and focuses our attention on the main problem of the play. When old friends, Count Freberg and his wife, arrive, De Monfort exclaims, 'O! many varied thoughts do cross our brain, / Which touch the will, but leave the memory trackless', alluding to the passion or disturbance of his mind. The 'morning sun' and 'light and cheerful' atmosphere seem to reassure De Monfort that he will feel freedom; yet as he utters words expressing a sense of inner peace, he also refers to 'abhorred serpents' crossing his way. Beneath the exterior manners of man, De Monfort says, we should be aware of 'a sore disease', a serpent sting of some secret guilt at the soul which is manifested in external appearance and not understood: 'We mark the hollow eye, the wasted frame, / The gait disturb'd of wealthy honour'd men, / But do not know the cause' (1.2). The cause of De Monfort's changed appearance, however, will soon be revealed as his diseased mind, tormented with guilt and repressed hatred. As spectators we understand De Monfort's suffering because of what Baillie calls our universal 'sympathetic propensity'. Baillie argues, 'There is, perhaps, no employment which the human mind will with so much avidity pursue, as the discovery of concealed passion, as the tracing the varieties and progress of a perturbed soul' (*A Series of Plays*, p. 11). As spectators, however, when we witness De Monfort's anguish and see his suffering, we wonder about Rezenvelt's character. Who is this man who is capable of engendering so much hatred? We feel empathy toward De Monfort in the scene in which he anticipates the arrival of Rezenvelt (1.2). We are not yet aware that De Monfort is deluded; we have willingly partaken of the illusion that Rezenvelt's arrival on the scene will reveal his villainous nature. In the opening scenes, Baillie has played with our expectations, for we erroneously expect the villain's actions to reveal all. Ironically, however, when Rezenvelt appears, his actions reveal little about him, but much about De Monfort's perception. The very worst we can say about Rezenvelt is that he taunts De Monfort. The audience and the reader see De Monfort's vision of Rezenvelt because Baillie paints us a lively portrait. We are not told about Rezenvelt's hair colour, his mode of dress, or any other detail. Rather, we see 'the side glance of that detested eye! / That conscious smile! / that full insulting lip' (1.2). We see only his essence, the coloration of darkness, the natural hue of malignant evil. We do see him before our inner eye. When Rezenvelt appears on the stage and confronts De Monfort, whether we are reading the scene or witnessing it, we compare in our imagination the insulting tone of the character we see now with what we envisioned earlier.[4]

As the play progresses, De Monfort's hatred is fed by a deluded belief that Lady Jane has become betrothed to Rezenvelt. The idea that his hated alter-ego could take his place in his sister's love, in her bed, drives De Monfort to the edge of insanity. The intensity of his delusions becomes unbearable. At the end of scene two, tossing his arms distractedly, De Monfort cries, 'Hell hath no greater torment for th'accurs'd / Than this man's presence gives – / Abhorred fiend . . . it makes me mad' (1.2). But his raving passion is comprehensible, understandable and dark. It is representative of the world of the unseen, the invisible seething world.

After the deed is done toward the end of the play, De Monfort feels self-exiled and alienated from nature: 'the filmy darkness on mine eyes has clung / And closed me out from the fair face of nature' (5.4). He realizes, too late, that he had been compelled by his own anxieties to hate Rezenvelt. Completely alone, he sees himself as a man deluded only by himself, noble in his alienation from himself, given stature by his intense suffering. Repeating a Job-like utterance, 'I am because I suffer', he promotes a Romantic sensibility. For De Monfort, there is no external guidance, no solace in powers or structures larger than himself, no alleviation from the alienation and torment of his hatred. Old systems of thought, old patterns of belief, whether Christian, moral or rational, are of no consequence to him. Some critics have objected to Baillie's focus on De Monfort's internal struggles and what seems to them to be a fault: the simplicity of plot as a means to delineate one passion throughout a play. However, another way of looking at this drama might be to argue that it is precisely this kind of seeming lack of action which constitutes the actual strength of her work. The real 'action' in this play is predominantly psychological, reflecting proairesis rather than praxis. In fact, Baillie incorporates narration as a dramatic trope to slow down the action, to allow the audience to envision the behind-the-scenes action and causes which precede the on-stage situation. She frequently collapses time and space, as she creates what we would call a *tableau vivant*, particularly as we have seen De Monfort describe Rezenvelt earlier. The audience responds to De Monfort's suffering because of what Baillie calls our universal 'sympathetic propensity'.

In the same *Series of Plays* we see Basil as a victim of love at first sight; he chooses to get one more look at his love, forgets his duty to his country, his duty to his soldiers and to his friend. When he realizes the folly of his decision, that he is responsible for the death of many soldiers, his suffering becomes intense. Another of Baillie's plays which was performed in Scotland at the Edinburgh Theatre Royal with the help of Sir Walter Scott is *The Family Legend*, which incorporates the same artistic techniques which we saw in *De Monfort*, and in which she dramatizes the legendary rivalry of two Scottish clans. Scott, like his friend Baillie, felt that the means of understanding the present was to till cultural legends, cultivate imagination and give new life in the present to the absent world of the legendary past. Often, Baillie insists that a hero's belief in a system or idea which is not supported by the commonly accepted opinion makes that hero appear delusioned, haunted by a visionary kind of madness. *The Family Legend*, in its reliance on myth and cultural history, resembles Greek tragedy's emphasis on feudal or family animosity; this play dramatizes the transcendence of human imaginative values over political power, giving priority to values based on tradition and individual sensibilities. Additionally, Baillie's dramatization incorporates framed moments of great passion reminiscent of Greek stagings.

The play was a hit because it evoked Scotland's historical past and illustrated 'a bold and gen'rous race' who have undauntingly maintained the 'rights and freedoms of our native land' (*The Family Legend*, 5.4). Scott set the tone and theme in the Prologue when he refers to 'the legends of our native land, / Link'd as they come with every tender tie, / Memorials dear of youth and infancy'. The past is brought to life again, 'dear illusions rise' to bring passions, feelings and pride once more to Scotland's theatre audience.

The strength of this play lies in Helen's and Maclean's characters, in their nobility of spirit striving against those clansmen whom they also respect with a sense of national pride. When Argyll speaks the last words of the play, he anticipates that future generations, 'looking back on these our stormy days', will 'pity, admire, and pardon / The fierce, contentious, ill-directed valour / Of gallant fathers, born in darker times'. The curtain then drops, reminding the audience that it is man alone who can look back toward the past and forward to futurity.

Political upheaval, visions in dreams, cultural destruction, psychological turmoil and illusions of power permeate another of Baillie's plays: *Constantine Paleologus: The Last of the Caesars*. In this play, she exploits the Romantic theatrical scenic display, the vastness of the theatres, and the taste of current theatre-going audiences. The subject of the play is Gibbon's account of the May 1453 siege by the Turks of Constantinople, a haven for science and learned men. Baillie made alterations to the Gibbon account: she introduced the character of Valeria, Constantine's wife, a strong, insightful female, as well as other characters. But her main achievement is her treatment of the growth and development of character resulting from the ordeals which the figures of her story undergo. Baillie's interest in Constantinople as the last remnant of a refined and learned civilization overthrown by violent pagan forces is part of her long-standing interest in human dignity in the face of seemingly uncontrollable passions and advancing barbarism. She was attracted to periods of 'discord, usurpation, and change' (*Works*, p. 8) which throw individuals into boundary situations that test the fibre of their being and the meaning of their lives, both personally and in a social, cultural environment. Always presented with choices, characters hover on the edge of indecision, facing annihilation and non-meaning, or action, suffering and meaning. Marshalling inner strength, they illustrate tragically that accepting death ultimately defines life. Affirming their existence, they declare victory of individual choice and will over circumstances. This is the Romantic spirit Baillie's drama exemplifies.

She draws heroes and heroines of convincing complexity who desire peace, not violence; stability, not anarchy; individual spirit, not mass submission. In her depiction of a hero, she concentrates upon the character's struggle against her/himself. For example, in *Ethwald*, she defines ambition as one of those passions that acquires 'strength from gratification and the dominion which it usurps over the mind is capable of enduring from youth to extreme age' (2.ix). Her heroes' moods seem often 'dark', portraying a hero's tragic tensions and conflicts within his consciousness, 'the passions of his mind', mirrored through language. Baillie's dramatic portrayal of martyrdom in *The Martyr* (1826) illustrates just such tensions between Christian precepts and secular rules, religious and political power, personal desire and universal causes, and the nature of illusion and delusion. And in *Orra* (1812), her one play clearly named after a female protagonist, we see Orra going to any lengths to avoid being married to a man she doesn't love. We see her preference for a 'darkness, peopled with its hosts unknown'. However, like De Monfort, like Constantine, and her other tragic protagonists, Orra willingly finds her own fate, accepts – in the abstract – her coming suffering and alienation, only to be confronted by the devastating actual experience. Even though, at the end of this play, 'Orra's mind within itself holds a dark world / Of dismal phantasies and horrid forms!' (5.2), she has attained a new kind of tragic stature, a new kind of Romantic freedom.

Baillie offered to the literary world a new way of looking at drama and poetry; yet, up to now, her plays and poems are not even anthologized in our studies of the Romantic period. Certainly, a playwright such as she, who was in her own day revered by poets on both sides of the Atlantic, will reward re-examination now, when we are finally coming to understand that the evolution of the received canon of literary studies may well have taken place under a gender bias that systematically marginalized women writers. It can at least be said that she initiates a Romantic perspective in the drama. And her psychoanalytical depictions of the human psyche influenced Romantic literature far more broadly than most critics have realized.

## NOTES

1  Baillie's tragedies account for her popularity during the Romantic period. Because of this, I have chosen to concentrate on them rather than on her comedies. Her comedies are enjoyable to read, and there are often satiric remarks on women's issues, particularly marriage. In 1992, *The Country Inn*, a comedy, was produced at the Wordsworth Summer Conference in Grasmere.

2  Baillie's dramatizations of psychological states, expressive of human hope and fear, may have influenced other Romantics' dramatic works. Coleridge's *Remorse* bears remarkable similarity to Baillie's play *The Beacon* (1812), which gained popularity on stage as a serious musical drama in 1812. Specifically, lines indicating Teresa's desire for Alvar to be alive, but fearing his return to see

her – with 'a brother's infant' in her arms – as wretchedness, are very similar to that of Aurora's longing for her lover in *The Beacon*. Francis Hodgson, in a review of Coleridge's play, notes the similarity to Baillie's *Orra* (*Monthly Review* 71 (1813): 82–93).

3  During the Georgian era, medicine could analyse the effects of morbidity in a number of different areas of the body, but to the physician, the workings of the mind remained an enigma. Medical cures involved leeching the blood, blistering the skin, purging the system. Whether morbidity of the nervous system, excess blood in the body, or hormonal imbalances caused madness was not known; what was known and feared was that madness, just as any excess of passion might suggest, rendered a person completely helpless. Common observations as remnants of eighteenth-century thought led to the belief that, when a person became completely dependent on imagination, on a world of visions or invisible forms of the mind, they must be mad.

4  Baillie describes in her Introductory Discourse how perception operates in the theatre, in terms which explain this shadowy vision: 'We behold heroes and great men at a distance, unmarked by those small but distinguished features of the mind, which give a certain individuality to such an infinite variety of similar beings, in the near and familiar intercourse of life. They appear to us from this view like distant mountains, whose dark outlines we trace in the clear horizon, but the varieties of whose roughened sides, shaded with heath and brushwood, and seamed with many a cleft, we perceive not' (I. 28).

## REFERENCES AND FURTHER READING

Allen, Elizabeth (ed.) *Hunterian Museum*, London, Royal College of Surgeons, 1974.

Anon., Review of 'Series of Plays on the Passions', *Critical Review* 24 (Sept. 1798) 13–22.

—— Review of 'Series of Plays on the Passions', *Monthly Review* 2nd series, 27 (Sept. 1798) 66–9.

—— Review of 'Series of Plays on the Passions', *British Critic* 13 (Jan. 1799) 284–8.

—— Review of 'Series of Plays on the Passions', *European Magazine* 37 (April 28, 1800) 384–5.

—— Review of 'Miscellaneous Plays', *Annual Register* 3 (July–Dec. 1805) 609–17.

Baillie, Joanna, *A Series of Plays on the Passions: in which it is Attempted to Delineate the Stronger Passions of the Mind*, 3 vols, London, T. Cadell, Jr. and W. Davies, 1798–1812.

—— *Miscellaneous Plays*, vol. 1, London, Longman, 1804.

—— *Miscellaneous Plays*, 3 vols, London, Longman, 1836.

—— *The Family Legend*, Edinburgh, Ballantyne, 1810.

—— *Metrical Legends of Exalted Characters*, London, Longman, 1821.

—— *The Dramatic and Poetical Works of Joanna Baillie*, London, Longman, 1851.

Baillie, Matthew, *The Morbid Anatomy of Some of the Most Important Parts of the Human Body*, London, J. Johnson and G. Nichol, 1795; 2nd edn J. Johnson, 1797.

Berry, Mary, *Extracts of the Journals and Correspondence of Miss Berry*, ed. Lady Theresa Lewis, 2 vols, London, Longman, 1865.

Boaden, James, *Memoirs of the Life of John Philip Kemble*, London, 1825.

Burroughs, Catherine Beau, *The Characterization of the Feminine in the Drama of the English Romantic Poets*, dissertation, Emory University, 1988.

Burwick, Frederick, *Illusion and the Drama: Critical Theory of the Enlightenment and Romantic Era*, University Park, Pennsylvania State University Press, 1991.

—— *Poetic Madness*, University Park, Pennsylvania State University Press, 1996.

Campbell, Thomas, Review of 'Series of Plays on the Passions', *New Monthly Magazine* 5 (Sept. 1798) 507–9.

—— *Memoirs of Mrs Siddons*, 2 vols, London, n.p., 1834.

Carhart, Margaret, *The Life and Work of Joanna Baillie*, New Haven, Yale University Press, 1923; Archon, 1970.

Carlson, Julie A., *In the Theatre of Romanticism: Coleridge, Nationalism, Women*, Cambridge, Cambridge University Press, 1994.

Cox, Jeffrey, *In the Shadows of Romance: Romantic Tragic Drama in Germany, England, and France*, Athens, Ohio, Ohio University Press, 1987.

Knight, David, *The Age of Science: The Scientific Worldview in the Nineteenth Century*, Oxford, Blackwell, 1986.

Patten, Janice, *Dark Imagination: Poetic Painting in Romantic Drama*, Ph.D. dissertation, University of California, Santa Cruz, 1992.

Ross, Marlon, *The Contours of Masculine Desire: Romanticism and the Rise of Women's Poetry*, New York, Oxford University Press, 1989.

Wordsworth, Jonathan, Introduction to *A Series of Plays: 1798*, Spelsbury, Woodstock Books, 1990.

# 16

# William Wordsworth, *The Prelude*

## *Jonathan Wordsworth*

*The Prelude* was written in four major stages, or versions, over a seven-year period, 1798–1805, but not published till after Wordsworth's death in 1850. It is the great epic of human consciousness, measuring Wordsworth's own position against the aspirations of Milton and the thinking of Coleridge. Milton saw his Christian epic, *Paradise Lost*, as replacing Homer and Virgil. Wordsworth noted the progression and, in an extraordinary passage of 1805, Book III, confidently added himself to the list. It is not that he regards his work as post-Christian, but that he has taken for his theme the human mind, a subject truly modern, without earlier parallel:

> Of genius, power,
> Creation and divinity itself
> I have been speaking, for my theme has been
> What passed within me! Not of outward things
> Done visibly for other minds – words, signs,
> Symbols, or actions – but of my own heart
> Have I been speaking, and my youthful mind. (1805: III. 171–6)[1]

Coleridge, in whose terms Wordsworth was 'at least a semi-atheist', must have found these lines disquieting. They have a bravura which exceeds his most outspoken Unitarian assertions, and hardly square with the Trinitarian orthodoxy he was by now trying to accept. Yet they are clearly related to his own claims for the grandeur of the human imagination. Wordsworth's tones are almost contemptuous as he speaks of his predecessors, who have written the old-fashioned epic of action, battle, 'outward things / Done visibly for other minds'. He himself has looked inward, and found 'genius, power, / Creation and divinity itself'. There could hardly be a grander assertion, but it is not the egotism that it might seem. Wordsworth is strongly aware of his own individuality – 'Points have we all of us within our souls / Where all stand single' (ibid., ll. 186–7) – yet rests his claim for the new epic on a godlike capacity that we are assumed to have in common: 'there's not a man / That lives who hath not had his godlike hours' (ibid., ll. 191–2).

Wordsworth is writing in January 1804, a week or two before completing *Ode, Intimations of Immortality from Recollections of Early Childhood*. *The Prelude* has been in abeyance for two years; he takes it up now, aware that it is going to be a longer poem than he had predicted, and announces as his theme 'the might of souls, / And what they do within themselves while yet / The yoke of earth is new to them' (ibid., ll. 178–80). 'This', he tells us, 'is in truth heroic argument / And genuine prowess' (ibid., ll. 182–3). Both halves of the sentence come as a surprise. The words are an allusion, however, and we are expected to notice the source. Faced with describing the Fall of Man in *Paradise Lost* Book IX, Milton had compared his task to those of Homer and Virgil:

> sad task, yet argument
> Not less but more heroic than the wrath
> Of stern Achilles on his foe, pursued
> Thrice fugitive about Troy wall; or rage
> Of Turnus for Lavinia disespoused . . . (13–17)

Prowess, shown in turn, by the *Iliad*, singing the deeds of Grecian heroes; by its sophisticated Latin counterpart, the *Aeneid*, telling of the founding of Rome and Roman values; and by Milton's seventeenth-century English adaptation of pagan form to Christian purposes, will be shown by Wordsworth himself in a revelation of the godlike nature of man – the 'majestic sway we have / As beings in the strength of nature' (1805: III. 193–4). Though quietly introduced, this is one of *The Prelude*'s major rethinkings of the Coleridgean higher imagination. For both poets, imagination is the godlike faculty unique in man's nature. Coleridge would not dissent from the view that it gives to man 'majestic sway' over the natural world. But the thought that it does so 'in the strength of nature' is essentially Wordsworthian. In exercising his 'sway' over nature, man demonstrates a power belonging to nature herself, of which he, man, is part.

Wordsworth's confidence in what he is doing is all the more astonishing if one looks back to the origins of *The Prelude*. The first brief version of October 1798, *Was It For This* (*WIFT*), begins fluently but tentatively. Wordsworth is thinking his way through a problem:

> Was it for this
> That one, the fairest of all rivers, loved
> To blend his murmurs with my nurse's song,
> And from his alder shades and rocky falls,
> And from his fords and shallows, sent a voice
> To intertwine my dreams? For this didst thou,
> O Derwent, travelling over the green plains
> Near my sweet birth-place, didst thou, beauteous stream,
> Give ceaseless music to the night and day,
> Which with its steady cadence tempering
> Our human waywardness, composed my thoughts
> To more than infant softness, giving me
> Amid the fretful tenements of man
> A knowledge, a dim earnest, of the calm
> That nature breathes among her woodland haunts?
> Was it for this . . . (*WIFT*, 1–16)

In the manuscript the poem starts not only in mid-line, but with a small 'w'. It is a very unobtrusive beginning – almost, it seems, accidental. Wordsworth doesn't know that he has embarked on a major poem. Yet his thoughts fall instinctively into blank verse. Coleridge and Milton are present already, looking over his shoulder: Coleridge in the quotation from *Frost at Midnight*, 'my sweet birth-place', at line eight; Milton in the urgent, rhetorical questioning – 'Was it for this... For this didst thou / O Derwent... Was it for this...?' The pattern had been used by others, Pope and Thomson among them, but it takes us more importantly to *Samson Agonistes*. 'For this', Manoah asks his blinded and imprisoned son,

> did the angel twice descend? For this
> Ordained thy nurture holy, as of a plant
> Select and sacred? (361–3)

Wordsworth, it seems, as he begins what turns out to be *The Prelude*, thinks of himself as having been singled out, and as failing. The task on which he should have been at work was *The Recluse*, the great philosophical poem that Coleridge had six months earlier persuaded him it was his duty to write. Looking back to his 'nurture' among the Cumbrian mountains, he felt reproached. With such a childhood to prepare him, surely he should have been able to get on? But as the reproaches prompt his memory, new and more productive questions are raised. What is the nature of these early experiences? How do they contribute to adult strength, consciousness, creativity? Moving on to ask, and answer, these questions, Wordsworth comes upon what is the great theme of *The Prelude* in all its stages and versions: education.

*Was It For This* is immensely important, showing us how quickly, and how inevitably, the theme of education is established. In 150 lines – just six paragraphs – Wordsworth creates a new idiom. In place of the public poetry and grand affirmations of *Tintern Abbey* (written only three months before), we hear the voice of *The Prelude*. *Tintern Abbey* is the seminal poem of the Romantic age, quoted, touched upon, imitated, again and again; yet it is a sequel to Coleridge's *Frost at Midnight*, and offers in its affirmations a version of Coleridge's early Unitarian faith. *Was It For This* is Wordsworth with no sources but the memory, imagination and speculative power of his own mind. At once we are offered 'spots of time' (isolated memories, made vivid by the imagination that is itself, in part, the subject of the poetry):

> Oh, when I have hung
> Above the raven's nest, have hung alone
> By half-inch fissures in the slippery rock
> But ill sustained, and almost (as it seemed)
> Suspended by the wind which blew amain... (*WIFT*, 37–41)

and at once we are offered the ruminative voice, that takes a larger, longer view, thinking things through as we listen. The forces that govern human education

> love to interweave
> The passions that build up our human soul

> Not with the mean and vulgar works of man,
> But with high objects, with eternal things,
> With life and nature, purifying thus
> The elements of feeling and of thought,
> And sanctifying by such discipline
> Both pain and fear, until we recognize
> A grandeur in the beatings of the heart. (*WIFT*, 50–8)

The final line might almost stand as a definition of imagination. As Keats put it, 'I am certain of nothing but of the holiness of the Heart's affections and the truth of Imagination' (to Bailey, 22 November 1817).[2] Wordsworth would have agreed, but as an instinctive follower of Burke on the sublime he tended to associate 'the beatings of the heart' with fear, pain, guilt. *Was It For This* contains not merely the birds-nesting episode, by the wood-cock-snaring; within a matter of days, Wordsworth would go on to write the boat-stealing, thus completing the first three 'spots of time' of the 1799 two-part *Prelude*, all of them showing the power of the sublime.

Not that he discounts the beautiful. At this stage (perhaps at all stages) he associates it with 'those first-born affinities which fit / Our new existence to existing things' (*WIFT*, 120–1), the bonding of the child and nature that precedes education through the sublime. The cadence of the River Derwent, blending its murmurs with his nurse's song, is our introduction to this way of thinking, but *Was It For This* includes, too, a unique passage ascribing the 'first-born affinities' to the work of a Platonic eternal spirit, the 'soul of things':

> he who painting what he is in all
> The visible imagery of all the worlds
> Is yet apparent chiefly as the soul
> Of our first sympathies (*WIFT*, 106–9)

It is the child's partaking of this world-soul that enables him, in this original *Prelude* version, to hold

> unconscious intercourse
> With the eternal beauty, drinking in
> A pure organic pleasure from the lines
> Of curling mist, or from the smooth expanse
> Of waters coloured by the cloudless moon. (*WIFT*, 127–31)

*Was It For This* did not simply grow into the 1799 *Prelude*. Wordsworth rethought his poem. Soon after Christmas 1798 he defined for himself a link between childhood imaginative experience and adult creativity:

> There are in our existence spots of time
> That with distinct preeminence retain
> A fructifying virtue, whence, depressed
> By trivial occupations and the round
> Of ordinary intercourse, our minds –

Especially the imaginative power –
Are nourished and invisibly repaired (1799: I. 288–94)

The key to this, and to the three 'spots' that cluster round Wordsworth's definition, appears in a link-passage that is, for no obvious reason, left out of the 1805 and 1850 versions of *The Prelude*. 'I might advert', Wordsworth writes, 'To numerous accidents in flood or field':

> tragic facts
> Of rural history that impressed my mind
> With images to which in following years
> Far other feelings were attached – with forms
> That yet exist with independent life,
> And, like their archetypes, know no decay. (Ibid., 279–87)

What is being described is an associative process within the mind that relies on Hartley's *Observations on Man* (reissued 1791), and ultimately on Locke, but which is peculiarly Wordsworthian in its application. Response to tragic occurrences in the region, traditional or recent, has the effect of 'impressing' (imprinting, stamping) images upon the mind – images of places where the occurrences took place, or where the poet heard of them. Over the years these images are visited, and revisited, within the mind, becoming the focus of new imaginative feelings, such as the child could not have had.

It is the process that is described in *The Pedlar* of spring 1798:

> In such communion, not from terror free . . .
> He had perceived the presence and the power
> Of greatness, and deep feelings had impressed
> Great objects on his mind with portraiture
> And colour so distinct that on his mind
> They lay like substances, and almost seemed
> To haunt the bodily sense. (30–4)

It is the process that leads on Wordsworth's first visit to Tintern Abbey to his storing-up of the 'forms of beauty' that later have such influence on his mind. And it is the process that underlies the imagery of association in *Was It For This*. More especially, it explains Wordsworth's reference to the 'characters' (handwriting) of 'danger and desire', which, 'impressed' through 'the agency of boyish sports' onto the Cumbrian landscape, have power to make

> The surface of the universal earth
> With meanings of delight, of hope and fear,
> Work like a sea. (*WIFT*, 69–75)

The new emphasis present in Wordsworth's *1799* link-passage is upon continuity and permanence: the 'forms' (images) stamped upon the mind *yet* (still, at the time of writing) exist, with their independent life, achieving within the mind a permanence comparable to that of their 'archetypes' (the landscapes, natural forms, from which they derive). With this as our introduction to the 'spots of time' definition, it is clear that we should expect the 'spots' to be not just memories where time stands still, but images, pictures in the mind, imprinted as the result of more than usually important emotional experience.

The final 'spot' of 1799 Part I shows the process at work. First we see the child, 'feverish, and tired, and restless', waiting on the hill above his school at Hawkshead for horses that will take him and his brothers home for the Christmas holidays. Then we cut to his father's sudden death:

> Ere I to school returned
> That dreary time, ere I had been ten days
> A dweller in my father's house, he died,
> And I and my two brothers (orphans then)
> Followed his body to the grave. The event,
> With all the sorrow which it brought, appeared
> A chastisement; and when I called to mind
> That day so lately passed, when from the crag
> I looked in such anxiety of hope,
> With trite reflections of morality,
> Yet with the deepest passion, I bowed low
> To God who thus corrected my desires. (1799: I. 349–60)

Revisiting the Hawkshead landscape in his remorseful mind, the child attaches to it 'far other feelings' than the hope with which it had so recently been associated. But Wordsworth is not merely writing about an episode in his past, he is telling us of its importance for the present. The details of the landscape become 'spectacles and sounds' to which he consciously returns to 'drink as at a fountain'. 'And I do not doubt', he concludes impressively,

> That in this later time, when storm and rain
> Beat on my roof at midnight, or by day
> When I am in the woods, unknown to me
> The workings of my spirit thence are brought. (Ibid., 368–74)

The Hawkshead landscape – associated first with 'anxiety of hope', next with guilty thoughts that the child is responsible for his father's death – changes, over the 15-year period before the poetry is written, into a source of strength, support for the workings of the adult poet's spirit. This time Wordsworth is no more able than we are to say what has taken place. These are experiences of the mind,

> Which, be they what they may,
> Are yet the fountain-light of all our day,
> Are yet the master light of all our seeing. (*Intimations*, 153–5)

1799 Part I has it in common with *Was It For This* that it deals primarily in terms of an education through the sublime. At a secondary stage, however, Wordsworth inserts the skating episode (lines 150–98) and the 'home amusements' section (lines 198–233), designed to show that his boyhood was not always lonely and subject to fear and guilt. And in Part II he takes his account of childhood through into adolescence, consciously offering beauty as a sequel to the sublime:

> But ere the fall
> Of night, when in our pinnace we returned
> Over the dusky lake, and to the beach
> Of some small island steered our course, with one,
> The minstrel of our troop, and left him there,
> And rowed off gently while he blew his flute
> Alone upon the rock, oh, then the calm
> And dead still water lay upon my mind
> Even with a weight of pleasure, and the sky,
> Never before so beautiful, sank down
> Into my heart and held me like a dream. (1799: II.204–14)

In Part II, as in Part I, we are offered vivid personal memories, intensified within the mind because they are associated with particular landscapes. Halfway through the part, however, Wordsworth becomes aware that he has unfinished business. Having dropped from his text the *Was It For This* sequence on the eternal spirit, he has left himself with no answer to the question, what *does* enable us to 'fit our new existence / To existing things?' What *are* the origins of the imaginative power seen so vividly in his remembered early experience? The 'spots of time' told of memories by which the mind, 'especially the imaginative power', is nourished and made fruitful by its own self-generated power; but where did the power come from? Wordsworth's thoughts took him once again to Coleridge and to Milton – to Coleridge, to whom 'The unity of all [had] been revealed' (1799: II. 256), and to Milton, who had in *Paradise Lost* offered the Christian myth of origins that no longer seemed sufficient.

No less than Milton, Wordsworth felt it to be his task to 'trace / The progress of our being' (1799: II. 268–9), but he did so, not from the Garden of Eden, but from an infant at the breast:

> blest the babe
> Nursed in his mother's arms, the babe who sleeps
> Upon his mother's breast, who when his soul
> Claims manifest kindred with an earthly soul
> Does gather passion from his mother's eye.

'Such feelings', Wordsworth continues,

> pass into his torpid life
> Like an awakening breeze, and hence his mind,
> Even in the first trial of its powers,
> Is prompt and watchful . . . (1799: II.269–77)

Clearly, he has *Was It For This* in his thoughts. 'Oh bounteous power', he had written, addressing the eternal spirit,

> In childhood, in rememberable days,
> How often did thy love renew for me
> Those naked feelings which when thou wouldst form
> A living thing thou sendest like a breeze
> Into its infant being. (*WIFT*, 109–14)

In each case the 'awakening breeze' of life is associated with love, but the Platonic eternal spirit gives place in the 1799 *Prelude* to the tenderness of a human mother. Along the child's 'infant veins are interfused', not the pantheist 'something far more deeply interfused' of *Tintern Abbey*, but

> The gravitation and the filial bond
> Of nature that connect him to the world. (1799: II.292–4)

As in *Was It For This* Wordsworth is concerned with 'those first-born affinities which fit / Our new existence to existing things', but now it is the gravitational pull of nature (personalized in the mother's love) that makes the infant part of the world in which he lives.

The mother's effect upon her child, it has to be said, is extraordinary. He becomes not merely 'prompt and watchful', capable (as we should expect) of the associative process of storing up images, but also 'powerful in all sentiments of grief, / Of exultation, fear, and joy' (1799: II.300–1). Two things are happening at once within the poetry: we are to see the child both as the credible human infant, and, symbolically, as the poet in embryo – one whose mind,

> Even as an agent of the one great mind,
> Creates, creator and receiver both . . . (Ibid., 302–3)

In the terms that Coleridge will later use in *Biographia Literaria*, the child is, from his earliest days, a fully imaginative being. Capable at once of creation and perception, he exercises the full powers of the primary imagination. At the day-to-day level he orders experience, builds the parts of his universe into a whole; as 'an agent of the one great mind', he performs the higher imaginative act that is 'a repetition in the finite mind of the eternal act of creation in the Infinite I AM' (God's eternal creative assertion of self, that brings into existence the other). As he grows, the child will develop – through the beautiful influence of his mother, through the more often sublime influence of nature – but already his imaginative capacity has been established.

That the two-part *Prelude* should end in a farewell to Coleridge is doubly appropriate. In the first place, Coleridge had decided in early December 1799, when Wordsworth was writing, to pursue his career as a journalist in London, leaving William and Dorothy to establish themselves in their new Lake District home at Dove Cottage, Grasmere. In the second, Wordsworth's poem had been from the outset addressed to his friend. The quotation from *Frost at Midnight* in Part I, line eight (originally *WIFT*, 8) had signalled this fact, and now, in rounding off Part II, Wordsworth alludes again to the same poem: 'Thou, my friend, wast reared / In the great city, mid far other scenes' (1799: II.496–7). Throughout Wordsworth's life *The Prelude* was to be known as 'The Poem' to Coleridge;

until the later revisions, each successive version is in some new way importantly bound up with him and his thinking. Each, it should be said, is also more strongly Miltonic than the last.

An effort was made in December 1801 to extend the 1799 poem into a third part, taking the study of Wordsworth's education up to his Cambridge days. After 167 lines, however (mostly old material, drawn from *The Pedlar*), the attempt broke down. It took the impetus of Coleridge's imminent departure for the Mediterranean in early 1804 to get Wordsworth restarted. On 4 January Coleridge records in his notebook a reading of 'the second part of [William's] divine self-biography' in 'the highest and outermost of Grasmere' (Easedale, perhaps?). Ten days later he leaves for London. Wordsworth falls to work, and by early March has at least nearly completed a *Prelude* in five books for Coleridge to take with him on his voyage. Then suddenly, around the tenth of the month, he takes it apart, and begins work on a still longer, and radically different, version. All texts of *The Prelude* (even the first edition) have their problems. *Was It For This*, however, is in the poet's hand, the 1799 and 1805 *Preludes* exist in duplicate fair-copies; the five-book poem has to be reconstructed from drafts and imperfect manuscripts. For all this, it is a poem of great importance. Broadly speaking, it consists of the first three books of the 1805 text, followed by a fourth containing the bulk of the material in 1805's Parts IV and V, and a fifth made up of the 'spots of time' sequence (revised and augmented as in 1805 Part XI), plus the Climbing of Snowdon (finally 1805: XIII.1–65). As always, education is Wordsworth's theme. Imagination, built up through childhood and adolescence among the mountains, is impaired by exposure at Cambridge to sophistication and artificiality. Through the workings of the 'spots of time', however, it is restored ('nourished and invisibly repaired'), and the poem shows it at its new adult height in the epiphany on Snowdon. With its Miltonic paradise-lost-and-regained structure, it is (or was, or would have been) a highly impressive work. Why, then, did Wordsworth dismember it? Not so much, probably, because he was dissatisfied, as because, like Penelope, he dared not finish his task. Coleridge had agreed that *The Prelude* should form part of *The Recluse*, but the central philosophical section still had to be written. An attempt to write it in *Home at Grasmere* (spring 1801) had merely shown how great was the problem. Wordsworth had no system to offer. Only Coleridge could supply such a thing, and he now (March 1804) was leaving for Malta, perhaps in fact dying. Hearing on the 29th that he has been dangerously ill, Wordsworth writes: 'I would gladly have given 3 fourths of my possessions for your letter on *The Recluse* . . . I cannot say what a load it would be to me, should I survive you, and you die without this memorial left behind.'

No notes on *The Recluse* were forthcoming (at one point Coleridge claimed that they had been written, and sent off, but unfortunately burnt when his messenger died of the plague). In their absence, Wordsworth reworked his material, sent Coleridge 1805 Books, I–V to take abroad, put Snowdon and the 'spots of time' on one side for future use, and embarked on Book VI. With the subject of his undergraduate travels through France in 1790, he introduced into his poem revolutionary politics. It is fairly certain that after completing Book VI in late March, he went on to write IX and the first half of X, carrying his readers up to the death of Robespierre. In the autumn of 1804 he added VIII (retrospect of childhood) and VII (London as Underworld), before completing X (politics and alienation in post-Revolutionary London). After a pause marking the death of

Wordsworth's brother, John, in February 1805, the poem was brought to a conclusion with three brief final books: XI (incorporating the 'spots of time', set aside from the five-book *Prelude*), XII (producing the poet's definition of 'the ennobling interchange / Of action from within and from without', lines 376–7) and XIII, with its climactic ascent of Snowdon.

*The Prelude* emerges as a poem not merely of different versions, but of essentially different structures. Though it is in a sense autobiography, it nowhere attempts to tell the story of Wordsworth's life. Even the 1799 version, where the division into childhood and adolescence appears straightforward, in fact disregards chronology. Of the major 'spots of time', the first takes place when the child is nine, the second when he is five, the third when he is thirteen. By the same token, in the 1805 version the Climbing of Snowdon should chronologically have been placed between Wordsworth's two visits to France, but is reserved to form a conclusion. Book VII (including London experiences of 1793–5) is placed for overall effect, as a descent into hell after the sublime of the Alps, and followed in VIII by a retrospect of childhood.

Four great similes show Wordsworth's awareness of the complexity of his structures. 'Who that shall point as with a wand', he demands in 1799 Part II, 'and say / "This portion of the river of my mind / Came from yon fountain?"' (lines 247–9). In 1805 Book V we see him 'Incumbent o'er the surface of past time', attempting from his boat to distinguish on the bottom of a lake 'The shadow from the substance' (lines 247–64). 'As oftentimes a river', Wordsworth writes at the opening of Book IX,

> Turns and will measure back his course – far back,
> Towards the very regions which he crossed
> In his first outset – so have we long time
> Made motions retrograde . . . (1–9)

And in Book XIII we have, in the last of these water-images of *The Prelude*, a tracing of the stream of imagination which is in effect a synopsis of the poem itself:

> we have traced the stream
> From darkness and the very place of birth
> In its blind cavern, whence is faintly heard
> The sound of waters; followed it to light
> And open day, accompanied its course
> Among the ways of nature, afterwards
> Lost sight of it bewildered and engulfed,
> Then given it greeting as it rose once more
> With strength, reflecting in its solemn breast
> The works of man and face of human life . . . (172–81)

Wordsworth is structuring his poem, telling us what to see and how to read.

Finally, the unity of *The Prelude* depends upon our sense of the mind that is at its centre, the consciousness of the adult poet looking into the deep that is his own identity, examining the emotions of the child whose mind is, and is not, his own. The Climbing of Snowdon is the ultimate achievement, and revelation, of this mind.

Ascending the mountain by night, the poet emerges into the moonlight above the clouds: 'on the shore / I found myself of a huge sea of mist, / Which meek and silent rested at my feet' (1805: XIII.42–4). For the last time in the poem the beautiful gives way to the sublime, as Wordsworth singles out from his moonscape the strange chasm at its centre:

> And from the shore
> At distance not the third part of a mile
> Was a blue chasm, a fracture in the vapour,
> A deep and gloomy breathing-place through which
> Mounted the roar of waters, torrents, streams
> Innumerable, roaring with one voice! (Ibid., 54–9)

In this 'dark deep thoroughfare', we are told, has 'nature lodged / The soul, the imagination, of the whole' (Ibid., 64–5). It is a strange, impressive claim, leading us to wonder at what seems to be Wordsworth's anticipation of modern concepts of the unconscious. The poetry needs no explication, but a year after composing the narrative of the ascent Wordsworth was prompted to add a gloss:

> A meditation rose in me that night
> Upon the lonely mountain when the scene
> Had passed away, and it appeared to me
> The perfect image of a mighty mind,
> Of one that feeds upon infinity,
> That is exalted by an underpresence,
> The sense of God, or whatsoe'er is dim
> Or vast in its own being. (Ibid., 66–73)

The landscape as a whole has become a mind 'that feeds upon infinity', but the infinity upon which it feeds comes from within, welling up through the 'deep and gloomy breathing-place' as 'the roar of waters, torrents, streams / Innumerable'. The streams, we have noticed, roar 'with one voice', achieving unity, wholeness. And Wordsworth has dignified them already in his reference to 'the soul, the imagination' that is 'lodged' in the cloud-rift. But nothing has led us to expect that he would gloss the 'underpresence' in terms of such grandeur, and such clarity. In words that show just how far he is prepared to go beyond Milton, beyond Coleridge, he tells us that it doesn't matter whether the highest achievement of the human imagination is a perception of God. It is equally important if it is a sense of that which is 'dim / Or vast in [our] own being'. Either way, it is the 'ennobling interchange / Of action from within and from without' that is his theme.

NOTES

1   All quotations from *The Prelude* are from the texts in *The Prelude: The Four Texts (1798, 1799, 1805,* *1850)*, ed. Jonathan Wordsworth, Harmondsworth, Penguin, 1995.

2   Rollins, I, 184.

## REFERENCES AND FURTHER READING

Gill, Stephen, (ed.) *William Wordsworth*, Oxford, Oxford University Press, 1984.

——*William Wordsworth: A Life*, Oxford, Oxford University Press, 1989.

Hartman, Geoffrey H., *Wordsworth's Poetry 1787–1814*, New Haven, Yale University Press, 1964.

Manning, Peter J., 'Reading Wordsworth's revision: Othello and the drowned man', in *Reading Romantics: Texts and Contexts*, New York, Oxford University Press, 1990, pp. 87–114.

Wordsworth, Jonathan, *William Wordsworth: The Borders of Vision*, Oxford, Clarendon Press, 1982.

# 17

# Poetry of the Anti-Jacobin

## John Strachan

During the 1790s, the impact of the French Revolution resounded through British intellectual life, in a debate initiated by Richard Price's enthusiastic *A Discourse on the Love of our Country* (1789) and Edmund Burke's antipathetic *Reflections on the Revolution in France* (1790) as to the merits or demerits of events across the Channel. On the radical side, the likes of Thomas Paine, William Godwin, Mary Wollstonecraft and Helen Maria Williams produced notable contributions to this 'Revolution Controversy'.[1] A new generation of poets also became identified with the pro-Revolutionary, or 'Jacobin', side: most notably Robert Southey and Samuel Taylor Coleridge, whom the Whig politician Lord Grey labelled 'interesting young enthusiasts in the Democratic cause'.[2] A number of periodicals, the most significant of which were the *Analytical Review* and the *Critical Review*, also propagandized for the radical interest. It is against this body of earnest, philanthropic, initially pro-French opinion that the satirical, Tory and vehemently patriotic journal the *Antijacobin* (1797–8) was aimed.

In the middle of the 1790s, the Tory government of William Pitt the younger, engaged in pursuing a war against the French which had begun in 1793, became increasingly concerned about the spread of radical ideas in England. August 1795 saw massive demonstrations in favour of radical reform and, in November 1795, the month after an anti-monarchical riot at the state opening of parliament, the government introduced the so-called 'Gagging Acts', which prohibited meetings of more than 50 people unless specifically licensed by a magistrate and introduced measures censoring the press. However, despite these attempts to control the dissemination of radical ideas, periodical publishing in the mid-1790s remained 'disproportionately "liberal"',[3] whether radical (the *Analytical*, the *Critical*) or Whiggish (the *Monthly*, the *Morning Chronicle*).[4] Though the *British Critic* campaigned vigorously against Whiggism and Jacobinism, and though Pitt's government had sponsored loyalist publications during the first half of the decade (*The True Briton* and *The Sun*),[5] these journals had comparatively little success. In response to what they saw as a dangerous oppositional press consensus, a group of young Tories initiated a new periodical, the *Antijacobin*, or *Weekly Examiner*, to redress the balance. Published weekly, on Mondays during the sitting of parliament, between 20 November 1797 and 9 July 1798, the *Antijacobin* was intended to expose what it uncompromisingly labelled the 'MISTAKES', 'MISREPRESENTATIONS' and 'LIES' of anti-governmental writing, be it journalistic, philosophical or poetical. The 'Prospectus' to the first number sets out the periodical's position clearly:

> in one word, of JACOBINISM in all its shapes, and in all its degrees, political and moral, public and private, whether as it openly threatens the subversion of States, or gradually saps the foundations of domestic happiness, We are the avowed, determined, and irreconcileable enemies.[6]

The *Antijacobin* stuck to these principles throughout its 36 issues, ceasing publication with the proud boast that 'The Spell of Jacobin invulnerability is now broken'.[7]

The main contributors to the paper were George Canning (1770–1827), George Ellis (1753–1815), John Hookham Frere (1769–1846) and William Gifford (1756–1826). The first three were Tory members of parliament. Canning, the *quondam* Whig who would go on to become a Tory prime minister during the 1820s, was undersecretary of state for foreign affairs. Ellis, who was a friend of Sir Walter Scott (and a fellow antiquarian), had achieved a literary reputation as the editor of the *Specimens of Early English Poets* (1790). Though now a Tory, Ellis had once been an oppositionalist and during the previous decade he had contributed to the *Rolliad* (1784–5), *ad hominem* satire on Pitt and his administration. Both Canning and Ellis were disillusioned Whigs who had transferred their political allegiance under the influence of Burke. Though Frere and Gifford were lifelong Tories, it is important to realize that the *Antijacobin* was, in part, prompted by the crisis in English liberalism caused by the Revolution. Canning, who according to Sir Walter Scott had been approached by William Godwin in the earlier 1790s to lead the English Jacobins,[8] was prompted into conservatism by the same motives as Burke and the Portland Whigs. Though it happens earlier, his trajectory into Toryism resembles that of Wordsworth and Coleridge. The *Poetry of the Anti-Jacobin* has much in common with that other landmark in the poetry of the late 1790s, Coleridge's *Poems of Political Recantation*.

Canning's school friend from Eton College, Frere, was also in the Foreign Office. Frere's most notable work is *Whistlecraft* (1817–18), a poem informed by Italian informal satire and written in *ottava rima*, which inspired Byron's *Beppo* and influenced that greatest of all radical satires, *Don Juan*. The *Antijacobin* was edited by William Gifford, a former apprentice cobbler who had some success with two neo-classical literary satires in the style of Pope during the earlier 1790s: *The Baviad* (1791) and *The Maeviad* (1795). Featuring largely in both poems is politically motivated, often spectacularly spiteful, satire on the Jacobinical poet Robert Merry and his Della Cruscan school.[9] Gifford would later go on to edit the High Tory *Quarterly Review*, where one of his main contributors was a former radical, Robert Southey, who had felt the lash of the *Antijacobin*'s parody.

The *Antijacobin* would only be of minor historical importance if its pages were solely limited to polemical journalism such as Gifford's intemperate repudiations of the liberal press. It is for its poetry, and in particular its satire and parody, that the periodical is significant. This body of writing, which from the first was recognized as the most innovative part of the *Antijacobin*, was collected by Gifford in 1799 as the *Poetry of the Anti-Jacobin*.[10] Not all of the poetry is humorous. There are, for example, patriotic verses in Latin and dull poetical diatribes against the French delivered *ex cathedra* by Tory correspondents. Hely Addington's *The Invasion; or, the British War Song* gives a flavour of this aspect of the *Antijacobin*:

> Let France in savage accents sing
> Her bloody Revolution;
> We prize our country, love our King,
> Adore our Constitution;[11]

However, such inanities are mercifully rare; what separates the *Antijacobin* from the bilious pro-ministerial stance of the *British Critic* or the later poor imitation, the *Antijacobin Review and Magazine* (which replaced venomous satire with venom, pure and simple)[12] is the verve and panache of its comic writing. The book offers a variety of comic styles: parodic imitations of contemporary authors, cod medieval ballads and imitations of classical, notably Horatian, satire. In particular, it is the politically motivated parody of the *Antijacobin*, what Canning called its 'Jacobinical imitations' of left-wing verse, which makes it significant.

The political targets of the *Poetry of the Anti-Jacobin* are manifold: the villainy of the French, the treachery of the Irish, the hypocrisy of the Whigs, the philanthropic cant of the radical:

> Liberty's friends thus all learn to amalgamate,
> Freedom's volcanic explosion prepares itself,
> Despots shall bow to the Fasces of Liberty,
>    Reason, philosophy, 'fiddledum diddledum'
>    Peace and Fraternity, 'higgledy, piggledy'
>    Higgledy, piggledy, 'fiddledum, diddledum'.
>      *Et caetera, et caetera, et caetera.*[13]

There is an extensive cast of villains traduced in this body of parodic and satirical writing: politicians (Fox, Grey, Sheridan and the Whig opposition); misguided clerics who support reform (Priestley, Wakefield); the radical Jacobins (Paine, Holcroft, Thelwall and Godwin). All are mockingly condemned for their enthusiasm for the French Revolution. As well as berating politicians and philosophers for their dangerous and irresponsible views, the contributors are also preoccupied with the repudiation of subversive, Jacobin poetry. They see no clear distinction between politics and imaginative literature. Contemporary poetry is inextricably placed within the context of the quotidian. The *Poetry of the Anti-Jacobin* parodies many of the popular literary forms of the age: Darwinian didactic couplets, Orientalism, sentimentalism, Gothic, antiquarian interest in balladry, German drama. All are politicized genres to the *Anti-Jacobin* parodists, who are acutely aware of the ideological subtexts of contemporary literature. For Canning, the muse is keeping bad company. Contemporary poetry is in the hands of the radical; Canning wryly laments in the first number 'that good morals, and what we should call good politics, are inconsistent with the spirit of true Poetry'.[14] Accordingly, the *Antijacobin* attacks the spirit of reform evident in contemporary letters. There are glances at non-poetical literature: Inchbald's translations of German drama and the Jacobin novel for example. However, the main emphasis is upon oppositionalist poetry. Poets are working in alliance with politicians to subvert the state. The *Antijacobin* attacked what it saw as the Jacobinical, pro-French position of many contemporary intellectuals and poets. *The Poetry of the Anti-Jacobin* targets the genteel liberals who pollute the Popean didactic poem with 'the coy Muse of *Jacobinism*':[15] Erasmus Darwin, author of *The Botanic Garden* (1792), and Richard Payne Knight, Whig MP and author of *The Progress of Civil Society, a Didactic Poem in Six Books* (1796). Inevitably, the philosopher and novelist Godwin, the whipping boy of numerous satirical novels in the late eighteenth and early nineteenth centuries,[16] figures as a major target of the *Poetry of the Anti-Jacobin*. Godwin becomes 'Mr Higgins of St Mary Axe' (glances at his wife and his supposed enthusiasm for the guillotine). Mr Higgins, poet and dramatist, supposedly writes some of the major parodies of the *Poetry of the Anti-Jacobin*: (*The Progress of Man, The Loves of the Triangles, The Rovers*). He is presented as an indefatigable radical who uses literature (didactic poetry, the currently modish German drama) to propagandize for the Jacobin cause. He boasts that his play, *The Rovers; or the Double Arrangement*, is a consummate piece of literary subversion: 'a Play: which, if it has a proper run, will, I think, do much to unhinge the present notions of men with regard to the obligations of Civil Society'. The work will foster 'a contemptuous disgust at all that *is*, and a persuasion that nothing is as it ought to be'.[17] Godwin/ Higgins, the philosopher and man of letters, is the representative of the twin-pronged assault on 'Civil Society'. As ever for the *Antijacobin*, politics and imaginative literature are inseparable.

As well as satirizing Godwin, the *Antijacobin* mocks the Jacobinical poets Southey and Coleridge, who fuse revolutionary politics with metrical experiment and thematic innovation. Parody is a key weapon in this attack on Jacobinical poetry. For Canning, contemporary poetry has become wedded to subversion. He lightheartedly worries that no right-thinking poetry can be found to leaven the pages of the *Antijacobin*: 'we have not been able to find one good and true poet, of sound principles and sober practice, upon whom we could rely for furnishing us with a handsome quantity of sufficient and approved verse'.[18] Accordingly, the periodical resolved to borrow from the 'Jacobin Muse' and offer 'imitations' (or parodies) of the 'Bards of Freedom'. Aware that one parody has more force than ten bromides on the iniquities of Jacobinism, Canning and his colleagues send up the range of liberal poetry of the 1790s.

They begin with Southey. The *Antijacobin* is sensitive to a nascent Romanticism, the as yet unnamed new poetical spirit of the age, with its 'love of all human kind',[19] millenarianism, and philanthropic animadversions on the injustice meted out to the poor. In the very first number of the *Antijacobin*, Canning writes of a 'NEW SCHOOL' of poetry and the early numbers parody its sympathy for the dispossessed. Southey's poetical efforts to discuss what he described in 1797 as the 'incalculable wretchedness of the poor'[20] are met with a resounding poetic raspberry from the *Poetry of the Anti-Jacobin*. 1798, the year of the *Lyrical Ballads*, is also the year of a marvellously assured counter-affirmation to the new valorization of the experience of the rural poor. In *The Friend of Humanity and the Knife-Grinder*, Canning and Frere's parody of Southey's *The Widow*, the philanthropist, in true Wordsworthian style, interrogates a ragged knife-grinder as to the antecedents of his dishevelled appearance and poverty. Inevitably, he assumes that the knife-grinder's poverty is the consequence of an unjust and tyrannical political regime and that his salvation lies in Paineite republican enthusiasm:

> Tell me, Knife-grinder, how came you to grind knives?
> Did some rich man tyrannically use you?
> Was it the squire? or parson of the parish?
> Or the attorney? . . .
> (Have you not read the Rights of Man, by Tom Paine?)
> Drops of compassion tremble on my eyelids,
> Ready to fall as soon as you have told your
> Pitiful story[21]

It turns out that the knife-grinder is a beggar and wastrel whose clothes were torn in a drunken brawl the previous evening. Enraged by the man's attempt to cadge sixpence for more drink, the Friend of Humanity assaults him:

> '*I* give thee sixpence! I will see thee damn'd first –
> Wretch! whom no sense of wrongs can rouse to vengeance –
> Sordid, unfeeling, reprobate, degraded,
> Spiritless outcast!'

[Kicks the Knife-grinder, overturns his wheel, and exit in a transport of Republican enthusiasm and universal philanthropy.][22]

The very first parody of the *Poetry of the Anti-Jacobin*, Canning's *Inscription*, well illustrates the volume's parodic methodology. Southey's *Inscription IV, For the apartment in CHEPSTOW-CASTLE where HENRY MARTEN the regicide was imprisoned Thirty Years* (first published in 1797) glorifies the Cromwellian Marten, describing his confinement in the following terms:

> For thirty years secluded from mankind,
> Here Marten linger'd. Often have these walls
> Echoed his footsteps, as with even tread
> He paced around his prison . . .
>   Dost thou ask his crime?
> He had REBELL'D AGAINST THE KING, AND SAT
> IN JUDGMENT ON HIM; for his ardent mind
> Shaped goodliest plans of happiness on earth
> And peace and liberty. Wild dreams! But such
> As PLATO lov'd; such as with holy zeal
> Our MILTON worshipp'd. Blessed hopes! awhile
> From man withheld, even to the latter days,
> When CHRIST shall come and all things be fulfill'd.[23]

Southey's sonnet is millenarian, idealist, republican, an able piece of Jacobin martyrology. Canning takes Southey's sentiments and debunks them, achieving this by replacing Marten with the repellent figure of the double murderer Elizabeth Brownrigg, a villain familiar to the eighteenth-century reader from the *Newgate Calendar*, awaiting her execution, cursing and screaming for strong drink:

> For one long term, or e'er her Trial came,
> Here BROWNRIGG linger'd. Often have these cells

> Echoed her blasphemies, as with shrill voice
> She screamed for fresh Geneva. Not to her
> Did the blithe fields of Tothill, or thy street,
> St Giles, its fair varieties expand;
> Till at the last, in slow-drawn cart, she went
> To execution. Dost thou ask her crime?
> SHE WHIPP'D TWO FEMALE PRENTICES TO DEATH,
> AND HID THEM IN THE COAL-HOLE. For her mind
> Shaped strictest plans of discipline. Sage schemes!
> 　　　　　. . . such as erst chastised
> Our Milton, when at college. For this act
> Did Brownrigg swing. Harsh laws! but time shall come,
> When France shall reign, and laws be all repeal'd![24]

Through the idealization of the infamous Brownrigg, Southey's liberal criminology is made to appear morally repellent and his millenarianism an endorsement of lawless anarchy.

　　The hapless Southey also features in one of the highlights of the *Poetry of the Anti-Jacobin*, *New Morality*, a collaborative effort by Canning, Frere, Gifford and Ellis which was published in the last number of the *Antijacobin*. The poem takes aim at what were, by now, the usual Jacobin suspects: Paine, Godwin, Priestley and Holcroft. The satire extends to the poetical side of Jacobinism, with Romantic writers paying homage to Lepaux, leader of the new Revolutionary religion of 'Theophilanthropy':

> And ye five other wandering Bards, that move
> In sweet accord of harmony and love,
> Coleridge and Southey, Lloyd, and Lambe and Co.
> Tune all your mystic harps to praise Lepaux![25]

Rather than a parody, *New Morality* is a satire in the manner of the *Dunciad*. It is also a literary manifesto which invokes 'Pope's satiric rage' and calls for a return to the 'days of Pope': 'Ah! where is now that promise? why so long / Sleep the keen shafts of satire and of song?'.[26] Frere writes, 'here, Satire, strike!'; the *Anti-Jacobin* works against 'the poetical, as well as [the] political, doctrines of the NEW SCHOOL'.[27] In *Don Juan*'s 'poetical commandments', Byron writes:

> Thou shalt believe in Milton, Dryden, Pope;
> Thou shalt not set up Wordsworth, Coleridge, Southey[28]

The anti-Jacobins share his feelings, endorsing a comic and satirical riposte to the earnest likes of the 'fine ear'd Democratic poet' Southey. Against the levelling muse of Romanticism, with its conscious provincialism and gestures towards originality and universality, the *Poetry of the Anti-Jacobin* valorizes neo-classical values: a metropolitan, highly educated imitation of literary precedent, whether classical or Augustan. Like that of Byron after them, the parody and satire of the contributors to the *Antijacobin* is the voice of a vibrant neo-classicism, engaging in debate with the new spirit of the age.

## NOTES

1 Paine, *The Rights of Man*, Part I, 1791; Part II, 1792; Godwin, *Enquiry Concerning Political Justice*, first edition, 1793; Wollstonecraft, *A Vindication of the Rights of Men*, 1790; Williams, *Letters from France*, vol. 1, 1790. See Butler, *Burke, Paine, Godwin* for a useful and accessible selection of prose dealing with the response to the French Revolution in England during the 1790s.

2 Cited in Crane Brinton's pioneering and unjustly neglected study *The Political Ideas of the English Romanticists*, p. 99.

3 The term is Butler's in *Burke, Paine, Godwin*, p. 214.

4 A press consensus satirized by the *Antijacobin* in *New Morality*:

*Couriers* and *Stars*, Sedition's Evening Host,
Thou *Morning Chronicle*, and *Morning Post*,
Whether ye make the Rights of Man your theme,
Your country libel, and your God blaspheme,
Or dirt on private worth and virtue throw,
Still blasphemous or blackguard, praise Lepaux!

For a fascinating account of the print culture of the 1790s, see Roper, *Reviewing Before the Edinburgh*.

5 Cf. Butler, *Burke, Paine, Godwin*, p. 214.

6 From the 'Prospectus' to the first number of the *Antijacobin*, 20 November 1797.

7 *Antijacobin, or Weekly Examiner*, no. 36, 9 July 1798.

8 Canning's biographer Wendy Hinde speculates that it was Canning's admiration for Burke which made him sever his links with the Whigs. See Hinde, *George Canning*, p. 24. The notion that Canning converted as a consequence of being approached by Godwin to lead a post-Revolutionary Britain is found in Douglas, *The Journal of Sir Walter Scott*, p. 575.

9 Brinton provides much evidence of Merry's jacobinism; Brinton, *Political Ideas*, pp. 23–9. Gifford's attack on the Della Cruscan poet Mary Robinson, who was crippled in later life, gives a flavour of what Leigh Hunt in *The Feast of the Poets* (1814) labelled his 'vile, peevish temper':

See Robinson forget her state, and move
On crutches tow'rds the grave to 'Light o' Love'.

Both Hunt (in *The Feast of the Poets* and his *Autobiography*) and Hazlitt (in *The Spirit of the Age*) specifically condemn this 'unmanly' attack.

10 The word was rendered 'Antijacobin' in the periodical's title. However, Gifford renders it 'Anti-Jacobin' in the 1799 first edition of the *Poetry of the Anti-Jacobin*. All quotations from the *Poetry of the Anti-Jacobin* are taken from L. Rice-Oxley's edition, hereafter referred to as *A-J*. Graeme Stones and John Strachan are currently preparing a scholarly edition of the *Poetry of the Anti-Jacobin* as part of their *Parodies of the Romantics* (five volumes, Pickering and Chatto, forthcoming).

11 *A-J*, p. 10.

12 See, for example, the index entry for its first volume, 1798: 'Prostitution: *See* Mary Wollstonecraft'. Under 'Mary Wollstonecraft', the reader is cross-referred back to 'Prostitution'. *The Antijacobin Review* also responded to Godwin's candid *Memoirs of the Author of a Vindication of the Rights of Woman* (1798) with its 1801 poem, *Vision of Liberty*:

William hath penn'd a wagon-load of stuff,
And Mary's life at last he needs must write,
Thinking her whoredoms were not known
     enough,
Till fairly printed off in black and white.

Quoted in Locke, *A Fantasy of Reason*, p. 158–9. The contributors to the original *Antijacobin* did not write for the *Review*.

13 From *The Soldier's Friend*, the *Antijacobin*'s parody of Southey's *The Soldier's Wife*, *A-J*, p. 15.

14 *A-J*, p. 1.

15 *A-J*, p. 4. *The Progress of Man* parodies Payne Knight and *The Loves of the Triangles* Darwin.

16 Most notably Charles Lucas's *Infernal Quixote* (1800) and Amelia Opie's *Adeline Mowbray* (1805). Locke's chapter, 'Apostasy and Calumny' ably summarizes anti-Godwinian rhetoric, both philosophical and literary. See Locke, *A Fantasy of Reason*, pp. 155–66.

17 *A-J*, p. 129.

18 *A-J*, p. 1.

19 The term is Canning's. *A-J*, p. 3.

20 Southey, *Life and Correspondence*, vol. 1, p. 317.

21 *A-J*, p. 8.

22 *A-J*, p. 9.

23 The *Antijacobin* obligingly reprinted Southey's poem above its 'imitation'; *A-J*, pp. 4–5. 'Imitation', the word used by Canning to describe the *Antijacobin*'s parodies, also invokes the journal's neo-classical literary values.

24   *A-J*, p. 5.
25   *A-J*, p. 185. The 'sweet accord of harmony and
     love' is surely an ironic glance at the antagon-
     isms then current between Southey, Lloyd and
     Lamb. Derek Roper argues that the fifth, name-
     less, bard is Wordsworth; see Roper, *Reviewing
     Before the Edinburgh*, pp. 109–10. The poem
     provides the inspiration for James Gillray in
     his cartoon of 1 August 1798, the 'New Moral-
     ity, or the Promis'd Instalment of the High-
     priest of the Theophilanthropes, with the
     homage of Leviathan and his Suite'. Gillray por-
     trays the devotees of Jacobinism (Godwin, Hol-
     croft and Tom Paine amongst them) bringing in
     offerings to the new creed of Theophilanthropy.

Southey and Coleridge, transformed into asses,
tender volumes of 'Dactylics' and 'Saphics' [sic],
whilst Lamb and Lloyd feature as a frog and a
toad, croaking selections from their *Blank Verse*
(1798). The hapless amphibians, who did not,
unlike Southey and Coleridge, produce incendi-
ary writing, were guilty only by association. As
Southey wryly commented on Gillray's cartoon,
'I know not what poor Lamb has done to be
croaking there'; Southey, *Life and Correspondence*,
vol. 1, p. 345.
26   *A-J*, p. 173.
27   *A-J*, p. 2.
28   McGann, V, 74.

## REFERENCES AND FURTHER READING

Brinton, Crane, *The Political Ideas of the English
     Romantics*, Oxford, Oxford University Press, 1926.
Butler, Marilyn, *Burke, Paine, Godwin and the Revolu-
     tion Controversy*, Cambridge, Cambridge University
     Press, 1984.
Douglas, David (ed.) *The Journal of Sir Walter Scott
     1825–1832, from the Original Manuscript at Abbots-
     ford*, Edinburgh, 1910.
Hinde, Wendy, *George Canning*, Oxford, Basil Black-
     well, 1973.

Locke, Don, *A Fantasy of Reason: The Life and Thought
     of William Godwin*, London, Routledge and Kegan
     Paul, 1980.
Rice-Oxley, L. (ed.) *Poetry of the Anti-Jacobin*, Oxford,
     Basil Blackwell, 1924.
Roper, Derek, *Reviewing Before the Edinburgh 1788–
     1802*, London, Methuen, 1978.
Southey, C. C. (ed.) *The Life and Correspondence of the
     Late Robert Southey*, 6 vols, London, 1849–50.

# 18

# Mary Tighe, *Psyche*

## *John M. Anderson*

Mary Tighe's *Psyche, or, the Legend of Love* (1805) begins like an epic, *in medias res*:

> Much wearied with her long and dreary way,
> And now with toil and sorrow well nigh spent,
> Of sad regret and wasting grief the prey,
> Fair Psyche through untrodden forests went. (I. 1)

We do not know who 'fair Psyche' is, where she is going, how she found herself alone in the woods, what might be causing her such regret and grief.

Readers of *Psyche* are likely to find themselves beginning 'in the middle of things' as well – unburdened (and unaided) by critical preconceptions like those that prepare our way for poems by Wordsworth or Keats – though *Psyche* has thus far received perhaps more critical attention than any other long poem written by a woman in the Romantic period.[1] These readers will also find things they know well from Edmund Spenser: poetry full of adventure, Gothic settings, and magic, narrated in lush, painterly language. Tighe has artfully employed a polished modernized version of Spenser's language to invent a subjective epic from a woman's perspective.

The story of Mary Tighe (1772–1810) is surprisingly familiar as well, in many ways the story of a typical Romantic poet. She died (like Keats, of tuberculosis) at the young age of 37 (a year older than Byron at his death) and (as with Keats, Byron and Shelley) the tragedy of her death brought poignancy and popularity to her work. Besides the epic which every Romantic found essential for admission into what was tellingly called the 'fraternity' of poets, she wrote sonnets, inscriptions and ballads. She wrote, as Keats would later do, a poem apostrophizing autumn; like Coleridge, she wrote a poem to her local river and another about her harp; before Byron (in *Cain*) took up the cause of a maligned biblical character, she had done it in *Hagar in the Desert* (herself anticipated by Elizabeth Hands's *The Death of Amnon*, 1789). It is impossible for a *woman* poet to be a typical Romantic, however, and *Psyche* is built upon that difference. Tighe retells a male-authored story from a new (woman's) perspective, and with epic aspirations.

Not that she was the only woman poet writing ambitious poetry at the time. The conservative Anna Seward had already written *Louisa: A Poetical Novel* in 1784, the same year that the very progressive Helen Maria Williams wrote her epic, *Peru*. Hands's *Death of Amnon*, a biblical epic about incestuous rape, anticipates some of the risks Tighe would take in treating issues of sexuality. Like Tighe, Charlotte Smith – in *The Emigrants* (1793), an epic about the French Revolution – returns repeatedly to the challenges faced by a woman poet. But Tighe's two main sources are men. In Spenser's style, she reshapes from a second-century work in Latin prose called *Metamorphoses*, by Lucius Apuleius, the story of Psyche and Cupid.[2]

Mortal Psyche's beauty leads her admirers to compare her inappropriately to the Goddess of Beauty. Venus sends Cupid to avenge her by pricking Psyche with an arrow poisoned with love's miseries. The plot backfires; Cupid, scratched with his own arrow, falls as deeply in love with Psyche as she with him. He whisks her off to his Isle of Pleasure but keeps her literally in the dark – she must never see him. When Psyche visits home, her envious sisters say she has married a monster. Looking upon him while he sleeps (killing him when their fears prove true) is only prudent, they say, providing lamp and dagger for the purpose. Psyche thus spies the beautiful Cupid – and stands lost in astonishment till he wakes to discover her deceit. He leaves her desolate, but she seeks and at last receives the blessing of Venus, and they live happily ever after. To this classical fairy tale Tighe adds a Romantic quest. Before making her conciliatory offering at the altar of Venus, Psyche (assisted by Cupid disguised as a knight) must pass through an array of allegorical hazards – battling Credulity and Vanity, getting lost on the Island of Indifference. The poet's own story breaks through at times, adding unexpected depths to the narrative.

Throughout, Tighe modestly but persistently asserts her membership in the culture's most exclusive literary club – the epic tradition – by deliberately employing a host of epic conventions, modifying each device in ways deriving from her status as a woman poet.[3] The epic catalogue – invented for lists of warriors and battleships – is one example; Tighe puts this convention to her own uses in a passage in Canto V celebrating the heroines of Chastity (stanzas 22–37). She employs the convention of the Homeric simile with still more skill – exploiting ambiguities which enrich the form. Often these similes describe Psyche herself, as when she is compared early on to 'the wintry flower, / That, whiter than the snow it blooms among, / Droops its fair head submissive to the power / Of every angry blast which sweeps along' (I.9). This extended simile is ambivalently related to its subject. Psyche, flower-like, is remarkable for her beauty – the source of all her trouble – and she does bloom in a hostile environment. But the whiteness of this flower allows it to blend into that environment, to be invisible in the snow. Psyche (unlike Wordsworth's Lucy, the object of a similar comparison) always attracts flattering attention. There is something jarring in the idea of submitting to 'every angry blast which sweeps along'; fortunately, Psyche is very rarely so passive. A later Homeric simile, bringing out precisely these suppressed characteristics, illustrates the dexterity and range with which Tighe employs this device. Psyche is no longer a tiny flower, hiding itself among the snows; her cheek is now compared to the Northern Lights, upon whom 'with awe the astonished rustics gaze' (II. 15)!

Some epic conventions seem fundamentally inappropriate to a female perspective. Consider the misogynist convention – essential, from Homer's Helen and Circe to Milton's

Eve – of the treacherous woman who causes all the trouble. In Apuleius the role is played by Psyche's sisters, and Tighe preserves their evil character for her plot. But she dwells on their treachery at much less length than Apuleius, paying far more attention than he to the treachery of Venus. This important change allows Tighe to explore the allegorical possibilities of this epic convention (Love and Beauty are notoriously fickle), while avoiding the misogynist lesson about the supposed treacherousness of women.

Her reconsideration of the convention of the Muse – a figure with implications for her calling as well as her gender – is more extensive. Writing across so much space and time, the epic poet often needs access to omniscience. In the Homeric tradition, Muses represent an 'objective' perspective. Muses, like a historian's documents, provide a writer with the data that his or her experience alone could never provide. They bridge the particular and the universal.

Nevertheless, Tighe identifies them with solitude. Psyche only dabbles in the arts, while she waits for night and Cupid to arrive; yet Tighe, the artist, returns to the idea of the Muses again and again, starting with the proem which precedes even the *in medias res* opening. In the first stanza she warns (implicitly male) readers not to

> scorn the lighter labours of the muse,
> Who yet, for cruel battles would not dare
> The low-strung chords of her weak lyre prepare;
> But loves to court repose in slumbery lay. (P.1)

This outline of a 'slumbery lay' is not an accurate depiction of *Psyche*; it is only courteously modest, and decorously 'feminine' – a device to disarm the critics. Tighe identifies herself with her own Muse, for these references to a 'weak lyre' and 'lighter labours' can hardly describe a goddess. She refers again to the feminine weakness and fickle moodiness of her Muse when she refuses a perspective which would allow her to describe the anguish of Psyche's parents, in favour of one focused on Psyche's own experience. Her parents lament Psyche's fate,

> But on such scenes of terror and dismay
> The mournful Muse delights not long to dwell;
> She quits well pleased the melancholy lay,
> Nor vainly seeks the parents' woe to tell:
> But what to wondering Psyche then befel
> When thus abandoned, let her rather say. (I.38)

This view of the Muse presents the opposite of that earlier avoider of 'cruel battles'. In such stanzas Tighe performs her most unexpected and effective reversal of the Muse convention. This Muse's ironically delicate preference of epic action scenes over more wrenching scenes of profound lyric melancholy leads her to make Tighe's own choice of genre.

Like Jane Austen (who said she 'could no more write a romance than an epic poem ...under any motive than to save my life'), Tighe marries her heroine off in a happy ending, but simultaneously undercuts this convention. Tighe achieves both feats in two stanzas, the poem's last. The happy ending has rarely been more luxuriously absolute: 'a thousand voices, joined / In sweetest chorus, Love's high triumph sing...While she enraptured lives in his dear eye, / And drinks immortal love from that pure spring / Of never-failing full felicity, / Bathed in ambrosial showers of bliss eternally!' (VI.59). The sublime optimism of this ending is more problematic than it appears, because it contradicts many of the dry, clear-eyed, almost cynical psychological insights that Psyche has been at such pains to earn. Such closure may fit the fairy-tale form Tighe has chosen, but as we have seen, the fairy tale is not the only story Tighe has been telling in this poem, and this apotheosis is not the last word in *Psyche*.

Tighe in fact ends with a farewell to her book that is troubled with undertones of old age, loss of inspiration, blindness and death. The intimate tone of this final stanza contrasts starkly with the formal conventions of the passage which precedes it.

> Dreams of Delight farewel! your charms no more
> Shall gild the hours of solitary gloom!
> The page remains – but can the page restore
> The vanished bowers which Fancy taught to bloom?
> Ah, no! her smiles no longer can illume
> The path my Psyche treads no more for me;
> Consigned to dark oblivion's silent tomb
> The visionary scenes no more I see,
> Fast from the fading lines the vivid colours flee! (VI.60)

The unexpected dying fall in this final stanza subverts pretty completely the optimism that immediately precedes it; what is more, this last cry from the heart of the artist subverts the allegorical structure of the whole poem. The 'Dreams of Delight' and the 'vanished bowers' through which Psyche moves are often the flimsy disguises covering horrible realities;[4] the reluctance with which Tighe now bids these bowers goodbye contradicts much of the poem's purported message.

By ending *Psyche* this way, Tighe raises to epic importance those apparently digressive portions of the poem which convey autobiographical content. She affirms the primary significance of profoundly felt though ambiguous experience – especially artistic experience – over the tidy lessons of didactic allegory. This final destabilizing stanza confirms the importance of unstable elements like those we have traced throughout, undercutting the apparent firmness of inherited traditions. *Psyche* is a Romantic epic after all, as only the feminine perspective could have conceived it; its lines will not fade so fast again.

## NOTES

1   See references, below.

2   But if Tighe gets the story from Apuleius, classical scholarship indicates that Apuleius, in his turn, may well have appropriated it from women. See Scobie, *Apuleius and Folklore*, p. 39.

3   The epic tradition is not the only one that Tighe revises; see, for example, the variations she plays on the Petrarchan tradition in her astonishing blazon of Cupid in Canto II.

4   When 'each silken veil is thrown aside' – as in the climax to the 'Bower of loose Delight' section of Canto III – 'foul deformity, and filth obscene, / With monstrous shapes appear on every side' (III.29).

## WRITINGS

Henchy, Patrick, *The Works of Mary Tighe, Published and Unpublished*, Dublin, At the Sign of the Three Candles, 1957.

Tighe, Mary, *Psyche, with Other Poems*, facsimile, Oxford, Woodstock Books, 1992.

## REFERENCES AND FURTHER READING

Apuleius, Lucius: *The Golden Asse of Lucius Apuleius* trans. William Adlington, London, Westhouse, 1947.

Ashfield, Andrew (ed.) *Romantic Women Poets, 1770–1838: An Anthology*, Manchester, Manchester University Press, 1995.

Feldman, Paula R. and Kelley, Theresa M. (eds) *Romantic Women Writers: Voices and Countervoices*, Hanover, University Press of New England, 1995.

Kucich, Greg, *Keats, Shelley, & Romantic Spenserianism*, University Park, Pennsylvania State University Press, 1991.

Mellor, Anne K., *Romanticism & Gender*, New York, Routledge, 1993.

Ross, Marlon, *The Contours of Masculine Desire: Romanticism and the Rise of Women's Poetry*, New York, Oxford University Press, 1989.

Scobie, Alex, *Apuleius and Folklore*, London, University College, 1983.

Weller, Earle Vonard, *Keats and Mary Tighe*, New York, Century, 1928.

Wilson, Carol Shiner and Haefner, Joel (eds) *Re-Visioning Romanticism: British Women Writers, 1776–1837*, Philadelphia, University of Pennsylvania Press, 1994.

# 19

# Charlotte Smith, *Beachy Head*

## *Jacqueline M. Labbe*

### Poetry and Authority I: Cultural

In her contemplative blank-verse poem *Beachy Head*, published posthumously in 1807, Charlotte Smith locates herself and her reader atop Beachy Head, investing the poem with the authority culturally allied to the prospect view and making use of her vantage-point to explore nature in all its 'multitudinous, uncanny particularity', in Stuart Curran's words.[1] *Beachy Head* participates in the Romantic revival of the prospect poem; it arises from the same impulse that produced *Tintern Abbey* and that would produce, for instance, *Mont Blanc*. In it, Smith creates a tableau fixing her own place – as poet, as woman – in a cultural, social, natural and poetical landscape, utilizing tropes of height, vision and dispossession; and inserting self-confidence and authority via the poem's footnotes, which act as a kind of running commentary on her own work. It is important to note *where* Smith situates herself and her poem: the prospect view, allied as it was with political and cultural power and dominance, and allied also with masculinity and breadth of vision, is not common property. Smith's daring opening move is to claim the prospect, but to do so in typically Smithian fashion; that is, she gestures towards power but cloaks her moves in decorous propriety. Again, as in so much of her work, she gradually unfolds to the reader's eyes a more assertive, authoritative persona. This essay will sketch out the different methods Smith chooses to preserve a persona reliant on a multiplied sense of self; characterized by a keen awareness of the suitability of voice, tone, self-construction, self-placement and even self-promotion; ultimately, cognisant of the necessity of strategy and skilful self-manoeuvring in a culture itself dependent on increasingly rigid gender roles.

A reader's first indication of Smith's technique is the cleverness of the poem's opening lines. *Beachy Head* begins in an interesting way: 'On thy stupendous summit, rock sublime! / That o'er the channel rear'd, halfway at sea / The mariner at early morning hails, / I *would* recline' (1–4, emphasis added). Although Smith invokes the masculine viewpoint and even the sublime, she does so subjunctively, conditionally: this is the position she *would* assume, if.... The answer is never given, while such a linguistic manoeuvre introduces uncertainty, leaving the reader unable to fix on Smith's authorial attitude. The second stanza, however, begins 'The high meridian of the day *is past*': imperceptibly, weaving in detail descriptive of place and passing time to mask her movement, Smith is now where she *would be*, on the cliff, overlooking Beachy Head – 'Imperial lord of the high southern coast!' (11) – and by extension *Beachy Head*. Her upward movements unobtrusive and decorous, even self-effacing, the very fact that Smith achieves her eminence transforms her subtle 'would' into an open, even assertive, claim to rightful access. Confidently, once on the eminence, she performs more poetic sleight-of-hand, assuming a historian's voice and a botanist's, as well as a poet's. Vales are invested with vision, and fancy with sublimity: 'Fancy fondly soars, / Wandering sublime thro' visionary vales' (85–6). She moves the poem from day into night, a period variously described as a 'blot', uninteresting and unmeaning by contemporary male writers but which Luce Irigaray subversively reads as representing the '*very shadow of [woman's] gaze*' (193, Irigaray's emphasis), even that which invests her with vision. Sheltered by darkness from prying eyes that may otherwise detect her strategy, in this way invisible and 'beyond [masculine] theoretical contemplation',[2] Smith is free to outline and, in essence, take possession of Beachy Head. The poem is unfinished, ending with the destruction of a male hermit, and since it is never resolved, Smith herself remains atop Beachy Head, while her poem becomes the 'mournful lines' 'chiseled' in rock the end of the poem inscribes: permanent, a landmark, perhaps even a proof of ownership.

## Poetry and Authority II: Poetical

Wordsworth is Smith's opponent in the body of the text, and his *Tintern Abbey* is her most sustained target. In delineating her own reactions to nature and culture, she often rewrites Wordsworth's, challenging his creation of a hierarchy of perception with her own description of a spectrum of experience. Throughout the poem-proper, she alludes to a variety of Wordsworth's poems, many of which appeared in *Lyrical Ballads*, as if she is deliberately setting out to debunk the poet whom most modern readers consider the father of British Romanticism. But her prescient challenge to what will become Wordsworth's authority is restrained, oblique: she never names names, but relies on her reader's knowledge of his poems to make her point. Never does she directly quote him. Rather, she builds a composite picture of her rival poet through reference and allusion; the thrust here is literary, and contemporary, and her challenge, though serious, is also off-hand, harnessed through poetic language and imagery. Language becomes not a tool for communication, but for obfuscation, as the knowledgeable reader builds up a picture of a deflated poet who is none the less merely shadowy and fragmented. Smith depends on indirection and hints in the main body of her poem – it allows for suggestion precisely because readers are accustomed to metaphor and allusion in poetry. Further, because Smith openly concentrates on building a poetic version of Beachy Head from its bottommost layers up to herself reclining on its headland, images of Wordsworth take their place among the other aspects of Beachy's history that she draws in: fossils, its importance to past invaders, its security for present smugglers, its natural beauty that takes her mind back to her own happy childhood in nature. Beachy Head becomes a vehicle for contemplation, reception, memory and anticipation, and she anchors her thoughts and descriptions in its soil.

The result is that Wordsworth, too, is buried in *Beachy Head*. But, as with her fossils, botany, geology and history, Smith uncovers enough of her fellow poet to allow her readers a glimpse of him and, as mentioned, his work, especially that from 1798. *Tintern Abbey* and a poeticized Wordsworth-figure are most prominent: in their sections Smith seems to answer Wordsworth back, proposing viable alternatives to the ideology he has begun to formulate in the *Lyrical Ballads*. Alongside brief allusions, then, to such poems as *To My Sister* (643–8), *The Last of the Flock* (197–9) and *Lines left upon a Seat in a Yew-Tree*' (573–7), Smith uprears a rewriting of *Tintern Abbey* and a pastiche version of Wordsworth as solitary, introspective country hermit. She takes on *Tintern Abbey* mainly in lines 282–389, embedding Wordsworth's delineation of the growth of the mind and the poetic imagination in a synopsis of her own youth. Like Wordsworth, she ranges through memory ('Haunts of my youth! / Scenes of fond day dreams, I behold ye yet!': 297–8); dwells on the prospect view although, unlike Wordsworth, giving prominence to detail ('Advancing higher still / The prospect widens': 309–20); and advances straight to her own understanding of her 'glad animal movements' and their place in her imaginative development ('An early worshipper at Nature's shrine / I loved her rudest scenes': 346–7). For Smith, unlike Wordsworth, it is her attachment to vision and sensation that allows her to recreate her past in poetry; unlike Wordsworth, she feels no need to subordinate or demonize the 'tyranny of the eye' and substitute 'something far more deeply interfused'. Wordsworth's famous inexactness becomes, in Smith's rubric, as much an indication of uncertainty and confusion as a sign of completed poetic maturation. And when, towards the end of *Beachy Head*, Smith offers her readers a hermit who leaves lines of poetry 'scatter'd' about 'one ancient tree' (574, 573), who wanders the public way alone at night disturbing dogs (566–72); and another who has rejected society because 'his heart / Was feelingly alive to all that breath'd' but who 'still acutely felt / For human misery' (687–91), one recognizes the portrait of her fellow (rival?) poet painted directly onto his own poetry. Even as Smith celebrates these hermits for their piety and their model behaviour, she reproaches them, too: the one through a subtle dissection of his naive idealism, the other through death. Such allusions and hints suggest that Smith rewrites and re-presents Wordsworth, in the process establishing her own poetic position. An intriguing clue that Wordsworth read and absorbed *Beachy Head* lies in line 649, in the middle of the first hermit's song to his beloved: 'Ye phantoms of unreal delight / Visions of fond delirium born!' he laments. *Beachy Head* was published in 1807, the same year as Wordsworth's *She Was a Phantom of Delight*. Late in his life, in 1833, Wordsworth remarked that 'English verse is under greater obligations [to Smith] than are likely to be either acknowledged or remembered'.[3] Considering that *Beachy Head* also contains lines reminiscent of *The Discharged Soldier* and *With Ships the Sea was Sprinkled*, one may conclude that Wordsworth elides his own great obligation when he speaks of the debt of English verse as a whole.

## Poetry and Authority III: Personal

When Smith focuses on the multitudinous particularity of nature (and culture) in *Beachy Head*, she manoeuvres her persona into a double vantage-point, and in so doing she invests her poem with a multivocality that suggests her awareness of the nature of the poetic voice itself. Smith underpins the personal exploration she situates at the heart of her poem with layers of history – history in all *its* particularity – making use of general allusion in the body of the poem while transferring detailed historical narratives to the copious footnotes that produce the poem's base, much as Beachy Head itself supports Smith's reclining persona. Smith actively questions established authority in her footnotes, while assuming the self-confidence this grants in subsequent lines of the poem proper. She thus establishes an interrelation between the poetic and the factual that informs her implied links between the personal and the historical, in a strategy that both gives added importance to the *personal* history she embeds in *Beachy Head* and confirms the legitimacy of her persona's voice.

Even as *Beachy Head* itself rewrites many of the conventions of the standard prospect poem, updating the topographically based versions of earlier years, so, too, her notes enlarge the possibilities open to the poetic voice. Smith's notes present her readers with a figure commenting on her own poetry, as well as anticipating the objections and requests for information of her potential readers. In *Beachy Head* Smith constructs a persona who is, in Shari Benstock's words, 'unrelentingly self-aware and therefore divided against itself'.[4] Benstock refers to the dual personality created in a fictional text when the author adds notes; in Smith's case, importing the prosaic device of footnotes into her poetic text also divides the text against itself. She self-consciously suits her tone and her treatment of subject to its placement in the text, and in doing so she underpins the poem with a factual base that substantiates the more flowery, more colourful, even more fanciful – in short, more poeticized – lines in the poem proper. I have already suggested ways in which *Beachy Head* functions outside of customary discourse, predicating an alternative ideology – in its grammar, its manipulation of the prospect view, its decorous yet telling jabs at Wordsworth. This continues in the notes, so that, for instance, Smith can display a historical knowledge not usually accepted in a woman in a culture that emphasized the virtues of passivity, piety and accomplishments over the 'hard' disciplines. Smith posits a self in her notes who is outside her own culture, who challenges its authorities and its conclusions, and who supports her own poetry with a voice that is confident and knowledgeable and yet hidden. Smith's notes allow, even command, her readers to attend to her display of knowledge, and to wander from poem to note to poem, constructing an ever-more-complex web of knowledge, historical, poetical and personal. The notes lead us outwards to the writing poet who strategically comments on her own poeticizing and who upholds her own authority by denying that of others.

Poetry, then, provides the forum wherein Smith can imaginatively examine the elements of Beachy Head that correspond to her search for a coherent poetic identity: it allows her to recreate for her readers the Beachy that she seeks to know in all its formations. She does this by opposing her writing self to those others who have written before her, endorsing the creation of an alternative authority. The footnotes, however, perform her own background voice, providing a space for her to enlarge on her own poetry. For example, 125 lines into the poem Smith has spanned the length of a day and in so doing has anchored her poetic persona firmly on and in Beachy Head, and thus finds the freedom to situate Contemplation as its resident genius. She now begins her survey of Beachy's past, beginning in distant ages with description of its earliest invaders, using language that is self-consciously poetic; she prepares her readers for her recital of history by invoking Contemplation, then moves slowly backward in time, but she also mythologizes this history in her use of archaic place-names and evocative brevity. As with her allusions to Wordsworth, here she depends upon a knowledgeable readership, those who know about Dogon, Trinacria, Parthenope. However, this allusive poetry has a footnote attached, and it is anything but brief: and here she gives us all the details we could wish for.[5] Place-names are defined, historical figures contextualized; what this note gives us is a mini-history, written in factual, informative language, fleshing out the sparse poetic narrative and displaying Smith's knowledgeable grasp of history. The dialogue that is implied, between poetry and note, allows Smith to explore different levels of the place she inhabits: she is poet and historian, dreamer and reasoner.

Smith follows a poetic trajectory that depends on the gradual construction of a personal voice, but she must do so unobtrusively. Accompanying the educational constrictions that make it difficult to combine propriety with the public display of knowledge are the restrictions attendant on the married woman. Although Smith's husband has abandoned the family (and in so doing rejected his role as family protector and bread-winner), Smith herself none the less remains married, and she uses her position as abandoned wife and mother to garner sympathy and support from her readers.[6] But this also means that she must be careful to preserve her decorum, publicly and poetically, and the declaration of a fully formed and independent personal self in her poem, while it may conform to Romantic expectations, clashes with cultural ideology. She therefore, as she does in her other poetry, approaches her goal of full personhood subtly, meanderingly, establishing herself as uncertain, self-doubting, detached, until the point in the poem when she has arrived at her first 'I' since line 12: line 282, well into the poem and sufficiently well-guarded by effusive praises of England's martial past, the glory of its present, the hardiness of its rustics. '*I once was happy*', she opens this section by saying, and leads her reader deep into her past, to instances of personal communion with nature, to a recognition that society disadvantages many of its members to advantage only a few, but most importantly to an understanding of her place in her culture: 'Early [evil] came, / And childhood scarcely passed, I was condemned, / A guiltless exile, silently to sigh, / While Memory, with faithful pencil, drew / The contrast'. Smith rejects Wordsworth's triumphant declaration in *Tintern Abbey* that 'other gifts / Have followed, for such loss, I would believe, / Abundant recompense'. As if unpacking the latent uncertainty in Wordsworth's own use of the subjunctive, Smith rejects specious hope and presents a stark picture of exile. This exile, however, is also what empowers Smith, for banishment to the fringes of culture entails an engagement with the liminal and the marginal; and once she has established herself as *willingly* on the margin – as a woman, as a poet, as a figure on a headland – she fearlessly takes on the authorities she has hitherto allowed to dominate her voice. So we see her notes challenging, in turn, 'late and excellent authorities' (unnamed), 'books', Linnaeus, Gilbert White and even Shakespeare; and the last appears in what can only be seen as an ironic self-reference. 'Poets have never been botanists', she remarks in her note, and in the next sentence coolly reveals the Latinate name of the Cuckoo flower. Smith, as poet, relocates her botanical knowledge in the notes she appends to her own poem, a more 'congenial soil' for the knowledge she clearly has, whether as poet or as botanist. Her comment becomes, not an admission of her own lack of knowledge, but a dismissal of Shakespeare's inexact and 'poetic' licence with the facts of nature; underlying her comment is the clear, though unspoken aside: 'Poets have never been botanists (until now)'.

## Poetry and Authority IV: *Beachy Head*

*Beachy Head* represents a compilation: it displays Smith's multivocal self-presentation. Poetry and history, the personal and the public, intermix, even as she carefully keeps them separate. Derrida's notion of the marginal allows us to see that *Beachy Head* embodies a hybrid poetry, where facts are grafted onto verse, where history takes on different guises depending on its placement, where culture impedes the writer unless she deliberately rewrites it. The copiousness of the notes, their position as appendage to the body of the poem, suggests that they signal the marginal nature of the text itself. Smith is not content to speak in only one voice, that of poet; after a 20-year career and a public reputation as poet, novelist, children's writer and possibly even playwright, she seems to seek, with *Beachy Head*, something new: the creation of a composite poem based on and around an experimental self-questioning, self-supporting chorus of voices. Beachy Head juts out to sea; the poet reclines on its edge and claims its authority; the poem recreates its surface, its depth, its inhabitants; the notes embody the knowledge necessary to comprehend all the facets of Beachy and its composition (and I use the word in all its meanings). Smith constructs her voices according to the space they inhabit in the text, and she ends her poem by metaphorically joining the margin and its enclosed centre. Her last vignette of a drowned hermit allows her to situate the text of *Beachy Head on*, or even *in* Beachy Head: the poem ends

> Those who read
> Chisel'd within the rock, these mournful lines,
> Memorials of his sufferings, did not grieve,
> That dying in the cause of charity
> His spirit, from its earthly bondage freed,
> Had to some better region fled for ever. (726–31)

*Beachy Head*, we are told in its 'Advertisement', 'is not completed to the original design. That the increasing debility of its author has been the cause of its being left in an imperfect state, will it is hoped be a sufficient apology'.[7] And yet, as Stuart Curran notes, 'a work that begins atop a massive feature of the landscape and ends immured within it bears a remarkable coherence'.[8] Smith's final lines may well refer to some part of the poem she did not complete, but their significance redounds onto the poet herself, and her poem. The text is 'chisel'd within the rock', and as such joins the poem and its notes inside the landmass of Beachy. In placing herself, her poem and her notes in layers of margins, however, Smith encodes her awareness of the cultural reliance on the marginality of women, the covered nature of wives and the bounded realities of their lives. Poetry, history, nature and the personal collude across textual space in *Beachy Head*, but time reserves for itself the ultimate marginality. Smith died before *Beachy Head* was conclusively finished, and although the text that remains is coherent, sustained and suggestive, it is also, like *Kubla Khan*, a self-designated fragment.

NOTES

1   In Smith, *Poems*, p. xxvii.
2   Irigaray, *Speculum*, p. 193.
3   Smith, *Poems*, p. xix.
4   Benstock, 'At the margin', p. 205.

5 Stuart Curran's edition of Smith's poetry has arranged the notes to *Beachy Head* as footnotes; the reader is, therefore, presented with pages in which long notes dwarf the few short lines of poetry the layout allows. This emphasizes the authority the notes hold: they begin to colonize the physical space more usually allotted to the poetry.

6 For a more detailed look at Smith's strategy of self-positioning, see Labbe, 'Selling one's sorrows'.

7 Smith, *Poems*, p. 215.

8 Ibid., p. xxvii.

## WRITINGS

Smith, Charlotte, *The Emigrants*, London, Cadell, 1793.

——*Elegiac Sonnets*, 2 vols, London, Cadell and Davies, 1800.

——*Beachy Head, with Other Poems*, London, Joseph Johnson, 1807.

——*The Poems of Charlotte Smith*, ed. Stuart Curran, Oxford, Oxford University Press, 1993.

## REFERENCES AND FURTHER READING

Benstock, Shari, 'At the margin of discourse: footnotes in the fictional text', *PMLA* 98 (1983) 204–25.

Brooks, Stella, 'The sonnets of Charlotte Smith', *Critical Survey* 4 (1992) 9–21.

Curran, Stuart, 'The I altered', in *Romanticism and Feminism*, ed. Anne K. Mellor, Bloomington, Indiana University Press, 1988, pp. 185–207.

——'Women readers, women writers', in *The Cambridge Companion to British Romanticism*, ed. Stuart Curran, Cambridge, Cambridge University Press, 1993, pp. 177–95.

Derrida, Jacques, 'Living on: *Border Lines*', in *Deconstruction and Criticism*, ed. Geoffrey Hartman, New York, Seabury, 1979, pp. 75–176.

Irigaray, Luce, *Speculum of the Other Woman*, trans. Gillian C. Gill, Ithaca, Cornell University Press, 1985.

Kelley, Paul, 'Charlotte Smith and *An Evening Walk*', *Notes and Queries* 29 (1982) 220.

Labbe, Jacqueline M., 'Selling one's sorrows: Charlotte Smith, Mary Robinson, and the marketing of poetry', *The Wordsworth Circle* 25 (1994) 68–71.

Mellor, Anne K., *Romanticism and Gender*, New York, Routledge, 1993.

Pascoe, Judith, 'Female botanists and the poetry of Charlotte Smith', in *Re-Visioning Romanticism: British Women Writers 1776–1837*, ed. Carol Shiner Wilson and Joel Haefner, Philadelphia, University of Pennsylvania Press, 1994, pp. 193–209.

Phillips, Judith Stanton, 'Charlotte Smith's "Literary business": income, patronage, and indigence', *The Age of Johnson* 1 (1987) 375–401.

Ross, Marlon, *The Contours of Masculine Desire: Romanticism and the Rise of Women's Poetry*, New York, Oxford University Press, 1989.

Zimmerman, Sarah, 'Charlotte Smith's letters and the practice of self-presentation', *Princeton University Library Chronicle* 53 (1991) 50–77.

# 20

# Walter Scott, *Waverley*

## *Fiona Robertson*

In the first chapter of *Waverley* its anonymous author remarks:

> I must modestly admit I am too diffident of my own merit to place it in unnecessary opposition to preconceived associations: I have therefore, like a maiden knight with his white shield, assumed for my hero, WAVERLEY, an uncontaminated name, bearing with its sound little of good or evil, excepting what the reader shall be hereafter pleased to affix to it.[1]

This 'uncontaminated name' has accumulated associations ever since, not all of them conducive to the kind of reading which Scott envisaged in 1814. Scott wrote his 26 subsequent novels (and several long tales) under various disguises, but the most constant was as the 'Author of Waverley', the officially faceless originator of the most widely read novels of the Romantic period. In consequence, the name came to indicate all the other novels which followed it, seeming to give *Waverley* a special defining place among Scott's works. *Waverley* is not, however, the start of a sequence; nor are the 'Waverley Novels' a special sub-category of Scott's prose fiction. These common assumptions, like so much else, separate modern readers' first experience of the novel from that of readers in 1814, for whom it was an entirely independent venture, an unmarked page.

The interpretation of *Waverley* offered here places it in a wider aesthetic, intellectual and historical context, then examines the following issues: the role of the curiously passive hero and his relationship to the implied reader of the novel; the relationship between art and politics, and the way in which this is mediated by women and through 'translations' of ancient culture; and the novel's structure, seen as a series of approaches and delays. This final section includes a detailed reading of one chapter which brings readers closer to the distinctive texture of Scott's writing.

*Waverley* was the first significant novel to deal with mainland Britain's last civil war, the Jacobite uprising of 1745–6. Beginning in the summer of 1744, it tells of the adventures of a young English officer, Edward Waverley, heir to a great fortune and entangled in the Jacobite uprising for reasons which are always more emotional than ideological. It describes his experiences as a volunteer in the army of Charles Edward Stuart, the 'Young Pretender', before ending, controversially, with his pardon, social reinstatement, and discordantly happy marriage amid the wreck of post-Culloden Scotland. The timing of the novel's publication in June 1814, in the months during which Britain's war against Napoleonic France seemed to be at an end, helps to explain its emphasis on reconciliation, but only the context of Scottish history fully accounts for its complex attitude towards cultural loss. The subtitle of the work (*Or, 'Tis Sixty Years Since*) subtly indicates not just its historical setting, but also the importance of the relationship between past and present. *Waverley* does not attempt simply to reconstruct the past. Its complexity lies in the fact that the past, while still politically and morally contentious, has also become an aesthetic object, something to be gazed at from a distance (see the particularly revealing disquisition upon distance, p. 143).

In 1814 the secret author of *Waverley* was a famous poet and a respected antiquarian, editor and lawyer. Scott had first attracted readers in 1802–3 with his ballad collection *Minstrelsy of the Scottish Border* and had then won a large audience for his long narrative poems (*The Lay of the Last Minstrel* in 1805, *Marmion* in 1808, *The Lady of the Lake* in 1810, *Rokeby* in 1813). He was a prominent figure in the literary circles of Edinburgh, publishing editions of Swift and Dryden, contributing articles to the leading periodicals, championing the attempted revival of Scottish theatre, and entering into secret partnership with the publisher John Ballantyne and his elder brother James, whose printing house produced Scott's works and enabled him to preserve his anonymity until 1827. He had begun work on *Waverley* in 1805, returned to it in 1810, and produced the finished version for publication in June 1814. Although reports of its instant fame have been exaggerated, it established itself by the end of the year as the major publishing event of 1814, and reviews, though far from uncritical, highly praised its originality, the freshness of its characters and its skilful, innovative, blend of history and romance. The 'white shield' of the 'maiden knight', meanwhile, rapidly acquired new bearings. Later in 1814 Scott wrote a new preface for the third edition, entering more fully into the game of his anonymity by giving a series of possible reasons for it, and taking the opportunity to defend characters and incidents in the work from objections raised by reviewers. This preface initiates a system of self-defence which was to become increasingly important in the various frame-narratives and different layers of introductory and explanatory material in subsequent novels. In addition, towards the end of his life Scott revised and wrote new introductions and notes for the so-called 'Magnum Opus' edition of his novels (1829–33). Influential new authorial directions for the interpretation of *Waverley* – including a romanticized version of Scott's 'accidental' rediscovery of the 1805 manuscript – are offered in both the 'General Preface' of 1829 and in the new Introduction to *Waverley* itself.

Although *Waverley* makes use of many well-established novelistic conventions, notably Henry Fielding's style of intrusive narration (see the passage about Mr Dent's dog-bill, p. 33) and the evocative accounts of landscape for which Scott praised Ann Radcliffe, it presents itself from the start as a distinctive new kind of fiction. The opening chapter, one of the most self-conscious introductions in literary history, is an elaborate process of dissociation. Fielding had begun *Tom Jones* with a 'bill of fare', setting out what readers were to expect, but *Waverley* begins by setting out what it is *not* to be: not a 'Tale of Other Days', 'A Romance from the German', a 'Sentimental Tale' or a 'Tale of the Times'. This level of literary allusiveness continues throughout the novel. The opening of chapter 5 discusses whether or not the work imitates Cervantes; the provokingly pedantic start of chapter 19 cites Francisco de Ubeda and notes that his work is a rarity in the antiquarian book trade; in chapter 20 two references to the *Odyssey* contextualize Waverley's introduction to clan life at Glennaquoich, obliquely registering at the same time the high cultural polish of Fergus and Flora MacIvor; Shakespeare and Spenser are cited frequently, subtly creating for the work a place in a much older tradition of British writing; while Scott's contemporaries have their place too, a quotation from Coleridge's *Ancient Mariner* clinching the message of Waverley's sentimental education (p. 296) and parallels with Wordsworth's *Idiot Boy* helping to sketch David Gellatly's relationship with his mother (p. 301).

Characters within the novel, moreover, quote extensively: in the case of the Baron of Bradwardine, indeed, quotation becomes its own private language, self-consciously introducing to the novel fragments and reminders of Roman and military history, the law, and other alternatives to the novel's central narratorial voice. The experiences of Waverley himself, meanwhile, are fundamentally and explicitly shaped by his reading. His first vision of Tully-Veolan is modelled on Ariosto, and it is entirely appropriate that when Waverley transfers his affections from Flora MacIvor to Rose Bradwardine he is reading aloud at the time from a comparable transfer in *Romeo and Juliet*. The intensively literary culture of *Waverley* is appropriate in a novel which is so centrally concerned with the relationship between politics and art (see further, below). Scott's concern with his own place in literary tradition, meanwhile, continues. In contrast to the process of differentiation and dissociation observable in the opening chapter, the end of the novel gives 'A Postscript, which should have been a Preface' in which the author praises other writers, suggests a debt to the regionalist fiction of Maria Edgeworth, and closes with a dedication page, to Henry Mackenzie, 'Our Scottish Addison'. The author who had begun in opposition to the norm appears to have established secure ground on which to end, from which he is able to suggest literary allegiances and similarities. The shift in attitude towards other writers is not the only difference between the start of the work and the end. Scott had begun by claiming that his focus is more on men than on manners, and that human nature stays essentially the same in all historical periods. In the 'Postscript', however, he uses the parallel with Maria Edgeworth to insist on historical and national specificity.

The technical innovation of *Waverley* is to tell a story of national history through the *Bildungsroman* (a novel tracing an individual's growth into adulthood), a form of fiction popularized by Goethe's *Wilhelm Meisters Lehrjahre* (1795–6). In order to investigate the events of 1745 Scott invents a hero who, as his name indicates, is inclined to waver in his political loyalties. One of the most important details the narrator gives about Edward Waverley as a child (apart from his desirous grasping at the trappings of aristocracy, a grasp amply rewarded by the end of the novel) is that he adapts to the ways of two distinct households and that his education 'was regulated alternately by the taste and opinions of his uncle and of his father' (p. 11). Scott's own childhood was comparably divided between his father's house in Edinburgh and his grandfather's in the Scottish Borders, but more important than this biographical link is the fact that Scott's depiction of Waverley introduces a marked degree of psychological probability to literature's long tradition of displaced, often foundling, heroes. As in so many ways, *Waverley* takes seriously the way in which ideas and personalities are formed. Its interest in education is usually read in relation to Scott's own experiences (that is his own interpretation, suggested in the 1829

'General Preface'), but Scott's own four children were growing up in the years of *Waverley*'s composition, and his soldier son Walter was the same age as Waverley when the novel was begun in 1805.

In a novel in which young men stand in for the cause of their fathers (as Charles Edward Stuart does most notably of all), the question of manliness is anxiously debated. Waverley endures at least one sneer about the effeminacy of southerners (p. 77), and his struggle away from the authoritative wing of Fergus MacIvor is an important part of his coming to know his own mind (to use the language of Fergus's amused denigration, p. 275). Nor are his later fortunes unambiguously grown-up, for Colonel Talbot's letter announcing his pardon tells him: 'You are therefore once more a free man, and I have promised for you that you will be a good boy in future, and remember what you owe to the lenity of government' (p. 313). He repeatedly likens his Scottish experiences to dreams, pleasurable for a while but in the thick of battle suddenly strange, horrible and unnatural. He sleepwalks rather than acts, reflecting in the Castle of Doune on 'the strangeness of his fortune, which seemed to delight in placing him at the disposal of others, without the power of directing his own motions' (p. 186): the plot, however, colludes with this, its strange improbabilities governed by Scott's desire to place his hero in a situation for which he cannot be held responsible. As a result, he is carried around, tended secretly by Rose Bradwardine, beset by spells of speechlessness and immobility. He is given the clue to Bean Lean's machinations against him when Alice places the mysterious packet of papers in his portmanteau, but forgets to look at it. Perhaps the most telling moment in Waverley's history is when, during the march through Lancashire, 'attracted by a castellated old hall, he left the squadron for half an hour, to take a survey and slight sketch of it' (p. 268). Waverley, like the reader, is a tourist and an observer.

The bonds between implied reader and hero are crucial to *Waverley*. The young English officer with his impressionable mind and heart carries the reader with him on his journey into the further reaches of Scottish society. He proceeds in stages to the Baron of Bradwardine's mansion of Tully-Veolan on the borders between Highland and Lowland, then to the cave of the robber, Donald Bean Lean, then to Glennaquoich where he sees clan life, or rather Fergus's politic restoration of clan life, apparently going on as it had for hundreds of years. There are other stages in his journey; but these first three are enough to show Scott's technique of gradually drawing Waverley and the reader further from the cultural norms which it is assumed they share. As always, the difference between the implied reader and the historical or actual reader complicates this relationship. (The actual reader may be a Highlander, or one of the Amerindians to whom so many references are made, or indeed an English reader who shares the prejudices of Colonel Talbot, who 'could not have endured Venus herself, if she had been announced in a drawing-room by the name of Miss Mac-Jupiter' (p. 247).) Scott's work is aimed, however, at an imagined reader much of Waverley's knowledge and tastes, which allows for a double process of education into Scottish customs, phrases and topography. When the Jacobite army marches south into England, Waverley notices that 'Of such [armchair Jacobites] as remained, the ignorant gazed with astonishment, mixed with horror and aversion, at the wild appearance, unknown language, and singular garb of the Scottish clans' (p. 264). The implied reader's position in such a sentence is complex. The narrator of *Waverley*, making use of but not confined to the observations of his nominally 'romantic' hero, has taken care to explain the appearance, language and garb of the intruding insurgents. Readers have already, in the course of the novel, picked up key phrases which complicate their assumed Hanoverian loyalties. The stages into which Scott organizes his depictions of different aspects of Scottish society also serve another, related, purpose. The steps away from the implied English centre are simultaneously steps back in time, as Waverley gradually approaches a more 'primitive' past. They are fictional equivalents of the 'stages' of society by which Scottish Enlightenment historians understood the progress of history. The complication in *Waverley* is that the 'primitive' is a construction designed to meet modern tastes.

The tales of his adventures and of 'old Scotch manners' which Waverley tells the Englishman Frank Stanley towards the end of the novel are enough to send Frank into a 'tartan fever' (p. 339). *Waverley* had much the same effect on English readers of Scott's day, and the narrative is alert throughout to the power of art to change the way in which cultures are understood. When Waverley first visits Scotland, the focus of the *Bildungsroman* is on the misjudgements he makes because of his tendency to interpret life according to the fictional models offered by his romantic reading. When he visits Fergus and Flora MacIvor at Glennaquoich, however, he is confronted with a way of life which is apparently authentic and ancient but is actually a careful modern reconstruction designed to serve Fergus's political ambitions. Significantly, during the banquet which inaugurates the Glennaquoich scenes, Waverley stands for the first time outside the literary culture he observes. The clan listens enraptured by their bard Mac-Murrough's Gaelic recitation, in which Waverley catches his own name but understands nothing else. The discussions about this recitation and its artistic worth are central to this crucial part of the novel. By falling in love with Flora, Waverley is committing himself to the Jacobite cause, and this already displaced commitment is mediated by Flora's role as the enticing representative of ancient Gaelic culture.

Chapter 22, 'Highland Minstrelsy', develops these ideas with considerable care. Throughout it, Flora is an artist pursuing a political goal: even the Highland scenery which so impresses Waverley has been improved by Flora's judicious landscaping (p. 106). The romantic scenes which move Waverley to 'dizziness' are under her control, although the narrator prevaricates over the precise degree to which she is conscious of this. Just as Charles Edward's Jacobite mission depends on the accession of English sympathizers like Waverley for its success, so the ancient culture apostrophized by Mac-Murrough needs to be translated for a new audience. Speaking in 1745, Flora clearly anticipates the Europe-wide success of James Macpherson's 'translations' from Ossian in the 1760s: 'Some of these [Celtic poems] are said to be very ancient, and, if they are ever translated into any of the languages of civilized Europe, cannot fail to produce a deep and general sensation' (p. 103). Scott, who in university days had written a dissertation on Ossian, was acutely aware of the questions of origin, authenticity and modern reinvention which his depiction of the scenes at Glennaquoich are designed to prompt. This is part of the political as well as the artistic texture of *Waverley*, for the source of political legitimacy and authenticity – that is, the claim of the exiled Stuarts to the throne – is also a matter of interpretation. (A miniature lesson in this is given in the history of the origins of the MacIvor clan in chapter 19.) Moreover, the underlying message, that culture and indeed nature are shaped by art, has important implications for Scott's presentation of his own art as well as Flora's. Here, the structure of the 'Highland Minstrelsy' chapter is revealing. Flora promises Waverley a translation of a song which he has already heard, but has not understood, in the original Gaelic; sets it amid impressive scenery; and is interrupted before she reaches the part mentioning Waverley, which she then gives hastily in prose. The chapter works by two main principles: translation and delay.

The structure of *Waverley* is characteristic of Scott, and in chapter 70 he attempts to account for it, likening his narrative to a stone rolling downhill, slow-moving at first but rushing furiously over all obstacles by the end. It is one of the many details which incline readers to accept the work as a 'natural' progression, something not shaped by an author but moving with its own life. In the 1829 'General Preface' Scott claims that *Waverley* was 'put together with so little care, that I cannot boast of having sketched any distinct plan of the work' (p. 354). His hero simply wanders around the country, contrasting picturesque scenes. The novel makes no claim (and has none) to the tight plotting of *Tom Jones*, but it is organized in a way which is crucial to its effect, and highly involving. This is the structure of approach and delay, followed by a bewildering rush of emotion and swiftly delineated detail. The English chapters at the beginning, which are full of comic detail and sharp observation of character, improve on second reading. It has often been argued that the beginning of *Waverley* prepares for a tale puncturing the hero's romantic interpretation of the world; that Scott begins in satire and ends with an entirely different type of novel. This is a simplification, as the humorous episode of the Baron, Baillie Macwheeble, and the 'international concern' of the money repaid to Sir Everard shows. The episode foreshadows the novel's subsequent investigation of the economic differences between England and Scotland, in the process giving a clear introduction to characters who are to play a major part in Waverley's subsequent fortunes. In other words the first chapters achieve more than is usually allowed, and they also set up a method of narration which underlies much of the novel's power. The languor of the scene-setting is expressive. Waverley is a bright and fanciful child, mercurially introduced to a large house in which ageing relatives tell long stories. The novel, like its hero, waits for a world it cannot imagine. That this other world should come to life in the way that it does strikes readers, and Waverley, as strange, marvellous and always just about to seem real. As many critics have pointed out, the alternative world is only finally, and most ironically, fixed when it is translated during the restoration of Tully-Veolan at the end of the novel into a 'spirited painting' of Waverley, Fergus and the clan MacIvor, at which those plucked from the rebellion can gaze sentimentally.

Another significant factor in the structure of *Waverley* is the use of historical prolepsis. Two stories are being told in the novel. One, the personal story of Edward Waverley, is not yet known to the reader. The other, the story of the '45, is perfectly well known, at least in outline. At the end of chapter 21, when Charles Edward looks to the future on the eve of the battle of Prestonpans, the narrator observes: 'When the Baron of Bradwardine afterwards mentioned this adieu of the Chevalier, he never failed to repeat, in a melancholy tone . . . "Ae half the prayer wi' Phoebus grace did find, / The t'other half he whistled down the wind"' (p. 211). The narrative future of the novel is already fixed in the past. In addition, the landscape through which the characters pass is already replete with historical meaning: before Prestonpans, for example, the eventual fate of the Stuart cause is anticipated by a half-sentence noting that Carberry-Hill was 'already distinguished in Scottish history as the spot where the lovely Mary [Queen of Scots] surrendered herself to her insurgent subjects' (p. 216).

One chapter from the middle of the novel clearly demonstrates the significance of structure and the use of historical anticipation and recollection. At the beginning of chapter 39, Waverley is a prisoner in the Castle of Doune, waking up to the significance of the documents hidden in his portmanteau just as his guard whisks it away for the next stage on his journey. He is then marched south by the motley troop of his old enemy the Laird of Balmawhapple, from whose quarter-master he attempts to inveigle details of his situation. The frustrated exchange recalls scenes in Radcliffe's novels in which garrulous servants never quite get to the point. The party skirts round Stirling Castle, which Waverley is not inclined in his present situation to sketch, then in six paragraphs of heady and dense historical allusion sweep on to Edinburgh and to the halls of Holyrood Palace itself. In the sentences about Bannockburn, Falkirk and Linlithgow the past, present (1745) and future (1814) are combined to make Waverley's approach feel like a passage through all Scottish history. Edinburgh is first seen at a distance, with toy flashes of smoke and toy skirmishes visible at the castle; then Waverley walks towards the chamber in which (in the next chapter) he is to kneel at the feet of Charles Edward, through a long gallery hung with fake portraits of possibly imaginary Scottish kings. The chapter is cunningly entitled merely 'The journey continues', preserving the surprise of Waverley's ejection into the centre of the rebel court. In a concentrated combination of historical, geographical and emotional approach Scott clears the ground for Waverley's sudden capitulation to the grace and dignity of his exiled prince.

As the novel enters its third volume, the narrator's anxiety to limit the significance of his tale becomes palpable. The beginning of chapter 56 introduces the strange claim, 'It is not our purpose to intrude upon the province of history. We shall therefore only remind our reader, that about the beginning of November the young Chevalier, at the head of about six thousand men at the utmost, resolved to peril his cause upon an attempt to penetrate into the centre of England' (pp. 263–4). These gestures towards a story beyond the confines of his own novel register the narrator's increasing helplessness in the face of facts which he might embroider, but cannot alter. This is what lends the ending of *Waverley* the elaborate defiancy which has so often been censured as sentimental evasion. Scott is a complex writer, but he is often taken at face value. So, when he lightly explains in the 'Postscript, which should have been a Preface' that his own flighty disorganization has produced such an inelegant end, readers tend to believe him. The 'Postscript' is there, however, because Scott knew that he could not end with Waverley's personal happiness. He therefore distances and contextualizes it, discusses his own literary allegiances in a way which is alien to the skittish first chapter of the novel, and so marks the entire closing fantasy as fictional. This does not prevent the ending from having cultural consequences beyond its control, and Scott has been found guilty by many readers of whitewashing Hanoverian actions in Scotland and offering up as artistic entertainment an oppression which was still going on as he wrote. The Highland Clearances, as Scott well knew, were not over in 1814. This painful context is not elided in the novel; but the best way of recognizing this is not to be seduced into the 'tartan fever' against which Scott so clearly warns his readers, but instead to give proper weight to the investigations *Waverley* makes into the entanglement and interdependence of art and politics.

NOTE

1   *Waverley*, ed. Claire Lamont, Oxford, Clarendon
    Press, 1986, p. 3: all subsequent references are to
    this edition.

## REFERENCES AND FURTHER READING

Duncan, Ian, *Modern Romance and Transformations of the
    Novel: The Gothic, Scott, Dickens*, Cambridge, Cam-
    bridge University Press, 1992.

Ferris, Ina, 'Re-positioning the novel: *Waverley* and
    the gender of fiction', *Studies in Romanticism* 28
    (1989) 291–301.

Garside, P. D., '*Waverley*'s pictures of the past', *English
    Literary History* 44 (1977) 659–82.

—— 'Popular fiction and the national tale: hidden
    origins of Scott's *Waverley*', *Nineteenth-Century Lit-
    erature* 46 (1991) 30–53.

Hennelly, Mark M., '*Waverley* and Romanticism',
    *Nineteenth-Century Fiction* 28 (1973) 194–209.

Kerr, James, *Fiction Against History: Scott as Storyteller*,
    Cambridge, Cambridge University Press, 1989.

Millgate, Jane, *Walter Scott: The Making of the Novelist*,
    Edinburgh, Edinburgh University Press, 1984.

Orr, Marilyn, 'Real and narrative time: *Waverley* and
    the education of memory', *Studies in English Litera-
    ture* 31 (1991) 715–34.

Raleigh, John Henry, '*Waverley* as history; or 'Tis One
    Hundred and Fifty-Six Years Since', *Novel: A Forum
    on Fiction* 4 (1970) 14–29.

Robertson, Fiona, *Legitimate Histories: Scott, Gothic,
    and the Authorities of Fiction*, Oxford, Clarendon
    Press, 1994.

Welsh, Alexander, *The Hero of the Waverley Novels with
    New Essays on Scott*, Princeton, Princeton University
    Press, 1992.

Wilt, Judith, *Secret Leaves: The Novels of Walter Scott*,
    Chicago, Chicago University Press, 1985.

# 21

# Jane Austen, *Pride and Prejudice*

## *Beth Lau*

If a book called *A Companion to Romanticism* had been compiled earlier in the twentieth century, it probably would not have included an entry on Jane Austen. Austen has long been recognized as a writer of genius, but critics in the past had difficulty placing her work within the traditional literary periods and movements. Although she lived and wrote during the years designated as the Romantic period (she lived from 1775 to 1817, and *Pride and Prejudice* was published in 1813), she was not for most of the last two centuries considered a Romantic writer. The major Romantic poets, so the traditional view went, celebrate emotion, nature, and the rights and experiences of the individual, whereas Jane Austen writes about a social world, where individual desires are regulated by an elaborate code of manners and decorum. In addition, the Romantic movement is allied with revolutionary politics – the overthrow of monarchs and resistance to authority and hierarchy of all kinds, including, for women, patriarchal authority – whereas Jane Austen was considered either apolitical or conservative in her views, since her novels are not directly concerned with the great revolutionary upheavals of the day and do not appear to challenge traditional institutions or conventions.

In recent years, however, many long-standing assumptions about both Jane Austen and the Romantic period have been questioned, and it is now possible to read *Pride and Prejudice* as not only a work of universal appeal, but also as one that participates in the concerns and developments of its age. This view can be supported by pointing out important similarities between *Pride and Prejudice* and the work of the major male Romantic poets, and also by noting ways in which Austen, like many other women writers of the day, differed from the male poets in her outlook and emphases.

What evidence supports the claim that *Pride and Prejudice* does not participate in the Romantic celebration of powerful feeling? One point is that Elizabeth, like her father, frequently adopts a detached, ironic tone in assessing human motives and behaviour. Unlike her sweet, trusting sister Jane, Elizabeth is alert to selfishness, foolishness and other foibles in the people she meets. She therefore seems to have more head than heart and to maintain a certain critical distance between herself and others.

To the extent that Elizabeth does allow herself to be guided by her feelings, moreover, she falls into error. Both her initial dislike of Mr Darcy and her attraction to Wickham prove misguided and result chiefly from Elizabeth's wounded pride, since Darcy scorned to dance with her at their first meeting, whereas Wickham singled her out for attention and intimate conversation during their first social encounter. Impulsive subjective feelings, whether of love or of hatred, are untrustworthy, the novel seems to suggest. Instead, one ought to form one's opinion of another person gradually, after sufficient evidence has been gathered about that person's character, background and relationships with family members, dependents and friends. Thus, Elizabeth comes to respect Darcy after she sees his tasteful and well-managed estate and learns that he is a good brother, master and landlord, whereas her regard for Wickham dissipates when she finds out that he has been dishonest and unscrupulous in his dealings with others.

Besides suggesting that informed judgement rather than impulsive emotions ought to guide women in their choice of a husband, other aspects of the novel's depiction of courtship and marriage appear anti-romantic. The fact that each character's income and net worth largely determine his or her eligibility as a mate gives the novel a crass, mercenary quality for some readers. Aunt Gardiner, one of the most positive characters in the novel, warns Elizabeth not to get attached to Wickham because he is too poor to support a wife, and even the warm-hearted, impractical Jane censures Lydia's alliance with Wickham as financially 'imprudent' (p. 273). Moreover, there are no passionate love scenes in *Pride and Prejudice*. When Elizabeth and Darcy finally come to an understanding and agree to marry (vol. 3, ch. 16), the emotional intensity of the scene is downplayed; Elizabeth's and Darcy's words are briefly summarized, rather than presented verbatim, and no embraces or kisses are mentioned. One can even question how passionate Elizabeth's feelings for Darcy are at the end of the novel. Her love is said to be based on 'gratitude and esteem' (p. 279), which may strike some readers as rather bland impulses.

Although all of these observations have validity, the idea that *Pride and Prejudice* advocates reason, practicality and self-control over emotion can be challenged and qualified. First, if Elizabeth learns in one sense to temper her impulsive first impressions with more objective evidence and sober judgement, she also learns to distrust ironic wit and become more emotionally involved with other people. As Susan Morgan argues, Elizabeth at first is much like her father, who has withdrawn from other people in disappointment over his flawed marriage and now derives a bitter amusement from laughing at his neighbours and even his own wife and daughters. After reading Darcy's letter, however, Elizabeth realizes that her criticism of Darcy was misguided and that ironic detachment may not be the best mode of relating to other people after all. As she tells Jane, 'I meant to be uncommonly clever in taking so decided a dislike to [Darcy], without any reason. . . . One may be continually abusive without saying any thing just; but one cannot be always laughing at a man without now and then stumbling on something witty' (pp. 225–6). From this point on in the novel, Elizabeth is less judgemental and detached. She urges her father to prevent Lydia from going to Brighton and possibly causing harm to herself and her family, instead of joining him as an amused spectator of Lydia's folly. Moreover, she begins to interact with Darcy less guardedly and defensively when she encounters him at Pemberley. In the process, she becomes more vulnerable and uncertain, both of how to assess Darcy and even of her own feelings (see, for example, vol. 2, ch. 2). She is not as clever and incisive in judging others, nor as cool and composed as she was at the beginning of the novel, but she is more open to others and more emotionally engaged. One could say that Elizabeth's progress in the novel is away from intellectual, ironic detachment like her father's and toward more emotional, complex and committed relationships with others.

In addition, Elizabeth always regards love as an important element in a marriage. She condemns Charlotte Lucas for agreeing to marry Mr Collins for purely practical reasons, and she herself refuses Mr Collins on the ground that 'My feelings in every respect forbid' her acceptance of him as a husband (p. 109). She also rejects Darcy's first proposal, despite the wealth and status this alliance would bring her, because she does not at this point love and respect him.

If the novel's representation of romantic love still appears rather subdued to some modern readers, Jane Austen's situation as a woman writer may help to account for this impression. Male Romantic writers were revolutionary in their celebration of powerful emotion, in contrast to the eighteenth-century emphasis on reason as the most important human faculty. Women, however, have traditionally been associated with emotion rather than intellect, and feminist writers from the Romantic period, such as Mary Wollstonecraft in her *Vindication of the Rights of Woman*, insisted that women were capable of rational thought. When Elizabeth appeals to Mr Collins to 'not consider me . . . as an elegant female intending to plague you, but as a rational creature speaking the truth from her heart' (p. 109), she echoes Wollstonecraft, who declares that her *Vindication* will 'treat [women] like rational creatures, instead of flattering their *fascinating* graces' (Perkins, *English Romantic Writers*, p. 226). For women of the Romantic period, rational behaviour was more revolutionary than emotionalism.[1]

In addition, for women of Austen's day, surrendering to passionate feelings was dangerous, as Lydia's example proves in *Pride and Prejudice*. Not only could women, unlike men, get pregnant if they engaged in illicit passion; they were also held to stricter codes of decorum than men, and a woman who lost her reputation for virtue might never gain a husband. Moreover, marriage was, as Charlotte Lucas recognizes, 'the only honourable provision for well-educated young women of small fortune' (p. 122), since almost no opportunities existed for women to work and support themselves and women often could not inherit family estates, as is the case with the Bennet sisters. As a result, women necessarily regarded marriage as a practical as well as an emotional connection, and female characters' cool calculation of a prospective husband's financial profile in *Pride and Prejudice* may be understood as an essential survival tactic rather than as callous materialism.[2] For a number of reasons, then, women in the Romantic period, while still valuing emotion, were less likely than some of their male peers to celebrate it unreservedly.

Finally, it is worth noting that most of the major male Romantic poets also advocate a balance of emotion and reason or judgement, rather than strong feeling alone. For example, William Wordsworth's Preface to *Lyrical Ballads* makes the well-known claim that 'all good poetry is the spontaneous overflow of powerful feelings', but it then qualifies that remark by insisting that a worthy poet must also have 'thought long and deeply' (*Romanticism*, p. 253). Similarly, Samuel Taylor Coleridge in *Biographia Literaria* defines the imagination as a power that combines and balances all human impulses and faculties, including 'a more than usual state of emotion, with more than usual order; judgement ever awake and steady self-possession, with enthusiasm and feeling profound or vehement' (*Romanticism*, p. 577). Jane Austen's concern with maintaining a balance of sense and sensibility is therefore not fundamentally different from the outlook of her most famous male contemporaries.

The major male Romantic poets are unquestionably known for their love of nature, whereas Austen writes novels of manners which portray men and women in social settings. None the less, nature can be seen to play a significant role in *Pride and Prejudice*. Elizabeth's delight at the prospect of touring the Lake District with her Aunt and Uncle Gardiner makes clear her love of nature, and her appreciation of the beautiful grounds at Pemberley, where 'natural beauty' is not 'counteracted by an awkward taste' (p. 245), is instrumental in changing her opinion of Darcy. Several other key scenes involving Elizabeth and Darcy take place outdoors: she reads his important letter while walking about the park at Rosings, and Darcy's second, successful proposal occurs outdoors on a walk, unlike his first, unsuccessful proposal which was made in the Collins's drawing room. Outside in nature, men and women can often communicate more directly and honestly than they can indoors, where codes of manners regulate behaviour and often inhibit intimacy. Elizabeth and Darcy are associated with nature in other ways. Elizabeth offends the Bingley sisters' sense of feminine propriety both when she walks across the muddy countryside to visit Jane at Netherfield Park and when she shows up at Pemberley 'brown and coarse' or suntanned from her summer travels (p. 270). In each situation, however, Elizabeth's outdoor exercise enhances her attractiveness for Darcy, who himself enjoys fishing and tending the grounds of his estate. In fact, as Alison Sulloway points out, although Darcy may seem to be the epitome of a civilized, society man, he is actually uncomfortable among strangers in drawing rooms and more at ease at home in the country, alone or with a few close friends. This fact, along with Darcy's pride and aloofness, allies him with Mr Rochester in Charlotte Bronte's *Jane Eyre*, a character who is usually considered a quintessential Romantic hero (Sulloway, *Jane Austen*, pp. 206–7).

Along with nature, Wordsworth's poetry describes 'incidents and situations from common life', rather than sensational or exotic people, scenes and events.[3] Similarly, Jane Austen presents ordinary, provincial people in their day-to-day lives, which usually consist of family routines and visits to nearby neighbours, with an occasional ball or trip 50 miles from home as significant events. In fact, for many years Jane Austen's focus on '3 or 4 Families in a Country Village' was considered a liability, making her novels limited and inferior to works with more varied casts of characters and more dramatic plots. Austen's concern with ordinary, humble, domestic life, however, is a quality she shares with other Romantic writers, especially Wordsworth.[4]

The Romantic movement as traditionally defined is more interested in solitary human experience than in the affairs of people in society; it is also allied with the democratic belief in individual rights, which gained currency in an era that witnessed the American and French revolutions. Once again, *Pride and Prejudice* may not at first appear to share these concerns, since it depicts a world in which people are portrayed as members of families and communities rather than as autonomous individuals, and characters are almost never alone. In addition, the novel may seem to promote a hierarchical rather than a democratic society, since its hero is a wealthy aristocrat.

In a number of ways, however, *Pride and Prejudice* participates in the Romantic period's celebration of individualism and democracy. Elizabeth Bennet is unquestionably a distinctive individual. Darcy declares that what drew him to her was 'the liveliness of [her] mind', or her unique and vital personality (p. 380). As Robert Polhemus points out, this emphasis on personality rather than status, wealth, or even beauty as the essence of Elizabeth's appeal for Darcy illustrates a belief in the worth and uniqueness of each individual; 'the need to be noticed and loved for your own distinctive self', Polhemus remarks, 'expresses the passion of modern individualism' (Polhemus, *Erotic Faith*, p. 45; see also pp. 31, 54). Polhemus further observes that one trait of flawed characters in the novel, such as Mr Collins, Mr Bennet, Wickham and Lydia, is that they select partners indiscriminately, instead of valuing or even perceiving the other person's distinctive personality (ibid., pp. 45–6). As several other critics note, the very notion that marriage ought to involve love, compatibility between partners, and personal fulfilment is associated with the growth of individualism and a belief in the validity of personal happiness (Johnson, *Jane Austen*, pp. 90–1; Brown, 'Social history', pp. 60–1).

Elizabeth clearly asserts her revolutionary right to 'the pursuit of happiness' when she tells Lady Catherine, who wants Elizabeth to promise that she will never marry Darcy, 'I am only resolved to act in that manner, which will, in my own opinion, constitute my happiness, without reference to *you*, or to any person so wholly unconnected with me' (p. 358).[5] In the process, Elizabeth defies the aristocratic Lady Catherine and asserts her own equality with Darcy, even though Lady Catherine considers her an 'upstart . . . young woman without family, connections, or fortune' (p. 356). Indeed, all of the snobbish upper-class characters – Caroline Bingley and Mr Darcy himself, along with Lady Catherine – are humbled in the novel, and Elizabeth's marriage to Darcy can be read as the story of a middle-class girl who, through the force of her own personality and merits, rises above the liabilities of her family background and gains wealth, prestige and happiness. It should be noted, too, that the Bingleys themselves are not originally from the gentry class but acquired their money through trade; Mr Bennet, a gentleman, married a lawyer's daughter; and Sir William Lucas was originally a tradesman who was knighted after making an address to the king. In various ways *Pride and Prejudice* portrays a society in which rigid class barriers are breaking down and where the bourgeoisie especially are merging with the landed gentry.

Of course, as Johnson notes (*Jane Austen*, pp. 89, 93), the aristocrats in *Pride and Prejudice* are not seriously challenged or overthrown; their insolence is rebuked, but they retain sufficient power and dignity to make joining their ranks highly desirable. It is 'something', as Elizabeth comes to appreciate, 'to be mistress of Pemberley' (p. 245). In addition, individualism and the right to personal happiness have limits in the novel. Lydia's selfish hedonism is not condoned, and Elizabeth's marriage to Darcy provides pleasure and benefit to a number of people besides herself: Georgiana Darcy, Kitty and Mr Bennet, and the Gardiners, in addition the servants and tenants of Pemberley.

Moreover, Elizabeth's 'lively mind' seems checked and subdued in the second half of the novel. Susan Fraiman argues that Elizabeth's humiliation and self-castigation after she reads Darcy's letter mark a turning point, after which Elizabeth grows more passive and uncertain of her judgement and Darcy assumes greater power and authority as he 'magically set[s] everything straight', arranging Lydia's marriage, reuniting Jane and Bingley, and transporting Elizabeth to Pemberley (Fraiman, *Unbecoming Women*, p. 79). Readers may feel that Elizabeth's distinctive personality is repressed as she evolves from witty antagonist to grateful admirer of the proud and powerful Mr Darcy.

Many critics believe that *Pride and Prejudice* exposes the hardship and injustice of nineteenth-century women's lives. According to these critics, the loss of authority and confidence Elizabeth experiences after reading Darcy's letter, along with other episodes in the novel, reveal problems in courtship and marriage for women in Austen's society.[6] Other critics, however, do not regard Austen's depiction of marriage and family life in *Pride and Prejudice* as problematic. Brown, for example, argues that Austen's gender induced her to value family, marriage and community in a way that men traditionally have not (Brown, *Jane Austen's Novels*, pp. 6–7, 11, 17). According to this view, Austen does not lament women's lack of power and independence but celebrates their connectedness to other people. Anne Mellor asserts that women Romantic writers generally are less prone to the egotism and individualism of male Romantic writers and instead endorse an ethic of care that values community and human bonds (Mellor, *Romanticism and Gender*, pp. 1–11).

Although this point of view has validity, one should keep in mind that the major male Romantic poets also struggled with the competing claims of personal fulfilment and interpersonal or social obligations. In a number of poems, Wordsworth describes his initial penchant for solitary nature worship giving way to love of other human beings (e.g. *Lines Written a Few Miles above Tintern Abbey, The Prelude, Elegiac Stanzas, Suggested by a Picture of Peele Castle in a Storm*). Coleridge's *Rime of the Ancient Mariner* is one of the most powerful works ever written on the horrors of solitude and the problems inherent in overweening individualism, and Shelley's *Alastor* is also a cautionary tale about the dangers of solipsism. John Keats increasingly wished to do 'some good to the world' instead of merely writing lush, escapist poetry.[7] Even Byron, whose early poems featured such gloomy, misanthropic, solitary heroes as Childe Harold, the Giaour and Manfred, ended his career with the comic satire *Don Juan*, which is very much concerned with people in society. Clearly, the male Romantics, like Jane Austen, struggled to work out a balance between duty to self and to others, or between the pleasures of solitude and the pleasures of relationship.

*Pride and Prejudice* is a rich and complex novel, and many of its themes, conflicts, motifs and key episodes can only be touched on in a short essay like this. What I hope this essay has established, however, is that *Pride and Prejudice* can unquestionably be considered a Romantic work. It is so in the way it participates in beliefs and values expressed by the major male Romantic writers – the importance of emotion, love of nature and common life, a celebration of individualism, and endorsement of democratic sentiments – and also in beliefs and values conveyed by other women writers from the period, such as the need to balance emotion with reason and the importance of family and community relationships as well as individual rights. A study of *Pride and Prejudice* further suggests that, in the end, the concerns of male and female writers in the Romantic period may not be fundamentally different.[8]

NOTES

1   Margaret Kirkham and Alison Sulloway relate Austen's attitude toward reason and feeling to Wollstonecraft and other eighteenth-century feminist writers.

2   Julia Prewitt Brown (*Jane Austen's Novels*, pp. 13–14) and Robert Polhemus (*Erotic Faith*, p. 43) remark the dangers of passion for nineteenth-century women. Brown (*Jane Austen's Novels*,

pp. 12–13) and Lillian Robinson (*Sex, Class, and Culture*, pp. 178–99) discuss the importance of marriage for women's financial and social survival.

3 Preface to *Lyrical Ballads* (*Romanticism*, p. 252).

4 The phrase '3 or 4 Families in a Country Village' comes from Austen's letter of 9 September 1814 to her niece Anna Austen (Austen, *Letters*, p. 275). Stuart Tave (*Jane Austen*) notes the similarity between Wordsworth's and Austen's celebration of common life. For a lively and convincing refutation of the idea that Austen's novels are limited in scope, see Greene, 'The myth of limitation'.

5 'Life, Liberty, and the pursuit of Happiness' are among the 'unalienable Rights' vouchsafed to all people, according to the United States Declaration of Independence – a revolutionary document in the late eighteenth and early nineteenth centuries.

6 See, for example, Robinson, *Sex, Class and Culture*; Gilbert and Gubar, *Madwoman*; Newton, *Women, Power and Subversion*; Kirkham, *Jane Austen*; Newman, 'Can this marriage be saved?'; Johnson, *Jane Austen*; Sulloway, *Jane Austen*; and Fraiman, *Unbecoming Women*. These writers characterize Austen's outlook in a variety of different ways, but all regard her as a critic of her society's treatment of women.

7 From Keats's letter of 24 April 1818 to John Taylor (Perkins, *English Romantic Writers*, p. 1,279).

8 For further discussion of parallels between Austen and other Romantic writers see Morgan, *In the Meantime*, and the essays in Ruoff, *The Wordsworth Circle*.

## WRITINGS

Austen, Jane, *Pride and Prejudice*, 3rd edn, ed. R. W. Chapman, Oxford, Oxford University Press, 1932.
——*Jane Austen's Letters*, 3rd edn, ed. Deirdre Le Faye, Oxford, Oxford University Press, 1995.

Perkins, David (ed.) *English Romantic Writers*, Fort Worth, Harcourt Brace, 2nd edn, 1995.

## REFERENCES AND FURTHER READING

Auerbach, Nina, *Communities of Women: An Idea in Fiction*, Cambridge, Mass., Harvard University Press, 1978.

Brown, Julia Prewitt, *Jane Austen's Novels: Social Change and Literary Form*, Cambridge, Mass., Harvard University Press, 1979.

—— 'The "social history" of *Pride and Prejudice*', in *Approaches to Teaching Austen's Pride and Prejudice*, ed. Marcia McClintock Folsom, New York, MLA, 1993, pp. 57–66.

Butler, Marilyn, *Jane Austen and the War of Ideas*, London, Oxford University Press, 1975.

Fraiman, Susan, *Unbecoming Women: British Women Writers and the Novel of Development*, New York, Columbia University Press, 1993.

Gilbert, Sandra M. and Gubar, Susan, *The Madwoman in the Attic: The Woman Writer and the Nineteenth-century Literary Imagination*, New Haven, Yale University Press, 1979.

Greene, Donald, 'The myth of limitation', in *Jane Austen Today*, ed. Joel Weinsheimer, Athens, University of Georgia Press, 1975, pp. 142–75.

Johnson, Claudia, *Jane Austen: Women, Politics, and the Novel*, Chicago, University of Chicago Press, 1988.

Kirkham, Margaret, *Jane Austen, Feminism and Fiction*, Brighton, Harvester Press, 1983.

Knuth, Deborah, 'Sisterhood and friendship in *Pride and Prejudice*: need happiness be "entirely a matter of chance"?', *Persuasions* 11 (1989) 99–109.

Mellor, Anne K., *Romanticism and Gender*, New York, Routledge, 1993.

Morgan, Susan, *In the Meantime: Character and Perception in Jane Austen's Fiction*, Chicago, University of Chicago Press, 1980.

Newman, Karen, 'Can this marriage be saved? Jane Austen makes sense of an ending', *ELH* 50 (1983) 693–710.

Newton, Judith Lowder, *Women, Power, and Subversion: Social Strategies in British Fiction, 1778–1860*, Athens, University of Georgia Press, 1981.

Paris, Bernard, *Character and Conflict in Jane Austen's Novels*, Detroit, Wayne State University Press, 1978.

Polhemus, Robert M., *Erotic Faith: Being in Love from Jane Austen to D. H. Lawrence*, Chicago, University of Chicago Press, 1990.

Robinson, Lillian S., *Sex, Class, and Culture*, Bloomington, Indiana University Press, 1978.

Ruoff, Gene (ed.) *The Wordsworth Circle*, vol. 7 (1976). Special issue on Jane Austen.

Sulloway, Alison G., *Jane Austen and the Province of Womanhood*, Philadelphia, University of Pennsylvania Press, 1989.

Tave, Stuart, 'Jane Austen and one of her contemporaries', in *Jane Austen: Bicentenary Essays*, ed. John Halperin, Cambridge, Cambridge University Press, 1975, pp. 61–74.

# 22

# Mary Shelley, *Frankenstein*

## *John Beer*

When Coleridge visited William Godwin's family during the Christmas of 1799 he was oppressed by the 'cadaverous silence' of his children by comparison with the boisterousness of his own. Despite her reserve, however, one of them, the two-year-old Mary, proved to have an extraordinary receptivity – activated strongly, no doubt, six years later when she heard the poet read *The Rime of the Ancient Mariner* to them.

Such receptivity proved to be the hallmark of her literary career, never more amazingly demonstrated than in her fictional achievement *Frankenstein, or the Modern Prometheus*, a novel which has rightly been said to contain an *excess* of significance. This story of a scientist whose overreaching intellectual ambitions led him to attempt an assault on the greatest problem of all, that of making a new life, only to discover that his creation had an unforeseen liberty of its own, was to become a potent myth in the hands of all who were apprehensive at the dangers of the scientific explorations that had just begun to show their potentiality; Chris Baldick has demonstrated its influence on Carlyle, Dickens and many other writers, along with the presence of the larger myth in the writings of Karl Marx ('A spectre is haunting Europe . . .'). Its fascination remains to the present day for readers who may never have read the novel or even seen the film but still know its barest outline.

Mary Shelley's own account of how she came to write the novel has often been reprinted and there is no space to reproduce it at length here; it is sufficient to recall how having listened silently to many conversations between Byron and her husband, particularly on the nature of life and the probability that its principle might be discovered and commun-icated, she became so excited that during the subsequent night her thoughts rose up in visionary form: she saw 'the pale student of unhallowed arts' kneeling behind the thing he had put together until it began to stir with life and then, when he went to sleep hoping that it would die again, continued to live and to haunt him. When her companions planned that each should write a ghost story she realized that she had one already to her hand and set to work on *Frankenstein*.

In the detail of its writing the novel breaks little new ground: its incidents, though sometimes surprising, would be readily recognizable to readers who had been brought up on a diet of Gothic fiction. But its overall organization bears the stamp of the Romantic mind, particularly through its interplay of narrators. In this it follows *The Ancient Mariner*, where three distinct tellers may be discerned (the Mariner, the narrator of the ballad and the compiler of the marginal glosses) and looks forward, by way of the narrators in works such as *Bleak House*, *Wuthering Heights* and *The Turn of the Screw*, to the varying points of view in a novel such as *A Passage to India*. Such narrative complexities reflect the interplay of different strains of thought in the new situation that came into existence during the time of the French Revolution. It is significant that the composition of this novel took place during a period of intensive intellectual discussion.

Anne Mellor has pointed to the atmosphere of scientific optimism that followed the writings of Erasmus Darwin and surrounded figures such as Humphry Davy in the earliest years of the century, while Marilyn Butler has drawn attention to the relevance ten years later of the vitalist controversy, connected particularly with the lectures of the Shelleys' friend William Lawrence. The fact that Lawrence was suspended by the Royal College of Surgeons and not reinstated until he withdrew his *Lectures on Physiology, Zoology and the Natural History of Man*, published in the year after *Frankenstein*, illustrates the dangers of the path trodden by anyone whose work might be held to support a materialist version of vitalism and probably helps to explain why, in the 1831 version, Mary introduced changes likely to tilt the reader's balance of sympathies further in favour of Frankenstein by reinforcing his religious and moral attitudes.

As a story-teller Mary Shelley proved to be marvellously inventive at times, even if her use of some devices was on occasion unduly repetitive. The true power of the story, however, lies in the quality of the ideas around which it was constructed. At one level its technique ranges between a matter-of-factness, which she handled with care, and an element of the miraculous. No one is expected to take seriously the monster's powers of knowing exactly where to find his victim at any particular juncture, or his powers of self-transportation (including even, apparently, a power to appear or disappear at will), while his account of his own self-education in language through overhearing other people's conversations beggars belief; yet the story's plausibility is unaffected. It is driven less by such matters than by the ideas it transmits and generates, and the complexity of their working. It soon becomes evident that Mary Shelley had lighted on a theme ranging well beyond her immediate ends, enabling her not only to reflect, consciously or unconsciously, on her own personal history, but also to explore the moral implications of events in recent political history and pressing current themes, both in society and in contemporary thought.

The respective narratives of Frankenstein and the monster that take up much of the book afford quite different perspectives on the events described. Frankenstein sees the nature of his monster as unambiguously evil, corresponding to the foulness of his appearance and the crimes he commits; yet when the monster tells his own story his behaviour is represented as explicable in terms of the treatment he has received. It is not clear whether Mary Shelley herself took either side in this implicit debate, but her husband Percy Bysshe Shelley was primarily sympathetic to the monster's version. In an unpublished review produced at the time he wrote (affecting not to know the author) that the moral of the story was 'perhaps the most important, and of the most universal application, of any moral that can be enforced by example':

> Treat a person ill, and he will become wicked. Requite affection with scorn; – let one being be selected, for whatever cause as the refuse of his kind – divide him, a social being,

from society, and you impose on him the irresistible obligations – malevolence and selfishness.

Shelley's further analysis of the means by which 'his original goodness was gradually turned into inextinguishable misanthropy and revenge' goes far towards acceptance of Frankenstein's horror at the behaviour of his creation as carrying within it its own necessity; but the language of the analysis betrays its true origin. As Laurence Lipking has contended, the most plausible among the sources that have been cited for the thinking in *Frankenstein* is Rousseau's *Emile*, owing to its unusual position as a site of the contradictions with which it is riven. In a writer whom they found almost obsessively attractive, both Mary and Percy Bysshe Shelley came to appreciate the power of those contradictions, but Mary was sceptical – the more so since from one point of view her husband's behaviour, particularly to his first wife, showed how idealism could result in behaviour that seemed, as with Rousseau himself, monstrous.

The novel's subtitle, *The Modern Prometheus*, reflects the fascination of this figure for contemporary writers, including her husband, who in fact entitled his major poetic drama *Prometheus Unbound*. Romantic writers in general, with their concern for human liberty, developed a natural fellow-feeling for the great protagonist of humanity. Instead of a Son of God made to suffer by his contemporaries, as promulgated in Christianity, they were drawn to the idea of a man with sufferings directly attributable to his Creator. Why, they asked, should humankind be made to feel guilty for breaking a code which was imposed in the first place by God? Why should not they be allowed simply to protest against their plight, retaining in the circumstances a dignity and nobility? Prometheus on his rock became their emblem for such feelings.

Something of the kind was in Mary Shelley's mind when she produced as epigraph for her novel the words of Adam's protest in Milton's *Paradise Lost* after the Fall:

> Did I request thee, Maker, from my clay
> To mould me man? Did I solicit thee
> From darkness to promote me?

It is not surprising, therefore, that some readers have regarded the monster as himself a Prometheus, condemned to a life not asked for, though it is more likely that in selecting her subtitle Mary Shelley actually had in mind another part of the Prometheus myth: having stolen the heavenly fire, Prometheus implanted it in clay and so brought about the creation of humanity. Her Dr Frankenstein, usurping the creator's prerogative, had brought down on himself the same curse.

It is another mark of the novel's power that it has prompted so much discussion and interpretation among critics. Ellen Moers, for instance, in her study of the novel as a piece of 'Female Gothic', has pointed out that Mary Shelley was unusual among major female novelists of the nineteenth century in having borne children. Jane Austen, the Brontes, George Eliot, were all childless. During the months before she conceived and composed *Frankenstein*, moreover, Mary's life, which had originally been overshadowed by the tragedy of her mother's death at her own birth, was dogged by event after event in which pregnancy, childbirth and child-death were intermingled. The main ones were that in February 1815 she gave birth to a premature female child, who died twelve days later. Thirteen days after that she dreamt that her baby had come to life again, having simply been cold and that they had rubbed her back to life in front of the fire. In January 1816 she gave birth to her son William; in October, Fanny Imlay, Mary's half-sister, discovering that her father was not Godwin but Mary Wollstonecraft's American lover, committed suicide, followed on 10 December by Harriet Shelley, who was then pregnant by another man. The Shelleys married three weeks later and in March 1817 were joined at Marlow by Claire Clairmont, who had recently had a child by Byron. The composition of the novel was taking place meanwhile, between the summer of 1816 and the following April.

During the months before and during the writing of the novel, then, Mary Shelley had good cause to reflect on life and death in ways that would bring very firmly to her mind questions of growth and decomposition. Being brought close to the premature death of a child induces consciousness of the intricacy of the processes involved – far more so than with a healthy birth, where most of them remain invisible. Mary's preoccupation comes out in the descriptions of Frankenstein's visits to charnel-houses as he worked on the creation of his human beings. A sense of doom directed at her and those whom she loved may well have coloured much of the later part of the novel also, where Frankenstein receives blow after blow by way of disaster to those whom he loves, and always in an unexpected manner. In particular, one notices the stress on impending doom when, marrying his Elizabeth, he is haunted by the monster's words, 'I will be with you on your wedding night'. Mary's own marriage was, as we have seen, shadowed by the very recent death of Harriet.

Mary Shelley's relationship to her father, who brought her up, suggests further depths in the gestation of the novel. U. C. Knoepflmacher has pointed out that the sympathetic element in Mary's portrayal of the monster may well owe something to her curious position in childhood when, as she herself said, she suffered from a 'total friendlessness', a 'horror of pushing' and an 'inability to put myself forward unless led, cherished, and supported'. There may also have been a concealed aggressiveness: to her own father she appeared 'singularly bold' and 'somewhat imperious'. In the first edition of *Frankenstein* the epigraph from Milton quoted above is followed on the next page by the dedication 'To WILLIAM GODWIN / Author of Political Justice, Caleb Williams, &c. / These Volumes / Are respectfully inscribed / By / The Author'. Knoepflmacher may be right in detecting a bitter irony, a similar questioning directed to her father, in this juxtaposition. It is equally possible, however, that Mary is simply presenting herself to her father as someone worthy of her intellectual forebears. The most fascinating feature of *Frankenstein* from this point of view is the degree to which it actually echoes Godwin's own first novel. In *Things as They Are, or Caleb Williams*, as here, we have the incident of a false step, the attempt to do something forbidden which yet seems innocuous and a subsequent precipitation into sequences of persecution and flight. When Godwin wrote his work he began by conceiving these, then looked for a situation of sufficient interest and power to account for them. He settled on the ambiguous figure of Falkland, noblest yet also proudest of men, unable to face the disclosure of his guilt and so driven to persecute the man whose knowledge of it has given him power over him. This image of flight and relentless persecution, followed by the reversal, when the pursued turns into the pursuer and finally hunts him down, provides the point of greatest contact between the two novels. But there is also a further dimension, created by the subtle bond of affection between the two and consummated in both cases in the last scene. When Falkland finally acknowledges that he is wrong, Williams is left full of remorse at his own triumph and ends acknowledging Falkland's nobility. The monster, similarly, having destroyed everything that Frankenstein holds dear and lured him on to his own destruction, falls on his body at the end in a fit of uncontrollable grief and affection.

The major difference between the two novels is equally remarkable. The very code of chivalry according to which Falkland acts is seen as something outdated and belonging to the past, Caleb Williams's ultimate concern being with what has actually happened and with the need for justice. The forbidden knowledge he stumbles upon is the truth of past fact. That which Frankenstein discovers belongs to a coming world, in which man may be freed from dependency on the past and given control over his destiny. It is as if Mary Godwin is confronting her father and showing him how she has complemented his nightmare of the past with one of the future. 'Things as They Are' have now been supplemented by 'Things as They Will Be'.

There is also a running reference to the political writing of the time. As Lee Sterrenburg has pointed out, the image of the monster out of control was not uncommon. Edmund Burke had written in *Letters on a Regicide Peace* (1796),

> Out of the tomb of the murdered monarchy in France has arisen a vast, tremendous, unformed spectre, in a far more terrific guise than any which ever yet have overpowered the imagination, and subdued the fortitude of man. Going straight forward to its end, unappalled by peril, unchecked by remorse, despising all common maxims and all common means, that hideous phantom overpowered those who could not believe it was possible she could at all exist.

This image of the monstrous was equally available to writers on either side of the political spectrum. Mary's father had used it for the feudal system, which he saw as a ferocious monster, destroying, wherever it came, all that the friend of humanity regarded with attachment and love. He himself had in turn been seen in the same light. Burke had called his opinions 'pure defecated atheism ... the brood of that putrid carcase the French Revolution', while Horace Walpole called him 'one of the greatest monsters exhibited by history'. In 1799, the *Anti-Jacobin* published a parody of Fuseli's famous painting 'The Nightmare', showing the opposition Whig leader Charles James Fox asleep on his bed, while a grinning French Jacobin monster, resurrected from the dead, rode across his chest. At the foot of the bed lay a copy of Godwin's *Political Justice*. Mary Godwin grew up with a father constantly presented to the world in monstrous form, and knew how difficult it was, once it had been given currency in the public mind, to break such an image. It cannot have been a welcome development to her when, years later, Thomas De Quincey clinched the comparison further by declaring that Godwin had been regarded with the same alienation and horror as 'the monster created by Frankenstein'.

It was the French Revolution nevertheless that figured primarily as monstrous and the Shelleys shared the general fascination. Sterrenburg tells further how in the year she began *Frankenstein* they toured the revolutionary landmarks in France. They not only studied systematically the works of English radicals such as Thomas Paine and Mary's parents, but read widely in the works of conservatives and anti-Jacobins, including Edmund Burke, Abbé Barruel, John Adolphus and the anonymous French Revolutionary Plutarch, where the revolutionary mobs were often depicted as demons and monsters. Another telling point he makes is that in the Abbé Barruel's book on the history of Jacobinism, which Mary Shelley studied, Ingoldstadt, the city where Frankenstein made his monster, was cited as the place in which the 'monster called Jacobin' was conceived.

Before the making of this novel's themes is given over entirely to political influences, however, it should be recalled that in literature the relationship between actual life and any novel that may be written in its wake is always a complicated one, and more complex the better the novelist. The work of the imagination is by no means necessarily driven directly by the past, whether recent or remote; it may provide a means of escape. Much in *Frankenstein* belongs rather to Mary's reading of contemporary imaginative literature and her desire to contribute to it in her turn. Her very decision to throw in her lot with Shelley and live, first and foremost, in the life of the mind could be viewed in this light.

Three works are particularly relevant here. At one point the monster, living in a humble cottage in Germany, keeps watch on the family next door without their realizing it and is deeply attracted by their effortless affection towards one another. The description here is reminiscent of the German writing of the time, and particularly of *The Sufferings of the Young Werther*, where the key image is that of a young hero forced to look on at a family happiness he knows he can never share. The monster, in his own way, is in precisely that position. Just after relating these strong impressions he himself reveals how Goethe's novel was among three books he stumbled across and read: the others were Milton's *Paradise Lost* and Plutarch's *Lives*. The significance of the latter, in which uprightness of character in non-Christians is constantly displayed, should not be overlooked. The crucial figure, however, is Milton:

> But *Paradise Lost* excited different and far deeper emotions. I read it as I had read the other volumes which had fallen into my hands, as a true history. It moved every feeling of wonder and awe that the picture of an omnipotent God warring with his creatures was capable of exciting.

There had been rumblings of discontent with Milton's God in Pope's poetry, and Blake believed that Milton had written so well about the devils and so colourlessly about the angels because he was a true poet and therefore of the devil's party without knowing it; it was left to Mary Shelley's husband, however, to write of Milton's God as 'one who in the cold security of undoubted triumph inflicts the most horrible revenge upon his enemy, not from any mistaken notion of inducing him to repent of a perseverance in enmity, but with the alleged design of exasperating him to deserve new torments'.

Percy Bysshe Shelley's comments were not written until 1821; they may reflect Mary's views, or some further communal discussion. When the monster goes on to say that he found an affinity in himself to Satan, he is helping to establish the degree to which he also is a Promethean figure – and more directly in some ways than Frankenstein himself, being bound to the rock of a deformity which means that he can never hope for anything but hostility and fear from human beings.

The figure of Faust is also relevant. Whether Mary Shelley knew the first part of Goethe's drama is not clear, but it is very likely indeed that she knew Marlowe's version. The element of dabbling with forbidden knowledge has obvious links with that story. Instead of suffering an overtly divine vengeance, however, Frankenstein is punished through the necessary working out of the very process he has set in motion by creating his monster.

The element of the supernatural in the novel, signalled by events which are increasingly unbelievable on any other basis, brings us back to Wordsworth and Coleridge and most notably to *Lyrical Ballads*. In *The Rime of the Ancient Mariner*, a tale of the supernatural is presented not just as a work of pleasing terror in the Gothic style, but (rather as Godwin had hoped with *Caleb Williams*) in a way that might change the reader's view of the world. Even the elements of firm logic in her plot remind one of the naturalistic way in which the voyage is described in Coleridge's poem.

There can be no doubt of its presence since (apart from the fact that she herself had heard Coleridge read it aloud) it is quoted by Frankenstein himself to describe his state of mind when he has just run away from the monster he has created:

> Like one, that on a lonesome road
>   Doth walk in fear and dread,
> And having once turn'd round, walks on
>   And turns no more his head;
> Because he knows, a frightful fiend
>   Doth close behind him tread.

It is there also at the very beginning; in his second letter Walton writes:

> I am going to unexplored regions, to 'the land of mist and snow', but I shall kill no albatross, therefore do not be alarmed for my safety, or if I should come back to you as worn and woful as the 'Ancient Mariner?' You will smile at my allusion; but I will disclose a secret. I have often attributed my attachment to, my passionate attachment for, the dangerous mysteries of ocean, to that production of the most imaginative of modern poets.

Fourteen years later, when Mary Shelley was looking back on the creation of the novel and particularly of the monster, her description of his appearance in her original dream, 'I saw the hideous phantasm of a man stretched out, and then, on the working of some powerful engine, show signs of life, and stir with an uneasy, half-vital motion', recalls that of the ship in Coleridge's poem:

> But in a minute she 'gan stir
> With a short uneasy motion

These ready quotations show how intimately the images and language of Coleridge's poem had entered her imagination; we are also reminded that the poem's figure of Death has features akin to the monster's. Both the underlying preoccupation with the nature of life and the incidental imagery (the phantasmagorial travellings of the Mariner passing like night from land to land, for instance, being very like the behaviour of her own figures at the end of the story) betray the continued working of the poem in her imagination. The resemblances to Wordsworth are almost as telling. In chapter 18 Frankenstein pays tribute to his friend Clerval in the words: 'He was a being formed in the "very poetry of nature". His wild and enthusiastic imagination was chastened by the sensibility of his heart.' This could serve as a summary of Wordsworth's aims in *The Prelude*, where the workings of sublime feelings which separate him from the rest of mankind are constantly counter-pointed by the interventions of a quiet sensibility that reunites him again with the human race, 'Love of nature leading to love of man'. Mary could not of course have known *The Prelude*, but she knew the rest of Wordsworth's poetry, and a few lines later she actually quotes from *Tintern Abbey* – a poem describing his progress from a childhood of aching joys and dizzy raptures to the humane vision of the adult man. Precisely the kind of alternation that Wordsworth describes, between feelings of awe and fear in nature and feelings of unusual beauty and sympathy, characterizes Mary's novel. The monster is fearsome and tender by turns. There are long sequences in which he tells his own story and strikes a note of sympathy; there are others when we are aware of him only as an external and looming threat; the two can alternate rapidly.

At this point we have moved away from Mary's personal life and political concerns to her literary medium and to her Wordsworthian ideal of persuasion through fear and tender-ness. In these respects she participates in the development from a late eighteenth-century indulgence in Gothic terrors and cultivation of sensibility to a more fully realistic and human view. She also shares something of Coleridge's fascination with symbolic inter-pretations of the world. Andrew Griffin has shown how extraordinarily predominant in this novel is its imagery of fire and ice. The monster seems always to be encountered in frosty regions – but also often at times when a lightning storm is playing. Twice he expresses his despair by making a fire – the first time when he burns down the cottage vacated by the family from whom he had hoped for friendship, the second, at the end of the novel, when he sets himself on fire. Griffin further shows how Percy Bysshe Shelley's use of similar imagery – particularly in *Prometheus Unbound* – suggests a fascination with the extremes of nature displayed in these phenomena. In this sense, and given the patent improbability of the events, one may think of the novel as bordering on symbolic myth.

In considering the general impact of the novel this symbolic element must be given due weight. Yet if one follows its texture closely, paying attention to its proportions as it unfolds, the major power found to be constantly at work is that alternation between tenderness and domesticity on the one hand, and fear and violence on the other, which has been traced in the work of Wordsworth and Coleridge. It both penetrated her current relationships, where attempts to live by an ideal of love were constantly thwarted by events of an extraordinarily melodramatic nature, and was the most burning issue in contempor-ary politics, where movements towards humane reform were dogged by the effects of violence. It even lurked in the interstices of her relationship with her husband, where a notably tender and idealistic nature combined with a tendency to extremes that predicted his future fate and would leave some future students with the impression of him as a monstrous figure.

It is part of the power of her fiction, however, that she leaves the final implications of the future open. For many readers the effect of the novel remains primarily one of terror, the image of the monster haunting the imagination because we are most likely to identify ourselves with his creator. But it is also the case that Frankenstein drives the monster to despair by breaking his promise that he will create a mate for him. The monster's complaint throughout is that he was made needing and yearning for affection and benevolence, and these had been denied him. If he was right, then the gamble of making a mate for him would have paid off, leaving him, satisfied, to go away and stop troubling the human race. Frankenstein was not prepared to take the risk, but a modern audience that has read *The Elephant Man* may be more sympathetic to the monster.

On this larger scale the novel retains its potency by very reason of the fact that the questions it raises are unresolved. The monster becomes a symbol of the various terrors that lie beneath the surface of a rational civilization – fears of war, oppression, violence – and of the moral question that remains unanswered: whether or not it is the case that a failure of love and affection within the human race is the ultimate reason that those terrors abound. Because the questions are left open, they can be explored by each reader in his or her own way, while the basic issue, the Faustian question concerning the value to human beings of knowledge beyond a certain point, remains to tease further. She allows both elements of the Promethean myth, sharing them out between creator and creation. Frankenstein is Prometheus, stealer of fire and implanter of it in human clay; but it is the monster he created, forever to be tortured by the contradictions of his being, who exhibits most fully the Promethean predicament. If, as is sometimes claimed, Prometheus is the greatest saint in the Romantic calendar, Mary Shelley may be credited with having seen more fully than her Romantic contemporaries into the possibilities of his canonization and in so doing to have exposed some of the tensions inherent in Romanticism itself.

She also showed how fully she had absorbed the impact of *The Ancient Mariner*. From Coleridge's poem she had learned a means of handling nightmare in a way that could override more facile strategies of the time by incorporating an element of the contradictory. Just as the 'crime' of the Mariner looks more like a misdemeanour, so Frankenstein is punished by events that seem quite out of proportion to the act that initiated them. In both cases the reader is invited to question further. And since the issues conjured up take the reader to the very core of the problems besetting humanity in a post-Enlightenment world, her novel remains, even more than Coleridge's poem, infinitely reinterpretable.

## WRITINGS

Shelley, Mary, *Frankenstein, or the Modern Prometheus*, London, 1818; World's Classics edition ed. Marilyn Butler, Oxford and New York, 1994; Norton critical edition ed. J. Paul Hunter, New York and London, W. W. Norton, 1996.

## REFERENCES AND FURTHER READING

Baldick, Chris, *In Frankenstein's Shadow: Myth, Monstrosity, and Nineteenth-century Writing*, Oxford, Oxford University Press, 1987.

Bann, Stephen, *Frankenstein, Creation and Monstrosity*, London, Reaktion Books, 1994.

Botting, Fred, 'Frankenstein's French Revolutions: the dangerous necessity of monsters', in *Making Monstrous: Frankenstein, Criticism, Theory*, New York, St Martin's Press, 1991, pp. 139–63.

Brooks, Peter, 'What is a monster? (according to Frankenstein)', in *Body Work: Objects of Desire in Modern Narrative*, Cambridge, Mass., Harvard University Press, 1993, pp. 199–220.

Griffin, Andrew, 'Fire and ice in *Frankenstein*', in *The Endurance of Frankenstein*, ed. George Levine and U. C. Knoepflmacher, Berkeley, University of California Press, 1979, pp. 49–73.

Hume, Robert D., 'Gothic versus Romantic: a revaluation of the Gothic novel', *PMLA* 84 (1969) 282–90.

Kiely, Robert, *The Romantic Novel in England*, Cambridge, Mass., Harvard University Press, 1972.

Jacobus, Mary, 'Is there a woman in this text?', in *Reading Women: Essays in Feminist Criticism*, New York, Columbia University Press, 1986, pp. 83–109.

Levine, George, '*Frankenstein* and the tradition of Realism', *Novel* 7 (1973) 14–30.

—— 'The ambiguous heritage of *Frankenstein*', in *The Endurance of Frankenstein*, ed. George Levine and U. C. Knoepflmacher, Berkeley, University of California Press, 1979 pp. 3–30.

Lipking, Lawrence, '*Frankenstein*, the true story; or Rousseau judges Jean-Jacques', in *Frankenstein*, Norton critical edition, ed. J. Paul Hunter, New York and London, W. W. Norton, 1996, pp. 313–31.

Mellor, Anne K., '*Frankenstein*: a feminist critique of science', in *One Culture: Essays in Science and Literature*, ed. George Levine, Madison, University of Wisconsin Press, 1987, pp. 287–312.

—— *Mary Shelley, Her Life, Her Fiction, Her Monsters*, New York and London, Routledge, 1988.

Moers, Ellen, 'Female Gothic', in *The Endurance of Frankenstein*, ed. George Levine and U. C. Knoepflmacher, Berkeley, University of California Press, 1979, pp. 77–87.

Richardson, Alan, 'From *Emile* to *Frankenstein*: the education of monsters', in *Literature, Education and Romanticism: Reading as Social Practice, 1780–1832*, Cambridge, Cambridge University Press, 1994.

Spivak, Gayatri Chakravorty, 'Three women's texts and a critique of imperialism', in *'Race', Writing and Difference*, ed. Henry Louis Gates, Jr, Chicago, Chicago University Press, 1986, pp. 262–80.

Sterrenburg, Lee, 'Mary Shelley's monster: politics and psyche in *Frankenstein*', in *The Endurance of Frankenstein*, ed. George Levine and U. C. Knoepflmacher, Berkeley, University of California Press, 1979, pp. 143–71.

# 23

# John Keats, *Odes*

## *John Creaser*

Keats's odes can tempt us to either a mindless or a single-minded response. One temptation is to surrender to the richness of texture and perfection of utterance in a stupor of admiration. Keats himself seems a victim of the other when he writes: 'Poetry should be great & unobtrusive, a thing which enters into one's soul, and does not startle it or amaze it with itself but with its subject.'[1] He is envisaging a deep and undivided response, uncomplicated by effects of alienation. Yet, while the odes do lack the ostentatious virtuosity of earlier poems such as *Endymion*, their writing remains 'startling', disconcerting and anything but monotone to an alert reader.

It can be difficult to trust oneself to the complexity of textual play in the odes. For example, the first three stanzas of *Ode on a Grecian Urn* address the urn with unhesitating and mounting rapture. In its silence, the urn is praised for transcending the narratives of poetry. Initially, the insistent questions which complete the first stanza – 'What men or gods are these? What maidens loth' – seem of a rhetorical tendency: they are not enquiries, but expressions of wonder at the energy and attitudes portrayed. The second and third stanzas celebrate a world which is 'for ever new': the urn's silent portrayal of music is set above music itself, while the perpetual eagerness of the lovers is far superior to the cloying of normal earthly desire. But in the third stanza the writing becomes over-heated and over-insistent, and some fine critics have censured the six repetitions of both 'happy' and 'ever', the chiming of five present participles, the contorted word-order of the eighth line, 'All breathing human passion far above', and the frenetic images of warm and panting marble.[2] They assume that Keats has blundered into crude emphasis rather than 'unobtrusive' authority.

Yet the surface of unquestioning rapture at what the urn offers is always accompanied by a sceptical and questioning response, for the urn also invites genuine enquiry. The first two lines can be read as tantalizingly enigmatic. In what way is the urn 'still unravish'd'? Will it somehow 'always' be so, or has it only escaped 'so far', or is it merely 'unmoving'? In what sense is the urn the bride 'of quietness'? How can an urn be an 'unravish'd bride'? An urn can certainly be imagined as suggesting a female form, and an urn receives and contains, but what is its marriage-night? A bride is traditionally *virgo intacta* and this urn is remarkably intact. But a bride 'puts on perfection, and a woman's name'[3] by losing her 'intact' state, whereas once an urn is no longer intact it is no longer perfect. Ignore such questions, and 'unravish'd' presumably means not yet enraptured by the love-making of the marriage-night. But if 'quietness' is the groom, perhaps the marriage will remain perpetually unconsummated? And what groom thinks of himself as 'ravishing' his bride, as if he were violating her? None the less, the term admits the elements of possessiveness and dread within sexual joy, as when Porphyro steals into Madeline's bedroom and melts into her dream, or when Lycius, cruel in his passion, imposes his will on Lamia until 'she burnt, she lov'd the tyranny' (II, 81). So where an unquestioning response sees only rapturous expectation in 'unravish'd bride', a more reflective response sees the vulnerability of both art-object and love-object.[4]

The foster-parents emphasize the mystery: with its maker dead, we have the 'silence' of inscrutability left by the slow passage of time. To the reflective onlooker, its mysterious beauty also brings home a loss of historical immediacy and shared understanding. It cannot even tell us whether it is a funerary casket or a domestic ornament. Now the questions in the first stanza are real questions, not just expressions of wonder. We cannot be sure what is happening in the orgiastic frenzy shown on the quiet surface of the urn, since we do not know who is taking part, or where they are. Is it a holy rite, a ceremony of fertility? Or, since the maidens are 'loth', is it a scene of mass-rape? Or do the women share in the 'wild ecstasy' and is their 'struggle to escape' there merely to heighten the excitement?

This implies reservations about the urn as a 'sylvan historian' which 'sweetly' tells 'a flowery tale'. At the simplest, historians both tell and interpret stories. Perhaps the urn can 'express' itself 'more sweetly than our rhyme' precisely because the last thing it can do is tell, let alone analyse, a story. Instead, it gives a moment of 'ecstasy', of action just before consummation, without having to present or examine the consequences. As a 'sweet' and 'sylvan' historian, its pastoral art works through simplification and idealization. The touch of menace in the legend which 'haunts about' its shape and in the struggle of the 'maidens loth' is perceived only by the reflective consciousness. In a letter, Keats writes: 'Though a quarrel in the streets is a thing to be hated, the energies displayed in it are fine; the commonest Man shows a grace in his quarrel.'[5] The urn can represent the momentary fineness of such energies, but not the moral realities in which they are displayed.

There are, therefore, antithetical ways of reading the first stanza, and neither can be rejected. The immediate, absorbed response of the speaker is to the beauty of the urn – its remoteness makes its survival the more wonderful. It is the excitement of the scene which matters, not what it signifies. But from a reflective viewpoint, the urn is frustratingly enigmatic. Now the urn will always remain 'unravish'd' in another sense, that it will never be possessed by the understanding. The urn is perpetually novel and perpetually tantalizing.

In the next two stanzas, there are exclamation marks, not questions, because the urn portrays the universal pleasures of music and of accepted courtship. Now the only questions are begged. Why are unheard melodies sweeter than heard? Why is a being of arrested motion happier than a being whose life is process? The immediate response still approaches the urn in a spirit of wishful thinking, responding to its art as if it were life. But as the stanzas proceed, the 'dull brain perplexes and retards', and the enthusiasm becomes a vehement and implausible assertion. For, to the reflective mind, if the lovers on the urn are imagined as alive – 'For ever warm, and still to be enjoy'd' – then their state is as much frustration as vital promise, to be pitied as much as envied. The address to the 'fair youth' has hardly begun when the note turns from joy to limitation: 'never, never, canst thou kiss'. The advice not to grieve suggests he resembles Tantalus in Hades. The blessing of immortality condemns the lovers to sterility. The speaker strains to persuade himself that such a state is blissful and desirable, and the strain shows in the heated language, as if he is desperate to believe it possible to be 'happy' and live 'for ever'.

The contradiction between the rapturous and sceptical responses can be accommodated by reading the ode as a subtle kind of dramatic monologue – a form which turns on a discrepancy between what the speaker proclaims and what the author implies. Keats's ode distinguishes between the immediate utterance of the poet as speaker and his reflective consciousness – between (to take phrases of Wordsworth out of context) the spontaneous overflow of powerful feeling and emotion recollected in tranquillity. The enthusiastic speaker is so oppressively conscious of the frustrations and transience of mortal living that he projects his own fantasies of timeless passion onto the carved images. With almost cruel illogic, Keats the questioning poet undermines the desires of his speaking self by having him claim that the 'panting' love on the urn is far superior to 'breathing human passion'. The ideal is modelled on the reality of flesh, and the more alive the urn seems, the less ideal it becomes. Nor is it self-evident that being perpetually 'near the goal' is superior to having a 'heart high-sorrowful and cloy'd', since that implies there has been some fulfilment, something worth having.

So the immediate, speaking self is aching to attain a state of passionate arrest which the poet's reflective self sees as scarcely more desirable than it is attainable. Keats's odes are at their strongest – in *to a Nightingale*, *To Autumn* and here *on a Grecian Urn* – precisely where they most exploit this distinction, separating or merging the selves in response to the flow of emotion and recollection. Read sequentially, much in these poems is the utterance of a speaker carried away by images of perfection. But read spatially, as integrated wholes, they are the work of a poet who has already been through the experience and is recreating it judiciously. Speaker and author are different phases of the same mind, answering to different needs and impulses within the same consciousness.

At first sight it is strange that mental division should be expressed through a traditional form such as the ode, which has its roots in ancient religion and festival. As the most exalted of lyric forms, the ode was a self-conscious creation of Renaissance Humanists, but its origins lie in the cult-hymns of ancient Greece and in the songs where Pindar, the great lyric poet of fifth-century Greece, celebrates victors in the ancient games. By definition, a hymn is an act of religious worship, while Pindar not only links ephemeral human deeds to what is enduring and divine, but also embodies social solidarity, because his songs, written for public performance, made him literally the voice of the community. Out of these ancient forms develops the act of rhetorical celebration which is the 'Pindaric' or 'Great' or 'sublime' ode of the seventeenth and eighteenth centuries.[6]

A cult-hymn has the tripartite structure of prayer: invocation of a deity by his or her several names; celebration of the divine origins, deeds and powers; a vow of service and petition for favour.[7] This simple pattern remains clear in Keats's *to Psyche* or Shelley's *Ode to the West Wind*. The formal elaboration of most odes owes more, however, to Pindar, whose songs are intricately symmetrical in form, densely allusive in phrasing, and given to abrupt transitions of subject and steep changes of tone.[8] The result is the most ceremonious, elevated and complex of lyric forms, clearly distinguishable from the more urbane and colloquial odes in simpler forms which descend from the Latin poet Horace, and from the slighter Anacreontic odes of wine, women and song. The 'Greater' ode aims at sublimity and amplitude; its celebration comes from a mind 'transported' by enthusiasm and fervour, expressing itself through bold imagery and volatile transitions. Decorum and dignity are not sacrificed, however, because an ode is also a self-reflexive demonstration of the poet's rhetorical authority. It is no coincidence that the odes most acclaimed in the eighteenth century are Dryden's *Alexander's Feast; or the Power of Music* (1697) and Thomas Gray's *The Bard* (1755–7), both of which commemorate the powers of art and manifest them in the poetry itself. Even so, with its origins in worship and festivity, the ode remains pre-eminently a public rather than personal form, declamatory rather than intimate in expression.

By Keats's time, however, the ode was being transformed. The single-minded faith of the ancient hymn has become the inner division of the dramatic monologue; the ancient poet as an embodiment of social values has become an isolated individual (though he may often be representative in his isolation); the celebration of the power of poetry is becoming a concentration on the poet himself. As elaborate poems of address, Keats's odes belong in an exalted tradition, and yet within it they are untraditionally personal, intimate and reflective.

As is shown by Shelley's odes *to Liberty* and *to Naples* (both 1820), the tradition of the public and sublime ode remained alive when Keats was writing. Nevertheless, reading Coleridge's *Dejection: an Ode* (1802) after his odes of the 1790s, such as *to the Departing Year* (1796), shows how poets of the Romantic period could give the form a new inwardness. *Ode to the Departing Year* is traditional in its declamatory sublime; *Dejection*, which is based on a verse letter and begins not 'Lo!' but 'Well!', is addressed not to a deity or higher quality but to an equal, and is more conversational and equable in tone than a traditional ode. The subject is now personal, and the setting occasional and specific, while worship and celebration give place to meditation. This, together with Wordsworth's companion poem *Ode: Intimations of Immortality* (1802–4), initiates the ode of personal crisis, a poem of process rather than projection, more intimate and searching than even a personal neo-classical ode such as Gray's *on a Distant Prospect of Eton College*. Although quieter and more meditative than traditional odes, these poems are nevertheless more dramatic, because the speaker works his way through a crisis. They are not poems of confident exposition but of sustained exploration, while the speaker seeks to discover what can be retrieved from the damage done to his confidence in nature and his art. Keats shares this inwardness, and even *to Psyche*, an address to a goddess in traditional form, becomes highly subjective, locating her cult in a fane within a garden within a sanctuary within a mountainous landscape within 'some untrodden region of my mind'. Whereas the shepherds' hymn to Pan in the first book of *Endymion* worships that deity-in-nature with such naturalness that Words-worth anxiously dismissed it as 'a Very pretty piece of Paganism', *to Psyche* is written out of a nostalgic sense of exclusion from the ancient harmony of nature and the divine.[9]

Keats and the other Romantics remain traditional, however, in writing odes, like hymns, pre-eminently in the form of an address. The distinctive rhetorical figure of their odes remains apostrophe, direct address even to absent or dead persons, or things, or abstract ideas, as if they were alive and present.

At first sight it is paradoxical that many Romantic poems of crisis should be written in a mode apt for the expression of secure faith, but apostrophe can reveal alike the power and the powerlessness, the communal authority and the utter loneliness, of the poetic voice. On the one hand, the 'vocative' poet seems to enjoy a relationship commanding and familiar with the universe. On the other, the very act of invocation readily becomes more important than what is invoked, and reveals the impotent isolation of the speaker. As Jonathan Culler has argued, to utter an apostrophe is

> the pure embodiment of poetic pretension, . . . the attempt to bring about . . . the condition of visionary poet who can engage in dialogue with the universe . . . But one must note that it figures this reconciliation as an act of will, . . . and poems which contain apostrophes often end in withdrawals and questions . . . This figure which seems to establish relations between the self and the other can in fact be read as an act of radical interiorization and solipsism.[10]

This duality is much more explored by the Romantic ode of inwardness and its successors than by earlier odes speaking from a stronger sense of shared values. After Wordsworth and Coleridge, even the most passionate of invocations – of, say, the west wind by Shelley – can arouse no more than endlessly prolonged expectation. Significantly, Keats invokes figures – pagan deity, nightingale, urn and diverse personifications – which could never respond. Invoking such ideals only emphasizes how unattainable or incommunicable they are. Apostrophe is peculiarly apt for that state of alienation which Matthew Arnold was to define as the displacement of 'disinterested objectivity' by 'the dialogue of the mind with itself'.[11]

Just as Keats makes a pervasive distinction between the optimistic fervour of poet as speaker and the ironic reservations of poet as implied author, so he exploits the ambivalence of Romantic apostrophe: the poems make the highest claims for the evocative powers of the poetic voice, and also reveal its powerlessness in the face of external reality. This reflects a deep division in Keats's prevailing impulses, a division which can merely be sketched out here.

On the one hand, he aligns himself with liberal, progressive, and optimistic views, and, as David Perkins puts it, responds to religious and political dilemmas 'by constructing myths of progress'.[12] He rejects the Church and what he terms 'the pious frauds of Religion' but, as someone of keen religious sensibility, searches for a personal faith which could do justice to his spiritual intuitions. His most resourceful speculation comes in a letter where he rejects Christian notions of redemption and of the world as a 'vale of tears' in favour of what he terms 'The vale of Soul-making'. He outlines a theory in which a human being develops a soul and identity through suffering, so that a world of pain and death can be justified as necessary.[13]

There is a similar wresting of optimism from adversity in Keats's historical and political views. For example, he argues that Wordsworth has profounder insight into human experience than does Milton, not through having greater powers but through 'the general and gregarious advance of intellect'. Their equality as individuals 'proves there is really a grand march of intellect –, It proves that a mighty providence subdues the mightiest Minds to the service of the time being, whether it be in human Knowledge or Religion'.[14] For Keats, this means 'the gradual annihilation of . . . tyranny', the growth of 'popular privileges' and 'the . . . progress of free sentiments'.[15] Such a faith is the basis of the epic fragment *Hyperion*, where the Titans are being displaced by their descendants the Olympians, not through any failures as ruling deities, but through irresistible evolution.

Yet again, there is optimism in the shaping patterns of Keats's literary art. For example, his first major achievement, the sonnet *On First Looking into Chapman's Homer*, ends with a heart-stopping image of expanding horizons as Cortez stands silent on the skyline between two oceans, on the verge of articulating a discovery which will change the world. Keats's most charged poetry continues to dwell in this way on the liminal, on the 'still unravish'd' moment before a transforming experience. Moreover, he is very much a poet of 'epiphanies', of sudden, overwhelming manifestations. The pattern is again set by the irruption of Homer in the Chapman sonnet, is most fully developed in the diverse appearances of the loving goddess Diana to Endymion, and continues in endless modulation.

Yet such 'myths of progress' in Keats are stubbornly resisted by pessimistic impulses. Even the sketch of the 'vale of Soul-making' denies unqualified optimism: 'But in truth I do not at all believe in this sort of perfectibility'.[16] As Greg Kucich in particular has shown,[17] Keats laments the absence from his time of men of Milton's stature, and his account of social and political progress is complicated by acknowledged periods of reaction in England and France. Keats's maturer poetry is initiated by a verse-letter to J. H. Reynolds which sets out as an informal and jocose poem to cheer up an invalid, yet moves through nightmarish images into a terrible vision of destruction. The two versions of *Hyperion* which frame the writing of the odes in 1819 belie the evolutionary doctrine. The first lingers compassionately on the shock and suffering of the displaced Titans, while giving no more than an outline of Olympian Apollo's maturing into godhead. *The Fall of Hyperion* is a work of profound desolation, yet in his letters Keats makes no distinction between the two versions, as if his conscious intentions remained as progressive as before.

There is a similar conflict of impulses within the odes, although held now in conscious tension rather than merely juxtaposed in contradiction. The optimistic tendencies of both borderline and epiphanic experiences are clearly present. The Grecian urn, for instance, has a sense of perpetual promise, as the urn itself and its images are located on a series of borderlines – with winning 'near the goal' – moments or sequences which are alert with expectation because they are on the brink of transition from one state to another. In *To Autumn* the whole of nature and of seasonal labour is on the edge of repletion; all is 'last oozings', yet nothing is 'o'er-brimm'd' except the benign excess of honey; there is not even the overripeness of windfallen fruit. The poem locates itself in a blessed interval of plenitude, with the harvest safely gathered in and the swallows still only gathering before the onset of colder weather. Similarly, the apparitions of Psyche and the other revered presences in the odes bring inspiring images of perfection into focus.

Characteristically, however, these manifestations become subject to ironic, although never caustic, reservation and misgiving. The men and maidens on the urn, for example, recede into decorative details, worked over as a 'brede' or braid which all too clearly can never breed or even become 'overwrought'. As 'cold Pastoral' rather than 'warm and still to be enjoy'd', the marble urn can seem inhuman in its inviolable perfection – 'marble to the touch and to the heart', as Hazlitt describes ancient statues.[18] Similarly, the urn's faith in its aestheticism seems too comfortable, especially if one accepts the present consensus that the urn is to be imagined speaking the whole of the last two lines: '"Beauty is truth, truth beauty," – that is all / Ye know on earth, and all ye need to know.'[19] Old age's wasting of mortal generations is alone enough for us to realize that not all truths are beautiful. Indeed, the central impulse of Keats's art is to come to terms with ugly truths and realities. Although a beguiling and idyllic image of unity of being, the urn speaks only for itself, a beautiful illusion.

So despite the eager greeting of objects of veneration throughout the odes, the poems are elegiac and nostalgic in feeling. They speak of a state of wholeness and of old certainties out of a conviction of loss. The vocatives of greeting so characteristic of an ode are here balanced by 'farewell'. These are poems where Joy's 'hand is ever at his lips / Bidding adieu'; the cry 'Adieu' is heard in every poem except *To Autumn*,[20] and there everything is pervaded by the imminence of loss: the imagined fecundity of the first two stanzas is a time of 'last oozings', while the songs of autumn among the real stubble-plains of the last stanza are all songs of farewell, heard among the declining light of evening.

Read as grouped in *1820*, and even more if read in the likely chronological sequence, the odes present a progressive disenchantment and resignation. *Nightingale*, *Grecian Urn* and *Psyche* are grouped together, separated by four short and lighter poems from *Autumn* and *Melancholy*. The first group – which almost certainly contains the first odes of spring – attempts to bring images of perfection into focus and to present manifestations of time-lessness within time. The later poems of the second group acknowledge transience frankly.

On the surface, the earliest ode, *to Psyche*, is the most confident in its enthusiastic response to a vision of harmony. Cupid and Psyche embody both unity of being and, in view of the myth behind the poem, the union of the mortal with the divine. But the dominant feeling is nostalgia, as Psyche represents only the last glimmering of an age of 'happy pieties', when the material universe was instinct with divinity. The poem is not, as Ian Jack maintains, 'essentially a pagan act of worship',[21] but one of intense wish-fulfilment on the speaker's part, symbolized in the extreme subjectivity of the cult of Psyche in the closing stanza.

While the optimistic fantasies are moderated in *to a Nightingale*, the speaker is still passionately in search of an organic relation with nature which would also be a transcend-ence of time: 'Thou wast not born for death, immortal Bird!' Now, however, there is an explicit fear that the fancy has merely been cheating him. In *Grecian Urn* timelessness is sought not in divinity or nature but in something man-made: the grounds for confidence are shrinking, while confidence itself is being undermined. Whereas the speaker of *Psyche* remains within the enchantment and the speaker of *Nightingale* emerges only confusedly out of it, the speaker of *Grecian Urn* eventually achieves a state of critical although admiring detachment from his 'cold Pastoral'.

The broad pattern I am sketching out continues with the second group in *1820*, which, in acknowledging transience, does not attempt its arrest in an imagined timelessness, but instead seeks to prolong the evanescent. In *Melancholy* the speaker is a gourmet of experience, with the 'palate fine' of a connoisseur; he advises relishing the transience which earlier odes sought to transcend, luxuriating in what is passing because it is passing. *To Autumn* seeks a less hedonistic and ultimately less self-defeating awareness of transience, and achieves serene acceptance through abandoning hope. The deified presence of Autumn to whom the ode is supposedly addressed is consistently overwhelmed – first by natural fecundity, then by human presences, and finally by precise location in a landscape without numinous overtones. Nature is now loved for itself – even though the 'music' of autumn sounds always of farewell. The first three odes are marked by states of trance and rapture, though with each poem these are seen more clearly for what they were. *Melancholy* turns disenchantment to intoxication. In *To Autumn*, however, the drowsy repletion of the first two stanzas gives way to the sobriety of the third, while the melancholy music of the season is recorded with disenchanted affection.

In parallel with this, the central symbolic figures of the odes become less dominant. While the visionary figure of Psyche pervades her ode, the nightingale eventually deserts the listener and the urn becomes carved marble rather than impassioned life. The figure of Melancholy emerges only in the closing stanza, while the personified deity of Autumn is at last abandoned, now for the first time without reluctance, and devotion focused on the reality of the season.

Jonathan Culler has distinguished vocative and narrative writing in these terms: 'Apostrophe resists narrative because its *now* is not a moment in a temporal sequence but a *now* of discourse, of writing'.[22] The progress of disenchantment which marks Keats's finest odes brings them from the continuous present of vocative to the real time of narrative, as the sceptical poet emerges from the eagerness of the speaker. Tolled back to 'my sole self', the poet of *Nightingale* comes to acknowledge that the eternal song of the bird is 'now...buried deep / In the next valley-glades'. After the steadying meditation on the scene of sacrifice in the fourth stanza, the poet of *Grecian Urn* is able to face with equanimity the present wasting of 'this' generation, aware that not all is lost. *To Autumn* abandons its invocation of the personified season for 'now', a real moment, when the redbreast whistles and swallows twitter.

The return to present realities is not, however, a simple process of escape from illusion. The depth of perception within the richest passages means that the objects of veneration retain significance. The final crescendo in praise of the immortal bird in *Nightingale*, for example, is nonsense in the workaday world of ornithology and history, and becomes more fanciful with each example. Yet it also offers a concentrated symbol of continuity in human experience, for nightingale song can indeed touch the hearts of emperor and clown, past and present, home and abroad, and bring romance into the mundane. Although the nightingale plays no part in the biblical story of Ruth, the lines on her create an image of nostalgic loneliness which is as vivid and true to life as anything in the original. A sense of human solidarity is enhanced by the images which invoke common sources of joy and sorrow. Meanings are given *off* in these figures of community, compassion and yearning beyond the simple fantasies spelt *out* by the speaker. So an experience worked up in the speaker's fancy need not be rejected outright by the reflective poet. There has been 'vision' as well as merely 'a waking dream'.

Similarly, there is a vivid response to the real within the escapism of the speaker. Literally, the fifth stanza reinforces the acknowledgement in the preceding lines that his 'dull brain' prevents him from flying with the bird to the moon's heavenly light, and that his place remains with the darkness of earth. Symbolically, it is a benighted reality, and its 'embalmed darkness' prepares for the next stanza's brooding over the riches of death. Yet this dark reality is full of richly appreciated nature, in a palpable setting where light is felt to be 'blown' and scents rather than flowers 'hang' upon the boughs. The sense of smell tests each 'sweet' with a discrimination that is loving and not at all indulgent, and though the violets are fading (as does so much in this ode and all the odes), the musk-rose is 'coming' into bloom. There is a serene acceptance of natural process here which anticipates the ripeness of *To Autumn*, a poem which in its turn does not dismiss the abnormal fecundity of the opening stanzas when the reality of the stubble-plains is reached.

Helen Vendler rightly finds completion rather than disappointment in Keats's endings: 'The odd result of the desolations in *Nightingale* and elsewhere is that we feel, in those pained awakenings from Fancy, Keats's most solid poetic strength, a strength which eventually affirms not a vanishing but a discovery'.[23] That discovery is a process of discrimination: reflective judgement emerges from a trance of passion into a state of disenchantment and even desolation. Although the sceptical poet is only too aware that the imagination may 'feign', 'cheat' and 'tease', he is careful to preserve intimations of insight and value within the dissolved fantasies.

## NOTES

1   To J. H. Reynolds, 3 February 1818, Rollins, I, 224.
2   For example, Brooks, *The Well Wrought Urn*, p. 129; Vendler, *Odes*, p. 128.
3   John Donne, *Epithalamion Made at Lincoln's Inn*, line 96.
4   Feminist critics' distaste for this passage as 'obviously male . . . offensive and blinkered' (Kelvin Everest in Roe, *Keats and History*, p. 123), overlooks how the passage invites questioning.
5   To George and Georgina Keats, 19 March 1819, Rollins, II, 80.
6   On the nature and history of the ode, see Curran, *Poetic Form*; Maclean, 'From action to image'; Shafer, *The English Ode*; and Sheats, 'Keats'.
7   See, for example, Alcaeus, *The Dioscuri*, Sappho, *A Prayer to Aphrodite* and Cleanthes, *Hymn to Zeus*, reprinted and translated in *The Penguin Book of Greek Verse*, ed. Constantine A. Trypanis, Harmondsworth, Penguin, 1971, pp. 143–4, 283.
8   For Pindar, see Nisetich, *Pindar's Victory Songs*. Accomplished English imitations of Pindar include Ben Jonson, *To the Immortal Memory and Friendship of That Noble Pair, Sir Lucius Cary and Sir H. Morison* and Thomas Gray, *The Progress of Poesy* and *The Bard*.
9   Rollins, *Keats Circle*, II, 143–4.

10  Jonathan Culler, 'Apostrophe', in *The Pursuit of Signs: Semiotics, Literature, Deconstruction*, London, Routledge & Kegan Paul, 1981, pp. 143, 146.
11  'Preface to the First Edition of *Poems*', in *The Poems of Matthew Arnold*, 2nd edn, ed. Kenneth and Miriam Allott, London, Longman, 1979, p. 654.
12  Perkins, *The Quest for Permanence*, p. 197.
13  To George and Georgina Keats, 21 April 1819, Rollins, II, 101–4.
14  To J. H. Reynolds, 3 May 1818, Rollins, I, 281–2.
15  To George and Georgina Keats, 18 September 1819, Rollins, II, 193.
16  Ibid., p. 101.
17  In Roe, *Keats and History*, pp. 249–51; see also letters to George and Georgina, 14 October 1818 and 18 September 1819, Rollins, I, 396–7; II, 193.
18  'On Poetry in General' (1818), in Howe, V, 11. See also Howe, IV, 79.
19  This is the conclusion of both the Longman and Penguin editors. See also Stillinger, *Hoodwinking*, pp. 167–71. 'This crux now seems settled' (Vendler, *Odes of John Keats*, p. 312).
20  Sperry, *Keats the Poet*, p. 284.
21  Jack, *Keats and the Mirror of Art*, p. 204.
22  'Apostrophe', p. 152: see note 10.
23  Vendler, *Odes of John Keats*, p. 86.

## WRITINGS

Allott, Miriam (ed.) *The Poems of John Keats*, London, Longman, 1970.

Barnard, John (ed.) *John Keats: The Complete Poems*, Harmondsworth, Penguin, 1973.

Rollins, Hyder Edward (ed.) *The Keats Circle: Letters and Papers*, 2 vols, 2nd edn, Cambridge, Mass., Harvard University Press, 1965.

Stillinger, Jack (ed.) *The Poems of John Keats*, London, Heinemann, 1978. Quotations are from this edition.

## REFERENCES AND FURTHER READING

Bate, Walter Jackson, *John Keats*, Cambridge, Mass., Belknap Press of Harvard University Press, 1963. A major life-and-works survey.

Brooks, Cleanth, *The Well Wrought Urn: Studies in the Structure of Poetry*, London, Methuen, 1968. See chapter eight, 'Keats's sylvan historian'.

Creaser, John, 'From Autumn to autumn in Keats's ode', *Essays in Criticism* 38 (1988) 190–214. Fills out the references to the ode in this chapter.

Curran, Stuart, *Poetic Form and British Romanticism*, Oxford, Oxford University Press, 1986. See chapter four, 'The hymn and ode'.

Fraser, G. S. (ed.) *John Keats: Odes: A Casebook*, London, Macmillan, 1971.

Jack, Ian, *Keats and the Mirror of Art*, Oxford, Clarendon Press, 1968. Keats and his visual sources.

McGann, Jerome, 'Keats and the historical method in literary criticism', *Modern Language Notes* 94 (1979) 988–1,032. Influential attempt to set Keats in context.

Maclean, Norman, 'From action to image: theories of the lyric in the eighteenth century', in *Critics and Criticism: Ancient and Modern*, ed. R. S. Crane, Chicago, University of Chicago Press, 1952, pp. 408–60. Development of the ode in the century before Keats.

Mellor, Anne K., *English Romantic Irony*, Cambridge, Mass., Harvard University Press, 1980.

Nisetich, Frank J., *Pindar's Victory Songs*, Baltimore, Johns Hopkins Press, 1980. Makes a difficult but seminal ancient author accessible.

Perkins, David, *The Quest for Permanence: The Symbolism of Wordsworth, Shelley and Keats*, Cambridge, Mass., Harvard University Press, 1959.

Phinney, A. W., 'Keats in the museum: between aesthetics and history', *Journal of English and Germanic Philology* 90 (1991) 208–22. Valuable on Grecian Urn.

Rhodes, Jack Wright, *Keats's Major Odes: An Annotated Bibliography of the Criticism*, Westport, Conn., Greenwood Press, 1984.

Roe, Nicholas (ed.) *Keats and History*, Cambridge, Cambridge University Press, 1995. Keats in context: uneven but interesting.

Shafer, Robert, *The English Ode to 1660*, Princeton, Princeton University Press, 1918. Simple introduction to the ode.

Sheats, Paul D., 'Keats, the greater ode, and the trial of imagination', in *Coleridge, Keats, and the Imagination*, ed. J. Robert Barth, SJ and John L. Mahoney, Columbia, University of Missouri Press, 1990, pp. 174–200.

Sperry, Stuart M., *Keats the Poet*, Princeton, Princeton University Press, 1973. A fine general study.

Stillinger, Jack, *Twentieth Century Interpretations of Keats's Odes*, Englewood Cliffs, NJ, Prentice-Hall, 1968.

—— *The Hoodwinking of Madeline and Other Essays on Keats's Poems*, Urbana, University of Illinois Press, 1971.

—— 'John Keats', in *The English Romantic Poets: A Review of Research and Criticism*, 4th edn, ed. Frank Jordan, Modern Language Association of America, 1985), pp. 665–718. A discriminating appraisal of work on the poet.

Vendler, Helen, *The Odes of John Keats*, Cambridge, Mass. and London, Belknap Press of Harvard University Press, 1983. Richly perceptive, though can be perverse.

# 24

# George Gordon, Lord Byron, *Don Juan*

*Jane Stabler*

Unlike Romantic epics by Byron's contemporaries – Robert Southey's *Madoc*, William Blake's *Jerusalem*, William Wordsworth's *The Prelude* and John Keats's unfinished *Hyperion* poems – *Don Juan* was released volume by volume to its readership, so that consequent changes in Byron's relationship with the English public are foregrounded as a dynamic of the poem. Access to *Don Juan* is now usually through anthologized extracts, or through editions of Byron's complete works: increasingly, access will be through electronically retrievable texts. In all these cases, we lose the immediate impact that the circumstances of publication made on the poem's first audiences. In all readings of *Don Juan*, it is vital first of all to recover a sense of where we are in the history of the poem: whether we are reading one of the early cantos published by John Murray, or whether we are joining the poem in Canto VI or later, when Byron had passed over the business of publishing to the Radical John Hunt (who was associated with the Cockney School).

For the poem's first readers, the details of publication were part of *Don Juan*'s meaning. John Murray had established Byron's reputation in 1812, when the first instalments of *Childe Harold's Pilgrimage* made Byron famous and Murray rich. Since then, Murray had published Byron's work in handsome and highly collectable editions: referring to *The Giaour*, a reviewer commented on the costliness of 'four shillings and sixpence for forty-one octavo pages of poetry . . . very happily answering to Mr Sheridan's image of a rivulet of text flowing through a meadow of margin'.[1] During the 'years of fame' (1812–16) Byron's poetry was launched as a fashionable high-society commodity. Late in 1818, however, there was strong disagreement between Byron and his publisher and friends about whether *Don Juan* was publishable.

Byron had begun the poem in July 1818 while resident in Venice. After some debate about revisions, the first two cantos were published anonymously on 15 July 1819. The expensive quarto production and pre-publication rumours meant that the poem was instantly recognizable as another work by Byron published by Murray. *Don Juan* had a cautious welcome from some reviewers but it provoked outrage from other quarters: *Blackwood's* reviewer decided that

> The moral strain of the whole poem is pitched in the lowest key – and if the genius of the author lifts him now and then out of his pollution, it seems as if he regretted the elevation, and made all haste to descend again.[2]

Gradually, this tone of moral affront took firm hold amongst reviewers and public alike, and by 1822 Murray himself was no longer able to withstand it. He had reluctantly published a further three cantos (III–V) in 1821, but drew back from Cantos VI, VII and VIII because, as he wrote to Byron, 'they were so outrageously shocking that I would not publish them if you were to give me your Estate – Title and Genius – For Heaven's sake revise them'.[3]

When the next volume of *Don Juan* appeared under the imprint of John Hunt, many reviewers commented on Lord Byron's 'falling off' into a 'shilling's worth of dirty brown paper'.[4] These judgements in turn fuelled Byron's campaign against 'moral England' (VI.29). We may read *Don Juan*, therefore, as a series of skirmishes leading to outright confrontation with the sexually prudish, religiously orthodox and politically Tory parties in England. Robert Southey, the Society for the Suppression of Vice, Viscount Castlereagh and the Duke of Wellington are all directly accused of hypocrisy and concealment of vested interest: 'And I shall be delighted to learn who, / Save you and yours, have gained by Waterloo?' (IX.4).

The poem is aware, however, of more readers than its immediate enemies. Jerome McGann has shown how Byron's writing offers hints and allusions to his friends and his estranged wife: to these readers we could add his (estranged) publisher, London society, the women of London society, reviewers, and audiences past, present and future.[5] The narrator keeps all these groups in play and interrogates every reader individually about his or her allegiances. This challenge can be seen in the epigraph from *Twelfth Night, or What You Will* which Byron gave to the first set of cantos not to be issued by John Murray: ' "Dost thou think, because thou art virtuous, there shall be no more Cakes and Ale?" – "Yes, by St Anne; and Ginger shall be hot i' the mouth too!" '.[6]

*Don Juan* invites and anticipates a number of critical stances. For example, the narrator encourages us to read intertextually with reference to earlier poems by Byron and the Lake School poets he despised. We are acutely aware of gender relations whilst reading the poem and, as demonstrated by recent work, *Don Juan* is a rewarding text for feminist approaches.[7] *Don Juan*'s preoccupation with bodily functions – eating, drinking, indigestion – has encouraged Bakhtinian 'carnivalesque' readings whilst the poem's disruptions of genre anticipate Bakhtinian theories of novelistic discourse.[8] The poet's recurring mythopoeic and autobiographical references invite psychoanalysis, and the poem's versified awareness of the materiality of language applies a deconstructive technique with exhilarating *jouissance*.[9] What I hope to offer here is a focus on the digressive literary texture of the poem and its relationship with a variety of readers. I shall concentrate on the Dedication and Cantos I and II to discuss continuities and differences between the first volume of *Don Juan* and later episodes in the poem.

One main constant throughout the poem is Byron's choice of form. Every reader has to come to terms with demands made by the rhythm and rhyme of English *ottava rima*. Byron experimented with this form in 1816 in the *Epistle to Augusta*. There, it anchors a poem which is about personal loss; Augusta's absence is given shape and meaning by the coherence of the elaborately patterned language. In 1817, however, Byron's residence in

Venice led to his immersion in *ottava rima* verse from different Italian sources and an English mock epic, *Whistlecraft*, by John Hookham Frere, brought from England by a visiting friend. These examples showed Byron how *ottava rima* might be used for a mingled narrative yarn, offering the possibility of a rapid sequence of decasyllabic *ababab* appositions before the concluding couplet enabled an undercutting of the previous six lines (Romantic irony in performance), or an audacious lead into the next stanza.

Byron exploits the way that rhyme may be both a visual and an aural experience: the verse of *Don Juan* maximizes the reader's realization that pronunciation will have to be distorted to fit in with the rhyme. At the same time, Byron's use of quotation from other works and extensive *double entendres* insists on the multiple meanings of the same word, forcing the reader to acknowledge (if not to step into) other contexts. We can see this in action in the first stanzas of the Dedication written by Byron for *Don Juan*, but suppressed by John Murray:

> BOB SOUTHEY! You're a poet – poet Laureate,
>     And representative of all the race;
> Although 'tis true you turn'd out a Tory at
>     Last, – yours has lately been a common case: –
> And now, my epic renegade! what are ye at,
>     With all the Lakers in and out of place?
> A nest of tuneful persons, to my eye
> Like 'four and twenty blackbirds in a pie;
>
> 'Which pie being open'd, they began to sing' –
>     (This old song and new simile holds good)
> 'A dainty dish to set before the King,'
>     Or Regent, who admires such kind of food.
> And Coleridge, too, has lately taken wing,
>     But, like a hawk encumber'd with his hood,
> Explaining metaphysics to the nation –
> I wish he would explain his Explanation.
>
> You, Bob! are rather insolent, you know,
>     At being disappointed in your wish
> To supersede all warblers here below,
>     And be the only Blackbird in the dish;
> And then you overstrain yourself, or so,
>     And tumble downward like the flying fish
> Gasping on deck, because you soar too high, Bob,
>     And fall, for lack of moisture, quite adry, Bob!

In these stanzas, the shifts of tone and nuance complement the slipperiness of the 'epic convert', Robert Southey. At first, the shortened 'Bob' seems designed simply to belittle the poet, but the cheerful obscenity of 'adry, Bob' (slang for coition without ejaculation) shows how the verbal games of the poem can acquire a subversive momentum of their own, able to demolish not only the pretensions of the target but also the complacencies of the reader. Both Murray and Byron's best friend John Cam Hobhouse were horrified by this pun: they understood it, as most male readers of that time would, but they expected such discourse to be kept out of poetry. Byron regarded this compartmentalization as a form of English hypocrisy: it is against this that the poem is fighting. The point has been made before, but it is worth reinforcing, that Byron's *Don Juan* follows the imperative of William Wordsworth's Preface to *Lyrical Ballads* and brings poetry near to 'the language of men'. Wordsworth is, of course, the next target of the Dedication.

The rhymes 'poet Laureate / out a Tory at / what are ye at' create a miniature satirical narrative, uncovering an inevitable correspondence between Laureates and Tories which is inherent in the necessity of rhyme before Byron points out the 'common case' of this progression ('sing' and 'King' echo the idea in the second stanza). Hovering visually behind the accusation that Southey is now a Laureate / Toryeate is the idea that he has eaten rather well since his change of allegiance. This suggestion may account for the choice of simile 'like four and twenty blackbirds in a pie' – but the fun of this line as well is that Henry Pye was an earlier Poet Laureate.

The speed of *ottava rima* means that we don't have much time to savour the quip, for enjambment across stanzas (which is a recurring form of transgression in the poem) leads the reader onwards into whimsical play on the nursery rhyme 'Sing a Song of Sixpence'. Byron's parenthetical observation that '(This old song and new simile holds good)' introduces the self-reflexive nature of Byron's narration. Unlike the blank verse of *The Prelude*, *Don Juan* continually interrupts its own progression to share the risks of composition with the reader. Other Romantic poems, of course, refer to their own process, but *Don Juan* is the only Romantic epic which leads the reader to question the rhetoric of organic creation. Throughout, *Don Juan* foregrounds the delights of what Byron called elsewhere 'the superartificial'.[10]

In Canto I, Juan's first lover is introduced as a typical heroine:

> There was the Donna Julia, whom to call
> Pretty were but to give a feeble notion
> Of many charms in her as natural
> As sweetness to the flower, or salt to ocean,
> Her zone to Venus, or his bow to Cupid,
> (But this last simile is trite and stupid.) (I.55)

The same joke about the predictable nature of romantic description can be traced later in the poem in Canto VI when, for example, Byron invites the reader to choose which simile he (it probably is a 'he' at this point) would prefer to describe an attractive girl asleep in an Oriental harem:

> White, cold and pure, as looks a frozen rill,
> Or the snow minaret on an Alpine steep,
> Or Lot's wife done in salt, – or what you will; –
> My similes are gathered in a heap,
> So pick and chuse – perhaps you'll be content
> With a carved lady on a monument. (VI.68)

The superabundance of images invites the reader to become a voyeur of Oriental fantasy: simultaneously, the text is aware of its relationship with Byron's earlier bestsellers. 'I won't describe', the narrator claims in Canto V, 'description is my forte, / But every fool describes in these bright days / . . . And spawns his quarto, and demands your praise' (V.52). Asides like this remind readers that they share responsibility for creating fashionable literature – Byron's critical perspective on England from Italy allows the act of reading *Don Juan* to become a political gesture as the reader co-produces scandal and satire.

Byron's use of simile rather than metaphor is significant. Frequently, the poem works by asking the reader to hold disparate objects together. Metaphor suppresses the effort of comparison and creates a new totality; simile, on the other hand, leaves its mechanics on view. We do not see Byron's drafts and revisions unless we consult an edition which gives us these variants, but the narrator of *Don Juan* highlights the role of craftsmanship and talks about some of the devices at his disposal – which he expects his reader to praise. By appealing to us in parenthesis, Byron digresses from the immediate subject and dramatizes a dialogue with his reader. The sudden change of tone produced by these asides disturbed Byron's contemporary reviewers: many of them used pantomimic analogies to question Byron's sincerity:

> The most extraordinary . . . character of this poem is this, that it delights in extracting ridicule out of its own pathos. While it brings the tears of sympathy into the eyes of the reader . . . a heartless humour immediately succeeds, showing how little the writer participates in the emotion he excites. Skilful to play upon another's bosom, and to touch with mysterious art the finest chords of sensibility himself, he is all the while an alien to his own magical creation.[11]

In the first volume, two instances in particular unsettled the reviewers: the way in which Julia's farewell letter is upstaged by Juan's vomiting overboard, and the grotesque images of the shipwreck. In both cases, it is the effect of unstable shifting between different tones which offended. The *Investigator*, for example, described the 'mischievous levity' with which 'every finer and kindlier emotion of the heart is tacitly and insidiously neutralised with the ridiculous and the absurd'. The reviewer quoted Canto II stanzas 20 and 21, where Juan's 'beseeching' is interrupted by emetic 'reaching', and commented:

> We should be inclined to remark . . . that the whole circle of poetry does not contain a more striking contrast of beauty and deformity – exquisite feeling and the most disgusting want of it, – but that it is succeeded by a description of a shipwreck, wherein this forced and revolting union is carried to a height.[12]

Part of Byron's offence was the way in which verse undercut reverence for biblical authority. The *Investigator* identified 'sneers at Noah's ark and the Christian creed – comparisons of the rainbow to a kaleidoscope, or black eyes got in a boxing match – and allusions so grossly indecent, that none but minds the most debased could conceive them'. Implicit here is the reviewer's fear that he *had* been made to conceive them in reading the poem. *Don Juan* had a peculiarly 'palpable' effect on its readers: contemporary reviewers frequently responded to the poem's sudden turns and transitions as if they were being physically moved.

One of Murray's advisers, Francis Cohen (later Francis Palgrave, father to the Palgrave of the *Golden Treasury*), objected that the reader should not be 'drenched and scorched' at the same time. Byron answered this criticism in one of his most famous letters appealing to wordly *savoir-faire*:

> I will answer your friend... who objects to the quick succession of fun and gravity... Ask him these questions about 'scorching and drenching'. – Did he never play at Cricket or walk a mile in hot weather? – did he never spill a dish of tea over his testicles in handing the cup to his charmer to the great shame of his nankeen breeches? – did he never swim in the sea at Noonday with the Sun in his eyes and on his head – which all the foam of ocean could not cool?... Why Man the Soul of such writing is it's licence? – at least the *liberty* of that *licence* if one likes – *not* that one should abuse it – it is like trial by Jury and Peerage – and the Habeas Corpus.[13]

Byron's insistence on 'life' and 'the thing' in his poem is combined in his letters with an assertion of '*liberty*'. Both claims are an attempt to expel the Lake School's reliance on imaginary presence and transcendental meaning – allied for Byron with an orthodox deference to divinity; 'God will not be always a Tory', he wrote in 1821.[14] Not only in *Don Juan*, but in the historical dramas Byron wrote in 1820 and 1821, we can see a determination to deal with facts and things: 'this story's actually true', he claims in Canto I:

> If any person doubt it, I appeal
>     To history, tradition, and to facts,
> To newspapers, whose truth all know and feel,
>     To plays in five, and operas in three acts;
> All these confirm my statement a good deal. (I.203)

The blending of fact and fiction in journalism is both preoccupation and method in *Don Juan*, and it combines with the poem's concern with 'truth' in a scathingly satirical treatment of war:

> This is the patent-age of new inventions
>     For killing bodies, and for saving souls,
> All propagated with the best intentions;
>     Sir Humphrey Davy's lantern, by which coals
> Are safely mined for in the mode he mentions,
>     Tombuctoo travels, voyages to the Poles,
> Are ways to benefit mankind, as true,
> Perhaps, as shooting them at Waterloo. (I.132)

Having advertised his intention to produce a panoramic battle scene 'After the style of Virgil and of Homer, / So that my name of Epic's no misnomer' (I.200), Byron produced 'a little touch at warfare' in Cantos VII and VIII where Juan, having escaped from the harem, finds himself fighting with Russian forces to enter a Moslem fortress on the Danube. This episode was based on the siege of Ismail which took place in 1790. Byron refers his reader to a celebratory account of the siege by Castelnau, a Russian historian, although anyone consulting Castelnau would see how *Don Juan* emphasizes the horror instead of the glory of war. Implicitly criticizing jingoistic celebrations of Wellington as a hero after the Battle of

Waterloo, Byron employs the verbal resources of *ottava rima* to specify the atrocious violence of modern warfare.

> Thus on they wallowed in the bloody mire
>> Of dead and dying thousands, – sometimes gaining
> A yard or two of ground, which brought them nigher
>> To some odd angle for which all were straining;
> At other times, repulsed by the close fire,
>> Which really poured as if all Hell were raining,
> Instead of Heaven, they stumbled backwards o'er
> A wounded comrade, sprawling in his gore. (VIII.20)

The enjambment in this stanza recreates the onward effort of the soldiers: as one line runs into the next, mud and blood; dead and dying merge into each other. The final line of the couplet is a horrible summary of this confusion of outer ('o'er') and inner space ('gore'). Byron's technique is to keep the reader aware of scale, shifting between close-ups on his hero, Don Juan, and the broader view which is taken by the generals and the popular press:

> And therefore we must give the greater number
>> To the Gazette – which doubtless fairly dealt
> By the deceased, who lie in famous slumber
>> In ditches, fields, or wheresoe'er they felt
> Their clay for the last time their souls encumber; –
>> Thrice happy he whose name has been well spelt
> In the despatch: I knew a man whose loss
> Was printed *Grove,* although his name was Grose. (VIII.18)

There is a footnote to this stanza in which Byron emphasizes his point:

> A fact: see the Waterloo Gazettes. I recollect remarking at the time to a friend: – *'There is fame!* a man is killed, his name is Grose, and they print it Grove.' I was at college with the deceased, who was a very amiable and clever man, and his society in great request for his wit, gaiety, and 'chansons à boire.'

The footnote is a register of particular lucklessness which stands against the wholesale misfortune of Ismail. But Byron has, of course, another reason to be cynical about the haphazard apportioning of fame. His peculiar bitterness about 'Truths that you will not read in the Gazettes' (IX.10) has a great deal to do with the lurid insinuations about his own life in newspapers of his time. One satiric impulse of the poem is an attempt to correct the misconstructions of various texts: 'the best edition, / Expurgated' which distorts Juan's education (I.44), and the partisan nature of the magazines: 'I've bribed my grandmother's review – the British' (I.209–11), the 'unintelligible' Lake poets (I.90), laureate hymns 'so quaint and mouthey' (I. 205), and the sentimental rhetoric of Julia's farewell letter: '– forgive me, love me – No, / That word is idle now – but let it go' (I. 196). Different rhetorical strategies are teased apart and exposed by *ottava rima,* but the verse of *Don Juan* has another effect as well, which is a more open hospitality to the uncertainties of reading.

*Don Juan* quotes from a variety of literary sources. Sometimes this is for satirical purposes, as in the last stanza of Canto I:

> 'Go, little book, from this my solitude!
>     I cast thee on the waters, go thy ways!
> And if, as I believe, thy vein be good,
>     The world will find thee after many days.'
> When Southey's read, and Wordsworth understood,
>     I can't help putting in my claim to praise –
> The first four rhymes are Southey's every line:
> For God's sake, reader! take them not for mine. (I.222)

Byron's irreverent borrowing of Southey is another deflation of epic pretensions which at the same time renovates the material under attack.[15] This technique acquires a fiercer edge in the Siege Cantos where Byron attacks the ideological basis of Wordsworth's *Thanksgiving Ode*:

> 'Carnage' (so Wordsworth tells you) 'is God's daughter:'
> If *he* speak truth, she is Christ's sister, and
> Just now behaved as in the Holy Land. (VIII.9)

Again, a footnote insists that we read Wordsworth literally ('this is perhaps as pretty a pedigree for murder as ever was found') and as Anne Barton has pointed out, Wordsworth seems to have felt the force of the critique as the incriminating line was removed in later editions of the ode.[16] There is, however, a more genial form of quotation at work in *Don Juan*. We find it in Juan's farewell to Julia, which inspires the narrator to drop in a reference to Shakespearean tragedy:

> And Juan wept, and much he sigh'd and thought,
>     While his salt tears dropp'd into the salt sea,
> 'Sweets to the sweet;' (I like so much to quote;
>     You must excuse this extract, 'tis where she,
> The Queen of Denmark, for Ophelia brought
>     Flowers to the grave); and sobbing often, he
> Reflected on his present situation,
> And seriously resolved on reformation. (II. 17)

The pleasure of this quotation comes from a trail of aural association leading into conversational irrelevance: the alliteration of two 'salts' prompts a recollection of two 'sweets' in an elegiac context, though by referring the reader to the exact scene of the source quotation, the narrator interrupts Juan's drama and makes the reader aware of the difference between Juan's grief and Gertrude's.

Unlike some of his contemporaries, Byron's writing is usually aware of the context of his quotations from other works and his verse invites the reader to follow the trail left by allusion. In the Preface to *Adonais*, Shelley charges Gifford that his savage criticism has resulted in the death of John Keats: 'Nor shall it be your excuse, that, murderer as you are, you have spoken daggers, but used none'. Here, the allusion to *Hamlet* does not particularly assist the thrust of Shelley's argument. The ghost's counsel to Hamlet about his mother is that her faults should be left to her own conscience and this act of censure would transfer (unhappily) to Keats if we dwelt on the quotation for too long. When Byron accuses Wellington of murder, his use of Shakespeare is a more conscious deployment of theatrical resonance:

> You are 'the best of cut-throats:' – do not start;
> The phrase is Shakespeare's, and not misapplied:–
> War's a brain-spattering, windpipe-slitting art,
> Unless her cause by Right be sanctified. (IX.4)

The signalled quotation here is indeed from Shakespearean drama, where Macbeth addresses the murderers who have killed Banquo: 'Thou art *the best o' th' cut-throats*' (III. 4.16); but Byron has followed this up with an echo of the scene in Act I where Banquo detects Macbeth's guilty apprehension of the witches' greeting: 'Good Sir, why do you *start*, and seem to fear / Things that do sound so fair' (1.3.51–2). In both cases, the poem is fully aware of the context of the allusion and moves from the name 'cut-throat' to the verbal adjective 'windpipe-slitting' in order to realize Wellington's crimes. The shift backwards into *Macbeth's* plot illustrates the fragmentation of the source text which Byron often effects in his compound allusions. *Don Juan* raids well-known texts and estranges their familiarity.

One aspect of *Don Juan's* emphasis on 'fact' is a tendency to literalize quotations which appear from other sources. An example of this can be found in one of the poem's many topical references to Irish suffering and English indifference:

> Gaunt Famine never shall approach the throne –
> Though Ireland starve, great George weighs twenty stone. (VIII. 126)

The epithet for a ruler in so many panegyrics, 'great' has here been checked and balanced, so the rhyme ensures that the reader measures the grossness of the injustice. Though it was evident enough in cartoons by Gillray and Cruikshank, the corpulence of the English monarch was never mentioned in social columns – another taboo which Byron despised. Whilst he was in Italy, Byron kept up with events in England through newspapers, periodicals and letters from home. These account for the way that *Don Juan* conveys encyclopedia-like references to English life. Formerly, critics had assumed that the last seven cantos of *Don Juan*, set in an English country house where Juan falls under the influence of three women, are evidence of Byron's nostalgia for England. There are undoubtedly passages of reflection on his former life, but *Don Juan's* view of England is far from idealized and may be compared with Shelley's scathing satire on London in *Peter Bell the Third*.

Even before Juan reaches England in Canto X, throughout Cantos VII, VIII and IX Byron interrupts his narrative with snatches of current newspaper debate. By mentioning bishops 'taken by the tail' (VIII. 76), 'taxes, Castlereagh, and debt', 'Ireland's present story' (VIII.125), '"Gentleman Farmers"' and the falling price of oats (IX. 32), Byron offers a reflection of England as a sleaze-ridden and economically ruined country. What is interesting to consider in the light of our own times is Byron's critique of 'tabloid' xenophobia and sentimentality about home institutions. The precision of his attack may be seen at the end of Canto X, where the narrator makes one of his more didactic stands:

> Teach them the decencies of good threescore;
>     Cure them of tours, Hussar and Highland dresses;
> Tell them that youth once gone returns no more;
>     That hired huzzas redeem no land's distresses;
> Tell them Sir W[i]ll[ia]m C[u]rt[i]s is a bore,
>     Too dull even for the dullest of excesses –
> The witless Falstaff of a hoary Hal,
> A fool whose bells have ceased to ring at all. (X. 86)

This is a direct response to a newspaper report on George IV's stage-managed visit to Scotland in August 1822. George IV appeared for one public gathering in full Highland dress. Subsequent newspaper reports were appallingly sycophantic:

> It is a dress which requires a tall and robust figure to produce advantageous display, and the general opinion of the levee was, that this martial and picturesque dress was never worn to more advantage.... Next appeared in a similar garb Sir Wm Curtis; but the worthy Baronet's figure was anything but that of the hardy, swarthy Highlander.... The worthy Baronet laughed heartily himself at the merriment his presence excited.... Sir Wm., however, makes a better soldier than Falstaff, while he rivals him in the better part of his other gay qualifications.[17]

Byron had read this account and the verse of Canto X punctuates the excited report of the Highland Tour with an alternative point of view. Byron debases the newspaper's patriotic allusion to *I Henry IV* by casting Sir William's attendance on the monarch as an example of bad theatre: 'A fool whose bells have ceased to ring at all'. There is, of course, a risk that readers will not recognize the full extent of Byron's engagement with current affairs, but if we pick up the hint that there is more to the surface of the poem than first meets the eye, we have become receptive to new facts – whether the poem mobilizes the pleasure of gossip or the challenge of investigative journalism.

The references to George IV's weight and 'hoariness' contribute to *Don Juan*'s notorious references to the palpable effects of indigestion or drunkenness and the struggle between age and sexual desire. What this perspective offers is a counter to philosophic idealisms or even the comfortable beliefs of some types of liberal humanism. The shipwreck scene with its narrative of cannibalism in Canto II offers an unillusioned view of human life caught – like Beckett's characters – between bowl and pot. Yet *Don Juan* is also a poem which shares with the reader the anticipation of physical pleasures (or 'Cakes and Ale'): 'and all that, / A lobster-salad, and champagne, and chat' (I. 135). The flux of everyday life is not a way of escape, but a form of affirmation and it has something more to offer than 'I can't go on. I'll go on'.

In 1819 Francis Jeffrey attacked the poem for demonstrating 'how possible it is to have all fine and noble feelings, or their appearance, for a moment, and yet retain no particle of respect for them – or of belief in their intrinsic worth or permanent reality'.[18] It is open to twentieth-century readers, although it was not to Jeffrey, to distinguish relativity from cynicism. Byron's modes of digression and allusion materialize a modern awareness of contingency and, more importantly, accept this contingency and offer a hospitality to haphazard historical particulars.

> But for the present, gentle reader! and
>     Still gentler purchaser! the bard – that's I –
> Must, with permission, shake you by the hand,
>     And so your humble servant, and good bye!
> We meet again, if we should understand
>     Each other; and if not, I shall not try
> Your patience further than by this short sample –
> 'Twere well if others follow'd my example. (I.221)

The reader is a vital part of the poem who realizes the radical potential in *Don Juan*'s indeterminacy by creating the liberty of licence.[19] Despite its moments of misogyny and aristocratic *ennui*, I believe that *Don Juan* is an emancipatory poem. Even as it sifts, satirizes and seduces the men and women who make up its readers, its fictional handshake is warm.

## NOTES

1   Reiman, *The Romantics Reviewed*, Part BV, 2,134.
2   Ibid., I, 144.
3   Quoted in Hugh J. Luke, Jr, 'The publishing of Byron's *Don Juan*', *PMLA* 80 (1965) 199–209.
4   Reiman, *The Romantics Reviewed*, IV, p. 1,461.
5   McGann, 'Hero with a thousand faces'; *The Beauty of Inflections*, p. 287.
6   McGann, V, 293. All references are to this edition.
7   See, for example, Franklin, *Byron's Heroines*; Wolfson, 'Their she condition'.
8   See, for example, Philip Martin, 'Reading *Don Juan* with Bakhtin', in Wood, *Don Juan*; Graham, *Don Juan and Regency England*.
9   See, for example, Peter Manning, *Byron and His Fictions*, Detroit, Wayne State University Press, 1978.
10  Byron uses this word in his prose defence of Alexander Pope in 1821; see Andrew Nicholson, *Lord Byron*, p. 146.
11  Reiman, *The Romantics Reviewed*, I, 490.
12  Ibid., III, p. 1,182.
13  Marchand, VI, 207–8.
14  Ibid., VIII, 74.
15  See McGann, *Don Juan in Context*, pp. 77–8.
16  Barton, *Byron*, pp. 58–9.
17  *Galignani's Messenger*, no. 2,334, 26 August 1822.
18  Reiman, *The Romantics Reviewed*, II, p. 937.
19  For a revisionary account of Byron as champion of liberty, see Kelsall, *Byron's Politics*.

## WRITINGS

Nicholson, Andrew (ed) *Lord Byron: The Complete Miscellaneous Prose*, Oxford, Clarendon Press, 1991.

Steffan, T. G. and Pratt, W. W. (eds) *Byron's Don Juan: Variorum Edition*, 4 vols, Austin, University of Texas Press, 1957.

## REFERENCES AND FURTHER READING

Barton, Anne, *Byron: Don Juan*, Cambridge, Cambridge University Press, 1992.

Beatty, Bernard, *Byron's Don Juan*, New Jersey, Barnes & Noble, 1985.

Beatty, Bernard, 'Continuities and discontinuities of language and voice in Dryden, Pope, and Byron', in *Byron and the Limits of Fiction*, ed. Bernard Beatty and Vincent Newey, Liverpool, Liverpool University Press, 1988, pp. 117–35.

Beaty, Frederick L., *Byron the Satirist*, De Kalb, Northern Illinois University Press, 1985.

Bone, J. Drummond, 'The art of *Don Juan*: Byron's metrics', *Wordsworth Circle* 26 (1995) 97–103.

Cochran, Peter, 'The domestic reception of *Don Juan*', in *Romanticism*: (forthcoming).

Cooke, Michael G., *The Blind Man Traces the Circle: On the Patterns and Philosophy of Byron's Poetry*, Princeton, Princeton University Press, 1969.

England, A. B., *Byron's Don Juan and Eighteenth-century Literature: A Study of Some Rhetorical Continuities and Discontinuities*, London and New Jersey, Associated University Press, 1975.

Franklin, Caroline, *Byron's Heroines*, Oxford, Clarendon Press, 1992.

Graham, Peter W., *Don Juan and Regency England*, Charlottesville, University of Virginia Press, 1990.

Keach, William, 'Political inflection in Byron's *ottava rima*', *Studies in Romanticism* 27 (1988) 551–62.

Kelsall, Malcolm, *Byron's Politics*, Brighton, Harvester, 1987.

McGann, Jerome J., *Don Juan in Context*, London, John Murray, 1976.

——— *The Beauty of Inflections: Literary Investigations in Historical Method and Theory*, Oxford, Clarendon Press, 1985.

——— 'Hero with a thousand faces: the rhetoric of Byronism', *Studies in Romanticism* 31 (1992) 295–313.

Marshall, L. E., '"Words are things": Byron and the prophetic efficacy of language', *Studies in English Literature 1500–1900* 25 (1985) 801–22.

Reiman, Donald H. (ed) *The Romantics Reviewed: Contemporary Reviews of British Romantic Writers*, 9 vols, New York, Garland, 1972.

Ridenour, George M., *The Style of Don Juan: Yale Studies in English*, volume 144, New Haven, Yale University Press, 1960.

Wolfson, Susan, '"Their she condition": cross-dressing and the politics of gender in *Don Juan*', *English Literary History* 54 (1987) 585–617.

Wood, Nigel (ed) *Don Juan*, Buckingham, Open University Press, 1993.

# 25

# Percy Bysshe Shelley, *Prometheus Unbound*

## *Michael O'Neill*

*Prometheus Unbound*, Shelley's most ambitious poem, was written between September 1818 and December 1819 (with later additions) and published in August 1820 as the title poem of one of the finest collections of Romantic poetry. Regrettably, the text of the poem in the 1820 volume was full of errors.[1] Other poems in the same volume were *Ode to the West Wind* and *To a Skylark*, both of which participated in the volume's overall ambition to be 'The trumpet of a prophecy' (*Ode to the West Wind*, line 69).

Like the ode, *Prometheus Unbound* is much more than a piece of libertarian propaganda. Just as the ode lays bare Shelley's fears and hopes as a poet living in exile in Italy, ignored or reviled by reviewers (principally on account of his heterodox religious views), so *Prometheus Unbound* practises what in its Preface it forcefully preaches: 'abhorrence' of 'Didactic poetry'. Shelley asserts that 'nothing can be equally well expressed in prose that is not tedious and supererogatory in verse' (p. 879).

Four features of *Prometheus Unbound* deserve emphasis. There is the fact that it offers itself as a cross between genres, a 'lyrical drama' in the words of the subtitle. There is the allusive, inventive sophistication with which it operates, signalled by the epigraph, '*Audisne, haec Amphiarae, sub terram abdite?*' (Do you hear this, Amphiaraus, in your home beneath the earth?), a quotation from Aeschylus extant in Cicero's *Tusculan Disputations*. This mischievously disdainful epigraph reminds us of Shelley's aristocratic origins and education, and can be read as a challenge to a number of authors, including Aeschylus, Milton (whose *Paradise Lost* is an epic model continually revised and ideologically questioned by *Prometheus Unbound*) and Byron, especially in his proto-Nietzschean lyrical drama, *Manfred* (1817). There is the twining together, through the poem's deftly spun webs of imagery, of multiple strands of suggestion and significance, so that an image – that of the volcano, say – will have political, scientific, psychological and spiritual dimensions. And, lastly, there is the fact that though the poem offers a vision that is affirmative, sometimes rapturously so, it is realistically alive to forces that challenge such a vision.

All four features intermesh, but here I shall briefly discuss each one in turn. The first, the poem's hybrid generic nature, illustrates its author's very Romantic ability to draw from literary tradition yet to make something new. Aeschylus's *Prometheus Bound* supplies details in Prometheus's opening speech and elsewhere. But Shelley writes in the Preface that he was 'averse from a catastrophe so feeble as that of reconciling the champion with the oppressor of mankind' (p. 877), the supposed eventual outcome of Aeschylus's treatment of the subject, and the Greek drama's idiom and mode are not merely reproduced in the Romantic poem. *Prometheus Unbound* is written 'in the merest spirit of ideal Poetry, and not, as the name would indicate, a mere imitation of the Greek drama' (Jones, II, 219); employing 'characters & mechanism of a kind yet unattempted' (ibid., p. 94), it seeks to retain the variety of perspectives important in drama, even as it is propelled by the wish to make of its materials a lyrical embodiment of that 'stream of sound' (IV, 506) which is a key metaphor in the work. As an example of 'ideal Poetry', the work is consciously sublime. So the evocation of 'Terrible, strange, sublime, and beauteous shapes' (I, 202) reworks Edmund Burke's remark that in Milton's lines on Death (*Paradise Lost*, II: 666–73) 'all is dark, uncertain, confused, terrible and sublime to the last degree' (*Romanticism*, p. 4). The 'beauteous', Shelley's addition, is to the fore in a work that aspires towards an ideal of a redeemed society, an aspiration whose point of departure is William Godwin's notion of 'perfectibility' in *Political Justice*. From this work Shelley derived the philosophical anarchism at the heart of his politics, the notion, not that human beings can be made perfect, but that they can continually be made better by learning mastery over themselves and resisting the authority of others, especially as invested in governments and systems of religious belief.

In his Preface, Shelley hints at the implications for his poetic practice of the fact that his is a 'lyrical drama': 'The imagery which I have employed will be found, in many instances, to have been drawn from the operations of the human mind, or from those external actions by which they are expressed' (p. 877). (Here the third aspect listed above comes into play.) The 'Spring' which brings with it intimations of change for the better descends on Asia at the start of the second act:

> like a spirit, like a thought which makes
> Unwonted tears throng to the horny eyes,
> And beatings haunt the desolated heart
> Which should have learnt repose (II, i, 6, 2–5)

In this example mental and physical states are involved in one another; Spring comes to Asia both 'like a spirit' external to her and 'like a thought' within her. The state described is provisional, a step along the road towards transformation. Asia will advance beyond the inhibited lack of expectation suggested by her reference to 'the desolated heart / Which should have learnt repose'. Central to the subtlety with which Shelley uses 'the operations of the human mind' is his keen interest in the fact that most moments or states are Janus-faced, simultaneously open to optimistic or pessimistic interpretation.

Though some commentators (notably Earl Wasserman) have seen the lyrical drama as a psychodrama staged within the theatre of one mind (Prometheus's), it is crucial to recognize that *Prometheus Unbound* is fascinated by the role played by 'the operations of the human mind' in creating a climate conducive to political and historical change. World and mind interpenetrate. If the mind can shape the world, the world can condition the mind, as is the burden of much of Act 1: the Furies, for instance, taunt Prometheus with the failure of the French Revolution in terms which are at once political and psychological:

> See how kindred murder kin!
> 'Tis the vintage-time for Death and Sin;
> Blood, like new wine, bubbles within,
>     Till Despair smothers
> The struggling world, which slaves and tyrants win. (I, 573–7)

'Despair', in Romantic literature, frequently suggests the giving-up of political hope in the aftermath of the French Revolution. Certainly Shelley sees 'Despair' as implicated in the political coma which descended on Europe after the defeat of Napoleon.

For all its apparent optimism, the work stops short of implying a straightforward causal relationship between state of mind and political change. Shelley says, in the Preface,

> The great writers of our own age are, we have reason to suppose, the companions and forerunners of some unimagined change in our social condition, or the opinions which cement it. The cloud of mind is discharging its collected lightning, and the equilibrium between institutions and opinions is now restoring, or is about to be restored. (p. 878)

Though he values them, Shelley does not ascribe to artists ('companions and forerunners') a directly causal role in any 'change'. The metaphor of the 'cloud of mind . . . discharging its collected lightning' at once affirms 'mind' and represents its operations as governed by materialist laws. Demogorgon, 'a mighty darkness / Filling the seat of power' (II, iii, 2–3), is a figure resisting definition – which has not prevented many critics from seeing it as standing for Necessity, defined in a note to *Queen Mab* (1813) as the conviction conveyed to one who

> contemplating the events which compose the moral and material universe . . . beholds only an immense and uninterrupted chain of causes and effects, no one of which could occupy any other place than it does occupy, or acts in any other place than it does act.[2]

Too allegorical an equation between any of the dramatis personae and an abstraction fails to do justice to the sharply particularized ways in which the lyrical drama works. But Demogorgon's inclusion shows Shelley's awareness that neither the right disposition of the will nor the solicitations of feeling can, of themselves, bring about a desired alteration in the course of history; someone else, or, rather, given Demogorgon's genderless state (see II, iv, 5) some *thing* else needs to be present, a concatenation of favourable events and circumstances.

Many of these points deriving from the work's status as a lyrical drama are linked directly to the second feature adumbrated above, the poem's allusive, highly sophisticated inventiveness. Shelley was aware that this allusiveness would restrict the work's appeal, speaking in the Preface of his desire 'to familiarize the highly-refined imagination of the more select classes of poetical readers with beautiful idealisms of moral excellence' (p. 879). In other works composed during the period when he was working on *Prometheus Unbound*, Shelley sought to reach a wider audience: *The Cenci*, a play concerned, like *Prometheus Unbound*, with the ethics of revenge, but bleak enough to be read as the lyrical drama's pessimistic shadow, was written during the summer of 1819, and intended to be performed in a major London theatre; *The Mask of Anarchy*, Shelley's response to the

Peterloo Massacre of 16 August 1819, is composed in a cunningly deployed populist ballad form and aimed at an altogether different audience from that envisaged for *Prometheus Unbound*. In a letter in which Shelley says that the work 'is my favourite poem' and that *The Cenci* 'is written for the multitude', he remarks wryly that 'if I may judge by its merits, the "Prometheus" cannot sell beyond twenty copies' (Jones, II, 174). It is part of *Prometheus Unbound*'s Utopianism to address an audience which is created by the work itself. To be a fit reader of the work is to be obliged to recognize and thus, to some degree, transcend the 'mind-forg'd manacles' enslaving consciousness.

The work can be seen as a heretical *summa*, a gathering together, revisionary in intent, of many strands and traditions of philosophical, theological and poetic thought. Greek and Christian traditions combine, but they do not do so uncomplicatedly. Shelley's Prometheus must be released from what is worst in the Aeschylean handling of his story, namely, his final compromise with and preceding hatred for Jupiter. Nor, though Shelley admires the figure of Christ (whose teachings he thought were distorted by the Church into a series of rigid dogmas), is his Prometheus related to Christ in a simple fashion. Prometheus, endowed with Christ's willingness to suffer for others, is ready to be 'The saviour and the strength of suffering man' (I, 817), but the echo of religious language does not so much express allegiance as suggest that Christ's example is a valuable foreshadowing of Prometheus's labours for human beings.

In *A Defence of Poetry* Shelley argues that Dante's and Milton's 'distorted notions of invisible things' 'are merely the mask and the mantle in which these great poets walk through eternity enveloped and disguised' (p. 962). The remark indicates how *Prometheus Unbound* reads past literatures and cultures, seeking to suggest that beneath their masks and mantles lies a frustrated, approximate, but potentially beautiful idealism of moral excellence. The lyrical drama can be seen as fulfilling Wordsworth's claim, in his Preface to *Lyrical Ballads* (1802), that 'Poetry is the breath and finer spirit of all knowledge; it is the impassioned expression which is in the countenance of all science' (*Romanticism*, p. 259) – if one adds to it the proviso that the 'knowledge' embodied in previous works is redefined in the light of the 'finer spirit' breathed by Shelley's poem. So Byron's Prometheus might be 'a symbol and a sign / To mortals of their fate and force', the fact that 'man in portions can foresee / His own funereal destiny' (45–6, 49–50). But Shelley obliquely questions this view as too pessimistic when he has the tormented Prometheus address Jupiter with the words:

> The sights with which thou torturest gird my soul
> With new endurance, till the hour arrives
> When they shall be no types of things which are. (I, 643–5)

Byron's Prometheus typifies the fact that human beings can occasionally foresee their 'funereal destiny'; Shelley's Prometheus seeks to break the cycle of disappointment and suffering into a redeemed world that will demand new symbols and forms of representation – such as the use of negative epithets that tell us, say, that in the changed dispensation,

> The loathsome mask has fallen, the man remains
> Sceptreless, free, uncircumscribed – but man:

Equal, unclassed, tribeless, and nationless,
Exempt from awe, worship, degree . . . (III, iv, 193–6)

Again, the tradition of classical pastoral, drawn on in the speech between the two Fauns in
Act 2, scene 2, is transformed to accommodate a vision that makes pastoral no temporary
refuge from the difficulties of living. Rather, it becomes a space, like the poem itself, that
imagines how reality itself might be; hence, the Fauns look forward to Silenus singing
about 'the chained Titan's woeful doom, / And how he shall be loosed, and make the earth /
One brotherhood' (II, ii, 93–5). In the final act, Panthea's intricately exhilarating evocation of 'A sphere, which is as many thousand spheres' (IV, 238) has as its point of departure
Milton's account of the Chariot of Paternal Deity in *Paradise Lost* (Book VI). True to
his more human-centred vision, however, Shelley's emphasis is placed on a poetic-
cum-scientific re-imagining of the earth.

The third feature listed above, the multilevelled significances possessed by the writing's
imagery, is illustrated by the passage just discussed. The speech belongs to an act that has
left behind the first act's grimly epic struggle (the lyrical drama is a compendium of
brilliantly remodelled genres) for what amounts, in its sustained lyric beauty and persuasive quality of celebration, to a cosmic masque. Ione and Panthea each has a vision, Ione of
the Moon, Panthea of the Earth. Panthea's vision, like Ione's, is informed by Shelley's
interest in science, an interest shaped by the fact that early nineteenth-century science was
fascinated by the idea that matter, far from being lifeless and inert, was made up of a dance
of molecules, a fluid interplay of energies. Such a vision is evoked by Panthea, as is science's
Promethean offer of expanded awareness. The sphere, embodiment of the transformed
Earth, is governed by the 'Spirit of the Earth' from whose forehead 'Vast beams' lay bare
the earth's secrets and past history, including 'the melancholy ruins / Of cancelled cycles'
(IV, 265, 274, 288–9) out of which the earth has sprung, renewed. That such 'cancelled
cycles' are called to mind even as they are overthrown indicates the writing's self-
awareness, its recognition that the vision offered takes place in a poem. Indeed, so richly
has Shelley made over the language of contemporary science into his own poetic idiom that
the passage has been read by critics as implicitly self-reflexive, about the poetic process
itself. Similarly, throughout Act 2, Shelley uses images that work in multiple ways to
suggest the coming about of desired change. Asia describes in exquisite detail how 'The
point of one white star is quivering still / Deep in the orange light of widening morn /
Beyond the purple mountains' (II, i, 17–19). But beyond the satisfying metereological
accuracy is the evident symbolic import of the passage. Hard to paraphrase, quick to
communicate, such import is bound up with the fate and function of ideals; here the
apparent swallowing up of the star by the 'widening morn' suggests optimistically that the
ideal has found a home in the real; at the same time, the moment belongs to a stage of
wistful longing that must give way, as it does, to a more complex process of participation
in historical change.

The fourth aspect sketched above, the fact that the poem's vision, though optimistic,
does not overlook difficulties, is central; Shelley's glimpse of a better way takes a full look
at the worst. The tortures to which Prometheus is subjected by the Furies culminate in a
shrewd, harrowing depiction of the ineffectual acquiescence by many in the post-Napoleonic status quo (I, 618–31). Shelley's language is alive to the mental impasse of those

'who dare not devise good for man's estate, / And yet they know not that they do not dare' (I, 623–4). Even at the lyrical drama's close, Demogorgon reminds us that the change from bad to good is reversible and that should tyranny reassert itself it will only be defeated by those able to 'hope, till Hope creates / From its own wreck the thing it contemplates' (IV, 573–4): an injunction which, coming at this late stage and in the midst of general jubilation, is acutely clear-sighted and affecting.

In what remains I shall offer a brief outline of the lyrical drama's structure, plot and aesthetic achievement, highlighting the way in which the work is full of ideas given poetic form, for all its dislike of the didactic. Act 1 begins with Prometheus 'Nailed to [a] wall of eagle-baffling mountain' (I, 20) in the Indian Caucasus, possibly selected by Shelley as the scene for his drama because it was thought to be the cradle of civilization. The scene is important in symbolic terms. A stage direction observes that 'During the scene, morning slowly breaks', and what we witness in the work is the coming about of the long-awaited millennial day. Though Prometheus, punished by Jupiter for giving succour to human beings, endures heroically, the start of Act 1 is concerned with the proper mode of resistance to tyranny. In his Preface Shelley finds in favour of Prometheus rather than Milton's Satan, because the former is 'the type of the highest perfection of moral and intellectual nature, impelled by the purest and the truest motives to the best and noblest ends', while the mixture in the latter of 'faults' and 'wrongs' 'engenders in the mind a pernicious casuistry' (p. 877). But Prometheus, too, undergoes complex changes of feeling. The opening speech is dominated by expressions of resistance to Jupiter, the embodiment of 'ill tyranny' (I, 19), and there is a suggestion in the following lines that Prometheus runs the risk of being caught up in a vicious cycle of hatred:

> Whilst me, who am thy foe, eyeless in hate,
> Hast thou made reign and triumph, to thy scorn,
> O'er mine own misery and thy vain revenge. (I, 9–11)

The hoveringly positioned 'eyeless in hate' might describe Prometheus as well as Jupiter; certainly, it is vital that Prometheus should not, in resisting Jupiter, succumb to the 'hate' which Shelley regarded as a major cause for the apparent failure of the French Revolution.

*Prometheus Unbound* seeks to re-imagine recent historical events, to stage in its mental theatre a drama of how things should be that takes account of how things have been and how things are. A crucial moment, the reversal on which subsequent optimistic unfoldings depend, is I, i, 53, where Prometheus expresses 'pity' for Jupiter. Prometheus 'would recall' (I, 59) the curse he laid on Jupiter in the past, and the double sense of 'recall' – meaning to remember and to take back in order to annul – motivates the complicated machinery of what follows. Prometheus conjures up the Phantasm of Jupiter, a ghostly double of his former self, to repeat the curse. In so doing he is able to come to terms with and to overcome, as in a session of psychotherapy, his feelings of hatred for Jupiter. There is a fine contrast established in the plotting between what I have called the 'machinery' of the passage (the Phantasm is called up from a vast underworld 'where do inhabit / The shadows of all forms that think and live' (I, 197–8), a kind of cultural unconscious) and the terse plainness with which Prometheus rejects his former anger.

However, his struggles are by no means over. Mercury, one of the work's truly dramatic creations, a hand-wringingly sorrowful and reluctant servant of Jupiter, calls up the Furies to tempt Prometheus to despair. The Furies embody destructive emotions, at once political and psychological in origin, of 'pain and fear, / And disappointment, and mistrust, and hate' (I, 452–3). As already suggested, their torturing of Prometheus results in some of the first act's most memorable writing. A continual strength of Shelley's poetry is its vigilant empathy with states of despair beyond which he seeks to move. These states never vanish, growing in force and eloquent irresistibility in two of his finest works, *Adonais* and *The Triumph of Life*. In both of these late poems the ardent flame of trust in the possibility of social redemption threatens to burn out. In the lyrical drama, however, Prometheus outfaces despair, and hope's emissaries, the Spirits of the Human Mind, utter consolation in lyrics which include an account of a poet able to 'create' from natural particulars symbolic structures (such as *Prometheus Unbound*) that enshrine 'Forms more real than living man' (I, 747, 748): here, as elsewhere in the lyrical drama, Plato's language of enduring value is adapted to Shelley's quite different outlook, an outlook embracing the world of mutability and process rejected by Plato. Even these songs conclude with a lyric that is as much warning as promise. 'Ah sister! Desolation is a delicate thing' (I, 772) evokes the bitter-sweet state of 'Desolation', that is, disenchantment with the possibilities of hope, and Prometheus's final state in the act is one of exhaustion mixed with trust in 'love' (I, 824).

'Love', like most such abstractions in Shelley's poetry, carries a freight of suggestions. In *A Defence of Poetry* 'Love' is said to be 'The great secret of morals' and is defined as 'a going out of our own nature, and an identification of ourselves with the beautiful which exists in thought, action, or person not our own' (p. 961). Act 2 of *Prometheus Unbound* is full of such transfers out of the self, movements towards the 'beautiful'. At its centre is the figure of Asia, Prometheus's beloved and feminine counterpart; without her involvement Prometheus's endurance would come to nothing. The scene shifts from the bleak crags of the opening of Act 1 to 'A lovely vale', as the stage direction to the second act has it, and throughout Act 2 there is, by contrast with the first act's emphasis on stasis and suffering, a proliferating strain of lyric celebration, as the characters and natural world share in a sense of coming transformation. 'Some good change / Is working in the elements' (II, v, 18–19), remarks Panthea in the presence of Asia's 'transfiguration'. This 'good change' is registered through favourable portents in the poetry's imagery, culminating in the great lyrics concluding the act in which Asia is addressed as an ever-changing, elusive and indefinable principle of beauty, and then replies, in lines that capitalize on the images of music and voyaging which have suggested quest and transformation in Act 2, 'My soul is an enchanted boat' (72–110).

The lyric, like the act, ends with a journey 'Through death and birth to a diviner day' (II, v, 103), into what might be regarded as a pastoral paradise, a delightful resting-place rather than a final goal. Here the miracle of change and mutual happiness is hymned by 'shapes too bright to see, / ... Which walk upon the sea and chaunt melodiously!' (108, 110), the last line's internal rhyme a mirroring in the poem's form of its concern throughout the act with harmony and creative doublings. In the first scene Panthea records a dream of quasi-sexual union with a transformed Prometheus; a second dream of hers, about leaves stamped with the words 'Oh follow, follow!' (II, i, 141), induces in

Asia a comparable memory. The theme is picked up by spirit-echoes who draw the characters down towards 'the world unknown' where 'Sleeps a voice unspoken' (II, i, 190, 191). Shelley deliberately places his 'world unknown' not above this world but below, in accord with the lyrical drama's humanist vision. Very beautifully the scene shows the emergence out of amnesia (a state with political implications) into enquiry.

The second scene, made up of choral lyrics sung by spirits and a dialogue between Fauns, is a lyric interlude, during which the implications of the previous scene are dwelt upon; the entrance into history of ideals is suggested by the account of dew and starlight piercing the forest's 'interwoven bowers' (6), while the collective nature of the awakening described in the act is intimated in the evocation of the nightingales sustaining one another's song. And the lyrical drama's concern with free will and necessity is the subject of a typically haunting, delicate and equivocal lyric (41–63). The lines imply that 'Demogorgon's mighty law' (43) is at work in the descent of those who 'Believe their own swift wings and feet / The sweet desires within obey' (55–6). Such 'desires' are both necessary and in themselves insufficient, the lines seem to say, to bring about change. Shelley's concern is, however, with the state of mind that will make the best use of the revolutionary moment when it comes; hence, the act's emphasis on the figure of Asia and the importance of love. In the third scene, Asia and Panthea have reached 'the realm / Of Demogorgon' (1–2), represented as the crater of a volcano. Before they descend into it and activate its power, Asia, in a sharply controlled blank verse, praises the Earth's beauty and finds in a 'sun-awakened avalanche' (37) an emblem for the coming about of revolution. In the fourth scene Asia puts to Demogorgon a series of finally unanswerable questions about the source of life and evil, then embarks on a creation narrative that consciously ducks the question of whether there is an ultimate power, focusing, instead, on Prometheus's interventions on behalf of human beings and betrayed giving of power to Jupiter. Both she and Demogorgon come face to face with human ignorance about ultimate questions. Shelley's sceptical idealism is prominent here, the scepticism memorably embodied in Demogorgon's 'the deep truth is imageless' (116), the idealism apparent in the affirmation of the supremacy, in the face of 'Fate, Time, Occasion, Chance, and Change' (119), of 'eternal Love' (120). The metaphysical decks thus cleared, the moment is ripe for the 'destined hour' (128) when revolutionary change will come and Prometheus be released. Shelley's inventiveness, prodigally in evidence throughout, shows in the arrival of two spirits representing the 'destined hour': one with a 'dreadful countenance' (142) suggestive of the violence inseparable from the overthrow of tyranny, one with 'dove-like eyes of hope' (160).

The fifth scene dwells on the transfiguring effects of achieved hope. But the third act begins with a scene that depicts Jupiter's overthrow by Demogorgon. Jupiter reverts to an emptily vaunting Miltonic style, his very images undercutting themselves; so the image of his curses falling 'flake by flake' (III, i, 12) echoes Asia's image of revolutionary thoughts falling 'Flake after flake' 'till some great truth / Is loosened' (II, iii, 39, 40–1). He thinks he has begotten, by sexually overpowering Thetis, 'That fatal child, the terror of the world' (19) – possibly some reactionary doctrine such as Malthus's idea that the rate of population increase made dreams of perfectibility untenable. In fact, what arrives is Demogorgon to take Jupiter 'down the abyss' (53). The overthrow is effectively understated, the only sound and fury being Jupiter's unavailing melodramatics. The second scene, a dialogue between Ocean and Apollo, moves from discussion of Jupiter's passing to Ocean's imagining of how its realms will no longer be stained by human evil.

From here on the poetry devotes itself to finding a language for the barely thinkable, a world in which human beings are liberated to participate in the creativity described by Prometheus in the third scene of act three. He and Asia leave the lyrical drama after the next scene, having borne 'the untransmitted torch of hope', as Earth puts it, 'To this far goal of time' (III, iii, 171, 174). 'Untransmitted', there, reminds us that the 'torch of hope' has to be continually rekindled, and the fading from the action of Prometheus and Asia is best understood as signifying the transfer of the burden for keeping hope alive to the reader. In the fourth scene, the Spirit of the Earth and the Spirit of the Hour report on changes in the physical and human worlds, the Spirit of the Hour describing with urbane yet impassioned clarity a world which negates the negations that make up fallen experience; so, for example, 'None wrought his lips in truth-entangling lines / Which smiled the lie his tongue disdained to speak' (142–3). In fact, despite the gladness with which it depicts the collapse of religious dogma, moral repression and political tyranny, the speech is imbued with a sense of the contradictions, lies and hypocrisies of things as they are; it builds to a crescendo in which humans are imagined exempt from moral evil, though still subject to 'chance, and death, and mutability' (III, iv, 201). These are said to be, in words that show Shelley's ability to maintain a cool head in the midst of imagined raptures, 'The clogs of that which else might oversoar / The loftiest star of unascended Heaven, / Pinnacled dim in the intense inane' (III, iv, 202–4).

These lines, poised between an acceptance of an as yet 'unascended Heaven' and a glimpse of a 'Pinnacled' star, give way to a fourth act that makes up in its lyrical ecstasies for the restraint of the blank verse closing the third act. Here the lyrical drama becomes at once paradisal ballet and aria-filled opera. Choruses of hours and spirits divide and combine in metres that are swift and elated to 'weave the web of the mystic measure' (IV, 129) and affirm the intoxicating joy proffered by 'the new world of man' (IV, 157). Ione and Panthea then describe their visions of the transformed Moon and Earth, visions followed by a remarkable lyrical duet between the Earth and Moon in which the 'love' (IV, 369) between them is at once electromagnectic and erotic, and emerges as a force infusing itself through the entire creation. Shelley's syntax is richly interwoven in places, yet some of the finest moments in the lyrics are quietly delighted simplicities: 'Familiar acts are beautiful through love' (IV, 403), for instance, or the definition of 'Man' as 'one harmonious soul of many a soul, / Whose nature is its own divine control' (IV, 400–1), a couplet that expresses the central drive of the lyrical drama to transfer 'control' from any non-human, though humanly created, authority to human beings themselves. When Demogorgon comes forward at the end to preside over the general joy, his admonitions on how to cope with any change for the worse movingly spell out a credo at the heart of which are the virtues, profoundly humanist in implication, of hope, defiance of tyranny, and endurance. And yet the lyrical drama matters as poetry because it embodies and imagines problems and solutions with great resourcefulness and originality; in Shelley's own words about poetry from *A Defence of Poetry*, *Prometheus Unbound* 'awakens and enlarges the mind itself by rendering it the receptacle of a thousand unapprehended combinations of thoughts' (p. 961).

## Notes

1  Unless indicated otherwise, all quotations in this essay are taken from *Romanticism*, to which page references are made in the case of prose. Duncan Wu the editor chose to take as his copy-text 'the flawed printed text of 1820 corrected and emended from Shelley's fair copy' (see p. xxxv for a full account of the editor's practice). See also Reiman and Powers, *Shelley's Poetry and Prose*, the standard scholarly edition, for an excellent text. Shelley's letters are quoted from Jones.

2  Quoted from Matthews and Everest, *The Poems of Shelley*, p. 375.

## Writings

Fraistat, Neil (ed.) *The 'Prometheus Unbound' Notebooks: A Facsimile of Bodleian MSS, e. 1, e. 2, and e. 3*, The Bodleian Shelley Manuscripts, vol. IX, New York and London, Garland, 1991.

Matthews, Geoffrey, and Everest, Kelvin (eds) *The Poems of Shelley, Volume 1, 1804–1817*, London and New York, Longman, 1989.

Reiman, Donald H. and Powers, Sharon B. (eds) *Shelley's Poetry and Prose*, Norton Critical Edition, 3rd printing, New York and London, Norton, 1977.

Webb, Timothy (ed.) *Percy Bysshe Shelley: Poems and Prose*, London and Vermont, Dent and Charles E. Tuttle, 1995.

## References and Further Reading

Abrams, M. H., *Natural Supernaturalism: Tradition and Revolution in Romantic Literature*, New York and London, Norton, 1971.

Bloom, Harold, *Shelley's Mythmaking*, Ithaca, Cornell University Press, 1969.

Cameron, Kenneth Neill, *Shelley: The Golden Years*, Cambridge, Mass., Harvard University Press, 1974.

Clark, Timothy, *Embodying Revolution: The Figure of the Poet in Shelley*, Oxford, Clarendon Press, 1989.

Cronin, Richard, *Shelley's Poetic Thoughts*, London and Basingstoke, Macmillan, 1981.

Curran, Stuart, *Poetic Form and British Romanticism*, New York and Oxford, Oxford University Press, 1986.

Everest, Kelvin, '"Mechanism of a kind yet unattempted": the dramatic action of *Prometheus Unbound*', *Percy Bysshe Shelley: Special Issue*, ed. Michael O'Neill, *Durham University Journal*, new series 54:2 (1993) 237–46.

Hogle, Jerrold E., *Shelley's Process: Radical Transference and the Development of His Major Works*, New York and Oxford, Oxford University Press, 1988.

Leighton, Angela, *Shelley and the Sublime: An Interpretation of the Major Poems*, Cambridge, Cambridge University Press, 1984.

McGann, Jerome J., *The Romantic Ideology: A Critical Investigation*, Chicago and London, University of Chicago Press, 1983.

O'Neill, Michael, *The Human Mind's Imaginings: Conflict and Achievement in Shelley's Poetry*, Oxford, Clarendon Press, 1989.

——*Percy Bysshe Shelley: A Literary Life*, Basingstoke and London, Macmillan, 1989.

Pulos, C. E., 'Shelley and Malthus', *PMLA* 67 (1952) 113–24.

Reiman, Donald H., *Percy Bysshe Shelley: Updated Edition*, Boston, G. K. Hall, 1990.

Scrivener, Michael Henry, *Radical Shelley: The Philosophical Anarchism and Utopian Thought of Percy Bysshe Shelley*, Princeton, Princeton University Press, 1982.

Sperry, Stuart M., *Shelley's Major Verse: The Narrative and Dramatic Poetry*, Cambridge, Mass. and London, Harvard University Press, 1988.

Tetreault, Ronald, *The Poetry of Life: Shelley and Literary Form*, Toronto, University of Toronto Press, 1987.

Wasserman, Earl R., *Shelley: A Critical Reading*, Baltimore and London, Johns Hopkins University Press, 1971.

Webb, Timothy, *Shelley: A Voice Not Understood*, Manchester, Manchester University Press, 1977.

Weisman, Karen A., *Imageless Truths: Shelley's Poetic Fictions*, Philadelphia, University of Pennsylvania Press, 1994.

# 26

# Thomas De Quincey, *Confessions of an English Opium-Eater*

## Damian Walford Davies

In December 1820, Thomas De Quincey (1785–1859), by that time an opium-eater for over 16 years and an addict for over eight, arrived in Edinburgh from Grasmere to write for *Blackwood's Magazine*. He was, more accurately, an opium-*drinker*, taking the drug in the form of laudanum, alcoholic tincture of opium. His friend John Wilson, editor of *Blackwood's*, had been trying for some time to recruit him for 'the Maga', but had received nothing but promises from a man who had recently begun to make a habit of drawing bills on him. De Quincey was himself no stranger to the trials of editorship: he had recently served his journalistic apprenticeship as the editor of the *Westmorland Gazette* (from which, however, he had been dismissed the previous year). It was for *Blackwood's*, then, that De Quincey began what he referred to at the time as an 'Opium article'. 'Opium', he wrote to William Blackwood, the publisher, 'has reduced me for the last six years to one general discourtesy of utter silence. But this I shall think of with not so much pain, if this same opium enables me (as I think it will) to send you an article'.[1] For the first time, he was turning the pains and pleasures of his opium experience to account. But the distinction of publishing what became the *Confessions of an English Opium-Eater* was not to be *Blackwood's*; the procrastinating De Quincey infuriated the publisher with his tardiness (and tartness), went to London, and offered his services to *Blackwood's* arch-rival, the *London Magazine*. He set to work on the 'Opium article', and the *Confessions*, signed 'X.Y.Z.', was published in the September and October 1821 issues of the *London Magazine*, appearing in book form in 1822.

It was written in inauspicious circumstances. Harried by creditors (a constant feature of his untidy life), De Quincey had to leave his lodgings and write parts of it on the run, in the coffee-rooms of coaching-inns. He was also homesick and ill. Reviewing this period 16 years later in his *Recollections of Charles Lamb* he recalls: 'I was ill at that time, and for years after – ill from the effects of opium upon the liver...I began to view my unhappy London life – a life of literary toils, odious to my heart – as a permanent state of exile from my Westmoreland home'.[2] He armed himself with increased doses of opium which afforded him 'artificial respites' in which he could write, but which were purchased, he recalls, 'at a heavy price of subsequent suffering'. The 'narrative part' – that is, the 'Preliminary Confessions' – were written, he claimed, 'with singular rapidity', while the accounts of his dreams in the second part 'had been composed more slowly... at wide intervals of time'. Indeed, he may already have had the dream-passages to hand; since 1818, he had made a point of noting down his opium dreams.

*Confessions of an English Opium-Eater* would have struck De Quincey's readers as a novel title. It evokes the *Confessions* of St Augustine and perhaps the 'conversion accounts' of contemporary evangelical tracts on the one hand, and Rousseau's *Confessions* on the other, thereby suggesting both spiritual soul-searching and scandalous secular autobiography. But Rousseau's work is rejected as a model for the *Confessions* as De Quincey, anxious guardian of the 'delicate and honourable reserve' which 'restrains us from the public exposure of our own errors and infirmities',[3] glances contemptuously at the 'gratuitous self-humiliation' of French literature. The autobiographical passages were much expanded in De Quincey's 1856 revision, making the *Confessions* into a more recognizably 'autobiographical' piece of writing; the earlier *Confessions*, however, are selective, sometimes secretive, with regard to the life: De Quincey reminds us that 'To tell nothing *but* the truth – must, in all cases, be an unconditional moral law: to tell the *whole* truth is not equally so'.[4] 'Not the opium-eater, but the opium, is the true hero of the tale', he famously declares, modifying the statement in later years only to place more emphasis on the dreaming faculty, 'the one great tube through which man communicates with the shadowy'.[5]

One model for the *Confessions* is Wordsworth's autobiographical poem, *The Prelude*. It remained unpublished until 1850, but De Quincey had the honour of reading it in manuscript. Just as Wordsworth's *Prelude* analyses how the foundations of a poet's mind were laid in childhood, so De Quincey's 'Preliminary Confessions' are an 'introductory narrative of the youthful adventures which laid the foundation of the writer's habit of opium-eating' – and opium-dreaming – 'in after-life'.[6] In the great works of his later years, *Suspiria de Profundis* ('Breathings from the Depths' – a 'sequel' to the *Confessions*) and *The English Mail-Coach* (clearly related to *Suspiria*), De Quincey was to analyse with great insight the relation between childhood, grief, time and the imagery of dreams – between the child who suffers and the man who dreams.

From the outset of the *Confessions*, De Quincey strikes up an affable acquaintance with the reader, seeking to enlist his understanding and support. The persona of the learned opium-confessor, which De Quincey slips in and out of, has much wry humour about him, and the address 'To the Reader' is a perfect piece of casuistry. De Quincey is hedging on the question of his guilt as an opium-eater and ambivalent in his reaction to opium, which is presented as both a key to divine enjoyment and a tormenting chain. Moreover, his statement that 'I... have untwisted, almost to its final links, the accursed chain which fettered me', repeated at the end of the *Confessions*, is untrue. An appendix to the 1822 *Confessions* and a passage in the 1856 revision were to modify this rather too sanguine statement.[7]

Before launching into the narrative of his 'youthful adventures' in Wales and London, De Quincey is careful to make a point that should guard us against ascribing the terrifying magnificence of his dreams solely to the agency of opium:

> If a man 'whose talk is of oxen' should become an opium-eater, the probability is, that (if he is not too dull to dream at all) – he will dream about oxen: whereas ... the reader will find that

the opium-eater boasteth himself to be a philosopher; and accordingly, that the phantasmagoria of *his* dreams (waking or sleeping, day-dreams, or night-dreams) is suitable to one who in that character,

> *Humani nihil à se alienum putat.*
> [He deems nothing human alien to him][8]

This was repeated in *Suspiria*; 'Habitually to dream magnificently', De Quincey added there, 'a man must have a constitutional determination to reverie'.[9] He was to admit in *Suspiria* that opium had a '*specific* power... not merely for exalting the colours of dream-scenery, but for deepening its shadows; and, above all, for strengthening the sense of its fearful *realities*',[10] but in De Quincey's case, the opium seems to have been a catalyst, not a cause. It has been suggested that he would have 'dream[ed] magnificently' even if laudanum had never passed his lips. Moreover, this 'constitutional determination' to dream and reverie was something he had consciously cultivated in youth. In March 1803, he drew up in a notebook a 'system of education' which included physical exercise, but which was to fulfil its aims by 'relieving – varying – and so rendering more exquisite those fits of visionary and romantic luxuriating'.[11] At this time he was also allowing his powerful visual imagination free play in waking reveries, noting that 'striking descriptions' were 'always paintings' to him,[12] and on 18 August 1806, under the title 'constituents of Happiness' (the *Confessions* was to provide another famous 'analysis of happiness'),[13] he listed 'abstraction and reverie'. Indeed, glancing back at the *Confessions* in later works, De Quincey was to shift the balance of things: in *Suspiria* he states that 'The *Opium Confessions* were written with some slight secondary purpose of exposing this specific power of opium upon the faculty of dreaming, but much more with the purpose of displaying the faculty itself'.[14]

De Quincey is concerned in the 'Preliminary Confessions' to emphasize that it was pain, not self-indulgent pleasure, that drove him to addiction. In 1856, he inserted a passage comparing his own case-history as an addict with that of Samuel Taylor Coleridge, strenuously denying Coleridge's claim (published in Gillman's 1838 *Life of Coleridge*) that his own addiction sprang from 'voluptuousness in the use opium'. He was forever analysing Coleridge's own motives in taking opium[15] – part, perhaps, of his eternal fascination with the idea of the 'double', on which he was to write so powerfully in *Suspiria*.

De Quincey's description of his education at 'various schools, great and small' is amplified in 1856 by an account of his two years (1800–2) at the 'great school on an ancient foundation' – Manchester Grammar – and his relationship with his fellow pupils and Charles Lawson, the headmaster. His flight from Manchester, early on the 'cloudless' morning of 20 July 1802, was to be represented in 1856 as 'inexplicable', a 'fatal error', and narrated with a far greater sense of ominous brooding.[16] The later *Confessions* fill in many gaps, making it explicit that De Quincey's original plan of proceeding to Westmorland was on account of the 'deep deep magnet' that was William Wordsworth (whose poetry provides much of the material for the *Confessions*' allusive method). De Quincey's description of his wanderings in Wales is also much extended in 1856. These later *Confessions* can be long-winded at times, but a marvellous passage describing De Quincey's experience in the empty ballroom of a Shrewsbury inn as he waited, with a storm raging outside, for the Night Mail for London, dramatically fills out the scant link between the Welsh and London sections of 1821:

> And at intervals I heard...the raving, the everlasting uproar of that dreadful metro-
> polis.... The unusual dimensions of the rooms...brought up continually...the mighty
> vision of London waiting for me far off...that unfathomed abyss...into which I was now so
> wilfully precipitating myself.[17]

The earlier *Confessions* now throw us into his hunger-bitten experiences in London, which he reached in late November 1802. The 'poor friendless child, apparently ten years old' with whom De Quincey shares a bed in the draughty house in Greek Street, Soho of a shifty attorney named in 1856 as Brunell, *alias* Brown, is the first of many suffering female figures – outcasts or 'pariahs' – encountered in De Quincey's writings. We are soon introduced to another 'pariah woman': 'noble-minded' Ann, the fifteen-year-old prostitute who saved De Quincey's life and became his 'youthful benefactress' by reviving him with 'a glass of port wine'. Following these tales of suffering, De Quincey turns to contemplate what he calls the 'hieroglyphic meanings of human suffering' – his main concern in the *Suspiria*. The remainder of the 'introductory narrative' concerns De Quincey's journey on the mail coach (the central, apocalyptic image of *The English Mail-Coach*) to Eton as part of his effort to borrow money, and ends with his reconciliation with his guardians, his removal to Oxford, and the swallowing-up of Ann in the 'mighty labyrinths' of London. He was to search for her, in various forms, for the rest of his life.

De Quincey first took opium in the autumn of 1804 in London, where it was recommended, perfectly responsibly, by an Oxford friend as a cure for his toothache. His humorous account of the 'immortal druggist' who first 'laid open to [him] the Paradise of Opium-eaters' marks the beginning of what is referred to as the 'honeymoon stage' of his opium-use (he called it his 'noviciate'): a period when the drug affords pleasurable sensations and physical dependence has not yet begun:

> I took it: – and in an hour, oh! heavens! what a revulsion! what an upheaving, from its lowest
> depths, of the inner spirit! what an apocalypse of the world within me! That my pains had
> vanished, was now a trifle in my eyes: – this negative effect was swallowed up in the
> immensity of those positive effects which had opened before me – in the abyss of divine
> enjoyment thus suddenly revealed. Here was a panacea...for all human woes: here was the
> secret of happiness.[18]

What De Quincey is describing here is serene freedom from anxiety, immense emotional relaxation. His terminology is significant: he often speaks of his opium experiences in terms of descent into interminable depths and abysses.[19] Adopting the religious termino-logy which also marks his opium *patois*, he now proclaims 'the doctrine of the true church on the subject of opium', of which, he says, 'I acknowledge myself to be the only member – the alpha and omega' (he took a demotion in 1856 by referring to himself as the 'Pope'), and launches into a lecture on the physical effects of the drug.

All the 'Pleasures of Opium' recorded in the *Confessions* are waking reveries. In 1805, De Quincey began to combine his visits to London with his opium debauches, indulging in the drug on a Tuesday or Saturday night whilst at the King's Theatre or the opera house, where he used to listen, rapt, to the divine voice of the celebrated contralto Josephina Grassini. Rather, he records that he *saw* the music (which also provides De Quincey with much opium-terminology) displayed before him as 'a piece of arras work'.[20] On Saturday nights he also used to join the poor of London on the streets to view them 'laying out their wages'. He was to pay a heavy price for these enjoyments: his journeys homewards through the 'sphynx's riddles' of London's streets and the sea of faces rose up later in his opium nightmares to terrify him. He ends his account of the pleasures of opium with a picture of himself (around 1805) sitting in an opium-trance at the open window of a cottage at Everton overlooking Liverpool bay. In this passage, which has affinities with Wordsworth's 'meditation' on the summit of Snowdon in Book XIII of the 1805 *Prelude*,[21] De Quincey draws a parallel between the 'tranquillity . . . resulting from mighty and equal antagonisms; infinite activities, infinite repose' observed in the external scene and the action of opium upon the mind in reverie. The famous apostrophe which concludes this section – 'thou hast the keys of Paradise, oh, just, subtle, and mighty opium!' – ominously marks the end of the 'Pleasures of Opium' and heralds the beginning of its 'Pains' in the echo of Sir Walter Raleigh's apostrophe to Death in the *History of the World* – 'O eloquent, just, and mighty Death!'

We are now moved on to spring 1812 to find De Quincey, still an opium-eater (but still not an addict), 'tolerably well, thank you'. But now comes a heavy change. De Quincey states that in the summer of 1812 he 'had suffered much in bodily health from distress of mind connected with a very melancholy event' – the death of three-year-old Catharine Wordsworth, on whom he doted. The following year, he remarks, whether as a result of the 'illness' of 1812 or not, he was 'attacked by a most appalling irritation of the stomach', which he saw as the reactivation of the stomach pains he had endured as a youth in London.[22] It was this illness of 1813, he claimed, that forced him to have recourse to opium and become an addict. He was thus able to argue that it was bodily suffering that drove him to dependence. But it is likely that dependence began soon after the death of Catharine in 1812 as De Quincey took opium to combat depression of spirits and as a prophylactic against the effects of damp and cold (he was in the habit of sleeping on little Kate's grave). The 'year of brilliant water' ('water' referring to the lustre of a gem) which he places in 1816 or 1817 – a year 'set . . . in the gloom and cloudy melancholy of opium' in which he claims to be enjoying the benefits of having reduced his dosage by a massive 7/8ths from 8,000 to 1,000 drops a day – is probably another fiction. It is in this 'intercalary year' of contentment that he roots his 'analysis of happiness' – the picture of domestic cosiness at Town End, Grasmere – and the comic meeting with the fearful opium-eating Malay who was to return to torment De Quincey in his nightmares of 1818. But there probably was no such year of happiness; the struggle to reduce his dose during this, his first 'prostration before the dark idol',[23] must have resulted in all the misery of opium withdrawal (which was generally marked in De Quincey's case by an upsurge of dreaming activity).

An ill-omened epigraph from Shelley's *Revolt of Islam* fittingly introduces De Quincey's final collage of terrifying opium experiences. An acute observer of his own dream processes, De Quincey now relates how the troubling hypnagogic visions of 'vast processions' and 'friezes of never-ending stories' which in 1817 rose up as he began 'painting, as it were, upon the darkness, all sorts of phantoms' were resurrected in 'insufferable splendour' by the 'fierce chemistry' of his dreams; how time and space were both terrifyingly amplified; and how incidents from his childhood and the 'secret inscriptions on the mind' were revealed again in dreams (a resurrection he was to analyse brilliantly in *Suspiria* by taking the 'Palimpsest' as an image for the human mind). He likens the 'power of endless growth and reproduction' which governed his architectural dreams to the endless flights of stairs represented in Piranesi's *Carceri d'Invenzione* ('Imaginary Prisons') engravings, which had been described to him by Coleridge.[24] Dreams of 'seas and oceans' succeeded dreams of 'lakes – and silvery expanses of water' (De Quincey lived in constant fear of hydrocephalus, which he believed killed his sister Elizabeth in 1792), to which was linked the 'tyranny of the human face' which he traced back to his experiences on the streets of London.[25]

During 1818 his dreams were tormented by the Malay and the gods, architecture, landscape, mythical tortures, and monsters of the East – a region which he contemplated with profound horror and loathing:

> I ran into pagodas: and was fixed, for centuries, at the summit, or in secret rooms; I was the idol; I was the priest; I was worshipped; I was sacrificed. I fled from the wrath of Brama through all the forests of Asia: Vishnu hated me: Seeva laid wait for me. I came suddenly upon Isis and Osiris: I had done a deed, they said, which the ibis and the crocodile trembled at.[26]

The origin of opium in the East, De Quincey's wide reading of travel literature, and fashionable *chinoiserie* seen in England, all contribute to the imagery of these dreams. But it was the crocodile that terrified him most; he was to be horrified by the beast once again in the bestial 'involute' (De Quincey's term for 'perplexed combinations of concrete objects') of *The English Mail-Coach*.[27]

'Noble-minded Ann' is found, lost, and found again, in a more poignant dream of 1819 in which De Quincey gazes from the door of Town End at Catharine's grave in Grasmere churchyard on Easter Sunday: 'the day on which they celebrate the first-fruits of resurrection. I will walk abroad; old griefs shall be forgotten today'.[28] The scene becomes an Oriental one, and Ann is seen sitting under 'Judean palms'. 'So then I have found you at last', De Quincey cries, but he loses sight of her only to find himself with her again, walking 'by lamp-light in Oxford-Street'. In contrast, however, the final dream related in the *Confessions* ends, not with recovery and resurrection, but with reverberating 'everlasting farewells'.

Although he declares at the end of the *Confessions* that he has 'triumphed' over opium, De Quincey was to remain an addict for the rest of his life. He describes the *Confessions* as 'an appeal to the prudence and the conscience of the yet unconfirmed opium-eater', stating that 'enough has been effected' if the opium-eater is 'taught to fear and tremble'.[29] But in November 1821 he was to consider 'very just' the objection that there is in the *Confessions* 'an overbalance on the side of the *pleasures* of opium; and that the very horrors themselves . . . do not pass the limits of pleasure', and promised to remedy this in a third part (which was never written).[30] He repeatedly denied, however, that what others saw as his 'wee wud wicked work'[31] had a pernicious influence on others: 'Teach opium-eating! Did I teach wine-drinking? . . . no man is likely to adopt opium or lay it aside in consequence of anything he may read in a book'.[32] But he did acknowledge that the *Confessions* had undeniably 'sharpened the attention . . . [and] pointed a deeper interest, to this perilous medicine'.[33]

It is certainly as the high-priest of opium that De Quincey is remembered. Baudelaire, Branwell Bronte, Edgar Allan Poe and Francis Thompson, opium-eaters all, were to become his disciples. But he should also be remembered as the high-priest of the shadowy world of dreams, whose 'resurrections' and 'fierce chemistry' he analysed so powerfully 70 years before Freud came to write *The Interpretation of Dreams*.

## NOTES

1  Eaton, *Thomas De Quincey*, p. 262.
2  Masson, III, 71.
3  De Quincey, *Confessions*, ed. Hayter, p. 29 (hereafter, Hayter).
4  Ibid., p. 119; see also pp. 163–4.
5  De Quincey, *Confessions*, ed. Lindop, p. 88 (hereafter, Lindop). See also Lindop, *The Opium-Eater*, pp. 269–70 for William Maginn's cruel exposé of the private details which the *Confessions'* blurred chronology hides.
6  Hayter, p. 33.
7  Ibid., pp. 121–3, 215.
8  Ibid., p. 33.
9  Lindop, p. 87.
10  Ibid., p. 88.
11  Eaton, *A Diary*, p. 143.
12  Ibid., pp. 153–4, 156–7.
13  Hayter, pp. 93–6.
14  Lindop, p. 88. For similar statements from *Suspiria* and the 1856 *Confessions* on the relative importance in De Quincey's design of dreams and opium, see Lindop, pp. 89 and 93–4; Hayter, pp. 136–7, 146–7, 205.
15  For De Quincey on Coleridge's case-history, see Hayter, pp. 128–30 ('Coleridge and opium-eating') and pp. 139–47 (1856 *Confessions*). See also De Quincey, *Recollections*, ed. Wright, pp. 55–7, 74–5, 77–8, 97–8. For Coleridge on De Quincey, see Masson, III, 225.
16  See Hayter, pp. 172–6.
17  Ibid., pp. 193–7.
18  Ibid., pp. 71–2.
19  Cf. ibid., p. 103.
20  Ibid., pp. 78–9.
21  See Wordsworth, *The Prelude* (1805), XIII, 66–119.
22  Introducing the 'Pains of Opium' section in the 1856 revision, De Quincey, fascinated by the 'natural links of affiliation' that connect distant periods of our lives, justifies the architecture of the *Confessions*: the 'early series of sufferings' in Wales and London, he says, 'was the parent of the later. Otherwise, these Confessions would break up into two disconnected sections' (Hayter, p. 204).
23  Lindop, p. 89.
24  De Quincey wrongly refers to the *Carceri* as Piranesi's *Dreams*. He is also wrong in describing Piranesi's halls as 'Gothic'; they are classical.
25  In 1856 De Quincey stated: 'Perhaps some part of my London life (the searching for Ann amongst fluctuating crowds) might be answerable for this' (Masson, III, 441).
26  Hayter, p. 109.
27  See Lindop, pp. 198–201.
28  Hayter, p. 111.
29  Ibid., pp. 114, 115. Cf. his later statements: 'I deny the opening to any large range of mischief; and . . . equally I deny the opening to any compensating power of detaining men from opium' (ibid., p. 131); and 'I have elsewhere explained, that it was no particular purpose of mine, and *why* it was no particular purpose, to warn other opium-eaters' (Lindop, p. 91).
30  Hayter, pp. 119–20.
31  *Blackwood's Magazine*, XIV (1823), p. 495.
32  See Hayter, pp. 130–2; Lindop, p. 248; and Masson, III, 225n. In a comic exchange in the issue of *Blackwood's* cited above, John Wilson's dramatic persona 'Christopher North' asks the 'Opium-Eater': 'Pray, is it true, my dear Laudanum, that your "Confessions" have caused about fifty unintentional suicides?', to which De Quincey's persona replies: 'I should think not. I have read of six only; and they rested on no solid foundation'.
33  Hayter, p. 131.

## WRITINGS

De Quincey, Thomas, *Confessions of an English Opium-Eater in both the Revised and the Original Texts, with its Sequels, Suspiria De Profundis and The English Mail-Coach*, ed. Malcolm Erwin, London, Macmillan, 1956.

—— *Recollections of the Lakes and the Lake Poets*, ed.

David Wright, Harmondsworth, Penguin, 1970.
——*Confessions of an English Opium-Eater and Other Writings*, ed. Grevel Lindop, Oxford, Oxford University Press, 1985. Including *Suspiria de Profundis* and *The English Mail-Coach*.

——*Confessions of an English Opium-Eater*, ed. Alethea Hayter, Harmondsworth, Penguin, 1986. The 1822 text, with excerpts from the 1856 revision and other material.
Japp, A. H. (ed.) *Posthumous Works of De Quincey*, 2 vols, London, Heinemann, 1891.

### REFERENCES AND FURTHER READING

Barrell, John, *The Infection of Thomas De Quincey*, New Haven, Yale University Press, 1991.

Baxter, Edmund, *De Quincey's Art of Autobiography*, Edinburgh, Edinburgh University Press, 1990.

Bilsland, John W., 'De Quincey's opium experiences', *Dalhouse Review*, autumn 1975.

*Blackwood's Magazine*, Edinburgh, Blackwood, XIV (1823).

Davies, Hugh Sykes, *Thomas De Quincey*, London, Green, 1964.

De Luca, V. A., *Thomas De Quincey: The Prose of Vision*, Toronto, University of Toronto Press, 1982.

Devlin, D. D., *De Quincey, Wordsworth, and the Art of Prose*, London, Macmillan, 1983.

Eaton, Horace A., *A Diary of Thomas De Quincey, 1803*, London, Noel Douglas, 1927.

——*Thomas De Quincey: A Biography*, London, Oxford University Press, 1936.

Hayter, Alethea, *Opium and the Romantic Imagination*, Wellingborough, Crucible, 1988.

Holstein, Michael E., '"An apocalypse of the world within": autobiographical exegesis in De Quincey's *Confessions of an English Opium-Eater* (1822)', *Prose Studies, 1800–1900* 2: 2, 1979.

Jack, Ian, 'De Quincey revises his *Confessions*', *PMLA* LXXII (1957).

Jordan, John E., *Thomas De Quincey, Literary Critic: His Method and Achievement*, Berkeley, University of California Press, 1952.

——(ed.) *De Quincey as Critic*, London, Routledge and Kegan Paul, 1973.

Lever, Karen M., 'De Quincey as Gothic hero: a perspective on *Confessions of an English Opium-Eater* and *Suspiria de Profundis*', *Texas Studies in Language and Literature* XXI (1979).

Lindop, Grevel, *The Opium-Eater: A Life of Thomas De Quincey*, Oxford, Oxford University Press, 1985.

McFarland, Thomas, *Romantic Cruxes: The English Essayists and the Spirit of the Age*, Oxford, Clarendon Press, 1987.

Miller, J. Hillis, *The Disappearance of God: Five Nineteenth-century Writers*, Cambridge, Mass., Harvard University Press, 1963.

Ramsey, Roger, 'The structure of De Quincey's *Confessions of an English Opium-Eater*', *Prose Studies, 1800–1900*, 1: 2 (1978).

Sackville-West, Edward, *A Flame in Sunlight: The Life and Work of Thomas De Quincey*, London, Cassell, 1936.

Snyder, Robert L. (ed.) *Thomas De Quincey: Bicentenary Studies*, Norman and London, University of Oklahoma Press, 1985.

Spector, Stephen, 'Thomas De Quincey: self-effacing auto-biographer', *Studies in Romanticism* 18 (1979).

Whale, John C., *Thomas De Quincey's Reluctant Autobiography*, London, Croom Helm, 1984.

Woolf, Virginia, 'De Quincey's autobiography', in *The Common Reader*, 2nd series, London, 1932.

Wordsworth, William, *The Prelude*, ed. Jonathan Wordsworth, M. H. Abrams and Stephen Gill, New York and London, Norton, 1979.

# 27

# Charles Lamb, *Elia*

## Duncan Wu

Gorgons, and Hydras, and Chimaeras – dire stories of Celaeno and the Harpies – may reproduce themselves in the brain of superstition – but they were there before. They are transcripts, types – the archetypes are in us, and eternal.[1]

This sentence, dropped casually into the midst of Charles Lamb's essay, 'Witches, and Other Night Fears', is one of those seminal statements that define what was once considered 'High' Romanticism. Lamb's 'transcripts' invite comparison with 'The types and symbols of eternity, / The first, and last, and midst, and without end',[2] which Wordsworth 'reads' in the ravine of the Simplon Pass in *The Prelude*, and the emotions that, in De Quincey's account of the 'palimpsest of the human brain', are inscribed indelibly in the mind: 'Everlasting layers of ideas, images, feelings, have fallen upon your brain softly as light. Each succession has seemed to bury all that went before, and yet in reality not one has been extinguished'.[3] This is curious enough, until you realize that Lamb's claims are greater than De Quincey's, who argues only that the brain stores everything it experiences; for Lamb, the imagination contains emotions embedded *before* birth. Having quoted *Ancient Mariner* 451–6,[4] he elucidates:

That the kind of fear here treated of is purely spiritual – that it is strong in proportion as it is objectless upon earth – that it predominates in the period of sinless infancy – are difficulties, the solution of which might afford some probable insight into our ante-mundane condition, and a peep at least into the shadow-land of pre-existence.[5]

The 'shadow-land of pre-existence'? It is a startling comment, and ought to give us pause, especially if we had been inclined to write Lamb off as the prize exhibit of the 'jolly-good-chap' school of criticism that, despite honourable intentions, has done more to destroy his artistic credibility than could any, more hostile, intellectual act. The assertion of pre-existence refers back to that manifesto of Romantic thought, Wordsworth's *Ode*, which takes the view that 'Our birth is but a sleep and a forgetting'.[6] Lamb follows Wordsworth also in regarding everything that follows childhood as decline; he is in dialogue with a pre-natal past, the source of those clouds of glory the fading glow of which illuminates the ideal Romantic childhood.

'God help thee Elia, how art thou changed!'[7] That exclamation, with all its chilly horror at the undeceived sophistications of adulthood, could serve as a motto for the essays as a whole. The Elian golden age lies in the dim, only partially retrievable past, in which Stackhouse's Bible illustration of the witch of Endor raising up Samuel[8] so possessed the boy Elia that he could not expel it from his mind:

> It was he [Stackhouse] who dressed up for me a hag that nightly sate upon my pillow – a sure bed-fellow, when my aunt or my maid was far from me. All day long, while the book was permitted me, I dreamed waking over his delineation, and at night (if I may use so bold an expression) awoke into sleep, and found the vision true.[9] I durst not, even in the day-light, once enter the chamber where I slept, without my face turned to the window, aversely from the bed where my witch-ridden pillow was.[10]

'Credulity', as Lamb remarks, 'is the man's weakness, but the child's strength'. Why strength? Because being scared of what isn't there is more than mere credulity; it is proof of an instinct from which the adult has long been cut adrift – a sense of the numinous and magical. If the disbelieving sensibility of the adult strips the Bible story of its power, the child's lack of scepticism restores it, and even reasserts the force of those convictions that give witchcraft its power. We are a long way from the empiricist tendencies of such Enlightenment worthies as John Locke, for whom imagination, and particularly the susceptibilities of the infant mind, were a source only of derangement:

> The Ideas of Goblins and Sprights have really no more to do with Darkness than Light; yet let but a foolish Maid inculcate these often on the Mind of a Child, and raise them there together, possibly he shall never be able to separate them again so long as he lives; but Darkness shall ever afterwards bring with it those frightful Ideas, and they shall be so joined, that he can no more bear the one than the other.[11]

Lamb would have sympathized more with the 'foolish Maid' than with the schoolmasterish dominie who kept the volumes of fairy tales and myths out of her reach. Nor was he alone in declaring war on such strictures; as early as 1797 Coleridge had told Tom Poole that, 'from my early reading of fairy tales and genii etc. etc., my mind had been habituated *to the Vast*'.[12] Locke's larger argument is against the associative tendencies of the mind, and it was these that Wordsworth and Coleridge placed at the centre of the philosophical complex to be enshrined in *The Recluse*. In short, the author of the *Essay* represents a school of thought that Lamb, as a believer in the redemptive force of the imagination, would have resisted; to Locke, such concepts as pre-existence, credulity and childhood vision would have been claptrap or, at best, of questionable value. Why? Because they lie beyond the reach of human reason; they appeal to our appetite for the immaterial. Locke is, in fact, a type of what Lamb terms the 'Caledonian' intellect:

> You never witness his first apprehension of a thing. His understanding is always at its meridian – you never see the first dawn, the early streaks. – He has no falterings of self-suspicion. Surmises, guesses, misgivings, half-intuitions, semi-consciousnesses, partial illuminations, dim instincts, embryo conceptions, have no place in his brain, or vocabulary.[13]

The Caledonian is the exemplary anti-Elian not just because he lacks negative capability, but because of his claims to certainty. He is also the arch-materialist, embodying the ever-present fear that time is unstoppable and relentless, the horrible suspicion that pre-existence might be no more than wish-fulfilment, and that everything is doomed to degrade into chaos. Despite the tone of light-hearted whimsicality by which his writing is often thought to be characterized, there was in Lamb a deeply religious streak that led him early in life to become (like Coleridge and Hazlitt) a devout Unitarian, and which found expression in such serious works as *Living Without God in the World*.[14] That religiosity can only have been intensified by the tragic events of 22 September 1796, when his sister Mary stabbed their mother to death in a manic-depressive seizure, and wounded their father, embedding a fork in his forehead.[15] Lamb was only 21; he was probably responsible for the humane treatment Mary received, both in court and at the Islington asylum, Fisher House. He nursed her at home for the rest of his life, despite suffering from spells of mental illness himself, and it is likely that his lengthy tenure (1792–1825) of a clerical job at the East India Company in the City of London was intended partly to keep him on an even keel. The belief that great art is created by the mad is the stuff of Hollywood myth. *Elia* is the creation of a supremely sane man – but that sanity was hard-won in the face of unspeakable personal hardship, and his Unitarian convictions played their part in enabling him to face a future in which neither his, nor his sister's, mental stability, could be depended on. As late as July 1829 he is to be found telling Bernard Barton of how he looks forward to bringing Mary home from the asylum at Fulham; she was, he wrote, 'looking better in health than ever, but sadly rambling, and scarce showing any pleasure in seeing me, or curiosity when I should come again'.[16]

For Lamb, therefore, there may have been a powerful emotional and psychological motive for preserving the imaginative freedom celebrated in *Elia*; a note of urgency creeps into his voice when he tells us, 'I must have books, pictures, theatres, chit-chat, scandal, jokes, ambiguities, and a thousand whim-whams'.[17] In this mood he becomes the advocate of play as therapy – of which the very persona of Elia, engaged in an occasional cat-and-mouse game with the reader, is an example.[18] Similarly, Sarah Battle's prominence in the Elian pantheon derives from her conviction that whist was more than a card-game; it was a complex ritual invoking 'the gay triumph-assuring scarlets – the contrasting deadly-killing sables – the "hoary majesty of spades" – Pam in all his glory!'[19] Without their regalia, the '*beauty* of cards would be extinguished for ever. Stripped of all that is imaginative in them, they must degenerate into merely gambling'.[20] Lamb is talking less about cards than about spiritual need. Behind the apparent ease and assurance of the Elian manner, he harbours a deep apprehension that the materialist nightmare might turn out to be all there is – that card games might be no more than a form of gambling, and that the world, stripped of magic and beauty, might be only matter in motion. Such a vision comprises the Elian hell, confronted in one of the *Last Essays*, 'Popular Fallacies', when he describes how poor parents have no choice but to 'drag up' their baby: 'It was never sung to – no one ever told to it a tale of the nursery. It was dragged up, to live or to die as it happened. It had no young dreams. It broke at once into the iron realities of life'.[21]

Against those 'iron realities', which Lamb no doubt felt closing in on him every time his sister suffered a relapse, he mediates constantly in his writing between moments of illumination and the 'real', as if to assert the interdependence of the two. What could be more devastating than the burning down of the home of the 'great lubberly boy', the Chinese Bo-bo, who stoops to feel the family pig which has been roasted in the inferno?

> Some of the crums of the scorched skin had come away with his fingers, and for the first time in his life (in the world's life indeed, for before him no man had known it) he tasted – *crackling*! . . . The truth at length broke into his slow understanding, that it was the pig that smelt so, and the pig that tasted so delicious; and, surrendering himself up to the new-born pleasure, he fell to tearing up whole handfuls of the scorched skin with the flesh next it, and was cramming it down his throat in his beastly fashion, when his sire entered amid the smoking rafters, armed with retributory cudgel, and finding how affairs stood, began to rain blows upon the young rogue's shoulders, as thick as hail-stones, which Bo-bo heeded not any more than if they had been flies.[22]

As the helter-skelter rhythms of that last sentence gather pace, you realize that the 'history' Lamb relates could not be more authentic in its evocation of the raw exhilaration of newness. It is his rewriting of the Fall – one which, in true Romantic fashion, surrenders us not to evil, but to a kind of rediscovered innocence. If the violence of Bo-bo's father, Ho-ti, represents the Lockean imperative knocking loudly at the door, it is firmly silenced by his own appetite for the extraordinary and the new. Invited to share the roast pork,

> Ho-ti trembled every joint while he grasped the abominable thing, wavering whether he should not put his son to death for an unnatural young monster, when the crackling scorching his fingers, as it had done his son's, and applying the same remedy to them, he in turn tasted some of its flavour, which, make what sour mouths he would for a pretence, proved not altogether displeasing to him. In conclusion . . . both father and son fairly sat down to the mess, and never left off till they had despatched all that remained of the litter.[23]

Father and son are united in a peculiarly physical and secular ecstasy not unlike that experienced elsewhere in the essays by April fools ('I love a *Fool* – as naturally, as if I were of kith and kin to him')[24] and those who receive Valentine cards.[25] In each case, Lamb reposes his faith in an ability to transcend the strait-jacket of materialism to which the human condition confines us. And yet such moments are the exception rather than the rule. 'Lawyers, I suppose, were children once', he comments, in 'The Old Benchers of the Inner Temple', 'Why must every thing smack of man, and mannish? Is the world all grown up? Is childhood dead?'[26] It is symptomatic of how thoroughly he has been misrepresented that Lamb is often regarded as a sort of court-jester to the Romantics – Haydon's sentimental account of the 'immortal dinner', so beloved of his admirers, declares as much.[27] But the Elian manner is typically elegiac, not jocular, for much the same reason that *The Prelude* is pervaded not by the high hopes that conclude it, but by the spirits of the drowned man, the Winander boy, and the poet's deceased father. Both Wordsworth and Lamb lament the passing of 'a glory from the earth'.[28] Elia is constantly communing with the dead – Sarah Battle, 'the souls of all the writers' in the Bodleian Library,[29] and long-forgotten theatre-stars ('On Some of the Old Actors') – in an attempt to regain the flawed paradises they once inhabited.

I cannot think of a writer who speaks more urgently or with greater relevance to those who face the dawning of a new millennium, with all its attendant anxieties and aspirations.

And yet, of all the Romantic essayists, Lamb remains one of the least fashionable:[30] to the hard-nosed critics of the cold war era, he was insufficiently 'serious'; to modern tastes, he seems either complacent or conservative. Such judgements are misconceived. The prose still crackles with an inventive, mischievous wit, and can be as inspired as anything in De Quincey, Hazlitt or even Melville, such as this valedictory effusion from 'The Old Benchers of the Inner Temple':

> Fantastic forms, whither are ye fled? Or, if the like of you exist, why exist they no more for me? Ye inexplicable, half-understood appearances, why comes in reason to tear away the preternatural mist, bright or gloomy, that enshrouded you? Why make ye so sorry a figure in my relation, who made up to me – to my childish eyes – the mythology of the Temple? In those days I saw Gods, as 'old men covered with a mantle', walking upon the earth. Let the dreams of classic idolatry perish, – extinct be the fairies and fairy trumpery of legendary fabling, – in the heart of childhood, there will, for ever, spring up a well of innocent or wholesome superstition – the seeds of exaggeration will be busy there, and vital – from every-day forms educing the unknown and the uncommon. In that little Goshen there will be light, when the grown world flounders about in the darkness of sense and materiality. While childhood, and while dreams, reducing childhood, shall be left, imagination shall not have spread her holy wings totally to fly the earth.[31]

## NOTES

1  Lamb, *Elia* (1823), p. 155.
2  *Thirteen-Book Prelude*, VI. 571–2.
3  *Romanticism*, p. 692.
4  Like one that on a lonesome road
      Doth walk in fear and dread,
    And having once turned round walks on
      And turns no more his head
    Because he knows a frightful fiend
      Doth close behind him tread.
5  *Elia* (1823), p. 156.
6  Line 58. Jonathan Wordsworth writes illumin-atingly about this aspect of Wordsworth's poem in *William Wordsworth: The Borders of Vision*, Oxford, 1982, pp. 90–4.
7  'New Year's Eve', *Elia* (1823), p. 64.
8  This story is told at 1 Samuel 28.
9  The expression is 'bold' because it recalls Adam's dream, during which God created Eve out of one of Adam's ribs (Genesis 2:21–2); Keats had used the same reference to discuss the imagination in his letters (*Romanticism* p. 1,014). Keats and Lamb were acquainted, and might have dis-cussed this.
10  *Elia* (1823), pp. 153–4.
11  John Locke, 'Of the Associations of Ideas', *An Essay Concerning Human Understanding*, 16th edn, 2 vols, London, 1768, i. 369.

12  *Romanticism*, p. 514.
13  *Elia* (1823), p. 137.
14  See, notably, Jonathan Wordsworth, 'Lamb and Coleridge as One-Goddites', pp. 37–47.
15  This incident is described and analysed in detail by Mary Blanchard Balle, 'Mary Lamb: her men-tal health issues', *Charles Lamb Bulletin* NS 93 (1996) 2–11.
16  *The Letters of Charles and Mary Lamb*, ed. E. V. Lucas, 3 vols, London, 1935, iii. 224.
17  *Elia* (1823), p. 143.
18  The strategy is explained partly in a letter to his publisher, John Taylor (*Romanticism*, p. 616). Jonathan Bate discourses on this in his introduc-tion to *Elia and the Last Essays of Elia*, Oxford, Oxford University Press, 1987.
19  *Elia* (1823), p. 78.
20  Ibid.
21  *Elia and The Last Essays of Elia*, ed. Jonathan Bate, Oxford, Oxford University Press, 1987, p. 300.
22  *Elia* (1823), p. 278.
23  Ibid., pp. 279–80.
24  Ibid., pp. 99–100.
25  In the essay, 'Valentine's Day'.
26  Ibid., p. 193.
27  *Romanticism*, pp. 706–8.

28  *Ode* 18.
29  Ibid., p. 20.
30  A detailed account of why this has happened is given by Bill Ruddick in a posthumously pub-

lished article in the *Charles Lamb Bulletin*, April 1997.
31  Ibid., pp. 205–6.

## WRITINGS

Lamb, Charles, *Elia and The Last Essays of Elia*, ed. Jonathan Bate, Oxford, Oxford University Press, 1987.

——*Elia 1823*, introduced by Jonathan Wordsworth, Oxford and New York, Woodstock Books 1991.

Morpurgo, J. E. (ed.) *Charles Lamb and Elia*, Manchester, Carcanet, 1993.

## REFERENCES AND FURTHER READING

Courtney, Winifred F., *Young Charles Lamb 1775–1802*, London, Macmillan, 1982.

Park, Roy (ed.) *Lamb as Critic*, London, Routledge and Kegan Paul, 1980.

Prance, Claude A., *Companion to Charles Lamb: A Guide to People and Places 1760–1847*, London, Mansell Publishing 1983.

Trott, Nicola, '"The Old Margate Hoy" and other depths of Elian credulity', *Charles Lamb Bulletin* NS 82 (1993) 47–59.

Wordsworth, Jonathan, 'Lamb and Coleridge as One-Goddites', *Charles Lamb Bulletin* NS 58 (1987) 37–47.

# 28

# William Hazlitt,
## *The Spirit of the Age*
### *Bonnie Woodbery*

William Hazlitt's *The Spirit of the Age*, published in 1825, began as a journalistic endeavour for the *New Monthly Magazine*. Entitled 'Spirits of the Age', the string of essays was launched with 'Jeremy Bentham' in January 1824, 'Rev. Mr. Irving' in February, 'The Late Mr. Horne Tooke' in March, 'Sir Walter Scott' in April, and 'Lord Eldon' in July. Hazlitt added 18 sketches to this group for the first edition of the book, including essays on Wordsworth, Byron, Coleridge, Southey, Godwin, Malthus and Lamb. As a culmination of over a decade of critical endeavour, Hazlitt's assessments of the representative figures and their impact on the age have been very influential in shaping subsequent characterizations of Romanticism.[1]

Critics disagree over whether Hazlitt's book is united under a single unifying trope or person – some believe that Hazlitt meant Wordsworth to be the figure most representative of the spirit of the age – or whether a spirit of contradiction and resistance to simplification governs the book.[2] Still another point of view says that *The Spirit of the Age* is Hazlitt's requiem for the failure of Romantic poetry and the imaginative spirit.[3] As such it recapitulates Hazlitt's distrust of the age's tendency toward abstraction embodied in any kind of speculative theory – philosophical, historical, scientific, religious, economic or aesthetic – at the expense of the imaginative, the spiritual and the poetic. Hazlitt feared the erosion of the poetic sensibility by the abstract because he believed that at least to some extent the age and its tendencies shape the imaginative capacity of its people. Thus, he claims that Shakespeare could not have been born in the early nineteenth century, an age Hazlitt characterizes as 'one dull compound of politics, criticism, chemistry, and metaphysics' ('On Modern Comedy', Howe, IV, 12).[4]

Hazlitt's choices for representatives of his critical age have long been puzzled over, his omissions even more so. One key to his choices is his epigraph from *Hamlet*: 'To know another well, were to know oneself'. As self-discovery his choices would out of necessity be based on those whose careers he had followed as a political journalist and literary critic, public figures who had, over the years, helped define Hazlitt's sense of himself as a writer and as a person. On the public level, these figures offered the urbane journal-reading audience a survey of the popular and the profound, the failed and the famous, but all were public figures whom his readers would recognize as at least reflecting, if not being wholly representative of, the intellectual, artistic and political atmosphere of the age.[5]

As for his omissions – Keats, Shelley, Wollstonecraft, Inchbald, Dacre, Austen, Hemans, Baillie, Edgeworth, Burney and endless others – for whatever reason, they were not part of Hazlitt's idiosyncratic vision of the spirit of the age. He does include Keats as an ironic contrast to William Gifford's failed attempts at poetry in the essay on Gifford, and he adds a homage to Wollstonecraft and Inchbald at the conclusion of William Godwin's portrait. The way many read Hazlitt today depends more on his omissions than on his inclusions. The rejection of a masculine vision of Romanticism for which Hazlitt has been dubbed one of the chief spokesmen has for some time characterized the debates over the politics of canon formation and the adequate representation of women writers in Romantic studies.[6] However, Hazlitt always imagined himself to be an unpopular critic. In an 1826 essay 'On Knowledge of the World' he complains about the neglect of *The Spirit of the Age*, which he attributes to the public's exclusive spirit:

> If you do not attach yourself to some one set of people and principles, and stick to them through thick and thin, instead of giving your opinion fairly and fully all round, you must expect to have all the world against you, for no other reason than because you express yourself sincerely. (Howe, XVII, 300)[7]

Hazlitt's method of proceeding is different for each individual portrait; however, they are all models of compression that attempt neither to condense nor to collate a philosopher's system or a writer's fiction. Instead, in each sketch Hazlitt with wit and accuracy reveals what he believes are the essential traits of his subject's mind and work. In spite of or because of this intuitive style, the effect seems haphazard as 'descriptions of physical appearance, dress, and personal habits jostle with philosophical analysis, critical comment-ary, and anecdotal reportage'.[8] A contemporary reviewer of *The Spirit of the Age*, although fascinated by Hazlitt's idiosyncratic style, concludes that its unfortunate result is 'that we retain nothing distinctly of what he says. It is a sort of confused memory of sounds, like the clashing of musical instruments'.[9] What follows attempts to make sense of this brilliant confusion by condensing and collating (what Hazlitt identifies as Bentham's plodding strengths) the major themes that characterize the spirit of the age as represented in Hazlitt's chosen writers, philosophers and politicians.

The character and quality of genius was for Hazlitt a lifelong preoccupation. Thus, it is not surprising that we should find Hazlitt returning to various reincarnations of this theme in *The Spirit of the Age*. In his essay from *Table-Talk*, 'On Genius and Common Sense', Hazlitt defines genius or originality as 'some strong quality in the mind, answering to and bringing out some new and striking quality in nature' (Howe, VIII, 42). In this essay, Hazlitt distinguishes between two kinds of genius.[10] On the one hand, there is the genius best exemplified in Shakespeare, who was the least egotistical of authors: 'His genius consisted in the faculty of transforming himself at will into whatever he chose: his originality was the power of seeing every object from the exact point of view in which others would see it' ('On Genius', Howe, VIII, 42). In *The Spirit of the Age* Scott's prose novels and romances come closest to embodying this kind of genius. Scott has achieved the ability to 'borrow of others' and in so doing has 'enriched his own genius with everlasting variety, truth, and freedom' and has enriched his audience with 'a new edition of human nature' (Howe, XI, 61, 64). Hence, Scott, like Shakespeare, has the potential to lose his authorial-self in his subject. On the other hand, there is what Hazlitt identifies as 'genius in ordinary', a genius which is exclusive, self-willed, egotistical, and reflects the author more than the object he looks upon ('On Genius', Howe, VIII, 42). This kind of genius Hazlitt finds typical of Wordsworth, who 'stamps [his] character, that deep individual interest, on whatever he meets', which in *Lyrical Ballads* includes ingrafting 'his own conscious reflections on the casual thought of hinds and shepherds' (Howe, XI, 89). Between these two definitive poles, however, Hazlitt comprehends many varieties of genius.

Hazlitt dwells on the foibles of unfocused genius as he sees them manifested in Coleridge's aborted career. In an age when the 'accumulation of knowledge' has surpassed all that has gone before and 'distracts and dazzles the looker-on' (29), Hazlitt reasons that it is understandable that Coleridge, with his 'tangential mind' and an understanding 'fertile, subtle, expansive . . . beyond all living precedent', touches on all subjects, but rests on none (Howe, XI, 29). Hazlitt praises the *Ancient Mariner* as the one work by Coleridge that is 'unquestionably a work of genius – of wild, irregular, overwhelming imagination', but this work was done 20 years earlier, when Coleridge was infused with the ideas of liberty (34). Since then, Hazlitt believes that Coleridge has done little of note, and rather than ridicule Coleridge, Hazlitt sadly records his fall:

> Alas! 'Frailty, thy name is Genius!' – What is become of all the mighty heap of hope, of thought, of learning, and humanity? It has ended in swallowing doses of oblivion and in writing paragraphs in the *Courier*. – Such and so little is the mind of man! (Howe, XI, 34)

To underscore this great waste of genius, Hazlitt draws an interesting contrast between Coleridge's unfocused genius and the plodding talent of William Godwin, who Hazlitt believes has accomplished much in spite of his lack of natural capacity and few acquired advantages. While Mr Godwin's faculties have approached a task with diligence and carried it out as a 'matter of duty', Coleridge 'delights in nothing but episodes and digressions, neglects whatever he undertakes to perform, and can act only on spontaneous impulses, without object or method' (ibid., p. 36). Of the two kinds of genius, Hazlitt must finally commend Godwin for his 'determined purpose' that enabled him with less natural talent than Coleridge to finish works like the *Enquiry into Political Justice* (1793) and *Caleb Williams* (1794), which Hazlitt believes will ensure his lasting fame. Coleridge, on the other hand, is in jeopardy of not being remembered at all.[11] For, as Hazlitt points out, Coleridge is the opposite of the egotist and 'in him the individual is always merged in the abstract and general' (Howe, XI, 31). But this abstraction is not the disinterested genius of Shakespeare. Rather, it is the abstract principle that underlies all speculative philosophies that Hazlitt refers to here and that he finds troubling.[12] Hazlitt illustrates Coleridge's intellectual peregrinations from the poet's prize-winning Greek epigrams at Cambridge University, where he was renowned for his knowledge of the Classics, to the Hartz Forest of Germany, where Hazlitt pictures a rather dazed Coleridge wandering among the 'cabalistic names of Fichte and Schelling and Lessing and God knows who' (Howe, XI, 34). From Hazlitt's point of view, the influence of German transcendental philosophy greatly contributed to Coleridge's decline as a poet and critic. Hazlitt sees Coleridge as a counterpart to the age's propensity for abstraction and critique, and he laments Coleridge's failure because, like the age itself, he had not fulfilled his early promise.

In contrast, the writers who would get the most votes for the 'greatest geniuses of the age' are Sir Walter Scott and Lord Byron; the character of their genius, however, could not be more opposite. Throughout the essay on Lord Byron, Hazlitt uses Scott's impersonal genius, rather than his conservative politics, as a touchstone against which to measure the extent and form of Byron's genius. Byron is a complete contrast to Scott in poetry, prose, politics and temperament (Howe, XI, 69). Their only similarity seems to be that their political identities are notoriously inconsistent with their moral and literary values: 'Lord Byron, who in his politics is a liberal, in his genius is haughty and aristocratic: Walter Scott, who is an aristocrat in principle, is popular in his writings, and is . . . equally servile to nature and to opinion' (Howe, XI, 70–1).

In terms of talent, no two men could be more different. Lord Byron's genius is governed by nothing other than his own will, while the genius of Sir Walter is essentially imitative (ibid., p. 71). Hazlitt admits that he prefers the genius of Scott to that of Byron since Scott 'casts his descriptions in the mould of nature, ever-varying, never tiresome, always interesting and always instructive', in contrast to Byron who 'makes man in his own image, woman after his own heart; the one is a capricious tyrant, the other a yielding slave' (ibid.). Hazlitt blames Byron's shortcomings on his being an 'anomaly in letters and society, a Noble poet', enabling him to claim both the 'pride of birth and genius' (ibid., p. 77). The ruling motives of one with such fierce pride are vanity, distinction and contempt (ibid.). Thus, Hazlitt detects a splenetic contempt behind most of Byron's productions. He admits that *Don Juan* has great power but sees that power undercut by Byron's penchant for mortifying and shocking the public (Howe, XI, 75–6). In *Childe Harold*, too, Byron assumes a 'lofty and philosophic tone', but it turns out that a petulant disdain for his contemporaries is the stimulus behind his escape into the past (Howe, XI, 74). This supreme egotism, however, increases the particular intensity of Byron's poetry, which is propelled by a 'feverish and irritable state of excitement' and the 'electric force of his own feelings' (ibid., p. 72). Byron's genius is therefore an example of 'genius in ordinary'. He achieves a great intensity and force in his poetry because of his ego, not without it. In contrast, Scott's genius arises from his ability to completely get 'rid of the trammels of authorship' (ibid., p. 61).

Another theme that is central to many of the sketches in *The Spirit of the Age* is the opposition between anti-Jacobin politicians and writers and their reformist counterparts. Two representatives of the anti-Jacobin camp are George Canning (1770–1827) and William Gifford (1756–1826). Both were writers for the newspaper the *Anti-Jacobin; or, Weekly Examiner* (1797–8), and both were associated in later years with the conservative *Quarterly Review*.

George Canning, a Tory member of the House of Commons, was a writer for the short-lived *Anti-Jacobin*, whose main purpose was to make the radical reformers represented by the Opposition politicians look ridiculous. Canning was also an intimate of Sir Walter Scott, and said to be, along with Scott, a founder of the *Quarterly Review*. In *The Spirit of the Age*, Hazlitt criticizes Canning for his blatant sophistry which the public admires because his clever, empty rhetoric soothes and pleases the public mind. His success as an orator, Hazlitt says, is in fact due to the 'genius of the age, in which words have obtained a mastery over things, "and to call evil good and good evil", is thought the mark of a superior and happy spirit' (Howe, XI, 157). Hence, Mr Canning can praise the Constitution but in reality violate it, can commend religion and social order but mean 'slavery and super-stition' (ibid.). Hazlitt mocks Canning's rhetorical evasions when he identifies Canning's parodies for the *Anti-Jacobin* as some of his best writing. Since any sort of poetry or heart-felt sentiment is alien to Canning, he is, according to Hazlitt, ready-made for parody: 'Any thing more light or worthless cannot well be imagined' (ibid., p. 158).

William Gifford was also a writer for the *Anti-Jacobin* newspaper. However, Hazlitt finds him most obnoxious as the editor of the *Quarterly Review*, a Tory journal well known for its political bias. As editor from 1809–24, Gifford bowed to 'authority and ministerial influence by slanderously denouncing the poetry or prose of any member of the opposite party and ignoring such critical principles of fairness and truth'. According to Hazlitt, Gifford's 'happy combination of defects' – low breeding, pedantry, a dependency on the great – make him a perfect editor of the *Review* (Howe, XI, 114). Thus, there is not a single statement in the *Quarterly* that can be trusted, due to his misrepresentation of the facts.[13]

Hazlitt also condemns Sir Walter Scott for his association with the *Quarterly Review*. The contradiction between the Scott who is the 'finest, the most humane and accomplished author of his age' and the Scott who associates himself with Legitimacy and power as represented in a 'venal press' (particularly the *Quarterly*) that deluges the public mind with 'offal garbage' under the mask of 'literary criticism and fair discussion' is, for Hazlitt, an anomaly which only Britain could produce (Howe, XI, 68). He is sure that in no other age or country could 'such genius . . . have been so degraded' (ibid.).

For the most part, Hazlitt's political sympathies align with the humanitarian causes of the reformers. Therefore, Hazlitt praises Godwin for his legal acumen that helped save the lives of the 'twelve innocent individuals', including John Horne Tooke, John Thelwall and Thomas Holcroft, charged with treason in 1794. Here Hazlitt refers to Godwin's pamphlet *Cursory Strictures on the Charge delivered by Lord Chief Justice Eyre to the Grand Jury*, which helped turn the trial, thus keeping the men from being found guilty and hung for high treason (Howe, XI, 26).[14]

A liberal politician whom Hazlitt very much admires is Sir Francis Burdett (1770–1844), a parliamentary reformer who was twice imprisoned for his support of humanitar-ian causes. According to Hazlitt's sketch of Burdett, he is a man of impeccable honesty and one who is warmly admired by his constituency. Hazlitt pays tribute to Burdett for his unflagging support of oppressed individuals, exclaiming that Burdett's 'love of liberty is pure, as it is warm and steady: his humanity is unconstrained and free' (ibid., p. 141).

Hazlitt claims that Francis Jeffrey (1773–1850), editor of the *Edinburgh Review*, a journal known to be sympathetic to the Whig party, is William Gifford's opposite in education, politics and temperament. Under Jeffrey's direction, the political and critical articles of the *Review*, and the tone of 'manly explicitness' in which they are delivered, are 'eminently characteristic of the Spirit of the Age', in contrast to the *Quarterly*, whose object it is to extinguish that spirit (Howe, XI, 127). Hazlitt admires Jeffrey's ability to judge a work on its literary merits rather than on 'ignorance', 'prejudice' and 'personal malevol-ence' (ibid., p. 128).

The early work of Wordsworth and Coleridge also reflects a reformist spirit for Hazlitt. He describes the *Lyrical Ballads* as partaking of 'the revolutionary movement of our age', in that the poems 'proceed on a principle of equality' that mirror the 'political changes of the day' (Howe, XI, 87). As for the young Coleridge, the *Ancient Mariner*, that work of a 'wild, irregular, overwhelming imagination', sprang from those years when Coleridge 'hailed the rising orb of liberty' and sang the 'joy' of the French Revolution (Howe, XI, 34). Although Hazlitt dislikes what he views as Byron's 'preposterous *liberalism*', affecting 'the principles of equality', but resuming at will the 'privilege of peerage', his concluding requiem for Byron, written shortly after the poet's death, rises above petty invective. Here Byron receives Hazlitt's highest praise for his efforts in the cause of freedom: 'Lord Byron is dead: he also died a martyr to his zeal in the cause of freedom, for the last, best hopes of man. Let this be his excuse and his epitaph!' (ibid., p. 78).

Another theme which is central to Hazlitt's spirit of the age is reason vs. the imagination. For Hazlitt this opposition takes many forms. Hazlitt believed that any creed, dogma, theory or system, when it restricted feeling and man's imaginative spirit, was a threat to the individual's awareness of his relation to the rest of humanity.[15] His portraits of Jeremy Bentham (1748–1832) and Thomas Malthus (1766–1834) represent the danger of theories that are taken to extremes.

In his portrait of Jeremy Bentham, Hazlitt emphasizes the Utilitarian's neglect of poetry and the natural, both of which have a basis in man's affective nature. Hazlitt points out that Bentham 'has no fondness for poetry and can hardly extract a moral out of Shakespeare. . . . He is one of those who prefer the artificial to the natural in most things . . . and is for referring everything to Utility. There is a little narrowness in this' (ibid., p. 28). Hazlitt's understatement here characterizes the whole of his portrait of Bentham, a man who on the one hand plays the organ, admires the prints of Hogarth, and dissipates part of a handsome fortune on 'plausible projectors', while on the other lives like a monk 'with the dust and cobwebs of an obscure solitude', writing a 'barbarous philosophical language' that 'darkens knowledge' and talks of nothing except his grand theme of Utility' (ibid., pp. 6, 14, 15). While these two characterizations could not be farther apart, they both describe a man who is naive and ignorant of the world, but one who ironically enough proclaims his doctrine of Utility as the foundation of the world's just laws and moral and political reasoning.

Hazlitt questions the right of Bentham or, indeed, any empirical philosopher to legislate for the future good of man when their doctrines rely on a faulty view of human nature.[16] As Hazlitt sees it, Bentham's doctrine of self-interest and its favourite dictum that every pleasure is equally a good whether it 'arise from the exercise of virtue or the perpetration of crime' fails to take 'into account the varieties of human nature, and the caprices and irregularities of the human will' (ibid., p. 8). Bentham's blindness to the realities of human nature results in his narrowness of vision, a vision that excludes the natural and sympathetic.

Thomas Malthus's principle of population as advanced in his *Essay on the Principle of Population as it affects the Future Improvement of Society* (1798) was for Hazlitt an 'irresistible monster' that was meant not only as an argument against Godwin and the Utopian philosophers, but also as a rationale for opposing governmental reforms.[17] Hazlitt begins his sketch on Malthus by grudgingly pointing out that Malthus has managed to become something more than a mere name: 'One has not to *beat the bush* about [Malthus's] talents, his attainments, his vast reputation, and leave off without knowing what it all amounts to' (Howe, XI, 254). What it all amounts to, according to Hazlitt, is a single principle: 'population cannot simply go on increasing without pressing increasingly on the food supply, and thus a check of some kind must oppose it sooner or later' (ibid., p. 255). According to Malthus, the only possible checks to this inevitable growth are vice and misery: an unfortunate conclusion for the poor, who under this principle are doomed to starve for the greater good. Herein lies Hazlitt's greatest disagreement with Malthus. Hazlitt argues that the principle of uncontrolled growth is an error to which even Malthus later admitted, but has never taken the sufficient pains to dispel, thus allowing the general public to believe that the increase in population is an unqualified evil that can be stopped only by vice and misery. Hazlitt views this 'error' as comprising a false but powerful argument against humanitarian reforms and as keeping existing prejudices and interests in place (ibid., p. 271). In so doing Malthus has sunk in Hazlitt's estimation from scientific philosopher to sophist and party writer (ibid., p. 272).

The development of man's imaginative spirit was, Hazlitt believed, one way to offset the bias of the age toward reason in all its forms as it denied man's affective nature. In 'On Genius and Common Sense' Hazlitt defines the imagination as 'the power of carrying on a given feeling into other situations, which must be done best according to the hold which the feeling itself has taken of the mind' (Howe, VIII, 42). This ability to stamp one's feelings on external objects through association is the great strength of Wordsworth's poetry. In his sketch of the poet, Hazlitt explains that what Wordsworth does in his poetry is set up an opposition between the 'natural and artificial; between the spirit of humanity, and the spirit of fashion and of the world' (ibid., XI, 87). It is thus the natural world combined with the spirit of humanity in Wordsworth's poetry that give it the power to combat the utilitarian systems and theories that would arrest man's emotional development. Hence, Hazlitt praises the *Lyrical Ballads* for proving the inherent truth or beauty of 'even the lichens on the rocks' (Howe, XI, 87, 89). For these reasons Hazlitt calls Wordsworth the 'most original poet now living' (ibid., p. 89). His inartificial style and his ability to translate the thoughts and feelings of the human heart effect in his poetry a 'return to the simplicity of truth and nature' (ibid., p. 87).

However, Hazlitt criticizes Wordsworth's later work, most notably *The Excursion*, as a falling off from his early poetry, and satirizes the pomp which accompanied the poem's publication when he compares the raised expectations with the actual event to 'being ushered into a stately hall and invited to sit down to a splendid banquet in the company of clowns, and with nothing but successive courses of apple-dumplings served up' (Howe, XI, 91). Hazlitt also criticizes Wordsworth's severe standards for others' poetry, admitting of 'nothing below, scarcely of anything above himself' (ibid., p. 92). But his weakness – a tendency toward egotism – is simply the underside to his strength, a fine and original poetry, and Hazlitt admits that without the egotism he might simply have been a common man.

With his novels and romances, Sir Walter Scott also manages to provide relief to the mind of the age with its 'fastidious refinement . . . rarefied as it has been with modern philosophy, and heated with ultra-radicalism' (ibid., p. 61). Hazlitt commends Scott the novelist as having no tendency toward the theoretical and speculative. It is Scott's memory, 'teeming with life and motion', rather than his speculations, 'flacid, poor, and dead', that make his novels almost universally admired. Hazlitt attributes Scott's success to his ability to lose his individuality in his writings, which convey 'the romance of real life' and 'all is fresh, as from the hand of nature' (ibid., pp. 61, 63). Scott's genius is his power to recreate human life in all its variations and complexities and thus to reassert the power of the imagination over the abstract and mechanical.

Another aspect of this central opposition, reason vs. imagination, is the rage of the age for novelty, fashion and prejudice, again to the detriment of the emotions and the authentic. For Hazlitt, the Revd Mr Irving (1792–1834), a charismatic, Calvinistic divine, is an example of the 'preposterous rage of the age for novelty' (ibid., p. 83).[18] Combining the poetry of Shakespeare with the doctrine of eternal punishment, Irving, Hazlitt ruefully admits, has gained an almost 'unprecedented popularity' (ibid. 83). Hazlitt believes the secret to Irving's overwhelming success is his height: he remarks that 'If Rev. Irving were five feet high he would never have been heard of', but 'with all his native wildness he adds uncommon height, a graceful figure and action, a clear and powerful voice, a striking if not a fine face, a bold and fiery spirit' (ibid., p. 40). The fact that Irving in his sermons demands a renunciation of all worldly improvements and a return to a *tabula rasa* of Calvinism' seems to have little affect on his listeners who allow themselves to be 'bullied' out of their wits by this imposing and handsome speaker.[19]

Thomas Moore (1779–1852) is a writer whose popular poetic creations also exhibit the love of the age for the artificial, and Hazlitt criticizes Moore for his attempts to pander to the artificial taste of the age which result in his 'effeminate' and 'meretricious' productions (ibid., p. 170). Hazlitt includes an excerpt from the *Lalla Rookh* to support his claims that Moore's poetry is all glitter with no depth of thought, singling out the description of the warrior Mokanna in a fight to the death as 'fantastic and enervated', and 'a mere piece of enigmatical ingenuity and scientific mimmineepimminee' (Howe, XI, 173, 174). Hazlitt regrets that the same censure applies to the *Irish Melodies* which 'if they do indeed express the soul of impassioned feeling in his countrymen, then the case of Ireland is hopeless' (Howe, XI, 174).[20]

In opposition to the spirit of the age and its love of novelty and prejudice, Hazlitt presents Elia, alias Charles Lamb, whom he praises for succeeding 'not by conforming to the Spirit of the Age, but in opposition to it' (ibid., p. 178). Thus, what Hazlitt admires most in Lamb's essays is his defiance of the age's propensity for novelty and the fashionable. Lamb's *Essays of Elia* recognize and have the ability to soothe the 'frailties of human nature' with their descriptions of characters, places, and manners of the last age (Howe, XI, 180).

For Hazlitt, Lamb is the reverse of the love of the age for the 'obtrusive and common-place', whether these be found in the sophistry of Canning or the poetry of Moore. Hazlitt congratulates Lamb's ability to shun 'grand' theories and fashionable and novel topics that would attract 'the thoughtless and the vain' (ibid., pp. 179, 180). He commends Lamb's descriptions of London, its inns and courts of law, its streets, its avenues and playhouses as having 'gusto', a term Hazlitt reserved for the best and most passionate art in which truth of character proceeds from truth of feeling.[21] Indeed, Hazlitt identifies Lamb's originality as partaking both of egotism and disinterestedness, a peculiar blend of the two poles of genius: the Shakespearian ability to lose oneself in its object and 'genius in ordinary', exemplified by the egotistical sublime of Wordsworth.

In contrast to Lamb, whom Hazlitt views as successfully opposing the prejudices of the age, William Godwin (1756–1836) is the writer that Hazlitt identifies as the most lamentably affected by the fickle spirit of the age and 'its love of paradox and change, its dastardly submission to prejudice and to the fashion of the day' (ibid., p. 16). That

Godwin could have enjoyed an unprecedented popularity only 25 years ago and now have dropped from sight almost entirely to 'repose on the monument of his fame' can only be explained by the overly ambitious nature of Godwin's project. According to Hazlitt, Godwin's celebrated *Enquiry Concerning Political Justice* (1793) 'raised the standard of morality' to 'airy and romantic heights', quite out of reach of the general run of humanity (Howe, XI, 18). The 'Modern Philosophy', as it was called, rejected sentimental emotions, like guilt, gratitude, affection and charity, in favour of the general good which took priority over individual pleasures. Like Bentham's theories, Godwin's appeals to utilitarian principles fail to take into account 'the amiable weaknesses of our nature' by imposing the impossible task of pursuing universal benevolence while forsaking all emotional and private attachments (ibid., p. 19). However, unlike Bentham, Godwin's strength lies in his weakness. Hazlitt praises Godwin's work which like all original thinking 'discovers the truth, or detects where error lies' (ibid., p. 23). In doing this, Godwin illustrates the limits of the human character to resist the affections and the force of habit. The failure of Godwinianism supports Hazlitt's belief in the strength of the feelings and caprices of human nature.

Hazlitt praises Godwin as 'an indefatigable and accomplished author', who, if not spontaneous, makes up for it with a focused and voluntary exercise of talent (ibid., p. 26). In spite of the defect of his natural imagination which makes Godwin's powers of conversation 'but limited', Hazlitt points out that he has kept the best company of his time: Mr Sheridan, Mr Curran, Mrs Wollstonecraft and Mrs Inchbald, all of whom Godwin has outlived. Hazlitt's sad refrain, 'Frail tenure, on which human life and genius are lent us for a while to improve or to enjoy' (ibid., p. 28), ends this requiem for Godwin's diminished fame and could also serve as a postscript to Hazlitt's last and perhaps greatest critical work, in which he presents the spirit of the age in all its glories and failures.

## NOTES

1 The first edition of *The Spirit of the Age: or Comtemporary Portraits* (London, 1825) has recently been reprinted by Woodstock Books, ed. Jonathan Wordsworth, (Oxford, 1989). P. P. Howe reprints the second English edition of the text also dated 1825 for Howe, XI. For his second edition, Hazlitt slightly rearranged the order of the essays and added a sketch of William Cobbett. Howe substitutes the sketch of Mr Canning for Cobbett since that portrait had already been included in volume eight as part of *Table-Talk*. I use Howe's edition for the present essay.

2 See James Chandler's 'Representative men, pp. 104–32. Chandler summarizes the varying viewpoints on what exactly Hazlitt meant by the 'spirit of the age'. He notes that M. H. Abrams in *Natural Supernaturalism* is one of the main advocates for Wordsworth as the representative spirit of the age in Hazlitt's book. Chandler dis-

agrees. He argues that a spirit of contradiction and resistance to simplification governs the book.

3 See Park, *Hazlitt and the Spirit of the Age*, p. 236. Park defines Hazlitt's 'spirit of the age' as an opposition between abstraction and the particular. Park's work places Hazlitt's critical thought within the philosophic contexts of the late eighteenth and early nineteenth centuries.

4 See ibid., p. 214.

5 See Gaull, *English Romanticism*, for a good summary of *The Spirit of the Age*.

6 See Ross, *The Contours of Masculine Desire*, p. 259, who argues that Hazlitt is the 'supreme romantic apologist' who represents the 'contours of romantic masculine desire that we as critics have been taught to echo'.

7 However, Hazlitt did have his staunch admirers. For instance, early in 1818, John Keats writes to Benjamin Robert Haydon (1786–1846): 'I am

convinced that there are three things to rejoice at in the Age – The Excursion, Your Pictures, and Hazlitt's depth of Taste' (Rollins, I, 203).

8 See Park, *Hazlitt and the Spirit of the Age*, p. 214.

9 See *Monthly Review* (May 1825), 107:2.

10 See Natarajan, 'Power and capability'. Natarajan identifies two types of genius in Hazlitt's critical perception: the Shakespearean genius, 'isolated from the ordinary human condition', and the egotistical 'genius in the ordinary', 'characteristic of a determined selfhood' (p. 66).

11 For a full discussion of Hazlitt's admiration and disappointment with Coleridge see McFarland, *Romantic Cruxes*.

12 Park argues that Hazlitt viewed Coleridge's reliance on the general and abstract as more insidious than Bentham's because it was a less widely recognized danger (Park, *Hazlitt and the Spirit of the Age*, p. 76).

13 For an alternative view to Gifford's personality see Clark's *William Gifford*, and Montluzin's *The Anti-Jacobins*, pp. 22–4. Montluzin reports that Gifford's physical deformity – he was a dwarf and a hunchback, with one eye turned outward – and his poverty-stricken youth were part of his rabid anti-Jacobinism. He strongly believed in keeping in place a social system that permitted him to rise as he did (he eventually graduated from Oxford).

14 In the spring of 1794 radical activities, involving demands for parliamentary reform, particularly universal suffrage and annual parliaments, increased in conjunction with the guillotining of leaders in France for their excessive moderation. The British government, in order to quell suspected violence, suspended Habeas Corpus on 17 May, and arrests of alleged radicals soon followed, a group that included

Godwin's close friend Thomas Holcroft. Godwin's pamphlet *Cursory Strictures* appeared anonymously in the *Morning Chronicle* on October 21, and dealt a serious blow to the prosecution's case when the trial opened four days later on 25 October. On legal grounds Godwin argued that political demands for parliamentary reform are not equivalent to plots to assassinate the king, the only offence for which one could be found guilty of high treason. See William St Clair's *The Godwins and the Shelleys*, pp. 129–33, for an account of Godwin's role in freeing the 12 men.

15 See Park, *Hazlitt and the Spirit of the Age*, who argues that Hazlitt believed that self, bias and prejudice 'vanished in the individual's awareness of his inter-relatedness with the rest of humanity and nature' (p. 74).

16 See Park, ibid., p. 74.

17 Hazlitt was so infuriated with Malthus's theories that he published a reply in 1807, *A Reply to the Essay on Population* (see Howe, vol. one) in which he makes many of the arguments that he summarizes in his sketch of Malthus for *The Spirit of the Age*.

18 As John Kinnaird in *William Hazlitt: Critic of Power* (p. 313) points out, Hazlitt could not have predicted the imminent and unjust persecution of Irving by the Church of Scotland: he was effectually driven to his death by heresy-fearing elders.

19 For a sympathetic view of Irving, see Thomas Carlyle's *Reminiscences*.

20 See excerpts from 'Irish Melodies' in *Romanticism*, p. 664.

21 See Hazlitt's essay 'On Gusto' for a discussion of gusto and its relationship to the imagination in *Romanticism*, pp. 641–3.

## WRITINGS

Hazlitt William, *The Spirit of the Age* (London, 1825), in Howe, vol. XI.

Sikes, H. M. et al. (eds) *The Letters of William Hazlitt*, New York, New York University Press, 1978.

## REFERENCES AND FURTHER READING

Abrams, M. H., *Natural Supernaturalism*, New York, Norton, 1971.

Baker, Herschel, *William Hazlitt*, Cambridge, Mass: Harvard University Press, 1962.

Bromwich, David, *Hazlitt: The Mind of a Critic*, New York, Oxford University Press, 1983.

Carlyle, Thomas, *Reminiscences*, London, 1881; reprinted London, J. M. Dent & Sons, 1932.

Chandler, James, 'Representative men, spirits of the age, and other Romantic types', in *Romantic Revolutions*, Bloomington, Indiana University Press, 1990, pp. 104–32.

Clark, Roy Benjamin, *William Gifford: Tory Satirist, Critic, and Editor*, New York, Columbia University Press, 1930.

Gaull, Marilyn, *English Romanticism: The Human Context*, New York, Norton, 1988.

Jones, Stanley, *Hazlitt: A Life*, Oxford, Clarendon Press, 1989.

Kinnaird, John, *William Hazlitt: Critic of Power*, New York, Columbia University Press, 1978.

McFarland, Thomas, *Romantic Cruxes: The English Essayists and the Spirit of the Age*, Oxford, Clarendon Press, 1987.

Montluzin, Emily Lorraine de, *The Anti-Jacobins, 1798–1800*, London, Macmillan Press, 1988.

Natarajan, Uttara, 'Power and capability: Hazlitt, Keats and the discrimination of the poetic self', in *Romanticism* 2:1 (1996) 54–67.

Park, Roy, *Hazlitt and the Spirit of the Age*, Oxford, Clarendon Press, 1971.

Review, '*The Spirit of the Age; or Contemporary Portraits*. 1825.' *The Monthly Review* 107 (May 1825): 1–15.

Ross, Marlon, *The Contours of Masculine Desire*, Oxford, Oxford University Press, 1990.

Ruddick, William, 'William Hazlitt', in *Handbook to English Romanticism*, ed. Jean Raimond and J. R. Watson, New York, St Martin's Press, 1992.

St Clair, William, *The Godwins and the Shelleys*, London, Faber & Faber, 1989.

Story, Patrick, 'Hazlitt's definition of the spirit of the age', *The Wordsworth Circle* 6 (1975) 97–108.

# 29

# Letitia Landon (L.E.L.), *The Improvisatrice*

## Adam Roberts

It might seem, from a cursory glance, that the traditions of nineteenth-century female authorship constitute a chain whose links are forged together out of mournful elegies for the premature death of women. Letitia Landon wrote *Stanzas on the Death of Mrs Hemans* in 1835; and when she herself died young three years later, younger female poets picked up the torch. Elizabeth Barrett's *L.E.L.'s Last Question* (1839) finds its own 'vocal pathos' with which to mourn the premature death of the poet. Landon, in this poem, is a desolately isolated figure, alone on the African coast (where she had moved with her military husband soon after her marriage), asking her 'last question': 'do you think of me as I think of you, / My friends, my friends?' Barrett insists upon the 'passionate response' of the sisterhood of poets in England ('We think of thee'), but Landon is deaf to this. Her place is 'in the dust'.

> Was she content with that drear ocean's sound,
> Dashing his mocking infinite around
> The craver of a little love, beneath
> Those stars, content – where last her song had gone?
> *They*, mute and cold in radiant life, as soon
> Their singer was to be, in darksome death? (37–42)

This theme of female isolation is one to which later nineteenth-century women poets returned; for instance, Christina Rossetti's *L.E.L.* (1859) which envisages the doomed poetess mournfully cut-off from normal human intercourse: 'All love, are loved, save only I; their hearts / Beat warm with love and joy... My heart is breaking for a little love'. The creation of a myth of isolated and doomed feminine beauty, the linkage of the poet and death, might seem to be an exact correlative of the sorts of myths of the poet dying young that are so familiar from mainstream Romanticism – Keats, Shelley, Byron, Chatterton. But there is something particular about the configuration of youth, beauty and death that is so strongly associated with Landon. Not only is it specifically gendered (which is to say, it not only depends fundamentally upon the fact that Landon was a woman, but it also goes towards defining what a certain sort of woman – a woman poet – ought to be), but it is also linked to notions of self-destruction in ways that are not true of male Romanticism. It was Landon's first great success, *The Improvisatrice* (1824) that set the tone for all her later popularity. In this long poem we find, not once but repeated many times in a variety of different narrative guises, those elements that were to coalesce in to the potent 'myth' of L.E.L.

*The Improvisatrice* represents, in a sense, the offspring of two particular literary parents. One is *Corinne* (1807), a novel by the French Romantic writer Madame de Staël, and a text that had a wide-ranging influence on a number of female writers in the nineteenth century. This is chiefly because it provided, in its tale of a beautiful female poet living a free-spirited, uninhibited and exciting life in Italy, a role-model, howsoever idealized. *Corinne* is not a particularly good novel. Angela Leighton describes its plot, which she calls 'pedantically high pitched', as consisting of 'a lengthy walking tour round Italy, as the heroine journeys from one historical site to another, reciting her verses to the adoring crowds and meanwhile catching the eye of her English lover, Lord Nevil'.[1] When Nevil leaves her for the more conventional Lucile, Corinne dies, grief-stricken. But the point is that this was virtually the only literary work to suggest what life as a female poet might be like. Women writers of the period seized on the possibilities of de Staël's fiction, often writing poems based on or directly alluding to this novel. In fact, the plot of *The Improvisatrice* is really nothing more than an adaptation of the plot of *Corinne*; only the names, and the nationality of the male love-interest, have been changed. The Improvisatrice has a large and admiring audience for her extemporized poetry. She falls in love with the handsome Lorenzo, is heartbroken when he marries another, pines away and dies – although, at the end, Landon inserted her own twist on the Corinnean narrative, when it turns out that Lorenzo has actually loved the Improvisatrice all along, and only married Ianthe out of duty because he had been betrothed to her since childhood. His bride conveniently dies after the wedding and Lorenzo returns to the Improvisatrice to claim her as his wife – but it is too late, she has sunk too far, and she dies anyway. *The Improvisatrice* follows *Corinne* in one formal aspect as well; the frame narrative of both works serves as an excuse to include several, often lengthy, examples of the protagonist's poetic works; in Landon's work this means three fairly long narrative poems, all tragic love stories ('Leila and Abdalla', 'The Indian Bride', 'Leades and Cydippe'), as well as various shorter lyrics.

The other literary parent for this confection of versified sentiment and death was Byron; not the Byron chiefly remembered today, the author of the witty and sophisticated *Don Juan*, but the earlier Byron of pot-boiler verse-tales in rhymed octosyllables that treated of Oriental and Mediterranean adventures, and centred usually on a doomed love affair between star-crossed lovers. In the 1820s it was Byron's colossal popularity that chiefly dictated the literary tastes where poetry was concerned; a writer like Landon, who was writing to earn money, could not afford to ignore the public demand for Byronic verse tales – especially in 1824, the year of Byron's death. But there is something awkward in the yoking together of *Corinne* and Byronism. There is nothing empowering for women in Byron's verse tales, whose heroines are exclusively spiritless and passive girls, whose usual recourse is to lie down and die. De Staël's novel, on the other hand, does at least provide a model of an active woman, in charge of her own voice and productivity, for all that the novel ends tragically.

Something of this contradiction is at the core of *The Improvisatrice*. The eponymous poet enjoys some of the advantages of a Corinne; she (apparently) has independent wealth, she is

without the ties of family or other responsibilities, she is able to pursue her poetic calling
without hindrance. Yet her poetic style, improvisation, tends to downgrade the resulting
work; her verses are not brain-work (as male poets considered their poetry to be), but the
spontaneous outpourings of emotion. At the beginning of her narrative we find her
downplaying her poetic skills: 'my power was but a woman's power' she rather disparag-
ingly says; 'I poured my full and burning heart / In song' (25–9).[2] Moreover, she makes
clear that despite growing up 'mid radiant things / Glorious as Hope's imaginings' (9–10)
her mind was none the less drawn to melancholy tales of death, to the extent of anticipating (rather like Landon herself) her own premature demise:

> Sad were my shades; methinks they had
>     Almost a tone of prophecy –
> I ever had from earliest youth,
>     A feeling what my fate would be. (37–40)

'Shades' here means 'paintings', since the Improvisatrice paints as well as writes poetry; but
both her visual and her poetic productions are fascinated with the figure of the suffering and
dying (or dead) young poetess. One of Landon's recurring themes is that the female poet
must suffer even unto death for her art, precisely because that art is predicated upon a
greater susceptibility to feeling (the feminine heart, rather than the supposedly masculine
head). But another way of looking at it might be to suggest that Landon seems to want the
female poet (herself included) to be *punished* for daring to give herself and her sex a voice.

   Immediately after introducing herself, the Improvisatrice describes some of her work for
us; first of all, a painting of Petrarch, 'pale, dark-eyed, beautiful and young' (53),
pondering in solitude his unconsummated passion for Laura, 'Love's long catalogue of
tears' (108). After this, we are told of the Improvisatrice's portrait of Sappho, that primal
symbol of the female poetic.

> Her head was bending down
> As if in weariness, and near
> But unworn, was a laurel crown.
> She was not beautiful, if bloom
> And smiles form beauty; for, like death,
> Her brow was ghastly; and her lip
> Was parched, as fever were its breath.
> There was a fever upon her dark
> Large, floating eyes, as if each spark
> Of minstrel ecstasy was fled,
> Yet leaving them no tears to shed;
> Fixed in their hopelessness of care,
> And reckless in their great despair. (116–29)

As an example of the verse of *The Improvisatrice* this is fairly typical; most of the work is
made out of this fluid, onwards-moving, rather unstructured poetry, only occasionally end-
stopped, punctuated chiefly with commas and semi-colons. This is, in other words, a style
appropriate to its subject, verse improvised and flowing directly from the poet. Landon

herself was fond of improvising poetry, and supposedly wrote all 1,578 lines of *The Improvisatrice* in under three weeks. Angela Leighton argues that Landon's style represents something distinctively female, 'poems whose language *sounds* improvised, and whose very structureless length mimes the notion of woman's unstoppable flow of creativity'.[3] But this is true only up to a point. The rolling passage quoted above is a description of a picture; when the narrator inserts one of her own lyrics (in this case the much anthologized 'Sappho's Song'), the verse becomes markedly more stationary.

> Farewell, my lute! – and would that I
>     Had never waked thy burning chords!
> Poison has been upon thy sigh,
>     And fever had breathed in thy words.
>
> Yet wherefore, wherefore should I blame
>     Thy power, thy spell, my gentlest lute?
> I should have been the wretch I am,
>     Had every chord of thine been mute.
> . . .
> If song be passed, and hope undone,
>     And pulse, and head, and heart, are flame;
> It is thy work, thou faithless one!
>     But, no! – I will not name thy name!
>
> Sun-god! lute, wreath are vowed to thee!
>     Long be their light upon my grave –
> My glorious grave – yon deep blue sea:
> I shall sleep calm beneath its wave! (132–51)

This does stand out from its surrounding poetry; it is much more restrained in tone, more poised in expression. In place of the rushing onward-cascade of lines and the profusion of exotic adjectival qualification the diction is almost plain, and the emotion correspondingly more affecting. The contrast in the final stanza between the fiery life of the (male) sun-god on the one hand, and the watery grave of the (female) poet on the other, effectively and simply articulates the chief contrast of Landon's verse. The men ('but no! I will not name thy name!'), nefarious or otherwise, survive; the women, in their fluidity and vulnerability to the emotions, die.

This simple imagistic equation between fire/male and water/female resonates through-out the whole of *The Improvisatrice*. The narrator is repeatedly invoked in proximity to water, from the 'fountain . . . sprinkling its scented waters round, / With a sweet lulling sound' in her palatial home, to the waters of the Arno, over which she glides as she extemporises the 'Moorish Romance', her first major interjected verse-tale. Water figures prominently in this tale, too; the sea over which the Moorish Leila and her Christian lover Abdalla set sail, in order to elope to Italy and find happiness; the sea, in fact, which drowns them in a storm (they are washed up on an Italian beach in one another's arms). Fire, on the other hand, is the dominant feature of the second of the three interpolated tales (not counting the briefer lyrics and other interludes), that which the Improvisatrice sings at Count Leon's ball: 'The Indian Bride'. Here the Improvisatrice captivates her audience (and one member of that audience in particular, Lorenzo the male love-interest) with a touching tale of the Indian custom of burning the wife on the dead husband's funeral pyre. To put it another way, on the other hand, we might refer to Germaine Greer's sardonic description of the narrator 'blight[ing] the festivities with an appalling tale of suttee'. Greer's account of the whole poem is never very far away from this sort of sarcasm. Of the narrator's description of her hall, with its 'blue and fretted roof' and 'marble floors', its 'sprinkling fountain' and orange plants 'like Eastern gold', Greer wonders 'how the oranges and roses grow under the fretted roof and through the marble floor, and what the running rose water did to the frescoes and the curtains'.[4] But, flippancy aside, there is some point in Greer's reaction. *The Improvisatrice* frequently *is* banal and rather rubbishy in its sentimentalism, and the reader can often find his or herself responding facetiously to the poet's earnestness. 'The Indian Bride' exactly captures the mix of morbidity and genuine pathos, of sausage-machine versification and moments of genuine power, that are typical of Landon as a poet. There certainly are moments of really bad poetry:

> This looks not a bridal – the singers are mute,
> Still is the mandore and breathless the lute;
> Yet there the bride sits. Her dark hair is bound
> And the robe of the marriage floats white on the ground
> Oh! Where is the love, the bridegroom? – Oh! Where?
> Look under yon black pall – the bridegroom is there! (851–6)

The 'breathless' lute involves an inappropriate ambiguity between 'lacking breath' and 'panting with excitement'; and the reiterated 'oh's' and the peek-a-boo revelation of the corpse are miserable lapses of taste. But a few lines later, Landon can rise considerably, describing the actual moment of immolation of the bride in a genuinely striking fashion.

> At once there came
> A mingled rush of smoke and of flame:
> The wind swept it off. They saw the bride, –
> Laid by her *Azim*, side by side.
> The breeze had spread the long curls of her hair
> Like a banner of fire they played on the air.
> The smoke and the flame gathered round as before
> Then cleared, – and the bride was seen no more. (881–8)

Here, the three stressed syllables of 'side by side' slow the otherwise trotting iambic metre right down, helping to impart a more funereal pace; and the comparison of the bride's hair 'like a banner of fire' hovers achingly between the merely metaphorical and the grim possibility that her hair is actually alight. More than this, it identifies her body with the fiery medium it occupies, an identification so complete that the bride seems in the final lines to vanish literally in a puff of smoke. That final image, which might have smacked bathetically of prestidigitation, in fact manages an almost mythic weight, as if the bride has undergone some strange apotheosis, become one with the flames that surround her.

The third interpolated tale, 'Leades and Cydippe', concerns another doomed marriage. Leades is to marry Cydippe, but he leaves her to take one last farewell of his native land. She waits for him, hopefully at first, but eventually 'the heart's decay / Wasted her silently away' (1,162–3). When the tardy lover returns, he finds his bride-to-be dead and buried under a cypress – a tree which had symbolically wilted when the body was buried underneath it. In a strange touch, Leades kisses the dead tree ('For wild he kissed the withered stem': 1,211), magically restoring it to life – until, that is, he dies of his own broken heart and is buried with his love, when it wilts once again.

These interpolated verse-tales and lyrics all, without exception, point to the moral that a woman falling in love is dooming herself to misery and death. It is hardly surprising that the frame narrative itself also embodies this death-fixated theme. The huge success of the volume presumably traded on precisely that conjunction of female beauty and heart-wrenching death; an early nineteenth-century weepie, if you like. As several critics have pointed out, Landon, who helped bolster up a certain, restrictive conception of woman as passive, a feeling rather than a thinking creature, defined by love not reason, was also trapped within this ideology. Anne Mellor argues that Landon's limitations as a poet are a direct result of this conception:

> Once Landon accepted her culture's hegemonic definition of the female, she could only repeat the same story over and over. Her poetry obsessively details every nuance of female love, of female sympathy, of female imagination in the service of the affections, always arriving at the same narrative conclusion: such love is futile.[5]

In Mellor's reading the very obsessiveness of Landon's treatment can be, as it were, its own reward; it can function as a critique of the ideology of romantic love, just as much as a celebration of it. But actually we need to be more precise; if it functions as anything, *The Improvisatrice* is a critique not of love but marriage. The connection is made less between love and death, and more between death and the official sanction of that love. The Improvisatrice herself dies only *after* she has been reconciled with her lover, after he has promised to marry her. The tale is not one of love abandoned, but one that equates marriage with death. The interpolated tales magnify the point; Leila and Abdalla elope together so that they can marry, but their marriage becomes the two of them drowned in one another's arms; the Indian bride literally dies at the moment of marriage, burnt in suttee; Leades and Cydippe are likewise betrothed to be married, a marriage that can only be consummated (as it were) in the grave. The point seems to be one of opposites; the linking of incompatibles, as in the marriage of Byronic form and Corrinean subject, of fire and water.

The anticipation of Landon's own deadly marriage, and the establishment of a celebrity in death, is striking. It is perhaps not surprising that Landon's contemporaries were moved but not shocked by the news of her death. 'Poor L.E.L.!' the young Elizabeth Barrett wrote to a friend; 'I had a *prophet in my thoughts* about her ever since she went away. It is a fatal climate, and the longest years do not seem to go to the lives of poetesses.'[6] Barrett's prophet had been prompted by Landon's own poetry.

## Notes

1   Leighton and Reynolds, *Victorian Women Poets*, p. 23.

2   *The Improvisatrice* is quoted from Landon's *Poetical Works*, ed. William Scott, 1873; quotations are followed in the text by line numbers.

3  Leighton and Reynolds, *Victorian Women Poets*, p. 32.
4  She calls the poem as a whole 'a phantasmagoria of sentimental silliness', although she does concede it 'a certain gnashing dramatic power'; Greer, 'Success and the single poet', p. 279.

5  Mellor, *Romanticism and Gender*, p. 114.
6  Letter from Elizabeth Barrett to Mary Russell Mitford, 5 January 1839; Kelley and Hudson, (eds), *The Browning's Correspondence*, Wedgestone Press, 1986, vol. 4, page 116.

## REFERENCES AND FURTHER READING

Blain, Virginia, 'Letitia Elizabeth Landon, Eliza Mary Hamilton, and the genealogy of the Victorian poetess', *Victorian Poetry* 33 (1995).

Greer, Germaine, 'Success and the single poet: the sad tale of L.E.L.', in *Slip-shod Sibyls: Recognition, Rejection and the Woman Poet*, Viking, 1995.

Leighton, Angela, 'L.E.L.', in *Victorian Women Poets: Writing Against the Heart*, Harvester, 1992.

Leighton, Angela and Reynolds, Margaret (eds) 'L.E.L.', in *Victorian Women Poets: An Anthology*, Blackwell, 1995.

Mellor, Anne, *Romanticism and Gender*, Routledge, 1993.

Ross, Marlon, *The Contours of Masculine Desire: Romanticism and the Rise of Women's Poetry*, Oxford, 1989.

Stephenson, Glennis, 'Letitia Landon and the Victorian improvisatrice: the construction of L.E.L.', *Victorian Poetry* 30 (1993).

Stevenson, Lionel, 'Miss Landon: "The milk-and-watery-moon of our darkness", 1824–30', *Modern Language Quarterly* 8 (1947), 355–63.

# 30

# John Clare, *The Shepherd's Calendar*

## John Lucas

In 1820 John Clare's first collection of poems, *Poems Descriptive of Rural Life and Scenery*, was published to enthusiastic reviews and sold spectacularly well. Clare became famous. But the fame did not last and by 1827, when *The Shepherd's Calendar* finally found its way into book form, it had virtually disappeared. Nor did the *Calendar* help to restore it. In *The Right to Song: A Life of John Clare*, Edward Storey tells us that despite some favourable reviews 'only 425 copies were bought in the first two years and eventually the publisher was to offer the remaining stock at cost price to the poet in the hope that he could sell more locally'.[1] Clare, who had hoped that publication of the poem would return him to public favour and also provide much-needed money, was mortified. His publisher, John Taylor, was no better pleased. The original firm of Taylor and Hessey, which had handled Clare's two previous volumes, had been dissolved in 1825, and Taylor, who had been under increasingly severe financial stress, would soon afterwards decide to publish no more poetry.

But then he had not been especially enthusiastic about publishing *The Shepherd's Calendar*. One reason seems to have been that he had come to the conclusion that the 'vogue' for poetry was now over. In this he may well have been right. Lee Erickson has argued that the shortage of paper supply during the Napoleonic wars gave poetry a natural edge over prose.[2] This strikes me as a dubious argument, not merely because *The Excursion*, say, is longer than *Sense and Sensibility*, but because prose aplenty was published in the first decade-and-a-half of the nineteenth century. It is, however, true that during the 1820s new magazines and publishing ventures tended to favour fiction over poetry. And new technology made mass printing easier and cheaper.[3] Equally important, for Clare at least, is the fact that he had from the first been marketed as a 'peasant poet'. The 1820 volume identified him as 'A NORTHAMPTONSHIRE PEASANT', and peasant poetry had been fashionable ever since Burns had hit on the idea of presenting himself as a 'natural genius', an 'unlettered' poet of inspiration, and had as a result made money and reputation out of the publication in 1786 of his *Poems, Chiefly in the Scottish Dialect*, in the Preface to which he had claimed an inability to commence 'Poet by Rule'. A similar inability had been imputed to Clare by his publishers, who had provided a Preface to *Poems Descriptive*, in which they remarked that

> The following Poems will probably attract some notice by their intrinsic merit, but they are
> also entitled to attention from the circumstances under which they were written. They are the
> genuine productions of a young Peasant, a day-labourer in husbandry, who has had no
> advantages of education beyond others of his class. . . .

Taylor and Hessey had no right to claim that the poems are Clare's 'genuine productions'.
As I and others have pointed out, there was heavy, even excessive, interference with what
Clare had written; and although in his *Revision and Romantic Authorship* Zachary Leader has
argued a sophisticated case for the propriety of Taylor's editorial intrusions, I remain
unconvinced. To say which brings me to the complicated subject of the text of *The
Shepherd's Calendar.*

The full title of the collection which appeared in 1827 was *The Shepherd's Calendar: with
Village Stories and other Poems.* There were four such stories: *The Sorrows of Love; or, the Broken
Heart, Jockey and Jinney; or, The Progress of Love, The Rivals; A Pastoral*, and *The Memory of
Love: a Tale.* The stories might be thought of as make-weights and as independent of the
*Calendar* itself. In 1822 Clare seems to have hit on the idea of writing a 'Poem for each
Month', which both his publishers warmly supported. This is the genesis of *The Shepherd's
Calendar.* He had also, however, been writing narrative poems; and in 1823 Taylor wrote to
Clare outlining his proposal for a new collection:

> Talking the other day with Hessey it occurred to me that a good Title for another Work
> would be – 'The Shepherd's Calendar' – a Name which Spenser took for a Poem or rather
> Collection of Poems of his. – It might be like his divided into Months, & under each might be
> given a descriptive Poem & a Narrative Poem – nay I don't know why 'the last of March' &
> such like Pieces might not as well be introduced. But if you like the Thought we can easily
> settle a Plan.
>
>    It would do very well to call the next Volume by such a Name, adding '& other Poems' to
> take in such at the End as would not come well in under the Months. But such as Jockey &
> Jenney would find their places under those particular Months in which the Story is laid.

From this it would seem that the plan for the volume as it evolved was to link the stories to
the *Calendar* in a manner far closer and more supportive than could be sensed from the
published collection, and this is borne out by further letters to Clare from Hessey and from
Clare's own proposals, which are helpfully set out by Robinson, Powell and Dawson in
their edition of *Cottage Tales.*[4] Yet even while this planning was going on, Taylor and
Hessey began to voice doubts about Clare as poet. Or rather, they worry that the way he
writes and what he writes about won't do. Having created a 'peasant poet', and having
realized from the comparatively poor sales of Clare's second collection, *The Village Minstrel*,
that this fashion is now *démodé*, they want to turn Clare towards what for want of a better
phrase I will call Wordsworthian reflectiveness. I do not suggest that this was a cynically
exploitative decision, nor that they were fully conscious of the implication of their advice.
But I do not see how you can read the following letter, from Taylor to Clare, without
feeling that the publisher is telling his poet that it's time for a change:

> I have often remarked that your Poetry is much the best when you are not describing common
> Things, and if you would raise your Views generally, & speak of the Appearances of Nature

each Month more philosophically (if I may say so) or with more Excitement, you would greatly improve these little poems; some parts of the November are extremely good – others are too prosaic – they have too much of the language of common everyday Description; – faithful I grant they are, but that is not all – 'What in me is low, Raise & refine' is the way in which you should conceive them as addressing you.

That letter was written in March, 1826. Earlier, in January of the same year, Taylor had protested angrily that the poems out of which he was trying to make the collection 'are not only slovenly written, but as slovenly *Composed*, & to make Good Poems out of some of them is a far greater Difficulty than I ever had to engage with in your former Works'. *July* in particular was beyond saving. Clare was informed that he would have to produce another version. Clare did as he was told. And at Taylor's bidding he wrote a Preface in which he apologized 'for the long delay in publishing these Poems, which, I am sure will be readily forgiven when it is known that severe illness was the cause'. Between 1822 and 1827 he had indeed suffered from illnesses of various kinds, but as the repeated delays in publishing *The Shepherd's Calendar* were entirely due to Taylor, it isn't surprising that the excuse Clare was made to offer should have stuck in his craw. Nor was he better pleased to discover that the editing of his manuscripts had been taken over by a young poet friend of Taylor's called Harry Stoe Van Dyk, and he was still more upset by the fact that between them Taylor and Van Dyk proposed to cut almost half of his original manuscript and that *Valentine Eve*, a tale by which he set great store, was to be omitted. As Edward Storey remarks, 'little wonder that [Clare] wrote in his journal on 30 April, 'if Doctors were as fond of amputation as they are of altering & correcting the world would have nothing but cripples' ".

In the introduction to his 1993 edition of *The Shepherd's Calendar* Eric Robinson remarks that 'Taylor's treatment of Clare's poetry is like an encloser destroying local custom', and he adds for good measure that the *Calendar* 'was more than Taylor understood'.[5] More recently, however, Zachary Leader has argued that although Taylor certainly made unwarrantable cuts in *The Shepherd's Calendar*, these have to be seen in the context of a relationship in which Taylor did his best to advance the cause of Clare's poetry and that Clare was on the whole grateful to Taylor for the publisher's editorial work. It may be that some of us have been too hard on Taylor, but after all he did considerable damage to Clare's first collection; and he did even more to *The Shepherd's Calendar*. Leader suggests that Clare himself liked to mingle linguistic registers and would shift between the local to the urbane from 'a simple love of language'. But a love of language isn't simple. Clare's 'urbanity' often comes across as inauthentic because the switch of linguistic registers all too clearly suggests that he is trying on a style for which he has little aptitude. More woundingly, it implies an attempt to speak from a social and cultural position with which he is in truth ill-at-ease. And this has an especial relevance to *The Shepherd's Calendar*, where moments of linguistic uncertainty, of what feels like loss of tonal control, few though they are, may well indicate an attempt on Clare's part to ingratiate himself with his publishers by responding to their wish that he should raise his views and speak more philosophically. It doesn't matter that on occasions Clare echoes other poets. In *June* he takes over and makes good use of Herrick's phrase about 'a sweet disorder of the dress'. (He speaks of bindweed which 'round each bush in sweet disorder run'.) A passage in *July* about the 'oven heated air' in which 'Not one light thing is floating', is patently derived from some lines in *Hyperion*, and Keats is also behind a line in *Jockey & Jinney*, where Jockey thinks of himself as Jinney's lover and of 'How would I pillow on her panting breast'. (Compare Keats's 'Pillowed for ever on her ripening breast'.) Even Crabbe, whom Clare effected to despise, is echoed in *September*. At all events when Clare's bees 'threaten war to all that come', I am inevitably reminded of the thistles in *The Village* which 'to the ragged infant threaten war'.

So I could go on. But to point out these echoes, borrowings and stealings is interesting only in so far as it shows how confidently Clare could absorb his wide reading into his own work. This is very different from moments when he adopts a tone of lofty or condescending humour towards his chosen subject matter. Some years ago John Barrell importantly remarked that Clare differed from most pastoral poets in that, to adapt some words Burns applied to himself, he did not look down for a rural theme. His experiences as a day labourer meant that he was on the level, within the scene, rather than surveying it from a distant, lofty, prospect. In this he is therefore markedly different from James Thomson, whose *The Seasons* (1748) he had read while young and which, he famously said, made his heart 'twitter with joy'. Thomson frequently apostrophises 'Labour' in his expanded Georgic: 'Labour', lusty, brown, contented, is the visible emblem of an industrious and healthy nation. This, we might say, is the quintessential raised view. In *The Shepherd's Calendar* Clare also apostrophises Labour. In *March*, 'The little daisey in the wet grass lye / That to the peeping sun enlivens gay / Like Labour smiling on an holiday'. Here, the comparison of Labour to the 'little' daisy is not meant to diminish the lives of labourers, but it undoubtedly implies their low social status as well as the fugitive nature of their pleasures. (Which are then all the more intensely to be enjoyed.) Clare has a more socially exact sense of the lives of the labouring poor than Thomson; and this also comes out in *June* where he writes that 'Labour pursues its toil in weary mood'. He has just catalogued some of the tasks that make up toil and he will go on to instance more. He has also made much of June heat and of the ceaseless stir of the natural world:

> Now summer is in flower and natures hum
> Is never silent round her sultry bloom
> Insects as small as dust are never done
> Wi' glittering dance and reeling in the sun
> And green wood fly and blossom haunting bee
> Are never weary of their melody

That is how *June* opens and it partly echoes the opening of Thomson's *Summer*, although there Summer is personified as a young ardent lover, 'attended by the sultry Hours, / And ever-fanning Breezes', and this then gives way to the human scene where 'swarms the village o'er the jovial mead; / The rustic youth, brown with meridian toil, / Healthful, and strong . . . While heard from dale to dale,/ Waking the breeze, resounds the blended voice / Of happy labour, love, and social glee' (324–42). Thomson's village 'swarms', for all the world like insects, and insects are, Clare remarks, 'never weary'. But Labour is.

It is therefore all the more surprising that very occasionally in *The Shepherd's Calendar* Clare should appear to demean the people about whom he writes, by sticking on them the labels derived from the line of pastoral poetry which takes for granted an idealized, deeply conservative, 'settled' view of rural circumstance, in which the 'natural' order is as agreeable as it is agreed. To this line belong such terms as 'clown', 'Hodge' and 'Goody', all of which find their way into Clare's poem. To some extent such terms are wished on Clare, as I have argued elsewhere, simply because there was no accepted or acceptable way of referring to rural labourers as a class, not anyway if you were of that class (hence, of course, the abstraction 'Labour'). Clare can use the exact terms of occupation: milkmaid, foddering boy, hedger, ditcher, shepherd, blacksmith and so on. But a term under which all these occupations can find identification is simply not available – unless, that is, you take the raised view. Then, and only then, you can use such terms as 'clown' or 'peasant'. If there are moments when Clare is prepared to use these terms it can only be because by doing so he opens up a gap between himself and those about whom he writes. And at such moments Clare's viewpoint is not, as Eric Robinson and others maintain, 'on the flat'. Quite the reverse. It strives to elevate itself.

So does *April*. *The Shepherd's Calendar* is remarkable for metrical variety. Clare deploys pentameter couplets in, for example, *June* and *September*; *May* and *July* are among those written in octosyllabic couplets; for *February* and *December* he uses the eight-line octosyllabic stanza he will later put to such wonderful effect in his great poem, *The Flitting*; and *November* is written in the Spenserian stanzas he had earlier appropriated for *The Village Minstrel*. (This had been conventional for pastoral poetry at least since Shenstone's *The Schoolmistress*, 1737.) As to *April*, Clare here makes use of an eight-line stanza of alternate four- and three-stress lines. A variation on common measure, we might say, the staple ballad form. But *April* is no sort of ballad. Instead, Clare apostrophises the month in a manner that feels as faded as it does tiresomely literary:

> The infant april joins the spring
> And views its watery skye
> As youngling linnet trys its wing
> And fears at first to flye
> With timid step she ventures on
> And hardly dares to smile
> The blossoms open one by one
> And sunny hours beguile

'Youngling' is the kind of coinage you find in Chatterton's imitations of medieval ballads, and the sense of tried-on, even perhaps tongue-in-cheek mannerisms is sharpened by Clare's invocation to the 'fairey month of waking mirth / From whom our joys ensue / Thou early gladder of the earth / Thrice welcom here anew', behind which it is impossible not to hear Wordsworth's address to the cuckoo as 'Thrice welcome, Darling of the Spring!' whose coming has made the earth 'an unsubstantial, faery place'. And *To The Cuckoo* is written in common measure.

*April* is poor stuff. Elsewhere in *The Shepherd's Calendar* there are undue repetitions. The 'downy plumb and luscious pear / That melt i'th mouth' at lines 186/7 of *August* become at line 209 'pears that melt ith' mouth like honey'; and the opening of *July* is marred by the fact that 'sultry' turns up twice in ten lines, as does 'dewy' / 'dew'. There are also scattered throughout the poem lines which I find difficult if not impossible to scan, although given

Clare's customarily exact ear and his flexible but secure rhythms it may be that the problem in these cases is one of transcription. But whoever is responsible for line 504 of *July*, 'To rest till the sun comes again', has made a line in which, although it certainly has eight syllables, I simply cannot hear four stresses. Add to these flaws some awkward narrative transitions as well as decidedly odd enjambments (for example, 'While he will urge wi' many a smile/ It as a strength' – lines 85/6 of *July*), a few dull thumpers ('And the while the shepherd stayd') and you have virtually the sum total of the poem's failings. These chokepears apart, it is praise to the end.

In what follows I shall consider *The Shepherd's Calendar* as we now have it restored to us through the labours of Eric Robinson and others. I shall also bring into consideration their edition of those tales which appeared with Taylor's mangled edition of *The Calendar*, together with *Valentine Eve*, which, as I have already remarked, Clare desired to have included in the 1827 volume. *Valentine Eve* is indeed as good a poem as any with which to begin. In their edition of *Cottage Tales* Robinson et al. note that 'The story . . . came to Clare in two versions sent to him, independently, by John Taylor and by Taylor's cousin, Edward Drury. . . . One version was a fairly well-known real event, namely the courtship and marriage of the future Marquis of Exeter to Sarah Hoggins, who became known as "The Cottage Countess"'. In 1820 Drury told Clare that he thought the story of 'the actual circumstances of our present Marquess of Exeter's grandfather marrying a country girl of humblest life', would make an excellent subject for 'A Dramatic Poem like Allan Ramsay's Gentle Shepherd'. Despite initial doubts as to whether his gifts were suited to such a narrative, Clare seems to have begun work on the poem in 1822 and to have finished it early in January, 1824. Taylor, however, did not much like the finished product. 'I have considerable Doubts whether anything good enough can be made of Valentine's Eve', he wrote to Clare on 8 April 1826, although the editors of *Cottage Tales* note that the motive for his writing in such discouraging terms may well have been that he had mislaid the manuscript of Clare's poem. Clare made another copy, but to no avail. It was not to appear in the 1827 collection.

This matters, not merely because *Valentine Eve* is a good poem, but because it is in a way an act of homage to Robert Bloomfield. Bloomfield, whom Clare admired hugely, perhaps extravagantly, had died in 1824, two years after the publication of his finest work, *May Day With the Muses*. The setting for this book-length work is Oakley Hall, home of the aged Sir Ambrose Higham, who decides to spare his tenants from payment of their tithes on condition that each agrees to tell a tale before the assembled company. *May Day With the Muses* is thus a kind of medley, a way of telling tales within a tale; and it will be obvious that the evolving plans for *The Shepherd's Calendar* owe much to a strategy which, in its more modern format at least, Bloomfield seems to have invented and which later in the century would be used by Tennyson among others. (I am thinking in particular of such idyls as *Edwin Morris* and *Audley Court*, although *The Princess* also comes into the reckoning.) It is to be noted that in *Valentine Eve* the country girl turned Madam Meers 'now lives at Oakley Hall / With coach & four & footmen at her call' (18–19).

This may be an unconscious debt. But elsewhere in tales of the 1820s Clare makes clear his admiration for Bloomfield. In *Opening of the Pasture – Love & Flattery*, written between

1823–4, one of the female protagonists tells her friend that a young man has tried to woo her by getting her to read Bloomfield's poems:

> they were sweet indeed
> He turned a leaf down where he bid me read
> It was a story called 'the broken crutch'
> 'Theres luck' said he 'your face might get as much'
> —I loved the poems & the story too . . .
> . . . .Bloomfields Poems theyre so sweet to hear
> They live with me like neighbours all the year (*Cottage Tales*, 294–308)

*The Broken Crutch* had appeared in Bloomfield's 1806 volume, *Wild Flowers*. It tells a tale very similar to that of *Valentine Eve*, of a poor girl whose face and disposition are her fortune. She leaves home to work for a squire, one of the old school, a man of benevolence. He keeps a 'kitchen table, never clear of beef, / Where hunger found its solace and relief'. The squire falls in love with the girl, Peggy, and so far from exploiting her vulnerability, makes her his wife. The tale is set in a past which, the narrator makes clear, is very different from the present. For now, 'In Gain's rude service and in Pity's spite', the axe has despoiled a sweet, especial rural scene; and this act of despoliation has to be read as indicative of a newly aggressive acquisitiveness which brings with it a new form of social relations, of class separateness, of lost community. Where once squires had mingled with their men and the marriage of squire Herbert and Peggy could be taken as an image of social cohesion, desire for gain now works against Pity. (I take it that pity here has overtones of charity and hence *caritas*.)

It hardly needs saying that Clare was also preoccupied with what he saw and, more importantly, felt to be the deep contrast between past and present. *June* of *The Shepherd's Calendar* ends with an evocation of a land of lost content:

> And the old freedom that was living then
> When masters made them merry wi their men
> Whose coat was like his neighbors russet brown
> And whose rude speech was vulgar as his clown
> Who in the same hour drank the rest among
> And joind the chorus while a labourer sung
> All this is past – and soon may pass away
> The time torn remnant of the holiday
> As proud distinction makes a wider space
> Between the genteel and the vulgar race
> Then must they fade as pride o'er custom showers
> Its blighting mildew on her feeble flowers

Such laments for a destroyed world occur frequently in the 1827 collection, as they do throughout Clare's work. And the destroyer is, in a word, enclosure. As he said in a poem usually called *Helpstone*, which appeared in his first collection, *Poems Descriptive of Rural Life and Scenery*, 'Accursed wealth o'er bounding human laws / Of every evil thou remainst the cause'. Wealth is accursed because it sets no store by community: like Milton's Satan who 'oe'r leapd all bound', wealth is no respecter of the rights of others. Its invasive power takes away those rights, rights held in common. Needless to say the lines in question did not survive Taylor's cutting. He had appointed Lord Radstock to be Clare's patron and at Radstock's insistence removed what his lordship perceived to be 'radical slang'. But Clare went on uttering such slang. To take one example. In *The Sorrows of Love* he has his narrator recall a time 'Ere vile enclosure took away the moor / & farmers built a workhouse for the poor'. The tale appeared in 1827 but predictably enough it was shorn of these lines. Taylor also cut many other lines from the tale, nearly all of them ones which provide details of village life. Out goes the narrator's account of how she would see the village Lothario 'start / Up from his chair to offer girls the quart'; out goes a particularly vivid description of the magpie kept by an old woman which would 'unbidden run its gabble o'er / While she would twirl the tea grounds round the cup / Or take the pack to cut or shuffle up'; out goes the recollection of fairground gifts brought to children: 'Clay sergants broken armd wi' faded sash / & one ey'd dolls & churns wi' out a dash'; and out goes much else beside.

Nor does Taylor confine his cutting to this tale. As I have already noted, he savaged *The Shepherd's Calendar* itself. He was especially hard on moments in the poem which are most Clare-like. Not only does he guard against Clare's protests at enclosure and its consequences (the last four lines of *June*, quoted above, were taken out); he as regularly excises passages where Clare is at his most uninhibitedly ready to use the language and idiom he had acquired from his upbringing and work as a day labourer. And if we ask why Clare set such store by this language, this idiom, and why he wanted to detail the daily lives of the people about whom he writes, part of the answer can be found in his praise of Bloomfield. 'Our English Theocritus' he called the poet, whose biography he at one time contemplated writing, and he also said that he adjudged Bloomfield 'our best pastoral poet'. To understand this aright, and to pay due attention to why he should have been so delighted when Bloomfield called him 'brother bard' and why he should have said that Bloomfield was a poet for whom 'I feel more than admiration', we have to take the measure of the kind of poet he considered Theocritus to have been.[6]

Theocritus and Virgil were famous throughout the eighteenth century as the two leading poets, even the founding fathers, of pastoral poetry. But there was a general feeling that whereas Virgil's *Eclogues* were to some extent 'artificial', Theocritus could be relied on to tell the plain, unvarnished truth. In 1692 Richard Polwhele, the translator of *Idyllia, Epigrams and Fragments of Theocritus, Bion and Moschus*, claimed that 'The pieces of Theocritus are the result of his own accurate observation. He described what he saw and felt. His characters, as well as his scenes, are the immediate transcript of nature'. This reading of Theocritus became a commonplace and was certainly taken for granted by Clare himself. We know this because in his *Essay on Landscape* he claims that the landscape painter Rippingille is 'the Theocritus of English painting'. Rippingille's works, he explains,

> are as true as if nature had just left them & none of the ridiculous imaginings of fashion hung about them – the dewy morning is not more fresh in her features than the air & the sky & the very grass of the pastures – tis summer the very air breathes hot in ones face we see nothing but natural objects not placed for effect or set off by other dictates of the painters fancys but they are there just as nature placed them.[7]

Bloomfield, like Rippingille, is therefore to be valued for his willingness to tell the truth about the nature of rural life, its labouring and social activities, its customs, pleasures, hardships; and he is equally to be valued because in some poems at least he allows his country people to speak their own language. Clare's avowed love of *Richard and Kate*, which was included in Bloomfield's *Rural Tales* (1802), and *The Horkey* from *Wild Flowers* (1806), undoubtedly owes much to the fact that both make use of Suffolk dialect and that the former is about a fair day, while the latter deals with a Suffolk custom explained in the 'Advertisement' placed immediately before the poem:

> In Suffolk husbandry the man who (whether by merit or by sufference I know not) goes foremost through the harvest with the scythe or the sickle, is honoured with the title of *Lord*, and at the Horkey or harvest-home feast collects what he can, for himself and brethren, from the farmers and visitors, to make a 'frolic' afterwards, called 'the largess spending.' By way of returning thanks, though perhaps formerly of much more, or of different signification, they immediately leave the seat of festivity, and with a very long and repeated shout of 'A largess,' the number of shouts being regulated by the sums given, seem to wish to make themselves heard by the people of the surrounding farms. And before they rejoin the company within, the pranks and the jollity I have endeavoured to describe, usually take place. These customs, I believe, are going fast out of use; which is one great reason for my trying to tell the rising race of mankind that such were the customs when I was a boy.[8]

Clare's own devotion to country customs is evident not merely in his poetry, especially *The Shepherd's Calendar*; it can be found in his prose of the period. There is, for example, a long letter he sent to William Hone, in April 1825, in which he instances some 'superstitions & shadows of customs almost worn out here' and tells among much that is fascinating of the 'dumb cake' made by young women on the eve of St Marks, which they must eat 'silent. . . . when they have done they walk up to bed backwards & those that are to be married see the likeness of their sweet hearts hurrying after them', a custom which Clare draws on in *The Sorrows of Love*. But then throughout the *Calendar* there are references to such customs, superstitions and old wives' tales, especially perhaps in the haunting lines of *January: A Cottage Evening*, with their account of how 'dames the winter night regales / Wi' wonders never ceasing tales' while children 'Quake wi' the ague chills of fear / And tremble while they love to hear / Startling while they the tales recall / At their own shadows on the wall' (199–208). Clare then sums up in a manner which seems at first glance to belong to that nostalgic evocation for lost childhood fast becoming an orthodoxy of the time. 'O spirit of the days gone bye / Sweet childhoods fearful extacy / The witching spells of winter nights / Where are they fled wi' their delights' (233–6). This surely echoes Charles Lamb's lines on *Childhood*: 'In my poor mind it is most sweet to muse / Upon the days gone by; to act in thought / Past seasons o'er, and be again a child'.

But there is a difference. For Clare is not merely lamenting the loss of early days. He is aware of *different* days, of time's alteration.[9] Grieving over the inevitability of loss, of decay, is part of the picturesque tradition with which Clare has nothing to do. On the contrary, he understands change in terms of human agency. So did his brother bard. In 'Summer', the second section of *The Farmer's Boy*, Bloomfield points a contrast between past and present social relations as they affect farmers and labourers, and he does so in terms that closely anticipate lines from *June* quoted earlier. Bloomfield comments on how 'once a year

Distinction low'rs its crest, / The master, servant, and the merry guest, / Are equal all', and then goes on to say that he is speaking of 'days long past'. Nowadays it is the custom,

> to violate the feelings of the poor;
> To leave them distanced in the maddening race,
> Where'er refinement shows its hated face:
> Nor causeless hated; – 'tis the peasant's curse,
> That hourly makes his wretched station worse;
> Destroys life's intercourse; the social plan
> That rank to rank cements, as man to man:
> Wealth flows around him, Fashion lordly reigns;
> Yet poverty is his, and mental pains.

We have seen that Taylor omitted the last four lines of *June*. He also took out some key lines on *The Sorrows of Love*, where Clare, as so often in his poetry, lashes out against enclosure. Here, the female narrator of the poem has been talking of country customs:

> For we on sabbath days in pleasant weather
> Went still to walk & talk of love together
> & often sought a hut beside the wood
> That from the town a gossips minute stood
> Twas calld the herdsmans hut for when her spouse
> Walkd wi out sticks he kept the village cows
> Ere vile enclosure took away the moor
> & farmers built a workhouse for the poor (167–74)

The cutting of lines 171–4 means that the contrast between past and present is made to seem a part of that 'principle of change' which is at the root of the aesthetic of the picturesque. It also amounts to a de-naturing of Clare's intent.

Taylor's editing has the effect of denying his readers a full understanding of the intensity of Clare's recall of past customs and of the imaginative reach of his language. And this matters most of all because Clare's greatness as a poet is inseparable from such language. When he says in *May* that 'My wild field catalogue of flowers / Grows in my rhymes as thick as showers' (193–4) he is making a vivid claim for the fecundity of both rhyme and what nourishes it. Nature and art here interpenetrate each other. The last lines of *June* recall this moment, as they pick up and surpass the lines from Bloomfield's *Summer* quoted above. Holiday will pass, Clare says, 'as pride o'er custom showers / Its blighting mildew on her feeble flowers'. Pride is here linked to a new world of 'distinction', a severing of social relations which goes with, is prompted by and endorses, the evils of enclosure. And how with this rage shall custom hold a plea, whose action is no stronger than a flower? Clare's use of the imagery of mildew and blight draws attention to the destruction of what has grown out of more natural relations, of what in the eighteenth century was called a natural oeconomy. When Taylor suggested to Clare that he take a more 'philosophical' view of nature I find myself thinking that somewhere at the back of his mind he may have intended Clare to understand the word as carrying the implied meaning of 'resigned to circumstances', a meaning which according to the *OED* had acquired currency as early as the mid seventeenth century. But Clare was not prepared to be so resigned. At the end of the twentieth century, as environmental issues press upon us with peculiar urgency, his detestation of and rage at the wrecking of custom, the loss of common rights, ought to speak to us with a like urgency.

## NOTES

1  Edward Storey, *The Right to Song*, p. 202.
2  Lee Erickson, 'The poet's corner: the impact of changes on printing English poetry, 1800–1850', *ELH*, 52, 4, winter 1985.
3  See John Feather, 'Technology and the book in the 19th Century', *Critical Survey*, 2, I, 1990.
4  Clare, *Cottage Tales*, edited by Eric Robinson, David Powell and P. M. S. Dawson. This excellent edition contains letters from Taylor and Hessey to Clare about their often changing thoughts on the progress of *The Shepherd's Calendar*, as well as a helpful account of different plans and proposals for what eventually became the 1827 volume.
5  Clare, *The Shepherd's Calendar*, edited by Eric Robinson and David Powell. This is an improved version of the 1964 edition prepared by Geoffrey Summerfield and Eric Robinson which formed a landmark in making available Clare's poetry in its original form.
6  See Clare, *Letters*, pp. 302, 321, 437.
7  Tibble and Tibble, *Prose*, p. 212. The essay was written in 1825, at a time, therefore, when Clare was deeply exercised over *The Shepherd's Calendar*.
8  There is no modern edition of Bloomfield's work, although John Goodridge and John Lucas are preparing a selection. The quotations in this essay come from the edition of 1867, published in London by Routledge.
9  For an account of the implications contained in this phrase see an important essay by Alun Howkins and I. C. Dyck, '"The Time's Alterations": popular ballads, rural radicals and William Cobbett', *History Workshop*, 23, spring 1987.

## WRITINGS

*John Clare: The Oxford Author Series*, edited by Eric Robinson and David Powell, 1984

Clare, John, *The Shepherd's Calendar*, edited by Eric Robinson and Geoffrey Summerfield, Oxford, Oxford University Press, 1993.

——*Cottage Tales*, edited by Eric Robinson, David Powell and P. M. S. Dawson, Northumberland, MidNAG / Carcanet, 1993.

Grainger, Margaret (ed.) *The Natural History Prose Writings of John Clare*, Oxford, Oxford University Press, 1983.

Storey, Mark (ed.) *The Letters of John Clare*, Oxford, Clarendon Press 1985.

Tibble, J. W. and Tibble, Anne (eds) *The Prose of John Clare*, London, Routledge and Kegan Paul, 1951.

## REFERENCES AND FURTHER READING

Barrell, John, *The Idea of Landscape and the Sense of Place, 1730–1840: An Approach to the Poetry of John Clare*, Cambridge, Cambridge University Press, 1972.

——*The Dark Side of Landscape*, Cambridge, Cambridge University Press, 1980.

Chilcott, Tim, *A Real World and a Doubting Mind: A Critical Study of the Poetry of John Clare*, Pickering, Hull University Press, 1985.

Chirico, Paul, 'Writing misreadings: Clare and the real world', in *The Independent Spirit: John Clare and the Self-taught Tradition*, edited by John Goodridge, Helpston, The John Clare Society and The Margaret Grainger Trust, 1994.

Clare, Johanne, *John Clare and the Bounds of Circumstance*, Kingston and Montreal, McGill-Queen's University Press, 1987.

Goodridge, John, *The Rural Tradition of Poetry in the 18th Century*, Cambridge, Cambridge University Press, 1995.

Haughton, Hugh and Phillips, Adam (eds) *John Clare in Context*, Cambridge, Cambridge University Press, 1994.

Leader, Zachary, *Revision and Romantic Authorship*, Oxford, Clarendon Press, 1996.

Lucas, John, *John Clare*, Plymbridge, Northcote House and The British Council, 1994.

——*England and Englishness: Ideas of Nationhood in English Poetry, 1688–1900*, London, Chatto & Windus, 1990.

Neeson, J. M., *Commoners: Common Right, Enclosure and Social Change in England, 1700–1820*, Cambridge, Cambridge University Press, 1993.

Storey, Edward, *A Right to Song: The Life of John Clare*, London, Methuen, 1982.

Storey, Mark, *John Clare: The Critical Heritage*, London, Routledge and Kegan Paul, 1973.

Thompson, E. P., *Customs in Common*, London, Merlin Press, 1991.

Tibble, Anne, *John Clare: A Life*, London, Michael Joseph, 1972. This is an updated version of the biography first produced by the Tibbles in 1932.

Williams, Raymond, *The Country and the City*, London, Paladin, 1975.

# 31

# Felicia Hemans, *Records of Woman*

## *Adam Roberts*

According to her biographer, Hemans's *Records of Woman* was the collection by which she was 'most universally known'.[1] These poems are certainly characteristic; all of them inflect the tension in a woman's life between the domestic and the heroic. Or, to put it another way, the keynote, here as in all of Hemans's work, is that very nineteenth-century but nowadays rather out-of-fashion quantity, Duty. It is a hymn to duty, even unto death, that remains the one poem of Hemans's still in general currency today – *Casabianca*, with its wincingly famous opening: 'The boy stood on the burning deck / Whence all but he had fled.' The duty of this boy, or of any of the military male characters in Hemans's output, is usually straightforward. What the 19 poems in the *Records of Woman* attempt to establish, to define by example, is woman's duty. Some of the characters of these various poems are famous or otherwise prominent women (Joan of Arc, the great sculptress Properzia Rossi, Arabella Stuart with her royal blood), some are ordinary or low-born (Edith, Imelda), some are without even a name (the speaker of the *Indian Woman's Death Song*). But regardless of birth they all, in one form or another, have to face trials, and must do what Hemans considered to be the right thing. The duties of woman turn out to be constancy, endurance, championing the domestic, turning away from the public. By today's standards, there is something reactionary in Hemans's view of gender roles. As Anne Mellor puts it, Hemans 'constructed her self and her poetry as the icon of female domesticity, the embodiment of the "cult of true womanhood." As she wrote to her friend, Mary Russell Mitford, "there is *no* enjoyment to compare with the happiness of gladdening hearth and home for others – it is a woman's own true sphere".'[2] The immense popularity of Hemans in her heyday – and she outsold even Byron with some volumes – seems to reflect the appeal that these poetic restatements of conventional domestic ideology had for the readership of 1820s Britain.

Of course, to suggest that Hemans wrote poetry in the service of a monolithic and to modern sensibilities rather repellent domestic ideology is hardly going to recommend her to present-day readers. The interest in Hemans's poetry – and she *is* an interesting poet – lies in the fruitful tension that exists in her best work between its surface concerns and its buried subtext. Tricia Lootens argues that what Hemans's readership found in her work was 'a fragmented, compelling, and complex range of [feminine] patriotic positions, and the verses this audience favoured – such as the silly, sinister, and explosive "Casabianca" – were often among the most disturbing'. It is possible to read Casabianca's boy, who dies on the burning deck rather than abandon his post, as a heroic embodiment of a patriotic ideal; but as Lootens points out, this poetic treatment of a real military circumstance (The Battle of the Nile, during the Napoleonic wars) places 'the tragically unnecessary death of a child at the heart of Britain's victory . . . [and] never fully defuses the horror of the history it evokes'.[3]

*Records of Woman* presents us as readers with similar dilemmas. The 19 poems give us 19 women, each facing the death or desertion of a male loved one, or some other crisis connected with love or family ties. All uphold the ideal of a specifically feminine heroism, rooted not in the public sphere, but rather in an exaggerated capacity for love and self-sacrifice as wife, mother or lover. The collection's first epigraph, from Wordsworth, insisted that the love found in 'feeble woman's breast' is 'mightier far / Than strength of nerve or sinew'. But the second epigraph, from Schiller, suggests the mournful cast of many of the poems, the moral that female love leads often as not to death and misery: 'Das ist das Loos des Schonen auf der Erde!' Such is the lot of Beauty in this world! There is a contradiction here, and it resonates through *Records of Woman*. When women suffer, particularly when they suffer because of men, is their plight tragically heroic or just wastefully unnecessary?

*Records of Woman* begins with four instances of women's constancy (even to death) to their husbands. The heroine of *Arabella Stuart* is separated from her husband William Seymour, never to meet again, but her monologue reveals the depths of her hopeless love. Eudora, the heroine of *The Bride of the Greek Isle*, bids a tearful farewell to her family in order to marry Ianthis; but when he is murdered by pirates during the wedding feast she carries out a resolute and pyrrhic revenge, going aboard their ship and setting fire to it. *The Switzer's Wife* rouses her otherwise vacillating husband to fight for his Swiss homeland, even though it may mean her death. *Gertrude* is subtitled *Fidelity Till Death* and tells the grisly story of (to quote Hemans's epigraph) how the Baron Von der Wart was 'bound alive on the wheel' by the wicked Emperor, and was 'attended by his wife Gertrude throughout his last agonizing hours with a most heroic devotedness'. Gertrude's words certainly sound heroic ('And bid me not depart' she tells him; 'My Rudolf say not so! / This is no time to quit thy side'), but the poem leaves a very peculiar taste in the mouth. In part this is because the husband's torture is dissociated from any cause or rationale, and is not in itself described, so that the wife's ministrations take on oddly tormenting overtones:

> She wiped the death-damps from his brow,
>     With her pale hands and soft,
> Whose touch upon the lute-chords low,
>     Had still'd his heart so oft.
> She spread her mantle o'er his breast,
>     She bathed his lips with dew,
> And on his cheeks such kisses press'd
>     As hope and joy never knew. (41–8)[4]

It is difficult to shake the sense that Gertrude's caresses might actually be a particularly exquisite form of torture, adding to the husband's sufferings rather than alleviating them. The last two lines almost suggest that she kisses her husband more passionately *because* he is in terrible pain. But husbands throughout the collection are rarely delineated as anything other than ciphers, blanks against which the heroism of the wives can be more strikingly portrayed.

More importantly, perhaps, in the collection as a whole, *Gertrude*, the fifth poem in the sequence, is the last to portray female heroism in terms of duty to husband. In other words, to read the opening poems of *Records of Woman* sequentially sets up an expectation (that a woman's duty is chiefly to her husband) which the rest of the collection rather contradicts. With *Properzia Rossi*, the collection's fourth poem, we are given a different model of woman's suffering. Rossi is a martyr to Love in the abstract, despite rather than on account of the man in her life. Hemans's epigraph summarizes the situation of the poem:

> Properzia Rossi, a celebrated female sculptor of Bologna, possessed also of talents for poetry and music, died in consequence of an unrequited attachment. – A painting by Ducis, represents her showing her last work, a basso-relievo of Ariadne, to a Roman Knight, the object of her affection, who regards it with indifference.

Once again, we learn nothing of the Knight, although the vigour and power of Rossi's artistic talent is suggestively related:

> It comes, – the power
> Within me born, flows back; my fruitless dower
> That could not win me love. Yet once again
> I greet it proudly, with its rushing train
> Of glorious images: – they throng – they press –
> A sudden joy lights up my loneliness – (25–30)

The imagery of fluidity, of the rushing outpour of female creativity, is one Hemans frequently resorts to in *Records of Woman* (*Madelaine*, for instance, 'pour'd forth her own sweet solemn vesper-song': 38). More significant is the cameo of talented and/or beautiful woman abandoned by man, the situation that informs most of the remaining poems in the collection. Three poems that follow *Properzia Rossi* describe heroines who are in a sense abandoned by men, left alone because their love is dead: *Imelda* (whose lover is murdered by her brothers, and who poisons herself to join him on a marriage bed that is also a deathbed); *Edith* (an English girl in the New World whose lover is murdered by Indians, and who, after an interlude with a more kindly native tribe, climbs into a canoe to sing her swan-song, drifting down the river, and die); and *The Peasant Girl of the Rhone* (who continues placing wreaths on the tomb of the warrior she loved, even after the fellow's parents have got over their grief and forgotten him – until she herself dies of a broken heart). But the *Indian Woman's Death Song*, the tenth, and in some senses, the key poem in the sequence introduces the notion that a man does not need to die to desert and betray a woman. This brief lyric is sung by a heroine 'driven to despair by her husband's desertion of her for another wife'. Rather than endure this slight, the Indian Woman commits suicide by rowing her canoe, with herself and her daughter in it, over a waterfall. In place of the usual overheated bombast and adjectival-overload that so often characterizes Hemans's style, this lyric is really quite dignified in its restraint. The misery of the protagonist – her sleepless nights, her fading looks and increasing age, are hinted at rather than explicitly invoked:

> Thy mother bears thee away, young Fawn! from sorrow and decay
> She bears thee to the glorious bowers where none are heard to weep,
> And where th'unkind one hath no power again to trouble sleep;
> And where the soul shall find its youth, as wakening from a dream, –
> One moment at that realm is ours – On, on, dark rolling stream! (39–43)

After the *Indian Woman's Death Song*, the model of female duty to a sexual partner is never again introduced into *Records of Woman* as a noble or praiseworthy aim. *Juana*, who sits by her husband's corpse, refusing to believe that he is really dead, is forced to concede that the same husband, who had 'treated her with uniform neglect' when alive, never loved her. *Constanza*, now a nun, is able to nurse the warrior who had betrayed her before she took holy orders, and to listen to his blubbing apologies ('I *cannot* die / Without forgiveness from that mournful eye!': 101–2) before he expires in her arms – a fitting punishment, it seems, for one who had been 'lured' from her side by 'hollow splendour' of the martial life. *Madelaine*, similarly, praises the 'true and perfect love' between mother and daughter, a love interrupted by the husband who leaves the wife and carries the child away, but which survives to be reunited at the poem's end with the fortuitous death of the man. Anne Mellor argues that this trope of the deserting man has its roots in Hemans's own experience of men, and that *Madelaine* in particular 'is arguably the most autobiographical poem in this self-revealing volume'.[5] Hemans was herself abandoned by her husband, Captain Alfred Hemans of the King's Own Regiment, who went to live alone in Italy, leaving his wife to bring up their five sons by herself. Hemans managed this task thanks largely to the income she derived from her writing, but her own experience bitterly contradicted the conventional pieties of married love.

But if the love of a husband was not dependable, familial love emerges in Hemans's work almost as the replacement of such passion. The *Indian Woman's Death Song* hints at this transformation, when its heroine, abandoned by her husband, throws herself upon a metaphorical father: 'Father of the ancient waters, roll! And bear our lives with thee!' (2). 'Father of waters' was, as Hemans acknowledges in a note, the Indian name of the Mississippi; but the fact that the heroine seeks solace in the arms of a metaphorical father marks an important shift of allegiance in the tenor of the collection. The poem that follows, *Joan of Arc, In Rheims*, is also a hymn to the nobility of the father, first in the figure of the symbolic fatherhood of the king, in all his splendour of his coronation; and second in the person of Joan's actual father, and the comfort Joan can find in what the epigraph calls 'les bras d'un père vertueux'. But even the saintly figure of the father 'in the calm beauty of his silver hair' (64) cannot match the potency of the figure of the mother in Hemans's poetical imagination. It is the mother, and the love of mother for child (and particularly daughter) that dominates the last eight poems of *Records of Woman*. In *The Indian City*, a Muslim boy is murdered by Brahmins for daring to swim in one of their pools; his mother is able to whip up such outrage at this story that she can gather together an army and overthrow the Brahmin city, and have herself and her son buried together in the ruins that she has herself created, 'the work of one deep heart wrung!' In *Pauline* a mother refuses to leave a burning palace without her daughter, and both are burnt to death:

> But bore the ruins no recording trace
> Of all that woman's heart had dared and done?
> Yes! there were gems to mark its mortal place,
> That forth from dust and ashes dimly shone!
> Those had the mother on her gentle breast,
> Worn round her child's fair image, there at rest. (79–84)

Fire is invoked here as a medium of change, almost of apotheosis; as if the mother and the daughter she loved so strongly are actually transformed in death into these jewels. Death by fire, with its suggestions of suttee (the *Bride of the Greek Isle* who sets fire to the pirate ship in revenge for her husband's death is described amongst the flames as standing 'proudly...like an Indian bride / On the pyre': 215–16) is reclaimed, feminized by Hemans's poetic imagination.

*Madelaine*, as we have seen, celebrates the love between mother and daughter, a love that triumphs over the interference of the husband:

> Love, true and perfect love! – Whence came that power,
> Uprearing through the storm the drooping flower?
> Whence? – who can ask? – the wild delirium passed,
> And from her eyes the spirit looked at last
> Into her *mother's* face, and wakening knew
> The brow's calm grace, the hair's dear silvery hue,
> The kind sweet smile of old! (85–91)

This is perhaps rather hackneyed, but there is no denying the sincerity of Hemans's paean to the maternal. *The Queen of Prussia's Tomb* again celebrates a woman in maternal terms:

> She was a mother – in her love
> How sorrowfully true!
> Oh! hallow'd long be every leaf,
> The record of her children's grief! (27–30)

The penultimate poem is also about the love between mother and daughter. *The Memorial Pillar* stands between Penrith and Appleby, and records the last parting of Ann, Countess Dowager of Pembroke, and her mother, Margaret, Countess Dowager of Cumberland, in 1616. Hemans is moved by this monument to apostrophise 'Mother and child! whose blending tears / Have sanctified the place'. And the final poem in *Records of Woman*, *The Grave of a Poetess*, is also about motherhood, although more obliquely realized. Here the narrator, identifiable with Hemans herself in this Coda to her collection, stands by the grave of a poetess, a poetic 'mother'. The collection as a whole is dedicated to another poetic 'mother' figure, the poet Joanna Baillie. In fact, Hemans's own mother (with whom she had been very close) died in 1827, the year before *Records of Woman* was published.

In other words, what we have in this collection is a conception of female duty that moves away from involvement with husbands and lovers, and ultimately from family, and which ends up asserting strength in the relationship between mother and daughter. Of course, *Records of Woman* is full of expressions of conventional pieties with respect to marriage and heterosexual love, but the effect of reading the collection *sequentially* is the gradual exclusion of the masculine. Angela Leighton suggests that 'in *Records of Woman* [Hemans] does forge a sense of the woman's voice as historically significant, and, in its own sphere, self-determining and self-asserting'.[6] But, this notwithstanding, the most arresting passages in the collection come not in the conventional pieties of the mother-loving final poems, but in the ambiguous ways in which men are represented in the earlier poems. Loving one's mother, of course, is a totally conventional and laudable virtue; Hemans can present it without conflict. But her anger at the masculine is not something sanctioned by convention, and accordingly it must be veiled.

One of the most striking things about the men in *Records of Woman* is that they seem to *bleed* all the time, usually profusely. Imelda finds the body of her lover, and asks of it, 'On thy breast / Is the stain, – yes, 'tis blood!' (*Imelda*, 81–2); *Edith*'s dying lover puts out more than just a stain:

> Heavily she felt his life-blood well
> Fast o'er her garments forth, and vainly bound
> With her torn robe and hair the streaming wound. (28–30)

The mother of the Muslim boy in *The Indian City* faces a similar flood:

> Breathless she knelt in her son's young blood,
> Rending her mantle to staunch its flood:
> But it rushed like a river that none may stay. (87–9)

This poetic bloodlust can become so intense that the strangest images become connected with the flow. *In Bride of the Greek Isle* Eudora sees her husband slain before her very eyes:

> She saw but Ianthis before her lie,
> With the blood from his breast in a gushing flow,
> Like a child's large tears in its hour of woe. (140–2)

This is so clumsy an analogy as to be almost powerful in its surreal oddity. But what are we to make of all this (male) blood, gushing so copiously upon Hemans's pages? Resisting the temptation to read all this male carnage as a crude expression of buried anger at the masculine (she doesn't like men so she has them all killed off), it is possible to read all this outpouring blood as a menstrual reappropriation of the male in terms of the female. There seems to be a sort of transference at work. All the men in *Records of Woman* who die, die bloodily. Plenty of the women die too, but none of them bleed so much as a drop; either they die of that vaguest of ailments, the broken heart, or else they are burnt to death in the fire (*Bride of the Greek Isle, Pauline*). The one man who faces this fate, about to be immolated by savages (the English youth in *The American Forest Girl*), is saved by the intervention of the young Indian girl. The ostensible moral of the collection – that women have an emotional strength to compensate them for their lack of physical strength – becomes blurred; the women recorded by Hemans cannot, it seems, be scratched or made to bleed. Physical frailty is transformed to the masculine, and women adopt heroism in a more than metaphorical sense. It is in these ways that a reactionary writer carries through a subtext far more revolutionary.

## NOTES

1  Henry Chorley, *Memorials of Mrs. Hemans, with illustrations of Her Literary Character from her Private Correspondence*, London, 1838, I: 103.
2  Mellor, *Romanticism and Gender*, p. 123.
3  Lootens, 'Hemans and home', p. 5.
4  Hemans's poetry is quoted from her *Poetical Works*, edited by W. M. Rossetti, 1878.
5  Mellor, *Romanticism and Gender*, p. 132.
6  Leighton and Reynolds, 'Felicia Hemans', p. 32.

## REFERENCES AND FURTHER READING

Greer, Germaine, *Slip-shod Sibyls: Recognition, Rejection and the Woman Poet*, Viking, 1995.

Leighton, Angela, 'Felicia Hemans', in *Victorian Women Poets: Writing Against the Heart*, Harvester, 1992.

Leighton, Angela, and Reynolds, Margaret (eds) 'Felicia Hemans', in *Victorian Women Poets: An Anthology*, Blackwell, 1995.

Lootens, Tricia, 'Hemans and home: Victorianism, feminine "internal enemies" and the domestication of national identity', in Angela Leighton (ed.) *Victorian Women Poets: A Critical Reader*, Blackwell, 1996.

Mellor, Anne, *Romanticism and Gender*, Routledge, 1993.

Ross, Marlon, *The Contours of Masculine Desire: Romanticism and the Rise of Women's Poetry*, Oxford, 1989.

Sweet, Nanora, 'History, imperialism, and the aesthetics of the beautiful: Hemans and the post-Napoleonic moment', in Favret and Watson (eds) *At the Limits of Romanticism: Essays in Cultural, Feminist and Materialist Criticism*, Indiana University Press, 1994.

# PART THREE
# Genres and Modes

# 32

# The Romantic Drama

## Frederick Burwick

The drama in every generation is swayed by the currents of social and political change affecting the theatre-going public. In the Romantic period the theatre audience grew more rapidly than at any previous period in British history. With the urban influx brought about by the Industrial Revolution, London had by 1800 become the world's largest city. Theatres were rebuilt to house larger audiences. Drury Lane under David Garrick's management seated 2,000 spectators; under Richard Brinsley Sheridan's management, it seated 3,600. The larger audience also more broadly represented the growing middle class, who were prompt to riot for 'Old Prices' when, in 1809, Kemble endeavoured to recoup expenses of rebuilding Covent Garden by raising seat prices and converting the third tier from open gallery to expensive private boxes. Dramatic performance in the period was influenced by middle-class values, tastes and political convictions, as well as by the physical demands of performing in vast auditoriums unaided by electronic amplification.

Because subtleties of vocal modulation and nuances of facial expression could not be perceived beyond the first few rows, the acting style that evolved to meet the demands of the large playhouses was declamatory with emphatic physical gesturing. When John Philip Kemble rehearsed a performance, he choreographed every pose, every gesture, every step that he would make upon the stage. The result was a highly-wrought formalism that gave a quality of cautious deliberation to whatever character he might play. It was an acting style not inappropriate to the tragic roles in which he gained acclaim: his Richard III was cold and calculating, his Coriolanus haughty and aloof, his Hamlet burdened with grief, intense yet preoccupied. By all contemporary accounts his sister, Sarah Siddons, was the superior performer. She, too, relied on a formal, declamatory style, but she had the skill of making even stylized gesture seem spontaneous. Her vocal delivery was at once more forceful and more natural. She was also capable of a wider range of modulation that enabled her to adapt to comedy or melodrama, although she was at her best in tragic roles that allowed her to show the heroic powers of the feminine emotions. Her performance in the title role contributed to the continuing popularity of Nicholas Rowe's *Jane Shore*; she was bold and innovative in her interpretation of Lady Macbeth; as Belvidera in *Venice Preserved*, according to James Boaden's account, she conveyed more passion than the audience had thought possible in a woman, perhaps more passion than the prim Boaden thought proper.

Boaden disapproved of Siddons's 'display of the figure' as Imogen in *Cymbeline* or Rosalind in *As You Like It*. Boaden's censure, of course, did not prevail against the popularity of 'breeches parts'. It was not merely a provocative display of the female form in breeches, however, that contributed to the acclaim of Dorothy Jordan. She appealed, as well, to the women in her audience for the high-spirited and competitive feminine temperament exhibited in her interpretation of Peggy in *The Country Girl*, or Miss Hoyden in Sheridan's *A Trip to Scarborough*.

The formalized declamatory style of Kemble and Siddons held sway for the first half of the period, then, in 1814, Edmund Kean brought to the stage a new style of acting in which improvisational spontaneity replaced the thoroughly choreographed delivery. While Kean could not imbue his performance with the statuesque dignity of Kemble, he displayed far more intense energy. As Sir Edward Mortimer in George Colman's *The Iron Chest*, William Hazlitt reported, Kean conveyed the abrupt and erratic changes of a troubled mind: 'from calmness to deep despair, from concealed suspicion to open rage, from smooth decorous indifference to the convulsive agonies of remorse'. William Charles Macready's acting apprenticeship commenced when, at the age of 17, he was enlisted of necessity as a 'stand-in' for his alcoholic father, not simply to play the role, but to play his father playing the role. By the 1820s Macready had gained increasing popularity for his 'familiar' style, in which he seemed to obliterate the proscenium barrier and speak personally to the audience. In the 1830s Madame Vestris (Eliza Lucy Bartolozzi) introduced 'drawing-room' performances at the Olympic Theatre to restore a sense of closeness between performer and spectator that had been lost in the larger theatres.

The audience, which included many uneducated in the literary tradition of the drama, had little patience with complexity of character, flourishes of wit and rhetoric in dialogue, or the interweaving of subplots. They wanted vigorous action, and they expected virtue to be rewarded and vice punished. Responding to these conditions, melodrama emerged as a new dramatic form during the 1790s and held sway throughout the nineteenth century. Melodrama had its antecedents in the sentimental tragedies of the mid-eighteenth century. Edward Moore's *The Gamester* (1753), an indictment of gambling as social evil, was originally performed with Garrick as the honest but weak-willed Beverley, Hannah Pritchard as the wife who suffers the poverty of his gambling losses, and Thomas Davies as Stukely, the false friend who urges Beverley to wagers that result in his financial ruin. The play was revived in 1783, with Kemble in the role of Beverley, Siddons as his wife, and John Palmer as Stukely. Imprisoned for debt, Beverley inflicts his own sentence upon his folly by swallowing poison. Even as this draught works its fatal effect, news arrives that he has inherited a fortune from his uncle. His final interview with Mrs Beverley, and her confrontation with the villainous Stukely, are scenes in which Sarah Siddons played her character with a fervour that stunned contemporary audiences. While some contemporary critics would maintain that the role of Mrs Beverley was 'beneath her powers', Sarah Siddons was exceptionally skilled in transforming the 'suffering heroine' into a sublime statement of feminine strength.

Among the first playwrights of the period to alter the conventions of sentimental drama by adding the comic relief and happy ending that were essential to melodrama was Thomas Holcroft, whose *Duplicity* (1781), *Seduction* (1787), and *The Deserted Daughter* (1795) combined strong emotional appeal with the high moral sentiment that gave domestic tragi-comedy its melodramatic shape. With *The Road to Ruin* (1792), which was performed a record-setting 38 times during its opening season at Covent Garden, Holcroft also attained success in sentimental comedy. Harry Dornton, a wayward gambler, is a comic version of Beverley. The comedy is heightened by the company he keeps: Sophia, the light-hearted, light-witted heroine; Widow Warren, the overripe, overzealous coquette; Goldfinch, the foppish young man of fashion; Silky, the usurer; Sulky, the morally sententious family friend. The scenes between father and son, with their emotional emphasis, are pure melodrama.

Other successful plays during these formative years were George Colman's *Inkle and Yarico* (1787) and *The Heir at Law* (1797), Richard Cumberland's *The Wheel of Fortune* (1795), Thomas Morton's *Speed the Plough* (1800), and James Kenney's *Raising the Wind* (1803). Colman's *The Iron Chest* (1796), adapted from William Godwin's *Caleb Williams* (1794), opened at Drury Lane with Kemble playing the lead role and with the historical setting in accord with Colman's own instructions: as the curtain rose, 'the great actor was discovered as Sir Edward Mortimer in his library – gloom and desolation sat upon his brow, and he was habited from the wig to the shoestring with the most studious exactness – had one of King Charles the first's portraits walked from its frame upon the boards of the theatre, it could not have afforded a truer representation of ancient and melancholy dignity' (Baker, *John Philip Kemble*, pp. 197–200). Although pleased with 'the picture', Colman was less pleased with the acting. Just prior to the performance, Colman had witnessed Kemble 'in his dressing-room seemingly very unwell, and swallowing opium pills'. Kemble's 'soporific monotony', bereft of the almost psychopathic turbulence with which Kean was later to play the part, did not undermine the gloomy character of Mortimer, who is tortured by guilt over a murder he committed in his youth. Mortimer's guilty secret is not simply concealed within his own breast, it is also documented in a letter narrating the deed which, together with the bloody knife, is kept in the iron chest entrusted to Mortimer's friend Wilford. A man whose own moral principles keep him on the rack of guilt and despair, Mortimer's character is an antecedent to the self-persecuting Byronic hero.

Typically in melodrama, the villain has a much stronger role than the hero or the heroine. The hero's follies or frailties render him an easy prey to the villain's stratagem to gain wealth, power and, not incidentally, control over the hapless, helpless, uncompromisingly virtuous heroine. With its machinations of villainy, melodrama opened the theatre to the Gothic, which had already gained popularity in such novels as Horace Walpole's *The Castle of Otranto* (1764) and Ann Radcliffe's *The Mysteries of Udolpho* (1794). Gothic villainy, an acceptable venue for exploring sexual taboos and darker passions under the guise of the supernatural and demonic, could be carried to even further extremes than the greed and lust of mere domestic melodrama.

For crime to be properly exposed in Gothic drama, a bloody weapon or a written confession would not suffice. The ghost of the victim must reveal the deed. In Matthew Gregory Lewis's *The Castle Spectre* (1797), the ghost of Evilina, murdered by Osmond 16 years earlier, returns to prevent Osmond from forcing Angela to submit to his will. In his effort to prevent Evilina's murder, Reginald, Osmond's brother, was severely wounded and thrown into a dungeon. Ostensibly to help Angela escape from Osmond, Father Phillip has led Angela into the dungeon. There, in a repetition of the events of the past, Reginald comes to her defence. When Osmond lifts his dagger to stab Reginald, Evilina's ghost appears between them. Startled by the apparition, 'Osmond starts back and drops his sword', according to the stage directions, and 'Angela springs suddenly forward and plunges her dagger into Osmond's bosom'. The ghost vanishes. During the phenomenal opening run of 47 performances, Dorothy Jordan played Angela and Jane Powell played the spectral Evilina.

The sudden appearances and disappearances of the ghost could be managed much more effectively after gas-lighting was introduced in 1802. When *The Castle Spectre* was revived at Covent Garden in 1804, the appearance and disappearance was manipulated by brightening and dimming Argand burners equipped with a concave mirror reflector and coloured glass to cast a ghostly beam upon the actress previously obscured in the shadows. Oxygen-fed spirit lamps, introduced 15 years later, provided an incandescence bright enough to allow projection with the magic lantern in the huge theatres. The new lighting technology also made it possible, with concave mirrors, to cast onto the stage phantom images of actors actually concealed in the wings. David Brewster and Thomas Young were among the contemporary scientists commissioned to provide the theatres with optical devices for producing these stunning stage illusions.

Stage designs became more elaborate: back-lighting and magic-lantern projection expanded the possibilities of stage illusion; historical costumes enhanced the pretences of authenticity. As playbills of the period reveal, innovative stage effects were often featured in bolder type than the performers. Many plays were little more than spectacles. Colman's *Blue Beard* (1798) created mounting excitement among spectators anticipating the opening of the 'secret room' with its sadistic horrors. William Thomas Moncrieff's *Rochester, or Charles The Second's Merry Days* (1818) delighted those few in the audience who could interpret the risqué allusions, but for most the entertainment was provided by the elaborate recreation of Restoration costumes. *Tom and Jerry* (1821) was Moncrieff's 'street comedy', appropriated from Pierce Egan's novel, *Life in London*, in which Corinthian Tom brings Jerry Hawthorn, his country cousin, to the city. As originally performed at the Adelphi, the backdrops were well-known scenes from London. The humour relies on Jerry's initiation into 'city' ways: the slang taught by Bob Logic, the lesson in horse-trading at Tattersall's, the 'genteel' society at Almack's, the fight with the watchmen in Fleet Street, the descent into a gamblers' Hell, and the encounter with beggars in the Back Slums.

James Robinson Planché, a playwright who also possessed great ingenuity in stage design, produced *The Vampire* (1820), using the newly developed stage trap, which allowed Ruthven, the vampire, played by Thomas Potter Cooke, to pass magically through solid objects on stage. Planché's greatest illusionist effects were created for the Covent Garden premiere of Carl Maria von Weber's *Oberon* (1826), for which Planché had also written the libretto. Planché adapted several novels for stage performance with elaborate settings, including *Maid Marian* (1822), from the novel by Thomas Love Peacock, and *Kenilworth* (1824), from the novel by Sir Walter Scott. Madame Vestris called upon Planché's skills to create the 'drawing-room' settings at the Olympic.

In *Maid Marian*, T. P. Cooke played the role of King Richard, but he was especially successful in the macabre role of the vampire. He also played the monster in *Presumption; or, the Fate of Frankenstein* (1824), adapted by R. B. Peake from the novel by Mary Shelley.

Cooke's most memorable role, in which he appeared no less than 765 times, was William in Douglas Jarrold's *Black-Eyed Susan* (1829). When Captain Crosstree makes immodest advances to William's beloved Susan, the good-hearted burly sailor knocks his superior officer to the ground, for which offence William is sentenced to hang. But this is melodrama, so it has a happy end.

The changes that had given rise to the melodrama in London were also at work in theatres on the Continent, and there was an active interchange among acting groups travelling to and from Paris, Berlin and other metropolitan centres. Successes in French or German theatres were quickly adapted for the English stage. By far the most popular foreign playwright of the period was August von Kotzebue, 36 of whose plays were performed in English adaptations. *Pizarro* (1799), Sheridan's adaptation of *Die Spanier in Peru*, remained a box-office success when revived in 1803, but in 1816, when Charles Young played Rolla, the politically charged rhetoric had lost its immediacy. Amidst fears of French invasion during its opening season in 1799 (with Kemble as Rolla, Siddons as Elvira, Jordan as Cora, Barrymore as the ruthless Pizarro), it was easy for an English audience to identify with the Peruvian natives in their resistance to the Spanish *conquistadors*. Rolla's address to the soldiers was clearly designed to stir popular sentiments in reaction to the French Revolution. Another favourite on the stage was *The Stranger* (1798), adapted by Benjamin Thompson from Kotzebue's *Menschenhaß und Reue*, in which Kemble played the misanthropic 'stranger', moved in the climactic scene with their children to forgive his long-suffering wife, Siddons as Mrs Haller, for an infidelity she committed many years before.

In France, the main purveyor of melodrama was Guilbert de Pixérécourt, 'le Corneille des boulevards', who supplied the stage with over one hundred plays between 1798 and 1835. His *Cœlina, ou L'Enfant du mystère* was adapted by Thomas Holcroft as *A Tale of Mystery* (1802). The mystery centres on Francisco, who, like Lavinia in *Titus Andronicus*, has been wounded and had his tongue cut out. Rescued by a passing servant girl, Francisco is received into the house of Bonamo. The plot depends on the gradual revelation of identity: who is he? who attacked him? Francisco belonged to a noble family; his daughter is the woman whom Bonamo's son wishes to take as a bride; he recognizes Romaldi among the wedding guests. Accused of the attempted murder, Romaldi is condemned to death. As the archers prepare to shoot him, Francisco stands in front of the condemned man, whom he reveals to be his brother. Holcroft softened the anti-aristocratic revolutionary polemics, and emphasized the plight of the mutilated victim. Melodrama was to make frequent use of a mute or blind character to arouse pity. Pixérécourt also relied on dogs and children to achieve sentimental appeal. The first 'dog melodrama' to attain theatrical success was *Victor, ou L'Enfant de la forêt*, adapted by Pixérécourt from a novel by Ducray-Duminils and introduced by Charles Dibdin at Covent Garden as *The Forest of Bondy* (1814).

If an audience would weep for a dog in a melodramatic predicament, then a child in a similar dilemma ought to solicit at least as much pathos. When Sarah Siddons returned to the London stage in 1782 after six years in Bath and York, she appeared as Isabella in an adaptation of Southerne's *The Fatal Marriage*. To enhance the sentimental appeal of her performance, she introduced her eight-year-old son, Henry Siddons, to play the role of Isabella's son in the play. The following season, she played Constance in Shakespeare's *King John*, with Henry Siddons as little Arthur, imprisoned in the Tower and condemned to have his eyes burnt out. The appeal of children on the stage led to the sensational reception of William Henry West Betty, 'the Infant Roscius'. The applause he had won with his performances in Birmingham secured the 13-year-old prodigy a place at Covent Garden for the 1804–5 season, where he played, not in child's roles, but in such 'manly' parts as Achmet in John Brown's *Barbarossa* (1756), Norval in John Home's *Douglas* (1757) and Frederick in Elizabeth Inchbald's *Lovers' Vows* (1799). The public enthusiasm was not sustained through a second season. Betty's attempt as an adult to stage a comeback at Covent Garden in 1812–13 proved a dismal failure. Nevertheless, other children, as well as horses and dogs, continued to receive brief fame by exciting the spectators' delight in novelty.

Several women playwrights, notably Aphra Behn, Susanna Centlivre, Mary Manley, Mary Pix and Catherine Trotter, had gained success in the theatre during the century preceding. Many women authors contributed to the drama during the formative years of the Romantic period: Ann Yearsley, *Earl Goodwin* (1789), Mariana Starke, *The Widow of Malabar* (1790), Maria Barrell, *The Captive* (1790), Lady Eglinton Wallace, *The Ton* (1787), *The Whim* (1792). Many novels by women authors were adapted for the stage: notably Amelia Opie's *Father and Daughter* (1801), which enjoyed a successful run in Moncrieff's play of 1829; Ann Radcliffe's *The Italian*, given stage life in Boaden's *The Italian Monk* (1797); and Mary Shelley's *Frankenstein* in Peake's stage version (1824). Women authors also dominated the comedy of courtship and domestic life, a popular genre in which they were clearly more adept than their contemporary male rivals at giving in their dialogue a sharp satirical edge to the dynamics of male–female relationships. The leading women playwrights of the period were Hannah Cowley, Elizabeth Inchbald, Joanna Baillie and Mary Mitford.

With the Covent Garden production of *The Belle's Stratagem* (1780), Cowley convincingly demonstrated her command of character, dialogue and intrigue. Letitia Hardy, perceived as a pretty yet brainless female by Hardy, Flutter, Saville and Courtall, is actually astute and capable. *Which is the Man?* (1782) is a clever comedy of errors in which Julia, secretly married to Bellville in Paris, is called home by her guardian, Fitzwilliam, who is unaware of her marriage. Nor does Bellville know that she is Fitzwilliam's ward. Thus ensues a series of complications that result in Julia's being decoyed by the lecherous Lord Sparkle. She is rescued and properly wed to Bellville, and Lord Sparkle is happily paired with the equally lecherous Lady Bell Bloomer. *The Town Before You* (1794), performed at Covent Garden, was Cowley's thirteenth success on the London stage; eleven of her plays appear in her posthumously published *Works* (1813).

Elizabeth Inchbald was the author of 19 dramatic works: satirical farces, such as *Animal Magnetism* (1788); melodrama, including the frequently revived *Such Things Are* (1787), which was on the London stage as late as 1824; comedies, of which *Wives as they were, and Maids as they are* (1797) had the most enduring popularity, playing at Covent Garden in 1825. Her *oeuvre* also includes successful adaptations from Kotzebue, including *Lovers' Vows* (1799). Drawing upon her own experience as an actress, she crafted her plays with lively dialogue and effective control of scenes and sequence. Of significant value to historians of the drama is her edition of plays, *The British Theatre* (1806–9) in 25 volumes, with critical and biographical commentaries.

Although tragedy had traditionally used outbreaks of derangement to dramatize the emotional suffering of a character, the plays of the Romantic period began to trace more carefully the causes and effects of madness. The more detailed literary attention to the 'case history' of madness followed a new medical interest in nervous disorders and the rise of psychology as a scientific discipline. Joanna Baillie, in her *Plays of the Passions* (1798–1812), sought to dramatize the obsessive and compulsive hold of one dominant passion on the life and mind of a character. Her brother, Dr Matthew Baillie, who had focused on the brain and abdominal organs in his *Morbid Anatomy* (1793; 2nd edn 1797), was encouraged by Joanna to pursue his studies on the effects of disease on the spinal cord and nervous system. In 1797 he became physician extraordinary to George III, who had already suffered spells of raving violence. Joanna Baillie attempted in her plays to dramatize the pathology of an *idée fixe*. This meant, of course, that she must somehow reveal internal motivation and contrive to make her dialogue express the inner turmoil of her characters. Scene and setting serve to provoke the mimetic activity of her characters who project their psychological experience onto the people and things with whom they interact. The sense of external reality is gradually transformed by the inner vision. Baillie dramatizes the process by which a character succumbs to delusion: the supernatural fear that victimizes Osterloo in *The Dream*, the paranoic fear that grips the title characters in *Orra* and *Ethwald*, the compulsive hatred that drives De Monfort to kill an imagined enemy, the honest Rezenvelt. For an audience attuned to the stereotype villains of melodrama, Baillie's hints of a progressive aberration were too subtle. Elizabeth Inchbald, commenting on the first performance of *De Monfort* (1800) at Drury Lane with Kemble in the title role, Talbot as Rezenvelt, Siddons as Jane de Monfort, observed that 'the most attentive auditor, whilst he plainly beholds defects, asks after causes; and not perceiving those diminutive seeds of hatred, here described, till, swollen, they extend to murder, he conceives the hero of the tragedy to be more a pitiable maniac, than a man acting under the dominion of a natural propensity'.

During the last decade of the period, Mary Mitford wrote a series of historical tragedies with strong melodramatic scenes: *Julien* (1823), *The Foscari* (1826), *Rienzi* (1828), *Inez de Castro* (1831) and *Charles I* (1834). The most popular was *Rienzi*, based on Edward Gibbon's account of the revolutionary leader who, in 1347, established a Tribune of the People and endeavoured to liberate Rome from the factions of Ursini and Colonna. With Charles Young in the title role, *Rienzi* was acted 34 times in its opening season at Drury Lane. When Angelo Colonna is taken prisoner, his wife Claudia pleads with Rienzi to spare his life. Rienzi pardons Angelo, but the pardon comes too late. With the execution of Angelo, the nobles resume arms and the people abandon Rienzi. In the final scene, Rienzi surrenders alone and unarmed, but is killed on the spot, and Claudia, who cries in vain for mercy, throws herself on his body.

Few of the translators of German plays could match the work of Anne Plumptre for the polish and precision of language. Her adaptations from Kotzebue include *The Count of Burgundy* (1798), *The Natural Son* (1798), *The Force of Calumny* (1799), *The Virgin of the Sun* (1799) and *The Widow and the Riding Horse* (1799); Bell Plumptre, Anne's sister, based *The Foresters* (1799) on Iffland's *Die Jäger*. Maria Geisweiler also supplied the London stage with English versions of Kotzebue's *The Noble Lie* (1799), *Poverty and Nobleness of Mind* (1799), *Joanna of Montfaucon* (1800), subsequently altered by Cumberland for production, and August Wilhelm Iffland's *Crime from Ambition* (1799). Constantin Geisweiler provided a turn-about translation by rendering Sheridan's *Pizarro*, freely adapted from Kotzebue, back into German. A selection of the popular adaptations from Kotzebue and Iffland appeared in Thompson's *The German Theatre* (1801).

The playwrights who found success on the contemporary stage catered to the prevailing taste for spectacle and melodrama. While most of the prominent poets of the period wrote plays, few of those plays were performed. It might seem tenable, therefore, to attribute the emergence of 'closet drama', plays written to be read rather than performed, to a refusal to compromise literary quality by a vulgar appeal to display and sensation in theatrical production. William Blake's *King Edward the Third* (1783), William Wordsworth's *The Borderers* (1796), John Keats's *Otho the Great* (1819) and Percy Bysshe Shelley's *The Cenci* (1819) shared the common fate that they were never accepted for performance during the poets' own lifetimes, a fate that may have had more to do with their lack of theatrical awareness than the audience's lack of literary sophistication. Wordsworth, Shelley and Keats certainly intended their efforts for the stage rather than the closet. Furthermore, they by no means rejected the sentimental manners of the popular melodrama. Wordsworth created in the character of Rivers a villain of more complex psychological motivation than was typical of the period, and the lines given to Rivers are among the most powerful that he wrought as a poet. His Mortimer, however, is an ineffective hero, not because he is easily led, but because his role has little action. The plot is built of the improbabilities typical of melodrama. After convincing Mortimer that Herbert, the blind father of Mortimer's beloved Matilda, has sold his daughter into the clutches of the evil Baron Clifford, Rivers then persuades him that he must kill the aged Herbert.

Shelley intended *The Cenci* to be performed at Covent Garden, declaring that 'the principle character Beatrice is precisely fitted for Miss [Eliza] O'Neill, & it might even seem to have been written for her' (to Thomas Love Peacock, 20 July 1819). It played at the end of the century, and on several occasions in this century. The father–daughter incest plot is developed with the efficiency of Jacobean tragedy: Count Cenci rapes his daughter Beatrice, and she plots his death in revenge. With the exception of a few poetic mono- logues too long for performance, the dialogue is poignant and powerful, and the moral issues, fully charged with Shelley's assault on hypocrisy, are effectively dramatized.

There was good reason for a poet to turn to drama: successful theatre performance was a lucrative venue. Coleridge, when *Remorse* was performed at Drury Lane in 1813, 15 years after Sheridan had rejected the version originally entitled *Osorio*, earned more from its ten- day run than he earned from all of his other literary endeavours put together. Working directly with the actors during the rehearsals, Coleridge altered lines to improve dialogue and delivery. Robert William Elliston played the role of Alvar, appropriately mysterious in his disguise as the Moor and Sorcerer. Ordonio, played by Alexander Rae, was not as effective a villain as Coleridge wished, but the fiery Alhedra was well played by Julia Glover. The Epilogue was especially composed by Coleridge for Miss Smith, who played Teresa. Because of his desire for Teresa, betrothed to his brother, Ordonio sent Isidore, a Moorish chief, to kill Alvar. Isidore reports Alvar's death, but Alvar lives and returns, disguised as a Moor. In the meantime, Ordonio attempts to convince Teresa to give up her false hope in Alvar's return and to marry him. He commissions the mysterious Moor to play the Sorcerer and to conjure proof of Alvar's death. Before the conjuring scene commences, however, Teresa grows impatient with the mockery and walks out. As she exits, the moorish Sorcerer whispers to her that she is right to reject such mawkish displays. This is precisely the rejection of stage trickery that Coleridge had recommended to those who attended his lectures on Shakespeare. In the production of *Remorse* at Drury Lane, he has Alvar repudiate mawkish displays and then proceed to perform one. It was, in fact, precisely this *coup de théâtre* that most impressed the audience at Drury Lane. Conjuring at his altar with smouldering incense, the Sorcerer reveals in a bright phosphorescent flash a painting of the attempted assassination. Ordonio, who sought to convince Teresa of Alvar's death, suddenly is confronted with the truth of his own crime.

The one poet of the period to achieve repeated success in his dramatic endeavour was George Gordon, Lord Byron, who became a member of the Drury Lane subcommittee in May 1814, and continued to read plays for the theatre even after his departure from England in April 1816. The only play to be performed during his lifetime, and that in spite of his protests, was *Marino Faliero*, which opened at Drury Lane on 25 April. After Marino, the old Doge, had taken a young wife, the scurrilous Steno had written on the Doge's chair, 'others kiss her, but he keeps her'. The Council reprimands Steno with such a mild punishment, that Marino angrily conspires to overthrow the government, fails in the endeavour and is executed. The plot is slight, but the dialogue is vigorous. It was Macready, playing the title role, who brought *Werner* to the stage in 1830 and kept it there throughout his career. Having opposed his father's wishes by eloping with Josephine, Werner is disinherited. The estate falls into the hands of the Baron of Stralenheim. Werner's son Ulric becomes engaged to Ida, Stralenheim's daughter, and thus has the prospect of regaining the estate. Impatient for wealth he murders Stralenheim, and casts suspicion on Gabor, who manages to vindicate himself. Ulric, disclaiming all regard for his father confesses his crime to Ida, who falls senseless. Although Macready was not happy with the title role in *Sardanapalus*, it was a play that gained even greater popularity. Structurally, it is a well-crafted drama of the effete king, in the tradition of Marlowe's *Edward II* and Shakespeare's *Richard II*. But it no doubt owed its popularity on the stage more to sumptuous staging and ornate Orientalism. *The Two Foscari* was performed at Covent Garden in 1837 and again in 1839. *Manfred* was first staged at Covent Garden in 1834, with music by Henry Bishop, and during the latter part of the century it was performed in the operatic adaptation by Enrico Patrella (1874).

REFERENCES AND FURTHER READING

Baker, Herschel, *John Philip Kemble: The Actor in His Theatre*, Cambridge, Mass., Harvard University Press, 1942.

Boaden, James, *Memoirs of Mrs. Siddons*, 2 vols, London, H. Colburn, 1827.

——*Memoirs of Mrs. Inchbald*, 2 vols, London, R. Bentley, 1833.

Booth, Michael, *English Melodrama*, London, Herbert Jenkins, 1965.

——(ed.) *English Plays of the Nineteenth Century*, 5 vols, Oxford, Clarendon Press, 1969.

Booth, Michael, Southern, Richard, Marker, Frederick, Marker, Lise-Lone and Davies, Robertson (eds)

*The Revels History of the Drama, 1750–1880*, vol. 6, New York, Harper, 1976.

Burwick, Frederick, 'Romantic Drama: from Optics to Illusion', in *Literature and Science: Theory and Practice*, ed. Stuart Peterfreund, Boston, Northeastern University Press, 1990, pp. 167–208.

——*Illusion and the Drama: Critical Theory of the Enlightenment and Romantic Era*, University Park, Pennsylvania State University Press, 1991.

Cave, Richard Allen, *The Romantic Theatre: An International Symposium*, Gerrards Cross, Colin Smith, 1986.

Cox, Steven, *In the Shadows of Romance: Romantic Tragic Drama in Germany, England, and France*, Athens, Ohio, Ohio University Press, 1987.

Donehue, Joseph, *Dramatic Character in the English Romantic Age*, Princeton, Princeton University Press, 1970.

—— *Theatre in the Age of Kean*, Oxford, Blackwell, 1975.

Evans, Bertrand, *Gothic Drama from Walpole to Shelley*, Berkeley, University of California Press, 1947.

Fletcher, Richard, *English Romantic Drama, 1795–1843: A Critical History*, New York, Exposition, 1966.

Genest, John, *Some Account of the English Stage from the Restoration in 1660 to 1830*, 10 vols, Bath, H. E. Carrington, 1832.

Inchbald, Elizabeth, *The British Theatre*, 25 vols, London, Longman, Hurst, Rees and Orme, 1806–9.

McConachie, Bruce, *Melodramatic Formations*, Iowa City, Iowa University Press, 1992.

Nicoll, Allardyce, *A History of Late Eighteenth-century Drama: 1750–1800*, Cambridge, Cambridge University Press, 1927.

—— *A History of Early Nineteenth-century Drama: 1800–1850*, Cambridge, Cambridge University Press, 1930; 2nd edn 1960.

Patten, Janice, 'Joanna Baillie: passions of the mind', in 'Dark Imagination: Poetic Painting in Romantic Drama', dissertation UCSC, 1992, pp. 61–96.

Rees, Terrence, *Theatre Lighting in the Age of Gas*, London, The Society for Theatre Research, 1978.

Richardson, Alan, *A Mental Theatre: Poetic Drama and Consciousness in the Romantic Age*, University Park, Pennsylvania State University Press, 1988.

Thompson, Benjamin, *The German Theatre*, London, J. Wright, for Vernor and Hood, 1801.

Watson, Ernest B., *Sheridan to Robertson: A Study of the Nineteenth-century London Stage*, Cambridge, Mass., Harvard University Press, 1926.

# 33

# The Novel

## John Sutherland

In any period after 'the rise of the novel' there is more fiction than one can read and more, probably, than anyone will ever count. Historically, the sample becomes unmanageable by the usual machineries of critical description in the period 1780 to 1830 when, it is estimated, the population of England doubled from 7 million to 14 million and adult readers as a group quintupled from 1.5 million to over 7 million. Up to three-quarters of working-class British adults were in some sense 'literate' by 1830 and were catered for by a well-developed and complex fiction industry producing a diverse range of wares from the very sophisticated to the monotonously crude.[1]

Various strategies for making sense of fiction of the Romantic period may be devised. One can examine productive, distributive and reception systems – going behind the novels to the material apparatus that makes them.[2] One can compile chronological checklists.[3] One can identify a manageably small canon of texts, and analyse them as the best (and arguably typical) examples of the whole – this is the method favoured in most educational programmes. Or one can offer a typology of the fiction in terms of its major 'genres' or styles – which is what I propose to do here. I have mapped out the major genres along four main stems: *Gothic Fiction, Romantic Fiction, Domestic Fiction, National Tales*. Branching off are a variety of sub-genres. Any such schema will be arbitrary and I am aware of whole missing sections of the period's fiction (picaresque novels, 'Robonsoniads', children's literature and religious tracts, for example). And it is easy to point out loopholes (the protean Walter Scott, for instance, could be inserted into any of the four areas). None the less, the coverage is broad enough to make the exercise worthwhile.

## Gothic

The subsoil of late eighteenth-century Gothic fiction is the larger-than-life conceptions of Elizabethan and 'heroic' Restoration drama and the morbid musings of the 'Graveyard school' of poetry (Blair, Young, Gray). Deeper sources are found in medieval romances of chivalry. A convenient generic starting-point for the Gothic novel, as such, is Horace Walpole's *The Castle of Otranto* (1764). As Walter Scott noted, this was 'the first attempt to found a tale of amusing fiction upon the ancient romances of chivalry'.[4] Walpole spectacularly rehabilitated the term 'Gothic', rescuing it from its negative literary connotations in the Augustan period ('vandalistic' has not yet found its Walpole). He was inspired by

Bishop Richard Hurd's *Letters on Chivalry and Romance* (1762), which located the heart of chivalry in ancient Gothic civilization. Gothic fiction's rise was also boosted by Bishop Percy's *Reliques* (1765) and the cult of Ossian (Mrs Radcliffe was, like Walpole – and possibly for a while even Scott – a firm believer in the ancient Celtic Homer).

The European excitement about Goethe's *Werther*[5] significantly increased the production of novels in Britain. This coincided with the growing efficiency of the book trade in catering for the English reading public via a network of circulating libraries ('ever green trees of diabolical knowledge'). Riding these waves, the Gothic novel is, one might argue, the first mass-produced genre of English fiction. Demonstrably, *Otranto* pioneered most of the conventions of the genre – such as the pseudo-authentic documentary 'original' which the novel purported to transcribe. (Appropriately, the notorious Shakespearian forger, William Henry Ireland, was a successful second-rank Gothic novelist. He had a notable success with *The Abbess*, in 1799.) Like other Gothic practitioners, Walpole claimed the *donnée* for *Otranto* had come to him in a dream. (Allegedly, Mrs Radcliffe would eat indigestible food to give herself inspirational nightmares; Mary Shelley similarly claimed to have had the original idea for *Frankenstein* in a dream.)

Above all, Walpole's antiquarian enthusiasm for old castles was copied by his disciples. *Otranto* trade-marked many of the conventional devices of the Gothic tale – the ruined but menacing castle with its labyrinthine passageways, secret compartments, hideous dungeons, haunted suites, trapdoors, oratories and chambers of horrors. With the evident sense that it was all a rather frivolous game, Walpole was less nervous than some of his successors with the paraphernalia of ghosts and supernatural machinery. Unlike Mrs Radcliffe and her famous 'veil' in *The Mysteries of Udolpho*, for instance, he felt no need to give any rational explanation for such things as the gigantic helmet that flies from a nearby cathedral to crush malefactors. Walpole's narrative is ornamented by the languishing heroines and brooding knights who were to become standard Gothic decor, although the author remained, apparently, studiously uninterested in the erotic potential of the genre – the sexual perils, that is, which might befall the languishing heroines.

Clara Reeve proclaimed her (similarly unaphrodisiac) *The Old English Baron, A Gothic Story* (1778) to be a 'literary offspring of *The Castle of Otranto*'. So, too, were Charlotte Smith's *Old Manor House* (1793) and Charlotte Lee's surreal fantasia on the secret history of the Stuarts, *The Recess* (1783–5). Following Walpole, the Gothic pile was adopted both as a main element of Gothic romance and of the emergent historical novel – see, for instance, Scott's *Kenilworth* (1821); *Woodstock* (1826); and Victor Hugo's *The Hunchback of Notre Dame* (1830). The description of these romantic structures (in which a beautiful heroine was typically to be imprisoned) drew as much from Piranesi's *Carceri d'Invenzione* as actual monuments – although, ironically, the literature was to feed back into a style of British architectural folly of which Walpole's Strawberry Hill is a prime example.

From more domestic sources Ann Radcliffe introduced into Gothic fiction a vein of sentimentalism which is fundamentally Richardsonian in origin but drawn more closely from Henry Mackenzie's *The Man of Feeling* (1771). She also devoted much of her narrative space to exercises in the picturesque sublime, with plentiful allusion to the poetry of her admired Thomson. Mrs Radcliffe (who stresses the word 'romance' in her titles) gave Gothic fiction a more sensational impulse than Walpole. None the less her narratives, however thrilling, remained essentially moralistic and rationalistic. The Mysteries of Udolpho are all eventually explained to the patient reader.

Mrs Radcliffe (born Ann Ward, 1764–1823) is the undisputed queen of the English Gothic novel. Her father had been 'in trade' (a haberdasher), although the level of the Wards' family life was distinctly genteel. Ann was well educated (something she projects on to heroines like Emily St Aubert). In 1786 she married an Oxford-trained lawyer, William Radcliffe. A victim to lifelong ill-health, Ann Radcliffe never entered the literary life. One of the few vignettes which have come down to posterity describes her 'smilingly handing chapters to her husband which he shuddered to read'. She published a brief 'Highland Tale', *The Castles of Athlin and Dunbayne* in 1789, a melodrama set in 'Scotland, during the dark ages'. This was followed by the two-volume *A Sicilian Romance* (1790). She expanded to three volumes with *The Romance of the Forest* (1791). This, her most Gothic work to date, pleased the reading public. London booksellers offered £500 for *The Mysteries of Udolpho* (1794) and a massive £800 for its successor, *The Italian* (1797). These last two novels made Mrs Radcliffe the most popular novelist of the day, and a favourite with readers (increasingly juvenile readers) throughout the nineteenth century. Radcliffe was particularly admired for her pre-Byronic gloomy villains, La Motte, Montoni, Schedoni. Typically, her novels feature an incarcerated and persecuted heroine, and quiveringly described scenery (her grandiose Italian views, however, were taken from guidebooks and her favourite painters, Claude, Poussin and Rosa). She stops well short of the near-pornographic excesses of 'Monk' Lewis. For unknown reasons, Radcliffe left the field of popular fiction after her triumph with *The Italian*. She may have inherited money; she may have been disgusted with the extravagance of some of her imitators; she may have been influenced by her husband. Mrs Radcliffe was admired by Coleridge who called *Udolpho* 'the most interesting novel in the English language'. Scott called her 'the first poetess of romantic fiction'.

William Beckford's 'Arabian Tale', *Vathek* (1786), is a more transgressive work than anything to be found in Radcliffe's *oeuvre*. The hero of the title is a 'Calif' who sells his soul to the devil for the pre-Adamite treasures of the Sultans. Beckford's colourful fiction (it can hardly be called a novel) was Byron's 'bible'. *Vathek*'s Faustian theme was further explored by Godwin's *St Leon* (1799) and Mary Shelley's *Frankenstein* (1819). The exotic setting of *Vathek* fed into the Oriental tale brought to its highest level by James Morier.

A more 'masculine' vein of Gothic than either Radcliffe's or Beckford's was introduced by M. G. 'Monk' Lewis. Lewis, who had travelled widely in Europe, absorbed the influence of the German *Schauer-romantik* school. Through his German connection Lewis (and through Lewis a host of imitators) drew on a rich brew of paranoid suspicion about Freemasons, Illuminati and Rosicrucians that was to furnish innumerable fantasies about immortality (an aspect picked up by the German, E. T. A. Hoffman in *The Devil's Elixir*, 1815–16). The more rabid propagandist tendencies of Gothic were fuelled by popular prejudices against Catholic emancipation (Mrs Eleanor Sleath was unusual among Gothic novelists in being a Catholic who wrote sympathetically about her co-religionists).

*The Monk* (1796) is the most notorious product of 1790s English Gothic, representing a boundary through which fiction could not pass, except by the underground route of pornography. The work was begun during Lewis's stay in Germany, at a period when the author had just read *The Mysteries of Udolpho*. The novel also draws on traditionally scabrous

French 'Nunnery Tales', as spiced by Jacobin anti-clerical pornographic satire. In Lewis's novel, the dark villain (a peripheral figure in Radcliffe's narratives) is given front-of-stage prominence. The hero-villain Ambrosio owes something to the satanic hero of John Moore's *Zeluco* (1787). But the conception of a near-saint, tempted into sexually debauching under-age penitents, murdering his mother and raping his sister, is original in its tastelessness.

Following its triumph with middle-class readers there was a tidal wave of crudified chapbook versions of Lewis's novel (the 'Bleeding Nun' episode was a particular favourite with adapters) ballets, operas, and even a pantomime. The novel inspired a brief fashion for things Spanish. At a higher level, Coleridge reviewed the book in 1797 and professed to find it 'the offspring of no common genius'. Shelley's poem *The Wandering Jew* (1811) was clearly influenced, and Lewis was in the neighbourhood in Geneva when Mary Shelley conceived *Frankenstein*. De Sade saluted *The Monk* as the most perfect of all Gothic fictions. It may well have inspired Mrs Radcliffe to create her moralized monk, Schedoni, in *The Italian* (1797).

With *The Monk* Lewis popularized a vogue for what has been called 'Terror Gothic' as opposed to the 'Sentimental Gothic' of Radcliffe, Charlotte Smith, Regina Maria Roche, Eliza Parsons and Mrs Sleath, or the 'Intellectual (or Jacobin) Gothic' associated with William Godwin, Robert Bage and Thomas Holcroft.[6] However one categorizes, there was a wave of *Monk* imitations. One of the best is *Zofloya* (1806) by Charlotte Dacre ('Rosa Matilda'). Set in fifteenth-century Venice it climaxes with Zofloya, the supposed Moor, on the brink of an awful abyss, where he reveals that he is 'SATAN', and casts his deluded dupe, Victoria, down to her death (a slavish imitation of the ending of Lewis's novel).

Lewis's 'Terror Gothic' took deep regional root in 'German mad' (Scott's phrase) Edinburgh in the first decade of the nineteenth century. As cultivated by *Blackwood's Magazine* (founded in 1817), the Scottish tale of terror found its highest point in James Hogg's Calvinist shocker, *The Private Memoirs and Confessions of a Justified Sinner* (1824). More distantly, Lewis gave a lead to the 'bloods' and 'penny dreadfuls' which came into their own in the 1830s.

Two late and less contentious masterpieces of Gothic fiction are Mary Shelley's *Frankenstein* (1819) and Maturin's *Melmoth the Wanderer* (1820). Both draw on the intellectual or Jacobin branch of Gothic inaugurated by the philosopher William Godwin, who wrote six novels in the mode; notably *Caleb Williams* (1794), a novel designed to promote the author's 'Necessitarian' doctrines.[7] It is significant that in *Frankenstein* Shelley goes out of her way to stress that hers is not a novel in the degraded Radcliffe–Lewis style (although we know that she was reading *Udolpho* just before, and Lewis was a regular visitor). It is also significant that Maturin indicates in his preface to *Melmoth* that only utter penury could induce him to write a Gothic novel.

The decline in Gothic fiction's esteem was partly brought about by the theatre, which routinely popularized high-brow Gothics for the masses. But whatever the cause, by 1820 the genre was regarded as *déclassée*. The excesses of post-Radcliffe, post-Lewis Gothic were 'corrected' by such satire as that of the *Anti-Jacobin* magazine in the 1790s (which regarded the genre as sympathetic with French Revolutionary excesses) and most famously by Jane Austen in the depiction of Isabella Thorpe in *Northanger Abbey* (written in 1798, but still topical when published in 1818) and by Peacock in *Nightmare Abbey* (1818). By this date, anti-Gothic had become a genre (or a self-justifying narrative gesture) in its own right. See, for example, Scott's prophylactic jest in the opening paragraphs of *Waverley*: 'had my title borne, "*Waverley*, a Romance from the German," what head so obtuse as not to image forth a profligate abbot, an oppressive duke, a secret and mysterious association of Rosicrucians and Illuminati, with all their properties of black cowls, caverns, daggers, electrical machines, trap-doors, and dark lanterns?'

Gothic, if it became unfashionable among the middle-class readers of England, survived in what Louis James calls 'fiction for the working man'. It can also be seen to sow the seed of two mass-market modern fictional genres, science fiction and horror. Brian Aldiss has convincingly made the case that *Frankenstein* is the foundation text of Anglo-American 'sf'.[8] Shelley reinforced her claim to be the founder of science fiction with *The Last Man* (written in 1824, published in 1826), which is set in the twenty-first century, and depicts humankind wiped out by plague, leaving one Crusoe-like survivor.

John Polidori's *The Vampyre: A Tale* (1819) can similarly lay claim to have been the begetter of thousands of works of fiction in the horror genre. Literary legend has it that Polidori's tale was inspired by the same wet summer parlour games in Geneva that produced *Frankenstein* – thus were two of the most popular themes of popular entertainment simultaneously launched on their nineteenth-century career. *The Vampyre* (a much shorter work than Shelley's) tells the story of a young Englishman ('handsome, frank, and rich') called Aubrey, who is infatuated by a suave older nobleman (with a penetrating 'dead grey eye') called Lord Ruthven. Ruthven is, it emerges, a vampire with all the monster's foul appetites.

## Romance

In the mid-eighteenth century, romance denoted a specific corpus of sagas of chivalry (works such as *Amadis of Gaul*). Charlotte Lennox's anti-romance *The Female Quixote* (1752) satirizes the heroine Arabella's dangerous infatuation with these old tales (as do the opening chapters of *Waverley*). With Clara Reeve's authoritative distinction (in *The Progress of Romance*, 1785), 'romance' was identified as a narrative set in the past, as opposed to the 'novel' which is set in the present (this, broadly, seems to have been the definition accepted by Scott and his many followers). But, as the lexical ambiguities of the term suggest, 'romance' became a label applied to that huge volume of fiction concerned with love (whether in the present or in the past) and to fiction which 'romanticizes' the lives of the rich and famous.

The bread-and-butter formulaic 'love story' in the Romantic period is commonly identified (as is 'Mills and Boon' today) by the name of its principal producer. The Minerva Press was a London publishing house established in Leadenhall Street in 1790 which was the principal purveyor of novels to circulating libraries for 30 years. 'Minerva' became a synonym for a certain kind of popular fiction, aimed principally at the woman reader. Although it did not publish the hugely successful authors of the day (such as Radcliffe, Dacre or Lewis) it put out distinctively flavoured lines of romance and Gothic fiction, the bulk of it by women writers. The average price paid a Minerva author for her copyright was around £30. Minerva's best-known authors were Agnes [Anna] Maria Bennett, Mary

Meeke, Regina Maria Roche and Eliza Parsons. The imprint was later associated with the 'Minerva Public Library', Leadenhall Street, which advertised a stock of 11,000 volumes and charged five guineas a year for first-class membership.

The Minerva Press product was unambitious, anodyne in content and wearyingly formulaic. More interesting, from a literary (and a sociological) point of view, is the fashionable or 'silver fork'[9] novel. With titles such as *Matilda, A Tale of the Day* (1825), by Lord Normanby, or Mrs Gore's *Women as They Are, or the Manners of the Day* (1830), the fashionable novel of the 1820s offered a bulletin on what the *monde* was doing, for the delectation of the novel-reading middle classes. The genre was given its characteristic 'smartness' by Theodore Hook's ostentatiously witty *Sayings and Doings* (1828). Hook also pioneered the genre's characteristic indiscretion, and *roman-à-clef* aspect (it was common for fashionable novels' sales to be boosted by clandestinely circulated 'keys' to the identities of the principal characters.)[10]

'The fashionable novel' was a dominant line of fiction from the mid-1820s until the mid-1840s. The mastermind behind silver forkery was the publisher Henry Colburn. In 1825–6, at a time when the book trade was prostrated by a recession, Colburn embarked on a saturation campaign of publishing short-life bestsellers, exploiting post-Regency fascination with high life. His first hits were Hook's social comedies, Disraeli's romance of political life, *Vivian Grey* (1826, 1827), T. H. Lister's languidly Byronic *Granby* (1826) and Robert Plumer Ward's *Tremaine* (1825). Each of these works purported to be composed by an insider, privy to the intimate secrets of the aristocracy and willing to divulge all to a middle-class reading public. Colburn is estimated to have put his imprint on three-quarters of the 500 or so silver-fork novels subsequently published. He was happiest when he could recruit to his list actual aristocrats such as the Marquess of Normanby, Lady Bury, and the Countess of Blessington.

The most interesting of Colburn's silver-fork productions is *Vivian Grey*. Disraeli claimed to have written the story before he was 21, urged by financial need following the 1825–6 banking crash (the same catastrophe that ruined Sir Walter Scott and forced him into the furious novel-writing that killed him in six years). Disraeli received £200 for the first part of the novel and £500 for the second part, which Colburn persuaded him to add in 1827. *Vivian Grey* was an instant hit, assisted by its publisher's 'shameless puffery'. Colburn put out with the novel a supposedly clandestine 'Key', indicating the famous people introduced in the narrative under thin disguise. Colburn also whipped up huge speculation as to who the apparently omniscient insider author could be. There was universal rage when it was discovered that the author was a '22-year-old nobody, and a Jew!' Disparaging it as 'a book written by a boy', Disraeli attempted in later life to suppress *Vivian Grey*, whose inextinguishable popularity he saw as damaging to his political career.

Colburn's biggest success was Edward Bulwer's *Pelham* (1828). This portrait of a modish 'gentleman' (a Byronic coxcomb to his detractors) profoundly affected contemporary sensibility and fashion. (It led directly, for example, to the universal Victorian style of dark suiting for men.) The success of *Pelham* promoted Bulwer to the £1,000-a-novel rank, and second only to Scott as the best-paid novelist in Britain.

As a conduct book for young men about town, *Pelham* revived Beau Brummel's cult and established 'Pelhamism' as a social ideology, equivalent to Wertherism and even Byronism. In the short term, *Pelham* gave a huge boost to fiction of fashionable life. It affronted Tory critics, particularly. Pelham's obsession with his clothes (he has three glove makers) infuriated Carlyle, who constructed his great satire on the present age, *Sartor Resartus* (1834), on a repudiation of *Pelham*.

The novel of high life necessitated its polar opposite, the novel of low life and its offshoot, the sporting novel. The archetype of these sub-genres is found in Pierce Egan's *Life in London* (1820–1; the first issue of the novel was published monthly in serial parts, illustrated by the young George Cruikshank, among others). The full title is descriptive of the narrative contents: *Life in London, or, the Day and Night Scenes of Jerry Hawthorne, Esq., and his elegant Friend Corinthian Tom, accompanied by Bob Logic, the Oxonian, in their Rambles and Sprees through the Metropolis.* Egan's novel – which drew both on Smolletian picaresque and the energies of new London journalism – was hugely successful. The narrative is a loose series of 'scenes' set in all levels of the metropolis, with a plentiful supply of fashionable slang and (in the low-life episodes) 'flash', or criminal argot. The young men-about-town disport themselves in such London resorts as Rotten Row, Covent Garden, Almack's, Vauxhall Gardens, the Royal Academy and – at the very top of London society – Carlton House. They frequent dogfights (both are 'sportsmen' or 'bucks', in the Regency sense of the word), gin palaces and brothels – all in a spirit of high jinks. They drink immoderately, gamble, roger 'Cyprians' (whores), play pranks on watchmen and come up before the beak next morning. The novel celebrates London fun and the anarchic youth culture promoted by the postwar years of the Regency. *Life in London* was adapted for the stage in numerous 'extravaganza' or burlesque versions. 'Tom and Jerry' hats became all the rage, and Egan's *joie de vivre* survives to the present day in the antics of a cartoon cat and mouse.

Another offshoot from the fashionable novel, via the fertile pen of Edward Bulwer (later Bulwer-Lytton) was the detective novel. Bulwer introduces a famous actual murder (that by John Thurtell) and its detection into *Pelham*. Bulwer's interest in crime was ideological, and strongly influenced by the Godwinian novel of ideas and Godwinian opposition to capital punishment (the publication of the French detective Vidocq's *Memoirs* in 1828 was also influential, as was Hugo's vivid *The Last Day of a Condemned Man*, 1828). Bulwer plunged into crime as fictional subject matter with the first of the so-called Newgate novels (i.e. fiction whose subject matter is drawn from the *Newgate Calendar*) *Paul Clifford* (1830). This romance of a highwayman by night, dandy by day, was overwhelmingly popular. Reportedly, a larger first impression of *Paul Clifford* was printed than of any novel hitherto, 'and yet all sold out on the day of publication'. Bulwer proclaimed the novel's Godwinian motive in the prefaces to subsequent reprintings of the novel (of which there were very many). Specifically, he conceived the novel to be written against the severities of the pre-Peelite 'bloody' legal code, in the belief that 'circumstances cause crime'. As a potent element in an anti-capital punishment campaign, *Paul Clifford* can also be seen as one of English literature's first novels with a purpose – or social protest novels. (In the same week that *Paul Clifford* was published, Bulwer was elected to parliament as a radically inclined MP).

## Domestic Fiction

The polar opposite to the Romance and Gothic genres, domestic fiction and its various sub-genres created the channels through which realism was to evolve in the later nineteenth-century novel. In the last decades of the eighteenth and early nineteenth century, the domestic tale and the 'improving' ideals it inculcated exercised a strong influence on subsequent English fiction (particularly novels aimed at young people). A convenient starting place is Goldsmith's *The Vicar of Wakefield* (1766) and its panegyric on the Revd Primrose, a domestic paragon who 'unites in himself the three greatest characters upon earth; he is a priest, an husbandman, and the father of a family'. Celebration of the central virtues of middle-class family life, and its role as a haven against the vicissitudes of the world, was to be the central tenet of the domestic novel. The top layer of domestic fiction contains writers of the calibre of Fanny Burney, Maria Edgeworth and Jane Austen. At its base it merges into the voluminous tract and improving-tale industry. The evangelical writer Hannah More (1745–1833) set up a printing house, the Cheap Repository, to fight the 'immoral' popular novel's fire with fire. The Repository produced 114 narrative tracts between 1795 and 1798, of which More wrote 50 herself.

More later wrote an instructive novel, *Coelebs in Search of a Wife* (1809), which was to prove massively successful in Britain and (even more so) America for 50 years. Barbara Hofland (1770–1844) was obliged to turn to fiction to support her family when her first husband died and when her second lost his money. This enterprising woman wrote (among some 60 improving works of fiction) a batch of novels celebrating indomitable widows and mothers, including *The History of an Officer's Widow and her Young Family* (1809) and *The Clergyman's Widow* (1812 – a work which is recorded as selling 17,000 copies). Mrs Martha Sherwood (1775–1851), out of her experience as an officer's wife in India, wrote the much-reprinted *Little Henry and his Bearer* (1814) and the extraordinarily successful *The History of the Fairchild Family* (3 parts, 1818–47). Mrs Inchbald's (1753–1821) *A Simple Story* (1791) is another pioneer text of the domestic mode.

The early highpoint of the domestic tale is Fanny Burney's *Camilla: Or A Picture of Youth* (1796), the occasion of the most successful literary marketing operation in fiction in the 1790s. At a period when the routine payment to authors for a circulating-library romance was £10, Burney made from this one work a reported £2,000. Miss Burney had left the royal entourage in July 1791, having been second keeper of the robes to Queen Charlotte for five years (Charlotte was to be the dedicatee of *Camilla*). To establish a home for her family, Burney meditated a *grand ouvrage* and began serious work in August 1794. Together with her husband she set up a subscription for the new work (Jane Austen and Edmund Burke were among the signatories). Three months after *Camilla's* publication, Burney reported to a friend that 'The sale has been one of the most rapid ever known for a Guinea book'. She built a home, Camilla Cottage, on the earnings.

*Camilla* takes the form of the group story of the Tyrold family over some 20 years during which the children grow to moral maturity, exhibiting their latent qualities and the effect of the moral instruction their excellent parent, the Revd Augustus Tyrold, has instilled into them. A main theme in the novel – something that was to be immensely influential on subsequent fiction (especially fiction for women by women) – is the overriding importance of making the right marriage choices.

A significant offshoot of the domestic genre is the village tale. Idyllic celebrations of the beauties of village life form a line of popular fiction running from eighteenth-century pastorals to the latest instalment of *The Archers*. Goldsmith's *Vicar of Wakefield* and the nostalgic depiction of Auburn in *The Deserted Village* constitute the principal influences on the village tale. Quaker writers such as Mary Leadbeater (1758–1826) and Amelia Opie (1799–1888) were to cultivate a strong line in uplifting village tales. Elizabeth Le Noir's (1754–1841) *Village Anecdotes* (1804) and Elizabeth Hamilton's (1758–1816) *The Cottagers of Glenburnie* (1808) enjoyed considerable popularity, despite a paternalistic moralism. John Galt's depictions of Scottish provincial life (notably *The Annals of the Parish*, 1821) look forward to the 'Kailyard' sentimentalities later in the century. Mary Russell Mitford's five-volume *Our Village* (1824–32) was probably the most successful product in the sub-genre's bestsellers.

As will be evident from the names in the preceding paragraphs, domestic fiction was dominated by women writers. And it is feasible to connect with the genre the supremely great woman novelist of the Romantic period – Jane Austen. One could fancifully cast *Emma* (1816) as a novel of village (Highbury) life; *Sense and Sensibility* (1811) is, from one aspect, a plucky widow's tale; *Mansfield Park* (1814), like *Camilla*, is a 'Picture of Youth'. And all Austen's heroines are female Coelebs, in search of a husband. But like Walter Scott, the other supremely great novelist of the period, Austen transcends easy generic categor-ization, although it is clear that her genius drew nourishment from a myriad of lesser novelists.

## The National Tale

Fiction was routinely used in the late eighteenth and early nineteenth centuries to advance nationalist causes – principally by cherishing or inventing myths about the nation's glorious past. A useful starting-point for the English national tale in its modern (i.e. Romantic period) form is Thomas Leland's *Longsword, Earl of Salisbury, An Historical Romance* (1762). Set in the thirteenth century, it anticipates Walpole's *The Castle of Otranto* by a couple of years, but unlike that work is aggressively 'English' and un-Gothic. Clara Reeve's *The Old English Baron* (1778) was the most influential and reprinted work in this vein, and anticipates in some respects Scott's *Ivanhoe* (1819).

These national tales celebrate the peculiar virtues of English (specifically 'Saxon') democracy, as founded and defended by English knights and barons. In the immediate context, they served as a useful prophylactic against Jacobin infection and the horrors of French Revolution. Scott's *Kenilworth* (1821), which celebrated the cult of Queen Eliza-beth's glorious reign, was timed to coincide with George IV's coronation and is a high-point of the English-chauvinist sub-genre.

The Scottish national tale was popularized by Jane Porter's *The Scottish Chiefs* (1810), which derived much of its popularity from British belligerence against Napoleon, and the achievements of the Highland regiments in the Peninsular campaign. Porter's wooden eulogy on Scottish warrior nobility in the wars against the English re-emerges in the 1995 film *Braveheart* (as does, in very mangled form, Scott's *Rob Roy*). Porter's other great success was the Polish national tale, *Thaddeus of Warsaw* (1803). Initially boosted by the country's wartime mood, this tale of insurrection against the Russian oppressor was hugely popular in England.

An odd offshoot of the national tale is the Oriental tale. The first translations of the *Arabian Nights* began to appear in the early eighteenth century, and the apparatus of the eastern tale was used for philosophical disquisition (the most famous English example is Johnson's *Rasselas*, 1759). Exploitation of the setting in English popular fiction begins with Beckford's *Vathek* (1786). Poets like Southey (*The Curse of Kehama*, 1810; *Thalaba*, 1801), Thomas Moore (*Lalla Rookh*, 1817) and Byron (*Don Juan*, 1819–24) made florid use of Oriental episodes. In fiction, Sydney Owenson's (Lady Morgan's) *The Missionary* (1811) is set in India, and Maturin's *Melmoth the Wanderer* (1820) has an inset Indian tale. Scott used a Syrian setting for his tale of the Crusades, *The Talisman* (1825). But the Oriental tale was given its most characteristic turn by James Morier's enjoyably kitsch (and bestselling) *The Adventures of Haji Baba* (1824) and its successors.

After Scotland and England, Ireland furnished the richest crop of national tales. Sydney Owenson's *The Wild Irish Girl* (1806, subtitled 'A National Tale') has, at its centre, a long disquisition on the aboriginal culture of the pre-colonial Irish civilization, but finally – as does Hamilton's *The Cottages of Glenburnie* (1808) – accepts the reality of English land-lordism. The Irish national tale, a sub-genre which always sold well in England, was further popularized by the Banim brothers (John and Michael), whose first series of 'O'Hara Family' stories came out in 1825. The Banims claim attention as folklorists, Irish nationalists and pioneers of regional authenticity in early nineteenth-century fiction. Their fiction laid down many of the popular stereotypes of the Irish later exploited by popular fiction, stage and film.

The greatest of the Irish national tales produced during the period is, however, the earliest: Maria Edgeworth's *Castle Rackrent* (1800). This powerful melodrama of Irish life in the mid-eighteenth century was an influence which Scott acknowledged in his after-word to *Waverley* (1815). It is a moot point as to which of these novels, Edgeworth's or Scott's, is properly the first historical novel in English. Whichever, historical fiction was the most notable evolution of the national tale, and its great exponent was the 'Author of *Waverley*' (following common eighteenth-century practice, Scott wrote anonymously, revealing his authorial identity only in 1826).

Convenient as it is to bracket Scott as 'our greatest historical novelist' the categorization does him a disservice. Like Austen, he transcends the genres that he habitually draws on. But unlike her, he is the spawner of innumerable sub-genres. One could write a whole history of nineteenth-century fiction in terms of the styles Scott invented. The nautical tale, for instance, can plausibly be said to begin with Scott's *The Pirate* (1822), and James Fenimore Cooper's corrective response (drawing on his authentic experiences at sea), *The Pilot* (1824). Via Cooper's leatherstocking tales which begin with *The Pioneers* (1823), and are frankly derived from *Rob Roy* (1817), Scott can claim to be father of the 'Western'. *Guy Mannering* (1815) patents in one of its subplots the 'gipsy novel' (later to become immensely popular). The low-life London scenes in *The Fortunes of Nigel* (1822) were taken over by later Newgate writers. Through his connection with *Blackwood's*, Scott strongly influenced James Hogg's tale of terror, *Confessions of a Justified Sinner*. And the 'pawky' regionalized framework of the *Tales of my Landlord* had a formative influence on the 'parochial' fiction of John Galt. With the sequential *The Monastery* (1820) and *The Abbot* (1820) he invented the multi-novel saga (later to be exploited by Balzac and Trollope). One could go on, finding novelties in all Scott's fiction up to the disastrous year 1825 (when he was financially ruined). It is a source of wonder that the two undisputed giants of the novel in this period, Scott and Austen, should have expressed their genius so differently: she, working ever more scrupulously on her two inches of ivory, he, never repeating himself and throwing off new possibilities for fiction with every novel he wrote.

## NOTES

1 I take these figures from Louis James's *Print and the People, 1819–1851* (London, 1971).

2 A pioneer example of this kind of literary sociology is Q. D. Leavis's *Fiction and the Reading Public* (London, Chatto and Windus, 1932). Leavis's notion of a kind of postlapsarian fall, with a concomitant nineteenth-century 'industrialization' of fiction, was questioned and denied by J. M. S. Tompkins's *The Popular Novel*.

3 Gary Kelly has compiled an excellent chronological checklist as an appendix to his *English Fiction of the Romantic Period*, which is currently the best book-length introduction to the subject. Other valuable catalogues of titles, authors and publication details can be found in Andrew Block, *The English Novel, 1740–1850: A Catalogue including Prose Romances, Short Stories, and Translations of Foreign Fiction* (London, Grafton, 1939); and A. J. M. A. Montague Summers, *A Gothic Bibliography* (London, Fortune Press, 1940).

4 Scott's views on Walpole and other (more contemporary) novelists are to be found in his 'Lives of the Novelists' (1821), conveniently collected by Ioan Williams (ed.), *Sir Walter Scott on Novelists and Fiction* (London, Routledge and Kegan Paul, 1968).

5 Goethe's *The Sorrows of Young Werther* (1774) sparked off what is probably the first 'mania' in the consumption of fiction. 'Wertherism' swept across Europe like a plague, leaving behind it a carpet of adolescent suicides. Less desperate devotees, it is reported, 'wore blue coats and yellow breeches in imitation of Werther; china tea-sets were produced with scenes from the novel depicted on them, and perfumes named after Werther were sold'.

6 A critical anatomy of the sub-genre is offered in Gary Kelly, *The English Jacobin Novel*. Marilyn Butler, in *Jane Austen and the War of Ideas*, chapter six, offers an extended analysis of Godwin's *Caleb Williams* and Robert Bage's *Hermsprong* (1796). Butler's book usefully contextualizes Austen among the intellectual controversies of her times.

7 *Caleb Williams*, with its crime and punishment plot, has been identified, *inter alia*, as the first detective novel in English (see, for instance, Julian Symons, *Bloody Murder*, London, Faber and Faber, 1972). Godwin's novel was crudely adapted as the play *The Iron Chest* (1796) by George Colman, Jr, and became one of the two or three most popular items in the nineteenth-century dramatic repertoire.

8 See Brian Aldiss, *The Billion-Year Spree* (London, Weidenfeld and Nicolson, 1973). Aldiss's science-fictional homage to Mary Shelley, *Frankenstein Unbound*, was published in the same year.

9 The term 'silver fork' derives from William Hazlitt, writing in the *Examiner*, 1827. The term, with its implied scorn, was picked up by *Fraser's Magazine*, which in the 1830s launched a savage campaign against the genre for its snobbishness and deference to aristocratic values.

10 The most notorious *roman-à-clef* of the period was Lady Caroline Lamb's *Glenarvon* (1816), which transcribes, under thin fictional disguise, her adulterous affair with Byron (Ruthven Glenarvon) in the novel. The book was scandalous and very popular. Ruthven is also (not coincidentally) the name of Polidori's *The Vampyre*.

## REFERENCES AND FURTHER READING

Altick, Richard D., *The English Common Reader: A Social History of the Mass Reading Public 1800–1900*, Chicago, University of Chicago Press, 1963.

Butler, Marilyn, *Jane Austen and the War of Ideas*, Oxford, Oxford University Press, 1987.

Kelly, Gary, *The English Jacobin Novel, 1780–1805*, Oxford, Oxford University Press, 1976.

——*English Fiction of the Romantic Period*, London, Longman, 1989.

Mayo, Robert D., *The English Novel in the Magazines, 1740–1815*, Evanston, Ill., Northwestern Press, 1962.

Punter, David, *The Literature of Terror: A History of Gothic Fiction from 1765 to the Present Day*, London, Longman, 1980.

Spencer, Jane, *The Rise of the Woman Novelist: From Aphra Behn to Jane Austen*, Oxford, Blackwell, 1986.

Tompkins, J. M. S., *The Popular Novel in England, 1770–1800*, (London, 1932; reprinted London, Methuen, 1961.

# 34

# Gothic Fiction

## David S. Miall

## Introduction

The rapid increase in the production of Gothic fiction in the 1790s and beyond is one of the more remarkable but also one of the less well understood phenomena of the British Romantic period. Before this, only a handful of novels in the genre had been produced, and readers and critics paid them little attention. Yet from 1800 onwards some 20–30 titles a year were being published, and the influence of the genre is readily apparent in the literary journals and in the writings of the Romantic poets. It is also an influence that persists long after its immediate efflorescence is over in the 1820s, extending into canonical works by authors such as Charles Dickens, Wilkie Collins, the Brontes and Henry James. This sudden rise of the Gothic is only the first of several intriguing issues involved in studying this genre.

A second question can be raised about the meaning of the term 'Gothic'. The term appears at the outset of the history of the genre, as part of the subtitle of the second edition (1765) of Horace Walpole's *The Castle of Otranto*, generally considered the first novel in the genre. While several features of this novel, such as the castle and the Gothic villain, recur frequently in later fictions considered Gothic (by Ann Radcliffe and Matthew Lewis), they are absent from other key texts considered to belong to the genre (Shelley's *Frankenstein* or Hogg's *Private Memoirs and Confessions of a Justified Sinner*). Thus, the Gothic cannot be defined simply as a certain type of setting or character.

At the same time, the Gothic is clearly a vehicle for aesthetic concerns. The term 'Gothic' was, after all, applied to a style of architecture long before it came into use in literature. Before Vitruvius and Palladio shaped English taste after Greek and Roman models, the dominant form of building, as in the great cathedrals, castles and abbeys of Northern Europe, had been Gothic for five centuries. Paradoxically, even while classical styles came to dominate British and colonial building in the early eighteenth century, rich landowners were beginning to commission Gothic 'follies' in their gardens. Walpole's mansion Strawberry Hill had an artificial origin of this kind in his own Gothic fantasies.

Unlike classical architecture, with its appeal to proportion, orderliness, light and reason, the appeal of Gothic architecture is to the sublime – to the forces of vastness, power, obscurity and terror described in Edmund Burke's highly influential treatment of the sublime, *A Philosophical Enquiry* (1757). In the gloomy receding depths of a Gothic cathedral, or below the crumbling battlements of an ancient castle, we begin with Burke's help to see the extraordinary resource that such architecture provides for elaborating psychological states. In a period conventionally said to pre-date the discovery of the unconscious, the hidden passageway, the vault and the dungeon began to provide suggestive analogues for mental states or passions for which only figurative expression was possible. However, several of the more notable writers later in the period emancipated themselves from these trappings. Shelley's *Frankenstein* and Hogg's *Confessions* require no ruined abbeys or dungeons: they find equivalent or perhaps more subtle means for intimating the hidden architecture of the mind.

While there is no doubt of the interest of most Gothic authors in states of the mind, there is some question about where this concern might lead. Understandably, psychoanalytic criticism has tended to focus on evidence for the 'family romance', as Freud called it, in the frequent generational conflicts in the fiction, or on the struggle between the Imaginary and Symbolic realms, in Lacanian terms (roughly, the pre-linguistic and the linguistic). Focus on the entrapment or passivity of the female characters has enabled feminist critics to examine questions of gender that seem to lie beneath the surface of many Gothic fictions.

In general, the Gothic at its best gives a sense of straining to exceed some limit. Unlike either the 'sentimental' fiction of the previous decades, out of which it partly emerged (such as Goldsmith, Sterne and Mackenzie), or the early 'realist' fiction of Burney, Edgeworth and Austen, which found a ready acceptance on the part of readers and reviewers, Gothic fiction led a curious borderline existence, widely read, but on the margins of both respectability and literariness. We confront the paradox most directly when we turn to consider the novels of Ann Radcliffe, arguably the most talented of the Gothic authors we will examine; but the sense of something off-limits and inchoate runs through all the most interesting Gothic fictions of the period. It is perhaps this that gives the disparate works of this genre such commonality as they possess.

In the discussion that follows, the Gothic themes I have just sketched will be elaborated in a broadly historical account of the Gothic, from its beginnings with Walpole to its close in the 1820s. This will also serve to raise further critical questions about the Gothic, but the order of discussion is determined by a provisional classification of the texts as conservative or radical Gothic.

## The Conservative Gothic: Walpole to Austen

A principle motive behind both Walpole's writing of *The Castle of Otranto* and his remodelling of Strawberry Hill to a Gothic mansion was nostalgia for a lost feudal past. But Walpole's appeal to the Gothic was part of a more general interest developing during the mid-eighteenth century in what opposed the orderly and rational. In his preface to the second edition of the novel, Walpole deliberately aligns his narrative technique with Shakespeare, 'That great master of nature', at the same time as he disparages Voltaire's strictures on Shakespeare. Thus, Walpole's work, like much that followed, can be seen as a reaction against the order and rules of the Enlightenment: with its privileging of classical models it excluded too much and could be seen as oppressive to the liberties of the poetic imagination.

But whereas Enlightenment thinking had begun to question the political systems of the time (thus preparing the ground for the French Revolution), Walpole, the son of a Prime Minister, clearly has no such intention. The function of the ghosts and portents in the novel is to restore the violated property rights of the 'true' owners of the province of Otranto, which requires that Manfred, the present occupant, be driven out. The helmet and other mysterious body parts glimpsed early in the novel act like the fragments of a Freudian super-ego that externalizes Manfred's conscience. In later Gothic fiction the supernatural will take on demonic meaning, but in *Otranto*, hovering between the sublime and the comic, it is the catalyst that helps restore Theodore, whose aristocratic origin shines through his peasant exterior, to his rightful place. The plot thus seems to argue for the perpetuation of the class values of a feudalist patriarchy. That this is not accidental is shown by the occurrence of comparable plot devices in later texts by Reeve, Radcliffe and Lewis.

Complicating issues, however, ensure that *Otranto* is more than a pure romance plot. Two features in particular endow it with its Gothic status: the figure of Manfred, and the use of the setting. In the energy and violence of Manfred we see the first example of a type: the Gothic villain who takes a variety of forms in numerous later texts, from Montoni in *The Mysteries of Udolpho*, through Falkland in *Caleb Williams*, to Melmoth in Maturin's novel, and who will evolve into a Heathcliffe or a Rochester in the hands of the Brontë sisters. As the literary offspring of Milton's Satan in *Paradise Lost*, the character is liable to be read as Blake read Milton: he forms the chief interest of the text besides which other characters may seem flat and bloodless. However, while Manfred's assumptions about marriage are drawn from earlier, conservative rules about the transmission of property rights through marriage, the younger characters are motivated by a later affectional view of marriage that, as historians of the family have shown, developed in uneasy opposition to the property view during the eighteenth century. Manfred's invocation of the earlier view, with its destructive effects, thus undercuts the conservative values apparently espoused by the novel.

Another important Gothic component also involves a second paradox: this lies in the use that the novel makes of its setting. When Isabella escapes from Manfred's advances into the underground passageways of the castle, her experience invokes the categories elaborated by Burke: darkness, obscurity, vastness and the terror arising from them which is the hall-mark of the sublime. The claustral imagery of these pages, together with the fact that Isabella, a defenceless virgin, is fleeing from male power, made this a particularly pregnant topos for later Gothic writers, although it was not to be taken up explicitly until Radcliffe's first novels 25 years later. Burke associated the sublime with classic male texts, such as the Bible, Shakespeare and Milton: his sublime is a thoroughly gendered concept. Yet for Gothic authors, both male and female, the underground setting becomes especially associated with the sexual ambience of female danger (as in *Otranto*) or discovery (e.g. Radcliffe's *Sicilian Romance*), and seems to call for a specifically female response not envisaged in the public discourse on the sublime. In this respect too, then, the conservative text seems to be troubled by a counter-current, although one that receives little serious attention in *Otranto*.

It is perhaps significant that the novels generally seen as central to the early Gothic, including Clara Reeve's *The Old English Baron* (1781) and Sophia Lee's *The Recess* (1783–5), each develop a plot that hinges on bringing family secrets to light, in particular the mysteries of birth. The supernatural interventions in Walpole and Reeve thus have some relation to Freud's important argument on the uncanny (1919). By showing that the German word for the uncanny, *unheimlich*, has its root in the word for home, *heimlich*, Freud was able to argue that the 'uncanny is in reality nothing new or alien, but something which is familiar and old-established in the mind and which has become alienated from it only through the process of repression'.

From Manfred's point of view, his illegitimacy as the holder of Otranto is clearly, in Freud's words, 'something which ought to have remained hidden but has come to light' (Freud, 'The Uncanny', p. 241). While Freud aims to uncover issues such as infantile sexuality and the Oedipal crisis, his framework for explaining the uncanny also points usefully to other relevant aspects: the 'omnipotence of thoughts' (ibid., p. 244) reminds us that Manfred's mere intentions (in proposing to marry Isabella) conjure up supernatural interventions analogous to those animate powers that once haunted us in early childhood; while Freud's 'repetition compulsion' (ibid., p. 238) will be seen most clearly in the uncanny story of the Bleeding Nun in Lewis's *The Monk*.

Although psychoanalytic insights offer an important avenue for understanding the Gothic (a point to which I return below), the latter's historical context also seems critical. It cannot be coincidence that major works by Radcliffe and Lewis and the rapid rise in popularity of the Gothic occurred during the 1790s while the French Revolution and the first European wars were unfolding (Godwin's work, of course, had an explicit relation to contemporary politics). Should Gothic be considered escapist fiction, a part of that out-pouring of 'frantic novels' of which Wordsworth complained in his Preface to *Lyrical Ballads* (1800)? Or is there, in Punter's words, a 'very intense, if displaced, engagement with political and social problems' (Punter, *The Literature of Terror*, p. 54)? The question is especially problematic when we turn to consider the work of Radcliffe, perhaps the most accomplished contributor to the Gothic genre during the Romantic period.

The novel that made Radcliffe's reputation, *The Romance of the Forest* (1791), was her third: it remained a touchstone for later criticism. Coleridge, for example, seems to have preferred it to the two novels that followed. Curiously, it is also the only novel in which a political dimension is clearly implied. In volume three the heroine Adeline takes refuge in Savoy with a Protestant minister, La Luc, whose character and principles are directly modelled on Rousseau's Savoyard vicar in *Emile*. Rousseau's name by 1791 was comprom-ised by association with the French Revolution, but Radcliffe deploys this character to illuminate the principles of simple living, charity and education (La Luc has two children), in contrast to the Epicurean corruption of the Marquis de Montalt from whom Adeline has fled. Although Radcliffe shares in the anti-Catholicism that is general to the Gothic, it is far from clear if we should attribute radical principles to her fiction.

A strong influence on Radcliffe is the sentimental tradition of Sterne or Mackenzie, especially, as we shall see, a significant debate about the role of sensibility which she inherits; but Shakespeare, Jacobean drama and Milton are also important contributors to her resources. In the attention she gives to landscape and what we might call an aesthetics of terror, she can be termed the first writer of poetic fiction. At the same time, aiming for poetic effects causes her some problems in narrative technique and plotting: awkward shifts in focalization occur, key characters are often stereotyped, and there is an undue use of coincidence. Even the poetic is somewhat repetitive, especially scenes of twilight and dusk, as critics of *Udolpho* (1794) in particular noted.

But Radcliffe's poetic stance is governed by a principle central to her achievement. In an essay published after her death, Radcliffe argued for the importance of obscurity. This, she noted, is an essential part of the terror of the sublime.

> Terror and horror are so far opposite, that the first expands the soul, and awakens the faculties to a high degree of life; the other contracts, freezes, and nearly annihilates them. . . . where lies the great difference between terror and horror, but in the uncertainty and obscurity, that accompany the first, respecting the dreaded evil?

Obscurity, in short, 'leaves the imagination to act upon the few hints that truth reveals to it' (Radcliffe, 'On the supernatural in poetry', pp. 149–50). Terror is thus seen as empowering, facilitating escape; horror in contrast freezes and incapacitates. Radcliffe's emphasis on obscurity is drawn from earlier writing on the picturesque, notably by William Gilpin, who also favoured the dusk. Radcliffe's development of this stance towards nature, as critics have often noted, anticipated the poetics of writers such as Wordsworth and Coleridge. But her distinction between terror and horror has also been adopted as a basis for contrasting two different kinds of Gothic fiction: the Terror Gothic of Walpole or Radcliffe on the one hand, with the Horror Gothic of Lewis or Maturin on the other (Hume, 'Gothic versus romantic'). It is only in the latter that events or objects intended to appal the reader are specified in detail. Such fictions seem to result in more pessimistic or cynical types of narrative.

Radcliffe's narratives, however, are essentially optimistic, although her heroines face severe and, across the course of her five Gothic novels, increasingly inward challenges to their fortitude before reaching the safe harbour of an appropriate marriage in the final chapters. To what extent the heroine's is an active or a passive virtue, however, is debatable. The sensibility with which Emily St Aubert is endowed in *The Mysteries of Udolpho* (1794) is made to seem a liability, to be reined in by reason, if the deathbed warning of her father is to be believed. At the same time, it is clear that only those possessed of sensibility are virtuous; those, like Madame Cheron or Montoni, who lack sensibility (shown in particular by a failure to respond to nature) are placed somewhere down the scale from the injudicious to the depraved. Moreover, the heroine's sensibility, when she is placed in situations of peril, equips her with a certain timely vigilance. If her surmises are often wrong (almost all the supernatural occurrences she seeks to interpret turn out, notoriously, to be explicable), in some cases they are appropriate, as when Ellena in *The Italian* (1797), acting on her suspicion that she is being poisoned at Spalatro's house, saves her life. Whether Radcliffe intended her readers to see this as a legitimate, if limited, claim to female power is not clear.

The vigilance of the Radcliffe heroine points to a larger cultural formation, a type of fiction that Anne Williams (in *Art of Darkness*) has termed the Female Gothic. The female protagonist, unlike the male, seeks to understand, not control; hence, Emily's explorations of Udolpho or Château-le-Blanc serve to bring the unknown within the boundaries of reason. In the Female Gothic, argues Williams, reason is overdetermined, a response to the standard patriarchal positioning of women as deficient in reason. This is represented by explicating the natural causes of apparitions and by bringing the unruly past to light and neutralizing its power to disturb. The male (e.g. Montoni or Schedoni) figures as the Other, a power to be overcome, rather than as the object of female desire he will become later (as in *Jane Eyre*).

The Male Gothic, in contrast, is said to have its basis in the Oedipal crisis, where the infant male self constitutes itself while the female (the mother) is defined as the Other. Since what the infant has seen and felt cannot be accommodated in the Symbolic, it remains a repressed potential, ready to reappear as the Spectral. Thus, the Male Gothic does not explain away its ghosts. For example, the Bleeding Nun of Lewis's *The Monk* (1796) is, in Williams's words, 'the female principle haunting the patriarchal Symbolic order: the baffling woman at once pure and bloody; chaste and violent' (*Art of Darkness*, p. 119). Although the Male Gothic, as Williams points out, was seen as revolutionary by de Sade, it actually argues the conservative case: like Walpole and Radcliffe, Lewis's plot serves to unravel a secret that, once again, argues the dangers of violating the principles of patriarchy and property.

Matthew Lewis, who wrote *The Monk* as a young man of 20, profits from the technical innovations of Radcliffe, but exploits them for depictions of violence and sexual disorder that would be inconceivable in a Radcliffe novel. Indeed, *The Italian* (1797) is often thought to be Radcliffe's sober response to this challenge. Lewis's novel offended many readers, including Coleridge who wrote in the *Critical Review*. Faced with possible prosecution, Lewis quickly republished the book in a watered-down version.

The violence of the crowd shown near the end of the novel, during which the prioress of St Clare is brutally killed, has been held to reflect events in London, such as the Gordon Riots of 1780, or the more recent disorders in France; but it also shows a distrust of the mob in Lewis that parallels that of the government, which had recently passed 'gagging' acts forbidding assemblies and censoring publication (December, 1794) after the king's coach was attacked by protesters at Westminster. In fact, the main disorders that Lewis puts on display are the result of violating the boundaries or proprieties of class: Antonia's anomalous position as a poor relation; the miscegenation of Ambrosio as the son of a shoemaker's daughter and a count; and Raymond's self-induced disasters, which come from travelling disguised as a lesser man than he is. Even the sexual licence that so shocked contemporary readers is treated with a profound conservatism: every act of male desire serves to invoke supernatural agency that eventually punishes it.

The popular success of the Gothic with Radcliffe and Lewis encouraged a host of imitators. During the same period Jane Austen also produced her satire on the Gothic, *Northanger Abbey*. Although written around 1798–9 the novel was not published until 1818, long after the Radcliffean genre at which it tilted had passed its prime. Austen appears to take for granted the ideology of realism, in which middle-class values prevail and in which the Gothic exists only in the fantasies of Catherine Morland. By 1818 this view was also thoroughly accepted by Austen's reviewers, who praised the novel for its fidelity to everyday life, and observed (in the words of the *British Critic*) that Austen was 'extremely deficient' in imagination, except, that is, for General Tilney, who was not considered a very probable character. However, while Catherine entirely misses the mark in suspecting General Tilney of being a Gothic villain on the Italian model, Tilney's weakness for class status and his abuse of power in dismissing Catherine, reveals him to be a tyrant of another kind – elaborated more fully in the figure of Falkland in Godwin's *Caleb Williams*. When Henry Tilney chides Catherine by asking her to see England as a place where 'every man is surrounded by a neighbourhood of voluntary spies, and where roads and newspapers lay everything open', he points to other forms of oppression, although these were not of a kind that Austen herself seemed prepared to explore. For this the radical Gothic was a fitter instrument.

## The Radical Gothic: Godwin to Hogg

The preceding novels seem to aim for a sense of closure. This is not evident in the novels now to be discussed, where a stable place from which moral judgements might be made is eroded or unavailable, leaving us uncertain about what the forces unleashed in the novel may mean. In addition, there is a more specific and intense focus on investigating mental states of terror, supported by a greater effort to situate such states circumstantially. The result often seems designed to show that acceptance of the realist assumption is equivalent to ideological collusion: just the type of unreflecting trust in reality, for example, that Austen's reviewers showed by claiming she had 'no imagination'. The radical Gothic, in other words, prepares us to see fissures within that comfortable middle-class world precisely because its assumptions about family, class or gender are the products of a certain kind of imagination, one with specific blindnesses and liabilities.

In Godwin's *Caleb Williams* (1794) there is neither a ghost nor an Italian castle. We find instead a novel that aims at great psychological realism. But its emphasis on the traumatic effects of Caleb's paranoia, together with the apparently omniscient persecutions of Falkland, serve to make the novel Gothic, and place Falkland in the Gothic tradition of Manfred or Schedoni. But Godwin insisted on the reality of the horrors that he shows: his prison scenes, he tells us in a footnote, are taken from observation (he knew Newgate Prison as a visitor) and from the documentary evidence of John Howard, the writer on prison reform. In fact, Godwin's novel arose directly out of his political understanding: he tells us that he sat down to write it in order to exemplify the principles of his *Enquiry Concerning the Principles of Political Justice* (1793), although how far he succeeded in this aim has been questioned. The object of Godwin's political critique in the novel is the monarchical system and the class differences and oppressions to which it gives rise. It is this system that is responsible for both Falkland's overweening and destructive sense of honour and Williams's morbid curiosity. The focus on terror, however, is so absorbing that the reader may overlook Godwin's political thesis.

*Caleb Williams* is the first major novel in which an uncanny doubling occurs. Caleb attempts to become Falkland by wanting to know what Falkland knows; but this in turn precipitates Falkland's persecution of Caleb which Caleb, wherever he flees, seems unable to escape, as though Falkland has privileged access to Caleb's plans. A similar situation is created in the first novel of Godwin's daughter, Mary Shelley: Frankenstein and his monster also become bound to one another in a persecutory relationship in which the monster eventually seems to have omniscient powers. In Hogg's *Confessions* Wringhim and the mysterious Gil-Martin not only share an intimate relationship, but Gil-Martin may even impersonate his companion. This is a Gothic topos later treated with striking effect in *Dr Jekyll and Mr Hyde* (1886) by Stevenson: here, the splitting of personality intimated in the earlier novels is realized literally.

*Frankenstein* (1818) carries forward Godwin's concerns in several other ways. The monster can be seen as a study in Godwinian Necessitarianism. Like Caleb, the monster is a victim of his environment. He might have been otherwise, being born with benevolent human impulses and without inherent evil; but he is dehumanized, not only in his treatment by everyone except the blind De Lacey, but more importantly by Frankenstein, who sees him as a demon, or as an insect to be crushed. Frankenstein, on his part, is the product of a flawed upbringing, as Shelley's detailed account emphasizes, one in which the domestic is divorced from the world of business, permitting Frankenstein to develop passions unrelated to any sense of social responsibility. The scientific dimension of the novel, however, is peculiarly Shelley's own: through the creature's depredations she explicitly rebukes the visionary role assigned to science by the young Frankenstein (whose inspiration is patterned after the actual discourse of such noted scientists as Humphry Davy and Erasmus Darwin). The novel also has a complex relationship with the feminist work of Shelley's mother, Mary Wollstonecraft. While it questions the patriarchal assumptions of the Frankenstein family, the women in the novel are oddly passive, dull creatures. At a deeper level, the novel has also been read as an exploration of women's fears over birth, or repressed sexual emotions, especially anxiety and guilt.

Charles Maturin (1782–1824) was an Anglican clergyman whose pronounced Calvinist beliefs are reflected in his Gothic masterpiece, *Melmoth the Wanderer* (1820). The plot is disrupted by a series of digressions, often lengthy, and often containing stories within stories; each, however, progressively casts light on the central character, the wanderer Melmoth. Melmoth, who combines features of both Milton's Satan and the Wandering Jew, not only embodies supernatural powers, but he is also their victim; only glimpsed at first as a disturbing presence, his suffering and distorted humanity becomes clear only towards the end of the story, in his love and betrayal of Immalee. Each of the novel's narrators seems to argue for the inevitability of the brutality, suffering and stupidity of the human condition, although the narrative voices are hardly to be distinguished from one another, given that Maturin's own impassioned voice seems continually to break through.

In contrast, James Hogg's *Private Memoirs and Confessions of a Justified Sinner* (1824) manages its double narrative with extraordinary virtuosity. The 'Private Memoirs' of Wringhim are prefaced by an editor's narrative amounting to nearly half the novel. Wringhim's narrative tells the same story, but with significant differences in point of view that serve to cast doubt on the reliability of both. This makes the advent in Wringhim's life of Gil-Martin, who may be the devil, all the more disturbing, since apart from his role as Wringhim's tempter (as one of the Elect, Wringhim is entitled to commit any sin he pleases), it is left unclear what role he plays. Wringhim's terrifying end is described with great circumstantial detail; so, too, is the final bizarre episode in which his corpse is dug up and Wringhim's narrative discovered. The editor, who has the last word, objects that Wringhim's story is too improbable to be believed.

The psychological issues raised by this and the previous radical Gothic fictions remain troubling, whether handled ineptly, as occurs at times in *Frankenstein*, or with paranoid intensity, as in Maturin. In each of the novels the suffering of the central characters seems out of proportion if intended as punishment for their rather venial sins. The moral balance sheet, to which the realist novels of the same period appeal, is significantly missing. Despite the frequent appeals to Providence, there is a darker wisdom glimpsed here, of a universe that is indifferent or hostile to human purposes, where humans prey upon one another, and in which the finest impulses only betray us to horror and destruction. This tendency can be glimpsed in the earlier fictions of Radcliffe and Lewis, but here at least a tenuous moral system frames the stories: villains are punished or removed, and heroines gain the long-deferred haven of their marriages (in Radcliffe's case, apparently bearing no psychic scars from their long-endured sufferings). But perhaps it is the psychological that, in the end, gives the Gothic such coherence as it has.

Thus, the Gothic has often been seen as a promising field for psychoanalytic speculation, by authors from Freud to Kristeva. For example, we might see its focus on terror and horror originating in the infantile process of individuation, where the nascent self casts off what is not-self, which then becomes alien and associated with the unclean (including the mother) as the infant enters the Symbolic order. If horror 'freezes', in Radcliffe's terms, this may be because it includes both the repulsion towards the Other (the Kristevan abject) and the assertion of separate selfhood, as Williams has proposed (*Art of Darkness*, p. 76). A problem with such views, however, is their lack of historic specificity: their proponents cannot easily explain why the Gothic arises when it does.

An alternative account of the Gothic would stress the historical dimensions of this process of symbolization. A key concern of the period in which the Gothic arose was the creation and flow of capital, and a consequent preoccupation with economic development – issues which only came clearly into focus for the first time with Adam Smith and David Ricardo. Those who impede the flow of capital, debtors unable to meet their liabilities, are removed from 'circulation' in the indefinite suspension of the debtors' prison, while the machinery of the prison, fetters, the stocks, or the gallows, comes into use for economic crimes more widely than for crimes against the person. In these circumstances, the stresses of forging a new human identity now correlate most strongly with fears of impedance, improgressiveness or stasis. This casts the Gothic obsession with castles, dungeons and incarceration in a rather different light. Ellena's captivity at the convent of San Stefano reflects her disruption of the economic order of which Vivaldi was to form a part. The persecution of Frankenstein's creature only begins when he is no longer able to participate in the economic order of the De Laceys' cottage. The Gothic does not reflect the economic order in any simple way, however. Rather, it resonates with a struggle for meaning in which economic man (the gendered term is intentional) evolves against alternative or older concepts of human purpose, including an ameliorating female vision which, as the nine-teenth century entered its second quarter, seemed more remote than ever.

## WRITINGS

Austen, Jane, *Northanger Abbey*, ed. John Davie, Oxford, Oxford University Press, 1990.

Godwin, William, *Caleb Williams*, ed. David McCracken, Oxford, Oxford University Press, 1982.

Hogg, James, *Private Memoirs and Confessions of a Justified Sinner*, ed. John Carey, Oxford, Oxford University Press, 1981.

Lewis, Matthew, *The Monk*, ed. Howard Anderson, Oxford, Oxford University Press, 1980.

Maturin, Charles Robert, *Melmoth the Wanderer*, ed. Douglas Grant, Oxford, Oxford University Press, 1989.

Radcliffe, Ann, 'On the supernatural in poetry', *New Monthly Magazine* 16 (1826) 145–52.

——*The Mysteries of Udolpho*, ed. Bonamy Dobrée, Oxford, Oxford University Press, 1980.

——*The Italian*, ed. Frederick Garber, Oxford, Oxford University Press, 1981.

——*The Romance of the Forest*, ed. Chloe Chard, Oxford, Oxford University Press, 1986.

——*A Sicilian Romance*, ed. Alison Milbank, Oxford, Oxford University Press, 1993.

Shelley, Mary, *Frankenstein: 1818 Text*, ed. Marilyn Butler, Oxford, Oxford University Press, 1993.

Walpole, Horace, *The Castle of Otranto*, ed. W. S. Lewis, Oxford, Oxford University Press, 1982.

## REFERENCES AND FURTHER READING

Botting, Fred, *Gothic*, London, Routledge, 1996.

Burke, Edmund, *A Philosophical Enquiry into the Origin of our Ideas of the Sublime and Beautiful*, ed. Adam Phillips, Oxford, Oxford University Press, 1990.

Day, William Patrick, *In the Circles of Fear and Desire: A Study of Gothic Fantasy*, Chicago and London, University of Chicago Press, 1985.

Ellis, Kate Ferguson, *The Contested Castle: Gothic Novels and the Subversion of Domestic Ideology*, Urbana and Chicago, University of Illinois Press, 1989.

Fleenor, Juliann E. (ed.) *The Female Gothic*, Montreal and London, Eden Press, 1983.

Freud, Sigmund, 'The Uncanny', in *The Standard Edition of the Complete Psychological Works of Sigmund Freud*, 24 vols, ed. James Strachey, vol. 17, *An Infantile Neurosis and Other Works*, London, The Hogarth Press, 1955, pp. 217–52.

Haggerty, George, *Gothic Fiction / Gothic Form*, University Park, Pennsylvania State University Press, 1989.

Howard, Jacqueline, *Reading Gothic Fiction: A Bakhtinian Approach*, Oxford, Clarendon Press, 1994.

Hume, Robert D., 'Gothic versus romantic: A reavaluation of the Gothic novel', *PMLA* 84 (1969) 282–90.

Miles, Robert, *Gothic Writing 1750–1820: A Genealogy*, London, Routledge, 1993.

Napier, Elizabeth R., *The Failure of Gothic: Problems of Disjunction in an Eighteenth-century Literary Form*, Oxford, Clarendon Press, 1987.

Punter, David, *The Literature of Terror*, 2 vols, vol. 1, *The Gothic Tradition*, London, Longman, 1996.

Sage, Victor, *Horror Fiction in the Protestant Tradition*, London and Basingstoke, Macmillan, 1988.

Williams, Anne, *Art of Darkness: A Poetics of the Gothic*, Chicago and London, University of Chicago Press, 1995.

# 35

# Parody and Imitation

*Graeme Stones*

*'Once', said the Mock Turtle at last, with a deep sigh, 'I was a real Turtle'.*
*Alice's Adventures in Wonderland*

'The exact imitation of a good thing', wrote Francis Jeffrey in 1812, 'it must be admitted, promises fair to be a pretty good thing in itself'.[1] This conventional, eighteenth-century view is what one would expect from the editor of the *Edinburgh Review*, notorious for his attacks on the Lake School radicalism of Wordsworth, Coleridge and Southey. 'This will never do', he thundered famously of the *Excursion* – not the most subversive of poems, but Jeffrey had long since convinced himself that the first generation of Romantic poets was a nest of vipers, whose every utterance must be stamped on. Emulation, not innovation, was the proper task of poets, who should comply with decorums founded in the Classics. He was always curmudgeonly. But Jeffrey was often a better critic than he is given credit for.

In 1812 he reviewed the *Rejected Addresses* of Horace and James Smith. Their collection encouraged him into a lengthy discussion of imitation, and then parody. It was an influential and startling article. Jeffrey begins commonly enough, probing the way ahead from ground he was certain of. Self-appointed arbiter of public taste, Jeffrey had brooded for years over the early nineteenth-century literary renaissance. However, like it or not, he was a man of his own time. Imitative strategies – deeply embedded in all arts, High and Low – were intimately involved in that resurgence, though rarely then investigated. Almost despite himself, while following his critical instincts into this new territory, Jeffrey's regard for imitation falls away. He becomes a most unlikely champion of parodic creativity.

The *Rejected Addresses* of the Smiths, spoofs on prominent writers, are the best-known parodies in the period. Discovering his impersonation within, Walter Scott remarked, 'I certainly must have written this myself, though I forget upon what occasion'.[2] The remark holds more than geniality. Separating author from imitator from parodist can be a tantalizing, teasing affair. This is particularly true of the *Addresses*, whose 21 parodies dance the line between imitative and parodic recreation. The 'Walter Scott' was much admired for a time, for its fidelity. Scott certainly could have written it himself, but perhaps this is less complimentary to the brothers than it seems.

In different voices each of the addresses tells the same story: the destruction of the Drury Lane Theatre by fire, and its rebuilding – reopened now with an inaugural speech chosen by competition from aspiring or established authors. The Smiths weave fact and fiction together, with perfect comic timing. Their 'Walter Scott' retells the tale as historical mock-epic:

> The summon'd firemen woke at call,
> And hied them to their stations all:
> Starting from short and broken snooze,
> Each sought his pond'rous hobnail'd shoes,
> But first his worsten hosen plied
> Plush breeches next, in crimson died,
> His nether bulk embraced;
> Then jacket thick, of red or blue
> Whose massy shoulder gave to view
> The badge of each respective crew,
> In tin or copper traced.[3]

Witty enough, and attentive to the source, this is however no more inventive than Scott himself might have been. Parody consists in two immiscible impulses: imitation, and opposition, a mirrored text but a buckled one, whose ripples unsettle an observing eye, inciting contrasts and comparison. The Greek root 'para' embraces two antithetical meanings: 'beside' and 'counter'. Fine parodies demand a fine balance, between what John Fowles called a kind of homage and a thumbed nose. Those that repeat their source too faithfully only genuflect. Those grown over-assertive topple into satire or caricature. The *Addresses*, as Scott's remark should hint, are soft-centred, usually too compliant to revise a reader's notion of originals.

Frowning over the double-demands of the art, Francis Jeffrey became acute. Because his article *is* an exploration, of a form never before adequately analysed, there is a difficulty of terms. Parody is a word he uses rarely, thinking it a synonym of travesty – which at the time, in many quarters, it was. Instead, he uses the word 'mimickry' to label repetition, and then investigates the merits of opposition-within-imitation. What matters is the approval, high praise even, given to a recreative mimicry equivalent to modern use of the term 'parody'.

He opens at the level of physical impersonation: 'There is no talent so universally entertaining as that of mimickry – even when it is confined to the lively imitation of the air and manner – the voice, gait, and external deportment of ordinary individuals'. Already Jeffrey is surprisingly receptive, in these low beginnings, to sympathies evoked, skills required, and faculties woken:

> Nor is this to be ascribed entirely to our wicked love of ridicule; for, though we must not assign a very high intellectual rank to an art which is said to have attained to its greatest perfection among the savages of New Holland, some admiration is undoubtedly due to the capacity of nice observation which it implies; and some gratification may be innocently derived from the sudden perception which it excites of unexpected peculiarities.

Contrast this with Coleridge – always hostile to parody – using the same parallels:

> The talent for mimicry seems strongest where the human race are most degraded. The poor, naked, half human savages of New Holland were found excellent mimics: and, in civilized society, minds of the very lowest stamp alone satirize by *copying*.[4]

Set a thief to catch a thief. Coleridge is among the greatest of authorial impersonators, although the form, an addiction stronger than opium, repelled him throughout the peaks and troughs of his dependence. Wondering where imitation leads, Jeffrey could afford to be dispassionate where Coleridge could not: '[Imitation] rises in interest, however, and in dignity, when it succeeds in expressing, not merely the visible and external characteristics of its objects, but those also of their taste, their genius and temper'. Still at the physical level, Jeffrey moves from imitation-as-repetition to imitation-as-recreation: 'but he is an artist of a far higher description, who can make stories or reasonings in his manner, and represent the features and movements of his mind, as well as the accidents of his body'.

'The same distinction applies to . . . mimickry', Jeffrey continues, using the word as one would use it now for parody. His beginning from this aping level seems long-winded, but is useful. Jeffrey's article obliquely recalls the ubiquity of the parodic impulse, its vaudeville vitality, clowning inversions, its disregard for probity and rank. All of these will be investigated, even celebrated, by later writers and theorists.

Jeffrey now moves directly into literature, using parallel divisions. Parody which repeats the obvious is but to mimic 'as a monkey might imitate a man' – the result is tedium or caricature.

> It is another matter, however, to be able to borrow the diction and manner of a celebrated writer to express sentiments like his own – to write as he would have written on the subject proposed to his imitator – to think his thoughts, in short, as well as to use his words – and to make the revival of his style appear a natural consequence of the strong conception of his peculiar ideas.

Jeffrey is so engaged in his subject, so certain of his instincts, that he seems not to have thought through the consequences of his argument – its potential for liberating writers from that emulative decorum he would normally insist upon. He persuades himself into a regard for parody no critic before had admitted; and few after, until well into the twentieth century:

> To do this in all the perfection of which it is capable, requires talents, perhaps, not inferior to those of the original on whom they are employed – together with a faculty of observation, and a dexterity of application, which that original might not always possess; and should not only afford nearly as great pleasure to the reader, as a species of composition, – but may teach him some lessons, or open up to him some views, which could not otherwise have been disclosed.

Unwary of the implications, he is absolutely clear about the parodic distortion this mimicry demands: 'The resemblance, it is obvious, can only be rendered striking by exaggerating a little, and bringing more conspicuously forward, all that is peculiar and characteristic in the model'.

These are not conservative judgements. Willy-nilly, Jeffrey is moved by the spirit of the age.

Had he thought things through, he might have retracted. At any time, parody is a provocative, flirtatious art, tempting readers into active response. In the Romantic period, when issues of originality, copyright and the proper reception of adventurous literature were highly sensitized, parody was a contentious form – loved and loathed. At this point, some distinctions need to be drawn.

Imitation, once a respectable art, could not long survive Romantic convictions about genius: its organicism, individuality and immediacy. Young's *Conjectures on Original Composition* are an early warning in 1759:

> An *Original* may be said to be of a *vegetable* nature; it rises spontaneously from the vital root of Genius; it *grows*, it is not *made*: *Imitations* are often a sort of *Manufacture* wrought up by those *Mechanics*, *Art*, and *Labour*, out of pre-existent materials not their own.[5]

Romantic idealizing of this 'vital root' meant nurturing and protecting the individual imagination. Imitation, no fit occupation for artists, passed down to artisans. Plagiarism's poaching imitation grew from age-old sport into sneak-thievery. Parody, poaching-by-daylight, now could only be the pastime of outright villains.

The situation was compounded by opportunist evolutions in copyright protection. It was natural for booksellers, initially those with most to lose, to insist on a place in burgeoning property legislation. Natural, but problematic. The arthritic fingers of the law are not well-made to rootle through a mess of ideas, separating those of one man from another. As Emerson said, even the originals are not original.

When authors, ambitious now for status as well as money, displaced booksellers as those with most to lose, they were able to exploit a public confusion between a material product – the book – and the ideas which generated it. The two cannot easily be separated, although – in cold scrutiny – one is clearly entitled to protection in law, the other only dubiously so.

It is Romantic greed, not idealism, which largely sponsored the notion – lingering on – that plagiarism is breaking-and-entering, a burglary of The Author's Imagination. It is nothing of the kind. As J. O. Urmson pointed out concisely, plagiarism is an act of imposture rather than theft.[6] Any crime committed is against the reader rather than the author. Even less against The Author, discovered deceased by Roland Barthes in 1969[7] and not (for Barthesians at least) entitled to sue from beyond the grave. However, many Romantics found it useful to revive the old cry of 'Hang the plagiary' with a new intensity. Parodists were to be drawn and quartered as well, preferably without fair trial. It was unsavoury ambition, not high ideals, which led the Lake School poets to band together and hound Peter Bayley (an innocent emulator) out of his literary existence, as a vile parodist. Or Coleridge to label Charles Lloyd a vicious ingrate, for borrowing incidents and inclinations gathered in their friendship and reworking them into an ingenuous novel of sensibility.

At the same time, Romanticism grew up together with the emulative arts in a kind of spliced twinning, looking askance, with mixed irritation and pride, at duplicate, duplicitous selves who subvert its own dogmas. Macpherson's ersatz folk-poetry, Chatterton's parodic medievalism, Blake's upendings, Coleridge's bulk-importations, the chameleon Keats, Byron's self-deflating postures – these are only the more visible manifestations of parodic energy, that primal re-ordering of spent material which testifies to both the creativity and amorality of genius.

In this Romantic fog, Jeffrey's comments are a beacon. Parody, at its finest, has wide-ranging effects. It may query over-statement, banish sentimentality, restore historical context, re-introduce social influences, dispense with outworn forms, revive discarded forms thought to have been exhausted, and rescue art from narcissism. It can discriminate between the shock and the schlock of the new. It can qualify idealism by returning to the real, and modify realism by uncovering its fictions – highlighting the fictionality of all discourse but never discouraged by it. It is, above all, a consummate vehicle of irony, carrying that into areas where it has been excluded. Finally, it invites participation, encouraging active, intelligent reading.

Its most vigorous function in the Romantic period is the rejection of authorial authoritarianism: the attempts of authors to control the interpretation and market of their work. The threat posed by parody in this area is measurable in agitations it provoked among writers determined to stage-manage their reception. Wordsworth is a clear example. His campaign to create the taste by which he wished to be judged began modestly enough, but became belabourings which wearied his readers. Parodic response to his early simplicity was muted, but Wordsworth's elaborations of his creed in the *Excursion*, and the prose essays of the 1815 *Poems*, eventually provoked parodists into concerted action. The result, for a time, was an abrasive relationship between author and much of his audience. Parody is the *lingua franca* of the Reader's Liberation Movement. It leads to a more mature conversation between text and reader, but the process has its uncomfortable stages.

The Smith brothers rarely reach the level of fine parody. Jeffrey takes their lightheartedness as cause, and rightly ranks them below the accomplishments of the *Anti-Jacobin*. Their efforts never achieve the penetration of Frederick Deacon's *Warreniana*, or P. G. Patmore's *Imitations of Celebrated Authors*, or the genius of James Hogg in the *Poetic Mirror*. The *Addresses* lack critical distancing, and play to the audience for easy laughs or fall back on simple imitation. But the collection has its moments.

A fair example of what can be done with substantive parody is their 'Hampshire Farmer', which brings Cobbett vividly to life. He comes stumping up to the apron, scorning poetry for his address: 'To the gewgaw fetters of *rhyme* (invented by the monks to enslave the people) I have a rooted objection'. Cobbett 'naturally butts at all obstacles', wrote Hazlitt, 'as unicorns are attracted to oak-trees'.[8] The Hampshire Farmer's instincts are equally pugnacious:

> I have therefore written an address for your theatre in plain, homespun, yeoman's *prose*; in the doing whereof I hope I am swayed by nothing but an *independent* wish to open the eyes of this gulled people, to prevent a repetition of the dramatic *bamboozling* they have hitherto laboured under.

Imitating the italics of Cobbett's weekly *Political Register*, this parody immediately recaptures both its tone and bull-necked intent – however various the opinions, always resolute in manner. It also nicely recovers his social intemperance:

> When persons address an audience from the stage, it is usual, either in words or gesture, to say, 'Ladies and Gentlemen, your servant'. If I were base enough, mean enough, paltry enough, and *brute beast* enough, to follow that fashion, I should tell two lies in a breath.

And his below-the-salt and salt-of-the-earth paternalism:

> In the first place, you are *not* Ladies and Gentlemen, but I hope something better, that is to
> say, honest men and women; and in the next place, if you were ever so much ladies, and ever so
> much gentlemen, I am not, *nor ever will be*, your humble servant.

As ever, the timing of the brothers was perfect. Cobbett was released from Newgate on 9
July 1812, just three months before the *Addresses*, his asperity with the leisured classes
unimproved by two years of imprisonment. The resurrection of the Drury Lane Theatre by
Sam Whitbread, a no-nonsense brewer, made a fitting frame for parody:

> And now, *most thinking people*, cast your eyes over my head to what the builder, (I beg his
> pardon, the architect), calls the *proscenium*. No motto, no slang, no popish Latin, to keep the
> people in the dark. No *veluti in speculum*. Nothing in the dead languages, properly so called,
> for they ought to die, ay and be *damned* to boot!

To observe, in this, what Jeffrey would have called the original's 'marking features . . . mag-
nified and disengaged in the copy', compare it with one of Cobbett's wonderful tirades in
the *Register*:

> If this be the meaning of the 'Uti Posseditis', why not give us that meaning in our own
> language at once? Do those who make use of such phrases, which the stupidest wretch upon
> earth might learn to use as well as they, in a few hours; nay which a parrot would learn, or
> which a high-dutch bird-catcher would teach to a bull-finch or a tom-tit, in the space of a
> month; and do they think, in good earnest, that this relick of the mummery of monkery, this
> playing off upon us of a few gallipot words, will make us believe they are *learned*?[9]

The Smiths had a particularly good ear for Cobbett's earthiness, the way, whatever his
subject, he turns to the solidly material in all his writings – his constant, all-too-nearly
literal rubbing of noses in the soil of Old England. 'Look at the brickwork, English
Audience! Look at the brickwork!' cries the Hampshire Farmer:

> All plain and smooth like a quakers' meeting. None of your Egyptian pyramids, to entomb
> subscribers' capitals. No overgrown colonnades of stone, like an alderman's gouty legs in
> white cotton stockings, fit only to use as rammers for paving Tottenham Court Road.

In this parody, unlike others in the volume, the effect is larger than its comedy. It has what
Jeffrey called 'the additional advantage of letting us more completely into the secret of the
original author, and enabling us to understand far more clearly in what the peculiarity of
his manner consists'. The result is a symbiosis of reading and reacting, which clarifies
critical instinct.

What Hazlitt admired in Cobbett was the gusto which overrides his inconsistencies – a
confidence fed by physicality and tradition – and the 'fine *sauce-piquante* of contempt they
were seasoned with'.[10] It is this appetite the parody most successfully recreates. Kitchen
images, ruddy cheeks and a hearty dinner-table scepticism come readily to mind with
Cobbett, and to Cobbett's mind:

The people of England have been famed, in all ages, for their good living; for the abundance of their food, and the goodness of their attire. The old sayings about English roast beef and plum-pudding, and about English hospitality, had not their foundations in *nothing*.[11]

When the Hampshire Farmer casts round for a metaphor to sum up the abuse of the labouring classes he, too, like the Cobbett of *Cottage Economy*, turns happily to cooking, to 'plain, wholesome, patriotic beef or mutton broth':

I will endeavour to explain this to you: England is a large *earthenware pipkin*; John Bull is the *beef* thrown into it; taxes are the *hot water* he boils in; rotten boroughs are the *fuel* that blazes under this same pipkin; parliament is the *ladle* that stirs the hodge-podge.

Here then, in his essence, is what one critic called the 'immoderately political animal' who once launched on his *Register* 'would find it difficult to discuss even a potato in non-political terms'.[12] Or politics without bringing in potatoes, this parody reminds us. Here, too, is the man of whom one could say, as Lamb did of Munden, that he could throw 'a preternatural interest over the commonest daily-life objects'. Like Munden's, Cobbett's pots and ladles are 'as grand and primal as the seething-pots and hooks seen in old prophetic vision'.[13] And, as Lamb in his parodic portraiture, the Smiths are able to arrest the eye and excite the critical imagination.

Substantive parodies offer a gradient to the reader, to 'open up to him some views, which could not otherwise have been disclosed' as Jeffrey put it. This distancing from the original has discomforts, demanding an effortful separation some will resent. The finest parodies return a fitter reader, able to greet the author on a strong footing. But the true value of substantive parody is not perspectives gained on individual authors. It lies instead in the quickening sense of omnipresence, of textual contours stretching away as far as the eye can see. Extant parodies are formal notice of the ubiquity of the parodic impulse.

The parodic process is a paradoxical mix of supercession and creation. This is positive, not detrimental, in literature. It is more than that. One definition of parody might be: the necessary suspiration of disbelief. In this it is party to the nature of literature itself: 'writing ceaselessly posits meaning ceaselessly to evaporate it'. Read too literally, Roland Barthes's teasing distillation would seem to threaten creativity. Some sterile criticism has sought authority from Barthes. However, Barthes has done no harm to imaginative energy. Meaning, like The Author, is tougher than Barthes pretended; but he and parody agree that meaning cannot be policed.

The separation of artist from parodist, of original from recreation, the purity of the imaginative impulse: these are among the Romantic period's enduring fallacies. As Mikhail Bakhtin, parody's most persuasive theorist, insists:

It is our conviction that there never was a single strictly straightforward genre, no single type of direct discourse – artistic, rhetorical, philosophical, religious, ordinary everyday – that did not have its own parodying and travestying double, its own comic-ironic contre-partie. What is more, these parodic doubles and laughing reflections of the direct word were, in some cases, just as sanctioned by tradition and just as canonized as their elevated models.[14]

Romantic creeds die hard. 'We need to stop thinking of any poet as an autonomous ego', wrote Harold Bloom in his pivotal study, 'however solipsistic the strongest of poets may be.'[15] Parody is deeply implicated in Bloom's 'revisionary ratios', but the message was slow to filter through. However, Bakhtin's interest in the 'dialogic' in literature, in textual conversations internal and external, and the centrality of parody for all his work, offer eloquent reparation.

Bakhtin's convictions have been underwritten by recent criticism. Scholars of the Romantics, more swayed by the period's misapprehensions than they usually admit, have been reluctant to take to the theory of parody. But transformations in reading are possible for critics who have exercised themselves on parodic gradients. Mark Jones's recent absorbing discussion of Wordsworth's *Michael*[16] is an example of light shed on individual authors – the merest hint that Wordsworth, of all people, is deeply engaged in parodic dialogues would have been unthinkable not long ago. For a wider vantage, Don Bialostosky's *Wordsworth, Dialogics and the Practice of Criticism* places Wordsworth at the heart of the academy's hopes and fears, and discovers in dialogics a language of resolution.

Lewis Carroll's Mock Turtle has a gap in his education. Unlike the Gryphon, he never went to the classical master to learn 'Laughing and Grief'. Perhaps because of this, he is an incurable romantic: tearful, humourless, nostalgic for the real, and impatient with his audience – 'Really you are very dull!' Had he read the Classics, he might have discovered there, as Bakhtin did in ancient parody, 'a common purpose: to provide the corrective of laughter and criticism to all straightforward genres, languages, styles, voices; to force men to experience beneath those categories a different and contradictory reality that is otherwise not captured in them'.[17]

## NOTES

1   This, and all following 1812 quotations by Jeffrey, from *Edinburgh Review* vol. 20 (July–November 1812), no. 40 (November 1812), pp. 434–51.

2   According to Horace, at least, in the Preface to the *Rejected Addresses*.

3   This and all subsequent quotations from the *Rejected Addresses* taken from the eighteenth edition of 1833. This, with additional interpolations from the brothers, is the most useful in their time.

4   CC *Biographia*, I, 76.

5   Edward Young, *Conjectures on Original Composition. In a Letter to the Author of Sir Charles Grandison* (London, 1759), p. 12.

6   In 'Plagiarism – a symposium', *Times Literary Supplement* 9, April 1982, p. 415.

7   This and subsequent quotations of Barthes from 'The Death of the Author' in *Image, Music, Text*, trans. Stephen Heath, Fontana, London, 1977.

8   Howe, VIII, 54.

9   Cobbett, *Political Register*, 10 January 1807.

10  Howe, VIII, 53.

11  Cobbett, *Cottage Economy* 1821–2; reprinted by Peter Davies, London 1926, p. 4.

12  Daniel Green, *Great Cobbett*, p. 202.

13  Charles Lamb, 'On the acting of Munden', *Elia. Essays which have appeared under that signature in the London Magazine*, London 1823, p. 341.

14  Mikhail Bakhtin, *The Dialogic Imagination*, p. 53.

15  Bloom, *The Anxiety of Influence*, p. 91.

16  *PMLA* 108, no. 5 (1993).

17  Bakhtin, *Dialogic Imagination*, p. 60.

## WRITINGS

Canning, George, with George Ellis and John Hookham Frere, *The Poetry of the Anti-Jacobin*, London, 1799; facsimile reprinted by Woodstock Books, Oxford 1991.

Deacon, W. F., *Warreniana; with NOTES, Critical and Explanatory, By the Editor of a Quarterly Review*, London, Longman, 1824.

Hogg, James, *Poetic Mirrors*, ed. David Groves, Frankfurt, Verlag Peter Lang, 1990.

Jeffrey, Francis, Review of the *Rejected Addresses, Edinburgh Review* vol. 20, July–November 1812; no. 40 November 1812, Article 10.

Patmore, P. G. *Imitations of Celebrated Authors: or, Imaginary Rejected Articles*, London, Henry Colburn, 1834.

## REFERENCES AND FURTHER READING

Bakhtin, M. M., *The Dialogic Imagination: Four Essays by M. M. Bakhtin*, trans. Caryl Emerson and Michael Holquist, ed. Michael Holquist, Austen, University of Texas, 1981.

Bauer, N. S., 'Early burlesques and parodies of Wordsworth', *Journal of English and German Philology* 74 (1975) 553–69.

——'Wordsworth's poems in contemporary periodicals', *Victorian Periodicals Newsletter* 11, 2, June 1978, 61–76.

Bayley, John, 'Keats and the genius of parody', *Essays in Criticism* 43, 2, April 1993, 112–22.

Bialostosky, Don, *Wordsworth, Dialogics and the Practice of Criticism*, Cambridge, Cambridge University Press, 1992.

Bloom, Harold, *The Anxiety of Influence: A Theory of Poetry*, Oxford, Oxford University Press, 1973.

Booth, Wayne C., *A Rhetoric of Irony*, Chicago, University of Chicago Press, 1974.

Bradbury, Malcolm, 'An age of parody: style in the modern arts', *Encounter* 55, 1 (July 1980) 36–53.

Fruman, Norman, 'Originality, plagiarism, forgery and Romanticism', *Centrum* 4 (1976) 44–9.

Green, Daniel, *Great Cobbett: The Noblest Agitator*, London, Hodder and Stoughton, 1983.

Hamilton, Paul, *Coleridge's Poetics*, Oxford, Blackwell, 1983.

Hannoosh, Michele, 'The reflexive function of parody', *Comparative Literature* 41, 2 (spring 1989) 113–27. .

Hutcheon, Linda, *A Theory of Parody: The Teachings of Twentieth-century Art Forms*, London, Methuen, 1985.

Jacobus, Mary, *Tradition and Experiment in Wordsworth's Lyrical Ballads (1798)*, Oxford, Clarendon Press, 1976.

Jones, Mark, 'Double economics: ambivalence in Wordsworth's pastoral', *PMLA* 108, 5 (1993) 1,098–113.

Kiremidjian, G. D., 'The aesthetics of parody', *Journal of Aesthetics* 28 (1969) 231–42.

Lelievre, F. J., 'The basis of ancient parody', *Greece and Rome* series 2, 1/2, 66–81.

Mellor, Anne K., *English Romantic Irony*, Cambridge, Mass., Harvard University Press, 1980.

Rose, Margaret A., *Parody/Metafiction*, London, Croom Helm, 1979.

——*Parody: Ancient, Modern, and Postmodern*, Cambridge, Cambridge University Press, 1993.

Urmson, J. O., and others, 'Plagiarism – a symposium', *Times Literary Supplement* 4, 123 (9 April 1982) 413.

Wordsworth, Jonathan, '"The Barberry-Tree" revisited', *Review of English Studies*, 37, 147 (1986) 371–7.

# 36

# Travel Writing

## James A. Butler

It was, wrote Dorothy Wordsworth in 1823, a 'writing and publishing (especially *tour*-writing and *tour*-publishing) age'.[1] Indeed, many – perhaps most – Romantic writers wrote or read travel literature. To give only a few examples from the hundreds of such works: William Wordsworth early in his career wrote his *Descriptive Sketches, in Verse, taken during a pedestrian Tour in the Italian, Grison, Swiss, and Savoyard Alps* and several decades later produced a Lake District guidebook; Mary Wollstonecraft's volume of *Letters written during a short Residence in Sweden, Norway, and Denmark* accompanied her 16-year-old daughter on her elopement journey with Percy Bysshe Shelley (records of that 1814 lovers' trip in turn contributed to Mary Wollstonecraft Shelley's first published book); William Blake engraved some of the shocking illustrations for John Stedman's *Narrative of a five years' Expedition against the revolted Negroes of Surinam* (1796); future Poet Laureate Robert Southey concocted a fake travel journal (*Letters from England: by Don Manuel Alvarez Espriella, translated from the Spanish*: 1807) to allow him more freedom to indict English bigotry and parochialism. According to the Bristol Library records from 1773–84, the borrowers' top two choices were books of travel literature;[2] the word 'tourist' itself first dates from the end of the eighteenth century.[3] 'Travel I must, or cease to exist', stated Thomas Gray in 1771,[4] and he also spoke for the literary generations which followed him.

Several features of travel literature made it a central Romantic genre. By its nature the form is personal and autobiographical; as Mary Wollstonecraft explained in the Advertisement to her Scandinavian journey, 'In writing these desultory letters, I found I could not avoid being continually the first person – "the little hero of each tale"'. At their best, the journals and letters most characteristic of the tour books took their wayfaring shape from the immediacy of personal experience rather than from any superimposed model of appropriate literary language and structure. The starting, the stopping, the steps between, could all be random choices through which one escaped the familiar in search of fresh sensations in lands more exotic than home. Although the 'voyage' had long been an archetypal pattern, many Romantic writers even more insistently used the journey as a quest for internal as well as external understanding, for a psychological journey inward, for experiences which provided – as the subtitle of Wordsworth's 1850 *Prelude* has it – for the 'Growth of a Poet's Mind'.

This popularity of the form makes 'travel literature' a particularly slippery genre to define. We may have little difficulty distinguishing among our era's *Frommer's Guides* (the facts on what to take, where to stay, whether you can drink the water), the journalistic work of a foreign correspondent, the travel writing of someone like Paul Theroux in *The Old Patagonian Express* (an autobiographical and highly idiosyncratic record), and such mainly ethnographic accounts as Margaret Mead's trips to Samoa. But Romantic travel literature made no such distinctions and frequently mingled several types in the same volume.

Sometimes a book mixed its structural components in ways that resist easy classification but show the varied personal expression and freedom of form that so appealed to Romantic travel writers. In the lively and captivating *History of a six weeks' Tour through a part of France, Switzerland, Germany, and Holland* (1817), for example, there are at least five strands: (1) Mary Wollstonecraft Shelley's travel journal, rewritten for publication, of an 1814 trip; (2) simulated travel letters written by her about an 1816 tour; (3) actual letters about this 1816 tour (but probably also written with an eye to publication) from Percy Bysshe Shelley to Thomas Love Peacock; (4) the first appearance in print of Percy's poem *Mont Blanc*; (5) a preface by Percy. Combined but not blended, these ingredients appeared anonymously at the end of 1817, just a month before the anonymous publication of Mary's *Frankenstein* – another volume with travel literature as a vital part of its skeleton.

Much as Wordsworth in his 'Preface to *Lyrical Ballads*' defined his work in opposition to his eighteenth-century predecessors, Romantic travel literature is best considered against the eighteenth-century Grand Tour. As capstone of a liberal education for the English upper-class male, the Grand Tour of Europe lasted up to three years, frequently in the presence of a tutor. Such a trip would, claimed Thomas Nugent in his *Grand Tour* (1749), 'in a word form the complete gentleman'.[5] Like Virgil's archetypal traveller Aeneas, the aspirant to this station of 'complete gentleman' had a goal – indeed, the same goal: Italy. Ruins with Virgilian and other ancient Roman associations were among the prized antiquities where travellers could see their Classical educations (and the origins of much of eighteenth-century English architecture, art and literature) in stone. This leisurely procession to the correct 'sights' – Paris, Rome, home through Germany and the Low Countries – inculcated communal values and manners. (A dollop or two of sexual licence sweetened educational duty.)

Intimations of a different kind of travel literature came as early as a letter of Thomas Gray written in 1739, though first published posthumously in 1775. At a time in which Switzerland was mostly considered an annoying barrier on the way to Italy, and the natural world admired principally for its classical associations, Gray found 'not a precipice, not a torrent, not a cliff, but is pregnant with religion and poetry'. Gray's response was emotionally transforming as he encountered 'certain scenes that would awe an atheist into belief'.[6] Similarly, when Gray visited the English Lake District in 1769, he found Grasmere in Westmorland to be a 'little unsuspected paradise'.[7] Gray therefore anticipates Wordsworth's enthusiasm for rural seclusion and marks the distance from such earlier writers on the Lake District as Daniel Defoe, who grumbled in his *A Tour through the whole Island of Great Britain* (1724–6), 'Here we entered Westmoreland, a country eminent only for being the wildest, most barren and frightful of any that I have passed over in England, or even in Wales it self'.[8] By 1786, William Gilpin in his *Observations, relative chiefly to picturesque Beauty* did not dispute that 'wildness', but his comment about the same countryside shows the Age of the Grand Tour crumbling before what became one of the central tenets of Romantic travel literature: 'a journey through these wild scenes might be attended perhaps with more improvement, than a journey to Rome, or Paris' (II, p. 68).

Romantic travel literature found its theoretical underpinnings in accounts of the beautiful, the sublime and the picturesque, especially in works by Edmund Burke and William Gilpin. Eighteenth-century upper-class travellers to Rome could there purchase oils and prints of such landscape artists as the pastorally beautiful Claude Lorraine, the horrifyingly sublime Salvator Rosa, and the majestically picturesque Gaspard Dughet (whom that century called 'Poussin', a name now more commonly used for his brother-in-law Nicolas). Early attempts to describe the landscape as a painting thus referenced these and similar artists; for instance, John Brown in his *Description of the Lake at Keswick* (1767) claimed that any portrayal of the '*beauty, horror,* and *immensity*' of this scene 'would require the united powers of Claude, Salvator, and Poussin'.[9] Gilpin's volumes of 'picturesque tours' of the Wye Valley, the Scottish Highlands and the Lake District opened the floodgates of domestic travel and travel writing. In such books as Thomas West's *Guide to the Lakes, dedicated to Lovers of Landscape Studies* (1778 and a dozen more editions over the next four decades), the diligent picturesque tourist could find the best 'Stations' for viewing the scene, perhaps beholding that landscape in a small, tinted, plano-convex mirror (a 'Claude glass') to compose the landscape as if it were a picture.

By the end of the eighteenth century, the political situation as well as the surge of domestic tour books encouraged more travel in England, Scotland and Wales. From 1789 to 1815 the French Revolution and subsequent Napoleonic wars limited Continental travel. Europe became, in Anthony Burgess's words, 'a battleground, not a glorified museum with bordello attached'[10] and what travellers there were frequently went north or south to avoid French and European strife. When Ann Radcliffe, in the year (1794) in which her Gothic romance *The Mysteries of Udolpho* appeared, set out with her husband on a Continental tour, they passed through military precincts, saw wagons of wounded soldiers, and at times felt themselves in danger. They turned back before they reached the Alps, but the consolation prize (so over the next two decades for thousands of other English travellers) became a tour of the Lake District. There Radcliffe found the scenery of her native land to be far superior to what she saw in Europe. Her *A Journey Made in the Summer of 1794* (1795) uses language picturesque (and, even more, Gothic) to 'paint' Lake District scenes: 'of size and shape most huge, bold, and awful', 'terrific as the wildness of a maniac', 'every possible form of horror', 'a strange fantastic summit'.[11] But beneath that heightened and panting emotionalism, one feels in reading Radcliffe the presence of someone who looked hard at natural phenomena.

At their worst, however, travellers in the grip of a sublime and picturesque fervour simply mouth formulaic language. Some picturesque travellers and the books they wrote cry out for ridicule, and by the end of the eighteenth century, Wordsworth could begin *The Brothers* by having the parish priest of remote Ennerdale fulminate, 'These Tourists, Heaven preserve us!' One sub-genre of Romantic travel literature thus became anti-tourist literature, like William Combe's satiric *Tour of Doctor Syntax in Search of the Picturesque, a Poem* (1812), accompanied by 30 even more biting (and humorous) aquatints by Thomas Rowlandson. Wordsworth's guidebook to the Lakes is another rejoinder to tourist literature in the poet's attempts to convince travellers (and the residents themselves) to look at the scenery with a fresh, rather than a 'picturesque', eye. Even more important, Wordsworth wanted his readers to see themselves, the land and its inhabitants in harmonious relations that we might call 'ecological'.

After the defeat of Napoleon at Waterloo in June 1815, pent-up demand sent a torrent of English travellers across Europe. But in the quarter century since the start of the French Revolution, writers had helped change the goal of European travel from the focused educational journey to the melodramatic experiences of frequently moody wanderers. Close thy Grand Tour, open thy *Childe Harold's Pilgrimage*! Byron's great travel poem (Cantos I and II, 1812) clearly caught the fancy of a generation who had not been able to travel to Europe. In the Albanian and Greek journeys in Canto II, Greece replaces Rome as the centre of imaginative appeal. The traveller also becomes more important than the travel as he imposes his melancholy egoism on all he sees. 'The wandering outlaw of his own dark mind' set out again in 1816, and Byron in Canto III decisively moved writings about European travel away from urban antiquities and towards isolated spots of sublime beauty: 'High mountains are a feeling, but the hum / Of human cities torture' (III, 20, 682–3). Ecstatic responses to solo experiences were, of course, fragile and endangered as hordes of other 'Byronic' tourists and travel writers tramped across Europe in search of the solitary.

Another characteristic of post-1815 Romantic travel literature was the number of publications by women. Like the emerging genre of the novel, travel writing was less fettered by set assumptions about either the nature of the work or the gender of its author. The writing of journals and letters – sometimes thought of in the eighteenth and nineteenth centuries as primarily female activities – also easily translated into travel literature. Among the best of a generation of women travel writers should be included Anna Brownell Jameson (America, Canada, Europe), Frances Anne Kemble (America), Harriet Martineau (America, Egypt, the Holy Land), Sophia Poole (Egypt), Lady Hester Lucy Stanhope (Egypt, the Holy Land, Turkey, Syria, Lebanon and elsewhere), Frances Trollope (America, throughout Europe) and Dorothy Wordsworth (Scotland, Europe). In particular, Dorothy Wordsworth's admirable travel writings are now beginning to receive the attention they deserve. Her works in that genre have the qualities of the more famous Grasmere journals: vivid, imaginative, spontaneous, with a frank but unanalytical recording of feelings.

About the time of Queen Victoria's coronation in 1837, the competing guidebooks of John Murray and Karl Baedeker began to appear, with their homogenized litanies of facts and travel advice. And by the time of Wordsworth's death in 1850, Thomas Cook, exploiting the new railway networks, had begun to offer travel packages for the masses. 'Heard YE that Whistle?' asked Wordsworth in an 1844 sonnet (*Proud were ye, Mountains*), protesting against the expansion of the railway into the Lake District. That whistle's shriek ended the age of Romantic travel literature.

Many of the recent critical approaches to travel literature have been concerned less with the aesthetic than with the ideological. Hence, travel books have been used by some modern critics not primarily for their documentary or literary value, nor as markers of intellectual or imaginative history, but for what those works reveal about the interrelationships of literary history and social, political, economic, racial and gender histories. Since travel literature resides somewhere near the intersection of creative writing, popular culture and attempted factual reporting – and consciously or unconsciously embodies the author's attitudes toward the 'other' – these writings have been particularly useful to postcolonial, feminist and new historicist critics. Carole Fabricant argues in an influential essay that we should read this literature 'subversively and deconstructively rather than accepting it at face value',[12] and many have done so.

All travellers carry as baggage the ideals of their home culture. Travel literature can thus be read either as expressive of those ideals or as an indication of how someone with those beliefs inevitably imposes them on others. As Northern Europe began to assert its codes as dominant for the world and as Britain began its march toward imperial power, travellers' tales show how their attitudes slanted judgements of what they saw. Ultimately, post-colonial critics argue, the values expressed in travel writing assisted in the colonization process. While much travel literature makes the point, analyses of such accounts as James Bruce's *Travels to discover the Source of the Nile* (1790), Mungo Park's *Travels in the Interior Districts of Africa* (1799) and John Barrow's *An Account of the Travels into the Interior of Southern Africa in the Years 1797 and 1798* (1801) have been used to assert that English biases, often unknown to the writer, led to imperialism, to political control and economic exploitation. Mary Louise Pratt's *Imperial Eyes: Travel Writing and Transculturation* focuses on travel outside Europe, but she expresses no surprise that writings about Europe show similar conventions and techniques: 'The discourses that legitimate bourgeois authority and delegitimate peasant and subsistence lifeways, for example, can be expected to do this ideological work within Europe as well as in southern Africa or Argentina'.[13] Or, perhaps, in Wales, Scotland or the Lake District.

Recent feminist criticism of travel literature often converges with postcolonial analysis, finding 'travel' to be a term retaining 'its historical associations with a Western, white, middle class and with a generally male, privileged ease of movement'.[14] Male travellers typically applied female pronouns to the natural world, and those writers' minglings with nature also gendered the landscape as female (as in Wordsworth's stealing of the boat in *The Thirteen-Book Prelude*, I. 363–428). But those unions of the perceiver with the natural world may become problematic, rooted as they are in male understandings of the female and of the 'proper' gender roles in male–female relations. Indeed, many English male travellers characterized as female the Mediterranean, Near and Far Eastern countries, leading to less-than-benign formulations of those lands and their peoples. Of those travel books written by women, Mary Wollstonecraft's *Letters written during a short Residence in Sweden, Norway, and Denmark* (1796) has some of the most forceful protests against society's treatment of women, as when she asks 'is not man then the tyrant of the creation?' and does not apologize for asking the question: 'How can I avoid it, when most of the struggles of an eventful life have been occasioned by the oppressed state of my sex' (p. 171). Mary Wollstonecraft is thus much discussed in recent feminist criticism, as is Helen Maria Williams, whose volumes of *Letters written in France* give a graphic account of the French Revolution and her reluctant loss of faith in it.

Travel literature can also provide the factual details (of poverty and of social oppression, for example, or of the effects of the Industrial Revolution and the Enclosure Acts) that may be imaginatively glossed over by writers working in more explicitly 'literary' modes. Thus, new historicist critics – in their attempts to recover the economic and political realities 'absent' or 'repressed' from creative writing (and to understand why the authors displaced them) – find that the less literary varieties of travel writing often provide truer pictures of a society. For instance, Arthur Young's *Six Month's Tour through the North of England* (1771) has among its major headings 'The Use, Expence, and Profit of several Sorts of Manure' and 'The Condition and Number of the Poor, with their Rates, Earnings, &c.' Travellers in search of picturesque scenery had little truck with 'the several Sorts of Manure', and most similarly blotted out 'The Condition and Number of the Poor'. When new historicist critics turn to the more creative forms of travel literature, such omissions become primary, as do questions about who owns and has access to the land, and how the discourses of these writings reinforce dominant societal structures. For example, Carole Fabricant contends that domestic tourism, especially to country estates, seduced travellers 'into an identification with the tastes and interests of the landed rich through the manipulation of voyeuristic delights and vicarious pleasures'.[15]

Sociologist Dean MacCannell asserts that in post-industrial culture 'leisure is displacing work from the center of social arrangements'.[16] Travelling and the writing and reading of travel literature have become ever-increasing components of leisure from Wordsworth's time to the present. Thus, the popularity of travel writing in the eighteenth and nineteenth centuries, and the renewed critical interest in it in our time, make that literature as consequential for us as it was for the Romantics.

## NOTES

1   *LY*, I, 181.
2   See Fussell, 'Patrick Brydone', p. 53.
3   Buzard, *The Beaten Track*, pp. 1–2.
4   Ruddick, 'Thomas Gray', p. 133.
5   Buzard, *The Beaten Track*, p. 98.
6   Ruddick, 'Thomas Gray', p. 129.
7   Ibid., p. 142.
8   Nicholson, *The Lake District*, p. 25.
9   Ibid., p. 93.
10   Burgess, *The Grand Tour*, p. 28.
11   See *Romanticism*, p. 156.
12   Fabricant, 'The literature of domestic tourism', p. 275.
13   Pratt, *Imperial Eyes*, p. 10.
14   Lawrence, *Penelope Voyages*, p. xii.
15   Fabricant, 'The literature of domestic tourism', p. 257.
16   MacCannell, *The Tourist*, p. 5.

## WRITINGS

Gilpin, William: *Observations, relative chiefly to Picturesque Beauty, Made in the Year 1772*, 2 vols, London, R. Blamire, 1786; reprinted in facsimile as *Observations on the Mountains and Lakes of Cumberland and Westmorland*, Richmond, Surrey, Richmond Publishing, 1973.

Nicholson, Norman, *The Lake District: An Anthology*, Harmondsworth, Penguin Books, 1978.

Shelley, Mary and Shelley, P. B., *History of a six weeks' Tour*, Oxford and New York, Woodstock Books, 1991.

Wollstonecraft, Mary, *A short Residence in Sweden, Norway, and Denmark* and William Godwin, *Memoirs of the Author of The Rights of Woman*, ed. Richard Holmes, Harmondsworth, Penguin Books, 1987.

Wordsworth, William, *The Illustrated Wordsworth's Guide to the Lakes*, ed. Peter Bicknell, Exeter, Webb and Bower, 1984; New York, Congdon & Weed, 1984.

## REFERENCES AND FURTHER READING

Andrews, Malcolm, *The Search for the Picturesque: Landscape Aesthetics and Tourism in Britain, 1760–1800*, Stanford, Stanford University Press, 1989.

Bermingham, Ann, *Landscape and Ideology: The English Rustic Tradition, 1740–1860*, Berkeley and Los Angeles, University of California Press, 1986. Chiefly on painting, but much is also applicable to travel writing.

Bicknell, Peter, *The Picturesque Scenery of the Lakes*, Winchester, St Paul's Bibliographies, 1990; Detroit, Omnigraphics, 1990. A comprehensive bibliography, with informative notes.

Bohls, Elizabeth A., *Women Travel Writers and the Language of Aesthetics, 1716–1818*, Cambridge, Cambridge University Press, 1995. Includes fine chapters on Helen Maria Williams, Mary Wollstonecraft, Dorothy Wordsworth, Ann Radcliffe and Mary Shelley.

Burgess, Anthony, *The Age of the Grand Tour . . . in the Letters, Journals, and Writings of the most celebrated Voyagers between the Years 1720 and 1820*, New York, Crown, 1967. A coffee-table book – for a *very* big coffee table.

Buzard, James, *The Beaten Track: European Tourism, Literature, and the Ways to Culture, 1800–1918*, Oxford, Clarendon Press, 1993.

Copley, Stephen and Garside, Peter (eds) *The Politics of the Picturesque: Literature, Landscape and Aesthetics since 1770*, Cambridge, Cambridge University Press, 1994.

Fabricant, Carole, 'The literature of domestic tourism and the public consumption of private property', in *The New Eighteenth Century: Theory, Politics, English Literature*, ed. Felicity Nussbaum and Laura Brown, New York and London, Methuen, 1987.

Fussell, Paul, Jr, 'Patrick Brydone: the eighteenth century traveller as representative man', in *Literature as a Mode of Travel: Five Essays and a Postscript*, New York, New York Public Library, 1963.

Gilroy, Amanda, '"Love's history": Anna Jameson's grand tour', *The Wordsworth Circle*, 27 (1996) 29–33.

Lawrence, Karen R., *Penelope Voyages: Women and Travel in the British Literary Tradition*, Ithaca, NY: Cornell University Press, 1994. Excellent chapter on Mary Wollstonecraft.

MacCannell, Dean, *The Tourist: A New Theory of the Leisure Class*, New York, Schocken Books, 1976.

Nicholson, Norman, *The Lakers: The Adventures of the First Tourists*, London, Robert Hale, 1955.

Pratt, Mary Louise, *Imperial Eyes: Travel Writing and Transculturation*, London and New York, Routledge, 1992.

Robinson, Jane, *Wayward Women: A Guide to Women Travellers*, New York, Oxford University Press, 1990. Two-page-or-so entries, giving good biographical and bibliographical detail.

Ruddick, William, 'Thomas Gray's travel writing', in *Thomas Gray: Contemporary Essays*, ed. W. B. Hutchings and William Ruddick, Liverpool, Liverpool University Press, 1993.

Stafford, Barbara Maria, *Voyage Into Substance: Art, Science, Nature, and the Illustrated Travel Account, 1760–1840*, Cambridge, Mass., MIT Press, 1984.

Woof, Pamela, 'Dorothy Wordsworth and the pleasures of recognition: an approach to the travel journals', *The Wordsworth Circle*, 22 (1991) 150–60.

# 37

# Romantic Literary Criticism

## *Seamus Perry*

It is one of the great ages of criticism; but if we are looking for a general consensus about the true aims and procedures of art, then I suppose that 'Romantic Literary Criticism' doesn't really exist, not even in the baggy way that, say, 'deconstructive criticism' or 'The New Criticism' does. Mentioning it might make us think at once of Coleridge's gigantic attempt to construct a complete theory of literature based on fundamental principles; but then, equally, it might suggest quite the contrary of such systematic ambitions, the occasional, essayistic genius exemplified by Hazlitt. Despite such diversity, however, some major themes recur, often in the form of common indecisions; and in this essay, I am going to take a few related issues which we might choose to see as underlying this great body of work: naturalness (and its opposite, artificiality), organicism (and its opposite, mechanism) and egotism (and its opposite, empathy). Any of these would deserve a long chapter to itself, so I hope only to be suggestive; and I restrict myself to the way these interests shape the criticism of Shakespeare, Milton and Pope, the three most significant authors for critics of the period, and then come to a head in the response to Wordsworth.

## Naturalness and Artifice

'Romantic' critical concepts do not spring from nowhere of course, and to understand them properly we must see the way they fit into a wider tradition. The idea that poetry should somehow be 'natural' and avoid 'artifice', for instance, while sounding very 'romantic' to modern ears, is in fact part of a much wider cultural investment made by eighteenth-century thought in the authenticity of the primitive and the unsophisticated. For one example, the epics of the supposed ancient bard Ossian, actually the work of James Macpherson, enjoyed enormous popularity ('All hail, Macpherson! hail to thee, Sire of Ossian!' Wordsworth proclaimed – *W: Prose Works*, III, 77), and apparently confirmed the view that, in Hugh Blair's words, 'many circumstances of those times which we call barbarous, are favourable to the poetic spirit'. The refinements of civilization are ruinous to the vigorous natural energies of untamed imagination and true feeling: Ossian's poetry, wrote Blair, 'more perhaps than that of any other writer, deserves to be stiled, *The Poetry of the Heart* . . . a heart that is full, and pours itself forth', making an art that is Homeric in its primitive genius – 'Homer and Ossian both wrote from nature'.[1]

In one sense, of course, Ossian had it made because he was genuinely primitive (or so Blair thought): he hardly had to *choose* nature because he had never been civilized away from her in the first place; but the situation is less straightforward for someone coming afterwards. As the philosopher Imlac observes in Johnson's *Rasselas* (1759), 'the early writers are in possession of nature, and their followers of art: . . . the first excel in strength and invention, and the latter in elegance and refinement';[2] and Hazlitt argues similarly in his great essay 'Why the Arts Are Not Progressive' that the 'natural genius' of art is evident in its first stage, when the 'state of society' is 'comparatively barbarous' and artists still have a 'reliance on the power of nature', a happy dependency lost in later periods, when genius is displaced by 'cultivated and artificial minds . . . of an inferior order' (Howe, IV, 161, 163, 162). Such distinctions between 'nature' and 'art' are commonly used in eighteenth-century discussions to describe the relationship between Homer and Virgil, the exemplary case of original and latecomer. Pope prominently includes it in his *Essay on Criticism* (1711): Virgil may have seemed to be drawing 'but from *Nature's Fountains*', but, in fact, 'when t'examine ev'ry Part he came, / *Nature* and *Homer* were, he found, the *same*'. The moral Pope draws from this is not that we may then turn as happily to Nature as Homer did, but that, on the contrary, we must 'Learn hence for Ancient *Rules* a just Esteem; / To copy *Nature* is to copy *Them*'.[3] Foremost amongst the effects of civilization, then, is a kind of literary self-consciousness, exemplified by the establishment of canons of criticism, the ancient rules derived by Aristotle or by French neo-classicists like Boileau. Ossian, like Homer, 'did not write, like modern poets, to please readers and critics', a happy state of affairs which Blair, a reader and critic, regards with paradoxical nostalgia.[4] Virgil, on the other hand, the representative modern poet coming late, couldn't hope to rise above 'the Critick's Law'; and this, for a consciously Classicist poet like Pope, is entirely proper – though Pope's own interest in natural originality was actually quite as great as Blair's (and it was Homer, not Virgil, whom he chose to translate).

The great home-grown example of primitive genius was Shakespeare, who everyone had always celebrated as 'the poet of nature', and whose plays displayed this in their happy disruption of the alien ('French') neo-classical unities of time and place. 'The books of one age gain such authority, as to stand in the place of nature to another', wrote Johnson, describing exactly the relationship between Homer and Virgil portrayed by Pope; but 'Shakespeare, whether life or nature be his subject, shows plainly, that he has seen with his own eyes'.[5] In *L'Allegro* (published in 1645), Milton calls him 'sweetest Shakespeare fancy's child, / Warbling his native wood-notes wild' (133–4); and similarly, Pope (making an allusion to his own *Essay*) reduces him to the condition of nature in the preface to his edition: 'If ever any author deserved the name of an *Original*, it was *Shakespear* [*sic*]. *Homer* himself drew not his art so immediately from the fountains of Nature . . . 'tis not so just to say that he speaks from her, as that she speaks through him'. Fountains and bird-song flow over the potential imprisonment of imposed regulation; or, to use another metaphor, 'more finish'd and regular' plays are like 'a neat Modern building', whereas Shakespeare's ruder talent produces drama like 'an ancient majestick piece of Gothick Architecture'.[6] (A similar triumph of nature is implied by Johnson's figure: 'The work of a correct and regular writer is a garden accurately formed and diligently planted . . . the composition of Shakespeare is a forest'.)[7] Critics like Voltaire, who violate Shakespeare's natural genius with neo-Aristotelian criteria, attempt acts of sabotage: in an engaging little poem (1783),

Thomas Holcroft imagines Voltaire 'stabbing and stabbing' the bard, asleep in a dreamy pastoral dell; but to no avail – 'Preserved by his own charms and spells divine, / Safely the gentle Shakespeare slept and smiled'.[8] (Wordsworth is still angry about 'French critics' attacking Shakespeare in 1815: *W: Prose Works*, III, 68.) Unsurprisingly, English writers who chose to follow the artificial, neo-classical models were judged to have made a bad mistake: 'What are the lays of artful Addison', Warton wrote after *L'Allegro* in his own *The Enthusiast; or The Lover of Nature* (1744–8 – a tell-tale title), 'Coldly correct, to Shakespear's [*sic*] warblings wild?'[9]

The consensus on this decline from nature is not entirely complete: Peacock's delightful *The Four Ages of Poetry* (1820) satirizes the attempt to return to a second childhood, and, placing himself firmly on the side of refinement, Peacock provocatively takes the modern poet at his word, dismissing him as 'a semi-barbarian in a civilized community'.[10] Byron, too, the other great exception here, championed the urbane cultivation of Pope over the emotive naturalism he saw in Wordsworth and Coleridge: when he describes poetry, he turns instinctively to the new imagery of primitive, natural flow, 'the lava of the imagination', a more sensational version of Pope's unchecked fountain, but in a derogatory spirit ('I by no means rank poetry or poets high in the scale of intellect').[11] Metaphors of fluidity, as opposed to the hard constrictions of enforced regularity, are a tell-tale sign of the naturalist aesthetic: Wordsworth, for example, spoke at one point of good poetry as the 'spontaneous overflow of powerful feelings' (*W: Prose Works*, I, 126); and while in 1764 Churchill, a satirist in the Popean tradition, had mocked the fluidity of unchecked spontaneity in one of his targets – 'Why may not Langhorne, simple in his lay, / Effusion on effusion pour away?' (*The Candidate*, 41–2) – Coleridge defiantly reclaimed the word as the fitting name for his own early poetry.[12] 'The great fault of a modern school of poetry', as Hazlitt complained, 'is, that it is an experiment to reduce poetry to a mere effusion of natural sensibility': not that he rejected the criterion of nature, nor even that he rejected the laudatory rhetoric of 'flowing' – for example, he reserves highest praise for 'the impassioned parts of Shakspeare's [*sic*] language, which flowed from the warmth and originality of his imagination, and were his own' (Howe, V, 53, 55).

The rule-bound artificiality of Pope becomes a stock of Romantic criticism, as the criterion of naturalness establishes itself as a critical norm: being at once urban and urbane, and perceived as drawing his inspiration from literature rather than from genuine feeling, Pope (to a lesser extent, Dryden) becomes the great counter-example to the natural aesthetic. Warton's *Essay on the Genius and Writings of Pope* (1756; 1782) praised Pope's ethical virtues, while at the same time making very clear that his genius was of a secondary kind, an example of the 'correctness' championed in the 'nauseous cant of the French critics', rather than the nature and passion followed by other writers.[13] Pope is 'a satirist, and a moralist, and a wit, and a critic, and a fine writer, much more than he is a poet', wrote Francis Jeffrey: 'there are no pictures of nature or of simple emotion in all his writings', the inevitable limitation of being 'the poet of town life, and of high life, and of literary life'.[14] If by 'a great poet', wrote Hazlitt, 'we mean one who gives the utmost grandeur to our conceptions of nature, or the utmost force to the passions of the heart, Pope was not in this sense a great poet'. The definitive natural poets he has in mind are, as we might guess, Homer and Shakespeare: 'the power of the imagination in them, is the representative power of all nature', but Pope 'saw nature only dressed by art' (Howe, V, 69, 70). Keats similarly deplored the Augustan deviation from a true English, Shakespearean line, calling it 'a schism / Nurtured by foppery and barbarism', whose perpetrators 'swayed about upon a rocking horse / And thought it Pegasus' (*Sleep and Poetry* [1817], 181–2; 186–7). The joke is Hazlitt's, who dismissed neo-classical aesthetic prescriptiveness by announcing: 'Dr Johnson and Pope would have converted [Milton's] vaulting Pegasus into a rocking-horse' (Howe, IV, 40). Leigh Hunt enthusiastically applauded Keats's view of the period between Milton's death and the present, using a metaphor which happily coupled unnatural transplantation *and* urbane artifice: 'People got shoots from France, that ended in nothing but a little barren wood, from which they made flutes for young gentlemen and fan-sticks for ladies'. In so doing, they ignored 'the rich and enchanted ground of real poetry, fertile with all that English succulence could produce'.[15]

Perhaps the most devoted and extreme spokesman for a natural aesthetic is Wordsworth: as M. H. Abrams remarks, his 'cardinal standard of poetic value is "nature"'.[16] Wordsworth also criticized Pope, who should have 'confided more in his native genius': instead of doing so, he 'bewitched the nation by his melody, and dazzled it by his polished style', the success of which finally 'tempted him into a belief that Nature was not to be trusted' (*W: Prose Works*, III, 72). Pope didn't follow nature, and modern poetry follows Pope, describing the sophistications of civil society instead of pastoral authenticity, and supplanting genuine emotions by artificial ones. This baleful influence is especially evident in that poetry in which true feeling should be most evident: epitaphs; and, scrutinizing the eighteenth century, Wordsworth declared himself able to find 'scarcely one which is not thoroughly tainted by the artifices which have overrun our writings in metre since the days of Dryden and Pope' (*W: Prose Works*, II, 80). 'I vindicate the rights and dignity of Nature', the third *Essay on Epitaphs* begins ringingly; yet the eighteenth century shows nature's rights to be strangely ignorable: this is not because nature is weak, Wordsworth insists, but because 'the adversary of nature, (call that adversary Art or by what name you will) is *comparatively* strong' (*W: Prose Works*, II, 83). And so we come to the clearest statement of a very paradoxical position: the artist's adversary is – art.


## Organicism and Mechanism

An important development of the appeal to 'nature' is to look to the perfect poem not merely as a vivid presentation of nature and natural emotions, but as *itself*, as a poetic object, somehow possessing the attributes of naturalness, such as 'life'. The deplorable French might study laboriously and apply the critic's rules, but the real work of genius has its own life: it arises naturally, and so, far from being worked up from its literary precursors, it is perfectly original, like a tree. As Edward Young wrote in his very influential *Conjectures on Original Composition* (1759): 'An *Original* may be said to be of a *vegetable* nature; it rises spontaneously from the vital root of Genius; it *grows*, it is not *made*'; meanwhile, '*Imitations* are often a sort of *Manufacture* wrought up by those *Mechanics*, *Art*, and *Labour*, out of pre-existent materials not their own'.[17] The adversary of vegetable nature here is 'Art', as it is for Wordsworth: works of mere 'art' have to be worked up by the diligent mechanic, while the products of true original genius (as it were) work up themselves. 'If Poetry come not as naturally as the Leaves to a tree', as Keats wrote, 'it had better not come at all' (Rollins, I, 238–9), a sentiment satirically endorsed by Lamb, horrified at seeing a Milton manuscript: 'I had thought of the *Lycidas* as a full-grown beauty – as springing up with all its parts absolute. . . . How it staggered me to see the fine things in their ore! interlined, corrected! . . . as if they might have been otherwise, and just as good!'[18] The target of Lamb's comedy here is probably his friend Coleridge, the most important English theorist of the way great art-works are like biological organisms. Borrowing from Schlegel, Coleridge contrasts the naturally 'organic' with the mechanically 'artificial':

> form is mechanic when on any given material we impress a pre-determined form, not necessarily arising out of the properties of the material – as when to a mass of wet clay we give shape whatever shape we wish it to retain when hardened – The organic form on the other hand is innate, it shapes as it developes [*sic*] from within, and the fullness of its developement [*sic*] is one & the same with the perfection of its outward Form. Such is the Life, such is the form (CC *Lectures on Literature*, I, 495; Coleridge's alterations not reproduced)

When the shape is 'superinduced', he writes in his notebook, it is 'the Death or the imprisonment of the Thing', the denial, that is, of its natural 'Life' (ibid., II, 224).

It is Shakespeare, we are not surprised to find, whose works Coleridge finds fulfil the organic test totally, happily controverting 'the old blunder. . . concerning the irregularity and wildness' of his plays repeatedly made by the French critics and their followers (ibid., p. 211): a blunder because, while they do indeed fail the test of the Aristotelian unities, by the higher unities of organic form the plays 'have their own laws or regulæ – and according to these they are *regular*' (CC *Marginalia*, I, 378). Shakespeare is the poet of nature in a much more profound way than the cliché of the 'mere child of nature' (CC *Lectures on Literature*, I, 209) whose rude, uncultivated genius produced works of unpolished power. Quite to the contrary, his plays exemplify more than any other works the *true*, inwardly derived unity of organic form, 'the power of acting creatively under laws of its own origination': like a living creature, the art-work grows to completion, 'but a living Body is of necessity an organized one – & what is organization, but the connection of Parts to a whole, so that each Part is at once End & Means!' (ibid., pp. 495, 494). This is a real unity, not the mechanistic impositions of the neo-classicists, that takes the constituent parts of a play (its characters, say) as means to an end – the fulfilment of the neo-classical rules.

'The work of a true Poet, in its form, its shapings and modifications, is distinguished from all other works that assume to belong to the class of poetry, as a natural from an artificial flower; or as the mimic garden of a child, from an enamelled meadow', Coleridge said, borrowing from Schlegel (ibid., pp. 515–16); and Pope, we are no more surprised to learn, fails the organic test. His poetry comes from an arbitrary imposition of form on an unnatural subject-matter: 'observations on man and manners in an artificial state of society, as its matter and substance: and in the logic of wit, conveyed in smooth and strong epigrammatic couplets, as its *form*'. In Pope, thoughts are merely '*translated* into the language of poetry', gathered together mechanically, and joined into 'a heap of sorites' (that is, something 'heaped together'), 'a *conjunction disjunctive*' of witty antitheses (CC *Biographia*, I, 18–19). Such failure is not peculiar to Pope, though: Coleridge similarly deplored the 'conjunction disjunctive' of Samuel Butler's lines, 'And like a lobster boil'd the Morn / From black to red began to turn' (*Notebooks*, II, 2,112), which he saw as the work, not of imagination, but of 'wit' – or, to give it another name, 'fancy', 'the *aggregating power*', as he puts it in a letter (Griggs, II, 1,034), the faculty, as he said late in life, that 'brings together images which have no connection natural or moral, but are yoked together by the poet by some accidental coincidence' (CC *Table Talk*, I, 489–90). Ben Jonson also fails the test, for while he offers 'an extraordinary opulence of thought', it is 'the produce of an amassing power in the author, and not of a growth from within' (CC *Lectures on Literature*, II, 154). Beaumont and Fletcher fail the organic test too: 'Sh[ake-speare] is the height, breadth, and depth of Genius: B[eaumont] and F[letcher] the excellent mechanism, in juxta-position and succession, of Talent' (CC *Marginalia*, I, 401). Their plays are merely mechanical aggregations of material, 'just as a man might fit together a quarter of an orange, a quarter of an Apple, and the like of a Lemon and of a Pomengranate, and make it look like one round diverse colored [*sic*] fruit' – a fake fruit (not a true vegetable), quite unlike those made by Nature, 'who works from within', and also unlike those fruits of Shakespeare's imagination, 'for he too worked in the spirit of Nature, by evolving the germ within by the imaginative Power' (CC *Lectures on Literature*, II, 147).

So, Coleridge's criticism involves a surprising change in the notion of 'nature', away from meaning the world of reality which art may seek to mirror, and towards meaning a kind of energy or a principle of poetic organization. Dr Johnson announces in his Preface to Shakespeare that 'nothing can please many, and please long, but just representations of general nature'.[19] For Coleridge, the criterion of excellence has turned from the accuracy of representation, and towards the insides of the poetic work: 'nothing can permanently please, which does not contain *within itself* the reason why it is so, and not otherwise' (CC *Biographia*, II, 12, my italics). This 'internalizing' tendency is not the whole truth about Coleridge's aesthetics, but it is one important truth about them; and, in a way, Shakespeare was always going to be the most difficult author to apply the principle to, because his art has always been celebrated as a portrait of real life ('nature' in its usual, external sense), a triumphant imitation of reality: such praise stresses the relationship between art and the external world, rather than the relationships internal to the art-work. Of course, the perfection of organic form need not rule out the simultaneous achievement of mimetic accuracy – the internal administration of the poem may be as harmonious as its foreign affairs – and Coleridge applauded Shakespeare's realism as loudly as anyone; but the two approaches implied by these very different kinds of praise are, at the least, likely to prove difficult to reconcile in critical practice. This is indeed the case in Coleridge's own criticism, and the two strains co-exist, which explains why he is celebrated (or deplored) by later Shakespeareans both as a practitioner of 'character' criticism and the forerunner of 'symbolic' or 'structural' criticism. The plays show 'nature *shakespearianized*' (*Notebooks*, II, 2,274), organized into the 'second nature' of an organic unity; yet they obviously succeed, too, in convincingly imitating life; and so Coleridge has to strike a paradoxical comprom-ise. Shakespeare's characters are tremendously realistic and entirely themselves (as evi-denced, for instance, by Coleridge's ability to deduce Polonius's successful past career as a statesman); and yet they are *also* parts of the organic life of the play: 'each [character] has indeed a life of its own & is an individuum of itself; but yet an organ to the whole' (CC *Lectures on Literature*, II, 151).

## Egotism and Empathy

This Coleridgean ambiguity over Shakespeare is a version of a much more general feature of Romantic criticism. We could put this ambiguity as a question: is the true hero of criticism to be the poet's art or the reality which that art discovers for us?

When Coleridge speaks of art as a 'second nature' – a notion he would have known from Philip Sidney's *Apologie for Poesy*, and which he also met in Kant – he is favouring the subjective 'improvement' of *first* nature (that is to say, 'nature') effected by the imagination. When he memorably calls poets 'Gods of Love who tame the Chaos' (*Notebooks*, II, 2,355), he is making this kind of point; as he is when he remarks, 'Shakespeare's characters from Othello or Macbeth down to Dogberry are ideal; they are not [the] things, but the abstracts of the things which a great mind may take into itself and naturalize to its own heaven' (CC *Lectures on Literature*, I, 351). As I say, Shakespeare is an unlikely hero for this aesthetic; but Milton is altogether more suitable. The best word for Milton, Coleridge thought, was '*Ideality*' (ibid., p. 145), the 'subject' (that is, Milton) so much greater than the characters Milton describes that, as Coleridge enthused, 'it is Milton himself whom you see; his Satan, his Adam, his Raphael – they are all John Milton, and it is a sense of this intense egotism that gives me the greatest pleasure in reading Milton's works' (CC *Table Talk*, I, 420). It is a radically counter-Shakespearean imagination; and like all modern poetry (in Coleridge's view), it exhibits 'an under consciousness of a sinful nature, a fleeting away of external things, the mind or subject greater than the object' (CC *Lectures on Literature*, II, 427–8).

External things do not always fleet away, however: one kind of imagination *returns* you to nature, the kind Coleridge praises in a counter-idealist moment (he is a very contradictory figure) as 'the power of exciting the sympathy of the reader by a faithful adherence to the truth of nature' which he found in Wordsworth, an adherence especially to those 'forms, incidents, and situations, of which, for the common view, custom had bedimmed all the lustre, had dried up the sparkle and the dew drops' (CC *Biographia*, II, 5; I, 80). This giving 'the charm of novelty to things of every day' (ibid., II, 7) is a kind of primitivism, an 'as if' primitivism: the reader is startled by the vivid accuracy of poetry into seeing things *as if* for the first time, 'ordinary things . . . presented to the mind in an unusual way', as Wordsworth puts it (*W: Prose Works*, I, 123 [1802 reading]), as a child might see them, for instance, or Adam, the earth's 'first-born birth' (*Expostulation and Reply*, 11).

Again, Shakespeare is the naturalistic model: 'nature is the poet here', Coleridge writes of *Venus and Adonis*, a handing-over of authorship which allows the poetry a complete freshness of perception, as if seeing things for the first time: Shakespeare 'writes exactly as if of an other planet' (CC *Lectures on Literature*, I, 70). This kind of freshly realizing imagination was one way a modern poet might return to the natural. ' "With what eyes these poets see nature!" ', as Hazlitt said to himself after hearing Wordsworth praise a light effect; 'and ever after, when I saw the sun-set stream upon the objects facing it, conceived I had made a discovery, or thanked Mr Wordsworth for having made one for me!' (Howe, XII, 118). 'Romanticism' is often associated with the triumph of kinds of subjectivism; but it might quite as well be credited with the discovery of the external and 'ordinary' as a just subject of literary attention: the two trends are mutually defining, of course. 'I do not know how without being culpably particular I can give my Reader a more exact notion of the style in which I wished these poems to be written than by informing him that I have at all times endeavoured to look steadily at my subject', as Wordsworth wrote of the *Lyrical Ballads* (*W: Prose Works*, I, 130–2); and elsewhere claimed proudly of *An Evening Walk* that 'there is not an image in [the poem] which I have not observed'. The fresh-eyed perception of one image especially, some oak branches against the sun, he recalled in old age, initiated his poetic career: 'I date from it my consciousness of the infinite variety of natural appearances which had been unnoticed by the poets of any age or country, so far as I was acquainted with them: and I made a resolution to supply in some degree the deficiency'.[20]

Coleridge attributes Shakespeare's realistic powers to a miraculous power of self-projection: he 'darts himself forth, and passes into all the forms of human character and passion, the one Proteus of the fire and the flood' while Milton 'attracts all form and things to himself, into the unity of his own IDEAL. All things and modes of action shape themselves anew in the being of MILTON; while SHAKESPEARE becomes all things, yet for ever remaining himself' (*CC Biographia*, II, 27–8). Wordsworth adopts a distinction to do similar work in the Preface to his 1815 *Poems*: the 'poetical' and the 'human and dramatic Imagination' (*W: Prose Works*, III, 34); and Hazlitt, too, has the same division of principles. 'The two principles of imitation and imagination . . . are not only distinct, but almost opposite', he writes (Howe, XVI, 63); and which he owns allegiance to himself remains uncertain. Both principles can claim 'nature' to be on their side. At one point Hazlitt writes that 'imagination is that faculty which represents objects, not as they are in themselves, but as they are moulded by other thoughts and feelings', adding, 'this language is not the less true to nature, because it is false in point of fact; but so much the more true and natural, if it conveys the impression which the object under the influence of passion makes on the mind' (ibid., V, 4). This is a subjective notion of naturalness; but this same subjectivity can be regarded elsewhere with some suspicion: 'the imagination is an exaggerating and exclusive faculty: it takes from one thing to add to another: it accumulates circumstances together to give the greatest possible effect to a favourite object', unlike the understanding, 'a dividing and measuring faculty' that properly represents the natural differences of objectivity (ibid., IV, 214). Hazlitt's anti-idealism expresses itself in the belief that 'the arts hold immediate communication with nature, and are only derived from that source'; and in a stirring simile, Hazlitt compares the arts to 'Antaeus in his struggle with Hercules, who was strangled when he was raised above the ground, and only revived and recovered his strength when he touched his mother earth' (ibid., p. 160). 'The fine arts . . . are true and unsophisticated, because they are conversant with real objects . . . and please by the truth of imitation only' (ibid., XII, 245), a pleasure given especially vividly by Shakespeare, who possesses the 'faculty of bringing every object in nature, whether present or absent, before the mind's eye' (ibid.). Shelley's error, for example, is to abandon the Antaeus principle: 'clogged by no dull system of realities, no earth-bound feelings', Hazlitt ironically puts it, Shelley's 'fancy, will, caprice, predominated over and absorbed the natural influences of things' (ibid., VIII, 149; XVI, 265). The failure of Coleridge's criticism, analogously, is the loss of this grounding touch: 'quitting the plain ground of "history and particular facts" for the first butterfly theory, fancy-bred from the maggots of his brain', as he put it, graphically; or, slightly more patiently, 'he is without a strong feeling of the existence of anything out of himself' (ibid., XVI, 118; VII, 117).

Hazlitt's Shakespeare (like Pope's) is not just a realist, he is a super-realist, a poet of universal subjectivity who possesses a self-abnegating power of total sympathy. 'His genius consisted in the faculty of transforming himself at will into whatever he chose', writes Hazlitt: 'he was the Proteus of human intellect' (ibid., VIII, 42). 'He had only to think of any thing in order to become that thing, with all the circumstances belonging to it' (Coleridge, we recall, added the important caveat, 'yet for ever remaining himself'); and the result of this extraordinary power is a dramatic art in which 'each of his characters is as much itself, and as absolutely independent of the rest, as well as of the author, as if they were living persons, not fictions of the mind' (ibid., V, 48, 50). Shakespeare, said Hazlitt, was 'the least of an egotist of any body in the world', 'the least of an egotist that it is possible to be' (ibid., XI, 92; V, 47); and against this, like Coleridge, he places the counter-example of Milton: 'you trace the bias and opinions of the man in the creations of the poet' (ibid., VIII, 42). When Keats writes of Milton, 'life to him would be death to me', he is following Hazlittian principles, as he is when celebrating Shakespeare for exemplifying a poetic self capable of an utter, self-extinguishing identification: 'it is not itself – it has no self – it is very thing and nothing – It has no character' (Rollins, II, 212; I, 387). Keats's Shakespeare, chameleon-like, becomes what is around him: it can hardly be a plausible account of the real man I suppose, nor of his methods of composition; rather, it is a hyperbolic way of insisting on the validity of the realist imagination.

## The Case of Wordsworth

The elements of Romantic criticism which I have been describing – the paradoxical appeal to nature, and the great symbolic distinction between Milton and Shakespeare – find their contemporary focus in the criticism of Wordsworth, who appears in his contemporaries' accounts as an oddly hybrid creature, at once a poet of nature and yet a poet of egotism.

I have already mentioned Wordsworth's emphatic naturalism: Peacock not unreasonably judged him 'the great leader of the returners to nature';[21] and, later in the century, Arnold was attributing Shakespearean powers to him – 'It might seem that Nature not only gave him the subject matter for his poem, but wrote his poem for him'.[22] Such judgements follow one strong line of Wordsworthian self-definition: his naturalist manifesto-statements are certainly ringing, including at one point the enthusiastic adoption of the sympathetic principle: the poet, he writes, should 'bring his feelings near to those of the persons whose feelings he describes, nay, for short spaces of time, perhaps, to let himself slip into an entire delusion, and even compound and identify his own feelings with theirs' (*W: Prose Works*, I, 138); and Keats for one praised Wordsworth for his ability to 'think into the human heart', a capacity which he thought Milton lacked (Rollins, I, 282). Elsewhere, the desire to be 'real' (the word recurs again and again in the Preface to *Lyrical Ballads*) expresses itself as the announced intention to write in 'the very language of men', to use 'a selection of the language really used by men' (*W: Prose Works*, I, 130, 137) and so on; and the model for this 'real' poetry, we are not surprised to hear, is the work of 'the earliest Poets of all nations' who 'generally wrote from passion excited by *real* events; they wrote naturally, and as men' in the language 'really spoken by men' (ibid., I, 160, 161). Wordsworth's ambition is to write 'Poetry in which the language closely resembles that of life and nature' (ibid., p. 152) – but in 'closely' lurks the intricacy. Coleridge, whose use of the natural paradigm was not simply one of imitation (as we have seen), thoroughly criticizes the philosophical inadequacy of Wordsworth's use of 'real' in volume two of *Biographia*; and justly rubbishes Wordsworth's forlorn attempt to locate this 'real' language in a particular social group (Cumbrian shepherds). On the other hand, when Wordsworth's desire for a 'natural' poetic language takes up the rhetoric of embodiment, as in the third *Essay On Epitaphs* ('an incarnation of the thought' not 'a clothing for it'), we see him getting closer to a Coleridgean organicism (*W: Prose Works*, II, 84).

Yet, for all his intent interest in the appearances of external nature, Wordsworth is also characterized by his contemporaries as an egotistical poet. For example, despite his enthusiasm for the recuperative 'perfect truth of nature in his images and descriptions as taken directly from nature', Coleridge evidently wanted to see Wordsworth as a Miltonic genius as well, and laments the '*matter-of-factness*' which spoils the ideality to which his imagination should have aspired, its power (in Wordsworth's own words) to 'add the gleam, / The light that never was, on sea or land' (CC *Biographia*, II, 126, 151). Coleridge criticizes Wordsworth's misguided attempts at dramatic verse, for which his un-Shake-spearean cast of mind renders him quite unsuitable, capable only of 'ventriloquism, where two are represented as talking, while in truth one man only speaks' (ibid., p. 135) – and we think of a Miltonic imagination again, the author readily identified with 'his Satan, his Adam, his Raphael'. For Keats, Wordsworth gave his name to 'the wordsworthian or egotistical sublime; which is a thing per se and stands alone' (Rollins, I, 387), a cast of poetry in direct (and unfavourable) contrast with the characterlessness of Shakespeare. 'Milton is [Wordsworth's] great idol', wrote Hazlitt, who knew a significant fact when he saw one, adding (to Wordsworth's fury), 'we do not think our author has any very cordial sympathy with Shakespear [*sic*]' (Howe, XI, 92): no sympathy, that is, with the prime exponent of poetic sympathy.

Hazlitt's criticism is strongly influenced by his own inclination toward the drama and visual art as a paradigm for the arts (he was himself an accomplished painter); and his running complaint was against the 'devouring egotism' of modern poetry, whose meanness of spirit and wholly insufficient grasp of nature, render 'nothing interesting, nothing heroical, but themselves' (ibid., V, 53): the modern he has especially in mind is Words-worth. Wordsworth's realistic, de-familiarizing aesthetic is ostensibly self-denying, not attracting the reader to the facility of the art, but to its simple translucence; but Hazlitt cleverly interprets Wordsworth's use of the ordinary as a kind of self-aggrandizement, another kind of egotism. 'It was in truth / An ordinary sight, but I should need / Colours and words that are unknown to man / To paint the visionary dreariness' (*Prelude*, XI. 308–11; *Romanticism*, p. 453): is the hero of a 'Spot of Time' the extraordinariness of the ordinary, or the might of the mind to create such extraordinary experience out of such humble raw material? Hazlitt couldn't have known those lines as it happens; but he found plentiful evidence of the imagination they display elsewhere in Wordsworth: 'he takes the common every-day events and objects of nature, or rather seeks those that are the most simple and barren of effect' so that his own mental contribution can be shown at its most striking – 'all other interests are absorbed in the deeper interest of his own thoughts' (Howe, IV, 120). This might just about fulfil one of Hazlitt's criteria of imaginative naturalness ('the impression which the object under the influence of passion makes on the mind'), 'things not as they *are*, but as they *appear*', in Wordsworth's formulation (*W: Prose Works*, III, 63); but evidently it quite fails another criterion, the excellence of that 'trembling sensibility which is awake to every change and every modification of its ever-varying impressions' (Howe, VIII, 83). For Wordsworth, says Hazlitt, 'the object is nothing but as it furnishes food for internal meditation, for old associations', and this magnificent egotism is a kind of blind introversion: 'he sits in the centre of his own being'. Like Milton, Wordsworth 'stamps [his] character, that deep individual interest, on what-ever he meets', and that stamp is so completely deforming of the object in itself that, Hazlitt rather madly goes on to say, 'if there had been no other being in the universe, Mr Wordsworth's poetry would have been just as it is' (ibid., p. 44).

It is hardly surprising, then, that Hazlitt's follower Keats could bring himself to like only 'half of Wordsworth' (Rollins, II, 69), for it is, pre-eminently, in the hybrid art of Wordsworth that the contradictory imaginative impulses which dominate Romantic criticism co-exist in creative tension – and to that extent, at least, we may concur with Hazlitt's judgement that 'Mr Wordsworth's genius is a pure emanation of the Spirit of the Age' (Howe, XI, 86).

## NOTES

1 Hugh Blair, *A Critical Dissertation on the Poems of Ossian* (1763; 1765); reprinted in James Mac-pherson, *The Poems of Ossian and Related Works*, ed. Howard Gaskill, Edinburgh, Edinburgh University Press, 1996, pp. 343–412, 345, 358.

2 Samuel Johnson, *The History of Rasselas, Prince of Abissinia*, ed. Geoffrey Tillotson and Brian Jen-kins, London, Oxford University Press, 1971, p. 27.

3 Pope, *An Essay on Criticism*, 133, 134–5, 139–40; in John Butt (ed.) *The Poems of Alexander Pope: A One-volume edition of the Twickenham Text with selected annotations*, London, Methuen, 1968, p. 148.

4 Blair, *Dissertation*, p. 356.

5 Preface to *The Works of Shakespeare* (1765); in John Wain (ed.) *Johnson as Critic*, London, Rout-ledge and Kegan Paul, 1973, pp. 149–77, 170.

6 Preface to *The Works of Shakespeare* (1725); in Paul Hammond (ed.) *Selected Prose of Alexander Pope*, Cambridge, Cambridge University Press, 1987, pp. 158–69, 158, 169.

7 Johnson, 'Preface', p. 166.

8 In Roger Lonsdale (ed.) *The New Oxford Book of Eighteenth Century Verse*, Oxford, Oxford Univer-sity Press, 1985, p. 680.

9 In Lonsdale, *New Oxford Book*, p. 390.

10 Thomas Love Peacock, 'The four ages of poetry', in H. F. B. Brett-Smith (ed.) *Peacock's Four Ages of Poetry {;} Shelley's Defence of Poetry {;} Browning's Essay on Shelley*, Oxford, Blackwell, 1972, pp. 1–19, 16.

11 Marchand, III, 179.

12 Preface to *Poems on Various Subjects* (1796); in EHC, II, 1,136.

13 Joseph Warton, *Essay on the Genius and Writings of Pope*; in John Barnard (ed.) *Pope: The Critical Heritage*, London, Routledge and Kegan Paul, 1973, p. 390.

14 *Edinburgh Review* (August, 1811); in Francis Jef-frey, *Contributions to the Edinburgh Review*, 4 vols, London, Longman, 1844, II: 292.

15 Review of *Poems*, in *The Examiner* (1 June, 1817); in G. M. Matthews (ed.) *Keats: The Critical Herit-age*, London, Routledge and Kegan Paul, 1971, p. 57.

16 Abrams, *ML*, p. 105.

17 Edward Young, *Conjectures on Original Composi-tion*, 1759; facsimile reprint, Leeds, Scolar Press, 1966, p. 12.

18 *London Magazine* (October, 1820); in Joseph Anthony Wittreich, Jr (ed.) *The Romantics on Milton: Formal Essays and Critical Asides*, Cleve-land, Press of Case Western Reserve University, 1970, p. 298.

19 Johnson, 'Preface', p. 151.

20 Fenwick, Note to *An Evening Walk*; in William Wordsworth, *An Evening Walk*, ed. James Averill Ithaca, Cornell University Press, 1984, p. 301.

21 Peacock, 'Four ages', p. 15.

22 'Wordsworth' (1879); in Matthew Arnold, *Selected Prose*, ed. P. J. Keating, Harmondsworth, Penguin, 1987, pp. 381–2.

## REFERENCES AND FURTHER READING

Appleyard, J. A., *Coleridge's Philosophy of Literature: The Development of a Concept of Poetry 1791–1819*, Cambridge, Mass., Harvard University Press, 1965.

Attridge, Derek, *Peculiar Language: Literature as Difference from the Renaissance to James Joyce*, London, Methuen, 1988, pp. 46–89.

Badawi, M. M., *Coleridge: Critic of Shakespeare*, Cambridge, Cambridge University Press, 1973.

Beer, John, 'Coleridge's originality as a critic of Shakespeare', *Studies in the Literary Imagination* XIX.2 (fall, 1986), 51–69.

Bialostosky, D. H., 'Coleridge's interpretation of Wordsworth's preface to *Lyrical Ballads*', *PMLA* 93 (1978) 912–24.

Bromwich, David, *Hazlitt: The Mind of a Critic*, New York, Oxford University Press, 1983.

Fogle, Richard Harter, *The Idea of Coleridge's Criticism*, Westport, Greenwood Press, 1978.

Garber, Frederick, 'Nature and the Romantic mind: egotism, empathy, irony', *Comparative Literature* 29 (1977) 193–212.

Park, Roy, *Hazlitt and the Spirit of the Age: Abstraction and Critical Theory*, Oxford, Clarendon Press, 1971.

Parker, G. F., *Johnson's Shakespeare*, Oxford, Clarendon Press, 1991. Chapter three (pp. 63–155) compares Johnson, Hazlitt, Coleridge and Schlegel as critics of Shakespeare.

Sharrock, Roger, 'Wordsworth's revolt against literature', *Essays in Criticism* 3 (1953) 396–412.

Wellek, René, *A History of Modern Criticism: 1750–1950. The Romantic Age* (vol. 2), London, Cape, 1970.

# PART FOUR
# Issues and Debates

# 38

# Romanticism and Gender

### Susan J. Wolfson

## What is 'Gender Criticism'?

Literature is shaped by cultural forces as well as individual imaginations; as Percy Bysshe Shelley put it (reversing the emphasis) in his Preface to *Prometheus Unbound* (1820), writers 'are in one sense the creators and in another the creations of their age'. This is true of the language of 'gender', the culturally generated, invested and disseminated values – political, social, psychological and emotional – attached to sexual identity and difference, and radiating from such words as 'masculine', 'feminine', 'manly' and 'effeminate'. Sexual identity, 'male' and 'female', is grounded in anatomy, while 'gender' is a socio-cultural product, a historically specific creation of the age. Critical attention to gender is not only a lively project today; gender criticism was also at work in the age of Romanticism, whose literature is one of its founding sites. Before turning to these sites, we need to define more specifically what gender criticism is today, and how it got there.

Following a vigorous decade or two of modern feminist criticism and theory (which affected the study of British Romanticism), gender studies emerged in the 1980s, sometimes as a corrective to earlier feminist agenda. In a landmark essay published in 1981, 'Archimedes and the paradox of feminist criticism', Myra Jehlen argued that the focus of feminist criticism on women's writing was unproductively narrow and even isolationist. Jehlen called for a feminist analysis of the dominant canon of 'men's writing' and, with this relativizing term, proposed situating it and women's texts in a radically comparative analysis of their contingency. This proposal was controversial at a time when work on women writers was still seeking academic legitimacy, but it proved prophetic. Gender criticism is now a consolidated emergence from feminist criticism.

What are the main differences? Most feminist critics were women; gender critics are a mixed company, one that started to gather in the 1980s as men began to write feminist-toned criticism and deploy feminist theory. Gender criticism addresses men's writing, applying the paradigms of feminist criticism to this canon, in order to read literary texts and the larger 'social text' for their reflections, embodiments and disseminations of pervasive attitudes about gender: the cultural definitions of 'manhood' and 'masculine', the political priority of male over female, the assumptions about the 'natural' weakness of female intelligence, women's 'natural' tendency to subservience, and so forth. Gender criticism has also evolved to include gay studies, which critiques the heterosexism of the dominant canon, investigates writing by homosexual men and women, and reads texts for their stereotypes and their (often closeted) representations of homo-social culture and homo-erotic relations. Sometimes called a 'post-feminist' criticism, gender criticism has absorbed and built on feminist premises, but shifts the emphases. The critique of 'patriarchal culture' that motivated feminist criticism meant to unsettle a field of discussion that had ignored the paradigms of sexism and misogyny in the 'masculine' literary tradition, one said to marginalize or silence female voices and experience, or submit female figures to stereotyping, from the demonic to ideal. Gender criticism tends not to view men's writing as a uniform tradition, a monolithic canon of male privilege and power. It is more likely to read a range of attitudes, ones often at odds with one another, and given to instabilities and divisions – not only about 'masculinity' as a cultural category but also its unstable difference from the 'feminine'. Gender criticism shows how some writing by men (even texts previously identified as arsenals of patriarchal values) reports anxieties about male power, questions the divine ordination and natural guarantee of male authority, unsettles dominant ideologies of gender and reflects on their cultural 'construction' as a system of understandings and values neither inevitable nor incontrovertible.

The emergence of gender criticism has troubled some feminist critics, particularly the pioneers who published in the 1970s and before, and those convinced of the political importance of maintaining a specifically feminist criticism. Even as some welcomed the entrance of men into feminist criticism as a signal of academic legitimacy, others regarded them as opportunistic appropriators, once the battle was won. 'Women generated feminist criticism, fought for its importance, and often suffered in their careers for being identified with a radical movement', one pioneer, Elaine Showalter, reminded readers of *The New Feminist Criticism* (1985). Feminist critics also worry that gender criticism will dilute hard-won gains: their laborious recovery of women's writing and literary traditions might be marginalized by an all-too-familiar male hegemony, one enlivened with a feminist critique of patriarchy, yet prone to male texts and male critics, and not particularly motivated by the political commitments that have infused feminist criticism by women.

Gender critics, both male and female, have answered that their work has not displaced but has grown out of feminist criticism, is gratefully indebted to it, and demonstrates its success; it was feminist criticism, after all, that established 'gender' as an important category of literary analysis and theory. Gender criticism is 'a new phase in feminist criticism, a significant and radical expansion of our work', Showalter herself would write a few years onward in her introduction to *Speaking of Gender* (1989); although she is still a political feminist, she now thinks of herself as a gender critic (her recent work has been on madness and hysteria in both its male and female embodiments). The issues first articulated in feminist criticism have proven so forceful that they have been exported, carrying the promise, in Showalter's optimistic estimation, of moving us 'a step further towards post-patriarchy'.

## What Does this Mean for British Romanticism?

Although Jehlen's essay indulged a regrettably simplistic reading of Romantic egotism as an expedient (it's a subordinate plank in her polemic), her overall analysis was an accurate enough measure of the then current situation of 'Romanticism' in classroom study, critical work and scholarship, and of the need for reform. The 'Romantic' canon from its first formulation in the nineteenth century until the mid-1980s was characterized by men's writing, taken, without question, to embody 'the spirit of the age'. With some shifts in popularity in various decades, the writers were Blake, Wordsworth (William), Coleridge, Byron, Shelley (Percy Bysshe), Keats, and in a secondary orbit, Lamb (Charles), Hazlitt and De Quincey. Some women earned attention, but in a very qualified economy: Wollstonecraft's *Rights of Woman* was read, but in 'Women's Studies' and not in Romanticism courses. Similarly, Austen's novels were read in the perspective of late eighteenth-century or early Victorian novels rather than of her own age; Shelley's *Frankenstein* was interesting to Romantic studies, but none of her other writing; Dorothy Wordsworth's journals were mined for information about her brother, and (this was just beginning) her poems examined for symptoms of her inhibition and arrest by the 'masculine tradition' he was said to embody.

The study of Romantic-era writing in the 1990s has been reinvigorated by gender studies, including the reading of female writers in relation to the formerly dominant male canon, and of male writers in relation to women's writing. The assumption of male dominance is even being re-examined in light of the burgeoning culture of female writing and publishing, the prodigious commercial success of some women (e.g. Hannah More, Ann Radcliffe, Maria Edgeworth, Felicia Hemans) and the popularity of many others, such as Helen Maria Williams, Mary Robinson, Austen of course, and L.E.L. (Letitia Landon). In this light, too, gender studies has questioned the validity of the label 'Romanticism' (even as publishers of some anthologies and encyclopedias like to retain it for its familiarity), for this term, it is argued, describes affective, aesthetic and political issues central primarily to men's writing, and diminishes the recurrent concerns in women's writing with (for instance) female heroism, female desire, domestic affections, home and family, community, female childhood and education, motherhood, and last but not least, women's careers, especially as writers, outside the home. Gender criticism does not denigrate the canon of remarkable writings that have established the prestige of the 'Romantic' literary movement, but it does question whether 'Romanticism' ought to have relative status rather than absolute privilege in describing the literature of the age.

The traditional 'Romantic' canon, moreover, has a new look in gender criticism. In the earlier feminist criticism, both Wordsworth's *Prelude* and Byron's *Don Juan* (for instance) tended to be cast as standard-bearers of 'the patriarchal tradition', the 'masculine tradition' and its attendant stereotypes – notwithstanding the poets' quite different temperaments and social relations with women. Gender criticism has focused on the crisis of manhood and the strong tendency to stereotypically 'feminine' attitudes that interrupt, or perhaps even shape, these poems, as well as many others in the male canon. Conceding the sexist evidence documented by feminist criticism, gender criticism adds to the inventory texts that reflect on the social structure of gender difference, destabilize its stereotypes and signifiers of difference, and even sometimes criticize the politics of gender – those arrangements of power based on sexual identity. Men's writing, it shows, can articulate and provoke gender critique – not only in the obvious way of stating critical and oppositional views, but also in the way writers allow instabilities and irresolutions to press against traditional values and understandings. At the same time, much women's

writing in the age of Romanticism was not subversive, but devoted to traditional understandings of gender, and was as sceptical, even to the point of outright hostility and
ridicule, of the new discussions of 'the rights of women'; women joined men in arguing
that women were blessed with a special mission, in a separate sphere, to serve God, man
and country with their 'domestic affections' and their domestic labour.

## Romantic-era Gender Criticism

This discussion was inevitable in an age whose inaugural decade was shaped by two key
issues, supercharged by the cataclysm of the French Revolution: the 'rights of man' and
'the rights of woman', both often taking as a reference a third key issue of the age, the
abolition of slavery and the slave trade. Politically progressive women in England were
optimistic about the founding ideas (if not their subsequent execution) of the revolution in
France. But as Wollstonecraft observed in *A Vindication of the Rights of Woman* (1792), the
enthusiastic discourse of liberty, equality and fraternity was gender specific, marginaliz-
ing, even excluding women. Her impassioned argument for respecting women as potentially rational beings and not treating them as mere sensual creatures, constitutes the first
major feminist polemic in English literature. It is also the first major feminist criticism *of*
English literature, for much of the discussion proceeds as a feminist critique of men's texts
– not only literary texts (Milton's *Paradise Lost*, Rousseau's *Emile*, Pope's *Moral Epistle II*)
but also cultural texts: the structure of patriarchal society, and the gendered vocabulary of
its social evaluations (the praise of women's 'delicacy' and 'innocence'; the stigma of a
woman's being called 'masculine').

   In addition to this feminist critique, a gender criticism also emerges in Wollstonecraft's
strategic sense of the mobility of gender vocabulary: the way 'masculine' and 'feminine'
may be applied with startlingly defamiliarizing effects to either men or women. No small
part of this criticism is the application of language that male authorities have traditionally
used to condescend to women ('weak', 'irrational', run by their 'senses', etc.) to men – in
effect casting them as 'feminine' in the normative cultural sense. Thus, kings, aristocrats,
rich men, soldiers, sensualists, gallants and society wits are 'feminized' by a default of the
rational faculty supposedly innate to men, and Milton's contradictory arguments on sexual
equality and sexual hierarchy in *Paradise Lost* earn her tart remark, 'into similar inconsistencies are great men often led by their senses'. Rousseau is faulted for 'nonsense!' and
'unintelligible paradoxes': 'when he should have reasoned he became impassioned'; and
Burke displays 'skulking, unmanly' hypocrisy (so she said in her earlier *Vindication of the
Rights of Men*, an answer to Burke's *Reflections on the Revolution in France*). The implied
argument of all these taunts is that if men can lack reason and a smart woman can see this,
then reason is not an innately male attribute. Measured by 'reason', 'masculine' and
'feminine' detach from sexual determination: rational women may be seen as 'masculine'
in a positive sense, and foolish boys and servile, or sense-driven men disdained as 'unmanly'
and 'effeminate'.

   At other times, her gender criticism refuses this language as culturally contaminated.
This refusal is influenced by Catherine Macaulay's sharp critique of Pope's *Epistle II, to a
Lady*, 'Of the Characters of Women' (1735), where he famously speculated that 'Heav'n' to

make woman 'but forms a softer Man'. In *Letters on Education* (1790), Macaulay deploys a gender criticism to examine the linguistic politics:

> When we compliment the appearance of a more than ordinary energy in the female mind, we call it masculine; and hence it is, that Pope has elegantly said *a perfect woman's but a softer man*. And if we take in the consideration, that there can be but one rule of moral excellence for beings made of the same materials, organized after the same manner, and subjected to similar laws of Nature, we must either agree with Mr Pope, or we must reverse the proposition, and say, that *a perfect man is a woman formed after a coarser mould*. The difference that actually does subsist between the sexes, is too flattering for men to be willingly imputed to accident; for what accident occasions, wisdom might correct. (Letter 22)

Impressed by this critique, Wollstonecraft refuses gendered terms, honouring Macaulay in the process: Macaulay, she proposes in *Rights of Woman*, displays 'intellectual acquirements supposed to be incompatible with the weakness of her sex. In her style of writing . . . no sex appears, for it is like the sense it conveys, strong and clear. I will not call hers a masculine understanding, because I admit not of such an arrogant assumption of reason'.

This gender criticism is all the more compelling for its emergence within a more pervasive, virulent retrenchment in British writing of the sex and gender binaries codified over the course of the eighteenth century. A potent site is the 'Revolution debate', during which male political opponents often tried to score points by hurling charges of effeminacy at each other. Thus, when Burke issued his oft-quoted dismay over the arrest of Marie Antoinette as the fall of chivalry – a 'mixed system of opinion and sentiment' – his opponents were quick to ridicule this idealism as no more than a servile, unmanly sentimentality. Here is Burke's lament:

> Little did I dream that I should have lived to see such disasters fallen upon her in a nation of gallant men, in a nation of men of honour and of cavaliers. . . . But the age of chivalry is gone. . . . Never, never more, shall we behold that generous loyalty to rank and sex, that proud submission, that dignified obedience, that subordination of the heart, which kept alive, even in servitude itself, the spirit of an exalted freedom . . . the nurse of manly sentiment and heroic enterprize is gone! (*Reflections*, p. 89)

Priestley flings Burke's sentimental language back at him with a polish on its gendering:

> What an *exalted freedom* would you have felt, had you had the happiness of being a subject of the Empress of Russia; your sovereign, being then *woman*? Fighting under her auspices, you would no doubt, have been the most puissant of knights errant, and her redoubted champion, against the whole Turkish empire, the sovereign of which is only a *man*. (*Letters to Burke*, 1791; Priestley's italics)

Priestley refutes Burke by recasting chivalric 'subjection' as unmanly subservience, and epitomizing the scandal with the queen whom Englishmen from Coleridge to Hazlitt to Byron trotted out as a pet horrific of female political power. This mere renaming of the rhetorical parts shows why Wollstonecraft had no trouble in *Rights of Woman* discerning the misogyny behind chivalric idealism: 'women are systematically degraded by receiving the trivial attentions, which men think it manly to pay to the sex, when, in fact, they are insultingly supporting their own superiority'. Burke's reverence for queenly 'elevation' is located on the same gender map as Priestley's satirical denigration of female sovereignty as a grotesquery by which modern men can only be unmanned.

## Gender Trouble

This rhetorical escalation implicitly concedes a shift in the conceptual ground of gender. Sometimes even the language of renewed legislation effects such a shift. Consider this passage from Hannah More's conservative essay, 'The Education of Daughters' (1777):

> The natural cast of character, and the moral distinction of the sexes, should not be disregarded, even in childhood. That bold, independent, enterprising spirit, which is so much admired in boys, should not, when it happens to discover itself in the other sex, be encouraged, but suppressed. Girls should be taught to give up their opinions betimes, and not pertinaciously to carry on a dispute, even if they should know themselves in the right.... It is of the greatest importance to their future happiness, that they should acquire submissive temper, and a forbearing spirit: for it is a lesson which the world will not fail to make them frequently practise when they come abroad into it.

The 'natural cast' of character that is the basis of this moral and cultural pedagogy is unintentionally challenged by the discipline it requires. The enterprising spirit in girls needs to be 'suppressed' and counter-taught; desired behaviour is to be 'acquired' against better self-knowledge, and it is a 'lesson which the world will...make them frequently practise' – a performative term that unwittingly engages the master-trope, 'natural cast', to cast a shadow of cultural scripting on what is taken to be a naturally guaranteed tendency.

Even so, More's sense of the cultural discipline is accurate enough. In a chapter of her conduct manual *Woman* (1831) entitled 'The Value of Letters to Woman', Mrs Sandford argues that one reason men resist 'the diffusion of knowledge to woman' is that lettered women tended to 'plea for assumption':

> The disciple of Wollston[e]craft threw off her [maidenly] hat, and called for a boot-jack; and imagined that by affecting the manners of the other sex, she should best assert her equality with them. The female pedant appears in a disordered dress, and with inky fingers; and fancies that the further she is removed from feminine grace, the nearer she approaches to manly vigour.

To Mrs Sandford, the disruption of gender signs (the cultural language) can yield only a travesty and a farce. Yet the impulse to contempt, like More's urgency of discipline, acknowledges an emerging female resistance. *Woman* was ridiculed in such progressive journals as *The Athenaeum* (1832), and during the Regency even 'Mrs Hemans', a poet celebrated for her iconic 'femininity', was establishing herself as a learned professional writer and publishing poems that pressed against contradictions in prevailing ideals of the 'feminine'. She admired Joanna Baillie's capable heroines for being 'perfectly different from the pretty "*unidea'd girls*", who seem to form the *beau ideal* of our whole sex in the works of some modern poets'. One of the strongest emergences in Romantic-era women's writing, in fact, is a distrust of emotional excess, or 'sensibility' – a resource that contemporaneous male poets, by contrast, were beginning to plumb with enthusiasm. Most of the polemics by female intellectuals – Macaulay, Wollstonecraft, More among them – urged the cultivation of reason and a restraint on emotional self-indulgence as a woman's best social and spiritual resource.

In the age of Romanticism, gender difference gets tested for new routes of exchange, and literary texts become fields of negotiation. Variously, and not atypically in the same work, traditional values are both subverted and reinforced, questioned and then defended from erosion. The syntax of gender tends to operate less by stable grammar than in agitation over 'key words', to use Raymond Williams's term for those charged bearers of culturally-laden meanings, ones as volatile as they are crucial. If some female writers were rethinking the 'beau ideal', some male writers were unsure about their own orientation on the traditional gender map. Wordsworth, for example (cast in early feminist criticism as an icon of the masculine tradition) remembers himself in formative subjection to the feminine, his mind 'stamped' and 'led' by a feminine-personified Nature; he even recalls feeling feminized under this sway, 'impregnated' with thoughts and feelings (*Prelude* Book 1, 1805). The poet of Shelley's *Alastor* (1816) begs the 'Mother of this unfathomable world . . . to render up the tale / Of what we are' and then unfolds the story of another poet whose peculiar androgyny – a compound of male questor and feminine-troped passivity – allegorizes his radical metaphysical alienation. Nature and dreams in Keats's *Endymion* (1818) are haunted by a female deity who dominates the passive hero with a calculated script of frustrations. And a sequence of artful women enthralls the hero of Byron's ironically named *Don Juan* (1819–24). This repeated erosion of masculine self-possession by feminine forces suggests that the 'feminine' in male Romantic writing, though it evokes a politically excluded or subjected 'other', may also, and more deeply, refer to sensations within masculine subjectivity itself of its difference from prevailing definitions of masculinity. These instances, moreover, emerge from several decades of writing by men, especially poets, who were refining, not always with impunity, a poetry of feeling, sensibility and other 'female' coded resources.

Gender criticism has shown how in Romantic-era writing, it is not the case that only men are ever (and only) authoritative, egotistical, and only and ever women who are given to doubt certainties of self and world. The literature is populated with perplexed, passive and swooning heroes and smart, capable, outspoken heroines; men of feeling and women of intellect; women who invite the adjectives (sometimes with admiration) 'manly' and 'masculine', men termed 'feminine' (sometimes with admiration) or 'effeminate' (never). It is no wonder that Revd Hubbard Winslow, writing in 1838, credited the influence of this writing with a veritable cultural crisis. Conceding that 'it may be difficult to trace the precise line of demarcation where the masculine character ends and where the female begins', he broadcasts a gendered (if not gender) cultural criticism:

> The man who partakes of the character appropriate to female . . . is *effeminate;* . . . the woman who partakes of the character appropriate to males . . . is *masculine*. These terms, we all know, are intended to designate something out of place, something undesirable and unlovely. We tolerate here and there an anomaly of this kind; but we wish to see such cases 'few and far

between'. We should wisely consider the end of all things not far distant should they become universal. (*Woman As She Should Be*)

Two of Wollstonecraft's female contemporaries use such language to preserve an economic place for women, both summoning the term 'effeminate' to describe men who wrest away positions for which women qualify – in particular, the trade in female clothing and goods. In *Reflections on the Present Condition of the Female Sex* (1798), Priscilla Wakefield calls the usurpers 'a brood of effeminate beings in the garb of men', and following suit in *The Female Advocate* (1798), Mary Anne Radcliffe repeatedly refers to them as 'effeminate' and 'unmanly' tradesmen. She even suggests nastily that if ladies refused on principle to be served by them, they would be compelled to the 'tragic-comic farce of wearing "the disguise of gown and petticoat"' – forced to impersonate the women they usurp, in a kind of counterpart to the travesty described by Mrs Sandford.

## Gender and the Literary Market-place

One of the ways that women in the age of Romanticism could make a respectable living was as writers, and women in the age were succeeding with a vengeance. Radcliffe, More, Edgeworth and Hemans were selling better than Wordsworth, Coleridge, Shelley and Keats, and closing in on Byron enough to provoke nasty remarks, especially about the closest competitor in his own field, Hemans. Writing in 1820 to their mutual publisher, he refers to her as 'your feminine *He-Man*' or 'Mrs. Hewoman's', the tags turning her commercial prowess into a monstrous mockery of sexual identity. He preferred women in their place and not his. 'I do not despise Mrs. Heman – but if [she] knit blue stockings instead of wearing them it would be better', he liberally declared. With the rise of literacy and the flourishing of circulating (lending) libraries, moreover, there were many women with the means, interest and leisure to read, and with the purchasing and word-of-mouth capacity to affect a writer's success, male and female.

Even so, the powers of production – the publishers, the booksellers, the reviews and the press – were men's domains and not always open to female authors. A further and related barrier was the pervasive attitude that a female writer who presumed authority, and even aspired to make a living as an author, was grossly immodest, decidedly 'unfeminine'. Thus, many women published anonymously, or adapted male pseudonyms, or deployed, as Austen did, an anonymous and socially proper signature, 'by a Lady'. Women also maintained propriety by sticking to subjects and genres deemed 'feminine' – not political polemic, epic poetry, science or philosophy; but children's books, conduct literature, travel writing (if it was clear they had proper escorts), household hints, cookbooks, novels of manners, and poems of home, patriotism and religious piety. Women who transgressed provoked harsh discipline, frequently in terms of gender redress. When, for instance, Anna Barbauld (who even disagreed with Wollstonecraft about the 'Rights of Woman') ventured one anti-imperialist poem, *Eighteen Hundred and Eleven*, she provoked the chief Tory magazine of the day, the *Quarterly Review*, into voicing a reproof precisely in terms of the gender–genre transgression:

Our old acquaintance Mrs. Barbauld turned satirist!...We had hoped, indeed, that the empire might have been saved without the intervention of a lady-author.... Not such, however, is her opinion; an irresistible impulse of public duty – a confident sense of commanding talents – have induced her to dash down her shagreen spectacles and her knitting needles, and to sally forth...in the magnanimous resolution of saving a sinking state, by the instrumentality of a pamphlet....Her former works have been of some utility; her 'Lessons for Children,' her 'Hymns in Prose,' her 'Selections from the Spectator,' et id genus omne...but we must take the liberty of warning her to desist from satire...writing any more pamphlets in verse. (*Quarterly Review*, vol. 7, June 1812)

Barbauld took this advice to heart, and published no more.

In *The Unsex'd Females*, Anglican arbiter Richard Polwhele viciously listed a whole set of contemporary female writers, with virulent animosity to Wollstonecraft, under the sign of the 'unsex'd woman' who 'vaunts the imperious mien', both adjectives implying contrariness to nature. 'Unsex'd' because they write like men and thus imaging what 'ne'er our fathers saw', they affront patriarchal propriety. Another kind of unsexing (also aimed at Wollstonecraft) was re-sexing praise or blame as 'masculine'. With an ambivalent regard of Madame de Staël's forceful intellect, Byron scribbles in his journal in 1813 that 'she ought to have been a man' and, writing to his publisher in 1817 about Joanna Baillie's accomplishment, he invokes Voltaire's remark that 'the composition of a tragedy requires *testicles*'; 'If this be true Lord knows what Joanna Baillie does – I suppose she borrows them'.

Protocols of gender and genre coloured Hemans's public reviews. *Tait's Edinburgh Magazine* commended her in 1847 with a decidedly faint praise that simultaneously disciplines other female writers, the terms recalling Mrs Sandford's antipathy:

We are reluctantly compelled...to deny her, in its highest sense, the name of poet – a word often abused, often misapplied in mere compliment or courtesy....A *maker* she is not....Mrs. Hemans's poems are strictly effusions. And not a little of their charm springs from their unstudied and extempore character...in fine keeping with the sex of the writer. You are saved the ludicrous image of double-dyed Blue, in papers and morning wrapper, sweating at some stupendous treatise or tragedy from morn to noon, and from noon to dewy eve....the transition is so natural and graceful, from the duties or delights of the day to the employments of her desk, that there is as little pedantry in writing a poem as in writing a letter, and the authoress appears only the lady in *flower*.

Mystified as the product of natural instinct ('the lady in *flower*'), women's writing is acceptable only as an 'unstudied' 'charm' – 'an extension and refinement of that element of female influence' emanating from and limited to 'the proper sphere and mission of woman' and not to be confused, in production or effect, with the intellect, rigour and real labour of men's art. Noting women's general 'absence of original genius, or of profound penetration, or of wide experience', this reviewer assures his public that he does not consider them 'entitled to speak with equal authority on those higher and deeper questions, where not instinct nor heart, but severe and tried intellect is qualified to return the responses'. Both the title of 'poet' and the spectacle of sweaty labour are cast as female travesties, an abuse and misapplication in the former case, and a farce in the latter.

Some years earlier, on the occasion of praising Hemans's excellence 'in painting the strength and the weaknesses of her own lovely sex' and the 'womanly nature throughout all her thoughts and her aspirations', *The British Critic* (1823) used the occasion to despise anything that advertised the intellectual and critical authority of women. Its review opens not with a discussion of Hemans but an assault on the world that was changing before its eyes, against which it invokes every counter-authority, from divine creation, to modern science, to Shakespeare, to the disciplines of ridicule and disgust:

> We heartily abjure Blue Stockings. We make no compromise with any variation of the colour, from sky-blue to Prussian blue, blue stockings are an outrage upon the eternal fitness of things. It is a principle with us to regard an Academicienne of this society, with the same charity that a cat regards a vagabond mouse. We are inexorable to special justifications. We would fain make a fire in Charing-Cross, of all the bas blus in the kingdom, and albums, and commonplace books, as accessaries [*sic*] before or after the fact, should perish in the conflagration.
>
> Our forefathers never heard of such a thing as a Blue Stocking, except upon their sons' legs; the writers of Natural History make no mention of the name. . . . Shakespeare, who painted all sorts and degrees of persons and things, who compounded or created thousands, which, perhaps, never existed, except in his own prolific mind, even he, in the wildest excursion of his fancy never dreamed of such an extraordinary combination as a Blue Stocking! No!

The extraordinary combination, however, was there to stay, reinforced by the lively and irrefragable representations of gender in Romantic-era writing, as well as by the gender criticism that constitutes an important activity of this literature.

This resistance echoes today in the complaints of some critics about the aesthetic inferiority of women's writing and the spectre of a Gresham's law of literary economy ('bad money drives out good'). As one critic (Virgil Nemoianu) sounded the alarm in 1991, 'Will the appreciation of Felicia Hemans be enhanced by the neglect of or contempt for Keats?' and stayed to answer, 'One can only shrug at such naiveties'. Gender criticism has put such concerns in a form less easy to shrug. Its question is, 'How can our appreciation of Keats be enhanced by attention to Hemans?' and, relatedly, 'How can our appreciation of Hemans be enhanced by attention to how Wordsworth and Coleridge, Byron, Shelley and Keats write about gender?'

## References and Further Reading

*Athenaeum* 236 (5 May 1832), Review of Mrs Sandford's *Woman*, pp. 282–3.

Battersby, Christine, *Gender and Genius: Towards a Feminist Aesthetics*, Bloomington, Indiana University Press, 1989.

*British Critic* NS 20 (July 1823), Review of Felicia Hemans's *The Siege of Valencia and The Last Constantine, with other Poems*, pp. 50–61.

Burke, Edmund, *Reflections on the Revolution in France*, 1790, Garden City, Anchor / Doubleday, 1973.

Butler, Judith, *Gender Trouble: Feminism and the Subversion of Identity*, New York, Routledge, 1990.

Chorley, Henry F., *Memorials of Mrs. Hemans, with Illustrations of her Literary Character from her Private Correspondence*, 2 vols, London, Saunders and Otley, 1836.

Claridge, Laura and Langland, Elizabeth (eds) *Out of Bounds: Male Writers and Gender(ed) Criticism*, Amherst, University of Massachusetts Press, 1990.

Clarke, Norma, *Ambitious Heights: Writing, Friendship, Love – The Jewsbury Sisters, Felicia Hemans, and Jane Welsh Carlyle*, London and New York, Routledge, 1990.

Crompton, Louis, *Byron and Greek Love: Homophobia in 19th-Century England*, Berkeley, University of California Press, 1985.

Curran, Stuart, 'Romantic poetry: the I altered', in *Romanticism and Feminism*, ed. Anne K. Mellor, Bloomington, Indiana University Press, 1988, pp. 185–207.

Dowling, Linda, 'Esthetes and effeminati', *Raritan* 12.3 (1993) 52–68.

Feldman, Paula and Kelley, Theresa M. (eds) *Romantic Women: Voices and Counter-voices*, Hanover, University Press of New England, 1995.

Franklin, Caroline, *Byron's Heroines*, Oxford, Clarendon Press, 1992.

Garber, Marjorie, *Vested Interests: Cross-Dressing & Cultural Anxiety*, New York, Routledge, 1992.

Hoeveler, Diane Long, *Romantic Androgyny: The Women Within*, University Park, Pennsylvania State University Press, 1990.

Hofkosh, Sonia, 'The writer's ravishment: women and the Romantic author – the example of Byron', in Anne K. Mellor (ed.) *Romanticism and Feminism*, Bloomington, Indiana University Press, 1988, pp. 93–114.

—— 'A woman's profession: sexual difference and the romance of authorship', *Studies in Romanticism* 32 (1993) 245–72.

Homans, Margaret, *Women Writers and Poetic Identity*, Princeton, Princeton University Press, 1980.

—— 'Keats reading women, women reading Keats', *Studies in Romanticism* 29 (1990) 341–70.

Jehlen, Myra, 'Archimedes and the paradox of feminist criticism', *Signs* 6.4 (1981) 575–601.

Johnson, Barbara, 'Gender theory and the Yale School', in *Speaking of Gender*, ed. Elaine Showalter, New York and London, Routledge, 1989, pp. 45–55.

Johnson, Claudia L., *Equivocal Beings: Politics, Gender, and Sentimentality in the 1790s: Wollstonecraft, Radcliffe, Burney, Austen*, Chicago, University of Chicago Press, 1995.

Kadish, Doris Y., *Politicizing Gender: Narrative Strategies in the Aftermath of the French Revolution*, New Jersey, Rutgers University Press, 1991.

Kamuf, Peggy, 'Writing like a woman', in *Women and Language in Literature and Society*, New York, Praeger Press, 1980.

Leighton, Angela, *Victorian Women Poets: Writing Against the Heart*, New York and London, Wheatsheaf / Harvester, 1992.

Linkin, Harriet Kramer, 'The current canon in British Romantic studies', *College English* 53 (1991) 548–70.

Macaulay, Catherine (Graham), *Letters on Education, With Observations on Religious and Metaphysical Subjects*, London, C. Dilly, 1790.

McGann, Jerome J., *The Poetics of Sensibility: A Revolution in Literary Style*, New York and London, Oxford University Press, 1996.

Mellor, Anne K. (ed) *Romanticism and Feminism*, Bloomington, Indiana University Press, 1988.

——*Romanticism and Gender*, New York, Routledge, 1992.

More, Hannah, 'Thoughts on the Cultivation of the Heart and Temper in the Education of Daughters', in *Essays on Various Subjects Principally Designed for Young Ladies*, 1777; rpt. *The Works of Hannah More*, 6 vols, London, H. Fisher, R. Fisher, and P. Jackson, 1834, vol. 6: pp. 317–31.

Nemoianu, Virgil: 'Literary canons and social value options', in *The Hospitable Canon: Essays on Literary Play, Scholarly Choice, and Popular Pressures*, ed. Virgil Nemoianu and Robert Royal, Philadelphia and Amsterdam, John Benjamins, 1991, pp. 215–47.

Page, Judith, *Wordsworth and the Cultivation of Women*, Berkeley, University of California Press, 1994.

Polwhele, Richard, *The Unsex'd Females* (1798).

Poovey, Mary, *The Proper Lady and the Woman Writer: Ideology as Style in the Works of Mary Wollstonecraft, Mary Shelley, and Jane Austen*, Chicago, University of Chicago Press, 1984.

Pope, Alexander, 'To a Lady, of the Characters of Women', *Epistle II* of *Epistles to Several Persons* (Moral Essays), in vol. 4, pt 2 of *Poems of Alexander Pope*, ed. F. W. Bateson, New Haven, Yale University Press, 1961.

Priestley, Joseph, *Letters to the Right Honourable Edmund Burke, Occasioned by his Reflections on the Revolution in France, &c*, Birmingham, Thomas Pearson, 1791.

*Quarterly Review* 7 (June 1812), Review of Anna Barbauld's *Eighteen Hundred and Eleven*, pp. 309–13.

—— 24 (October 1820), Review of several volumes by Felicia Hemans, pp. 130–9.

Radcliffe, Mary Anne, *The Female Advocate; Or an Attempt to Recover the Rights of Women from Male Usurpation*, London, Vernor and Hood, 1799.

Richardson, Alan, 'Romanticism and the colonization of the feminine', in *Romanticism and Feminism*, ed. Anne K. Mellor, Bloomington, Indiana University Press, 1988, pp. 13–25.

Ross, Marlon, B., 'Romantic quest and conquest: troping masculine power in the crisis of poetic identity', *Romanticism and Feminism*, ed. Anne K. Mellor, Bloomington, Indiana University Press, 1988, pp. 26–51.

Ross, Marlon, B., *The Contours of Masculine Desire: Romanticism and the Rise of Women's Poetry*, New York and London, Oxford University Press, 1989.

Sandford, Mrs John, *Woman, In Her Social and Domestic Character*, London, Longman, et al., 1832.

Sedgwick, Eve Kosofsky, *Between Men: English Literature and Male Homosocial Desire*, New York, Columbia University Press, 1985.

—— 'Gender criticism', in *Redrawing the Boundaries: The Transformation of English and American Literature*, ed. Stephen Greenblatt and Giles Gunn, New York, Modern Language Association of America, 1992, pp. 271–302.

Shelley, Percy Bysshe, *Shelley's Poetry and Prose*, ed. Donald H. Reiman and Sharon B. Powers, New York, Norton, 1977.

Showalter, Elaine (ed.) *The New Feminist Criticism: Essays on Women, Literature, Theory*, New York, Pantheon, 1985.

—— (ed) *Speaking of Gender*, New York and London, Routledge, 1989.

*Tait's Edinburgh Magazine* n.s. 14 (1847), 'Female authors. No. I – Mrs. Hemans', pp. 359–63.

Tayler, Irene and Luria, Gina, 'Gender and genre: women in British Romantic literature', in *What Manner of Woman*, ed. Marlene Springer, New York, New York University Press, 1977, pp. 98–123.

Wakefield, Priscilla, *Reflections on the Present Condition of the Female Sex; With Suggestions for its Improvement*, London, J. Johnson, Darton and Harvey, 1798.

Williams, Raymond, *Keywords: A Vocabulary of Culture and Society*, New York, Oxford University Press, 1983.

Wilson, Carol Shiner and Haefner, Joel (eds) *Re-Visioning Romanticism: British Women Writers, 1776–1837*, Philadelphia, University of Pennsylvania Press, 1994.

Winslow, Hubbard, *Woman As She Should Be*, Philadelphia, Henry Perkins, 1838.

Wolfson, Susan J., '"Their She Condition": cross-dressing and the politics of gender in *Don Juan*', *ELH* 54 (1987) 585–617.

—— 'Wordsworth and the language of (men) feeling', in *Men Writing the Feminine*, ed. Thaïs Morgan, New York, State University of New York Press, 1994, pp. 29–57.

—— 'Gendering the Soul', in *Romantic Women: Voices and Counter-voices*, ed. Feldman and Kelley, Hanover, University Press of New England, 1995, pp. 33–68.

Wollstonecraft, Mary, *A Vindication of the Rights of Men, in a Letter to the Right Honourable Edmund Burke; Occasioned by His 'Reflections on the Revolution in France'*, (2nd edn 1790; facsimile reprint Gainesville, Florida, Scholars' Facsimiles and Reprints, 1960.

—— *A Vindication of the Rights of Woman*, 1792, ed. Carol H. Poston, New York, Norton, 1988.

Wordsworth, William, *The Thirteen-Book 'Prelude'*, 2 vols, ed. Mark L. Reed, Ithaca, Cornell University Press, 1991.

# 39

# Romanticism and Feminism

*Elizabeth Fay*

Literary scholars and historians were examining women writers for several decades before feminism began to be applied to interpretive strategies and revisionist literary histories. Through the early and middle decades of this century, scholars published books on what were considered minor writers, many of whom were early women poets and novelists. Popular biographies and critical works that took the biographical approach were written about figures such as Anna Seward, Hester Thrale Piozzi, Letitia Elizabeth Landon (L.E.L.) and Charlotte Smith. The question was eventually asked of these studies, 'Is this enough, is this all these women writers mean to us?' In the years that led up to the Women's Movement of 1975, women scholars began to ask questions about the literary margins to which women writers' lives were consigned; after feminism began to influence critical thought, scholars began to ask even more interesting questions about what these women writers produced, the conditions under which they worked, and the genres that they found compelling for their artistic expression.

At the present time, feminist scholarship has achieved enough groundwork for us to ask a different kind of question: 'What is the value of feminist enquiry?' We can complicate this by adding, what kind of knowledge have we produced, and how does it help us understand literature, and more specifically Romantic literature? One answer is that it changes the way we read and interpret texts, and, in changing us, it changes what we value. One result of this is that feminist criticism and theory have shown women writers to be more worthy of being taught in literature courses. This is a remarkable achievement in itself, but much remains to be understood about women writers beyond a few admired ones; about what other women were writing during the Romantic period specifically; about how women thought about writing in this period; and about what kinds of influence existed between women and men writers during this period. I shall address only part of this unfinished and ongoing enquiry in order to show the direction that students of literature should consider as they read not just Mary Wollstonecraft, Jane Austen and Mary Shelley, but also Anna Laetitia Barbauld, Felicia Hemans, Dorothy Wordsworth, Elizabeth Inchbald, Anna Seward and L.E.L. More particularly, I want to address the essential question of value. What does the intervention of feminist thought and feminist critique bring to our understanding of the value of literature, and how do we value literature differently because of it?

Kate Millett wrote one of the early groundbreaking works of the feminist movement, *Sexual Politics* (1969). She begins her historical survey of her subject only in the 1830s, although she postpones British feminist thought until the 1860s with John Stuart Mill and his famous *The Subjection of Women* (1869). In addition, she conducts her argument through men's texts, such as her analysis of Mill's feminist treatise and the essay it counters, John Ruskin's patriarchal and condescending *Of Queen's Gardens* (1865). Although Millett mentions Wollstonecraft, she does not consider making her argument through this early feminist. Yet *Vindication of the Rights of Woman* (1792) was, like Mill's work, written as a fuller response (after her quickly written *Vindication of the Rights of Men*, 1791) to a patriarchal counter-text, Edmund Burke's *Reflections on the Revolution in France* (1790). What Millett does say about Wollstonecraft is that, while she is an important voice (because she translates the political thought of the French Revolutionaries into a corresponding version for British women), feminist activism 'did not emerge in any fullness until the 1830s' (Millett, *Sexual Politics*, p. 65). Wollstonecraft presents a figure to rebel against for later reactionaries, but she is not strong enough for Millett's purpose. It is also clear from her delimiting of Wollstonecraft's achievement that she does not take the earlier feminist's arguments to represent her own perspective or claims, that is, early feminist scholarly thought did not consider the Romantic period to contain the real awakening of the feminist imperative. This raises two crucial points: the first is that the real cry of passion is understood to emanate from the Victorian period; the second is that a man is understood to be able to emit this cry better than a woman writer. These are important points for us to consider, for they illustrate how feminist thought has impacted on Romantic period studies.

Let us consider the second point first. Millett's book is an excellent source for thinking about the issue of a writer's sex, since we see it not only in her choice of Mill over Wollstonecraft to make her argument, but also in her final section where she analyses the novels of several writers. Here she considers only male novelists: Henry Miller, Jean Genet, D. H. Lawrence, Norman Mailer. Why? In this early stage, the most obvious work to be done was an analysis of the male expression, whether of pro- or anti-feminist issues and representations. Quite simply, it was the male frame of mind, mode of expression and way of thinking that we were taught to respect and emulate, and it was that mental mode that had to be analysed and critiqued before anything else could be accomplished. It is as if Millett could not use Wollstonecraft because she did not have the language or the tools for understanding her. These were yet to be crafted out of the research and theoretical developments of feminist scholars and critics. Today, whole books are devoted to Wollstonecraft.

As these works, and even Millett's discussion of John Stuart Mill's work shows, men have always had a place in feminism, as readers, writers and critics who use, implement or promote feminist thought. At times, women have struggled with this paradox and argued that only women have the biological and social experience to carry out feminist research. However, the general consensus today is that if sexual difference is biologically based, not all men and women experience the same treatment according to their sex; that social experience is driven by gender rather than sex; that men can be subject to the same kind of treatment that women more generally are. Therefore, male critics can be experientially sensitive to the issues that arise from being female in a patriarchal environment, and from the social constraints issuing from that situation. The reverse of this notion should not be neglected: if men can speak convincingly of women's issues, so, too, can women speak of men's and of the nation's. I shall return to this point at the end.

Millett decides to work backward from examples of extreme patriarchal thought in order to make her claims about feminism, rather than begin with a feminist writer and work forward to what feminism can do. This is reflected in much of the early work feminist critics did, in which male writers of all kinds were studied for their representation of sexual difference. This could be enormously enlightening in the case of canonical authors such as Milton; for instance, Christine Froula's 'When Eve reads Milton' (1983) showed us how Milton's world was founded on the subjugation of Eve in a way we had not noticed before.

To return to the first point: why did earlier feminist critics turn to the Victorian but not the Romantic period?

Certainly, feminism was most strongly felt in Modernist and Victorian studies first. Several factors account for this. First, these are the closest periods to us historically, and the ones in which feminist struggle was most strongly and courageously articulated. And, because these periods are closest to our own, and because feminism was articulated so clearly in them, they are the likeliest places for us to hear the resonance of our own age. This is a historical and political relation that comes from our recognition of the Modernist character in all these periods; Victorian and Modernist women writers recognizably voiced the same concerns felt by women today. Romantic women seem at first glance somewhat less connected to our present experience. An example of this is Jane Austen, who maintains certain feminist principles, yet they are so coded that they are hard for twentieth-century readers to recognize. A widespread feminist reappraisal of Austen has taken place only recently.

The second factor comes out of the first: the Modern and Victorian literary periods contain strong voices that compel us in emotional as well as intellectual ways. Charlotte Bronte and Virginia Woolf offer strongly identifiable voices, characters and textual problems that twentieth-century readers find relevant in ways that Anna Seward's or Ann Radcliffe's are not. Why? First, their language is just a bit too old-fashioned, the literary tastes too sentimental; the politics should sound modern with all their emphasis on revolution and freedom, but they are still too involved with court life to feel very modern or accessible. Second, male Romantic texts have always constituted most of the Romantic period canon, and despite the acceptance of many women writers into the field of study, they continue to do so. Moreover, the most valued male texts of this canon were and are poetic. When feminist criticism began its work on the literary discipline, women's voices were simply too difficult to locate in the Romantic period, aside from Austen's novels, one work by Mary Shelley (*Frankenstein*) and occasional references to one work by Wollstonecraft (*Rights of Woman*). As none of these texts are poetic, and as none of the women poets of the period were easily available for study, the period did not appear as ripe for critique as later ones whose literary canons include novels in their first ranks. For these reasons much of the work done in the Romantic period was of male poetic texts and female novels. The male texts were examined for patriarchal or feminist bias, the female for their conformist or revolutionary politics. Even today, some of our most recent feminist critical studies are on male poets (such as Barbara Gelpi's *Shelley's Goddess*) or on women novelists (such as Anne Mellor's *Mary Shelley's Fictions*); however, Romantic studies has finally begun to study women poets as primary contributors to the literary culture of the day.

One figure who greatly contributed to Romanticism was Anna Laetitia Barbauld, best known today for her poems to Coleridge and William Wilberforce. In her *Summer Evening's Meditation* (1777) we find a strong presaging of Romantic themes:

> Fancy droops,
> And thought astonished stops her bold career;
> But oh, thou mighty mind, whose powerful word
> Said, 'Thus let all things be', and thus they were –
> Where shall I seek thy presence? (98–102)

The internal scene presented here, later associated more powerfully with Wordsworth, Coleridge and Keats, is that of the Romantic imagination struggling to understand its corollary in the external source of genius; this is Romantic expression, but the words themselves are impressive as poetry. Charlotte Smith's many sonnets on nature are less charged with the sublime, but they establish a meditative mood for the Romantic poet in nature that Dorothy Wordsworth is able to translate into her own idiom as brief lyric passages in her journals. Smith begins one sonnet with,

> Where the green leaves exclude the summer beam,
>     And softly bend as balmy breezes blow,
> And where, with liquid lapse, the lucid stream
>     Across the fretted rock is heard to flow,
> Pensive I lay . . . (*From Petrarch*)

Dorothy Wordsworth frequently begins at this moment, at rest in nature; she writes in a journal entry, for example, 'One beautiful ash tree sheltered with yellow leaves – one low one quite green. . . . Now rain came on' (16 November 1800). Both writers discover the essence of 'green' through the pensive rhythms and sound play of their word choice, in a manner we associate with the Romantic spirit. Smith's dreamy alliteration becomes Wordsworth's eclipse of the vision ('Now rain came on', the m/n repetitions calling us back to the present, to presence).

Our ability to read this spirit in these texts results from the changes feminist critique has made in the way we read and value literary texts. Clearly, considering how we hold our value and in what terms, becomes a productive literary undertaking.

WRITINGS

Wollstonecraft, Mary, *The Vindication of the Rights of Woman*, 1792.

REFERENCES AND FURTHER READING

Brown, Lyn Mikel and Gilligan, Carol, *Meeting at the Crossroads: Women's Psychology and Girls' Develop-* ment, Cambridge, Mass., Harvard University Press, 1992.

Chodorow, Nancy, *The Reproduction of Mothering: Psychoanalysis and the Sociology of Gender*, Berkeley, University of California Press, 1978.

Favret, Mary and Watson, Nicola J. (eds) *At the Limits of Romanticism: Essays in Cultural, Feminist, and Materialist Criticism*, Bloomington, Indiana University Press, 1994.

Feldman, Paula R. and Kelley, Theresa M. (eds) *Romantic Women Writers: Voices and Counter-voices*, Hanover, University Press of New England, 1995. Both Favret and Watson, and Feldman and Kelley contain essays that move in new directions for feminist Romantic studies. These studies are indications of the increasing shift in the way texts are being read, and in the kinds of writers and texts scholars are increasingly willing to study.

Froula, Christine, 'When Eve reads Milton: undoing the canonical economy', *Critical Inquiry* 10 (1983) 321–47.

Gelpi, Barbara Charlesworth, *Shelley's Goddess: Maternity, Language, Subjectivity*, New York, Oxford University Press, 1992.

Gilligan, Carol, *In a Different Voice: Psychological Theory and Women's Development*, Cambridge, Mass., Harvard University Press, 1982.

Homans, Margaret, *Women Writers and Poetic Identity: Dorothy Wordsworth, Emily Brontë, and Emily Dickinson*, Princeton, Princeton University Press, 1980. An important early feminist analysis of women's texts that remains relevant to literary research today. Homans's first study reveals how difficult it was for feminist critics trained in canonical literature to tackle the problems peculiar to women's artistic production.

Johnson, Claudia L., *Jane Austen: Women, Politics, and the Novel*, Chicago, University of Chicago Press, 1988.

Jump, Harriet Devine, *Mary Wollstonecraft, Writer*, New York, Harvester Wheatsheaf, 1994.

Kaplan, Deborah, *Jane Austen Among Women*, Baltimore, Johns Hopkins University Press, 1992.

Kelly, Gary, *Revolutionary Feminism: The Mind and Career of Mary Wollstonecraft*, New York, St Martin's Press, 1996.

Kirkham, Margaret, *Jane Austen, Feminism and Fiction*, New York, Methuen, 1986.

Mellor, Anne K., *Mary Shelley: Her Life, Her Fiction, Her Monsters*, New York, Methuen, 1988.

——(ed.) *Romanticism and Feminism*, Bloomington, Indiana State University, 1988. This volume of essays provided an important new step in feminist analysis of Romantic texts that continues to inform current critical practice.

Millett, Kate, *Sexual Politics*, Garden City, NY, Doubleday, 1969.

Sunstein, Emily W., *A Different Face: The Life of Mary Wollstonecraft*, Boston, Little, Brown, 1975.

# 40

# New Historicism

## David Simpson

It is a tribute to the captivating power and cultural currency of the new historicism that we should find ourselves writing about it in a companion to Romanticism. The movement usually thus described originated in the United States in the late 1970s and 1980s, dominantly in California, and is principally devoted to writing about the English Renaissance, with a secondary field in nineteenth-century American studies. Its foundation was specifically not in Romanticism; indeed, its claim to attention was very much premised on its providing an (unacknowledged) alternative to the Romanticism that had, for the previous 15 years or so, been dominant in the American literary academy. New historicism, I am suggesting, displaced Romantics-centred criticism and its methods, just as the Renaissance displaced the period of revolutions, as the favoured historical field. But because of the success of this very displacement, historical work in Romanticism has recently been obliged to define itself in relation to new historicism, and many Romanticists have had the title of 'new historicist' bestowed upon them, a process which has been to some degree resisted (in the interests of accuracy) and to some degree accepted (for the sake of appearing fashionable).

By now, the roster of the principal new historicists is more or less agreed. The Renaissance scholars Stephen Greenblatt and Louis Montrose and the Americanist Walter Benn Michaels, all working at the University of California in the early 1980s, formed the core group, although other names have accrued, especially in association with the journal *Representations*, founded in Berkeley in 1983. The matter of origins is a complicated one. Greenblatt himself is often credited with coining the term 'new historicism' in his edition of a group of foundational essays in *Genre*, 15 (1982). He himself soon declared a preference for 'cultural poetics' as a description of his own work (Greenblatt, 'Towards a poetics of culture'). And, anyway, the new historicism of 1982 was already a restrike. Wesley Morris had written *Toward a New Historicism* in 1972, and located what he meant by it in the context of a more general historicist inclination in American literary theory (p. viii). Like the later new historicists, Morris saw historicism as a commitment not just (if at all) to telling 'how it really was' but as recognizing both the incompletion and the foundation in the present of what we regard as the past. In other words, he recognized the instability of historical method as essential to that method, an insight he attributed to older historicists

(Meinecke, Dilthey) as well as to such contemporaries as Murray Krieger and Roy Harvey Pearce. Pearce's 1958 essay, 'Historicism once more', had also foregrounded the function of the present in bringing the past to light, by a process of existential conjunction: 'Poems . . . are not a means of transcending history. . . but rather of meeting it' (p. 33).

Brook Thomas's *The New Historicism* has done a useful job of explaining how much of the new historicism is in fact old historicism. But we miss the point if we address the question simply as a matter of methods and formal innovations (of which there are always very few). For the situation of the new historicism of the 1980s was different and thus arguably 'new'. More emphatically than other recent American historicisms, this work was focused on a period, the Renaissance. And both period and method evolved in unspoken reaction to another period and other methods: Romanticism. There is much debate about what holds together the new historicists; good introductions can be found in Howard's 'The new historicism', Cohen's 'Political Criticism' and Veeser's *The New Historicism* and *New Historicism Reader*. But a broad consensus can be suggested. New historicists are evasive on the question of theory, and prefer to operate by pleasure and surprise, putting together the familiar with the unknown, the literary and the 'non' literary, in unexpected ways. They are not obsessed with saying the final word on how wholes relate to parts, how 'culture' or 'the political' impact on literature or text; indeed, they are sceptical about whether there are social–historical wholes to be discovered in the first place. Their method is thus anecdotal and suggestive rather than ambitiously narrativized and exhaustive. Representation and circulation tend to replace cause and effect as the dominant mechanism of cultural energy; they are happier with Foucault than with Althusser or Marx(ism). And reflexivity, recognition of the present site of criticism, of the sort that Pearce and Morris had prescribed, tends to appear as biographical aside or analogy, as an opening of reference, rather than as an insoluble and anxiety-provoking interpretive puzzle leading to bewildering dead ends or (at the other extreme) a liberating opportunity for making a new world. The anecdote does indeed dramatize the place of the critic and thus of the present, as traditional historicism had prescribed that it should; but it does so by way of conversational ease rather than with theoretical rigour. Louis Montrose's admirably compact definition of the 'collective project' of new historicism specifies an ambition

> to resituate canonical literary texts among the multiple forms of writing, and in relation to the non-discursive practices and institutions, of the social formation in which those texts have been produced – while, at the same time, recognizing that this project of historical resituation is necessarily the textual construction of critics who are themselves historical subjects ('Renaissance literary studies', p. 6).

This task, to anyone looking at the world through a commitment to the problems raised by Romanticism, must seem extraordinarily daunting. Romanticism is anxious about these matters, and about whether we can get them right (see Simpson, *Irony and Authority*). Montrose seems relatively unflustered.

One might say, then, that the new historicism allows us to make peace with hermeneutics and get on with criticism, taking us out of the realm of theory into gloriously imprecise practice, and sidelining the ethical, political and historical legacies of (Romantic) interpretation in favour of what Adorno once called, in reference to something he did not like in Benjamin, the 'crossroads of magic and positivism' (Adorno, 'Letters', p. 129). Indeed, the famous exchange between Adorno and Benjamin on the topic of mediation and totality remains in my view unignorable for any adjudication of the new historicism as historical method (see Simpson, 'The moment of materialism'). But new historicism, while making an honourable exception of Foucault (who was a regular visitor at Berkeley) is defiantly anglophone in its self-designations. As such it not only sets itself up as an alternative to 'theory' in general, with its unavoidably non-English associations (principally French but also German); it also displaces psychoanalysis (Freud and his French interpreters) and feminism (with its psychoanalytic languages) – which Judith Newton has proposed as the unacknowledged precursor of the new historicism in America (Newton, 'History as usual?'). Comparisons and contrasts are more commonly made with British cultural materialism, a body of critical work loosely deriving from the (non-identical) paradigms of Raymond Williams, E. P. Thompson and Louis Althusser. Here the emphasis is more emphatically political, both in the analysis of the past (often construed as the site of class warfare) and in the adumbration of a present where the stakes are high and the struggle still worth having. In its most visible expressions (though there is some overlap) British cultural materialism has been more judgemental in its attitudes toward the great writers, and more inclined toward serious theoretical reflection on its materials than American new historicism has been.

New historicism also drew upon contemporary and analogous developments in the discipline of history itself, which was becoming more literary even as literary criticism sought to become historical: both processes looked to anthropology, and in particular to the case for local knowledge and 'thick description' made by Clifford Geertz, for inspiration. The French historians of the *Annales* school had, beginning in the 1920s, worked with the same emphases (see Cannon et al., *The Blackwell Dictionary*). Their methods had come into English in the work of such historians as Natalie Zemon Davis, who also worked in the Renaissance. And by 1989 Lynn Hunt (whose career began at Berkeley) could propose the existence of a 'New Cultural History' which conflated the Marxist and *annalistes* traditions with anthropological and literary critical insights into the power of language and symbol (Hunt, *The New Cultural History*). The new historicism was thus participating in strong interdisciplinary alliances; the common ground between historians, anthropologists and literary critics added to the visibility and credibility of each.

And what of Romanticism? I have said that new historicism and its Renaissance focus came along as a displacement of Romanticism. For Romanticism in the late 1970s and early 1980s was the most highly inspected historical period in departments of English and Comparative Literature in the United States. And Romanticism, at this time, stood for theory. Much of what was then recognized as 'literary theory' in fact appeared by way of critics based in Romanticism: Paul de Man, Geoffrey Hartman, Harold Bloom. In *The Literary Absolute*, first published in French in 1978, Lacoue-Labarthe and Nancy had argued that Romanticism *was* theory; that, in German Romanticism particularly, literature and philosophy had come together into a synthesis that remained constitutive for what we still know as 'literature'. Around 1980, the debates among Romantic scholars were very much phrased in terms of making choices between theory (including psychoanalytic theory) and history, whether it was the traditional literary history (and its humanist associations) identified principally with M. H. Abrams, or the about-to-be-born historical method that reflected life after May, 1968, after Althusser and (very belatedly) after Marx.

But theory could not be forgotten. And because there had been theory, theory has remained. It may seem cynical to suggest that only by displacing Romanticism could new historicism get away with its rediscovery of pleasure and methodological insouciance (not at all to be confused with naivety). But there is a visible appearance of starting afresh in its ingenuities, its illuminations of a different set of writers (the magisterial Shakespeare chief among them), and its friendlier and less defensive attitude to the 'capitalism' that had been the target of so much previous critique. Capitalism, for Greenblatt, was less the inevitable agent of human suffering or a 'malign philosophical principle' than a 'complex social and economic development' with 'contradictory historical effects' ('Towards a poetics of culture', p. 5). One might ponder the context of this position in a new 'American' world order, in a rhetoric of global culture, in a new professionalism or in a specifically Californian demography and economy – eight out of fifteen of the contributors to Veeser's *The New Historicism Reader* (1994) taught or had taught in California – though one would be unlikely to arrive at simple or single conclusions. But one should, in the context of this volume, consider the new historicism's relation to the English (not always British) Renaissance. And here we come to the appeal of Foucault, to the power–knowledge axis, and to the Elizabethan stage as the synecdoche for a national culture.

What does Foucault do that Derrida and Althusser do not do, or do much of? There are many priorities and emphases in Foucault's work, and my remarks are not intended to be comprehensive. But we can say that he does history, and lots of it, and that in doing history, he finesses the challenges of theory. One of his most influential books, *Discipline and Punish*, opens with two anecdotes and tentatively but firmly delineates modern society as a total disciplinary mechanism in which the delinquent are the products of the law just as, in the earlier *Madness and Civilization*, the insane are the necessary figments of the normal. Knowledge is not an enquiry into or critique of power but its product; power has made it what it is (*Discipline and Punish*, pp. 26–8). Foucault describes a 'carceral' society from which there is no escape, least of all in the gestures designated *as* escape. One can see an urgent and passionate protest in Foucault's book, a strong dissent from a world in which what is 'illegal' is invented as such to efface the presence of more profound and pervasive injustices, the 'illegality of the dominant class' (ibid., p. 282). But his message has often been taken to be a quietist message, encouraging an awareness that all protest is already permitted and co-opted, all critique itself and by virtue of its very expression an institutional product. Or, as Francis Fukuyama might say, there is only capitalism. This component of new historicism has led Walter Cohen, for example, to describe it as 'a form of leftist disillusionment' ('Political criticism', p. 36).

This emphasis has appeared in the new historicism (though it is not uncontested), as it has shown up also in much Romantic criticism written after the new historicism (of which more later). It is as methodologically liberating as it is politically depressing. For if there really is a social whole made up of similarly functioning parts, an 'entire social body' (Foucault, *Discipline and Punish*, p. 298), then any bit of it is as revealing as any other. There are no ultimate differences, everything gives the same message once the message is understood (see Simpson, 'The moment of materialism'). As critics, we are offered a cornucopia of texts, all of which are meaningful, and which new historicism has employed to show 'the sheer intricacy and unavoidability of exchanges between culture and power' (Veeser, *The New Historicism*, p. xi). What is effaced here is class, or critical difference. Society is not radically divided but organically involuted and interactive, kept going by the abstract circulation of energies.

Hence, a suggested answer to my second question: why the Renaissance? It matters that the Renaissance was over by 1640, at which point it becomes historiographically impossible to imagine that British society is not radically and fundamentally divided. I am not saying that there ever was an organic society; I am saying that it is easier to imagine one before the Civil War. Britain after 1789 becomes once again a visibly divided society. We have to work very hard, if we are doing historical criticism, to avoid both the apparent facts of that division (class, politics, religion) and their implications for any theorization of the period. The English Renaissance had a charismatic monarch (Elizabeth I) and an even more charismatic major writer (Shakespeare). It also had an apparently hegemonic metropolitan culture (London), where everyone could be imagined to be aware of or in contact with everything; and its favoured literary genre was the theatre, which depends upon an immediately apparent public, and one traditionally if debatably described as a cross-class assembly. Foucault and the Renaissance together image an unusual wholeness and simplicity. Foucault himself had written on the Renaissance as the last culture to be unified by a belief in the power of 'resemblance' (*The Order of Things*, p. 17). Romanticism cannot provide anything comparable either in its history or in its theorists. There are too many texts written by and for too many different kinds of people, and written in a world wherein no efforts at expressive circumscription (court culture, the aristocracy, the theatre) seem to suffice (see Klancher, 'English Romanticism'). Of course, I am simplifying new historicism, the Renaissance and Foucault. But the conjunction of the three can be said to create an image of sufficiency even as the notion of wholeness is being literally eschewed. Perhaps the new historicism can sidestep the compulsive need for theory and for justification – indeed, even deny its pertinence – precisely because no one doubts the importance of Shakespeare, the Globe Theatre and Elizabeth I to Renaissance culture and history. One can speak freely of other things because one knows that these icons are always there.

So what kinds of historical criticism have been generated around Romanticism? And has the appearance of the new historicism in the 1980s made a difference? Like the Renaissance, the Romantic period had been the object of distinguished historical criticism well before that time. Some of this earlier work had been motivated by a traditional desire to get things right, to explain what had not before been explained in the form of a coherent and disinterested historical narrative: the work of Carl Woodring comes to mind here. In other cases the urge toward empirical enquiry had been motivated by social and political commitments which did not at all negate but did clearly inspire the effort at history: E. P. Thompson, Victor Kiernan and David Erdman are examples. John Barrell's book on John Clare (*The Idea of Landscape*) can now be recognized as the first of the visibly new attempts at 'history' in Romanticism, but it was devoted to an uncanonized writer and significantly concerned with English painting, so that it never received the attention paid to later books, including those by Barrell himself. New historicism did not then arrive to confront a Romanticism innocent of history, notwithstanding the strong priority of the American version of 'theory' dominant in Romanticism at that time. And the history that was available was premised (especially among British critics) on an awareness of conflict and contention – about the French Revolution and the wars that followed it, about class struggle and industrialization.

For these reasons among others, neither of the two most influential works of historical criticism of Romanticism to appear at the inaugural moment of the new historicism were themselves 'new historical'. In Britain, Marilyn Butler published *Romantics, Rebels and Reactionaries* in 1981, attempting to complicate the debate about the politics of Romantic literature by bringing many more writers to the table than had traditionally been considered in the rush to judgements, and thereby offering a Romanticism that was not a 'closely coherent body of feeling' (ibid., p. 184) but rather a varied and historically nuanced response to a range of different kinds of history: cultural, political, economic, literary and others. Butler set the well-known writers in the same world as the largely unread, performing what we would now call an assault on the canon. But, in traditional British style, her theoretical ambitions went largely unannounced, and the book was not received (or perhaps intended) as a polemic. That role was embraced, in the United States, by Jerome McGann's *The Romantic Ideology* (1983), which boldly declared that criticism of the Romantics was dominated by 'an uncritical absorption in Romanticism's own self-representations' (ibid., pp. 1, 137). McGann recreated the canon that Butler had carefully disturbed in order to offer it up for critique, and once again raised the 'political' stakes and reintroduced the theoretical discussion (though he almost failed to mention his most testing challengers, Hartman and de Man). Among the precursors, McGann allows only Heine to stand as adequately self-critical and outside the Romantic ideology. Wordsworth is the chief poetic offender, writing poetry that 'annihilates' history (ibid., p. 90) and allows the poet (as Shelley and Browning, too, had suggested) to lose the world in order to gain his own 'immortal soul' (ibid., p. 88). Theoretically, McGann offered to cut through several Gordian knots traditional to historicism, both by proposing a monolithic (received) Romanticism and by suggesting that adequate, alternative self-critique is in fact possible, as in the case of Heine (ibid., p. 151).

Butler and McGann, then, represent two quite different responses to the question of how to do history in the early 1980s, and in so doing they neither mention nor replicate the new historicism that was becoming so influential in Renaissance criticism. Their respective local traditions go a long way toward explaining their differences. Butler writes for an already-polarized British literary academy in which 'politics' was a besetting critical term often far too loosely attached to any comprehensive reading of the past, while McGann faces a 'theoretical' American academy from which politics appeared to him to have been completely excluded. Neither introduced their work as 'new'; both are fully aware of writing within and for a pre-established debate about Romanticism. The rhetorical novelty of the new historicism is not available to them, nor do they attempt the anecdotal insouciance and casual hermeneutics of their contemporaries writing about the Renaissance. The same is true of most of the historical work that has been published since, which has tended toward a frontal engagement with the question of history and a theoretical earnestness not common among Renaissance new historicists. Historical criticism of Romanticism in the 1980s in the United States tended to be, in Marjorie Levinson's words, 'at once materialist and deconstructive' (*Wordsworth*, p. 9), committed to history but unable or unwilling to ignore theory, and often concerned to position each in terms of the other. Levinson identifies her own work and its companions as a 'new historicist criticism' (ibid., p. 13), but without invoking the Renaissance paradigm from which it visibly differs. Critics like James Chandler, Marjorie Levinson (both students of McGann), John Barrell, Jon Klancher, Alan Liu, David Simpson and Clifford Siskin have all been called new historicists, and of course there is no absolute division between their work and that of critics working in the Renaissance under the same nomination. But to read their work is to be reminded at almost all points of the shadow of Marx, Adorno, Macherey, Althusser, of Williams and Thompson, as well as of de Man, deconstruction and psychoanalysis. Their effort is eclectic and difficult, as it searches out what James Chandler called 'multiple incoherencies and contradictions' (*Wordsworth's Second Nature*, p. xviii) plotted in terms of both theory and history. Some of these writers are more outspoken in their theoretical concerns than others, but the emphasis is typically upon methodological self-consciousness, as befits a Romanticism that was itself conceived in such richly theoretical languages.

Looking back – and with the important exceptions of Levinson's book on Keats and Barrell's book on De Quincey – we may be struck by how much of the discussion of Romanticism and history in the 1980s was carried on by way of a debate about Words-worth. Chandler, Levinson, Liu, and Simpson, among others, all produced books in which the historical dimensions of Wordsworth were at issue. Much of this work carried on the case made by McGann, producing (in Levinson's words) 'demystifications of Romanticist readings as well as of Romantic poems' (*Wordsworth*, p. 1). Chandler read Wordsworth as poeticized Burke, and Liu wrote about 'his crowning denial of history: autobiography' (*Wordsworth*, p. 35). But it was also a longer-view response to Geoffrey Hartman's *Wordsworth's Poetry*, first published in 1964 and principally responsible for the rehabilita-tion of Wordsworth as a complex literary–theoretical figure, an assumption fully main-tained in M. H. Abrams's important *Natural Supernaturalism* (1971). Hartman especially established psychoanalysis as a key tool for a reading of Wordsworth, making it impossible to ignore in favour of any simple return to 'history'. Despite the centrality of Wordsworth, then, the new work of the 1980s never consolidated itself into a 'movement' or made a convincing claim for absolute novelty. The most explicit effort at a group manifesto, Levinson's editing of herself, Butler, McGann and Paul Hamilton in *Rethinking Historicism* (1989), did not have the effect of making familiar or marketing any widely recognized consensus either for Romantic criticism or for literary theory.

Perhaps by this time the field was being made over once again in response to the new primary concerns about gender and empire, concerns that had not been prominent in Romantic historicism thus far. The same issues have come to the fore in Renaissance studies, so that the question of the new historicism there, too, already has a somewhat dated aura. The historians up for adoption are no longer those of the *Annales* school and their successors, but the 'Subaltern Studies' group, based in India and frontally concerned with imperialism and with history 'from below' (see Guha and Spivak, *Selected Subaltern Studies*). But it must also be said that Romanticism was not especially sympathetic to representing a single movement so much as it was generative of debates. For all the reasons I have discussed, the Romantic period has simply not been prone to summary or charis-matic representation. The reasons for this lie partly in the history of Romanticism, partly in the history *in* Romanticism, and no doubt very considerably in the histories of our own times and places, of which it is so hard to speak.

## WRITINGS

Cohen, Walter, 'Political criticism of Shakespeare', in *Shakespeare Reproduced: The Text in History and Ideology*, eds Jean E. Howard and Marion F. O'Connor, London, Methuen, 1987, pp. 18–46.

Foucault, Michel, *The Order of Things: An Archaeology of the Human Sciences*, New York, Random House, 1973.

——*Discipline and Punish: The Birth of the Prison*, trans. Alan Sheridan, London, Allen Lane, 1977.

Greenblatt, Stephen (ed.) 'The forms of power and the power of forms in the Renaissance', *Genre* 15 (1982).

——'Towards a poetics of culture', in *The New Historicism*, ed. H. Aram Veeser, New York and London, Routledge, 1989, pp. 1–14.

Howard, Jean E., 'The new historicism in Renaissance studies', *English Literary Renaissance* 16 (1986), 13–43.

Morris, Wesley, *Toward a New Historicism*, Princeton, Princeton University Press, 1972.

Pearce, Roy Harvey, *Historicism once More: Problems and Occasions for the American Scholar*, Princeton, Princeton University Press, 1969.

Thomas, Brook, *The New Historicism and Other Old Fashioned Topics*, Princeton, Princeton University Press, 1991.

Veeser, H. Aram (ed.) *The New Historicism*, New York and London, Routledge, 1989.

——(ed) *The New Historicism Reader*, New York and London, Routledge, 1994.

## REFERENCES AND FURTHER READING

Abrams, M. H. *Natural Supernaturalism: Tradition and Revolution in Romantic Literature*, New York, Norton, 1971.

Adorno, Theodor, 'Letters to Walter Benjamin', in Ernst Bloch, Georg Lukács, Bertolt Brecht, Walter Benjamin, Theodor Adorno, *Aesthetics and Politics*, London, New Left Books, 1977, pp. 110–33.

Barrell, John, *The Idea of Landscape and the Sense of Place: An Approach to the Poetry of John Clare*, Cambridge, Cambridge University Press, 1973.

——*The Infection of Thomas De Quincey: A Psychopathology of Imperialism*, New Haven and London, Yale University Press, 1991.

Butler, Marilyn, *Romantics, Rebels, and Reactionaries: English Literature and its Background, 1760–1830*, Oxford, Oxford University Press, 1981.

Cannon, John, with R. H. C. Davis, William Doyle, Jack P. Greene (eds) *The Blackwell Dictionary of Historians*, Oxford, Blackwell, 1988.

Chandler, James K., *Wordsworth's Second Nature: A Study of the Poetry and Politics*, Chicago and London, University of Chicago Press, 1984.

Davis, Natalie Zemon, *Society and Culture in Early Modern France*, Stanford, Stanford University Press, 1975.

——*Fiction in the Archives: Pardon Tales and Their Tellers in Sixteenth-century France*, Stanford, Stanford University Press, 1987.

Geertz, Clifford, *The Interpretation of Cultures*, New York, Basic Books, 1973.

——*Local Knowledge: Further Essays in Interpretive Anthropology*, New York, Basic Books, 1983.

Guha, Ranajit and Spivak, Gayatri Chakravorty, *Selected Subaltern Studies*, New York and Oxford, Oxford University Press, 1988.

Hartman, Geoffrey H., *Wordsworth's Poetry, 1787–1814*, New Haven and London, Yale University Press, 1964.

Hunt, Lynn (ed.) *The New Cultural History*, Berkeley, Los Angeles, London, University of California Press, 1989.

Klancher, Jon P., *The Making of English Reading Audiences, 1790–1832*, Madison and London, University of Wisconsin Press, 1987.

——'English Romanticism and cultural production', in *The New Historicism*, ed. H. Aram Veeser, New York and London, Routledge, 1989, pp. 77–88.

Lacoue-Labarthe, Philippe, and Nancy, Jean-Luc, *The Literary Absolute: The Theory of Literature in German Romanticism*, trans. Philip Barnard and Cheryl Lester, Albany, SUNY Press, 1988.

Levinson, Marjorie, *Wordsworth's Great Period Poems: Four Essays*, Cambridge, Cambridge University Press, 1986.

——*Keats's Life of Allegory: The Origins of a Style*, Oxford, Blackwell, 1988.

——(ed.) *Rethinking Historicism: Critical Readings in Romantic History*, Oxford, Blackwell, 1989.

Liu, Alan, *Wordsworth: The Sense of History*, Stanford, Stanford University Press, 1989.

McGann, Jerome J., *The Romantic Ideology: A Critical Investigation*, Chicago and London, University of Chicago Press, 1983.

Montrose, Louis, 'Renaissance literary studies and the subject of history', *English Literary Renaissance* 16 (1986) 5–12.

Newton, Judith Lowder, 'History as usual? Feminism and the "New Historicism"', in *The New Historicism*, ed. H. Aram Veeser, New York and London, Routledge, 1989, pp. 152–67.

Simpson, David, *Irony and Authority in Romantic Poetry*, London, Macmillan, 1979.

—— *Wordsworth and the Figurings of the Real*, London, Macmillan, 1982.

—— *Wordsworth's Historical Imagination: The Poetry of Displacement*, London and New York, Methuen, 1987.

—— 'The moment of materialism', in *Subject to History: Ideology, Class, Gender*, ed. David Simpson, Ithaca and London, Cornell University Press, 1991, pp. 1–33.

Siskin, Clifford, *The Historicity of Romantic Discourse*, New York and Oxford, Oxford University Press, 1988.

Woodring, Carl, *Politics and English Romantic Poetry*, Cambridge, Mass., Harvard University Press, 1970.

# 41

# Romantic Ecology

## *Tony Pinkney*

'Romantic ecology' is a phrase given wide currency by Jonathan Bate's slim but incisive volume, *Romantic Ecology: Wordsworth and the Environmental Tradition*, published in 1991. Written in a lively and accessible style, and appealing over the heads of the professional critics to the 'common reader', Bate's book has been much discussed and highly influential. It intervenes effectively in two literary-critical debates, and this intersection of concerns has been a major factor in its success. First, it intervenes in the field of Wordsworth studies, where Bate grandly rejects the 'counter-intuitive' readings of Wordsworth offered by recent critics and theorists, and recommends a return to nineteenth-century approaches to the poetry: 'a primary aim of this book is to recapture something of what Wordsworth did for the nineteenth century'.[1] But to attend to Wordsworth in this fashion is to 'relearn [his] way of looking at nature' (p. 9), and this has wider implications, Bate suggests, for literary criticism in general. His book is not, after all, simply a study of Wordsworth, but a reflection on what literary criticism can be and do today, on what it has recently been and done, and what it *should* now be and do.

In terms of this second and broader debate, *Romantic Ecology* presents itself as a manifesto for a new ecological criticism: a 'green reading of Wordsworth' (ibid.), if successful, will teach us how to 'read greenly' in general. And this is no accident because Wordsworth himself, Bate argues, is a vital influence on the English 'tradition of environmental consciousness' (ibid.) which runs forward through John Ruskin and William Morris into our own century. *Romantic Ecology* therefore finds a benign mutual interaction between its subject and its critical approach: to read Wordsworth attentively is to learn to read greenly but, simultaneously, to practise ecological criticism (which I shall often hereafter abbreviate as eco-criticism) is to find the right approach to Wordsworth's verse. To read Romanticism correctly, on this showing, is to read it through the lenses of a contemporary ecological consciousness of which the Romantic writers were crucial pioneers. The very phrase 'Romantic ecology' points in two directions. Looking backwards, it affirms that the Romantic poets were ecological, or at least proto-ecological; looking forwards, it claims that contemporary ecology is a Romantic inheritance. I want, in what follows, to look in more detail at the debates in which Bate's volume intervenes: first, at the general question of what a 'green' literary criticism might be; second, at the particular reading of

Wordsworth and other Romantic poets which Bate and other like-minded critics have offered.

What then is 'literary ecology' or ecological criticism? Though Bate's book has been the focus for this literary movement in England, its origins in fact go a good deal further back in time and are mostly American. There are some stray English precursors, to be sure: Robert Waller wrote eloquently on 'Enclosures: the ecological significance of a poem by John Clare' in *Mother Earth, Journal of the Soil Association* in 1963, and Clare is certainly a figure we will have to consider in more detail below. But rather more eco-critical straws in the wind appear in America in the 1970s. Thomas Lyon has an important essay on 'The ecological vision of Gary Snyder' in the *Kansas Quarterly* in 1970; Glen A. Love, who has been a tireless propagandist for ecological criticism over the years, shifted the debate from poetry (Snyder) to narrative in his 'Ecology in Arcadia' in the *Colorado Quarterly* in 1972; and with the publication of the first book-length critical study in 1974, Joseph Meeker's admirable *The Comedy of Survival: Studies in Literary Ecology*, it might have seemed that the movement was well and truly under way. But it petered out again, and though one or two seminal articles continued to appear – William Ruekert on 'Literature and ecology: an experiment in criticism' in the *Iowa Review* in 1978, Don Elgin's brief 'What is "literary ecology"?' in *Humanities in the South* in 1983 – the eco-critical impulse seemed mostly lost in the 1980s, a decade divided between the continuing importation of literary theory from Europe and the emergence of 'new historicism'.

But as the environmental crisis our planet faces – global warming, holes in the ozone layer, population pressures, destruction of the rain forests, depletion of fish stocks, and so on – has both intensified and become more widely publicized in the last two decades, so both green politics in general, and its literary-critical off-shoot in particular, have seen a revival in their fortunes. The journal *Western American Literature* played a crucial role in this in the late 1980s and early 1990s. Glen A. Love wrote powerful general manifestos on 'Revaluing nature: toward an ecological criticism' in 1990 and '*Et in Arcadia Ego*: pastoral theory meets ecocriticism' in 1992, while Sue Ellen Campbell meditated profoundly on the relationship between literary theory and ecology in her 'The land and language of desire: where deep ecology and post-structuralism meet' in 1989. And for the next few years one could hardly pick up an issue of the journal without coming across titles such as 'Land and value: the ecology of Robinson Jeffers', ' "A relative to all that is": the eco-hero in Western American literature', 'Practising emptiness: Gary Snyder's playful ecological work', and so on. Out of this ferment of intellectual activity has since emerged the Association for the Study of Literature and Environment (ASLE). Founded in 1993, it now has some 600 members, and organizes an impressive programme of newsletters, journals, networks and conferences. Institutionally speaking, eco-criticism has now well and truly come of age.

But has it intellectually come of age? Could one summarize ecological criticism as a set of key principles, a relatively consistent programme that one could take from literary text to text to test it out against them? What are its fundamental orientations, and how does it situate itself in relation to the other brands of literary criticism and theory on offer in the academy today? As with any body of active and diverse writing, one risks being reductive and schematic in offering an 'x-ray' of eco-criticism's basic concerns. 'We murder to dissect', writes Wordsworth, and any definition of 'literary ecology' is likely to find itself instantly outdated by the nimble energies of its developing subject-matter. But it is still worth trying to pin down a few basics of eco-critical philosophy in order to orient the reader within this growing body of writing. Ecological criticism has always first and foremost been a call to *responsibility*. It has insisted that literary criticism should not simply be an esoteric pursuit, written by professionals for professionals, but should assume a wider social function, intervening in the great public debates of our epoch. This call to responsibility has often taken the form of hostility to literary theory. In the 1970s and 1980s, literary theory often seemed to undercut the notions of reference, representation and realism on which nature writing has traditionally depended. Complex theoretical arguments were elaborated to show that reference and realism, where art had once thought it could latch on to the external world, were merely rhetorical *effects*, illusions generated by the intricate internal *textuality* of literary works. The task of criticism, accordingly, was not to ponder the wisdom or otherwise of what the text told us about the world, but rather to analyse the complex pattern of tropes and devices whereby it created the illusion of an external world to talk about. Such positions have been anathema to some ecologically minded critics, for whom they represent criticism withdrawing into a narrow, highly specialized realm. Other, often younger, eco-critics have taken a more nuanced view of these matters. They have pointed out that some of the central tenets of literary theory are not unlike key principles of ecological thinking. Under the influence of Saussurean linguistics, for instance, literary theory has been a profoundly *relational* mode of thinking: it has insisted that nothing – whether it be a linguistic phoneme, a textual device or a whole literary work – has meaning or value by itself, but only by virtue of the system to which it belongs. This, of course, is uncannily like the *holistic* principles of green thinking, whereby we must understand each organism, not as a self-contained entity, but as a complexly interdependent unit of an entire ecosystem. Literary theory may begin by rejecting the notion of the 'organic unity' of the literary work, that biological metaphor for the text which derives ultimately from Romanticism, and yet it ends, in its dissolving of self-contained entities into wider, complex systems, in reinstating other Romantic impulses. Literary theory, these younger writers have argued, both reinforces *and* disturbs eco-criticism, and prolonged meditation about their relationship, rather than simplistically drawn battle lines, are the order of the day.

If theory, in the grip of deconstruction and poststructuralism, did indeed emphasize textuality rather than representation in the 1970s, it also, however, generated new kinds of politically responsible criticism in the 1980s. New, combative modes of criticism committed to the study of class, race or gender in literature emerged from the theoretical revolution; and eco-criticism now insists that the notion of responsibility at work here be extended to include the crisis of the natural environment, a universal crisis for our species which confronts us whichever class, race or gender we belong to. I propose to look briefly at two main areas of ecological 'responsibility' in literary criticism. First, the treatment in art of natural 'objects', both the environment as a whole and the diverse plants and creatures it contains; and second, the treatment in art of human interaction with this natural environment, both in actual and in projected Utopian communities. As the reader will see, there has been a tendency to map these two domains onto distinct literary modes – poetry for natural 'objects', narrative for the question of interaction – but this distinction is by no means watertight.

To what extent, ecological criticism will ask of any art-work put in front of it, are the flowers, birds, trees, animals represented in this work – the whole natural realm in general as it offers that to us – celebrated in and for themselves rather than being subjugated to human purposes, however benign the latter may seem? Let's take first two famous examples of how *not* to do it, of an exploitative rather than genuinely celebratory attitude to the natural world. Shelley's *To A Skylark* might seem to promise a Romantic openness to the life of natural creatures. Yet almost from the start another impulse intervenes: 'Hail to thee, blithe Spirit! / Bird thou never wert. . . .' That second line still has power to shock, surely; for the skylark's own identity, its actual autonomous being in its indigenous environment, is at once cancelled out. The bird instead is turned into a *symbol*, into a representative of the poet's own inner aspirations; it is folded back into the subjectivity of the author rather than respected in its objectivity and otherness. An equally notorious instance of such arrogant manipulations of nature comes in W. B. Yeats's *Coole Park and Ballylee, 1931.* Wandering in the grounds of Coole Park, the poet hears the 'sudden thunder of the mounting swan' and, turning towards the noise, exclaims, 'Another emblem there!' Once again, the distinctive being of the swans in nature is erased; they, too, metamorphose into an image for an aspect of the poet's own being rather than featuring in the poem in their own right.

Shelley and Yeats are not hacking down the rain forests in these poems, to be sure. And yet the humanistic arrogance that is casually prepared to exploit a living creature for its own symbolic or psychological uses is not in the last analysis different from that which exploits living organisms for its own economic purposes. For a properly ecological attitude to the natural world, we shall turn not to Wordsworth, who at once converts the living creature into 'Historian of my infancy' in *To A Butterfly*, but to John Clare, who has become such a pivotal figure in debates about Romantic poetry and ecology. The mode of attention to local flora and fauna in Clare's poetry has much in common with natural history writing in its devoted precision to the creature and habitat before it. The 'wonder' that invests such poems as *To a Snipe* or *The Pettichaps Nest* is not gained at any cost of natural-scientific observation; each, rather, movingly feeds into and reinforces the other. And the case of Clare makes it clear that an ecologically sensitive and responsible art must be open to the natural world it celebrates in terms of language and form as well as theme. Poetic language, one might suggest, should seek to attain the density and physicality of the natural objects and processes it describes (the verse of Gerard Manley Hopkins would be a good example); and poetic form should ideally be responsively open to its objects too, rather than imposing pre-given arbitrary structures upon them (sonnet, quatrain or whatever). The demands of literary ecology, that is, dovetail interestingly with some of the key prescriptions of literary modernism ('muscular', enactive language and free verse, say). In the premodernist epoch, Clare's creative deviations from the grammar, punctuation and diction of standard English, his use of regional and dialect forms, his mixing of popular with learned literary modes – all these create what James C. McKusick, in an excellent essay on Clare, has called 'a linguistic analogue to the natural world', an '"unenclosed" verse' which reflects and enacts the unenclosed, interdependent natural lives and habitats that his verse both celebrates and mourns.[2]

Mention of the parliamentary enclosures of the late eighteenth century brings me to the second aspect of an ecological poetics of responsibility: the question of human *interaction* with the natural environment. Perhaps no literary work can entirely avoid treating this issue, and yet clearly there is the world of difference between the intricate investigation of upper-middle-class consciousness in a late Henry James novel and Thomas Hardy's depiction of the fate of Clym Yeobright, Eustacia Vye and others on Egdon Heath in *The Return of the Native*. Consciousness is about as disembodied as it *can* be in a late James text, but it would be hard to imagine an environment more forcefully evoked and concretely active than Hardy's Egdon Heath. We can generalize out from this example to say that, within the canon, ecological criticism has certainly preferred realist texts to their experimental modernist or postmodernist counterparts, where the external world is indeed likely to be attenuated in favour of a searching attention to literary form and device. But eco-criticism has also sought to challenge the accepted canon more sharply than this, seeking to bring to the very centre of cultural debate such hitherto marginalized forms as 'nature writing', 'regional literature' (as with the 'Western American literature' I mentioned above) and 'travel writing'. For the eco-critic, it is a sign of how deeply mainstream criticism has retreated from its social responsibilities that such literary forms, in which the question of human relationship to the natural world is foregrounded from start to finish, should have been consistently treated as 'marginal' or 'sub-literary', with only very rare exceptions, such as Thoreau's *Walden*, being granted grudging acceptance into the standard canon.

One canonical genre in which eco-critics have shown sustained interest, however, is *pastoral*. Here more than elsewhere, they argue, can human interactions with our environment and biosystem be explored and reimagined. They would accept the conclusion of Marxist and feminist critics that traditional pastoral has often been an ideological tool, masking and furthering dominant class and gender interests. Yet ecological criticism insists that one should not throw out the baby – the pastoral impulse as such – with the bathwater of particular, socially exploitative uses of the genre. If pastoral has formerly presented a simplified, Edenic nature in which jaded city-dwellers could temporarily refresh themselves, we must now, Glen A. Love argues in his 1990 manifesto for ecological criticism, 'redefine pastoral in terms of the new and more complex understanding of nature' that twentieth-century ecology has brought us: 'a pastoral for the present and the future calls for a better science of nature, a greater understanding of its complexity, a more radical awareness of its primal energy and stability, and a more acute questioning of the values of the supposedly sophisticated society to which we are bound'.[3] Such a pastoral would no longer propose comfortable reconciliations of culture and nature in images of the garden; rather, it would now look long and hard at the radical *other* of culture, the wilderness, as a complex possible model for transforming human society.

With this defence of pastoral as a viable literary mode in eco-criticism, we can return to Jonathan Bate's attempt to construct a model of 'Romantic ecology' on the basis of Wordsworth's writings. *Romantic Ecology* also propounds the virtues of wilderness, as when it defends the consoling image of the weeds and spear grass which closes the tale of Margaret's sufferings in *The Ruined Cottage*. And it offers a vigorous defence of Wordsworth's uses of pastoral in *The Prelude*. 'A major count in the critical indictment of Wordsworth', Bate notes, 'is that he was among the many conspirators in the Great Pastoral Con Trick' (p. 18). But 'if there is to be an ecological criticism the "language that is ever green" [i.e. pastoral] must be reclaimed' (p. 19). Bate therefore mounts a spirited and many-sided defence of Wordsworthian pastoral. He demonstrates first its radicalism within the literary tradition itself, in its stress on labour, hardship, adverse weather and terrain in contrast to the indolent shepherds and idyllic settings of much Classical and Renaissance pastoral; Wordsworthian pastoral is 'hard', not 'soft'. But beyond this, in the wider realm of politics at large, the pastoral vision of Book VIII of *The Prelude* is 'republican pastoral' (p. 33) – as Thomas Macaulay had clearly grasped when he described the poem as 'to the last degree Jacobinical, indeed Socialist' (cited, p. 32). This radical vision of Grasmere rural life looks back as a critique of the alienated urban relationships of Book VII ('Residence in London') and forward to the revolutionary enthusiasms of Book IX ('Residence in France'). Whereas Marxist critics see pastoral as displacing politics or compensating for political disillusion, Wordsworthian 'hard' pastoral opens directly into a general radical politics, on Bate's reading.

However, this account is not without its problems. In a startling concession, Bate allows that it 'is easy to undermine the vision of book eight of *The Prelude*' (p. 28). The question of the actual economic record of the Lake District at the turn of the nineteenth century comes to the fore here. How many of the 'statesmen' whose proudly independent way of life Wordsworth so valued (Michael, in the poem of that name, is a memorable instance) were actually freeholders of their property? Faced with this searching query, Jonathan Bate uneasily shifts the grounds of his defence of Wordsworth. Having previously praised Wordsworthian pastoral for its 'hard' and gritty realism in contrast to the facile idealizations of earlier pastoral, he now asserts: 'For Wordsworth, to demand "realism" or "reportage" from poetry is to misapprehend its function; the purpose of book eight of *The Prelude* is not so much to show shepherds as they are but rather to bring forward an image of human greatness' (p. 29). This, frankly, is to have your cake and eat it, to construe Book VIII as simultaneously realist and idealist, toughly down to earth and inflatedly rhetorical. A second difficulty for Bate's republican reading of Wordsworth's pastoral vision is the fact that the most vivid images of shepherds in *The Prelude* are solitary rather than social. Far from being integrated participants in an egalitarian community, the poem's shepherds are awesome, larger-than-life figures perched on mountain tops or glimpsed through mists; if traditional 'soft' pastoral operates within the aesthetic convention of the 'beautiful', Wordsworth's awe-inspiring Solitaries clearly come within the more rugged ambit of the 'sublime'. But may it not be, Bate then suggests, that the poet 'makes the shepherd into a symbol of his personal sublime, what Keats called the "wordsworthian or egotistical sublime". He is not interested in the shepherd but in what the shepherd provides him by way of both inspiration and admonition' (p. 30)? Which is to ask whether Wordsworth doesn't do to his Grasmere shepherds what we earlier saw Shelley do to his skylark and Yeats to his swans, i.e. internalize them as an image for aspects of his psyche rather than respect them in their autonomy and otherness. Bate doesn't fully answer this objection to his reading of Wordsworth's pastoralism, but clearly he cannot let it stand, for it would be fatal to his case. Wordsworth's pastoral would then become 'soft' in a new sense – not because it envisaged an implausibly easy life for its subjects like the Classical tradition, but because it *dissolved* those very subjects, reducing them to the moveable chess pieces of some inner psychological drama. A similar objection can be raised to Bate's later and very positive account of the 'Naming of Places' sequence of poems from *Lyrical Ballads*. One can offer an eco-critical reading which stresses the benign reconciliation of poet and place, or language and nature, which is achieved in these texts; this is certainly how they themselves *want* to be read, after all. But it's also possible to suggest, in the light of Marxist and feminist criticism, that the educated, leisured, middle-class poet is unacceptably *appropriating* the locales he celebrates, erasing their accepted, public significances in favour of his idiosyncratic private associations.[4]

Jonathan Bate has produced a gripping account of the political implications of the depiction of Grasmere working life in Book VIII of *The Prelude*, but problems clearly remain. The next move in his construction of a 'Romantic ecology' based around Wordsworth's work is the canonical shift that I described above as general within ecological criticism: a moving to the very centre of critical attention of formerly marginalized genres such as 'nature writing', 'regional literature', 'travel writing', even 'natural history writing'. In Wordsworth's case, 'we must bring the *Guide* [*to the Lakes*] from the periphery to the centre' (p. 42). The *Guide to the Lakes* shows the Romantic writer moving beyond eighteenth-century analyses of the 'economy of nature', the systematic interconnectedness of all living things in the natural order, to the question of the relation of the *human* economy to that wider eco-system. This 'central Romantic text', as Bate provocatively describes it (p. 45), affords him a powerful answer to the kinds of objection I have been sketching to his earlier eco-critical analyses. Far from subjugating nature and shepherds to his own individual imaginative purposes, Wordsworth here immerses himself in the most detailed interactions of humanity and its environment – styles of rural architecture, modes of tree plantation, and so on. He celebrates traditional practices that integrate the inhabitants with their region, and berates contemporary innovations that threaten to disrupt this delicate balance. In contrast to Marxist critics who have claimed that the 'Romantic Ideology' involves a retreat from society into spiritual transcendence, Bate can now forcefully argue that 'the Romantic ecology has nothing to do with flight from the material world, from history and society – it is in fact an attempt to enable mankind the better to live in the material world by entering into harmony with the environment' (p. 40). In other ways, too, *Guide to the Lakes* is more of a collective than an individual text. Across its publishing history, it accreted components by other writers – botanical tables by Thomas Gough, letters on geology by Adam Sedgwick – to the point where, as Bate puts it, 'the very notion of this text having an individual author becomes unstable' (p. 45). Moreover, it is a work that has had very material effects on the world around it – its description of the Lakes as 'a sort of national property' being an inspirational slogan in the creation of both the National Trust in 1895 and the Lake District National Park in 1949.

As we move beyond Wordsworth's literary writings, so we enter that wider 'environmental tradition' which Jonathan Bate regards him as inaugurating. John Ruskin is a key figure in this lineage, and receives appropriately extended treatment in *Romantic Ecology*, where he figures as the 'exemplary English ecologist' (p. 59). So, too, does William Morris, whose attention to 'architectural style and town-planning' in his Utopian fiction *News from Nowhere* justifies Bate in once more asserting, *pace* the Marxist critics of Romanticism, that 'here the Romantic imagination is being used not to transcend nature but to reconstruct Trafalgar Square on ecological principles' (p. 56). Bate refers to 'the Wordsworthian ecology which Morris shared with Ruskin' (p. 59) and claims, provocatively, that 'Ruskinian texts, not Marx's *Capital*, were the inspirational force behind the socialism of Morris and others; English socialism is at root more "green" than it is "Marxist"' (p. 58). At this point, then, we should stand back from the detail of individual literary readings and reflect more generally on the politics of 'Romantic ecology' – particularly on its relation to another concept which in recent years has proved crucial in thinking about the politics of Romantic writers and their texts – 'Romantic anti-capitalism'.

Romantic anti-capitalism is a fierce critique of modern capitalist civilization, but the values in the name of which it launches that critique are backward- rather than forward-looking. It appeals to the supposedly 'organic' human communities of earlier historical epochs, integrated both internally within themselves (in contrast to the atomization and class division of society under capitalism) and in their relation to the natural environment (in contrast to the ruthless exploitation of nature for private profit under capitalism). Clearly, this is already a long way removed from socialism, which denounces capitalism in the name of a better future, not a golden past, in the name of the genuinely co-operative and classless culture we might create on the other side of working-class revolution – the social world of Morris's *News from Nowhere*, say. Romantic anti-capitalism tends to see the working class as more of a problem than a solution. The workers, in its view, are victims of the system, to be sure; but they are also passively integrated into it and are not seen to constitute, as they do for the socialist tradition, the *active* subject of political challenge and transformation. With no organized social force to attach itself to, the politics of Romantic anti-capitalism tend to be deeply unstable, veering erratically from one extreme to the other of the political spectrum. And Marxism too, for the Romantic anti-capitalist, is seen as part of the problem rather than part of the solution; it is seen as materialist, utilitarian, obsessively industrializing – just one further logical development, in fact, of the very system it claims to be challenging. The great and distinctive strength of the Romantic anti-capitalist tradition, however, is its profound interrogation of capitalism on *qualitative* rather than quantitative grounds. It doesn't ask about the statistics of economic deprivation so much as it enquires about the spiritual and cultural quality of life under capital, and that insistence on quality has always included a profound concern with ecological questions of the right relation between humanity and its natural environment – a relation which was benign and interactive, it is argued, under feudal or primitive societies, and which has gone disastrously wrong under the rule of capital.[5]

It doesn't seem to me to be helpful to say that William Morris is more 'green' than 'red': he is, surely, as green as he is red and as red as he is green. Which is to say that it was the unique genius of Morris to have held together the Romantic-ecological and the socialist critiques of capitalism at the very moment when, historically speaking, they were about to split ruinously apart. A vivid literary tradition of Romantic anti-capitalism then kept the ecological critique alive – think of D. H. Lawrence in *Lady Chatterley's Lover* pitting the joyous sexuality of Connie and Mellors in Wragby Wood against the pitiless mechanism of Clifford Chatterley's mines – but turned away from socialist politics (sometimes to the far right, as with W. B. Yeats). Meantime, official socialism, in the grip of Lenin's definition of communism as 'Soviets plus electrification', invested heavily in notions of industrial growth, productivity, modernization, and turned damagingly away from ecological questions. The only 'winner' in this splitting asunder of radical traditions has been capitalism itself, which saw Romantic anti-capitalism marginalized as 'nostalgic' and eccentric, and the communist movement degenerate into brutal authoritarianism. Only in the last few decades have there been sustained attempts to pull back together ecology and socialism,

Romantic anti-capitalism and a transformed Marxism. The writings of Raymond Williams, including his important essay 'Socialism and ecology' and his great study of *The Country and the City*, have been one such attempt at reintegration,[6] as are some of the red–green alliances that have been emerging within green politics recently. 'Literary ecology' or eco-criticism, as it defines itself across the coming years, may be another such venture. Jonathan Bate's *Romantic Ecology* is a pioneering effort which will remain influential for a long time to come. The role of Wordsworth within that 'environmental tradition' is, as we have seen, a problematic one, but no more so perhaps than 'Romantic ecology' in general. Contested and difficult though the concept of a Romantic ecology may be, however, its reactivation, in the ecological politics of our epoch, may be quite literally the measure of our common survival on this planet – ' "the very world which is the world / Of all of us, the place in which, in the end, / We find our happiness, or not at all", *Prel.* x. 725–7)' (*Romantic Ecology*, p. 33).

## NOTES

1 Bate, *Romantic Ecology*, p. 8.
2 McKusick, 'A language that is ever green'.
3 Love, 'Revaluing nature'.
4 For a fuller discussion, see my 'Naming Places'.

5 For an excellent brief synopsis of Romantic anti-capitalism, see Löwy, 'Marxism and revolutionary Romanticism'.
6 Raymond Williams, 'Socialism and ecology', in his *Resources of Hope*, edited by Robin Gable, London, Verso, 1989.

## REFERENCES AND FURTHER READING

Bate, Jonathan, *Romantic Ecology: Wordsworth and the Environmental Tradition*, London, Routledge, 1991.

Buell, Lawrence, *The Environmental Imagination: Thoreau, Nature Writing and the Formation of American Culture*, Cambridge, Mass., Belknap Press, 1995.

Campbell, Sue Ellen, 'The land and language of desire: where deep ecology and post-structuralism meet', *Western American Literature* 24 (1989) 199–211.

Elgin, Don, 'What is "literary ecology"?', *Humanities in the South* 57 (1983) 7–9.

Love, Glen A., 'Ecology in Arcadia', *Colorado Quarterly* 21 (1972) 175–85.

—— 'Revaluing nature: towards an ecological criticism', *Western American Literature* 25 (1990) 201–15.

—— '*Et in Arcadia Ego*: pastoral theory meets eco-criticism', *Western American Literature* 27 (1992) 196–207.

Löwy, Michael, 'Marxism and revolutionary Romanticism', *Telos* 49 (fall 1981) 83–95.

Lyon, Thomas, 'The ecological vision of Gary Snyder', *Kansas Quarterly* 2 (1970) 117–24.

McKusick, James, ' "A language that is ever green": The ecological vision of John Clare', *University of Toronto Quarterly* 61 (1991/92) 226–49.

Meeker, Joseph, *The Comedy of Survival: Studies in Literary Ecology*, New York, Charles Scribner's Sons, 1974.

Pinkney, Tony, 'Naming places: Wordsworth and the possibilities of eco-criticism', *News from Nowhere: Theory and Politics of Romanticism* 1 (1995) 41–66.

Ruekert, William, 'Literature and ecology: an experiment with criticism', *Iowa Review* 9 (1978) 62–86.

Waller, Robert, 'Enclosures: the ecological significance of a poem by John Clare', *Mother Earth, Journal of the Soil Association* 13 (1961) 231–7.

Williams, Raymond, *The Country and the City*, London, Chatto and Windus, 1973.

# 42

# Psychological Approaches

## Douglas B. Wilson

Freudian theory offers the one model of reading we have that can claim to make the text speak more than it knows.

Peter Hulme

Because of his literary and analytic skills, Sigmund Freud remains at the centre of psychological approaches to Romanticism. Although there is no evidence of direct influence of Wordsworth on Freud, both dominate their own spheres and deserve the primary focus of this study. Relying upon the premise that both psychoanalysts and literary critics exercise their interpretive powers on basically the same materials, Peter Brooks suggests that 'there ought to be, there must be, some correspondence between literary and psychic process, that aesthetic structure and form, including literary tropes, must somehow coincide with the psychic structures and operations they both evoke and appeal to' (Brooks, 'The Idea', p. 337). This essay, which begins and ends with Wordsworth, deploys Freud, Winnicott, Lacan and Kristeva for its theoretical arguments. Moving from private Oedipal to public historical contexts, the essay closes with Wordsworth's rhetoric of errancy.

Analysts and psychological critics are both sensitive to the many ways in which our readings defeat 'literal-minded expectations about meaning'. Both are wary of the 'referential fallacy' and look to dimensions beyond the literal for significance (see Skura, *The Literary Use*, p. 231). This brand of resistant reading begins with the study of mental structures, focusing in part upon unconscious subtexts. This approach is particularly well-suited to psychic space in Romantic discourse. Psychological criticism, beginning with family dynamics, can open doors to ethical and political questions instigated by cultural engagement. Space prohibits coverage of multiple approaches in this essay: I shall glance at a number of them, as they apply to individual poets, and suggest a wider scope in the notes and references.

In 'Creative Writers and Day-dreaming', Freud argues for the role of fantasy, of wish-fulfilment, as a model for the birth of fiction. The structure of dream formation is analogous to that of fictional narrative. Although, in Freud's theory, fantasy can provide the foundation for neurosis, it can also serve creative writers as a means of fashioning art out of unsatisfying reality. The writer discovers the secret of attracting a public audience to a private wish, and creates a formal dimension of aesthetic joy out of an egoistic fantasy:

We give the name of an *incentive bonus*, or a *forepleasure*, to a yield of pleasure such as this, which is offered to us so as to make possible the release of still greater pleasure arising from deeper psychical sources. In my opinion, all the aesthetic pleasure which a creative writer affords us has the character of a fore-pleasure of this kind, and our actual enjoyment of an imaginative work proceeds from a liberation of tension in our minds. (Freud, *Standard Edition* (*SE*) 9: 153).

An analysand's relation to an analyst in the interaction of transference also calls upon a play of fantasy: the analysands relive conflicts from their past experience in a present encounter, fostered by their analyst, with both emotionally invested at a deep level. The writer and the analyst call upon similar patterns of desire, one for the process of therapy, the other to induce pleasure in the reading public. Readers, in turn, enact their own transferences in interplay with the texts by engaging their own psychic dramas. Both rely upon dream formations that liberate unconscious energies implicit in the narratives.

Freud and Wordsworth have much in common in their reliance upon the process of recollection, a reliance that nicely reveals how psychoanalytic insights overlap with poetic ones. Where Wordsworth recalls episodes lodged with emotion, Freud's creative writer 'harks back to the memory of an earlier experience', usually one that deploys the subject's primary wish. Recalling a past fulfilment of this wish, the writer then constructs a future impulse framed upon this paradigm, 'a day-dream or phantasy, which carries about it traces of its origin from the occasion which provoked it and from the memory. Thus past, present and future are strung together, as it were, on the thread of the wish that runs through them' (*SE* 9: 147–8). As dialectical thinkers, both Wordsworth and Freud negotiate the interaction of past, present and future selves. In Wordsworth's formula for creation, *passion* rather than *wish* strikes the keynote for desire:

Poetry is the spontaneous overflow of powerful feelings; it takes its origin from emotion recollected in tranquility. The emotion is contemplated till, by a species of reaction, the tranquility gradually disappears, and an emotion kindred to that which was before the subject of contemplation is gradually produced, and does itself actually exist in the mind. (*Romanticism*, p. 263)

Whereas Wordsworth often brings together emotions that are antithetical, Freud makes the wish feed upon a discrepancy in reality that invites the projection of a fantasy world.

Both writers use memory as a matrix for the creative process, shaping the structures of fiction and poetry that are, in part, analogous to dream formation. Freud's paper on 'The "Uncanny"', for instance, illustrates how a psychological approach can make Romantic texts disclose a depth beyond their literal meaning. The uncanny, for him, forms a paradox, the conjoining of the familiar and the terrorizing. Wordsworth's affinity for incidents from common life, and his reliance upon the dream landscape of memory, suggest linkages with Freud's uncanny. Freud borrows his definition from Schelling: 'everything is *unheimliche* that ought to have remained secret and hidden but has come to light' (*SE* 17: 225). For Freud, *das Heimliche* (homely, familiar) becomes its opposite, *das Unheimliche* (unhomely, alien) when, as in Wordsworth, the commonplace is disrupted by the uncanny. In German dictionaries, extremes meet in the definitions of these two words: the *homely* shades into its opposite *unhomely*. 'This uncanny', according to Freud, 'is in reality nothing new or alien, but something which is familiar and old-established in the mind and which has become alienated from it only through the process of repression' (*SE* 17: 241). In the neurotic, the traumas of childhood often betray their guarded, secret presence by revealing themselves in deviant symptoms of compulsion; the poet, on the other hand, taps these unconscious energies and shapes them into fictions. Wordsworth's 'spots of time', for instance, with their very urgency of repetition, often disclose the turbulent depth of the uncanny rising to the surface of everyday life. Wordsworth deplores the 'gross and violent stimulants' needed to overcome 'the savage torpor' of modern humanity in cities; but he also disrupts the commonplace by releasing the turbulence of the uncanny.[1]

The most intricate passage in Wordsworth's *Immortality Ode* epitomizes the presence of the uncanny, the ghostly hauntings deployed within the 'spots of time',

> those obstinate questionings
> Of Sense and outward things,
> Fallings from us, vanishings,
> Blank misgivings of a creature
> Moving about in worlds not realized,
> High instincts before which our mortal nature
> Did tremble like a guilty thing surprised. (142–50)

In this passage from the ode, the disruption of the boundaries of the boy's self implies an intimation of immortality. What was a painful trauma to the child will become a paradoxical source of power to the adult. The phrase 'guilty thing surprised', of course, is an allusion to *Hamlet*, where the ghost of Hamlet's father lingers too long into the daylight and forgets the imperative call back to the underworld (I. i. 148–9).

We might have expected Wordsworth, who had lost his own father, to identify with Hamlet rather than with the ghost. On one level, the uncanny presence of this ghost may be a displacement for Wordsworth's own lost father. But the poet none the less shares the purgatorial guilt of the murdered king even while encountering an intimation of immortality. The boy's guilt triggers an intricate reaction: mortality discovers its own liability to death at the same time as it intuits the possibility of immortality. The uncanny shame that Wordsworth shares with the ghost is tantamount to a baffling of the mortal by the immortal. This psychoanalytic reading does not expunge the glimmer of immortality in the poet's ode: as D. W. Winnicott so aptly phrases it, the 'idea of eternity comes from the memory traces in each one of us of our infancy before time started' (Winnicott, 'The Five-Year-Old', p. 34). The hidden and secret sources of power for Wordsworth, like the enigmatic guilt of the old king's ghost, emerge from a no man's land on the border between this world and beyond. Wordsworth's own death-marked passages open new vistas on the ode, disclosing a turmoil that this poet of litotes struggles to hold at bay.

Although *Hamlet* is the classic literary text for critical application of Freud's Oedipus complex, Wordsworth's second spot of time, the one associated with his father's death, has also evoked extensive commentary based upon Freud's theory.[2] Perched on a crag at 'the meeting-point / Of two highways', – suggestive of Oedipus at the crossroads – Wordsworth overlooks a bleak prospect. In the latter spot, Wordsworth's father, lost in the darkness on Cold Fell, was exposed overnight and died later during these holidays. The 'visionary dreariness' of the scene, its storm and mist, infuses the spot with the memory of his father's death: 'The event, / With all the sorrow which it brought, appeared / A chastisement' (*Prelude*, 351–70). The Oedipal and the uncanny here both impinge upon the boy's sense of guilt. Writing of the primitive 'omnipotence of thoughts', Freud observes 'that an uncanny effect is often and easily produced when the distinction between imagination and reality is effaced, as when something we have hitherto regarded as imaginary appears before us in reality, or when a symbol takes over the full functions of the thing it symbolizes, and so on'. The Oedipus complex can intensify the feelings that occur in reaction to the death of a father toward whom one has had aggressive thoughts. A son's guilt can derive from the thought, ' "So, after all, it is *true* that one can kill a person by the mere wish!" ' (*SE* 17: 244, 248).[3] Oedipal dynamics illuminate Wordsworth's enigmatic need for chastisement.

Freud's Oedipus complex also informs Peter Manning's *Byron and his Fictions*. Psychoanalytic literary criticism may be defined by its 'object of attention': 'It can attend to the *author* of the work; to the work's *contents*; to its *formal construction*; or to the *reader*' (Eagleton, *Literary Theory*, p. 179). With Byron and Wordsworth, psychoanalytic focus can be placed either upon the author or upon the work's contents. Although recent scholars incline toward criticism of the text as a main priority, with Wordsworth's self-presentation in *The Prelude* and with Byron's projection of multiple selves into his works, both stances are fair game. Manning develops the recurrent pattern of Byron's mother/son tensions, which 'shade regularly into the triangular situation of hero, important woman, and dominating older man' (Manning, *Byron and his Fictions*, p. 16). The Haidée incident in *Don Juan* epitomizes a recurrent pattern in the canon of Byron's works: the 'enveloping protection' of woman 'becomes suffocation': 'no sooner does Byron endow a woman with extraordinary powers than she becomes a threat to the hero'. This pattern, going back to Byron's relationship to his own mother, is also coupled with an Oedipal tie with a dominating father figure: 'Juan has in effect stolen Haidée from Lambro, and his temerity incurs the wrath Byron invariably associates with any attempt to challenge a father' (Manning, *Byron and his Fictions*, pp. 186–7). In effect, any time Juan comes too close to a woman, the danger of suffocation requires such measures as the death of Haidée or the exposure of Juan's affair with Julia, forcing him into exile in quest of new encounters. By dealing with both biography and the text, Manning's reading exemplifies the power of a psychological approach to make the reader re-envisage Byron's narratives.

Feminists find that male gender bias subtends the concept of penis envy and castration, undermining the very foundation of Freud's Oedipal theory.[4] V. N. Vološinov, a Russian Marxist critic, on the other hand, objects to Freud's sexualizing of the family unit at the expense of the social: instead of the father's being an 'entrepreneur' and the son 'his heir', Vološinov sneers at Freud's family romance: 'the father is only the mother's lover, and the son is his rival!' (Vološinov, *Freudianism*, pp. 90–1). This Oedipal focus on the private and the sexual comes at the expense of the social and the political: 'All periods of social decline and disintegration are characterized by *overestimation of the sexual* in life and ideology, and what is more, of the sexual in an extreme unidimensional conception; its *asocial* aspect, taken in isolation, is advanced to the forefront' (ibid., p. 90). Although these critiques of Freud hit the mark, the Oedipus complex can also furnish the groundwork for a cultural criticism. The 'beginnings of morality, conscience, law and all forms of social and religious authority' derive, according to Freud, from the Oedipus complex (Eagleton, *Literary Theory*, p. 156). The very universality of the incest taboo in all cultures, throughout both space and time, has led to the well-known position of Claude Lévi-Strauss that this taboo marks the difference between nature and culture. This anthropological stance reinforces Freud's Oedipus complex.

The Oedipal and uncanny aspects of Wordsworth's spots of time tend to focus upon the individual poet and the family. The psychological approach of trauma theory, on the other hand, furnishes a wider historical perspective. One of the leading exponents of this theory, Cathy Caruth, defines trauma in 'its most general definition', as 'an overwhelming experience of sudden, or catastrophic events, in which the response to the event occurs in the often delayed, and uncontrolled repetitive occurrence of hallucinations and other intrusive phenomena' (Caruth, 'Unclaimed Experience', p. 181). In *Moses and Monotheism*, one of his cultural texts, Freud interprets Jewish history in terms of 'latency' and delay in responding to incomprehensible ordeals:

> It may happen that a man who has experienced some frightful accident − a railway collision, for instance − leaves the scene of the event apparently uninjured. In the course of the next few weeks, however, he develops a number of severe psychical and motor symptoms which can only be traced to his shock, the concussion or whatever else it was. He now has a traumatic 'neurosis'. (*SE* 23: 67)

In a brilliant extension of this idea from *Moses and Monotheism* to Jewish history, Freud shows how multiple private traumas become collective experience. There is a delay in response to certain painful events that occurred in another time and place: 'For history to be a history of trauma means that it is referential precisely to the extent that it is not fully perceived as it occurs; or to put it somewhat differently, that a history can be grasped only in the very inaccessibility of its occurrence' (Caruth, 'Unclaimed Experience', p. 187). Although the victims escape apparently unharmed from an accident, they do not fully absorb what has happened to them at the time of crisis and their history acquires a traumatic compulsiveness akin to Wordsworth's uncanny vestiges of memory.

Although controversy persists over exactly what symptoms constitute trauma, Coleridge's experience meets a number of the criteria. The question arises whether his opium addiction or his attempt to withdraw from it is the cause of his traumatic dreams. Coleridge's *Notebooks* and letters record his recurrent nightmares:

> God forbid that my worst Enemy should ever have the Nights & the Sleeps that I have had, night after night − surprised by Sleep, while I struggled to remain awake, starting up to bless my own loud Screams that had awakened me − yea dear friend! till my repeated night-yells had made me a Nuisance in my own House. As I live & am a man, this is an unexaggerated Tale − '*my dreams become the substances of my life*'. (Griggs, II, 1009)

Although Coleridge's condition is scarcely comparable to that of holocaust victims, his addiction, his compulsive nightmare life, and his alienation from his family establish his candidacy for trauma. Coleridge's nightmares, especially given his tendency to merge them with waking reality, invite a psychoanalytic reading. In ordinary dreams, unlike the nightmare, our judgement is asleep: we pass no verdict either way as to whether the dream images are real or not. We assent to the images without raising the question, 'Are they real?' In nightmares, on the other hand, Coleridge avers that the objects of dreaming are taken for reality. The nightmare, then, does not involve the full operation of the waking judgement: it stands, as it were, on middle ground between the sleeping judgement of ordinary dreams and the active judgement of the waking state. In the confusion between waking and sleeping, nightmares, incited by trauma, batten on the errant imagination with its capacity for ethical distortion.

Trauma theory can also be usefully applied to Coleridge's poems, especially those dealing with nightmare. In *The Rime of the Ancient Mariner*, for example, the protagonist mirrors the pattern of Coleridge's own existence, as the mariner's dreams become 'the substances of . . . [his] life'. Traumatic compulsion governs the repetitive storytelling: the mariner is doomed to 'pass, like night, from land to land' in search of yet another auditor. Readers of Coleridge's nightmare poems need to tune into the wave-length of oneiric logic and to rely less upon a hermeneutic of rationality. A psychological reading, taking into account the metonymic and symbolic play of language, affords a new perspective upon Coleridge's poems.

The nightmare poem *Christabel*, for example, also evolves under the auspices of trauma, under the sign of a surrogate mother and a rejecting father. When Bard Bracy recalls his dream of a dove coiled round by a 'bright green snake' (537–8), he identifies the bird in the dream as Christabel and seeks to exorcise the surrounding wood. Christabel's father the Baron Sir Leoline, however, perversely interprets the same dream, claiming that Geraldine is the victim of the snake. Torn between malice and dread, Geraldine looks 'askance' at Christabel with her eyes shrunk into a serpent's glare. Under the demonic possession of her double, Christabel shudders 'aloud with a hissing sound' (575–9). On her knees, she begs her father to send Geraldine away; instead, he spurns his daughter in anger and leads Geraldine off on his arm. As with the victim of a car crash, Christabel in her encounter with Geraldine does not so much forget, as in the period after an accident, but she is not completely conscious during the encounter itself, as if in a trance, her will is in abeyance.

This poem also invites a Kristevan reading, one that invokes the abject – an intense form of trauma. In her parasitic doubling, Christabel encounters *abjection*, the absence or collapse of boundaries that lead to the formation of the subject. Christabel's earlier vision of Geraldine's 'bosom and half her side – / A sight to dream of, not to tell' (246–7) discloses the abject, the horror created by the coalescence of the mother with the self. The undefined repulsion of Christabel for Geraldine's naked body here paralyses her ego. Geraldine as demonic, hostile mother causes Christabel to experience abjection. As Julia Kristeva puts it, 'I experience abjection only if an Other has settled in place and stead of what will be "me". Not at all an other with whom I identify and incorporate, but an Other who precedes and possesses me, and through such possession causes me to be'. As the binary between Christabel's innocence and Geraldine's evil breaks down, extremes meet: in a moment of nightmare menace they coalesce into a single figure. 'One thus understands why so many victims of the abject are its fascinated victims – if not its submissive and willing ones' (Kristeva, *Powers of Horror*, pp. 9–10). Kristeva's theory of abjection accounts for the moral complication that Geraldine is a part of Christabel's own psyche.

Abjection, of course, must be distinguished from mourning which bears upon Roman-tic melancholy. 'Mourning and melancholia' is a Freudian text, which so often adverts to the vagaries of dejection. In *Keats and the Silent Work of Imagination*, for example, Leon Waldoff uses Freud's paper both to disclose Keats's strain of gloom and to illuminate his conflicted relations to women. Freud's definition of 'the distinguishing mental features of melancholia' bears recalling:

> a profoundly painful dejection, cessation of interest in the outside world, loss of the capacity to love, inhibition of all activity, and a lowering of the self-regarding feelings to a degree that finds utterance in self-reproaches and self-revilings, and culminates in a delusional expectation of punishment. (*SE* 14: 244)

Mourning resembles melancholia in many respects, but it does not include diminishment of self-regard. Freud further defines the process of mourning as one of working through grief. When a loved one dies, that person's absence requires 'that all libido shall be withdrawn from its attachments to that object'. Because no one willingly abandons 'a libidinal position', the mourner may cling 'to the object through the medium of a hallucinatory wishful psychosis', and prolong with good reason the memory of inconsolable loss (ibid.). In normal circumstances, however, the libido is withdrawn from the lost object and frees the ego to carry on with life. Keats's very choice of the topic of melancholy for an ode implies an attempt to explore the psychology of loss: 'It is as if Keats turns on himself to confront his own melancholy, to examine the very mourning process that has all along been at the center of his imagination and thought, especially in the odes, even though he acknowledges it only occasionally in his letters' (Waldoff, *Keats*, p. 149).

Although Waldoff does not consider Keats a melancholic, he none the less reiterates the underlying moods of despair, disclosed from the contexts of the poet's letters, and he measures Keats's life-force against his potential melancholia (ibid., pp. 22–4). Keats's losses, including both parents and his brother Tom, coupled with his years of exposure to the unsanitary conditions of the London hospitals, now and then darken his psyche. The recurrent encounters of the poet's heroes with 'Goddesses' or 'feminine immortals' represent, for Waldoff, 'wish-fulfilling restorations of an image from the depths of his own psyche, an image that is ultimately related to a shadow of a lost maternal presence' (ibid., p. 111).

In his reading of *Lamia*, Waldoff notices that a 'feminine presence' – in figures such as Maia, Psyche, Lamia and Moneta – presides over Keats's exploration of the past or the future. This raises the question of how feminism can invigorate psychoanalysis as a critical approach. The death of Lycius in *Lamia*, provoked by Apollonius's exposure of Lamia as a serpent, epitomizes the poet's conflicted attitude towards women: Lycius's identity has become intertwined, for Waldoff, 'with the illusion of a feminine ideal behind which hides, in the nature of a serpent, the image of a phallic woman' (Waldoff, *Keats*, p. 169). The term 'phallic' here, of course, signifies the Medusa-like power of the female.[5] Lamia's death and Lycius's discovery of her serpent nature both unite, as Waldoff contends, 'to suggest that he dies because of a fatal wound to his male narcissism', indicating

> that the gordian complication in Keats's relation to women has all along been a form of castration anxiety, a deep suspicion that a woman, by her inconstant, abandoning, or deceptive behavior, or perhaps by some unnatural power that she possesses, could unman the poet and destroy him. (ibid., p. 170)

Recognizing that Lycius represents Keats only in a qualified way, Waldoff pinpoints the lost mother as the stimulus behind the poet's conflicted treatment of women in his poetry.

As an analyst who builds upon Freudian theory with his idea of object relations, D. W. Winnicott supplies a bridge from Freud to culture and society. Winnicott's *Playing and Reality* develops this path to culture by starting from the baby at its mother's breast and leading into the world of play in the patient's fantasy life. As in Wordsworth's *Tintern Abbey*, the infant half-creates what it perceives: 'Projection mechanisms and identifications have been operating, and the subject is depleted to the extent that something of the subject is found in the object, though enriched by feeling' (Winnicott, *Playing and Reality*, p. 88). The transitional object, as in Wordsworth's 'infant babe' passage in the *Prelude*, is imbued with human feeling. The Wordsworthian infant at the breast gathers 'passion from his mother's eye' and holds 'mute dialogues with . . . [his] mother's heart'. The baby derives the first poetic spirit of life by perceiving objects through its mother's love, both creating and receiving, 'Working but in alliance with the works / Which it beholds' (*Prelude* II. 243–83). Winnicott's object relations theory elegantly dovetails with Wordsworth's depiction of the child's bonding with the external world. For Winnicott, 'the essential feature in the concept of transitional objects . . . is *the paradox, and the acceptance of the paradox*: the baby creates the object, but the object was there waiting to be created and to become a cathected object' (Winnicott, *Playing and Reality*, p. 89).

Another paradox governs the identification of aggression by Winnicott (who builds upon the work of Melanie Klein) as an essential factor in the healthy growth of play, one that enables the proper relation to objects. The act of aggression begins with the baby's attack on the mother's breast, an attack that, because of its 'relative feebleness, can fairly easily be survived'. For the child to learn respect for otherness, it is necessary for the object in this case, the mother, to *survive* the infant's anger: '*There is no anger* in the destruction of the object . . . though there could be said to be joy at the object's survival' (ibid., pp. 92–3). Wordsworth's *Nutting*, in which a young boy ravishes a grove of hazelnut trees, epitomizes Winnicott's paradox of the child's discovery of otherness through aggression. First the boy comes upon a 'virgin scene', a bounty of hazel nuts; he lingers like a libertine, anticipating a conquest:

> Then up I rose,
> And dragged to earth both branch and bow, with crash
> And merciless ravage: and the shady nook
> Of hazels, and the green and mossy bower,
> Deformed and sullied, patiently gave up
> Their quiet being: and, unless I now
> Confound my present feelings with the past;
> Ere from the mutilated bower I turned
> Exulting, rich beyond the wealth of kings,
> I felt a sense of pain when I beheld
> The silent trees, and saw the intruding sky. (43–53)

In this vignette from childhood, the broken branches do not survive their rape, but the grove will renew its green in the ensuing spring. This scene of play leads to paradox: out of exultant pleasure comes pain. Nature has its own separate spirit, its *otherness* that earns the boy's respect, an ecological epiphany emerging from the destructive element. Through the transitional object the child finds the *other* and, hence, discovers a foundation for community. For Winnicott this move beyond aggression discloses the reality principle, a world that we all hold in common: 'It is these cultural experiences that provide the continuity in the human race that transcends personal existence' (Winnicott, 'Location', p. 8). Winnicott's culture thus derives from play, making it a fruitful focus of psychoanalytic criticism.

One further example of the cultural approach to psychological criticism of Romantic texts illustrates how Wordsworth's poetry contests his culture. David Collings in *Wordsworthian Errancies: The Poetry of Cultural Dismemberment* defines culture not as 'the question of intellectual cultivation or Arnoldian refinement but rather [as] . . . the institutional structure of human societies' (p. 2). Collings's argument takes as its starting-point Jacques Lacan's rescripting of Freud in ways relevant to all those concerned with the question of the child's relation to its community, and above all – as Lacan insists – its entry into culture, into the world of language. According to him, the subject must partly sacrifice his Imaginary stage of illusion in order to enter the Symbolic order. In Freudian parlance, the son, fearing the power of the father (a symbolic castration), defers to his authority, to his priority as a rival for his mother's love. The son gives up some of his Imaginary delusion in order to enter the cultural order: it is 'as if the son can receive the name of the father only if he submits to a symbolic violence even greater than castration and repudiates his native, nameless subjectivity' (ibid., p. 164).

Earlier we discussed Wordsworth as a poet of the commonplace, but also as even more bound to the turmoil of the uncanny. Collings's psychoanalytic reading moves a stage beyond the Freudian uncanny and even beyond the Lacanian Law of the Father, into the site of cultural dismemberment. For Collings, Wordsworth does not stake his poetic vocation upon the symbolic order of 'oedipal and phallic power', but instead 'aspires to embody the tempestuous energies that circulate around the site of cultural dismemberment. He embraces the poetics of errancy, unreadability, repetition, and even crime, abandoning himself to the unredeemed rhetoric of romantic error' (ibid., p. 155). Building upon Freud and especially Lacan, Collings deploys a new psychoanalytic approach to enrich our awareness of errancy – even a Gothic extravagance – in the early poetry of Wordsworth. The text and context of the poet's quarrel with culture change the focus of criticism from the individual imagination to a historical encounter that reveals Wordsworth's countercultural politics.

In a strategy that overlaps with Collings's cultural criticism of Wordsworth, Jane Gallop shows how psychoanalysis

> can unsettle feminism's tendency to accept a traditional, unified, rational, puritanical self – a self supposedly free from the violence of desire. In its turn, feminism can shake up psychoanalysis's tendency to think itself apolitical but in fact be conservative by encouraging people to adapt to an unjust social structure. (Gallop, *The Daughter's Seduction*, p. xii)

Like Jane Gallop's feminism, Romanticism bears a similarly unsettling relationship to psychoanalysis, a discipline which counters Romantic transcendence and reinforces Romanticism's strong ties to this world. With its rebellious energy, Romantic poetry corrects the psychoanalytic tendency, even in Freud's own work, toward authoritarian practice. In working with hysterics, for example, Freud finds it strange that his 'case histories should read like short stories', and he envies the way poets could come directly to the point while scientists discover the gist of mental processes only at the cost of intense labour (*SE* 2: 160–1). By recasting Romantic tropes as fundamental psychological processes, criticism opens a mutually enabling dialogue between Romanticism and psychoanalysis.

## NOTES

1   I thank the University of Nebraska Press for permission to adapt a few paragraphs for this article from *The Romantic Dream: Wordsworth and the Poetics of the Unconscious*. See chapter one, pp. 24–54, for extended use of the uncanny in reading Wordsworth's poetry, and for bibliography (p. 25, n4). I am indebted to Andrea Nightingale and María Antonia Garcés for excellent readings of this essay.

2   In *Hamlet and Oedipus* (p. 82), Ernest Jones gives a sharp epitome of the Oedipus complex in describing the predicament of Shakespeare's Hamlet, who, though unconscious of these family dynamics, finds the 'long "repressed" desire to take his father's place in his mother's affection is stimulated to unconscious activity by the sight of someone usurping this place exactly as he himself had once longed to do. More, this someone was a member of the same family, so that the actual usurpation further resembled the imaginary one in being incestuous'.

3   See Weiskel, *The Romantic Sublime*, pp. 167–204, for the Oedipal dynamics of the Wordsworthian sublime; Mitchell, *Psychoanalysis and Feminism*, pp. 377–81, for a discussion of how the incest taboo provides a foundation for the Oedipus complex; and Onorato, *The Character of the Poet*, pp. 209–11, for discussions of spatial Oedipal factors in the spots of time.

4   McLintock, *Imperial Leather*, pp. 191–2, opposes both the Freudian and Lacanian marginalization of women: 'In Lacan's texts, women are doomed to inhabit the tongueless zone of the Imaginary'. Following Jonathan Dollimore, McLintock finds the failure of Freudian theory to explain homosexuality as the result of an uncompleted Oedipal complex as inconsistent and absurd, which offers 'a challenge not only to the Oedipal law, but to the entire Oedipal drama as a theory' (ibid., p. 195).

5   Jane Gallop offers a feminist perspective upon the issue of the 'phallic mother': it is the 'insistence on the seemingly paradoxical term "phallic mother" which can most work to undo the supposedly natural logic of the ideological solidarity between phallus, father, power and man' (*The Daughter's Seduction*, p. 117).

## REFERENCES AND FURTHER READING

Brooks, Peter, *Reading for the Plot: Design and Intention in Narrative*, New York, Vintage Books, 1984.

——— 'The Idea of a Psychoanalytic Literary Criticism', *Critical Inquiry* 13 (1987) 334–8. Full of psychoanalytic insight.

——— *Psychoanalysis and Storytelling*, Oxford, Blackwell, 1994.

Caruth, Cathy, 'Unclaimed Experience: Trauma and the Possibility of History', *Yale French Studies* (1979) 181–92.

Collings, David, *Wordsworthian Errancies: The Poetics of Cultural Dismemberment*, Baltimore, Johns Hopkins University Press, 1994.

Eagleton, Terry, *Literary Theory: An Introduction*, Minneapolis, Minnesota University Press, 1983. Excellent theoretical introduction.

Ellis, David, *Wordsworth and the Spots of Time: Interpretation in 'The Prelude'*, Cambridge, Cambridge University Press, 1985.

Fields, Beverly, *Reality's Dark Dream: Dejection in Coleridge*, Kent, Ohio, Kent State University Press, 1967.

Freud, Sigmund, *The Standard Edition of the Complete Psychological Works of Sigmund Freud*, 24 vols, tr. James Strachey et al., London, Hogarth Press, 1953–74.

Gallop, Jane, *The Daughter's Seduction: Feminism and Psychoanalysis*, Ithaca, Cornell University Press, 1983. Superb feminist theory.

George, Diana Hume, *Blake and Freud*, Ithaca, Cornell University Press, 1980.

Hartman, Geoffrey H. (ed.) *Psychoanalysis and the Question of the Text*, Baltimore, Johns Hopkins University Press, 1978.

Hertz, Neil, *The End of the Line: Essays on Psychoanalysis and the Sublime*, New York, Columbia University Press, 1985.

Jones, Ernest, *Hamlet and Oedipus*, New York, Norton, 1976.

Kristeva, Julia, *Powers of Horror: An Essay on Abjection*, New York, Columbia University Press, 1982.

——*Strangers to Ourselves*, tr. Leon S. Roudiez, New York, Columbia University Press, 1991. Strong on self and Other.

Lévi-Strauss, Claude, *The Elementary Structures of Kinship*, tr. James Harle Bell, Richard von Sturmer and Rodney Needham, Boston, Beacon Press, 1969. Classic anthropological study.

McGhee, Richard D., *Guilty Pleasures: William Wordsworth's Poetry of Psychoanalysis*, Troy, NY, Whitston, 1993.

McLintock, Anne, *Imperial Leather: Race, Gender and Sexuality in the Colonial Contest*, New York, Routledge, 1995.

Manning, Peter J., *Byron and his Fictions*, Detroit, Wayne State University Press, 1978.

Mitchell, Juliet, *Psychoanalysis and Feminism: Freud, Reich, Laing, and Women*, New York, Random House, 1975.

Onorato, Richard J., *The Character of the Poet: Wordsworth in 'The Prelude'*, Princeton, Princeton University Press, 1971.

Shapiro, Barbara, *The Romantic Mother: Narcissistic Patterns in Romantic Poetry*, Baltimore, Johns Hopkins University Press, 1983.

Skura, Meredith A., *The Literary Use of the Psychoanalytic Process*, New Haven, Yale University Press, 1981.

Vološinov, V. N., *Freudianism: A Critical Sketch*, tr. I. R. Titunik, Bloomington, Indiana University Press, 1976.

Waldoff, Leon, *Keats and the Silent Work of Imagination*, Urbana, Illinois University Press, 1985.

Weiskel, Thomas, *The Romantic Sublime: Studies in the Psychology of Transcendence*, Baltimore, Johns Hopkins University Press, 1976.

Wilson, Douglas B., *The Romantic Dream: Wordsworth and the Poetics of the Unconscious*, Lincoln, Nebraska University Press, 1993.

Winnicott, D. W., 'The Five-Year-Old', in *The Family and Individual Development*, London, Tavistock, 1965.

——*Playing and Reality*, London, Tavistock Publications, 1971.

——'The Location of Cultural Experience', in *Transitional Objects and Potential Spaces: The Literary Uses of D. W. Winnicott*, ed. Peter L. Rudnytsky, New York, Columbia University Press, 1993.

# 43

# Dialogic Approaches

*Michael James Sider*

Introduced into Romantic studies by Don H. Bialostosky, the term 'dialogic' has its source in the writings of the Russian theorist, Mikhail Mikhailovich Bakhtin (1895–1975). 'Dialogic' literally means 'characterized by dialogue', and Bakhtin places the concept of dialogue at the centre of his work on language and textuality. For Bakhtin, the act of communication between two people at a specific moment in a particular place is a model of the way all language depends for meaning on its social context. He argues that words are traditionally treated as their own direct expressions, encountering in their attempt to make meaning only the object they seek to represent. But this seemingly direct relationship between a word and its object is mediated by other words which impinge on the attempt at representation. In 'Discourse in the novel', Bakhtin asserts that every word finds the object at which it is directed already 'overlain with qualifications' by 'alien words that have already been spoken about it' (p. 276). A word is shaped by dialogic interaction with the alien words that are already in its object, just as speakers shape their words in dialogue as rejoinders to what has been said and what they anticipate will be said. Although the communicative aspect of language is 'regularly taken into account when it comes to everyday dialogue', Bakhtin insists that 'every other sort of discourse' as well is 'oriented toward an understanding that is responsive' (p. 280). Thus, the responsiveness of dialogue stands as an image of the doubleness of all language in Bakhtin, where the word is directed not only toward its object, but also toward what other people have said and are saying about this object.

This context of other people's competing words on the same word forms a specific social environment for any discourse. Every linguistic act is shaped by the discourses which surround it, in much the same way as the speech of two people engaged in everyday dialogue is constrained by the social context in which their conversation takes place. Indeed, authors can only find their own style and generate meaning by struggling with the specific socio-ideological voices which surround their theme:

> The word, breaking through to its own meaning and its own expression across an environ-
> ment full of alien words and variously evaluating accents, harmonizing with some of the
> elements in this environment and striking a dissonance with others, is able, in this dialogized
> process, to shape its own stylistic profile and tone. (Ibid., p. 277)

In this sense, any text is shared or dialogic territory, a process of often conflicted negotiation with the many differing cultural voices that speak and have spoken on the author's chosen theme.

It is Bakhtin's insistence that language be studied dialogically, as communication between speakers, rather than monologically, as a unitary medium for the direct representation of objects, that structures the argument of Bialostosky's *Making Tales* (1984), a work which can be credited with popularizing the concept of dialogism among Romanticists.[1] Bialostosky argues that Wordsworth's experimental narratives in *Lyrical Ballads* have failed to find the recognition they deserve, because critics since Coleridge have read the poems within an Aristotelian poetics of imitated actions, rather than a poetics of speech. For Aristotle, poetic language represents not someone's words speaking about an object or action, but the action itself. Words belong to the poet, whose mastery is shown in the ability to assemble them as parts into a unified artefact which directly imitates its object. But in a poetics of speech, words are the property of certain speakers, so that the poet cannot approach them as neutral units of composition. Instead, the poet must orchestrate a dialogue between the voices to which words belong. As Bialostosky puts it, style, for the poet of speech, does not 'bespeak the artist, [but] the represented speaker, whether he is a lyric representation of the poet, a represented narrator, or a dramatic character' (Bialostosky, *Making Tales*, p. 15).

Looking to Wordsworth's ballad experiments for evidence of his ability to synthesize their language into an aesthetic whole, critics writing within an Aristotelian theoretical framework have generally agreed with Coleridge's complaint in the *Biographia Literaria* that Wordsworth's dialogue with the language of rustic speakers leads to an inconstancy of style which disturbs the poems' formal integrity. Their poetics cannot account for poems that 'subject the reader to an experience of sinking as they shift from the poet's elevated style to the character's low style', or that 'project language proper to the poet into the mouths of his characters' (Bialostosky, *Making Tales*, p. 35). However, a Bakhtinian poetics of speech, which envisions a text as a dialogue between different voices, replaces the search for Wordsworth's homogenization of poetic language with a critical goal more appropriate to Wordsworth's experimental aim.

This goal is to see the inconstancy of style in Wordsworth's ballads as an intended effect of Wordsworth's experimentation with narrative form. The real pleasure of Wordsworth's experiments, argues Bialostosky, is to be found in the reader's participation in a social dialogue which includes the voices of the poem's narrator, its assumed listener, and its hero (the subject of the narrator's story). Wordsworth's lyrical ballads are acts of communication between a speaker and a listener *about* the reported speech of a certain individual; they are, as Bialostosky writes, events in which 'someone tell[s] someone else that *someone said or did or experienced something*' (ibid., p. 63). Now, in order for the poem's speaker to communicate with the listener, the poet will have to assume between them a certain mutual understanding of values. Wordsworth's interest in rustic life 'makes sense in these terms as an interest in the language of speakers who can take the satisfaction of [shared values] for granted' (ibid., p. 40). The speaker's tone of voice, in this situation of communal values, carries great weight. Less needs to be said when speaker and listener share common ground:

> A 'simple and unelaborated' expression spoken under these conditions may carry evaluative weight in inverse proportion to its elaboration, for the less it is necessary to say, the more it is

assumed a listener will be able to understand of the situation that provokes the utterance. (Ibid.)

The less that is said, the more important it is for the listener to be attentive to the accents of what is being said. Consequently, for readers to understand the ballads, they must listen carefully for the tones that govern these simple expressions, tones which cultivate communication between Wordsworth's speakers and their assumed listeners.

Bialostosky's exploration of the importance of tone in Wordsworth's *Lyrical Ballads* – his exposition of the role tone plays in the communication between speaker, listener and poetic subject – involves him in a micrological analysis of each poem's dialogism. An example is his reading of Wordsworth's *Simon Lee*, a poem considered to be emblematic of Wordsworth's experimental project. The narrator in *Simon Lee* tells the story of his encounter with Simon, an old huntsman, a man who in his prouder days 'all the country could outrun' (41), but who has become lean and sick with age. The huntsman is struggling to cut a 'stump of rotten wood' (84) when the narrator appears. The narrator takes the mattock from Simon's hands and severs, with a single blow, the 'tangled root . . . / At which the poor old man so long / And vainly had endeavour'd' (94–6). Simon thanks the narrator for his help, but for a reason which goes unexplained, the speaker, in the concluding lines, is filled with regret at Simon's gratitude:

> The tears into his eyes were brought,
> And thanks and praises seemed to run
> So fast out of his heart, I thought
> They never would have done.
> – I've heard of hearts unkind, kind deeds
> With coldness still returning.
> Alas! the gratitude of men
> Hath oftner left me mourning. (97–104)

The poem's unresolved conclusion is typical of an uncertainty which disconnects the poem's parts throughout the story. The narrator's simple tale of his act of compassion for an old man is mixed with another story, the account of Simon Lee's past glory as a huntsman. The opening stanzas demonstrate this odd narrative mixture:

> In the sweet shire of Cardigan,
> Not far from pleasant Ivor-Hall,
> An old man dwells, a little man,
> I've heard he once was tall.
> Of years he has upon his back,
> No doubt, a burthen weighty;
> He says he is three score and ten,
> But others say he's eighty. (1–8)

The stanza leads us to expect a story with tragic overtones, about the fall into infirmity, but immediately the narrator shifts into what sounds like a romance about Simon's ability to resist change:

> Full five and twenty years he lived
> A running huntsman merry;
> And, though he has but one eye left,
> His cheek is like a cherry.
>
> No man like him the horn could sound,
> And no man was so full of glee;
> To say the least, four counties round
> Had heard of Simon Lee. (13–20)

It is as if the narrator cannot decide about what Simon Lee means, and as if Wordsworth is deliberately challenging the narrative conventions of direct imitation of an action by allowing his speaker to be so undecided. How are readers to understand this confusingly mixed (up) story?

The answer is that they need to listen carefully to the story as an act of communication between the speaker and his listener about his conversation with Simon Lee, an act of dialogue in which tone plays an essential role. The speaker tells two stories, because he is deeply embarrassed by his encounter with the old huntsman; hearing this embarrassment is central to understanding the speaker's halting delivery. The speaker is embarrassed, because when he came upon Simon toiling at the tree root, he could only see an old man working vainly at a task which age made impossible:

> The mattock totter'd in his hand;
> So vain was his endeavour,
> That at the root of the old tree
> He might have worked for ever. (85–8)

The listener can hear impatience in the speaker's voice here – impatience at Simon's frail chopping, but perhaps also at the human condition Simon represents, 'the image of futility and decay to which we are brought in our old age' (Bialostosky, *Making Tales*, p. 77). The speaker begins to transform Simon into a personification of mortality, and when he takes the axe and cuts the root, he positions himself patronizingly in relation to Simon as youth striking a redemptive blow against age:

> If he imagines himself striking a blow against the bitterness of our mortal deterioration, he does not think, until too late, that he is also severing the artery of Simon's self-respect and leaving the 'thanks and praises . . . to run / So fast out of his heart' that they seem to flow from a mortal, unstanchable wound. Realizing only after striking the blow that he has had this effect upon Simon and standing helplessly and embarrassedly listening to the excessive thanks and praises he had provoked, the young poet might be left with confused wishes to restore to Simon what he had taken from him (even to give back the mattock now is to give back something compromised) and to justify the impression under which he was moved to do what he now recognizes to be an unkind deed. (Ibid.)

The speaker's mixed narrative results from this confusion about his deed. Attempting to tell the story after the fact, and suffering from embarrassment at his actions, the narrator now attempts to relate 'the perspective from which Simon's suffering takes its place in a still vital framework of meaning' (ibid., p. 80). He strives to frame Simon's decrepitude in the meliorating context of Simon's continuing sense of his own strength and importance, endeavouring to restore to Simon the self-respect he took from him. But 'he cannot participate in that perspective to the exclusion of what . . . made him take the mattock from old Simon and strike the blow at the tangled root' (ibid.). He is, in effect, caught between these two discourses about the huntsman, unable to resolve the quandary about what his encounter with Simon means.

Simply put, he cannot tell the tale the reader expects. The appeal he makes to the listener immediately before he tells about his encounter with Simon indicates his awareness that he is having trouble resolving the situation into a focused story:

> My gentle reader, I perceive
> How patiently you've waited,
> And now I fear that you expect
> Some tale will be related.
>
> O Reader! had you in your mind
> Such stores as silent thought can bring,
> O gentle reader! you would find
> A tale in every thing.
> What more I have to say is short,
> I hope you'll kindly take it;
> It is no tale; but, should you think,
> Perhaps a tale you'll make it. (73–80)

The speaker's indecision asks that the listener make a tale where the speaker has failed. The story of Simon Lee becomes narrative ground shared between the speaker, Simon and the speaker's audience. The speaker assumes that his listeners can make a tale from his tellings, because he takes their sense of community for granted: their understanding of the problems of dignity, ageing and human mortality, and their esteem for the human kindness which the narrator temporarily forgot in his encounter with Simon Lee. Prompted to be aware of the need for this kindness by the speaker's own failings, the reader discovers a moral the narrator is too embarrassed to make.

By shifting the theoretical framework in which we read *Simon Lee* from a poetics of imitated action to a poetics of speech, Bialostosky is able to show the purpose behind the uncertainty that critics have deplored in the poem (the unresolved conclusion, the speaker's confusion, the mixture of languages). Seeing the poem as a *process* of communication between different speakers allows Bialostosky to relinquish the search for aesthetic wholeness – what Bakhtin would call the 'finalizability' (the complete unification of language and meaning) – that determines an Aristotelian poetics. Indeed, what Coleridge disliked so much in the *Lyrical Ballads* becomes in Bialostosky's reading the most generative aspect of the poems. Their lack of closure – Wordsworth's refusal, for example, in *Simon Lee* to finalize the dialogue between Simon and the narrator – becomes the means by which Wordsworth includes readers in the poems' making, thereby educating them in human values.

This view of the text as unfinalized is one of the most important interpretative consequences of a dialogic approach. It informs Bakhtin's entire theory of language. The context of other people's words on the same theme which every utterance must struggle with in order to achieve its own meaning is almost inexhaustible to Bakhtin. There are literally 'thousands of dialogic threads woven by socio-ideological consciousness around the given object of an utterance' (Bakhtin, 'Discourse in the novel', p. 276). A dialogized word (text) is always open to this context, always finding new resonance in its response to the inexhaustible array of words with which it comes into contact. Every word confronts us with its 'semantic openness', its 'capacity for further creative life', its 'unfinishedness and the inexhaustibility of our further dialogic interaction with it' (ibid., p. 346). Bialostosky's approach to Wordsworth locates this semantic openness within the dialogue between a poem's narrator, its subject and the reader, demonstrating how Simon's response to the narrator's action reveals to the narrator a new context for his deed – a new word, so to speak, on his theme – which forces him to rethink its meaning. Indeed, Simon's response comes so powerfully to inhabit the narrator's own word that the narrator finds resolution of his dialogue with the huntsman impossible. The narrator's uncertainty forces him to turn to the reader for the poem's resolution, thereby opening the poem to another context of response.

This sensitivity to the unfinalizability of the text as a communicative event helps to distinguish the dialogic approach to Romantic authors from other approaches which also seek to reveal the complexity of influence on the text. For example, both Paul Magnuson's book, *Coleridge and Wordsworth: A Lyrical Dialogue* (1988), and Gene Ruoff's *Wordsworth and Coleridge: The Making of the Major Lyrics 1802–1804* (1989), represent the two poets' mutual influence as a process of exchange. But Magnuson's dialogic method emphasizes the openness of this exchange, while Ruoff's approach accentuates the poets' attempts to suppress this dialogue through the deliberate misinterpretation of each other's words.

Magnuson grounds his study in a Bakhtinian poetics of speech, defining Wordsworth's and Coleridge's poetry as acts of communication between the poets (Magnuson, *Coleridge and Wordsworth*, p. 18). He argues that each poet attempts to find his own voice by opposing the other's words. The poems Magnuson studies form a dialogic sequence, in which the poet's opposition to the other's word becomes a transition toward further dialogue. Importantly, the oppositions which govern this sequence are not acts of parody. Parody, according to Magnuson, is intrinsically monologic, reducing the other's word to a caricature in order to stifle its potential for dialogue. These turns away from the other's word are instead a reflection of the interlocutor's discourse in which the invisibly present traces of this word determine the visible text. The speakers in these poems are listeners, presenting their words as a response to what has been said and is still being said within their texts by the other. They have one ear tuned to the other's past words as they live in their own present, the other ear to the potential for future words on the same theme. Wordsworth's and Coleridge's greatest poems are, in this sense, not individual texts, but a single work-in-process whose enabling condition is dialogue.

The success of this dialogic view of Wordsworth's and Coleridge's poetry depends on an interpretative practice that can accentuate each poem's contribution to the dialogic sequence it helps to form. Magnuson's reading of Coleridge's *Frost at Midnight* and Wordsworth's *Tintern Abbey* is a case in point. Magnuson argues that *Frost at Midnight* confronts the problem of the audibility and comprehensibility of nature's language for the adult poet. It separates a past, Coleridge's early childhood, in which there was 'an audibility and intelligibility', from a present in which Coleridge's developing self-consciousness obscures nature's voice (Magnuson, *Coleridge and Wordsworth*, p. 157). In contrast, Wordsworth's *Tintern Abbey* affirms nature's comprehensibility 'at all seasons of life' (ibid., p. 163), as a child and as an adult. Where Coleridge presents self-conscious, adult thought as the cause of discontinuity with an unreflective past in which nature's language was immediately transparent, Wordsworth argues that maturation transforms the thoughtless delight of the child with the natural world into something more valuable, 'the adult's power of insight and sympathy' (ibid., p. 175). But Wordsworth's optimistic response to Coleridge's assertion in *Frost at Midnight* that maturity means the loss of one's genial spirits is immediately qualified, in the context of the two poets' ongoing dialogue, by Wordsworth's early work on *The Prelude* and the Lucy poems, work which begins to see the affirmations of *Tintern Abbey* as an avoidance of the problems inherent to *Frost at Midnight*:

> Read in the context of 'Frost at Midnight' and the Conversation Poems, 'Tintern Abbey' is an optimistic affirmation of a continuity of personal growth grounded in nature's continuous ministry.... The seclusion that Coleridge could not completely overcome in 'Frost at Midnight' Wordsworth confidently affirms he can overcome by the retention of the natural images associated with his feelings. But read closely in the context of his early work on *The Prelude* and the Lucy poems, the calm assurances of 'Tintern Abbey' seem to be achieved by an evasion of the challenges of 'Frost at Midnight.' A dialogic reading of the sequence of Conversation Poems, 'Tintern Abbey,' and *The Prelude* (1799) reveals that each utterance is a momentary one, generative and valuable if it provides a turning point for further utterances. (Magnuson, *Coleridge and Wordsworth*, p. 177)

By tracing themes common to both Wordsworth and Coleridge through a sequence of their poems and reading each poem's treatment of these similar themes dialogically, Magnuson is able to reveal the fundamental openness of the poetry.

Ruoff's reading of Wordsworth and Coleridge is similar to Magnuson's, in that he is interested in the complexity of the poetic relationship between the two poets. For example, Ruoff demonstrates that Coleridge generated an early draft of his *Dejection Ode* in response to an early draft of Wordsworth's *Intimations Ode*. The overt sentimentality of Coleridge's response to Wordsworth's early draft bothered Wordsworth, who feared that Coleridge had found this maudlin tone in his own poem. A series of poems by both men follows Wordsworth's anxious reception of Coleridge's response, a sequence generated as a continuing dialogue about how Wordsworth's early poem should be read.

To the extent that Ruoff explores Wordsworth's and Coleridge's poetry as a sequence of responsive reinterpretation, his work is quite close to Magnuson's dialogic approach. However, Ruoff separates himself from dialogic criticism on the grounds that Bakhtin's insistence on the generative presence of one word within another does not adequately account for the role of parody in one poet's struggle with another poet's word (Ruoff, *Wordsworth and Coleridge*, p. 14). What Ruoff sees in the Wordsworth–Coleridge dialogue is the attempt by the poet to fix his interlocutor in a certain position, to make him inhabit an ideological territory in opposition to which the poet can express himself. Parody, in that it limits the resonance of the other's words, is an appropriate weapon for this monologization. Ruoff presents Wordsworth's *The Leech-Gatherer* in this context as a deliberately reductive answer to Coleridge's response to the early draft of Wordsworth's *Intimations Ode*.

Wordsworth reads Coleridge's poem 'as a lament of sensibility like those of Burns, all of which are predicated on the assumptions that poets are something different, finer, more fragile, less suited to bear the burdens of common life' (ibid., p. 135). In *The Leech-Gatherer*, Wordsworth deliberately travesties this idea in his presentation of the self-pitying poet who is made to laugh at himself when he confronts the contentment of the decrepit leech-gatherer. The cure *The Leech-Gatherer* offers to Coleridge's solipsistic complaint 'is that Coleridge remove himself from the company of poets and reintroduce himself to the company of men [like the leech-gatherer]' (ibid.), where, it is hoped, he will find the fortitude to endure his problems. But in order for Wordsworth to respond in this way to Coleridge's poem, he must hear less than is actually there. *The Leech-Gatherer* treats despair 'as wholly acute anxiety, denying it the dignity of the sense of chronic and permanent loss which echoes throughout [Coleridge's poem]' (ibid., p. 137). Wordsworth's anxieties about the sentimentality of his own poem cause him to misread and misrepresent Coleridge's response.

Thus, what differentiates Ruoff's model of influence from a dialogic approach is his presentation of the psychodynamics of influence as a struggle for domination based on deliberate misreading (a view of poetic dialogue influenced by Harold Bloom's *Map of Misreading* (1975)). The poet finds meaning in Ruoff's approach by parodically reducing the potential for dialogue inherent to an interlocutor's words, whereas a Bakhtinian dialogism insists that this potential is irreducible. Put another way, Ruoff's intertextual approach posits dialogue as a general paradigm for poetic influence, but his view of dialogue reduces the openness of a Bakhtinian dialogism.

The best current criticism grounded in Bakhtin's definition of dialogism conserves and indeed cultivates this textual openness. In 'Double economics: ambivalence in Wordsworth's pastoral' (1993), Mark Jones argues against the recent new historicist allegation that Wordsworth's pastorals sublimate the material reality of their subject matter. Jones points out that pastoral traditionally presents a split view of its object: the shepherd of the pastoral landscape cares for his sheep, but he also 'multiplies, trades, fleeces, and slaughters his animals to his own advantage' (ibid., p. 1,104). Instead of 'sublimating the material or "real" value of sheep, [pastoral] evaluates sheep in two contradictory systems at once' (ibid.). Pastoral, in this sense, is both real and ideal, smelling of fields and slaughterhouses; in pastoral poetry, 'lambs are dilemmas; one does not know whether to feed them or eat them' (ibid., p. 1,105). Jones argues that Wordsworth's pastorals are caught in this double bind between realism and idealism. *Michael*, for example, tells the story of an old shepherd who sends his only son, Luke, to the city to make the money the family needs to keep their land. Luke falls prey to urban temptations and never returns to the countryside. Realistically, Luke represents 'lucre' to Michael, a 'lamb' who must be sacrificed for the money he brings in. But Luke is also the last of Michael's flock, a lamb loved without thought of his exchange value. He is both of these things at once, the ideal figure of paternal love *and* the means to paternal security, just as any shepherd's sheep is both loved and sold for profit. Wordsworth's poem does not sublimate the realism of Michael's decision to send Luke to the city in order to preserve its ideal vision of the pastoral world. Rather, it shows that Michael's ideal pastoral world is also the world of profit and loss, and it exposes the terrible pain and uncertainty in which this double valuation places Michael: 'Michael survives his transaction only to brood on it, haunting the sheepfold he sought to secure by venturing the last lamb it was meant to enclose' (ibid., p. 1,108). This doubleness of meaning leading to an open and unresolvable tension Jones links to Bakhtin's view of dialogic parody, parody waged not against texts (as in Magnuson's view of parody), but against interpretation:

> The multiplication of viewpoint and valuation in Wordsworth's pastoral is equivalent to the multiplication of voice in Bakhtinian parody: the effect is not, ordinarily, to debunk one viewpoint, valuation, or voice but precisely to maintain more than one and thus problematize decision in the reader. (Ibid., p. 1,109)

Concentrating on the dialogue between contesting voices in Wordsworth's pastoral, Jones is able to reveal the fundamental restlessness of his poetry.

The difference between Jones's dialogic approach to Wordsworth and the approaches of Bialostosky and Magnuson is that Jones's dialogism is rooted in culture. Pastoral ambivalence is produced by the economics of rural life, the materiality of the slaughterhouse qualifying poetic idealism. Bialostosky contains dialogism to the narrative voices within a single poem, and Magnuson limits it to a specific scene of reading. Jones, however, suggests that a text's uncertainty is generated in response to historical conditions.

This expansion of the social environment which contextualizes and complicates the text might be taken to identify the trend in dialogic criticism in the 1990s. For example, Jacqueline Howard's *Reading Gothic Fiction: A Bakhtinian Approach* (1994) examines the Gothic novel as a highly uncertain feminist response to a masculinist cultural discourse of economic and political power.[2] Mary Shelley's *Frankenstein*, for example, interrogates the dominant, patriarchal language of Shelley's culture by placing Victor Frankenstein's male desire for knowledge and power in dialogue with a less prominent cultural voice – the discourse of sensibility. The language of sensibility, with its delicacy of feeling and its emphasis on domestic affections, expresses in the novel a female desire for social harmony in sharp contrast with Victor's destructive male ambitions. By giving voice in her novel to a marginalized feminist language, Shelley is able to relativize the authority of patriarchal discourse.

And yet the voice of sensibility is itself questioned in the novel. Victor's upbringing is everywhere informed by sensibility, but he fails to find in this context the antidote for his desires. Similarly, the De Lacey family, a sentimental example of domestic affection, reject Victor's creature at first sight: 'this again shows the limitations of the virtues of "domestic affection" and "sensibility" which Godwin . . . had argued would render people "more prompt in the service of strangers and the public"' (Howard, *Reading Gothic Fiction*, p. 280). A similar acknowledgement of the ineffectivity of sensibility as a critique of patriarchal norms is found in other Gothic novels of the time, as in Ann Radcliffe's *The Mysteries of Udolpho*, where the sentimental St Aubert and Emily can only withdraw from the worldliness represented by the Quesnels. Situated within a cultural context in which sentimentality was being presented as both empowering for the female author (Edward Young's *Conjectures on Original Composition*, 1759) and debilitating (William Duff's *Letters on the Intellectual and Moral Character of Women*, 1807), the Gothic answers this cultural dialogue with an internal dialogism about its own formative discourses.

By expanding the sphere of dialogism to include the discourses of Romantic culture, Howard is able to exploit the political ramifications of Bakhtin's theory of language for the purpose of ideology critique. The dialogic word, continually challenged by competing words, is never absolute or authoritative. If, as Bakhtin argues, all words are capable of dialogization, then even the apparently authoritative word will be undermined by other discourses (thus, in the Gothic novel, the discourse of sentimentality disrupts the official patriarchal discourse of Romantic culture). Defining culture as a dialogue of ideological voices and language as an inherently political dialogue, Howard's work demonstrates that the dialogic qualities identified by Bialostosky and Magnuson as definitive formal elements of Romantic literature contribute to this literature's political responsibility.

## NOTES

1   The concept has become particularly popular among Wordsworthians. Dialogic readings of Wordsworth's poetry represent the bulk of dialogic criticism in British Romantic literature. It is noteworthy that dialogism has been more often applied to Romantic poetry than to prose, because Bakhtin insists that the novel is a far more dialogic genre than the poem. Poets, he argues, often suppress the doubleness of language in their attempt to express the unity and uniqueness of their own poetic voice. Novelists, in contrast, coexist and interact with the many different voices that make up their novels. That Bialostosky and others can argue that dialogism is a definitive term for Wordsworth's poetry indicates not only that dialogism as a factor in determining meaning *can* be redefined as a poetic mode, but also that the emphasis on dialogue that distinguishes Romanticism as a literary period (seen, for example, in the use of dialogue by the Jena circle in their philosophical and critical writings and in Schleiermacher's editing of Plato) is also evident in British Romantic poetry.

2   See also Michael Macovski's book *Dialogue and Literature*, which uses Bakhtin to explore the way nineteenth-century authors employ dialogue to recover the history within their own pasts.

## WRITINGS

Bakhtin, Mikhail Mikhailovich, 'Discourse in the novel', in *The Dialogic Imagination: Four Essays*, ed. Michael Holquist, trans. Caryl Emerson and Michael Holquist, Austen, University of Texas Press, 1981, pp. 259–422.

Wordsworth, William, 'Simon Lee', in *Lyrical Ballads, with a Few Other Poems*, London, 1798; *Lyrical Ballads and Other Poems, 1797–1800*, ed. James Butler and Karen Green, Ithaca, Cornell University Press, 1992, pp. 64–7.

## REFERENCES AND FURTHER READING

Bialostosky, Don H., *Making Tales: The Poetics of Wordsworth's Narrative Experiments*, Chicago, University of Chicago Press, 1984.

—— *Wordsworth, Dialogics, and the Practice of Criticism*, Cambridge, Cambridge University Press, 1992.

—— 'Dialogic criticism', in *Contemporary Literary Theory*, ed. Douglas Atkins and Laura Morrow, Amherst, University of Massachusetts Press, 1989, pp. 214–28.

Bidlake, Stephen, '"Hidden dialog" in "The Mad Mother" and "The Complaint of a Forsaken Indian Woman"', *The Wordsworth Circle* 13 (1982) 188–93.

Howard, Jacqueline, *Reading Gothic Fiction: A Bakhtinian Approach*, Oxford, Oxford University Press, 1994.

Jones, Mark, 'Double economics: ambivalence in Wordsworth's pastoral', *PMLA* 108 (1993) 1,098–113.

Macovski, Michael, *Dialogue and Literature: Apostrophe, Auditors, and the Collapse of Romantic Discourse*, New York, Oxford University Press, 1994.

Magnuson, Paul, *Coleridge and Wordsworth: A Lyrical Dialogue*, Princeton, Princeton University Press, 1988.

Ruoff, Gene W., *Wordsworth and Coleridge: The Making of the Major Lyrics 1802–1804*, New Brunswick, Rutgers University Press, 1989.

Thomas, Gordon K., 'The *Lyrical Ballads* ode: dialogized heteroglossia', *The Wordsworth Circle* 20 (1989) 102–5.

# 44

# The Romantic Fragment

## Anne Janowitz

In 1813, Francis Jeffrey, the imposing editor of the *Edinburgh Review*, archly observed of Byron's narrative poem *The Giaour, A Fragment of a Turkish Tale* that 'The Taste for Fragments, we suspect, has become very general, and the greater part of polite readers would no more think of sitting down to a whole epic than to a whole Ox'. For Jeffrey, the fashion for fragments does not disturb the integrity of the epic genre, recognizable even in a part, and suffusing the part with the characteristics of the whole. And he goes on to produce a theory of the fragment vogue based in a psychology of dull writing and lazy reading: 'The truth is, we suspect, that after we once know what it contains, no long poem is ever read, but in fragments: and that the connecting passages which are always skipped after the first reading, are often so tedious as to deter us from thinking of a second'. But the relationship between fixed genres and the 'Taste for Fragments' was, in the early decades of the nineteenth century, less clear-cut than Jeffrey suggests, as the fragment came to be considered a genre in its own right. Furthermore, one of the peculiarities of the term 'Romantic fragment' and a reason for its prominent place in critical discussion of the characteristic poetic structures of the period, is that it not only refers to a 'kind' of Romantic poem, but it can also be used as a tool for opening up debates about the meaning of *genre* altogether within Romanticism. Coleridge's *Kubla Khan: or a Vision in a Dream. A Fragment*, Keats's *Hyperion. A Fragment*, Byron's *The Giaour, A Fragment of a Turkish Tale*, are just a few of the most renowned of the many Romantic poems which were published *as* 'fragments' and which, taken together, can be recognized as a genre. And at the same time, amongst the German writers associated with the Jena School and the journal *The Athenaeum* (1798–1800), the 'fragment' structure was held up by literary theorists as the model for a new kind of poetic originality freed from the constraints and forms of the classical genres. In the history of literary forms, the Romantic fragment poem, usually presented as a *partial whole* – either a remnant of something once complete and now broken or decayed, or the beginning of something that remains unaccomplished – is the precursor form to the modernist fragment poem, which, as in T. S. Eliot's *The Wasteland*, or Ezra Pound's *The Cantos*, or Louis Zukofsky's *A*, is structured as a *whole made of fragmentary parts* – the juxtaposition or concatenation of discrete poetic units. The Jena School theory of fragments lies at the origin of poststructuralist notions of all literary texts being in a state of incompletion and all literary language as insufficient.

The following observations, then, first set out the meanings and varieties of the Romantic fragment, and then aim to explain how the model of something either unfinished or broken came to be understood as both *a* genre within Romantic poetry and as *the* paradigm genre of Romantic literature. Given the importance of the fragment in both the theory and the practice of late eighteenth and early nineteenth-century Romantic poets in both England and Germany, it is surprising that within Anglo-American literary criticism and history, attention to the fragment as an identifiable and systematic *kind* of literary form is a fairly new one. In 1958, Robert MacAdams, a distinguished American critic, confidently wrote in *Strains of Discord* (p. 13), 'Fragments do not constitute a recognised literary mode, nor often, for that matter, so much as an interesting accident'. In 1963, Edward Bostetter recognized the abundance of unfinished poems amongst the work of Romantic poets, and argued that this was a symptom of the failure of the Romantic poetic project. But a few years later, in 1969, D. F. Rauber wrote an essay on the appropriateness of an unfinished structure to the themes of the Romantic mode. Rauber argued that the stance of Romanticism 'centred upon an aspiration for the infinite' renders an unfinished form particularly apt (Rauber, 'The fragment', p. 213). Since the appearance of Rauber's argument, other critics have turned to the large numbers of unfinished and fragment poems within the Romantic corpus and tried to make sense of the genre and its intentions.[1]

## The British Romantic Fragment

How is it that readers and critics came to accept the internally discontinuous, the unfinished and the apparently ruined poem as a publishable and meaningful kind of literary text and not just poetic filler? Marjorie Levinson has offered the intriguing suggestion that the groundwork for the general intelligibility of unfinished or internally fragmented texts such as Keats's *Hyperion* poems can be traced back to the 'hoax poem' scandals of the later eighteenth century; in particular, to counterfeit 'found' manuscript poems by Thomas Chatterton (1752–70) and to James Macpherson's (1736–96) putative 'translations' of the works of the blind poet Ossian. Chatterton asserted that he had found the fragmentary poems of a fifteenth-century monk named Thomas Rowley amongst a heap of manuscripts, and though Chatterton posed as the editor of these verses, they were, in fact, his own work. He was discovered in this ruse, humiliated, and he committed suicide in 1770. But the Rowley poems were reprinted in 1777, and, Levinson argues, a shift took place in the reception of the works, so that instead of reviling the poems because of their historical inauthenticity, they began to be judged positively because of their aesthetic beauty. This supercession of truth criteria by those of aesthetic value is a significant moment in the formulation of Romantic poetics.[2] It helps us, for example, to make sense of the claim made by Keats's *Grecian Urn* that 'beauty is truth, truth beauty' (*Romanticism*, p. 1,060). 'Chatterton, the marvellous boy', became the symbol of the starving, suicidal young Romantic poet, one of those who, as Wordsworth writes in *Resolution and Independence*, 'begin in gladness / But thereof comes in the end despondency and madness' (*Romanticism*, p. 271). The later eighteenth century also saw the rise in the popularity of collections of antiquities: anthologies of medieval songs and poems, such as Thomas Percy's *Reliques of Ancient English Poetry* (1764) and Charlotte Brooke's *Reliques of Irish Poetry* (1789). These collections were part of a more culturally widespread interest in history and the recovery of both objects and documents from the past. They were published alongside volumes of engravings locating and commenting upon ruins of castles and abbeys in the landscape.[3] The aesthetic taste for the picturesque, with its emphasis on irregularity, roughness and lack of conventionality, was a companionable habitat to nurture the growth of a ready audience for texts received only piecemeal or with a sense of ruination clinging to them. The taste for ruins in the landscape created a market for ersatz ones. The folly was a contemporary version of a ruin, added to create a frisson of antiquity right in one's own garden. If the ruin sentiment might give rise to sham ruins in the garden, then why should it not give rise to sham ruins in poetry as well? So it was that Romantic fragment poems found a congenial readership in an already-formed audience for poetic antiquities. Certainly, the Gothic elements in Coleridge's unfinished *Christabel* suggest that the poem might have been preserved in one of Percy's collections; *The Giaour* and *Kubla Khan* might be fragments from one of the collections of literary remains, called a Chrestomathy, gathered together by the newly developing discipline of Orientalism, and Keats's *Hyperion. A Fragment* seems almost a piece of the Elgin Marbles, the fragmented frieze from the Parthenon that had been brought to England by Lord Elgin in the very early years of the nineteenth century.[4] But compared with Chatterton's poems or with Macpherson's pseudo-antique *Fragments of Ancient English Poetry* poems, none of the Romantic fragment poems just cited so fully commit themselves to the past as to lose their flavour as contemporary, consciously created poems. The narrator of *The Giaour* is clearly an early nineteenth-century Englishman; the editorial apparatus that surrounds *Kubla Khan* insists on the poet's personal process of composition; and Keats's *Hyperion. A Fragment* is too crowded with Miltonisms and contemporary references to really pose as an 'authentic' Greek fragment. Significantly, though all these Romantic fragment poems might be assimilated to the general interest in antiquarian ruins, they also suggest that their incompletion may be more properly considered in thematic rather than historical terms. Observing how the 'Taste for Fragments' edges out that for ruins and for anti-quities, we can begin to distinguish between a ruin and a fragment. The crucial difference is that between a temporal and spatial construct. If something is ruined, then presumably it once had a full form that has eroded through time. A fragment, on the other hand, is simply part of a whole: temporal or visual. Unmoored from an antiquarian grounding, the fragment opens itself up to a new poetic matter: the relation between its own incompletion and the greater whole to which it alludes, and which it both aspires to and struggles against. In this de-historicizing and aestheticizing process, the fragment form becomes the place where the theme of incompletion is enacted. For example, many fragment poems take on the topic of how to build an equivalence between what one wants to figure in language, and what one can figure in language.[5] When Coleridge published a volume in 1816 comprising only the three poems, all fragments, *Kubla Khan*, *Christabel* and *The Pains of Sleep*, the third of these poems, which details the horrors of opium addiction, had neither real or sham antiquarian value, but could be read and made sense of in the ambience of the Orientalism of *Kubla Khan* and the medievalism of *Christabel*. But in addition to their sham-antiquarianism, these poems are also presented as examples of the inadequacy of language to vision. In the Preface to *Christabel*, Coleridge writes, 'I had the whole present to my mind, no less than the liveliness of a vision; I trust I shall be able to embody in verse the three parts yet to come'. The headnote to *Kubla Khan* similarly tells us that Coleridge had a vision in which 'all the images rose up before him as Things'. Unlike words, which lose the immediacy of vision, the 'Things' of the dream of *Kubla Khan* create the expectation of a whole which will exceed the boundaries of articulate poetry. Coleridge's statements are similar to Shelley's in his *Defence of Poetry*, where he contrasts poetic inspiration and poetic composition through the image of a 'fading coal' which dies out from the 'original composition in the poet's mind' (*Romanticism*, p. 966). When Coleridge's 1816 volume was reviewed, many readers made sense of the unfinished poems through the fragment sensibility: the reviewer in the *London Times* (20 May 1816) suggested that *Christabel* 'interests more by what it leaves untold than by what it tells', and suggests that 'wild . . . romantic and visionary as it is, the poem has a truth of its own, which seizes on and masters the imagination'. And Josiah Conder, reviewing the volume in the *Eclectic Review* (1816), explicitly uses the Romantic criterion of ineffable emotion when discussing what he cites as 'romantic fragments': he invokes 'the purely imaginative feeling, the breathless thrill of indefinite emotion of which we are conscious when in the supposed presence of an unknown being, or acted upon by some influence mysteriously transcending the notice of the senses'. In his next volume, *Sibylline Leaves*, published in 1817, Coleridge justified the title of the volume, 'in allusion to the fragmentary and widely scattered state in which the poems have long been suffered to remain', thereby classifying the entire work under the designation 'fragment'. In 1810, Percy Bysshe Shelley, playing with the idea of the fragment as the remnant of a life, published the fictional *The Posthumous Fragments of Margaret Nicholson*, whose Advertisement begins, 'the energy and native genius of the Fragments must be the only apology which the Editor can make for thus intruding them on public notice'.[6] A poignant counterpart to Shelley's volume is Mary Shelley's editing of her husband's own *The Triumph of Life*, a poem left unfinished at his death. In her Preface to the 1824 *Posthumous Poems*, Mary Shelley writes that the poem 'was his last work, and left in so unfinished a state that I arranged it in its present form with great difficulty'.[7] Her arrangement was deft, however, for she omitted $3\frac{1}{2}$ lines which existed in Shelley's manuscript, but which took the edge off a more suitably open-ended ending. Her re-edited version ends: ' "Then, what is life?" I cried . . .'. What might have been simply a break in the narration is now the entry into an unspecified answer to an overwhelming question!

The point I am making is that what begins as a historical fashion for antiquities with a particular structural form of fragmentariness becomes a poetic concern of thematic as well as spatial dimensions, entailing various outcomes within the practice of poem-making. These implications can be considered in relationship to traditional poetic topics, and in relation to poetic theories of language. For example, the most enduring service rendered by the sonnet form has been to bestow a memorializing immortality upon the transient objects of love and power. In Shakespeare's sonnets, flesh is redeemed by art; and further, verbal art can endure even after a material memorial has decayed: 'When tyrants' crests and tombs of brass are spent'. Yet one of the interesting things about the Romantic period is that the theme of the immortality of poetry is itself placed in jeopardy; that is, the argument that though objects in the world pass away, poetry remains and preserves and immortalizes the object of the poet's regard is placed under great stress in Romantic poetics. And this takes place in proximity to an assault upon the permanence of poetic genres, within increasingly subjective and individualized lyrics. Shelley's sonnet about statuary fragments, *Ozymandias*, while a complete poem in itself, takes up this theme of the growing insecurity of poetic permanence. In Shelley's sonnet, the theme of ruin and fragmentation alters this poetic intention, encapsulated in the irony of the slogan engraved on the shards of Ozymandias's now decayed statue (and empire): 'Look on my works, ye mighty, and despair'.[8] The transformation of the Egyptian Pharaoh's boast into an ironic epitaph points out to us that history not only confounds propriety by bringing down the mighty, but confounds verbal formulations themselves. What we find taking the place of the theme of the immortality of poetry is the theme of the inexpressibility of poetry; namely, a motif in which the poetic speaker asserts that he or she cannot express the full meaning of what they have to say. This topic gains ever greater currency within Romantic poetry as lyric privacy and the inadequacy of language appear as persistent themes: thoughts that lie too deep for words.

By the 1830s, the fragment as a structure and as a theme is an achieved and present part of the Romantic poetic. Readers had learned how to read the fragment as a generic possibility. The historical interest in antiquities contributed to a growing interest in poetic compilations, or anthologies, which in turn contributed to the fragment genre. Anthologies required the fragmentation of narrative poems into shorter, lyric forms, proving Jeffrey's point about reading habits. Tennyson's *In Memoriam* can be considered a fragmented epic or an anthology of lyric fragments, and Tennyson himself had originally planned to publish the poem under the title 'Fragments of an Elegy'. And from within the Romantic focus on individual growth and development, there came to be an increased interest in both poetic juvenilia – fragments of youthful compositions – and posthumous remains. Wordsworth's poem on the growth of his mind, published at his death in 1850 as *The Prelude*, was greeted by the press as 'a large fossil relic ... whose fragments will be valued as if they were a part of the ark' (*Eclectic Review* [1850], p. 551).

## Fragment Theory: Schlegel and The Athenaeum

The fragment poem has come to be granted its own integrity within our contemporary analytical classification system of Romantic genres, included amongst such other specific genres as the greater Romantic lyric, the internalized quest romance and the picturesque tour. But the category of the Romantic fragment has also served as an example of a larger critical investigation, characteristic of Romantic enquiry more generally, about the importance of *originality*. It was the pair of brothers, Friedrich and August Schlegel, who, in their short-lived but very influential journal *The Athenaeum* (1798–1800), discussed and reflected upon the fragment as a positive literary event, rather than as either an accident (for example, a poet dying before completing the poem – Shelley's *Triumph of Life*) or a failure (for example, the poet declaring that he has not the poetic wherewithal to complete the text – Coleridge's *Christabel*). Instead, they argued that what characterized what they called 'modern' poetry was that it refused to conform to the shape of traditional genres, and was the result of the self-activity, or coming into being, of thinking and feeling individuals, whose texts were marked by their individuality, not by conforming to their external laws of genre. Choosing to write in an aphoristic, fragmentary manner, Friedrich Schlegel argued that what characterizes the 'modernity' of the literary world he inhabited was the proliferation of genres, in which each poetic object took on its own appropriate shape – its own original genre. Schlegel's idea was an example of an *immanent theory* of poetry; that is, he argued that each poem has its own necessary shape, whose necessity is a function of the purpose of its poetic statement. Protesting against the *ancien régime* of genres, Schlegel writes, 'The customary divisions of poetry are only a dead framework for a limited horizon'.[9] One can recognize here the impact of the ideology of the French Revolution on this formulation of poetic independence. In fact, Schlegel specified the poetic revolution in political terms: 'Poetry is republican speech: a speech which is its own law and end unto itself, and in which all the parts are free citizens and have the right to vote'.[10] Another way to describe Schlegel's theory is to call it an *organic* theory of poetry, in which poems are understood as living and growing, rather than as built. His formulation is similar to Keats's poetic 'Axiom' 'That if poetry comes not as easily as leaves to a tree it had better not come at all'.[11] And Shelley writes something similar in his *Defence of Poetry*: 'All high poetry is infinite; it is as the first acorn, which contained all oaks potentially. Veil after veil may be undrawn, and the inmost naked beauty of the meaning never exposed' (*Romanticism*, p. 963). One of the implications of an organic, developmental theory of poetry is that the poem's value can be affirmed as potential rather than complete. So it is that Schlegel argues that 'All Romantic poetry is the poetry of becoming', 'Every poem is its own genre', and 'Romantic poetry is the art of poetry itself'.[12] This Schlegelian logic demonstrates that the fragment is the theoretical prototype of the genres of Romanticism as well as issuing in particular fragment poems. Every poem is its own fragment genre: each poem is individual and all poetry is incomplete. If Romanticism generally signalled the supercession of the genres of antiquity, then the fragment serves as the textual version of a ruin (the remnant of an antique genre), and as an incompletion (the never-to-be-achieved fulfilment of a potential): 'Many of the works of the ancients have become fragments. Many modern works are fragments as soon as they are written'.[13] Friedrich's brother August Schlegel writes,

> Romantic poetry... is the expression of the secret urge towards the chaos that is constantly labouring to bring forth new and wonderful creations, and that is hidden beneath, indeed within, the orderly universe.... Ancient poetry is simpler, clearer, and more like nature in the independent completeness of its individual works; romantic poetry, in spite of its fragmentary appearance, is closer to the secret of the Universe.[14]

What links the idea of the individuality of poetic endeavour with that of incompletion, of 'becoming', is that Schlegel also sees the Romantic poetic project as one which is aspirational: 'Romantic poetry is still in the process of becoming; this indeed is its very essence, that it is eternally evolving, never completed'.[15] This genre of modernity reaches towards the future, and importantly, reaches towards a mode of expression which is, paradoxically, unrealizable. Language, then, operates as a sort of necessary impediment to expression. Our contemporary literary theorists, Jean-Luc Nancy and Lacoue-Labarthe, in *The Literary Absolute*, have most impressively analysed the importance of the Schlegels' literary theory, and they note that this sense of incompletion always suggests an ineffable wholeness just out of reach, a perpetual 'beyond of literature' (ibid., p. 50). And so it is not surprising that there is a pervasive sense in the period of poets complaining that their projects are incompletable, and that no poem of the period can attain to its project or its ideal version. The issue of incompletion, then, operates as both a form and a theme within many Romantic period poems which are not formally unfinished. One might think, for example, of the conclusion to Shelley's *Epipsychidion*, which articulates a deep sense of the inadequacy between what the poet experiences and wishes to express, and what he is capable of performing: 'The winged words on which my soul would pierce / into the height of Love's Rare universe, / Are chains of lead around its flight of fire – / I pant, I sink, I tremble, I expire!' The fragment gives the most authentic spatial form to the problem of inexpressibility in poetry, but the problem pervades the Romantic poetic as a whole. And, of course, the theme of 'inexpressibility' has a long history as a rhetorical feature of poems in which the poet protests that the object of his writing far surpasses what he is capable of conveying in verse.[16] But in Romantic period poetry, where the subject matter of the poem is often extremely close to the subjectivity of the poem's speaker, the inexpressibility topic becomes an occasion for the poet to mourn the frailty of both himself and his poetic structure. For this reason, the fragment is often poised on the knife edge between euphoria and despair; and so it becomes linked to the problem of Romantic irony. Romantic irony, also theorized by Friedrich Schlegel in his fragments, is the simultaneous operation in literary productions of creation and destruction and joy and scepticism. This co-existent de-creative and re-creative action attests to the vitality of the imagination, and its ability to see the world as passing both into and out of form.[17] Schlegel writes that '[Irony] contains and arouses a feeling of indissoluble antagonism between the absolute and the relative, between the impossibility and the necessity of complete communication'.[18] In the early twentieth century, the philosopher and sociologist Georg Simmel thinks about ruins and fragments as a way of understanding universal human impulses, and we can hear his genealogy in the Jena School fragmentists at the cross-road of fragmentation and irony. The fragmentary ruin is, he writes, bounded by two impulses or instincts: on the one hand, the 'brute, downward-dragging, corroding, crumbling power of nature', and on the other, the advance or upward flight of the 'human will'.[19] One of the most significant of mid-twentieth-century philosopher-literary theorists, Maurice Blanchot, also assessed the importance of the Schlegel brothers' insights into the attachments between irony and fragmentation. 'Romanticism', he writes, 'is essentially that which begins, that which could only end badly'. Romanticism, then, as an entire literary formation, aims to be 'everything but without content', and so it affirms 'at once the absolute and the fragment-ary'.[20] His voice echoes Friedrich Schlegel's aphoristic remark: 'The overriding disposition of every writer is almost always to lean in one of two directions: either not to say a number of things that absolutely need saying, or else to say a great many things that absolutely ought to be left unsaid'.[21] More recently, Thomas McFarland, also working through the German tradition of fragment theory, writes about the general meaning of the fragment form, which he presents as an emblem of the necessary mortal limitations of all human productions, for the incomplete, he writes, 'seen from the larger truths of existence, is nothing less than the final shape of every man's effort'.[22]

Schlegel's Romantic fragment theory, we can see, encompasses more than simply the isolatable genre; it extends over the entire modality of Romanticism: 'the romantic kind of poetry [i.e. the poetry of becoming] is the only one that is more than a kind, that is, as it were, poetry itself: for in a certain sense all poetry is or should be romantic'.[23] So it is not surprising that the discussion of the poetic symbol, which, over the past 200 years, has been central to critical reflection upon poetic form, is illuminated by and interwoven with Schlegel's theory of the fragment. Coleridge's definition of the symbol is itself a theory of incompletion: for Coleridge the symbol is 'a translucence of the Eternal through and in the Temporal.... and while it enunciates the whole, abides itself as a living part of that Unity of which it is the representative' (CC *Lay Sermons*, p. 30). This notion is very close to August Schlegel's theory of the beautiful: 'The beautiful is a symbolic representation of the infinite, for from this formulation it becomes clear how the infinite can appear in the finite'.[24] The symbol, then, we might say, is the trope, or figure, of the fragment in poetic space.

As this discussion of the Jena School theory suggests, the fragment as the central structure and theme of Romanticism links not only issues of form and content, but also those of literary and philosophical texts. For the Schlegels, there was no clear distinction between writing poetry and reflecting upon the process of thought, since both were examples of the forms of incompletion: 'Whatever can be done while poetry and philosophy are separated has been done and accomplished. So the time has come to unite the two'.[25]

Jena School fragment theory not only links poetic practice to critical and philosophical reflection, it also links Romanticism to the present. In fragment theory, the pressure of the past makes itself felt even in our present. Lacoue-Labarthe and Nancy polemically write: 'Romanticism will always be more than a period ... in fact, it has not yet stopped in-completing the period it began'.[26]

In the light of this claim for the persistence of the Romantic modality into the present, it is worth concluding by returning to examples of the poetic genre of the fragment. For though we can hear amongst the modernist poetic fragmentists the Romantic irony of Pound's desire in *The Cantos* to make his fragments cohere, and in Eliot's desire to shore fragments against ruin, the modernist fragment poem, may, in fact, be recognizable within the fragment genre precisely by its different relation to both antiquity (the ruin) and the future (progressive incompletion). Modernist fragment poems are wholes made entirely of fragmentary parts, and not partial wholes. Pound, Eliot and William Carlos Williams all produced examples of the fragment epic in *The Cantos*, *The Waste Land* and *Paterson*. Antiquity is still invoked, but more often by way of making an ersatz or simulated version, as in Pound's ideal of ancient coherence which patterns the shape of the *Cantos*. But there are critical differences between the two kinds of fragment poem. The affirmation of the Romantic fragment poem is an affirmation of the ideal, and as such, it necessarily undervalues its own achievement in the face of its unachieved ideal completion, its 'beyond'. On the other hand, modernist fragment poems – collages built up out of the fragments and ruins of other texts – make their affirmation as a function of their visible juxtapositions. The modernist fragment collage poem does not allude to an invisible beyond, but instead generates new meanings out of visible and discrete remnants and ruins. The modernist fragment poem exhorts the poet to abandon a fruitless search for the 'beyond' and embrace the here and now. To conclude, we can return to the criterion of truth in poetry, and juxtapose, in the style of the Jena ironists, the poetic voices of a Romantic and a modernist fragmentist: Shelley's Demogorgon tells us that 'the deep truth is imageless'; the poet of *Paterson*, William Carlos Williams, says, 'Be reconciled, poet, with your world, it is the only truth'.

## NOTES

1 For example, Lacoue-Labarthe, 'Genre'; Lacoue-Labarthe and Nancy, *The Literary Absolute*; and Janowitz, Levinson and McFarland.
2 Levinson, *The Romantic Fragment Poem*, pp. 28–59.
3 Janowitz, *England's Ruins*, pp. 13–14.
4 Ibid.; Said, *Orientalism*, 127–9.
5 De Man, 'Intentional structure', pp. 65–77; Gleckner, 'Romanticism', pp. 173–89.
6 Shelley, *Poetical Works*, p. 861; Levinson, *The Romantic Fragment Poem*, p. 139.
7 Shelley, *Poetical Works*, p. xxvii.
8 Ibid., p. 550.
9 Athenaeum fragment 434, in Furst, *European Romanticism*, p. 112.
10 Critical fragments 65, in Wheeler, *German Aesthetic*, p. 42.
11 Furst, *European Romanticism*, p. 63.
12 Athenaeum fragment 116, in Schlegel, *Lucinde*; Wheeler, *German Aesthetic*, pp. 46–7; Furst, *European Romanticism*, pp. 4–5.
13 Athenaeum fragment 24, in Wheeler, *German Aesthetic*, p. 44.
14 'Essay on dramatic art and literature', in Furst, *European Romanticism*, p. 112.
15 Athenaeum fragment 116, in Wheeler, *German Aesthetic*, pp. 46–7; Furst, *European Romanticism*, p. 5.
16 Curtius, *European Literature*, p. 159.
17 Mellor, *English Romantic Irony*, p. 24.
18 Critical fragments 108, in Wheeler, *German Aesthetic*, p. 43.
19 Simmel, *Collection*, p. 261.
20 Blanchot, 'The Athenaeum', pp. 164–5.
21 Critical fragment 37, in Wheeler, *German Aesthetic*, p. 41.
22 McFarland, *Romanticism*, p. 8.
23 Athenaeum fragment 116, in Wheeler, *German Aesthetic*, p. 47; Furst, *European Romanticism*, p. 5.
24 Furst, *European Romanticism*, p. 94.
25 'Ideas' fragment 108, in Wheeler, *German Aesthetic*, p. 57.
26 *The Literary Absolute*, p. 2.

## REFERENCES AND FURTHER READING

Adams, Robert M., *Strains of Discord*, Ithaca, Cornell University Press, 1958.

Blanchot, Maurice, 'The Athenaeum', *Studies in Romanticism* 22 (1983) 167–72.

Bostetter, Edward, *The Romantic Ventriloquists: Wordsworth, Coleridge, Shelley, Byron*, Seattle, University of Washington, 1963.

Curtius, Ernst Robert, *European Literature and the Latin Middle Ages*, trans. Willard R. Trask, Princeton, Princeton University Press, 1973.

De Man, Paul, 'Intentional structure of the Romantic image', in *Romanticism and Consciousness: Essays in Criticism*, ed. Harold Bloom, New York, Norton, 1970, pp. 65–77.

Furst, Lilian R. (ed.) *European Romanticism: Self-definition*, London, Methuen, 1980. Readers will find selections from the Schlegels in this anthology.

Gleckner, Robert F., 'Romanticism and the self-annihilation of language', *Criticism* 18 (1976) 173–89.

Janowitz, Anne, *England's Ruins: Poetic Purpose and the National Landscape*, Oxford, Basil Blackwell, 1990.

Jeffrey, Francis, Review of 'The Giaour', *Edinburgh Review* 21 (1813) 299–309.

Lacoue-Labarthe, Philippe and Nancy, Jean-Luc, 'Genre', *Glyph* 7 (1981) 1–15.

—— *The Literary Absolute: The Theory of Literature in German Romanticism*, trans. Philip Barnard and Cheryl Lester, New York, State University of New York, 1988.

Levinson, Marjorie, *The Romantic Fragment Poem: A Critique of a Form*, Chapel Hill, University of North Carolina Press, 1986.

Macauley, Rose, *Pleasure of Ruins*, London, Thames and Hudson, 1953.

McFarland, Thomas, *Romanticism and the Forms of Ruin: Wordsworth, Coleridge, and the Modalities of Fragmentation*, Princeton, Princeton University Press, 1981.

Mellor, Anne, *English Romantic Irony*, Cambridge, Mass., Harvard University Press, 1980.

Rauber, D. F., 'The fragment as romantic form,' *Modern Language Quarterly* 30 (1969) 212–21.

Said, Edward, *Orientalism*, New York, Pantheon, 1978.

Schlegel, Friedrich, *Lucinde and the Fragments*, trans. Peter Firchow, Minneapolis, University of Minnesota Press, 1971.

Shelley, Percy Bysshe, *Poetical Works*, Oxford, Oxford University Press, 1971.

Simmel, Georg, *A Collection of Essays with Translations and a Bibliography*, ed. Kurt H. Wolff, Columbus, Ohio University Press, 1959.

Wheeler, Kathleen M. (ed) *German Aesthetic and Literary Criticism: The Romantic Ironists and Goethe*, Cambridge, Cambridge University Press, 1984. A good selection of Schlegel texts.

# 45

# Performative Language and Speech-act Theory

## Angela Esterhammer

The concepts of *performative language* and *speech acts* provide insight into the interaction that occurs among speakers, hearers, language and the world. Speech-act theory often works together with other critical approaches, from deconstruction to cultural studies to psycho-analytic theory, contributing to these approaches a focus on the 'performative' – that is to say, the active, dynamic or efficient – aspect of language. The speech-act critic is concerned with such questions as: how do spoken or written utterances affect the circumstances in which they take place? What gives these utterances and their speakers the authority necessary to alter reality? In what senses and under what circumstances can it be said that words change the world? These issues are addressed by Romantic writers themselves as well as by modern philosophers of language, and a speech-act approach to Romantic literature considers, among other things, the similarities and the differences in the way the issues are framed in the nineteenth and twentieth centuries.

The terms 'performative language' and 'speech-act theory' derive from a movement in the philosophy of language begun in the 1950s by the Oxford philosopher J. L. Austin and continued by his American student John R. Searle. In a series of lectures published after his death as *How to Do Things with Words*, Austin challenged the prevailing philosophical view of language, which he felt was overly preoccupied with reference and truth-value. He began by identifying a number of perfectly ordinary utterances which nevertheless refuse to fit into philosophers' ordinary ways of evaluating propositions – utterances such as 'Hello', 'I promise to come', or (his classic example) 'I do', uttered as part of a marriage ceremony. Because utterances of this sort seem to *perform actions* (e.g. greeting, promising, marrying) rather than describe or make statements about the world, Austin dubs them *performatives*, and over the course of the book he proposes different ways in which they might be distinguished from statements (or what Austin calls *constative* utterances). The most important of these distinguishing features is the *illocutionary* dimension of an utterance – that is to say, the act performed *in uttering* certain words. Thus, if one writes (as Wordsworth does in *Ode to Duty*) 'I myself commend unto thy guidance from this hour', the illocutionary dimension (or simply *illocution*) consists of the act of dedicating or making a vow, and the words themselves, rather than describing anything, create a new situation in which the speaker is henceforth under the guidance of the addressee.

One of the remarkable things about *How to Do Things with Words*, however, is that Austin ends by breaking down the very distinction between performative and constative that he began by establishing. *All* utterances turn out to have an illocutionary or performative dimension; even statements 'perform' the act of stating or describing, and identical statements may count as completely different acts if uttered under different circumstances. Austin is forced to conclude that 'performative' and 'constative' are not two different kinds of utterances, but simply possible dimensions of, or perspectives on, any utterance whatsoever. John Searle worked out the implications of this insight by analysing all aspects of ordinary utterances – including reference and predication as well as illocutionary acts such as promising, ordering or warning – as actions performed by a speaker. This project was begun in *Speech Acts: An Essay in the Philosophy of Language* (1969) and continued in *Expression and Meaning* (1979). Many linguists and literary theorists have found Searle's version of speech-act theory more accessible and applicable than Austin's, especially since he continues Austin's unfinished project of systematizing all possible illocutions in 'A taxonomy of illocutionary acts' and then attempts an application of speech-act theory to literary texts in 'The logical status of fictional discourse' (both these essays are in *Expression and Meaning*). However, Searle has also been criticized for substantially changing the emphasis of Austin's theory. Whereas Austin concentrates on *social* action and the conditions necessary for utterances to have illocutionary force in socio-political situations, Searle habitually emphasizes the conditions or rules of language itself and the individual speaker's intention to represent a specific meaning by his or her utterance, irrespective of societal context.

While the movement that goes by the name of 'speech-act theory' is mainly the creation of Austin and Searle, other scholars have made substantial contributions to the more diffuse concepts of 'performative language', 'the performative', or 'performativity'.[1] One of the most significant is the structuralist linguist Emile Benveniste, who, in essays such as 'Subjectivity in language' and 'Analytic philosophy and language', emphasizes the relation between verbal action and the first-person subject, or the way language and subjectivity in effect create each other when a speaker refers to him- or herself as 'I'. 'It is in and through language that man constitutes himself as a *subject*, because language alone establishes the concept of "ego" in reality', Benveniste writes; but equally, 'Language is possible only because each speaker sets himself up as a *subject* by referring to himself as *I* in his discourse' (Benveniste, *Problems*, pp. 224–5). Benveniste agrees that certain utterances count as actions, but he virtually restricts performative force to first-person utterances, which participate in the act of establishing individual subjectivity and determining the relation of the speaking self to the world.

What speech-act theory allows us to do, then, is examine the interaction of language with the world as well as the relationship between the speaker or writer and the world – whether in terms of the social conventions that allow certain utterances to perform successful actions in certain contexts (Austin), or the rules of language that allow a speaker to perform the act of expressing and meaning something (Searle), or the peculiarity of first-person utterance, which allows language to enact interpersonal relationships, beginning by establishing the very identity of an 'I' and a 'you' (Benveniste). These versions of speech-act theory are by no means distinct, and all of them contribute to the important observation that a speaker always takes on a social, political or other role when he or she enters into language – speaking, for instance, 'as' a professor or 'as' a supporter of free trade. It may in fact be more accurate to conceive of the speaker's identity as *shaped and determined, indeed performed by* his or her utterance, rather than regarding the utterance and its effect on the world as determined by the status of the speaker (as Austin does) or by the speaker's intention (as Searle does). Benveniste's theory goes in this direction, as does the work of Jean-François Lyotard (cf. *The Differend*, pp. 82, 145–7), but the effects of utterance on the speaker's subjectivity and status were already being addressed during the Romantic period as well. The Romantics were crucially interested in the way human identity is shaped through dialogue with other people or with nature, or even by the mind's dialogue with itself.

Until recently, the concept of the performative entered Romantic criticism primarily by way of the work of Paul de Man. In his *Allegories of Reading* (1979), de Man adopted Austin's distinction between performative and constative as a way of conceptualizing his own deconstructionist view of literary and philosophical language. De Man characterized language as always already divided within itself, so that a given text conveys a 'constative' (or 'cognitive') meaning via its grammar, or the reference of its signs within an abstract metaphysical context, but simultaneously conveys an irreconcilable 'performative' significance via its rhetoric, or the effect of its signs within a specific or immediate encounter with the reader. In de Man's formulation, 'performativity' is set in opposition to the Romantics' intentions; that is, the performative dimension of a text undermines what that text apparently wants (constatively) to say, in a way that is revealed by deconstruction but of which the Romantic author is presumably unaware.[2] Yet there is ample evidence that the Romantics were quite conscious of performativity, or at least that they were aware of and explored, in both their theory and their literary productions, the active and dynamic aspect of language that has been rediscovered by twentieth-century speech-act philosophy.

The central figure of a 'Romantic speech-act theory' must be Coleridge, whose extensive prose works on theology, philosophy and philology centre on a concept of *logos*, or the divine word which is also an action. Coleridge regarded all language as originating in the 'verb substantive', or the word/concept 'I am', which represents the ultimate union of verb and noun, since it simultaneously and equally expresses *existence* and *action*. According to Coleridge, since all language derives from 'I am', all words convey some degree of both action and existence: every noun is also a verb, and every verb is also a noun. Although J. L. Austin was working within a different philosophical context when he came to his conclusion that all utterances both state and perform, his principle and Coleridge's seem eminently reconcilable. Coleridge, indeed, regarded the verb-substantive 'I am' not only as the basis of language, but as the basis of all consciousness, human identity and the existence of reality as well. His theories are bound up with the influence of the German idealist philosophy that was at its height around 1800. Johann Gottlieb Fichte's concept of the beginning of all consciousness and existence in an *act* of self-positing was particularly influential; the implications of this transcendental philosophy were worked out in terms of language by Coleridge and his German contemporaries, such as the poet Novalis and the linguist Wilhelm von Humboldt. Humboldt's fascination with a concept of language as performative is reflected in his explicit and radical declaration that '*Language*, in the isolated word and in connected discourse, is an *act*, a truly creative *performance of the mind*' (*On Language*, p. 183). His ideas of dialogue and subjectivity are remarkably similar to those of Benveniste, and indeed the roots of the modern concept of performative language are very likely to be found in this constellation of German idealist philosophers and German and English philologists active in the early nineteenth century.

The idea of language as 'energy' (*energeia*), now associated primarily with Humboldt, was part of the Romantic spirit of the age, and not only in academic or philosophical circles. Romantic-period philosophy, as well as literature, received inspiration from the French Revolution and the ensuing political reorganization of Europe. Steven Blakemore has analysed some of the ways the revolution contributed to a forceful awareness of the effects of language, especially when language is used publicly to shape and transmit socio-political power. In their attempts to remould the structures of power, the French revolutionary forces had recourse to linguistic change: they abolished social titles and renamed years, months and other systems of measurement, as well as institutions. In the aftermath of the revolution, in England as well as France, numerous political events – censorship laws instituted by the English government, the framing of Declarations and Constitutions as well as public debates over the significance of such documents – brought home to the Romantics the extent and importance of actions performed by language and the conditions of utterance and types of authority by which these utterances function.

In my book *Creating States*, I proposed that the Romantic period saw not just a heightened awareness, but indeed a crisis, of performative language: the Romantics' experience of how socio-political authority is perpetuated and manipulated by public speech acts (declarations, constitutions, laws, censorship, etc.) clashed with traditional ideas about the effectiveness of an individual poetic voice. This latter concept, the performativity of individual utterance, is related to Coleridge's concept of the foundational 'I am', but it is also represented for the Romantics by what might be called the ideal paradigm of performative language, the biblical account of God creating a world through acts of speech (a traditional analogy for poetic creation). The juxtaposition of these concepts is evident, for instance, in William Blake, one of the most explicitly 'performative' of Romantic writers. In his *Songs of Innocence and of Experience*, the two 'Introductions' present contrasting models of the way language might have an effect on the world. In the Introduction to *Songs of Innocence*, the words of the Child on a cloud are mirrored in the actions of the Piper, and so bring about the creation of a book that will transmit inspired language into a universal context where it can have an effect on 'every child'. The process by which this creation occurs is represented in language reminiscent of the creation story in Genesis, with its simplicity, directness and exact correspondence between word and act:

> Pipe a song about a Lamb;
> So I piped with merry chear,
> Piper pipe that song again –
> So I piped, he wept to hear.

The Introduction to *Songs of Experience*, on the other hand, represents a very different kind of illocutionary act. The speaker here, who claims for himself the nationalistic title 'Bard', also claims that his words will have specific effects on the circumstances in which they are uttered. He claims the ability to prophesy, and he seeks to make the Earth and presumably the reader obey his pronouncements:

> Hear the voice of the Bard!
> Who Present, Past, & Future sees
> Whose ears have heard,
> The Holy Word,
> That walk'd among the ancient trees.

The Bard's utterance is an introduction to the way performative language functions in a socio-political context, where it is used by a speaker who claims authority but can only justify his authority by recourse to previous speech acts (e.g. the ambivalent 'Holy Word'). Later poems in *Songs of Experience* present further scenes of the way ideology is promulgated through socio-politically performative utterance. For instance, the Priest in *A Little Boy Lost* has the power not only to condemn a little boy to death through his official pronouncement but even, as it were, to control the meanings of the words in the poem:

> And standing on the altar high,
> Lo what a fiend is here! said he:
> One who sets reason up for judge
> Of our most holy Mystery.

While we may recognize that the Priest is manipulating the words 'fiend' and 'Mystery', we may also be seduced into accepting his definition of 'holy' or 'lost'. The poem thus asks us to reflect on how officially authorized pronouncements alter language itself, and alter people's lives by means of language.

As in Blake's *Songs*, so elsewhere in Romanticism, the creative utterance of the individual and the authoritative utterance of the state or society often intersect. In Coleridge's *Kubla Khan* the paradigm of God creating the world through performative language is disturbingly echoed by Kubla Khan's 'decree' – which also results in the creation of a world, but only because the bearer of the title 'Khan' has the ability to command workers or slaves to carry out his decrees. The socio-political performatives of Kubla are set alongside the performativity of the individual poet's voice ('I would build that dome in air'), a voice which indeed 'performs' the world of the poem, yet remains disturbingly ambiguous. With the fragment unfinished and the poet metamorphosed into an awful figure of enchantment, the reader is left to wonder about the extent to which Kubla's authoritative speech acts have imposed themselves on the poetic speech act, either invalidating or corrupting it in the process. Another representation of the performative, but one that posits the triumph of the individual voice over ideological pronouncements, occurs in Shelley's *Prometheus Unbound*. Here the condition of enmity between Prometheus and Jupiter has been brought about by an explicit performative: the curse of Prometheus, an utterance that enacts what it says. The turning point of the action occurs when this curse is recalled, in the double sense of being brought back to consciousness and of being recanted or rendered invalid (Act I, lines 303–5). Shelley thematizes the event-character of utterance by making the pivotal act of the drama a speech act, while allowing the ramifications of this focus on utterance to play themselves out on other levels of the text. In other words, by focusing our attention on illocutions (primarily Prometheus's curse, but also the highly charged questions posed by Asia to Demogorgon in Act II scene iv, and Demogorgon's cryptic answers, which seem somehow to bring about the hour of Jupiter's fall), Shelley also draws our attention to the performative quality of his own utterance (i.e. the drama itself) and how it might achieve a transformation of the conditions in which it is made public.

While self-reflexive works like *Prometheus Unbound* or *Kubla Khan* are especially interesting because of the interplay between the poet's and the characters' speech acts, a more complex representation of characters' performative utterances can be found in Romantic novels. Many of these are filled with the kinds of speech acts analysed by both Austin and Searle – performatives that alter relationships, power structures or dispensations of property, and that determine the fates of individuals, including proposals, engagements, marriages, wills, deathbed requests, and promises of all kinds. Jane Austen's *Sense and Sensibility*, for example, opens with classic performatives: marriages and wills. These speech acts having set the conditions within which the rest of the novel takes place, most of the action turns on when and whether the male characters choose to 'speak' – that is, to propose marriage – and on the difference between a private understanding (such as Willoughby's lovemaking to Marianne) and a formal proposal that would constitute a public engagement, the latter being a kind of utterance that only a man has the authority to make. The question of who has the authority to perform speech acts, and why, often comes to the fore in Romantic novels and often provides a focus for studying gender relations in these texts. One of the few performatives a woman can utter successfully is a promise, since the effectiveness of the promise depends not on socio-political authority but rather on subjective authority (i.e. by the very definition of what promising is, only I can make a promise on my own behalf). Perhaps for this reason, many novels, like Charlotte Smith's *Emmeline* and Susan Ferrier's *The Inheritance*, centre on a heroine's promises.

Both public and private performatives are thematized in the novels of William Godwin, a writer who also discussed performatives explicitly in his political writing. In the *Enquiry Concerning Political Justice*, Godwin expresses his opposition to the idea that promises could be the foundation of morality (pp. 216–30) or oaths the foundation of public duty (pp. 589–93). His objection might be explained, in the context of modern speech-act theory, as a distrust of the ability of language alone to govern future conduct; Godwin believes that promises or oaths, in reaching into an unknown future, disrupt temporality and misapply the power of language, which he prefers to regard as purely descriptive or constative. In his novel *Caleb Williams* Godwin portrays the disruption unleashed by Caleb's oath that he will guard Falkland's secret, as well as the destructive power of socio-political speech acts. Caleb's identity is, as it were, imposed on him by the force of laws, judgements, warrants, false versions of his biography, and other public documents. The narrative demonstrates again and again how different contexts for utterance, such as hearings, trials and the background of class difference, work to render false statements effective and true ones ineffective. Godwin's exploration of performatives in this novel takes place on several levels: the socio-political speech acts within Caleb's story colour and are coloured by his narrative itself, which is explicitly a 'performance', the self-creation of a character (Caleb Williams) who admits from the outset to regarding his life as a 'theatre'. If we consider the entire novel also to be the public utterance of the political activist Godwin, who in his original preface declares that the text is to perform the political act of exposing 'things as they are', *Caleb Williams* acquires yet another dimension of performativity.

This interplay between what utterances do *within* the text and what the text itself does *as* utterance in a public context is one of the most significant dimensions of speech-act analysis. To put it differently, one of the most important things speech-act theory can provide for the critic and interpreter is a way of bringing the text's thematization of what language does to bear on what the text, as a social and public 'act', actually does or tries to do. And the Romantics as well as the various schools of contemporary speech-act theory recognize a wide range of things that language may do. It may, as Coleridge and Humboldt, and more recently Emile Benveniste, have recognized, generate and set conditions for individual subjectivity. As many Romantic-period writers realized, and J. L. Austin made explicit, it may enact and perpetuate socio-political authority. It may also, in exceptional or revolutionary cases, allow individuals to challenge the conventions governing socio-political speech acts by making a successful declaration, by pronouncing a curse or a promise, or perhaps by writing and publishing a literary work. The particular applicability of speech-act theory to Romantic literature lies in the Romantics' attempts to both theorize and portray the operations of what later came to be called the performative, after the politics and the philosophy of their time combined to generate an awareness of the world-changing properties of words.

## NOTES

1   In addition to the versions of speech-act theory discussed in this essay, a number of important redefinitions of the performative derive from Jacques Derrida's deconstructionist critique of Austin and Searle. In *Limited Inc*, Derrida argues that speech acts cannot, as Austin implied, be unique utterances that depend on the conscious intention of the speaker and take place within an ideal, stable context, but that the performative must always be considered as an iteration or citation that incorporates the absence of intentionality and the possibility of non-ideal contexts. Along with Michel Foucault's work on discourse and power, Derrida's notion of speech acts contributes to recent redefinitions of the performative within cultural studies and gender theory, best represented by the work of Judith Butler. Butler's post-structuralist view of performativity is radically different from speech-act theory as presented here, however, since she does not consider how the individual speaker or the individual utterance interacts with the world, but rather the power of iterative discourse to construct social norms and identities.

2   For further ramifications of de Man's view of Romanticism and the performative, see the works by Chase and Warminski in References and Further Reading.

## WRITINGS

Erdman, David V. (ed.) *The Complete Poetry and Prose of William Blake*, revd edn, Berkeley, University of California Press, 1982.

Godwin, William, *Caleb Williams*, ed. David McCracken, Oxford, Oxford University Press, 1982.

——*Enquiry Concerning Political Justice and Its Influence on Modern Morals and Happiness*, Harmondsworth, Penguin, 1985.

Humboldt, Wilhelm von, *On Language: The Diversity of Human Language-structure and Its Influence on the Mental Development of Mankind*, trans. Peter Heath, Cambridge, Cambridge University Press, 1988.

## REFERENCES AND FURTHER READING

Austin, J. L., *How to Do Things with Words*, 2nd edn, ed. J. O. Urmson and Marina Sbisà, Cambridge, Mass., Harvard University Press, 1975. Idiosyncratic and unfinished, but the foundational text of speech-act theory.

Balfour, Ian, 'Promises, promises: social and other contracts in the English Jacobins (Godwin/Inchbald)', in *New Romanticisms: Theory and Critical Practice*, ed. David L. Clark and Donald C. Goellnicht, Toronto, University of Toronto Press, 1994, pp. 225–50. Exemplary essay on speech acts in the Jacobin novel.

Benveniste, Emile, *Problems in General Linguistics*, trans. Mary Elizabeth Meek, Coral Gables, University of Miami Press, 1971.

Blakemore, Steven, *Burke and the Fall of Language: The French Revolution as Linguistic Event*, Hanover, University Press of New England, 1988.

Butler, Judith, *Bodies that Matter: On the Discursive Limits of 'Sex'*, New York, Routledge, 1993.

Chase, Cynthia, *Decomposing Figures: Rhetorical Readings in the Romantic Tradition*, Baltimore, Johns Hopkins University Press, 1986.

De Man, Paul, *Allegories of Reading: Figural Language in Rousseau, Nietzsche, Rilke, and Proust*, New Haven, Yale University Press, 1979.

Derrida, Jacques, *Limited Inc*, trans. Samuel Weber and Jeffrey Mehlman, ed. Gerald Graff, Evanston, Northwestern University Press, 1990.

Edwards, Gavin, 'Repeating the same dull round', in *Unnam'd Forms: Blake and Textuality*, ed. Nelson Hilton and Thomas A. Vogler, Berkeley, University of California Press, 1986, pp. 26–48. A speech-act approach to Blake's poetry, especially *London*.

Esterhammer, Angela, 'Speech acts and living words: on performative language in Coleridge's 1798 poems', *Wordsworth Circle* 24 (1993) 79–83.

—— 'Wordsworth's "Ode to duty": Miltonic influence and verbal performance', *Wordsworth Circle* 24 (1993) 34–7.

—— *Creating States: Studies in the Performative Language of John Milton and William Blake*, Toronto, University of Toronto Press, 1994.

Fay, Elizabeth, *Becoming Wordsworthian: A Performative Analysis*, Amherst, University of Massachusetts Press, 1995. Not on speech-act theory per se, but develops a performative concept of imagination and poetic identity.

Lyotard, Jean-François, *The Differend: Phrases in Dispute*, trans. Georges Van Den Abbeele, Minneapolis, University of Minnesota Press, 1988.

Pechey, Graham, '1789 and after: mutations of "romantic" discourse', in *1789: Reading Writing Revolution*, ed. Francis Barker et al., Colchester, University of Essex, 1982, pp. 52–66.

Petrey, Sandy, *Speech Acts and Literary Theory*, New York, Routledge, 1990. A clear, readable introduction to speech-act theory and its literary-critical applications.

Pratt, Mary Louise, *Toward a Speech Act Theory of Literary Discourse*, Bloomington, Indiana University Press, 1977. The first extended attempt to apply speech-act theory to literary criticism, especially narrative.

Searle, John R., *Speech Acts: An Essay in the Philosophy of Language*, Cambridge, Cambridge University Press, 1969. A foundational text of speech-act theory; heavily philosophical.

—— *Expression and Meaning: Studies in the Theory of Speech Acts*, Cambridge, Cambridge University Press, 1979.

Warminski, Andrzej, 'Facing language: Wordsworth's first poetic spirits', in *Romantic Revolutions: Criticism and Theory*, ed. Kenneth R. Johnston, Gilbert Chaitin, Karen Hanson and Herbert Marks, Bloomington, Indiana University Press, 1990, pp. 26–49.

# 46

# Slavery and Romantic Writing

*Alan Richardson*

The half-century – roughly from 1780 to 1830 – that witnessed the literary movement we now call Romanticism was also an era of wrenching national debate, mass boycotts and political action, and writing of many kinds concerning Britain's role in the slave trade and the institution of slavery in the British colonies. Having won the *Asiento* (the right to carry African slaves to the Spanish colonies of the New World) as part of the Treaty of Utrecht in 1713, Britain had become the dominant slave-trading nation by the late eighteenth century, and depended on the trade to restock its own West Indian plantations, where brutal treatment together with disease led to high mortality rates among the enslaved labourers.[1] By the 1780s, British ships were carrying well over 30,000 slaves yearly from Africa to the Americas, often under conditions so inhumane that a third or more of the human cargo would perish at sea or in the critical early weeks of 'seasoning' in the West Indies. The horrors of the 'Middle Passage' across the Atlantic were augmented by such spectacular acts of cruelty as the *Zong* affair of 1781, when a slaver threw a shipload of diseased slaves into the sea in order to claim the insurance on them, a scandal still preying on the national conscience in 1840 when J. M. W. Turner painted his powerful *The Slave Ship*. Plantation conditions in the West Indian 'sugar colonies' were highlighted by a series of slave revolts and rebellions, from the 'Maroon wars' (involving escaped or 'maroon' slaves as well as plantation slaves) in Jamaica and Surinam beginning early in the eighteenth century, to the bloody 'Baptist War' or Jamaican Rebellion of 1831–2. At a time when sugaring one's tea carried political and moral overtones, few could remain unaware of one of the burning contradictions of British ideology in the Romantic era. The same nation that prided itself on individual liberties was the major European trafficker in human flesh, with a colonial system increasingly dependent on slave labour.

British writers, Romantics and others, registered their opposition to (and in some cases their collusion with) the slave trade and colonial slavery in diverse ways. In *The Task* (1785), William Cowper celebrated the landmark Mansfield Judgment of 1772, which held that the slave James Somerset must be considered free on English ground: 'Slaves cannot breathe in England'. Cowper (whose friend John Newton had, before his religious conversion, himself dealt in slaves) also asked what for many was the logical next question: 'We have no slaves at home – why then abroad?' Cowper wrote some of the most memorable lyrics of the anti-slavery movement, including *The Negro's Complaint* and *Sweet Meat Has Sour Sauce, Or the Slave Trader in the Dumps* (both 1788). Cowper's lyrics, which elude any simple distinctions between poetry and propaganda, 'high' art and popular writing, were distributed in the thousands in broadside form (printed single sheets) throughout Britain, as part of the massive Abolition campaign of 1788–9. Spearheaded by the Society for the Purpose of Effecting the Abolition of the Slave Trade (formed by a coalition of Quakers and political reformers in 1787), the Abolition campaign drew in numerous writers: radicals and conservatives, men and women, established writers like Cowper and relatively obscure 'labouring-class' poets like Ann Yearsley. Significantly, a number of anti-slavery poets were associated as well with educational innovation and writing for children: Thomas Day, Hannah More, William Roscoe and Anna Barbauld most prominently. Like the children's literature of the era, anti-slavery writing could be at once vivid and didactic, and propose needed reforms while condescending to those on whose behalf those reforms were advanced.

The main outlines of anti-slavery poetry can already be seen in *The Dying Negro*, published anonymously in 1773 and composed by Thomas Day (perhaps working from a draft by John Bicknell).[2] The poem is based on a historical event that points up the inadequate enforcement of the Mansfield Judgment: the very year after its passage, a slave wishing to marry his white fellow-servant was forced onto his master's ship and committed suicide rather than return to the West Indies. Day appeals to an Enlightenment conviction of the 'rights of nature' while employing a sentimental lexicon of tears and sighs; his protagonist is a version of the stock 'noble savage' and hails from the 'wild wastes of Afric's sandy plain', the imagined Africa of popular European stereotypes.[3] The deviousness of slave traders, the brutality of the plantations, and the religious hypocrisy of slave owners (who frequently refused to let their slaves become baptized as Christians) are all given stark expression, but the slave protagonist is (typically of the genre) portrayed as passive, chained and weeping, raising a weapon not in revolt or revenge but in self-slaughter. The same constellation of images and attitudes can be found in the major anti-slavery poems of More (*Slavery*) and Yearsley (*A Poem on the Inhumanity of the Slave Trade*), although (as critics like Moira Ferguson and Anne Mellor have argued) women's anti-slavery poetry tends to place greater emphasis on the domestic.[4] These domestic images and concerns include the forced separation of African families and couples by the slave trade, the impossibility of proper domestic life under the barbarous conditions of plantation slavery, and the threat to English domestic morality posed by the cruelty, corruption and the inherent ideological contradictions of the slave trade: 'Shall Britain, where the soul of Freedom reigns, / Forge chains for others she herself disdains?' (More, *Slavery*). There are also, of course, significant differences among the women writers. Ferguson, for example, finds More's portrayal of slaves relatively abstract and dehumanizing in comparison with the vivid narratives and vignettes found throughout Yearsley's poem, and Donna Landry has credited Yearsley with a more searching critique of 'custom', moving beyond the slave system to take in English political and domestic tyranny more generally.[5]

Not all anti-slavery poetry of the era adopts uncritically the governing oppositions of what Abdul JanMohamed calls 'Manichean allegory' and Ferguson 'Anglo-Africanist rhetoric': an ideological system or discursive code in which white and black, English and African, civilized and savage, Christian and pagan, self and Other constitute the ruling polarities and define white English Christians as the norm against which the colonial 'Other' is measured and found lacking.[6] Cowper, for example, denies the validity of racial hierarchies and affirms the (literal) superficiality of racial distinctions in *The Negro's Complaint* without (unlike More in *Slavery*) reasserting racist stereotypes elsewhere in the poem. His satirical lyrics, such as *Pity for Poor Africans* and *Sweet Meat has Sour Sauce*, highlight the venality, hypocrisy and lack of humanity of slave traders and their supporters, avoiding the portrayal of African subjects altogether. Chatterton, in his earlier *African Eclogues* (1770) had even attempted a reversal of 'Manichean' polarities, aligning beauty and nobility with black skin and describing white slavers as a 'palid race' of 'Daemons'.

Perhaps the most telling attempt, however, to challenge Anglo-Africanist rhetoric from within the anti-slavery tradition is Blake's complex lyric *The Little Black Boy*, from *Songs of Innocence* (1789). The poem begins disarmingly by seeming to confirm the very polarities it will end by seeking to dissolve: 'My mother bore me in the southern wild / And I am black, but oh, my soul is white!' Deftly employing the associations and resources of the genre – religious poetry for children – that he simultaneously extends and criticizes in the *Songs of Innocence*, Blake invites the reader to interpret such statements as 'mind-forg'd manacles': Blake's phrase (from *London*) for the internalized restraints imposed by such institutions as the school, the church and (here) the colonial mission. The remembered teaching of the boy's mother in Africa ('My mother taught me underneath a tree') does not so much undo as simply reverse the hurtful oppositions of the initial stanzas, portraying 'sunburnt' black skin as protective, a sign of God's love (identified with sunlight) rather than (as the boy fears in the first stanza) 'bereaved of light'. The very fact that the mother *is* instructing her child, however, represents a telling departure from the 'untutored savage' convention employed by poets like More and Yearsley. By the end of the lyric, the child speaker is, at least tentatively, able to see black and white skin as equivalent and imagine himself in a protective, even somewhat parental relation to the white English child, though the residual sense of servitude ('I'll shade him from the heat') and the need for the white child's approval ('and he will then love me') bring the reader back to a sense of social reality and forestall the false consolations of an 'innocent' reading. Blake would develop a different but similarly complex perspective on slavery in *Visions of the Daughters of Albion* (1793), placing slavery within a larger system of British imperial tyranny, equivalent to rape, and developing suggestive analogies between colonial slavery and the oppression of women.

The outpouring of anti-slavery verse in the years 1788–9 was only one aspect of a campaign that also included the distribution of thousands of prose tracts, the widespread purchase and display of the anti-slavery emblem (designed by Josiah Wedgwood), mass petitions, the parliamentary efforts led by William Wilberforce, and the relentless (and sometimes dangerous) pursuit of evidence on the slave trade by Thomas Clarkson. Clarkson published two important anti-slavery works in 1788–9 alone, the *Essay on the Impolicy of the Slave Trade* and the *Substance of the Evidence of Sundry Persons on the Slave-Trade*; notable prose tracts were contributed by John Newton (who could draw chillingly on his former career as a slaver) and by Clarkson himself, who abstracted his evidence on the slave trade for wider circulation in *A Summary View of the Slave Trade* (1787). Former slaves, thousands of whom settled in England, also wrote against the trade that had victimized them, claiming the authority of first-hand experience and, by the very act of writing, putting notions of African inferiority and mental 'savagery' into question. Ottabah

Cugoano's *Thoughts and Sentiments on the Evil and Wicked Traffic of the Slavery and Commerce of the Human Species* (1787) advances a number of abolitionist arguments on both rational and religious grounds, appealing to 'universal natural rights' as well as to Christian sentiment.[7] It also includes a brief and affecting account of Cugoano's childhood in Africa and his capture and deportation, which allows him to address some of the myths and exaggerations concerning Africa taken for granted by many abolitionist (not to mention pro-slavery) writers. Cugoano's associate Olaudah Equiano contributed a much more extensive autobiography in 1789, *The Interesting Narrative of the Life of Olaudah Equiano, or Gustavus Vassa, the African*, addressed to parliament, and detailing the 'horrors of [the] trade' as well as the author's pursuit of literacy and freedom. Equiano's engaging and popular book helped to codify a new genre, the slave narrative, that constitutes an important and frequently overlooked tradition within Romantic-era British literature, from the *Narrative of the Remarkable Particulars in the Life of James Albert Ukawsow Gronniosaw, An African Prince* (c. 1770) to the cogent and often harrowing *History of Mary Prince, a West Indian Slave* (1831).

The Abolition society and its many allies seemed on the verge of a parliamentary victory by the close of the 1780s, but the political unrest inspired by the French Revolution, greatly heightened in relation to the slavery question by the successful slave revolution in Saint Domingue (Haiti), contributed toward a new atmosphere of anxiety, caution and temporizing. Edmund Burke, who had compared the French revolutionaries to a 'gang of Maroon slaves' in his *Reflections on the Revolution in France*, withdrew his support of the Abolition movement, and by 1792 was arguing for a 'regulated and reformed' slave system.[8] Wilberforce's abolition bill was defeated in 1791, and the bill for gradual abolition passed the next year was calculated to preserve the status quo indefinitely. England would continue to trade in human flesh until 1807. The anger and dismay felt by the opponents of slavery starkly emerge in Anna Barbauld's *Epistle* to Wilberforce *On the Rejection of the Bill for Abolishing the Slave Trade* (1792): 'Still Afric bleeds; / Unchecked, the human traffic still proceeds'. Barbauld's epistle links the dehumanizing effects of West Indian slavery to the evils of British tyranny in India and the 'east', placing the slave system (as had Day in the preface to *The Dying Negro*) in the global context of British empire building. Like Day, too, Barbauld ends with a prophecy of vengeance on the part of the oppressed, brought about not through the direct political action seen in Saint Domingue, however, but through the corruption of the British themselves by the indirect effects of colonial domination: 'By foreign wealth are British morals changed / And Afric's sons, and India's, smile avenged'. In her concern with the 'contagion' of African slavery, with the 'voluptuous' habits of the West Indian planters and their 'monstrous' wives, with the 'luxurious plague' emanating from Britain's colonies in the 'gay east', Barbauld's condemnation of imperial domination can be seen as partly motivated by anxieties concerning Britain's 'exotic' colonial dependencies – and Britain's growing economic dependency on them.[9] Barbauld's republican fears for British morals should not be simply conflated with the reactionary hysteria of such as Clara Reeve, who worried in the same year that the West Indian slaves, having risen against their masters and 'cut their throats', would descend upon England, 'mix with the natives, and spoil the breed of the common people' (*Plans of Education*, 1792), nor prevent us from appreciating the sincerity and political courage with which the Abolition cause was fought.[10] But Barbauld's images of disease and contagion do help underscore how anti-colonial and anti-slavery ideologies in this period could include xenophobic and even racist elements, from condescending images of noble savagery to fears of racial contamination.

Nothing like this initial outpouring of anti-slavery literature followed the temporary defeat of the cause in 1791, but various writers helped keep the Abolition movement alive and in the public eye over the next 15 years. Robert Southey, for example, published a series of 'Poems Concerning the Slave Trade' from 1794 to 1798, supporting the popular boycott against West Indian sugar, celebrating the Haitian revolution in *To the Genius of Africa*, and refurbishing the less threatening Abolitionist icons of the weeping lover, the sinking slave ship, and the bound and dying slave. William Wordsworth also helped counter the widespread demonization of the Haitian revolutionaries or 'black Jacobins' in his admiring sonnet *To Toussaint L'Ouverture* of 1802, a powerful poem that can also be seen as a particularly complex variation on the 'dying slave' theme. Thomas Campbell roundly condemns slavery in *The Pleasures of Hope* (1799), though he includes a stock description of the black African as 'artless savage' and calls elsewhere in the poem for the global spread of European culture and 'Improvement' to sub-Saharan Africa and other 'wild' regions. Coleridge lectured against the slave trade – in Bristol, still an important slaving port – in 1795, and published a version of his lecture the next year in *The Watchman*. His great poem *The Rime of the Ancyent Marinere* (1798) which, as J. L. Lowes demonstrated long ago, is replete with references and allusions to colonial exploration, 'exotic' histories and travellers' tales, bears an oblique but demonstrable relation to British national guilt over the slave trade and imperial anxieties more generally. Southey's ballad *The Sailor who had Served in the Slave-Trade*, written later in the same year and evoking the sort of evidence collected and disseminated by Clarkson, also features a mariner who has 'done a cursed thing' at sea, has since lived in a restless agony of remorse, and compulsively tells his tale in hope of absolution. Southey's ballad asks to be read as a gloss on or rejoinder to Coleridge's much more celebrated poem, which can neither be reduced to an allegory of the slave trade nor altogether detached from the issues of colonial violence and British culpability that poems like Barbauld's *Epistle* and Southey's *The Sailor* address head on.

The long-deferred success of Abolition legislation in 1807 inspired a number of works that looked back on the efforts to end the slave trade – and forward to the renewed struggle for emancipation of slaves throughout the British colonies. Wilberforce published his *Letter on the Abolition of the Slave Trade*, explaining to his constituents of Hull (and to the nation at large) why he had devoted his career to Abolition. Wordsworth wrote a congratulatory sonnet to Clarkson, with its memorable line 'The blood-stained Writing is forever torn'. The next year, Clarkson himself brought out his *History of the Rise, Progress and Accomplishment of the Abolition of the African Slave-Trade by the British Parliament*, summing up two decades of Abolitionist work and laying the groundwork for the Emancipation agitation to come (he and Wilberforce would help found the Anti-Slavery Society in 1823). James Montgomery contributed his anti-slavery epic poem *The West Indies* to a collective volume published in 1809 to commemorate the Abolition bill; Montgomery portrays the sugar cane as the Tree of Good and Evil for his age, tracing the progress of slavery from the Spanish conquest of the Americas to British abolition in 1807, and prophesying continued slave revolts ('Tremble, Britannia') so long as colonial slavery persists.

After Montgomery, anti-slavery poetry markedly fell off. Byron and Shelley made their opposition to colonial slavery clear, but neither wrote a poem against slavery per se. It seems likely, however, that Byron's depiction of 'Oriental' slavery in poems like *The Giaour*, *Don Juan* and *Sardanapalus* can be meaningfully related to contemporary representations of slavery in the British colonies, and that the figure of Shelley's Prometheus, bound and tortured by a soulless tyrant, bears a more than incidental resemblance to the iconography of anti-slavery literature.[11] Keats, despite his liberal views, did not write against slavery; nor did Felicia Hemans, despite the global reach of her poetic subject matter. Perhaps colonial slavery seemed a less 'poetic' theme than had the slave trade, or Emancipation a less pressing cause than Abolition. More likely, as Montgomery suggested in the preface to *The West Indies*, 20 years of Abolitionist poetry had 'exhausted' the subject and left the reading public 'wearied into insensibility' by over-exposure to the horrifying and frequently 'disgusting' details of the slave system.[12] Popular sentiment against slavery remained strong, however, despite attempts (by William Cobbett among others) to turn the lower classes against the anti-slavery movement, which allegedly gave philanthropists and reformers a conveniently distant object of concern while obscuring the plight of the British working poor. Legislation ending colonial slavery was passed by parliament in 1833, and emancipation took effect the next year.

If the anti-slavery movement involved a contest for popular sentiment, it also became entangled in struggles over popular readerships. The full success of Abolitionist propaganda depended on its ability to appeal to the emergent mass reading audience as well as to the smaller existing audience for 'high' poetry and, as we have seen, poets like Cowper and Blake responded by writing (sometimes self-reflexively) in popular idioms. Others attempted a more wholesale adaptation of popular genres, especially the broadside ballad and the vernacular tale, both to disseminate a simplified version of anti-slavery ideology more widely across class lines, and to provide lower-class readers with a cause that entailed meaningful reform without (it was hoped) rousing the revolutionary spirit causing such spectacular upheaval in France – and Haiti. Hannah More, for example, included *The Sorrows of Yamba, or the Negro Woman's Lamentation* (c. 1795) in her series of 'Cheap Repository Tracts', a venture that also featured such patently reactionary titles as *The Riot; or, Half a Loaf Is Better Than No Bread* and *Patient Joe; or, The Newcastle Collier*. Written in imitation of the popular ballad, *The Sorrows of Yamba* seems intended to have a double effect on its (presumed) lower-class reader. It neatly points up the basic ideological contradiction of British slave trading ('Ye that "Never will be slaves", / Bid poor Afric's land be free') and raises Christian compassion for a superficially exotic other, in fact less 'savage' than the slavers who kidnap her. But it also underscores the consolations of religion, the passive acceptance of God's will ('Gracious Heaven's mysterious plan'), and the superiority of even a British labourer's harsh life to that of a slave ('Once I was as blessed as you'). This same dual purpose – raising equal measures of compassion and complacency, inspiring reformist zeal while preaching political quiescence – informs the prose tracts that More wrote or commissioned for the Cheap Repository from 1795–8, such as *The Black Prince*, a 'true story' of the life of an African prince transported to England in the early 1790s, which owes more to the popular Protestant conversion narrative than to writers like Cugoano and Equiano, and the *True Account of a Pious Negro*, which similarly softens the evils of slavery with the consolations of religion.

Maria Edgeworth also advances a dual agenda in her story *The Grateful Negro*, one of the *Popular Tales* she published in 1804 as an experiment in writing for new readerships (from the 'middling' as well as lower classes). Set in Jamaica with its history of slave rebellions and maroon revolts, the tale advocates the amelioration and gradual phasing out of the slavery system rather than 'sudden emancipation'. It contrasts the management styles of the enlightened and compassionate Edwards, who treats his slaves humanely and allows them plots to work on their own (to generate some spending money and give them their own small stake in the plantation system), with the cruel slave-driver Jeffries, whose harsh and shortsighted policies help foment plots of a different sort. Inspired by obeah, an Afro-Caribbean religion (roughly analogous to voodoo) that had become associated in the British mind with 'African' savagery and slave rebellion, the slaves on Jeffries' plantation band together to murder every white on the island. The 'grateful negro' of the title, however, reveals the plot to Edwards, who helps put down the insurrection and restore harmony to the island. The message to British labourers is obvious enough: violent rebellion is associated with African savagery, and political change should occur gradually, through reforms led by a paternalistic professional class working for the 'mental improvement' of slaves and free labourers alike.[13]

Harriet Martineau, in her *Illustrations of Political Economy* (1832–4), also sought to reach new reading audiences through adapting political and social ideas to fictional form. *Demerara: A Tale*, issued in 1832, is set in British Guiana and makes explicit allusion to the major slave insurrection there in 1823. It makes its case against slavery primarily on economic grounds, developing the arguments of Adam Smith and others that slavery is not only more brutal than a system based on free wage labour, but less efficient and more costly as well. Martineau takes a dim and demeaning view of the 'characteristics of Negro minds and manners', but attributes the slaves' alleged 'vices and follies' not to racial or cultural factors, but to the demoralizing effects of slavery itself. Like Edgeworth, Martineau emphasizes the need to appeal to the labourer's 'self-interest' by giving him a stake in the plantation enterprise (even if that stake is only to maximize his wages). Martineau also, with the consistency that is one of her more winning characteristics, argues on *laissez-faire* grounds against the sugar subsidy that helps maintain colonial slavery. Unlike Edgeworth, Martineau is willing to see a swift end to the slave system, and adds to her utilitarian arguments a Christian appeal, asking how slavery will appear 'at the end of time'.[14]

Slavery also left its mark on the novel and the popular stage of the era. In Edgeworth's *Belinda* (1801), for example, one of the heroine's suitors, Mr Vincent, is a West Indian heir who has been morally tainted by his colonial upbringing, though he is by no means without virtue (at one point he wins Belinda's approval by reciting Day's *The Dying Negro*); Vincent is accompanied by an excessively loyal, childlike slave named Juba, who (in a comic subplot) learns to control, if not quite overcome, his terror of obeah. Amelia Opie includes a more sympathetic former slave, Savanna, in *Adeline Mowbray* (1804), who is in many ways the book's most virtuous character, yet remains childlike in speech and in her very attachment to the heroine. Even in novels which do not feature slaves or former slaves or lengthy discussions of abolition, the slave system can make its presence felt: Jane Austen's *Mansfield Park* has been read (by Ferguson and Edward Said, among others) as an oblique response to the moral dilemma posed by slavery and colonialism, set as it is primarily in an English estate supported by revenues from an Antiguan plantation. Debates on slavery, abolition and emancipation were given dramatic form on the London stage, where popular audiences could be addressed directly, bypassing the medium of print. Plays like Thomas Bellamy's *The Benevolent Planters* (which premiered at the Haymarket in 1789) gave an idealized picture of plantation slavery and implied that slaves were better off in the hands of sentimental Christian proprietors than in the wilds of barbarous Africa. *Obi; or Three-Fingered Jack*, a popular melodrama (attributed to John Fawcett) first performed at the Covent Garden in 1800, capitalized on fears of slave revolts and features an escaped slave, living as a Maroon, who plunders the white community with the help of an obeah woman, though Jack (a rather sophisticated and unexpectedly sympathetic materialist thinker) holds himself above the superstitions he manipulates. *Furibond, or Harlequin Negro*, a Christmas pantomime performed at the Drury Lane in 1807, demonstrates how anti-slavery could become co-opted by patriotic propaganda, once legislation against the slave trade had been passed: it heralds the gradual phasing out of slavery under the aegis of a benign and morally regenerated 'Britannia', while simultaneously indulging in the sort of comic black stereotypes that would become staples of the minstrel show later in the nineteenth century.

Martineau's anti-slavery arguments in *Demerara* and the celebration of British moral ascendancy in *Furibond* look forward, as does Emancipation itself, to a new British imperial ideology, one that would stress commerce and free labour over slavery and other overt forms of coercion (though the practical administration of empire would continue to rely on force). It would be wrong, however, to conclude that the anti-slavery movement was merely cant, and that British writers and activists opposed slavery only or even primarily on economic and self-interested grounds. As David Brion Davis has argued, the Atlantic slave system 'had never appeared so prosperous' and profitable as during the late eighteenth century, when anti-slavery arguments (and literature) were first widely disseminated.[15] To argue that the acts of conscience embodied in anti-slavery work and writing can be largely reduced to anxieties concerning miscegenation or racial contamination would similarly do scant justice to the historical record.[16] Radicals and liberals promoting a universalistic conception of human rights, Quakers and Evangelical Christians (like Wilberforce and More) writing and acting from deep religious conviction, former slaves (like Cugoano, Equiano and Prince) working to help free those still in captivity, do not ask to be written off as cunning or unwitting apologists for an ascendant *laissez-faire* ideology. Nevertheless, the literature of the anti-slavery movement did register fear of racial contamination, promote demeaning stereotypes of Africa and Africans, and appeal to readers' crass economic self-interest. Anti-slavery literature was neither written in widespread collusion (naive or cynical) with the progress of empire, nor was it hermetically sealed off from the colonialist, racist and economic discourses and projects of its time. Considering anti-slavery writing in relation to British Romanticism similarly brings out contrasting aspects of the Romantic tradition: its association with individualism, democratic principles and human sympathy on the one hand, and such tendencies as primitivism, exoticism and the overvaluation of racial and cultural differences on the other. The anti-slavery writing of the Romantic era fully shares in the ambivalence and contradictions of its times, and reveals unique and important dimensions to the links between Romanticism and its social and historical contexts.

## NOTES

1  For a recent and comprehensive account of the Atlantic slave trade, anti-slavery agitation and slave resistance movements in this era, see Blackburn, *The Overthrow of Colonial Slavery.*

2  For surveys of anti-slavery literature in this era, see Sypher, *Guinea's Captive Kings,* and Dykes, *The Negro in Romantic Thought.*

3  Day, *The Dying Negro,* p. iii.

4  Ferguson, *Subject to Others;* Mellor, 'Am I not a Woman', pp. 311–29. For women's significant involvement in the anti-slavery movement, see also Colley, *Britons,* pp. 273–81.

5  Ferguson, *Subject to Others,* pp. 170–2; Landry, *The Muses of Resistance,* p. 238.

6  Ferguson, *Subject to Others,* p. 5; JanMohamed, 'The economy of Manichean allegory', pp. 78–106.

7  Cugoano, *Thoughts and Sentiments,* p. 30.

8  Burke, *Reflections on the Revolution in France,* quoted in Blackburn, *Overthrow,* p. 148.

9  See Coleman, 'Conspicuous consumption'.

10  Clara Reeve, *Plans of Education; With Remarks on the Systems of Other Writers,* ed. Gina Luria, New York, Garland, 1974, p. 91.

11  These issues remain largely unexplored by critics, though Joan Baum lays the groundwork, especially in relation to Byron, in *Mind-Forg'd Manacles.*

12  Montgomery, *Poetical Works,* pp. 16–17.

13  Maria Edgeworth, *Popular Tales,* 'New Edition', London, Simpkin, Marshall, 1854, pp. 399–414.

14  Harriet Martineau, *Demerara: A Tale,* Boston, Leonard C. Bowles, 1832.

15  Davis, 'At the heart of slavery'.

16  See, for example, Coleman, 'Conspicuous consumption'.

## WRITINGS

Cugoano, Ottabah, *Thoughts and Sentiments on the Evil and Wicked Traffic of the Slavery and Commerce of the Human Species,* London, 1787.

Day, Thomas, *The Dying Negro: A Poem,* 3rd edn, London, W. Flexney, 1775.

Equiano, Olaudah, *The Interesting Narrative of the Life of Olaudah Equiano;* and Mary Prince, *The History of Mary Prince, The Classic Slave Narratives,* ed. Henry Louis Gates, Jr, New York, New American Library, 1987.

Montgomery, James, *The Poetical Works of James Montgomery: Collected By Himself,* London, Longman, 1850.

More, Hannah, *Slavery: A Poem,* London, T. Cadell, 1788.

## REFERENCES AND FURTHER READING

Anstey, Roger, *The Atlantic Slave Trade and British Abolition 1760–1810,* London, MacMillan, 1975.

Baum, Joan, *Mind-Forg'd Manacles: Slavery and the English Romantic Poets,* North Haven, Archon Books, 1994.

Blackburn, Robin, *The Overthrow of Colonial Slavery 1776–1848,* London, Verso, 1988.

Coleman, Deirdre, 'Conspicuous consumption: white abolitionism and English women's protest writing in the 1790s', *ELH* 61 (1994) 341–62.

Colley, Linda, *Britons: Forging the Nation 1707–1807,* New Haven, Yale University Press, 1992.

Davis, David Brion, *The Problem of Slavery in the Age of Revolution 1770–1823,* Ithaca, Cornell University Press, 1975.

——'At the heart of slavery', *New York Review of Books,* 17 October, 1996, 51–4.

Dykes, Eva Beatrice, *The Negro in Romantic Thought: A Study in Sympathy for the Oppressed,* Washington, Associated Publishers, 1942.

Ebbatson, J. R., 'Coleridge's mariner and the rights of man', *Studies in Romanticism* 11 (1972) 171–206.

Empson, William, 'The Ancient Mariner', in *Argufying: Essays on Literature and Culture,* ed. John Haffenden, Iowa City, University of Iowa Press, 1987, 297–319.

Ferguson, Moira, '*Mansfield Park:* Slavery, colonialism, and gender', *Oxford Literary Review* 13 (1991) 118–39.

——*Subject to Others: British Women Writers and Colonial Slavery, 1670–1834*, New York, Routledge, 1992.

James, C. L. R., *The Black Jacobins: Toussaint L'Ouverture and the San Domingo Revolution*, 2nd edn, New York, Vintage, 1963.

JanMohamed, Abdul R., 'The economy of Manichean allegory: the function of racial difference in colonialist literature', in *'Race', Writing, and Difference*, ed. Henry Louis Gates, Jr, Chicago, University of Chicago Press, 1986, pp. 78–106.

Keane, Patrick J., *Coleridge's Submerged Politics: The Ancient Mariner and Robinson Crusoe*, Columbia, University of Missouri Press, 1994.

Landry, Donna, *The Muses of Resistance: Labouring-class Women's Poetry in Britain, 1739–1796*, Cambridge, Cambridge University Press, 1990.

Mellor, Anne K., '"Am I not a woman, and a sister"?: slavery, Romanticism, and gender', in *Romanticism, Race, and Imperial Culture: 1780–1834*, ed. Alan Richardson and Sonia Hofkosh, Bloomington, Indiana University Press, 1996, pp. 311–29.

Richardson, Alan, 'Colonialism, race, and lyric irony in Blake's "The Little Black Boy"', *Papers on Language and Literature* 26 (1990) 191–211.

——'Romantic voodoo: Obeah and British culture, 1797–1807', *Studies in Romanticism* 32 (1993) 3–28.

——'Darkness visible? Race and representation in Bristol abolitionist poetry, 1770–1810', *The Wordsworth Circle* 27 (1996) 67–72.

Said, Edward W., *Culture and Imperialism*, New York, Vintage, 1994.

Sypher, Wylie, *Guinea's Captive Kings: British Anti-Slavery Literature of the XVIII Century*, Chapel Hill, University of North Carolina Press, 1942.

Walvin, James, *England, Slaves and Freedom, 1776–1838*, Jackson, University Press of Mississippi, 1986.

Ware, Malcolm, 'Coleridge's "Spectre-bark": a slave ship?', *Philological Quarterly* 40 (1961) 589–93.

# 47

# Apocalypse and Millennium

## Morton D. Paley

In *A Discourse on the Love of Our Country* (1789), the address that drew Edmund Burke's rage in *Reflections on the Revolution in France*, Dr Richard Price represented the light kindled by the American Revolution as 'reflected to FRANCE, and there kindled into a blaze, that lays despotism in ashes, and warms and illuminates EUROPE!' Joseph Priestley's Unitarian sermon of 1794, *The present state of Europe compared with Ancient Prophecies*, viewed the millennial passages in Isaiah as close to historical fulfilment. The radical Thomas Holcroft, jubilant over the publication of *The Rights of Man*, wrote to William Godwin: 'Hey for the New Jerusalem! The millennium! And eternal beautitude be unto the soul of Thomas Paine'. In the late eighteenth and early nineteenth centuries, many sympathizers with the revolutions of their time (whatever their religious beliefs might be) found appropriate historical models in the biblical concepts of apocalypse and millennium, and this was also true of the poets. In the writings of all the major Romantics we find these themes, however much displaced, and the relationship between them as important subjects. *Apocalypse* is in this sense closely related to its etymological meaning, the Greek word for lifting a lid or a covering veil, as in the New Testament Book of Revelation. In that book, the Millennium signifies the thousand-year reign of Christ and his resurrected saints, prior to the loosing of Satan, Armageddon and the descent of the New Jerusalem. In the various works of the poets, however, the last of these events tends to be conflated with the Millennium, which no longer retains the meaning of a thousand years. Furthermore, the question of whether apocalypse will necessarily be succeeded by millennium becomes an important concern.

In William Blake's Lambeth books, written in the 1790s, apocalypse and millennium are seen as events taking place in the here and now and as inextricably linked with the revolutions of the late eighteenth century. *America: a Prophecy* (1793–4) is a prime example. The forces of revolution are personified in Orc, who in one of his aspects is the Christ of the Parousia predicted in Matthew 24: 30: 'And then shall appear the sign of the Son of Man in heaven . . . and they shall see the Son of Man coming in the clouds of heaven with power and great glory'. Orc appears flaming out of the sea at the beginning of the American Revolution:

> Intense! naked! a Human fire fierce glowing, as the wedge
> Of iron heated in the furnace; his terrible limbs were fire (4: 8–9)

In Orc's subsequent speech of deliverance, imagery associated with the resurrection of Jesus – 'The grave is burst, the spices shed, the linen wrapped up' (6: 2) – is used to figure the emancipation of humanity. Freed from chains and dungeons (images that, like much else in *America*, are more frequently associated with the French than the American Revolution), the former captives emerge into a millennial world where, Orc proclaims, 'Empire is no more, and now the Lion & Wolf shall cease' (6: 15). However, this declaration is proleptic: the Revolution remains to be fought and a millennial society achieved. The adversary in this conflict is Albion's Angel, at the same time the King of England and vice-regent to the principle of repression Blake calls Urizen. In a passage tinged with ironies, Albion's angel accuses Orc of being the great red dragon of Revelation 12: 3–4, who 'stood before the woman which was ready to be delivered, for to devour her child, as soon as it was born'.

> ... Art thou not Orc, who serpent-form'd
> Stands at the gate of Enitharmon to devour her children;
> Blasphemous Demon, Antichrist, hater of Dignities;
> Lover of wild rebellion, and transgressor of God's Law;
> Why dost thou come to Angels' eyes in this terrific form? (7: 3–7)

Part of the irony lies in the full-page design on which this text appears. We see two children sleeping with a ram under a graceful birch tree, with birds of paradise sitting on its branches against a radiant background. Vine leaves prominent at the left and right suggest, as often in Blake's iconography, Christ the True Vine (cf. John 15: 1). This is a foreshadowing of the world announced by Orc, undermining the Herodian fulminations of Albion's Angel. Yet in a further irony Orc does not deny his serpentine identity, but rather inverts the meaning conventionally associated with it:

> The terror answered: I am Orc, wreath'd round the accursed tree:
> The times are ended, shadows pass the morning 'gins to break ...

Blake appropriates the serpent to the cause of revolution, much as Shelley would do later, and perhaps with a nod to the Vermont Snake Flag with its legend 'Don't Tread on Me'. Orc in his human form appears as a Promethean firebearer; as a serpent twining round the tree bearing fruit denied to humanity in the Garden of Eden, he bears the promise of a new society as in Shelley's great 'Chorus' at the end of *Hellas*: 'The earth doth like a snake renew / Her winter weeds outworn'. These two aspects of Orc, human and serpent, seem compatible in *America*, both involved in the outbreak of apocalyptic revolution and the promulgation of millennial dawn.

Blake's confidence in the French Revolution as an apocalypse preceding an imminent millennium did not survive the Reign of Terror. In *Europe* (1794) a huge Orc serpent appears on the title page, its folds suggestive of the cycle of history into which revolutionary energy is now bound, and on the last pages of text

> ... terrible Orc, when he beheld the morning in the east,
> Shot from the heights of Enitharmon;
> And in the vineyards of red France appear'd the light of his fury. (14: 37–15: 2)

This is a travesty of the beginning of the part of the poem called *A Prophecy*, where, in imitation of Milton's *Ode on the Morn of Christ's Nativity*,

> The deep of winter came;
> What time the secret child,
> Descended thro' the orient gates of the eternal day:
> War ceas'd, & all the troops like shadows fled to their abodes. (3: 1–4)

Far from being a saviour bringing peace, Orc is now a participant in 'the strife of blood'. His association with the grape harvest indeed alludes to the angel of Revelation 14: 19 who 'thrust his sickle into the earth, and gathered the vine of the earth, and cast it into the great winepress of the wrath of God'. Yet the transformed world figured in the new heaven and new earth of Revelation 21 and prophesied in Orc's speech in *America* is no longer glimpsed in *Europe*, which presents apocalypse without millennium.

Nevertheless, Blake was not yet ready to abandon a linkage between the two. In the epic poem he began as *Vala* in the later 1790s and abandoned some ten years later, Orc begins once more as the hero who might bring in a new age for humankind. Before the end of the poem, however, he is once more transformed into a serpent as France follows the course of military expansion, and he is represented in terms of the beast of Revelation 17, upon whom rides 'the whore that sitteth upon many waters' (17: 1). In the great culmination of the poem, 'Night the Ninth / Being / The Last Judgement', Orc has no active role and is burned away, upon which 'The flames rolling intense thro' the wide Universe / Began to Enter the Holy City' (119: 16–17). Some of the verse describing the consequent millennial transformation is among the most magnificent Blake ever wrote; however, both apocalypse and millennium are now divorced from history. As Northrop Frye puts it, 'The Last Judgment simply starts off with a bang, as an instinctive shudder of self-preservation against a tyranny of intolerable menace' (*Fearful Symmetry*, p. 308). Blake himself must have seen the arbitrariness of such a solution, along with the impossibility of seeking a socio-political millennium in the early nineteenth century. Although his work never abandons contact with history, in his other two late long poems, *Milton* and *Jerusalem*, the emphasis is on the inner self. The regeneration of the world is now seen as a consequence of the regeneration of the human identity – individual in *Milton*, collective in *Jerusalem*.

The relation between Blake's two last great illuminated books has, because of the length and scope of each, been compared to that between Milton's 'brief epic', *Paradise Regained* and his twelve-book *Paradise Lost*. In *Milton* Blake himself is a protagonist, becoming one with Milton when the latter falls from the heavens as a star and enters Blake's left foot (his material identity). Taken up into the halls of Los, the poetic imagination, Blake is presented with a vision of the contemporary world in which 'there is no end to destruction' owing to the failures of the prophetic figures of the eighteenth century to effect its transformation. 'Swedenborg! strongest of men' became 'the Samson shorn by the Churches!' because he fell into the error of 'Shewing the Transgressors in Hell, the proud Warriors in Heaven: / Heaven as a Punisher & Hell as One under Punishment' (22 [24]: 50–2). Whitfield and Wesley, the founders of Methodism, performed 'Miracles' in devoting 'Their lifes entire comfort to intire scorn & injury & death' (23 [25]: 2), but, their faith rejected by society at large, they are identified with the two prophetic witnesses of Revelation 11: 3–12, who are to be killed by the beast from the bottomless pit. 'The Witnesses lie dead in the Street of the Great City / No Faith is in all the Earth: the Book of God is trodden under Foot' (22 [24]: 60). In such a world crying out to be delivered, Milton/Blake is the messenger of the Last Judgement.

The crucial visionary moment of *Milton* takes place in the garden of the cottage in Felpham, the Sussex village in which the Blakes lived from 1800 to 1803. Milton and his female aspect, the six-fold Emanation Ololon (comprising John Milton's wives and daughters) combine, Jesus the Saviour becomes manifest, and Blake undergoes an experience very like death:

> I fell outstretchd upon the path
> A moment, & my Soul returned into its mortal state
> To Resurrection & Judgment in the Vegetable Body (42 [49]: 25–7)

This apocalyptic episode in the little world of man is paralleled by external events, 'the Great Harvest & Vintage of the Nations' (43 [50]: 1) as in Revelation. Whether millennium – or anything else – may follow this apocalypse is not stated, nor is the cause-and-effect relationship between the individual and the social defined. True, *Milton* has a social texture. The French wars with their terrible human cost are linked with domestic repression:

> The Wine-press on the Rhine groans loud, but all its central beams
> Act more terrific in the central Cities of the Nations
> Where Human Thought is crushed beneath the iron hand of Power. (25 [27]: 3–5)

And on the penultimate page, 'Los listens to the Cry of the Poor Man: his Cloud over London in volume terrific, low bended in anger' (42 [49]: 34–5). We might say that the power of analogy is what yokes these two aspects of reality, as in Shelley's *Prometheus Unbound* the Moon becomes inhabitable after Jupiter's tyranny is overthrown. Although the structure of 27 'Churches' of history revolving in an eternal circle seems to condemn humanity to a nightmare of historical recurrence, there is nevertheless room for individual egress each time the Lark, Los's visionary messenger, mounts. A single line ending the poem – 'To go forth to the Great Harvest & Vintage of the Nations' – adumbrates what is to follow. Yet how we are to get from individual to collective illumination is a subject left to be developed in *Jerusalem*.

In *Jerusalem* history takes place during the sleep of the patriarchal giant Albion. Los, now William Blake in his prophetic mode, struggles to save the sleeper from destruction by his own sons and daughters, but Los is himself divided from his Spectre (reasoning power) and his Emanation (female counterpart). Only when Los's powers are unified can he bring about the awakening of Albion, and this does not occur until near the end of the poem. At this point Blake can exclaim with John of Patmos 'Time was finished' (cf. Revelation 10: 6). This apocalyptic moment is represented, as so often by Blake, in terms of morning:

> The Breath Divine went forth over the morning hills. Albion rose
> In anger: the wrath of God breaking bright flaming on all sides around
> His awful limbs: into the Heavens he walked clothed in flames
> Loud thundering, with broad flashes of lightning & pillars
> Of fire, speaking the Words of Eternity in Human Forms, in direful
> Revolutions of Action & Passion, thro the Four Elements on all sides
> Surrounding his awful Members. (95: 5–11)

Typical of Blake's imagination is the emphasis upon activity. The millennial world will be a place not of stasis but of the display of intellectual energy, as the dynamism of the syntax in the passage above and in the last pages of text generally indicates. Also typical is the persistence of the city. Like John's New Jerusalem in chapter 21 of Revelation, Blake's 'Spiritual Fourfold London', Golgonooza, does not fade away in the millennium but maintains its physical reality, and in the final design (plate 100) it forms the backdrop for the harmonious activity of Los, Enitharmon and the Spectre as they give material form to humanity and to the workings of the universe.

Blake was steeped in biblical tradition and symbols from the Old and New Testaments came to him as spontaneously as the imagery of his daily surroundings. The Romantic poet closest to him in this respect is the early Coleridge. Where Blake was by temperament a non-joiner – his only link with an association was a very brief and loose one with the Swedenborgians – Coleridge became a Unitarian and even preached as a Unitarian minister. Nevertheless, their poetic conceptions of apocalypse and millennium, especially in the 1790s, are remarkably similar. A case in point is Coleridge's *Religious Musings*, begun according to his account on Christmas Eve of 1794 and referred to early on as 'The Nativity'. Worked on over the course of the next year and into 1796, it became one of Coleridge's longest poems, an ambitious projection of modern secular history against the background of sacred history and prophecy. At certain points the text makes explicit contact with that of Revelation, as lines 304–15 with Revelation 6:

> The Lamb of God hath opened the fifth seal:
> And upward rush on swiftest wing of fire
> The innumerable multitude of wrongs
> By man on man inflicted! . . .
> . . .
> And lo! the Great, the Rich, the Mighty Men,
> The Kings and the Chief Captains of the World,
> With all that fixed on high like stars of Heaven
> Shot baleful influence, shall be cast to earth,
> Vile and down-trodden, as the untimely fruit
> Shook from the fig-tree by a sudden storm.
> Even now the storm begins . . .

Coleridge notes that this passage alludes to the French Revolution, but it's important to recognize that this passage, like Blake's Lambeth prophecies, is written retrospectively. Post-dating the Reign of Terror and coinciding with the Directory, the latter part of *Religious Musings* goes on to impose a Millennium upon recalcitrant history. 'While as the Thousand Years / Lead up their mystic dance, the Desert shouts!' (359–60). Milton becomes the angel who blows the trumpet of the first resurrection, and Newton and Priestley are among those who arise. One senses the poem rushing toward a willed climax when the throne of God descends 'flashing unimaginable day' (400), and no description of the New Jerusalem follows.

In other poems of the 1790s Coleridge elaborates on aspects of the linked themes of apocalypse, millennium and revolution. In *To a Young Lady, with a Poem on the French Revolution* (1794), Freedom is personified as if a female version of Orc, who 'With giant Fury burst her triple chain!' (18); while the poet imagines himself as a rider of the Apocalypse:

> Red from the Tyrant's wound I shook the lance,
> And strode in joy the reeking plains of France! (25–6)

Yet Coleridge had to confront the fact that in contemporary history there was plenty of material for apocalypse but very little for millennium. One solution he contemplated, with Robert Southey and other friends, was the establishment of a Utopia called Pantisocracy in America on the banks of the Susquehanna River, a society that would be a microcosm of the millennial community. This was never realized, but Coleridge continued for a time to attach millennial associations to personal relationships, and especially to his marriage to Sara Fricker. At the end of *Reflections on Having Left a Place of Retirement* (1794) his thought moves outward to the world from the cottage he and Sara shared:

> Ah! – had none greater! And that all had such!
> It might be so – but the time is not yet.
> Speed it, O Father! Let thy Kingdom come! (69–71)

By 1796 the last of Coleridge's millennial hopes had been abandoned. In his *Ode on the Departing Year* he envisages a world in which war, imperialism and slavery threaten to awaken an apocalyptic 'Strange-eyed Destruction' that will chasten Britain for committing atrocities on four continents. The ode ends with the poet, 'unpartaking of the evil thing', divorced from the society he condemns but facing utter solitude. The political road he had travelled in a few short years is mapped retrospectively in *France: An Ode* (1798), in which the early French Revolution is once more mythologized as a powerful figure who 'in wrath her giant limbs upreard' and 'Stamped her strong foot and said she would be free!' (22, 24). The poet had then foreseen a millennium in which 'conquering by her happiness alone', France would bring freedom to the nations, 'Till Love and Joy look round, and call the Earth their own' (60, 62). Undeceived by France's aggressive military policy culminating in its invasion of Switzerland, the poet now renounces his former revolutionary hopes and transfers them to the natural world, finding the spirit of Liberty in 'earth, sea and air' (103). *France: An Ode* thus terminates a period of close to a decade, early in which Coleridge had seen the French Revolution as an apocalyptic event leading to the political millennium foreseen by Joseph Priestley in his sermon of 1794.

William Wordsworth, too, once conceived of the French Revolution as realizing the Millennium, although his expression of this is further removed from sacred discourse than either Blake's or Coleridge's. In Book X of the 1805–6 *Prelude* he retrospectively evokes his view of the world after being converted to the Revolutionary cause by the charismatic Michel Beaupuis in 1792:

> Not favoured spots alone, but the whole earth
> The beauty wore of promise, that which sets,
> To take an image which was felt, no doubt,
> Among the bowers of paradise itself,
> The budding rose above the rose full blown. (701–5)

Yet the whole passage, governed by the vocabulary of dream and enchantment, acknowledges at the same time that this 'inheritance new-fallen' turned out to be no paradise regained. The themes of apocalypse and millennium are deeply embedded in *The Prelude*, but, distanced from the realm of the political, they are manifest in a sequence of visionary moments. Each of these involves an encounter of the poet with something outside himself that yet turns out to be, whether another person or an aspect of the natural world, within him; and each is further marked by the crossing of a threshold.

In the first of these episodes, that of the discharged soldier in Book IV, there is a transition from the quotidian world to the realm of imagination:

> I slowly mounted up a steep ascent
> Where the road's watry surface, to the ridge
> Of that sharp rising, glitter'd in the moon... (370–2)

The imagery of shining is, as so often in Wordsworth, liminal. Beyond the threshold is a figure who is at once Other and familiar. On a natural level, he could be one of the marginalized people of the *Lyrical Ballads* or *Salisbury Plain* poems, a soldier who had fought against the French in the West Indies and then been dumped at some English port to find his way home. Or 'Lank and lean', 'meagre', 'ghastly in the moonlight', he could be a terrestrial Ancient Mariner, ready to inculcate unsought-for self-knowledge in his normative listener. But this episode does not carry fully into revelation. Instead, we pass back into the natural world, encountering as it were the liminal imagery from the other side:

> ...every silent window to the Moon
> Shone with a yellow glitter. 'No one there',
> Said I, 'is waking, we must measure back
> The way which we have come...' (452–5)

The next expedition takes the reader much further into the apocalyptic. This time the figure we encounter has less natural substance, combining aspects of 'An Arab Phantom' of the *Arabian Nights*, Don Quixote and Wordsworth himself. This rider carries all human knowledge encapsulated as a Stone and a Shell, which are in the logic of the dream books.

The first contains the millennial possibilities held out by science: '[it] held acquaintance with the stars, / And wedded man to man by purest bond / Of nature, undisturbed by space or time' (5: 104–6). The other is the prophetic voice of poetry that, when held as a shell to the dreamer's ear, delivers its apocalyptic message:

> And heard that instant in an unknown Tongue,
> Which yet I understood, articulate sounds,
> A loud prophetic blast of harmony,
> An Ode, in passion uttered, which foretold
> Destruction to the children of the earth
> By deluge now at hand. (94–9)

First indicated by one of *The Prelude*'s liminal images – 'A glittering light' (129), the destructive element is declared to be 'the waters of the deep / Gathering upon us' (130–1). The Arab becomes an inversion of Moses, fleeing over the desert pursued by the sea, at which point the narrator awakens with *Don Quixote*, which he had been reading, at his side.

The 'ghastly' soldier is left safe (for the time being) in a labourer's cottage; the narrator of the Stone and the Shell 'wak'd in terror', but his terror is presumably dissipated at finding it was all a dream. In Book VI, the poet's visionary recollection of crossing the Alps in the summer of 1790 is provided with a different kind of buffering. He and his friend Jones landed at Calais 'on the very Eve / Of that great federal Day' on which the first anniversary of the Revolution was celebrated. The poet is indeed aware that this historical moment could have been celebrated in millenarian terms:

> . . . 'Twas a time when Europe was rejoiced,
> France standing on the top of golden hours,
> And human nature seeming born again. (352–4)

Yet if the revolution is figured as a clock face, the hands may – indeed must – descend from noon, at which point the emphasis of line 354 will be on 'seeming'. And as in the case of the imagery of enchantment in Book X, the descriptions of Revolutionary celebration are self-undermining. 'Gaudy with reliques of that Festival' appropriates diction typical of English Protestant denunciations of papist idolatry, and the 'Flowers left to wither on triumphal Arcs' (352–63) testify to a failure to appropriate nature to a political cause. Leaving political festivals behind them, the two Englishmen push on to the Simplon, where their famously anti-climactic crossing of the Alps occurs. In retrospect the poet recognizes that nature had become an unsealed text:

> Tumult and peace, the darkness and the light
> Were all like workings of one mind, the features
> Of the same face, blossoms upon one tree,
> Characters of the great Apocalypse,
> The types and symbols of Eternity,
> Of first and last, and midst, and without end. (567–72)

Whether or not we agree with Geoffrey Hartman's argument that 'An unresolved opposition between Imagination and Nature prevents him from becoming a visionary poet'

(*Wordsworth's Poetry*, p. 39), we can see that in Book VI Wordsworth himself acknowledges his inability to reconcile the apocalyptic and the natural or (at least potentially) millennial. When Wordsworth and Jones entered Switzerland, the first valley seemed like the earthly Paradise: 'A green recess, an aboriginal vale' (448). After crossing the Simplon Pass, they find at first a parallel experience:

> . . . Como, thou, a treasure by the earth
> Kept to itself, a darling bosomed up
> In Abyssinian privacy, I spake
> Of thee, thy chestnut woods, and garden plots
> Of Indian corn tended by dark-eyed Maids,
> Thy lofty steeps and pathways roofed with vines . . . (590–5)

However, as if to protect itself from those who have seen the great Apocalypse, nature closes itself against them. They get the time wrong, start out in the middle of the night, wander and get lost, and find the landscape anything but unfallen:

> . . . the sullen water underneath,
> On which a dull red image of the moon
> Lay bedded, changing oftentimes its form
> Like an uneasy snake . . . (635–8)

Tormented by stinging insects and terrified by the cries of nocturnal birds, the travellers find that they have as little place in the natural as in the political world. Millennium has become unavailable.

It was not Wordsworth's way to leave things so, and in the last book of *The Prelude* he attempts to bring apocalypse and millennium together again. The vision is once more retrospective, and it begins with the same elements as the crossing of the Alps: poet, friend (as it happens, the same Robert Jones) and a shepherd 'who by ancient right / Of office is the Stranger's usual Guide' (13: 7–8). The sullenness of nature reasserts itself, as if protecting a secret:

> It was a Summer's night, a close warm night,
> Wan, dull and glaring with a dripping mist
> Low-hung and thick that covered all the sky . . . (10–12)

Somewhat like Dante ascending Mount Purgatory, the poet stubbornly labours upward, 'With forehead bent earthward'. He is rewarded with a liminal moment, 'When at my feet the ground appeared to brighten' (36), followed by a 'flash' that simultaneously reveals the natural world and the universal mind. The 'sea of mist' transfigured by moonlight is simultaneously apocalypse and millennium, revelation and ongoing imaginative percep-tion. Wordsworth has conducted the reader to the view that characterizes his mature work. The millennium is now a version of the 'paradise within thee, happier far' that Michael promises Adam near the end of *Paradise Lost* (XII: 587). In M. H. Abrams's words, 'The recourse is from mass action to individual quietism, and from outer revolution to a revolutionary mode of imaginative perception which accomplishes nothing less than the "creation" of a new world' (*Natural Supernaturalism*, p. 338). It was left to the next generation to attempt to redefine history in terms of apocalypse and millennium.

The second generation of Romantic poets did not experience the trauma of the collapse of millennial hope attached to the fading of the French Republic and the rise of Napoleon. Byron was a little over one year old when the Bastille fell. For him and his younger contemporaries, what has come to be called the failure of the French Revolution was a given. Conscious of the importance of that failure in shaping the climate of opinion of their own time, Byron, Shelley and Keats had to adapt a rational explanation of what had happened in order to leave room for imagining a different kind of future. This they did, as Malcolm Kelsall argues in *Byron's Politics*, by adopting the Whig interpretation of history. The French people were incapable of self-governance because they had been disabled by centuries of oppression. An epitome of this explanation can be found in Shelley's Preface to *The Revolt of Islam*: 'If the Revolution had been in every respect prosperous, then misrule and superstition would lose half their claims to our abhorrence, as fetters which the captive can unlock with the slightest motion of his fingers, and which do not eat with poisonous rust into the soul'. With the trope of the internalized chain, Shelley hopes to show the inevitability of 'the atrocities of the demagogues, and the re-establishment of successive tyrannies in France', and by this means to leave room for a different outcome in an age that has learned from the mistakes of the past. Such a view was shared by Byron and Keats as well, and all three poets employed in their very different ways figurations of apocalypse and millennium in their interpretations of history.

Looking at the Jungfrau, Byron observed 'the torrent in shape curving over the rock – like the *tail* of a white horse streaming in the wind – such as it might be conceived would be that of the '*pale* horse' on which Death is mounted in the Apocalypse' (Marchand, 5, 101). This comparison found its way into *Manfred* (II, ii, 1–8). In Canto III of *Childe Harold's Pilgrimage* the apocalypse of nature mixes with that of history on the field of Waterloo, where Harold muses on 'How that rain hath made the harvest grow' (151); and that image is expanded three stanzas later with a reference to Napoleon as an Orc-like 'trampler of her [Europe's] vineyards' (175). Rousseau and 'his compeers' are seen as bearers of revelation: 'the veil they rent, / And what behind it lay, all earth shall view' (773–4). Such tropes are not casual; they reveal a deep characteristic of Byron's temperament, as Shelley recognized when he wrote '*Cain* is apocalyptic – it is a revelation never before communicated to man' (*Letters*, 2: 376). The Byronic hero strives to penetrate the barriers of nature and history, whether it be Manfred in the Hall of Arimanes, Cain with Lucifer in Hades, or Harold exploring the historical topography of Europe. However, the millennial has a less certain role. When the narrator of *Don Juan* fiercely declares 'I will teach, if possible, the stones / To rise against earth's tyrants' (Canto VIII, 1,076–7) and then addresses his future readers as 'in the great joy of your millennium' (1,082), we seem to see the familiar pattern of millennium following revolutionary apocalypse. Yet there is a difference in tone between the prophetic vehemence of the first part of the statement and the hopeful imagining of the second. How seriously are we to believe that the future will be so bright that 'our children's children' will hardly be able to believe '*what things were* before the world was free'? As so often in *Don Juan*, the answer is uncertain, especially as this passage follows the extraordinary detailed account of the horrifying siege and battle of Ismail. The ultimate expression of this disparity is in the powerful blank verse poem *Darkness*.

*Darkness* was written in Switzerland in the summer of 1816, which became known as 'the year without a summer' because of its extraordinary cold and darkness (not then known to have been caused by volcanic dust from the great Tambora eruption of the preceding year). These conditions led Byron to imagine the dying of the sun and the consequent destruction of life on earth. In doing so, he deliberately inverted the details of millennial prophecy. For example, Isaiah envisioned a world in which 'they shall beat their swords into ploughshares, and their spears into pruning hooks: nation shall not lift up sword against nation, neither shall they learn war any more' (Isaiah 2: 4), but in *Darkness* 'War, which for a moment was no more, / Did glut himself again' (38–9). Even where Byron parallels Isaiah, it is for ironic purposes. As in Isaiah 11:8, where 'the suckling child shall play on the hole of the asp', in Byron's poem vipers 'twined themselves among the multitude, / Hissing, but stingless' (36–7); and Byron's 'wildest brutes...tame and tremulous' (34–5) parallels Isaiah's 'The wolf also shall dwell with the lamb, and the leopard shall lie down with the kid' (11:6). However, in *Darkness* millennial images are consistently invoked only to be bitterly frustrated: these brutes and vipers are greedily devoured by the multitude, who next turn on each other. Instead of universal brotherhood, 'The meagre by the meagre were devoured' (46) until no one is left alive. In the year without a summer, which was also the year after the Congress of Vienna and the re-institution of the old political order in Europe, nature must have seemed to Byron as mirroring human events. Unlike apocalyptic poems of the 1790s like Blake's *America* and Coleridge's *Religious Musings*, *Darkness*, a true product of post-Revolutionary awareness, presents apocalypse but no millennium.

Percy Bysshe Shelley is in many ways the heir of Blake (whose work he did not know) and of Coleridge (whose work was very important to him) in trying to re-establish a socio-political mythos of apocalypse and millennium. In his first ambitious poem, *Queen Mab* (1813), he projected a millennial 'paradise of peace' (VIII, 238) in which tyranny, war and the eating of meat would not even be remembered. However, *Queen Mab*, as Shelley soon recognized, was too discursive; and in his next attempt his method was, as he announced in the Preface to *The Revolt of Islam* (1818), 'narrative, not didactic'. *The Revolt* tells the story of the rising of the people of the Golden City against the tyrant Othman, but it is analogically a retrospective account of the fortunes of the French Revolution. It begins with a vision of 'An Eagle and a Serpent wreathed in fight', a Shelleyan archetype of all revolutions. As in the early parts of Blake's Orc myth, conventional values are inverted, and it is the chthonic serpent who represents the cause of humanity. Wounded by the Jovian eagle, the serpent falls into the sea and is rescued by a beautiful dark-haired woman, at once Mary Godwin (to whom the poem is dedicated) and Cythna, the heroine of the poem to come. She inculcates the poet into a knowledge of the ongoing struggle between the powers of the serpent (originally the Luciferian morning star) and the 'Fiend of blood' who rules through 'King, and Lord, and God'. Their battle is continually renewed, and the revolt of the Golden City is an instance of it.

After the non-violent victory of the people over the Tyrant's army, a 'sacred Festival' is held, meant, with its 'Altar of Federation', to recall the great anniversary festival of the French Revolution that Wordsworth had glimpsed in Calais in 1790. A millennial age seems about to begin, but Othman returns with his army, supported by a confederation of kings similar to the first alliance against France in 1792. The people arm themselves with pikes, a weapon traditionally associated with British freedom, but the superior forces of the Tyrant triumph. As Laon is about to be executed, Cythna appears on horseback, reminding the crowd of apocalyptic destruction: 'All thought it was God's Angel come to sweep / The lingering guilty to their fiery grave' (4,522–3). She has come to share Laon's fate, but in the midst of their execution they are translated to the Temple of the Spirit. This outcome raises some important questions about apocalypse, millennium and history. Shelley hoped that when the revolution he expected came it would be by non-violent means, an instance of which is Laon's sparing of Othman's life (just as a large minority of French Revolutionary legislators, including Thomas Paine, voted to spare Louis XVI). Of course, this makes possible Othman's subsequent victory and his butchering of the people. Yet to adopt the methods of their enemies would bind revolutionaries into the cycle of history, as in the example of France. This dilemma of means and ends would be re-addressed in *Prometheus Unbound*.

In Shelley's *Lyrical Drama*, completed late in 1819, the apocalypse is literally an unveiling. Once more, its initiator is female. After Asia exclaims 'The veil has fallen!' (II, iv, 2), she finds that what she has revealed is, ironically, 'a mighty Darkness' possessing 'Nor form nor outline' (2, 6). This is Demogorgon, a mythologized version of Godwinian Necessity, which inexorably determines cause and effect. Demogorgon's power will dethrone the repressive sky-god Jupiter, the chained Prometheus will be freed and a new, Promethean age will begin. With its advent, all living things are transformed and – always a feature of Shelley's idea of the millennium – stop eating animal food. The angels' trumps of Revelation are transmuted to 'A long long sound, as it would never end', and paralleling the resurrection of the dead, 'All the inhabitants leapt suddenly / Out of their rest, and gathered in the streets' (III, iv. 57–9). However, Shelley is careful to characterize the millennium as a period in which the condition of mortality, though radically revised, is not abolished:

> The loathsome mask has fallen, the man remains
> Sceptreless, free, uncircumscribed – but man:
> Equal, unclassed, tribeless and nationless,
> Exempt from awe, worship, degree, – the King
> Over himself; just, gentle, wise – but man:
> Passionless? no – yet free from guilt or pain (III, iv. 193–204)

Furthermore, after a universal celebration of renewal in Act IV, Demogorgon considers what would happen if the cycle of history were reversed, as in *The Revolt of Islam*, and

> if with infirm hand, Eternity
> Mother of many acts and hours, should free
> The serpent that would clasp her with his length (IV, 566–8)

This would be analogous to the unloosing in Revelation 20 of 'that old serpent, which is the Devil and Satan' after his thousand years of imprisonment. The answer would be, as it also is in *The Mask of Anarchy* (1819), non-violent resistance: 'To suffer woes . . . To forgive wrongs . . . To defy Power. . . .' Only by such means could the millennium be re-attained, for as in Blake, violence would change the nature of even its righteous perpetrators. Yet, in the great Chorus of *Hellas*, prompted by the outbreak of the Greek Revolution against the Turks in 1821, Shelley despairs of such a possibility. After envisaging the rebirth of Greece and the return of the age of Saturn, Shelley suddenly asks 'must men kill and die?' The answer seems inescapable, for the poem breaks off, 'The world is weary of the past, / O might it die or rest at last!' The image of the snake renewing its skin that signifies regeneration at the beginning of the poem can also suggest the return of 'hate and death' in the cycle of history.

John Keats's interest in the history and politics of his time is amply demonstrated in his journal-letter to George and Georgiana Keats of 17–27 September 1819 (Rollins, II, 193–4): 'Three great changes', he wrote, 'have been in progress. First for the better, next for the worse, and the third for the better once more'. These begin with 'the gradual annihilation of the tyranny of the nobles, when kings found it in their interest to conciliate the common people, elevate them, and be just to them'. The second was 'a long struggle of kings to destroy all popular privileges'. This was resisted by the English in particular.

> The example of England, and the liberal writers of france and england sowed the seed of opposition to this Tyranny – and it was swelling in the ground until it burst out in the french revolution – That has had an unlucky termination. It put a stop to the rapid progress of free sentiments in England; and gave our Court hopes of turning back to the despotism of the 16 century. They spread a horrid superstition against all innovation and improvement.

However, like Shelley, Keats believes that there is room for hope in his own generation.

> 'The present struggle of the people of England is to destroy this superstition. What has rous'd them to do it is their distresses – Perhaps on this account the present distresses of this nation are a fortunate thing – tho so horrid in the[i]r experience. You will see I mean that the french Revolution put a temporary stop to this third change, the change for the better – Now it is in progress again, and I think it is an effectual one.

This is not so much a cyclical view of history as a series of pendulum swings, with the progressive swing carrying further at each of its strokes. Such a view is behind his first attempt at the epic *Hyperion*. The lament of the fallen Saturn over the loss of his power and with it of the Golden Age is answered by Oceanus with a fundamentally evolutionary view of history: 'We fall by course of Nature's law, not force / Of thunder, or of Jove' (181–2). Oceanus goes on to tell Saturn 'Thou art not the beginning nor the end' (190), an ironical contrast with One who is the beginning and the end, and who asserts it in Revelation 1:8: 'I am Alpha and Omega, the beginning and the end, saith the Lord'. The crude energies of the Titans are not the Omega of universal development, even though their fall involves losing the classical equivalent of the earthly paradise:

> So on our heels a fresh perfection treads,
> A power more strong in beauty, born of us
> And fated to excel us . . .
>
> . . . for 'tis the eternal law
> That first in beauty should be first in might (212–14; 228–9)

This is the theme of an epic of progress toward a millennial state that would more than compensate for the lost Golden Age. Yet Keats, while continuing to express in his letters political sentiments similar to those already mentioned, abandoned the project. One reason for this, as the poet stated, was that there were too many Miltonisms in it. However, there was also a deeper, structural problem. After the brilliant opening of Book III with Apollo's dying into life, what could have happened? The epic machinery could have been mobilized for a flashback war in heaven, but in the post-Waterloo world this would have presented even greater problems than it had for Milton. Hyperion could have made a noble speech of renunciation after recognizing Apollo's superior beauty, but that would hardly have carried the poem even one book further. And so *Hyperion* eventually appeared as 'A Fragment', capitalizing on a Romantic mode given renewed appeal by the publication of Coleridge's *Kubla Khan* in 1816; but this we know was not Keats's original intention. When he took up the subject again, he attempted first by beginning *The Fall of Hyperion* before what had been Book I, creating for it an apocalyptic introduction.

Keats had incorporated apocalyptic features into some of his previous poems. In verses Keats sent to his brother Tom, he found a comparison to the writing of the Book of Revelation appropriate in describing the rocks of Fingal's cave in Staffa:

> Not St. John in Patmos' isle,
> In the passion of his toil,
> When he saw the churches seven,
> Golden ailed, built up in heaven,
> Gazed at such a rugged wonder.

The reference here is to Revelation 1:20 – 'The seven stars are the angels of the seven churches: and the seven candlesticks which thou sawest are the seven churches'. Again, among the 'thousand things' that perplex Bertha in *The Eve of St Mark* (33–4) are 'Aaron's breastplate, and the seven / Candlesticks John saw in heaven'; and in *Lamia* (Part 2, lines 231–4) the 'awful rainbow once in heaven' and the 'angel's wings' allude to Revelation 10:1, where 'I saw a mighty angel come down from heaven . . . and a rainbow was upon his head'. Much more concentrated are the apocalyptic images that the narrator of *The Fall* employs in describing what he sees in Moneta's temple. Moneta tends a sacrificial fire that, 'Sending forth Maian incense, spread around / . . . And clouded the altar with soft smoke' (1: 102–5), and this is followed by the poet's hearing 'Language pronounc'd'. As J. L. Lowes ('Moneta's Temple,' p. 1,108) has shown, the furnishings of the temple and some of its architectural details are of biblical origin. Some derive from Revelation, especially the passage describing Moneta's ministering at the altar in 1: 95–107. This recalls several passages from Revelation, where 'Another angel came and stood at the altar . . . And the smoke of the incense . . . ascended up', 'And I heard a voice from the four horns of the golden altar', and 'The temple was filled with smoke . . . And I heard a great voice out of the temple' (Revelation 8:3–4; 9:13; 15:8; 16:1). These and other allusions create an aura of apocalyptic expectation, an expectation that is fulfilled when the poet looks behind Moneta's veils. This is an act rich in significance, for the uncovering of Moneta's face is literally and figuratively an apocalypse, recalling the Greek root *apokalupsis*, 'revelation', from *apokaluptein*, 'to uncover' (apo = 'away', kaluptein = 'to cover'). The face 'deathwards progressing / to no death' (260–1) may also echo a passage in a verse play by John Wilson, *City of the Plague* (Edinburgh, 1816), in which a victim of the plague of 1665 is described:

> I saw something in her tearless eyes
> More than a mother's grief – the cold dull gleam
> Of mortal sickness hastening to decay.

'Progressing to no death' extends mortality to endless process like 'woods decaying, never to be decayed' that Wordsworth recalled seeing when crossing the Alps in *The Prelude* (VI.557, a text Keats could not have seen). In this context, 'progressing' ironizes the theme of progress in the first *Hyperion*, and this is continued a few lines later when the poet adjures Moneta 'by the golden age' that we know to be irrecoverable and calls her 'The pale Omega of a wither'd race' (288), inviting contrast once more with the God of Revelation 1:8. Moneta is the vehicle of apocalypse, but it is now the poet who assumes the role of John of Patmos, describing the signs that appear to him in the light of Moneta's 'planetary eyes'. At this point it the poet's voice that becomes oracular, uttering a 'conjuration' that brings us to the point where the first *Hyperion* began.

Despite the power of this new beginning, when the narrative of *The Fall* breaks off with 'on he flared', we can no more see a suitable continuation for the second *Hyperion* than we could for the first. How is the 'progressive' theme of the earlier plot to be reconciled with the apocalyptic nature of *The Fall*? Grounding his narrative in the present, Keats could hardly proceed to a millennium within history. An alternative could be deflection by means of a frame story on the analogy of Last Man narratives, for we can see that in this respect *The Fall* resembles Wordsworth's dream of the Stone and the Shell and Byron's *Darkness*. Although *The Fall of Hyperion* is not literally a Last Man narrative, it almost might be, as the poet is the only human being in it. A typical strategy of such narratives, like Mary Shelley's *The Last Man* (1826) or its predecessor Grainville's *Le Dernier homme* (translated as *Omegarus and Sideria* in 1806), is to use a buffering frame that enables the reader to view the threatening apocalyptic content from outside. In *Darkness*, for example, the imagined speaker's 'dream, that was not all a dream' enables us to imagine both apocalyptic destruction and the poet's awakening to write the poem. Such a solution would not have been easy in *The Fall of Hyperion*, for there the frame narrative itself is apocalyptic. The nature of this dilemma is generic, involving an imaginative expansion and not necessarily a change of belief. Although we cannot know what further solution Keats might have attempted, we must recognize that in *The Fall of Hyperion* he did not succeed in connecting apocalypse and history.

With the end of the Romantic era, apocalypse and millennium recede as a major subject for poetry. It may have seemed that the subject had been taken as far as it could go. In addition, the historical events that had been perceived as potentially apocalyptic or millennial must have appeared distant in the age of the first Reform Bill and Queen Victoria. Yet the works that have been discussed here have retained their fascination for new generations of readers, perhaps never so much as today, when apocalypse and millennium are once more providing material for artistic expression.

## REFERENCES AND FURTHER READING

Abrams, M. H. *Natural Supernaturalism: Tradition and Revolution in Romantic Literature*, New York, W. W. Norton, 1971.

Coleridge, Ernest Hartley (ed.) *The Poems of Samuel Taylor Coleridge*, London, Oxford University Press, 1960.

Erdman, David V. (ed.) *The Complete Poetry and Prose of William Blake*, New York, Doubleday, 1988.

Frye, Northrop, *Fearful Symmetry: A Study of William Blake*, Princeton, Princeton University Press, 1971.

Gill, Stephen (ed.) *William Wordsworth*, Oxford, Oxford University Press, 1984.

Hartman, Geoffrey H., *Wordsworth's Poetry 1787– 1814*, New Haven, Yale University Press, 1964.

Hutchinson, Thomas (ed.) *The Poems of Shelley*, London, Oxford University Press, 1960.

Keats, John, *The Poems of John Keats*, Cambridge, Mass., Harvard University Press, 1978.

Kelsall, Malcolm, *Byron's Politics*, Brighton, Harvester, 1987.

Lowes, J. L., 'Moneta's Temple', *PMLA* 51 (1936).

Paley, Morton D., *The Continuing City: William Blake's Jerusalem*, Oxford, Clarendon Press, 1983.

Reiman, Donald H. and Powers, Sharon B. (eds) *Shelley's Poetry and Prose*, New York, W. W. Norton, 1977.

Roe, Nicholas (ed.) *Keats and History*, Cambridge, Cambridge University Press, 1995.

Woodman, Ross, *The Apocalyptic Vision in the Poetry of Shelley*, Toronto, University of Toronto Press, 1964.

Woodring, Carl, *Politics in the Poetry of Coleridge*, Madison, University of Wisconsin Press, 1961.

Wordsworth, Jonathan, *William Wordsworth: The Borders of Vision*, Oxford, Clarendon Press, 1982.

# 48

# The Romantic Imagination

## *Jonathan Wordsworth*

'Tis to create, and in creating live
A being more intense, that we endow
With form our fancy, gaining as we give
The life we image . . . (*Childe Harold*, III, 46–9)

Byron's famous lines, as he sets forward on Childe Harold's third 'pilgrimage' in April 1816, offer a beautifully concise view of the workings of imagination. We create because, in the intensity of creation, we lead a fuller life, losing ourselves in that which we are making. Elsewhere he makes the odd flamboyant assertion – 'Poetry is the lava of the imagination, whose eruption prevents an earthquake' (Marchand, III, 179) – but leaves theorizing to others. By contrast, his five great contemporaries – Blake, Coleridge, Wordsworth, Shelley, Keats – are preoccupied with imagination. Why they should have this in common is not at all obvious. They didn't know that imagination would come to be thought of as the hallmark of Romantic poets. And they didn't know they were Romantic poets. Given their differences of age, class and background, they would have been astonished to hear themselves described as a movement. Connections between them were few: Wordsworth learned from Coleridge, and perhaps to a slight extent Shelley did so too; Keats at times has Wordsworth in his thoughts. But by and large they were independent minds, drawn to a single way of thinking. It may be that one is forced back on the not very satisfactory concept of *zeitgeist* – Hazlitt's spirit of the age.

Aside from Byron all the Romantic poets attempted serious, complex definitions of imagination. Shelley tended to use the term 'poetry' instead, but it made little difference. It is as though they felt their creativity so strongly that they were urged to define it as something more, something above and beyond. Even Keats, who is normally so down-to-earth, can't seem to be simple on this particular subject. After making his famous, and attractive, statement – 'Imagination may be compared to Adam's dream – he awoke and found it truth' – he finds it necessary to start talking about the afterlife: 'Adam's dream . . . seems to be a conviction that Imagination and its empyreal reflection is the same as human Life and its spiritual repetition' (to Bailey, 22 November 1817; Rollins, I, 185). The dream is described in *Paradise Lost*, Book VIII. With closed eyes, Adam watches as God (painlessly) extracts a rib from his side and forms it into Eve. He then wakes, and finds Eve does exist, and is just as beautiful as she was when he was dreaming.

Keats's first statement makes a large enough claim for imagination: that which is imagined will be found to be real. His second one complicates this by suggesting that human imagination is in the same relation to its celestial 'reflection', as human existence is to heaven. It would be easier (as well as more traditional) to think of the human as 'reflecting' the divine, but Keats has it the other way round. Also, there is the problem as to whose 'conviction' he is referring to. Milton surely cannot think of the divine as reflecting the human? The train of thought is not at all easy to follow – and becomes no easier if one looks at the material between Keats's two references to Adam. He is not alone in entering into such complexities. Wordsworth often uses the word 'imagination' quite ordinarily: when he subdivides *Poems* 1807 into 'Poems of Fancy' and 'Poems of Imagination' we know what he means – as we do in the Preface to *Poems* 1815. But then suddenly in *Prelude* Book XIII he goes way over the top:

> imagination, which in truth
> Is but another name for absolute strength
> And clearest insight, amplitude of mind
> And reason in her most exalted mood. (167–70)

At the start Wordsworth sounds as if he is letting us into a secret ('which in truth / Is but another name for'), but he ends by calling imagination four different names, none of which we would ever have thought of in this context. So what is it all about?

Turning back to Book VI of *The Prelude*, we find again this impulse to turn imagination into something mysterious, beyond human experience. Wordsworth, in March 1804, is recalling his disappointment in 1790 at having crossed the Alps (which he'd imagined would be a splendid achievement) without noticing he'd got to the top – easily done, as he was walking through a long, bleak and nearly level pass. His imagination then (in 1804, not 1790) comes into its own. Instead of writing about past disappointment, he writes about his present mood:

> Imagination – lifting up itself
> Before the eye and progress of my song
> Like an unfathered vapour, here that power,
> In all the might of its endowments, came
> Athwart me! I was lost as in a cloud,
> Halted without a struggle to break through;
> And now, recovering, to my soul I say,
> 'I recognize thy glory.' (VI.525–32)

It is a sort of take-over. A cloud of the poet's own imagination envelops him, as a cloud on peak or pass might envelop the Alpine traveller he once had been. Coming out of the cloud, he gives thanks not to his imagination, but to his soul – the faculty that enables him to have such transcendent imaginings. Important in all this is the sense in which the experience, though it must logically be inward, is felt by Wordsworth to come from outside. 'In such strength of usurpation', he continues,

> in such visitings
> Of awful promise, when the light of sense
> Goes out in flashes that have shown to us
> The invisible world, doth greatness make abode,
> There harbours whether we be young or old. (VI.532–7)

What started as an imaginative moment in which the poet went back into an earlier mood, has turned into a mystical experience. Human 'greatness' is held to consist (as in *Tintern Abbey*) of a loss of bodily awareness, accompanied by a new insight into the 'invisible world' of the spirit.

It comes as no great surprise that Blake should have his version of all this. He of course thinks mythically, which makes him seem more complicated still. But in fact what he is saying is broadly clear, having as its basis the opposition we are all familiar with between imagination and reason. Wordsworth (depending on Kant, via Coleridge) confuses readers by alluding to imagination as 'reason in her most exalted mood'. Blake is unaware of this higher, German reason. Reason for him is the enemy. It is rationalism, associated with selfhood, with memory, with the philosophy of Bacon and Locke, with Newton and scientific enquiry, and (on a more personal level) with uninspired makers of paintings, poetry and music, who rely merely on technique. All these negate imagination. 'I come in self-annihilation', says Milton, who in Blake's prophetic book returns to earth to purge the rationalist self and find his true identity:

> I come in self-annihilation & the grandeur of inspiration
> To cast off rational demonstration by faith in the Saviour;
> To cast off the rotten rags of memory by inspiration;
> To cast off Bacon, Locke & Newton from Albion's covering;
> To take off his filthy garments, & clothe him with imagination;
> To cast aside from poetry all that is not inspiration
> That it no longer shall dare to mock with the aspersion of madness
> Cast on the inspired by the tame high-finisher of paltry blots
> Indefinite, or paltry rhymes, or paltry harmonies ...
> To cast off the idiot questioner who is always questioning
> But never capable of answering, who sits with a sly grin
> Silent plotting when to question, like a thief in a cave;
> Who publishes doubt, and calls it knowledge ...

The 'idiot questioner' is undermining faith, the imaginative view of things. He and his like are 'the destroyers of Jerusalem' (of the spiritual New Jerusalem, seen in the Book of Revelation) – they are

> murderers
> Of Jesus, who deny the faith & mock at eternal life,
> Who pretend to poetry that they may destroy imagination
> By imitation of nature's images drawn from remembrance. (*Milton*, plate 41)

Essentially the same pattern emerges. As we should expect, imagination is the quality that distinguishes the true poet from the uninspired (whom Blake sees as positively destructive). But it is also man's entrance to the larger world of truth. 'If the doors of perception were cleansed', Blake had said in *The Marriage of Heaven and Hell* (1790), 'every thing would appear to man as it is, infinite' (plate 14; *Romanticism*, p. 84). Imagination is vision of the infinite, possible to man in its highest form only when the senses (the 'doors' of our perception whilst we are part of the fallen, or mundane, world) have been cleansed, and selfhood is purged, or 'annihilated'. Attaining to imaginative vision, one strips Albion (who cannot be defined, but is partly England, partly humanity as a whole, even in some sense God – as the Great Humanity Divine) of the 'rotten rags' of rationalist thinking which have 'clothed' and crippled him.

Shelley, who regards himself as an atheist without ever seeming to be one, offers in the *Defence of Poetry* a version of Blake's cleansing of the doors, in which we have merely to substitute the word 'imagination' where he uses 'poetry'. It is not that the two are for him identical, but that he sees in poetry the embodiment (incarnation) of imaginative power:

> Poetry turns all things to loveliness. . . . It transmutes all that it touches, and every form moving within the radiance of its presence is changed by wondrous sympathy to an incarnation of the spirit which it breathes . . . it strips the veil of familiarity from the world and lays bare the naked and sleeping beauty, which is the spirit of its forms.
>
> All things exist as they are perceived – at least in relation to the percipient. 'The mind is its own place, and in itself / Can make a Heaven of Hell, a Hell of Heaven.' But poetry defeats the curse which binds us to be subjected to the accident of surrounding impressions. (*Romanticism*, p. 967)

Poetry/imagination transmutes all that it touches (one recalls Wordsworth's grand assertion, 'the midnight storm / Grew darker in the presence of my eye'; *Prelude* II.392–3), changing 'by wondrous sympathy' every form that comes within its influence into 'an incarnation of the spirit which it breathes'. The words are ambiguous. Given what follows, Shelley probably intends to say that the form becomes, as a result of the operation of poetry, an incarnation of its own indwelling spirit. It becomes perfectly itself, because poetry has laid bare 'its naked and sleeping beauty'. In the available second reading, the form becomes an incarnation not of its own perfect self, but of the spirit that is breathed by poetry. Perhaps there is no need to choose. Given the 'wondrous sympathy' existing between poetry and the essential forms of the universe, there would be little difference between the two readings. Poetry is an outgoing manifestation of an indwelling spirit that pervades the universe, and is found (to quote Wordsworth again) equally in 'the round ocean, and the living air, / And the blue sky, and in the mind of man' (*Tintern Abbey*, 99–100).

Atheist or not, Shelley is drawn like the others into definitions that use a religious frame of reference and (one might think) imply some degree of belief. 'Poetry redeems from decay the visitations of the divinity in man':

> We are aware of evanescent visitations of thought and feeling, sometimes associated with place or person, sometimes regarding our own mind alone, and always arising unforeseen and departing unbidden, but elevating and delightful beyond all expression, so that even in the desire and the regret they leave, there cannot but be pleasure, participating as it [pleasure] does in the nature of its object. It is, as it were, the interpenetration of a diviner nature through our own. (*Romanticism*, p. 966)

It is significant that Wordsworth's account of the process, quoted above:

> visitings
> Of awful promise, when the light of sense
> Goes out in flashes that have shown to us
> The invisible world

was in the unpublished *Prelude*, and not available to Shelley. To some extent *Tintern Abbey* may be regarded as a prototype of the Romantic imaginative experience, but the different poets seem to have lived it independently – and mused over its nature independently. Shelley's *Defence* was unpublished till 1840.

Coleridge, however, is a presence of whom all but Blake are aware. It seems likely that Shelley's use of the word 'interpenetration' ('the interpenetration of a diviner nature through our own') derives from the moment just before the great imagination definitions of *Biographia* chapter XIII, where Coleridge arrives at the concept of the *tertium aliquid*, a pantheist 'inter-penetration of counterating powers, partaking of both' (CC *Biographia*, I, 300). Pantheism, or Platonism, in one form or another, seems to be implied in all Romantic definitions of imagination. Effectively what is claimed is that human creativity is a sharing in the creative power of the godhead. Even Keats, of whom this seems least likely to be true, is prepared to write, 'Intelligences are atoms of perception – they know and they see and they are pure, in short they are God' (to George and Georgiana Keats, 3 May 1819; Rollins, II, 102).

For Coleridge alone, Platonism is an organized religion. He becomes a Unitarian at Cambridge in 1793, and despite many and prolonged attempts to talk himself into Trinitarian orthodoxy, he remains one, in all but name, until after the publication of *Biographia* in 1817. His definitions have caused problems to scholars who wished to deny his pantheism, and tended to read him in the contexts of German metaphysics. In fact his thinking on imagination emerges from staunchly Unitarian years in the mid-1790s, before he knew anything of Kant or Schelling beyond their reputation. The *Biographia* definitions are grander, more impressive, but they contain little that is not stated, or inherent, in a sequence of references that begins with *Religious Musings* (1794–6) and the Slave Trade lecture of 1795. The whole tenor of his thinking should lead us to expect that imagination would be for him (as it is, in different ways and at different times, for his fellow poets) a sharing in the divine.

In the event, Coleridge arrived at a distinction, which has seemed far more important to modern scholars than it did to his contemporaries, between a primary and a secondary imagination. There would be less to be said about this if scholars hadn't in the twentieth century more or less consistently got them the wrong way round:

> The IMAGINATION then, I consider either as primary, or secondary. The primary IMAGINATION I hold to be the living Power and prime Agent of all human Perception, and as a repetition in the finite mind of the eternal act of creation in the infinite I AM. The secondary Imagination I consider as an echo of the former, co-existing with the conscious will, yet still as identical with the primary in the *kind* of its agency, and differing only in *degree*, and in the mode of its operation. It dissolves, diffuses, dissipates, in order to recreate; or where this process is rendered impossible, yet still at all events it struggles to idealize and to unify. It is essentially *vital*, even as all objects (*as* objects) are essentially fixed and dead.

'FANCY, on the contrary', Coleridge goes on (and this third definition is of considerable importance),

> has no other counters to play with, but fixities and definites. The Fancy is indeed no other than a mode of Memory emancipated from the order of time and space; while it is blended with, and modified by, that empirical phenomenon of the will, which we express by the word CHOICE. But equally with the ordinary memory the Fancy must receive all its materials ready made from the law of association. (*Romanticism*, p. 574)

There is something to be said for reading these definitions from the bottom upwards. Fancy is clearly the most limited faculty. It handles bits of experience, bits of memory, which are brought to mind by the associative process, but it can't do much with them. They can be formed into patterns, but the individual components, because they remain fixed and definite, can take on no life of their own, and form no vital bonds with their neighbours. Coleridge, it has to be admitted, is down on fancy. Wordsworth sees it as enjoyable and charged with emotion.

For Coleridge, the secondary imagination is utterly distinct from fancy because its materials are alive. The imaginative mind has the capacity, which fancy lacks, to dissolve, diffuse and dissipate (strip its materials down, take them apart), but does so 'in order to recreate' (reassemble, make new wholes). Its inherent tendency is 'to idealize and to unify', which fancy cannot do. On the other hand, it has in common with fancy that it co-exists 'with the conscious will'. One can be deliberately imaginative at this secondary level, just as one can be deliberately fanciful – but it is not a good thing (watersnakes must be blessed 'unawares'). It resembles the primary imagination – indeed cannot be wholly distinguished from it – because it is alive. Its essential nature ('the *kind* of its agency'), as opposed to the way it works ('the *mode* of its operation), is identical. This being the case, it will at some point slide into the primary. It can be different only in degree. If we ask whether that means it is more, or less, important, than the primary, Coleridge tells us that it is an 'echo' – not the thing itself, but its echo.

A surprising number of twentieth-century scholars and critics (including the editors of the Oxford *Biographia* (1907) and Bollingen (1982)) have assumed that Coleridge called the secondary imagination 'secondary' (and placed it second) while meaning that it was primary. Logic is not on their side. Coleridge uses language carefully, and means what he says. So what is the primary imagination? Many things. Or rather, a whole spectrum. It is 'the living Power and prime Agent of *all* human Perception'. Everything we perceive, we perceive by virtue of the primary imagination – whether it is pleasant or unpleasant, physical or metaphysical, exalted or insignificant. But Coleridge's definition doesn't stop at this point. The primary imagination is also 'a repetition in the finite mind of the eternal act of creation in the infinite I AM'. It is not immediately clear what is being said, but the language has taken on a new grandeur. Coleridge is felt to be making a big claim. Like the other Romantics when they attempt to say how important the imagination is to them, he finds it necessary to use the language of religious experience. Man's creativity is a repetition – not merely an echo, but a repetition – of God's 'eternal act of creation'. And what is this divine act, that has always gone on, and will always go on? Coleridge has prepared an answer for the question in the previous chapter of *Biographia* –

and a very complicated answer it is, though it makes sense if one works patiently through it.

The eternal act of creation is God's self-naming. In affirming his own existence, saying I AM, he brings into existence that which he is not. *Thesis VI* concludes with the words:

> if we elevate our conception to the absolute self, the great eternal I AM [God], then the principle of being, and of knowledge; of idea, and of reality; the ground of existence, and the ground of the knowledge of existence; are absolutely identical: *Sum quia sum* – I am, because I affirm myself to be; I affirm myself to be, because I am. (CC *Biographia*, I, 275)

God is thus 'absolutely' self-conscious, aware of himself both as subject and as object. In *Thesis VII* Coleridge takes this important definition two stages further, defining God in his self-consciousness as Spirit, and defining Spirit as Act. As he does so (and not all his readers have followed him thus far), he links this discussion into the definitions of the human imagination that are to follow:

> It has been shown that a Spirit is that which is its own object; yet not originally an object, but an absolute subject, for which all, itself included, may become an object. It must therefore be an ACT; for every object is, as an *object*, dead, fixed, incapable in itself of any action, and necessarily finite. (Ibid., pp. 278–9)

Fortunately, one does not have to understand the finer detail to see that Coleridge has defined God *as* 'the eternal act of creation', absolute imagination. At the end of *Thesis IX* he slips in two nice, brief, easy sentences that tell the rest of us where we stand: 'We begin with the I KNOW MYSELF, in order to end with the absolute I AM. We proceed from the SELF, in order to lose and find all self in God' (ibid., p. 283). The ultimate act of the primary imagination, which is at once creative and perceptive, is the losing and finding of self in God. It is the self-annihilation of Blake's Milton:

> I will go down to self-annihilation & eternal death,
> Lest the Last Judgement come & find me unannihilate,
> And I be seized & given into the hands of my own selfhood. (*Milton*, plate 14)

Or, in a milder form, it is the moment in *Tintern Abbey* in which 'we are laid asleep / In body, and become a living soul' – and are thus enabled, creatively and perceptively, to 'see into the life of things'. Coleridge himself had written first of this losing and finding of self in *Religious Musings* (1796):

> 'Tis the sublime of man,
> Our noontide Majesty, to know ourselves
> Parts and proportions of one wond'rous whole . . .

Failure to accept this role delivers man (in Blakean terms) up to his own selfhood – as Coleridge puts it, describing the alienation of civilized man (the 'smooth Savage'),

> A sordid solitary thing,
> Mid countless brethren, with a lonely heart

> Thro' courts and cities the smooth Savage roams
> Feeling himself, his own low Self, the whole,
> When he by sacred sympathy might make
> The whole ONE SELF! (135–7, 163–8)

'Sacred sympathy' is an early and marvellous definition of the highest achievement of the human imagination – 'the sublime of man'. Everybody is capable of imagination in its primary form, and uses it all the time to make sense of day-to-day existence: it is the 'prime agent of *all* human perception'. The chosen few, who are capable of 'sacred sympathy', employ this same power to perceive themselves in relation to God, who, as pure spirit, is himself the continuing *act* of absolute imagination. The primary imagination is thus primary in two senses. It is shared by all, whereas the secondary is the imagination of the poet or creative artist. And it is, in its highest achievement, of infinitely greater importance.

Coleridge, though, in refusing to place a barrier between the primary and secondary imaginations, making them differ only in degree, has left open the possibility that the artist may in his work attain to the 'sacred sympathy' (synonymous of course with love) that loses and finds all self in God. He is encouraged in this by a passage of *Paradise Lost*, twice quoted in *Biographia*, which offers the source of his distinction between 'degree' and 'kind', and portrays existence as a ladder on which inanimate matter, vegetation, animals, human beings, move upwards towards reassimilation in the world of spirit. The passage is cited first in chapter X. Raphael (who, as archangel, has a spiritual existence, but is none the less on the ladder himself) is explaining the difference between angelic and human intelligence. The discursive mode, he tells Adam, 'is oftest yours', the intuitive 'most is ours, / Differing but in *degree*, in *kind* the same'. Man is *capable* of the angelic, higher reason (which is the topmost level of imagination), but, at this stage in his development, not usually. To make the point that we are ascending this ladder, Coleridge then quotes the Milton passage at length, beginning

> O Adam, one Almighty is, from whom
> All things proceed, and up to him return

as the epigraph to *Biographia* chapter XIII, *On the Imagination, or Esemplastic Power* (see CC *Biographia*, I, 295).

Essentially, the Romantic imagination is the wish of a number of creative geniuses (living at a certain period, but never a group) to 'lose, and find, all self in God'. In their inspired creativity they felt an analogy – or something more than an analogy – to the central mystical experience which they craved. Imagination in its highest moments appeared to them godlike, and, with differing degrees of assurance (Blake with certainty, Keats rarely and with hesitation), they dared to assert that it was indeed the link between man and God.

## REFERENCES AND FURTHER READING

Wordsworth, Jonathan, *William Wordsworth: The Borders of Vision*, Oxford, Clarendon Press, 1982, pp. 76–86.

——— '"The infinite I AM": Coleridge and the Ascent of Being', in *Coleridge's Imagination*, ed. Richard Gravil, Lucy Newlyn and Nicholas Roe,

Cambridge, Cambridge University Press, 1985, pp. 22–52.

Bate, Walter Jackson, 'Coleridge on the function of art', in *Perspectives of Criticism* 20 (Cambridge, Mass., Harvard University Press, 1950), pp. 125–59.

# 49

# England and Germany

*Rosemary Ashton*

Cultural phenomena are complex and difficult to explain, especially when the question of comparativism, or 'influence', between two or more national cultures is at issue. The difficulty is perhaps at its most acute when we contemplate the particular historical phenomenon known as Romanticism, for here definitions abound to the point of dizziness. Long ago the critic Arthur O. Lovejoy amusingly illustrated the problem of defining Romanticism in his essay 'On the discrimination of Romanticisms' (1948). He lists some of the candidates put forward by scholars as the originator(s) of Romanticism. These include Rousseau, Kant, Fénelon, Francis Bacon, the Reverend Joseph Warton, Sir Philip Sidney, medieval Anglo-French literature, St Paul, Plato, Homer and the serpent in the Garden of Eden. Rounding off this heterogeneous collection with a joke, Lovejoy writes:

> The inquirer would, at the same time, find that many of these originators of Romanticism – including both the first and last mentioned [i.e. Rousseau and Satan], whom, indeed, some contemporaries are unable to distinguish – figure on other lists as initiators or representatives of tendencies of precisely the contrary sort.[1]

One indisputable element in any definition of Romanticism – namely the important relationship between English and German literary culture in the years following the French Revolution of 1789 – is the subject of this essay. The discussion will focus in particular on the interest in ideas about poetic creation which emerged in Britain and Germany at the end of the eighteenth century.[2]

In both England (and Scotland) and Germany certain topics of critical interest arose at that time, questions about the nature of poetry, the poet and the faculty of Imagination. What is the origin of poetic activity? What is the relation of the subject to the object in perception and, by extension, in imaginative creation? In particular, what is the relation of the poet to external nature (the chief interest of Wordsworth in *The Prelude*, completed, though not published, in 1805)? A stress was now put on the 'organic unity' of a work of art, and the power and genius of the artist was an important object of attention. This represents a perceptible shift from the traditional emphases of the previous 'neo-classical' generation on questions of taste, judgement, decorum and the moral value of literature.[3]

Such 'neo-classical' interests do not disappear completely in the Romantic period, but a shift of emphasis privileges psychological and aesthetic, rather than moral, questions in relation to art. It was Coleridge who introduced the modern sense of the word 'aesthetic' – namely having to do with the art of criticism – into English in a letter published in *Blackwood's Magazine* in 1821 (the German writer Baumgarten having first used the word in this sense in his work *Aesthetica*, published in the 1750s).[4] And it is Coleridge who is the pivotal figure of Anglo-German relations in the Romantic period.

In keeping with the flourishing interest in psychology and the origins of perception and creativity in the later eighteenth century, much of the subject matter of English and German Romantic literature concerns the artist as hero. One thinks of Goethe's phenomenally successful work – translated into several languages and a tremendous success throughout Europe – *Die Leiden des jungen Werthers* (*The Sorrows of Young Werter*, 1774), which spawned a host of imitators, as well as a craze for Werter costumes, Werter china, Werter eau-de-Cologne, and Werter-like suicide among the young men of Europe.[5] One thinks also of the great characteristic English poem of the period, *The Prelude*, the subject of which is the growth of the poet's mind.

An intellectual climate obtained in which the poet was frequently the object of his own scrutiny. This is as true of the work of Friedrich Schiller, the brothers Friedrich and August Wilhelm Schlegel, E. T. A. Hoffmann, Novalis and others in Germany as it is of Coleridge, Wordsworth, Keats, Byron and Shelley in England.

About the middle of the eighteenth century a movement had arisen in Germany in response to the long political and cultural hegemony, or yoke, as it was felt to be, of France. Germany was not a political entity, but a heterogeneous group of petty principalities, which did not even share a common language. As is well known, Frederick the Great of Prussia refused to speak the 'barbaric' German tongue at his court, preferring French, the language of polite society and polite literature. Writers and critics such as Gotthold Ephraim Lessing and Johann Gottfried Herder began the cultural revolt. In their essays on literature and culture, they fought to free German language and literature from the foreign yoke.[6]

The battle was waged on two fronts. First, according to these writers, a literature should be truly national, indigenous, original, not dependent on foreign rules and examples (here Lessing and Herder had the neo-classical unities as applied to drama, with Racine and Corneille as models, chiefly in mind). Second, since Germans had more in common with the British than with the French in terms of their language and, especially according to Herder, their northern climate and culture, they should look to England, a country rich in original literature, for inspiration.

There was, of course, a contradiction here – though a fruitful one – for these German writers were calling on the new generation of German poets at once to be original, to throw off imitation of the French, and at the same time to imitate another model, the English one. With some ingenuity they solved the paradox by concentrating on one English author in particular – Shakespeare. For them, the point about Shakespeare was that he had freed himself from the dramatic unities; he was a great 'natural' genius, a 'Prometheus', a force of nature. In the flow of their enthusiastic rhetoric, Shakespeare and Nature became synonymous and as such the true model for striving German poets.

Both Herder and Goethe wrote rhapsodic essays on Shakespeare along these lines in the 1770s.[7] Goethe even answered his own call in his historical drama, clearly prompted by the example of Shakespeare's histories, *Götz von Berlichingen* (1773), as did Schiller in his Gothic tragedy of the good and bad brothers – strongly reminiscent of Edgar and Edmund in *King Lear* – *Die Räuber* (*The Robbers*, 1781). The young Coleridge read this play in translation in 1794 when his head was full of his new friend Robert Southey and their Utopian plan to set up a Pantisocracy on the banks of the Susquehanna. He dashed off a letter after midnight: 'My God, Southey, who is this Schiller, this Convulser of the Heart?' (Griggs, I, 122). He also sent his friend a rhapsodic sonnet, *To the Author of The Robbers*, which includes these stirring lines:

> Ah! Bard tremendous in sublimity!
> Could I behold thee in thy loftier mood
> Wandering at eve with finely-frenzied eye
> Beneath some vast old tempest-swinging wood!
> Awhile with mute awe gazing I would brood:
> Then weep aloud in a wild ecstasy![8]

The phrase 'finely-frenzied eye' echoes Theseus's line at the beginning of Act V of *A Midsummer Night's Dream* about 'the poet's eye, in a fine frenzy rolling'. Coleridge chooses it as a proper tribute to Schiller's genius, and perhaps also as an acknowledgement of the visible Shakespearean influence on Schiller.

Next most important to Shakespeare in the programme for the revival of German literature was the ballad literature of Germany. Encouraged by Bishop Thomas Percy's recent collection of English ballads, *Reliques of Ancient English Poetry* (1765), Germans sought out old German ballads, and – as had happened with James Macpherson's so-called 'discovery' and translation of an early Scottish epic by the bard 'Ossian' (1762), highly successful in Germany as well as in Britain – wherever they could not find original ballads they composed their own.

August Bürger's Gothic ballad of a ghostly ride by night, *Lenore*, loosely based on a Scottish ballad, *Sweet William's Ghost*, is the most celebrated example of how an influence could begin in Britain, with Percy's *Reliques*, inspire poetic activity in Germany, and travel back to Britain to have further literary success there. For *Lenore* was translated in the 1790s by several Britons, including the Poet Laureate, H. J. Pye; J. T. Stanley, whose translation was illustrated by Blake; and the young Walter Scott, who was to become the first popular and financially successful Romantic poet and novelist in Britain.[9]

Clearly, a sympathetic harmony existed between Britain and Germany in this revival of interest in ballads and old national literature. Wordsworth and Coleridge entered their famous collaboration on *Lyrical Ballads* in 1797, publishing the collection in 1798, the same year in which Goethe and Schiller published a collection of their own ballads. Scott's first literary efforts were in this mould too, and he was directly interested in literary events in Germany. Not only did he translate *Lenore* in 1797; he produced a translation (full of comic errors) of Goethe's *Götz von Berlichingen* in 1799. His contribution to British ballad literature began with an edition of Scottish border ballads in 1802–3, and continued in 1805 with his enormously successful ballad-like poem, *The Lay of the Last Minstrel*.

Important though Scott is in any story of the influence of German literature in Britain, there is one writer whose relationship with Germany was in every way more significant, though also fraught with complexities. This was Coleridge, who read widely in the literature, criticism and philosophy of Germany. The vexed question of his plagiarism from German sources, particularly the philosophers Kant and Schelling and the critics Schiller and A. W. Schlegel, has occupied observers from De Quincey and Hazlitt in Coleridge's own day to modern scholars and the editors of the Bollingen edition of Coleridge's *Collected Works*.[10] Suffice it to say that Coleridge did owe a debt to these writers, in some cases for philosophical insights which inform his own criticism, in others for the actual phrasing or examples he used. Sometimes he acknowledged his sources; sometimes not.

It must also be said that Coleridge was an astonishingly omnivorous reader, a walking compendium of ideas, of necessity not all of them original to him, and that he has a serious claim to be considered an 'original' thinker, since he brilliantly absorbed, adapted and extended various views which he found in his German – and other – reading. His critical theory and practice, particularly his remarks on Shakespeare, Milton and Wordsworth, have been enormously influential in their turn on subsequent generations of English poets and critics. The influence starts with Keats, whose critical remarks about Shakespeare and Wordsworth surely owe something to his own reading of Coleridge's *Biographia Literaria* (1817). Indeed, Keats's famous phrase 'negative capability', used in a letter of December 1817 to describe Shakespeare's genius, recalls two phrases in *Biographia Literaria*: 'negative faith' (chapter 22) and 'that willing suspension of disbelief for the moment which constitutes poetic faith' (chapter 14).[11] The Coleridgean critical influence extends to T. S. Eliot, I. A. Richards, and the American New Critics of the 1940s and beyond.[12]

In *Biographia Literaria* Coleridge asked the question 'What is poetry?' and, in a manner which illustrates what we may call the 'Romantic Revolution' in aesthetics, answered it as follows:

> What is poetry? is so nearly the same question with, what is a poet? that the answer to the one is involved in the solution of the other. For it is a distinction resulting from the poetic genius itself, which sustains and modifies the images, thoughts, and emotions of the poet's own mind. The poet, described in *ideal* perfection, brings the whole soul of man into activity, with the subordination of its faculties to each other, according to their relative worth and dignity. He diffuses a tone, and spirit of unity, that blends, and (as it were) *fuses*, each into each, by that synthetic and magical power, to which we have exclusively appropriated the name of imagination.[13]

These questions, and the answers which Coleridge gives, depend on a theory of knowledge, of the relations between the perceiving subject and the object of his/her perception, of the mind and nature. For much of his theory of knowledge Coleridge was indebted to German philosophy of the late eighteenth century, which enjoyed an astonishing flowering as part of the general upsurge in German culture. In particular, Coleridge drew on the work of Immanuel Kant, whom he called 'the illustrious sage of Königsberg', and on Kant's successor, Friedrich Wilhelm Joseph von Schelling.[14]

As was the case with German critics' appreciation of Shakespeare and the ballad form, so also with German philosophers. Those who were influential on English critical thinking, via Coleridge, were themselves steeped in the dominant British school of philosophy of the eighteenth century. This school had perfected the empirical method in philosophy, according to which one argues from the actual experience of the senses rather than from pure logic or notions of innate (inborn) ideas.

The empirical method had been applied by John Locke, in his *Essay Concerning Human Understanding* (1690). For Locke, the mind is a passive receiver of images imprinted on it by the senses, a 'mirror' which fixes the objects which it reflects, even a *tabula rasa* (blank tablet) on which sensations imprint themselves.

David Hume, in his *Treatise of Human Nature* (1839–40), took Locke's method to its logical extreme, finding that we have no mental mechanism for making any judgements which could claim to be universal or necessary, only the ability to build up a picture from the experiences we actually encounter through our senses. All we can know of cause and effect is that y follows x in all the situations we have observed. We have no faculty which tells us that y *must* follow x or that y *always* follows x. This argument attacks the claims of Idealist philosophers like Descartes, who argued that we are born with a faculty of Reason which intuits absolutes like the existence of God and immortality. With Hume, philosophy becomes separated from theology, and he, for one, embraced the ultimate logical position which flowed from his argument – atheism.

Though Hume's philosophy raised problems for theology, it was tremendously fruitful in the sphere of aesthetics, since it highlighted the immediate response of the senses, the feeling on the pulse, to use a Wordsworthian phrase. Moreover, though according to Hume we cannot have certain knowledge about ultimate questions regarding morality and spirituality, we do have faculties for building up our – albeit incomplete – knowledge. Among these are the imagination (or fancy) and the memory, both faculties which link experiences in the mind, imagination by a perceived similarity and by means of metaphor and simile, and memory by associations of time and place.

Following Hume came David Hartley, whose *Observations on Man* (1749) influenced Wordsworth, and also Coleridge in his brilliant youth. (So impressed was the latter with Hartley's ideas that he christened his eldest son Hartley Coleridge in 1796.) Hartley refined on Hume's ideas with his famous doctrine of the Association of Ideas by contiguity and succession. The mind absorbs impressions and orders them, not according to a faculty of pure reasoning, but according to their association in time and space with other impressions.[15]

A corollary of this thinking is that childhood is an important time for the moulding and developing of the eventual adult; this aspect of Associationism contributed to the increased interest in childhood in the period, and the flourishing of educational theories based on the idea that good teaching and training – or ensuring that the child encounters pleasant and morally beneficial experiences – will be a strong factor in the growth to civilized adulthood. *The Prelude* is the great poetic expression of this idea of the child being father of the man.

Associationism bore further fruit for the literature and criticism of the period. Memory plays an important part in Hartley's philosophy, and it does so also in the fine reflective poetry of Wordsworth, mingling there with that other linking faculty, Imagination, in a way which prefigures Freud, Proust and the stream of consciousness novel of the early twentieth century.

The poet's mind, in the light of the Hartleian doctrine, is a finely receptive but passive vehicle, ready to be worked on by external images. Coleridge's conversation poem of 1795,

*The Eolian Harp*, employs the suggestive symbolism of the lute of that name, which, if
hung at an open window, plays according to the movement of the wind through it:

> Full many a thought uncall'd and undetain'd,
> Traverse my indolent and passive brain,
> As wild and various as the random gales
> That swell and flutter on this subject Lute![16]

The mind, passive in ordinary perception, is also passive but receptive in poetic creation.

In 1799 Coleridge first began reading Kant, and he soon revised his philosophy of
mind, and with it his theory of literature. For Kant saw that for all its attractions the
Associationist philosophy of Hume and Hartley represented the mind as a slave to chance
external impressions. Hume had, Kant thought, brought philosophy to an impasse. He
and his fellow empiricists could not explain how it is that we *do* believe that every effect
has a cause and that its cause may be discovered. And they had relegated the mind to what
Coleridge described in a letter of 1801 as 'a lazy Looker-on on an external World'.[17]

On the other hand, Kant admired Hume's demolition of the Idealist school of Descartes
and Leibnitz, who started from a premise – that we have innate ideas such as God,
immortality, duty – which they had never investigated. Kant's own method was a
unique middle way between the idealists and the empiricists. He set out to criticize the
reasoning faculty itself – hence the titles of his most important works, *Die Kritik der
reinen Vernunft* (*The Critique of Pure Reason*, 1781), *Die Kritik der praktischen Vernunft* (*The
Critique of Practical Reason*, 1788) and *Die Kritik der Urteilskraft* (*The Critique of Judgment*,
1790).

Philosophy hitherto had assumed that the mind is dependent on the objects it encounters. The result, according to Kant, had been either uncritical, dogmatic assertions about
the power of reason when it encountered impressions, or the more honest position of the
empiricists that the mind merely absorbs impressions in a random way, and that it can
know nothing with certainty, including the existence of God. There was no way of solving
this stalemate, said Kant, except by means of a method he compared to the Copernican
Revolution in scientific knowledge. If we cannot reach a satisfactory conclusion by
assuming the subject to be dependent on its object, we should try turning the question
round and assume the object to be dependent for its validity on the perceiving subject:

> We must therefore make trial whether we may not have more success in the tasks of
> metaphysics, if we suppose that objects must conform to our knowledge. This would agree
> better with what is desired, namely, that it should be possible to have knowledge of objects *a
> priori*, determining something in regard to them prior to their being given. We should then
> be proceeding precisely on the lines of Copernicus' primary hypothesis. Failing of satisfactory
> progress in explaining the movements of the heavenly bodies on the supposition that they all
> revolved round the spectator, he tried whether he might not have better success if he made the
> spectator to revolve and the stars to remain at rest. A similar experiment can be tried in
> metaphysics, as regards the *intuition* of objects. If intuition must conform to the constitution
> of the objects, I do not see how we could know anything of the latter *a priori*; but if the object
> (as object of the senses) must conform to the constitution of our faculty of intuition, I have no
> difficulty in conceiving such a possibility.[18]

Kant accepts the empirical or sceptical premise that all knowledge begins with sense experience. But sense alone can yield no knowledge. Thus far he agrees with Hume. But he reverses Hume's conclusion. The mind applies categories of perception to the object, and has knowledge of it which goes beyond sense experience. Coleridge illustrates this idea with an example of his own in *Biographia Literaria*:

> By knowledge, *a priori*, we do not mean, that we can know any thing previously to experience, which would be a contradiction in terms; but that having once known it by occasion of experience (i.e. something acting upon us from without) we then know, that it must have pre-existed, or the experience itself would have been impossible. By experience only I know, that I have eyes; but then my reason convinces me, that I must have had eyes in order to [have] the experience.[19]

The mind is thus freed from the constraints imposed on it by the empiricists and from the unprovable and often absurdly subjective claims made for it by the idealists. The mind is, then, neither the slave of sense impressions nor the tyrant of innate ideas.

What holds good for a theory of knowledge could be helpful for a theory of literature too, as Schiller found when he adapted Kant's philosophy to a theory of literature in several essays on aesthetics written in the 1790s.[20] Kant, in *The Critique of Judgment*, described the imagination as the faculty which bridges the gap between the realm of the senses and the realm of ideas. Not only is the mind active in perception, but the creative mind is active in creation; the imagination is a synthesizing power, reconciling world and idea, mind and nature. As Coleridge adapts and extends the idea in *Biographia Literaria*, the poet brings 'the whole soul of man into activity', and the imagination is a 'synthetic and magical power' which

> reveals itself in the balance or reconciliation of opposite or discordant qualities: of sameness, with difference; of the general, with the concrete; the idea, with the image; the individual, with the representative; the sense of novelty, with old and familiar objects; a more than usual state of emotion, with more than usual order; judgement ever awake and steady self-possession, with enthusiasm and feeling profound or vehement.[21]

This is a fine analytical description of the ideal activity of poetic creation. It also enlightens us about the purposes, and the effects, of Coleridge's and Wordsworth's own poetry, as well as fitting well with his sympathetic insights into Shakespeare's genius. When Wordsworth writes in the Preface to *The Excursion* (1814) of a marriage between mind and nature and when in *The Prelude* he almost deifies the Imagination as a great power, he betrays the importance of his discussions with his fellow poet Coleridge, though he himself probably never read a page of Kant or Schiller. In the Preface to *The Excursion* he proclaims

> How exquisitely the individual Mind
> (And the progressive powers perhaps no less
> Of the whole species) to the external World
> Is fitted: – and how exquisitely too –
> Theme this but little heard of among men –
> The external World is fitted to the Mind;

And the creation (by no lower name
Can it be called) which they with blended might
Accomplish (*WPW*, V, 5)

In his appreciation of Shakespeare, for which he has become justly famous, Coleridge is close to the German critic A. W. Schlegel, from whom he undoubtedly borrowed, yet whom he outshone in the practical criticism of Shakespeare ('practical criticism' being a phrase coined by Coleridge in *Biographia Literaria*, taken up by I. A. Richards to describe his practice, and since then used to describe an important element in English literature courses in many universities). Schlegel, in his lectures on Shakespeare, published in 1809–10, went further than his predecessors Lessing and Herder. To their notion of Shakespeare as a child of nature (also commonplace in England, as in Milton's famous lines in *L'Allegro*, 'Sweetest Shakespeare, Fancy's child, / Warbl[ing] his native woodnotes wild') Schlegel added the idea of Shakespeare's judgement being as important as his genius, his active control equal to his native receptiveness: 'To me he appears a profound artist, not a blind and wildly luxuriant genius'.[22]

In his own Shakespeare criticism in lectures, letters and notebooks, as well as in passages of *Biographia Literaria*, Coleridge echoes Schlegel, and goes further with his definition of the reconciling qualities of the imagination, the faculty which resolves oppositions. In 1828 Coleridge said of himself, 'I still have that within me which is both Harp and Breeze', neatly encapsulating the change since his Hartleian youth, when he had used the metaphor of the harp to describe the poet's receptive but passive mind.[23] The mind in creation is now seen as active as well as receptive.

Kant had been indebted to Hume's criticism of dogmatic idealism, and in turn Coleridge owed much to Kant, Schelling, Schlegel and other German writers of philosophy and criticism, whom he read and absorbed alongside Classical philosophy and the works of many English thinkers of the seventeenth and eighteenth centuries.

As in Coleridge's individual case, so in the case of intellectual relationships between cultures and nations generally. One culture takes over, more or less consciously, elements from another to fit its needs and preoccupations. Thus, Kant built on eighteenth-century British empirical philosophy. Herder used Shakespeare as propaganda for a new German literature. The very German dramas and poems which resulted from his call to arms travelled back to England to energize British writers. This is true of the Gothic genre both in its glories, among which must be counted *The Ancient Mariner* as well as Mary Shelley's *Frankenstein* (1818), and its manifestations of absurdity and excess, such as Matthew Lewis's notorious works (in which he cheerfully acknowledges his borrowings from Schiller and other German writers of Gothic drama), *The Monk* (1796) and *The Castle Spectre* (1798).[24]

John Stuart Mill claimed in his *Westminster Review* essay on Coleridge (1840) that the latter exercised a seminal influence on the Victorians. What Mill calls the 'Germano-Coleridgean doctrine' in philosophy and criticism became a pervasive and fruitful presence in the thinking of the generation which came after.[25] As we have seen, the literary and philosophical renaissance in Germany, which was so important for Coleridge, and through him for many others, could not itself have taken just the form it did without the reception, absorption and imitation of British theory and practice, whether in the thought of Burke on the sublime and Hume and Hartley on the theory of association, or in the ballads collected by Percy and the plays of Shakespeare.

## NOTES

1   Lovejoy, 'On the discrimination of Romanticisms', in *Essays*, pp. 228–9.

2   See Abrams *ML*; E. S. Shaffer, '*Kubla Khan*'; Ashton, *The German Idea*; Marilyn Butler, 'Romanticism in England' and Dietrich von Engelhardt, 'Romanticism in Germany', in Porter and Teich (eds) *Romanticism in National Context*.

3   See Bate, *From Classic to Romantic*.

4   See Williams, *Keywords*, p. 27; Ashton, *The Life of Samuel Taylor Coleridge*, p. 337.

5   See Swales, *The Sorrows of Young Werther*, pp. 94–100.

6   See especially Lessing, *Briefe die neueste Literarur betreffend* (1759–65) and *Hamburgische Dramaturgie* (1767–9), in *Werke*.

7   Goethe, 'Zum Shakespeares Tag' (1771), in *Werke*, IV, 122–6; Herder, *Von deutscher Art und Kunst* (1773), in *Werke*, II, 498–521.

8   EHC, I, 72–3.

9   See Morgan, *Critical Bibliography*.

10   See Orsini, *Coleridge*; McFarland, *Coleridge*; Fruman, *Coleridge*; Ashton, *The German Idea*; Introduction and Appendix A to CC *Biographia*.

11   Keats to George and Tom Keats, 21 December 1817, in Rollins, I, 193–4; CC *Biographia* II, 134, 6.

12   See especially Richards, *Principles* and *Practical Criticism*.

13   CC *Biographia*, II, 15–16 (chapter 14).

14   Ibid., I, 153. See also Ashton, *The Life of Samuel Taylor Coleridge*, pp. 307–11.

15   See Willey, *The Eighteenth-century Background* and *The English Moralists*.

16   EHC, I, 101–2.

17   Coleridge to Thomas Poole, 23 March 1801, in Griggs, II, 709.

18   Kant, preface to second edition of *Critique of Pure Reason*, p. 22.

19   CC *Biographia*, I, 293n (chapter 12).

20   See, for example, Schiller's *Briefe über die Ästhetische Erziehung des Menschen*.

21   CC *Biographia*, II, 16–17 (chapter 14).

22   Schlegel, Lecture 26 of *Vorlesungen über dramatische Kunst und Literatur* (1809–10), in *Kritische Schriften und Briefe*, VI, 126.

23   Griggs, VI, 731n (marginal note on a letter from Lady Beaumont, 16 May 1828).

24   See Lewis's footnotes to *The Castle Spectre* (1798), in Cox, *Seven Gothic Dramas*, pp. 180n, 199n.

25   Mill, 'Coleridge', *London and Westminster Review*, 33 (March 1840), p. 263; reprinted in Leavis, *Mill on Bentham and Coleridge*.

## WRITINGS

Goethe, Johann Gottfried von, *Werke, Briefe und Gespräche*, Gedenkausgabe, ed. Ernst Beutler, 24 vols, Zurich, Artemis-Verlag, 1948–62.

Herder, Johann Gottfried, *Werke*, ed. Günter Arnold et al., 10 volumes in progress, Frankfurt am Main, Deutscher Klassiker Verlag, 1985–.

Kant, Immanuel, *The Critique of Pure Reason*, trans. Norman Kemp Smith, London, Macmillan, 1973.

Lessing, Gotthold Ephraim, *Werke*, ed. Herbert G. Göpfert et al., 8 vols, Munich, Carl Hanser Verlag, 1970–9.

Schiller, Friedrich: *Briefe über die Ästhetische Erziehung des Menschen*, parallel text with translation by E. M. Wilkinson and L. A. Willoughby, Oxford, Oxford University Press, 1967.

Schlegel, August Wilhelm, *Kritische Schriften und Briefe*, ed. Edgar Lohner, 7 vols, Stuttgart, W. Kohlhammer Verlag, 1962–7.

## REFERENCES AND FURTHER READING

Ashton, Rosemary, *The German Idea: Four English Writers and the Reception of German Thought 1800–1860*, London, Libris, 1994.

——*The Life of Samuel Taylor Coleridge: A Critical Biography*, Oxford, Blackwell Publishers, 1996.

Bate, Walter Jackson, *From Classic to Romantic: Premises of Taste in Eighteenth-century England*, New York, Harper & Row, 1961.

Cox, Jeffrey N. (ed.) *Seven Gothic Dramas 1789–1825*, Athens, Ohio: Ohio University Press, 1992.

Fruman, Norman, *Coleridge: The Damaged Archangel*, London, Allen & Unwin, 1972.

Lovejoy, Arthur O., *Essays in the History of Ideas*, Baltimore, Johns Hopkins University Press, 1948.

McFarland, Thomas, *Coleridge and the Pantheist Tradition*, Oxford, Clarendon Press, 1969.

Mill, J. S., *Mill on Bentham and Coleridge*, ed. F. R. Leavis, London, Chatto & Windus, 1950.

Morgan, B. Q., *A Critical Bibliography of German Literature in English Translation*, 2nd edn, New York and London, Scarecrow Press, 1965.

Orsini, Gian, N. G., *Coleridge and German Idealism*, Carbondale, Southern Illinois University Press, 1969.

Porter, Roy, and Teich, Mikulas (eds) *Romanticism in National Context*, Cambridge, Cambridge University Press, 1988.

Richards, I. A., *Principles of Literary Criticism*, London, Routledge & Kegan Paul, 1924.

——*Practical Criticism*, London, Routledge & Kegan Paul, 1929.

Shaffer, E. S., *'Kubla Khan' and The Fall of Jerusalem*, Cambridge, Cambridge University Press, 1975.

Swales, Martin, *The Sorrows of Young Werther*, Cambridge, Cambridge University Press, 1987.

Willey, Basil, *The Eighteenth-century Background*, London, Chatto & Windus, 1940.

——*The English Moralists*, London, Chatto & Windus, 1964.

Williams, Raymond, *Keywords: A Vocabulary of Culture and Society*, London, Fontana, 1976.

# 50

# Romantic Responses to Science

## Ian Wylie

In 1727 Sir Isaac Newton died at the huge age of 85. As a recent biographer has aptly described him, Newton was 'one of the tiny handful of supreme geniuses who have shaped the categories of the human intellect'[1] and the epitaphs of the day were equally fulsome in their praise. Alexander Pope's epitaph for Newton's tomb in Westminster Abbey captures the contemporary mood:

> Nature and Nature's Laws lay hid in Night.
> GOD said, *Let Newton be!* and all was Light.

In Newton's two seminal works, *Philosophiae Naturalis Principia Mathematica* (1687) and the *Opticks* (1704), the laws which governed the order of the natural world were comprehensively described for the first time. The universe was revealed as an ordered and rational economy in which things behaved the way they did because of a pre-established harmony that was comprehensible to humanity, or at least to a few individuals of genius, and could be communicated by these individuals to the rest of mankind. Those who looked deeply into nature, would see in its laws the hand of the beneficent lawgiver, who moved, or who had at one time moved, in all things. To Newton, 'nature . . . was an open book, whose letters he could read without effort', wrote the greatest scientist of our own century, Albert Einstein.[2] Thus, Newton led the civilized world into the age of reason, the age of optimism, the age of the best of all worlds:

> All Nature is but Art, unknown to thee;
> All Chance, Direction, which thou canst not see;
> All Discord, Harmony, not understood;
> All partial Evil, universal Good:
> And, spite of Pride, in erring Reason's spite,
> One truth is clear, 'Whatever is, is RIGHT'.[3]

Newton had been the first to admit that there was much science had to do to penetrate all the mysteries of the universe. 'I don't know what I may seem to the world, but, as to myself, I seem to have been only like a boy playing on the sea shore, and diverting myself in now and then finding a smoother pebble or a prettier shell than ordinary, whilst the great ocean of truth lay all undiscovered before me'.[4] This quote, shortly before his death, to an unnamed companion, was widely known, and could be read as an invitation to those who would pick up the Sage's mantle. Indeed, Newton had published 35 'queries' which he believed still needed answering in the second edition of the *Opticks* (1717). Some of these were not answered until Einstein's work at the beginning of the twentieth century (e.g. 'Query 30: Are not gross Bodies and Light convertible into one another?');[5] but other mysteries, particularly the chemical transformations of matter and the identity of the great forces of nature, might yield to the eighteenth-century natural philosopher, and so bring the age nearer to complete knowledge of nature's economy.

In 1749, 22 years after Newton's death, a printer from the New World, Benjamin Franklin, claimed Newton's mantle with a series of experiments which proved conclusively the identity of lightning and electricity, thus both describing and taming one of the great destructive forces in nature. The erection of lightning conductors on cathedrals and churches, an actual and symbolic representation of the ascendance of science, also signalled the advent of humanity's control over the natural world that would become the age of industrialization. When Franklin arrived in Britain as the chief emissary of the colonists of Pennsylvania to open negotiations with the British government over tax laws, he was one of the most celebrated men in Europe.

Ironically, the taming of the electrical storm occurred just before an event which ended the naive optimism of the 'best of all possible worlds' of the early eighteenth century and shattered the confidence of the rationalists. The Lisbon earthquake of 1754 hit the capital of Portugal at 11 o'clock on All Saints Day, causing the collapse of the cathedral and some 30 other churches with people at prayer on one of the principal days in the religious calendar. The earthquake was followed by a devastating fire and then a tidal wave, which drowned many of those who had escaped the shock and the fire.

News of the disaster reached London 11 days later, but many refused to believe the reports. Debate continued for months: should the earthquake be seen as the act of a just God, punishing his people for unspecified wrongs, or was nature itself bound by inexorable Newtonian laws to create such disasters? Was the deity amoral or even absent, leaving his machine-like universe to run without thought or compassion? The Lisbon earthquake ended the complacent view of the 'best of all worlds'. Voltaire buried it with *Candide* (1758), when his hero, battered and bereaved after being caught up in the Lisbon earthquake, declares in wonder: 'If this is the best of all possible worlds, what can the rest be like?'[6] In place, a new optimism arose. Nature cannot be described as perfect, because humanity, a part of nature, has not progressed to the state of perfect knowledge. But there are signs of providential progressiveness, and there will come about a state of harmony in nature and in society which will be the perfect millennial state predicted in the Bible. Joseph Priestley, the experimental philosopher, Unitarian minister, and early disciple of Franklin, expressed his confidence in the perfectability of the world in *An Essay on the First Principles of Government* (1768):

> In this state of things, it requires but a few years to comprehend the whole preceding progress
> of any one art of science ... nature, including both its materials and its laws, will be more at

our command; men will make their situation in this world abundantly more easy and comfortable; they will probably prolong their existence in it, and will grow daily more happy, each in himself, and more able . . . to communicate happiness to others. Thus whatever was the beginning of this world, the end will be glorious and *paradisaical*, beyond what our imaginations can now conceive.[7]

This is not mere rhetoric. Inspired and prompted by Franklin, Priestley had earlier written a *History of Electricity* (1767) and had begun to experiment in the 'science of airs'. He had also watched Franklin, the philosopher–sage, and the upstart colonists, win independence from the might of Britain. Priestley and a group of fellow radical thinkers began to wonder whether the progress in discoveries in the natural world might somehow be linked to progress in the social and political sphere, and whether similar progress might be made among the *ancien régimes* of Europe. They corresponded with philosophers and radicals in France. The answer came in March 1789 when the French chemist Anton Lavoisier published the results of 15 years of chemical experiments, inspired by Priestley, and laid the foundations of modern chemistry.[8] Four months later the fall of the Bastille signalled the end of the *ancien régime* in France. The radicals were delighted. Erasmus Darwin, the doctor–poet, wrote to the engineer James Watts: 'Do you not congratulate your grand-children on the dawn of universal liberty? I find myself becoming all french both in chemistry and politics'.[9] A new image was born of the philosopher–hero, moulding a new and better society through insights in the natural order; and the whole moving towards a future millennial state. Darwin celebrated the scientific and social advances in his poem *The Economy of Vegetation* of 1791. In rhyming couplets and copious footnotes, Darwin gave an authoritative overview of the state of science at the end of the century, and looked forward to the next scientific advances that would bring about the paradisiacal age:

> You led your FRANKLIN to your glazed retreats,
> Your air-built castles, and your silken seats;
> Bade his bold arm invade the lowering sky,
> And seize the tiptoe lightnings, ere they fly;
>
> . . .
>
> – The patriot-flame with quick contagion ran,
> Hill lighted hill, and man electrifed man;
> Her heroes slain awhile COLUMBIA mourn'd,
> And crown'd with laurels LIBERTY return'd.[10]

Coleridge, who mixed with many of the leading radicals in his troubled student days,[11] enthusiastically endorsed the notion of an elect group of philosopher–reformers, in an early poem, *Religious Musings* (1794–6):

> And the pale-featur'd Sage's trembling hand
> Strong as an host of armed Deities!
> From Avarice thus, from Luxury and War
> Sprang heavenly Science: and from Science Freedom. (235–8)

Written in the uncertain days of the mid-1790s, when Pitt's government was so concerned about the possibility of revolution that it passed emergency laws banning mass meetings,

*Religious Musings* sees the elect band of seers using their unique knowledge of the natural world to bring about the millennial state. Here the forces of disorder, the masses, are equated with chaotic nature devoid of laws to govern it:

> O'er waken'd realms Philosophers and Bards
> Spread in concentric circles (239–40)

> These hush'd a while with patient eye serene
> Shall watch the mad careering of the storm;
> Then o'er the wild and wavy chaos rush
> And tame th' outrageous mass, with plastic might
> Moulding Confusion to such perfect forms,
> As erst were wont, bright visions of the day! (256–61)

In Coleridge's two major poems, *The Rime of the Ancient Mariner* and *Kubla Khan*, the title figures have particular insight into the natural order, and use this insight to create new worlds: the recreated world of the glittering watersnakes in the *Ancient Mariner* and the miraculous pleasure dome of *Kubla Khan*.

Yet it was to Wordsworth that Coleridge turned for a contemporary example of the philosopher–sage. Coleridge's youth had been spent in the city, the natural world denied him, but Wordsworth's had been a privileged upbringing among the language of God. In Coleridge's exquisite conversation poem *Frost at Midnight*, after lamenting that he was brought up 'In the great city, pent', he anticipates the way he will bring up his first-born son, and so creates a vision of harmony between the child, nature and society:

> so shalt thou see and hear
> The lovely shapes and sounds intelligible
> Of that eternal language, which thy God
> Utters who from eternity doth teach
> Himself in all, and all things in himself. (58–62)

Nature as the expression of God was a traditional conceit in the eighteenth century, but the idea is given a more rigorous treatment in the poetry of Coleridge and Wordsworth. Wordsworth, tutored by the philosophical Coleridge, expressed his optimism in the unity of natural orders and social orders in *Lines Written above Tintern Abbey*:

> a sense sublime
> Of something far more deeply interfused,
> Whose dwelling is the light of setting suns,
> And the round ocean, and the living air,
> And the blue sky, and in the mind of man,
> A motion and a spirit, that impels
> All thinking things, all objects of all thought,
> And rolls through all things. (96–103)

Full of confidence that observation of the natural order would bring about the perfect state, Coleridge jotted in his notebook that the millennium might be brought about by 'progression in natural philosophy – particularly, meteorology, or science of airs & winds' and proposed to write a commentary on the Book of Revelation from 'late philosophical discoveries'[12] but he looked to Wordsworth to write the great philosophical poem of the age. Wordsworth, fired by Coleridge's optimism, but less than sure about his task, set himself to write *The Recluse: or, Views on Nature, Man, and Society*.[13] His lament that he could not make progress begins the poem which would become *The Prelude*. In the first version, Wordsworth begins by asking himself the rhetorical question why he is unable to write, when he had experienced a childhood full of the divine language of nature:[14]

> Was it for this
> That one, the fairest of all rivers, loved
> To blend his murmurs with my nurse's song
> And from his alder shades and rocky falls,
> And from his fords and shallows, sent a voice
> That flowed along my dreams?

The moral force of nature is most evident in *The Prelude*, in which Wordsworth develops the 'spots of time': moments when the natural world overwhelms the consciousness of the child and develops the moral sense. The philosophical parallel to this was William Godwin's *Enquiry Concerning Political Justice* (1793–5), written to expose the ills of societies governed by political structures, and the most thorough development of these ideas was in Shelley's poetry.

However, the discoveries in the natural world were not only providing philosophical ideas for transforming society, but were ordering and transforming the early industrial landscape. This period saw the improvement of the transport infrastructure with the building of the canal network, and the transformation of small market towns, like Birmingham and Manchester, into flourishing industrial centres. It is no accident that some of the most active social radicals of the period, Coleridge's 'elect band', were also some of the most successful industrialists, such as James Watt and Matthew Boulton, who created the Soho works in Birmingham and Josiah Wedgwood, chemist and potter, whose Etruria manufactory in the Potteries attracted visitors from across Europe. The manipulation of the natural world through the processes of industrialization was to prove a good source of material for the individual struggling to tame and better nature, and Mary Shelley's novel *Frankenstein* (1828) can be seen in a direct line from the electrical descriptions of Benjamin Franklin. And as London became the foremost industrial town in the world, it was the London poet, William Blake, whose imagery draws on the industrial scenes around him:

> And Urizen (so his eternal name)
> His prolific delight obscured more and more
> In dark secrecy, hiding in surging
> Sulphureous fluid his fantasies.
> The eternal prophet heaved the dark bellows,
> And turned restless the tongs, and the hammer
> Incessant beat, forging chains new and new,
> Numbering with links hours, days and years.[15]

In his prophet books, particularly *The First Book of Urizen* (1794) and *Vala, or the Four Zoas* (1797), Blake explicitly links the imagery of the manufactory with sexual energy and imagination, which all too easily are tamed by the intellectual, ordering, measuring mind. Reason without imagination is cold and dark, and it is in this context that Blake equates science with the tree of death. His plea for the 'tigers of wrath' to lead the 'horses of instruction' in the *Proverbs of Hell* is repeated in the revolutionary manifesto which precedes his later and difficult prophetic book *Milton*, where he calls for the world of imagination to overcome the world of memory.

Blake's magnificent colour print of Newton (1795), in which the naked figure (based on a figure in the Sistine Chapel) is composed formally, captures the growing ambivalence to Newton and experimental science. Blake's portrait evokes the spiritual form of Newton, a figure of energy and beauty who is fixed in a two-dimensional state, concerned only to pin down the heavens with measuring protractors. In the same year Coleridge suggested that Newton's philosophy might lead to atheism, because the experimental method described an ordered universe without admitting the need of an external Presence. Indeed, Coleridge came to see science as being only able to see 'little things', because its method was solely concerned with the world of the senses.[16] Keats, born into an age less certain about the place of scientific thought, is often quoted in support of this more sceptical attitude towards Newtonian science. In 1818 at a dinner at the house of Benjamin Haydon, and in the presence of Wordsworth and Lamb, Keats proposed a toast to Newton and the confusion to mathematics. His lines in *Lamia*, later that year, are often quoted:

> Do not all charms fly
> At the mere touch of cold philosophy?
> Ther was an awful rainbow once in heaven:
> We know her woof, her texture; she is given
> In the dull catalogue of common things.
> Philosophy will clip an Angel's wings,
> Conquer all mysteries by rule and line,
> Empty the haunted air, and gnomed mine –
> Unweave a rainbow (II, 229–36)

But Keats is on dangerous ground. In Book Five of *The Prelude* (1805), Wordsworth had retold a dream of Descartes: he is at the edge of a vast desert, when a Bedouin comes who carries under his arms two objects which will be the poet's guide across the desert. The Bedouin says these are books that contain the secrets of the natural world and the moral worlds, but the objects he actually carries are a *stone* and a *shell*: those two objects with which 'the great Newton' (*Prelude*, IV. 270) had been distracted.

Thus, in spite of Keats's rather superficial dismissal of science, for many, the charms and mysteries of nature were not emptied by philosophy but made sharper and were deepened. The great scientific advances of the late eighteenth and early nineteenth centuries fed both imagery and the intellectual excitement of writers, who articulated their visions in a natural world whose size and complexity continued to grow. Perhaps it was the increasing complexity and professionalism of the disciplines of science which finally broke the concord with writers like Coleridge and Wordsworth. By the 1820s the advances, specialisms and technical complexities made it impossible for those who had not trained in the specialism to understand.

It is perhaps an irony that the divorce was finally effected as a result of the work of the grandson of one of the proponents of the interrelation of science, society and literature. Charles Darwin, revolutionary author of the *Origin of Species* (1849), in describing how order in nature can arise from chance changes acted on by outside forces – the principle of natural selection – broke the link between nature and society. There was no moral force at work in nature, merely a blind interplay, and there was no correspondence between the social order and the natural order. Humanity had nothing to learn from nature about how to live, for as there was no intelligent design, there could be no intelligent progressiveness. Another poet, Tennyson, was there to signal the demise of the alliance:

> Are God and Nature then at strife,
> That Nature lends such evil dreams?
> So careful of the type she seems,
> So careless of the single life (*In Memoriam* A. H. H., lv)

## Notes

1  R. S. Westfall, *Never at Rest: A Biography of Isaac Newton*, Cambridge, Cambridge University Press, 1980, p. x.

2  Foreword to *Opticks, or A Treatise of the Reflections, Refractions, Inflections & Colours of Light*, Dover, New York, 1952, p. lix.

3  Alexander Pope, *An Essay on Man*, I, 289–94.

4  R. S. Westfall, *Never at Rest*, p. 863.

5  *Opticks*, p. 374.

6  Voltaire, *Candide*, trans. J. Butt, Harmondsworth, Penguin, 1947, p. 37.

7  *The Theological and Miscellaneous Works, etc., of Joseph Priestley*, ed. J. Rutt, 25 vols, 1817–31, XXII, p. 9.

8  *Traité Elémentaire de Chimie, présenté dans un ordre nouveau et d'après les découvertes modernes*, 2 vols, 1789.

9  Letter of 19 January 1790, quoted in I. Wylie, *Young Coleridge and the Philosophers of Nature*, Oxford, Oxford University Press 1989, p. 2.

10  Erasmus Darwin, 'The economy of vegetation', in *The Botanic Garden*, London, 1791, I, 83–6; II, 367–70.

11  See I. Wylie, 'Coleridge and the lunaticks,' in *The Coleridge Companion*, ed. R. Gravil & M. Lefebure, Macmillan, London, 1990, pp. 25–40.

12  *Notebooks*, I, 133.

13  See Stephen Gill, *Wordsworth: A Life*, Oxford, 1989, pp. 144–5.

14  *The Prelude 1799, 1805, 1850*, ed. J. Wordsworth, M. H. Abrams and S. Gill, New York, Norton, 1979, p. 1.

15  *Blake: The Complete Poems*, ed. W. H. Stevenson and D. V. Erdman, Longman, London, 1971; 'The First Book of Urizen,' pp. 176–83.

16  Letter to Thomas Poole, October 1797, Griggs, I, 354.

# 51

# Shakespeare and the Romantics

## Frederick Burwick

In describing William Shakespeare as 'Fancy's child' who would 'Warble his native wood-notes wild' (*L'Allegro*, 134), John Milton paid tribute to a poet without formal education who wrote from natural intuition. The advocacy of genius and originality among such eighteenth-century critics as Joseph Addison, Edward Young and William Duff prepared the way for the 'Bardolatry' in the Romantic reception of Shakespeare. When Addison (*Spectator* nos. 279 and 411–21; 1711) praised his 'great natural genius', he made it clear that 'natural' was the crucial attribute distinguishing Shakespeare's work from the sort of literary excellence achieved through imitation of established forms of art. Thus, Shakespeare's 'natural genius' was more evident in his creation of Caliban, shaped from his own imagination, than in his Julius Caesar, derived from historical sources. The concept was also part of a nationalist argument, as becomes apparent in Addison's assertion that works of 'natural genius' are 'infinitely more beautiful than all the Turn and Polishing of what the French call a Bel Esprit' (*Spectator* no. 160). As had John Dryden in his *Essay of Dramatic Poesy* (1668), Addison declared Shakespeare's superiority over the polished refinement of Pierre Corneille, Jean Racine and Jean-Baptiste Molière. Adherence to the unities of time, place and action, indispensable to the playwrights of French neo-classicism, failed to produce a drama that could rival the power of 'natural genius' in the works of Shakespeare.

The emphasis on Shakespeare's genius and originality brought with it an attention to Shakespeare's texts. When Nicholas Rowe produced his edition of Shakespeare's plays in 1709 he followed the fourth folio of 1685. Throughout the eighteenth, and well into the nineteenth century, Shakespeare's 'natural genius' could scarcely be manifest in the performance of versions revised to conform to neo-classical principles: William D'Avenant's *Macbeth*, Dryden's *The Tempest*, Nahum Tate's *King Lear*. To uphold the claims of Shakespeare's genius and originality, it was necessary to restore the texts of the first folio or the early quartos. Public interest in this enterprise was aroused with David Garrick's lavish 'Shakespeare Jubilee' celebrated in Stratford in 1769.

Scholars devoted not just years but entire careers to the task of editing the plays. Edmund Malone presented his chronology of the composition of the plays in 1778, and his restoration of the text was published, with explanatory notes, in the seven-volume Rivington edition of 1786–90. An intense devotion to Shakespearean scholarship resulted in six subsequent editions which furthered the principles of historical editing promulgated by Malone: Samuel Ayscough, recognized as the 'Prince of Indices', brought forth his edition in 1790 and prepared the first concordance to Shakespeare. George Steevens, who had reprinted 20 of the quarto editions in 1766, went on to provide commentary on the textual variants as well as on Shakespeare's sources. When John and Josiah Boydell planned 'a national edition of Shakespeare, ornamented with designs by the first artists of this country', they turned to Steevens to provide the text and annotation for the nine-volume edition published in 1802. The Boydells declared it was their purpose to 'establish an *English School of Historical Painting*'. 'No subject . . . could be more appropriate for such a national attempt, than England's inspired poet, and great Painter of Nature, Shakspeare'. Steevens, upon retiring among the 'dowager-editors', transferred his labours to Isaac Reed, whose copious annotations were posthumously published in the 12-volume edition of 1820. Two important editions appeared in 1825: one edited by William Harness; the other by Charles Henry Wheeler.

The availability of accurate historical texts brought with it two paradoxical consequences: the first was the discovery that the national Bard was too bawdy for 'polite' society; the second was the conviction that the greatest of all playwrights wrote plays inappropriate for the stage. The texts had been restored, but society and the theatre itself had undergone radical changes between the opening years of the seventeenth century and the closing years of the eighteenth. Addressing the moral values of the expanding middle class, Thomas Bowdler brought forth his *Family Shakespeare* in 1807. As explained in the subtitle to the 1818 edition, Bowdler expurgated 'those words and expressions . . . which cannot be read aloud in a family'. Felicia Hemans recalled her childhood experience in Wales when she hid in the branches of an apple tree, not to taste the forbidden fruit, but to peruse the forbidden pages 'Of him whose magic lays impart, / Each various feeling to the heart'. 'Led by Shakespeare, bard inspired', she confessed in her juvenile tribute, 'The bosom's energies are fired'. Bowdler's edition was an attempt to keep 'the bosom's energies' from becoming overly aroused. Shakespeare must be made accessible within the family, but accessible in a controlled manner. The very year in which Bowdler's *Family Shakespeare* was published, Charles and Mary Lamb produced their *Tales from Shakespear. Designed for the use of young persons* (1807), illustrated with William Blake's engravings from designs by William Mulready.

The second paradox, that Shakespeare plays were not suited for the stage, is considerably more complex than the conviction that they were not proper for children or young ladies. The problem was not that he was too raucous, but rather that he was too ingenious for the stage. In exalting Shakespeare's genius, Samuel Taylor Coleridge, Charles Lamb and William Hazlitt argued that his plays could not be adequately represented upon the stage. Shakespeare was thus acclaimed as the 'closet' dramatist *par excellence*. Because Shakespeare addressed his imaginative power to the mind rather than the senses, as Coleridge explained it, 'in the closet only could it be fully & completely enjoyed' (CC *Lectures on Literature* I, 254). In Lamb's opinion, 'the plays of Shakspeare are less calculated for performance on a stage, than those of almost any other dramatist whatever'. Lamb, too, explained the paradox in terms of their demands upon the mind: 'There is so much in them, which comes not under the province of acting, with which eye, and tone, and gesture, have nothing to do' (*On the Tragedies of Shakespeare, Considered with Reference to their*

*Fitness for the Stage*). The Romantic conviction that stage performance was 'an abuse of the genius of the poet' Hazlitt reiterated with even more vehemence than either Coleridge or Lamb: 'the reader of the plays of Shakespeare is almost always disappointed in seeing them acted; and, for our own parts, we should never go to see them acted if we could help it' (*A View of the English Stage*, Howe, V, 222).

Coleridge acknowledged conditions that made proper performance of the plays virtually impossible: the enormous size of the theatres was at odds with good acting; the elaborate settings detracted from imaginative appeal of the language; the language itself had been altered for 'modern ears'. The Globe Theatre, Shakespeare's 'wooden O', 'had no artificial, extraneous inducements – few scenes, little music'. Thus, as Coleridge reasoned, 'it was natural that Shakespeare should avail himself of all that imagination afforded' (CC *Lectures on Literature* I, 228, 254, 561). In the London theatres of the early nineteenth century, Coleridge lamented, acting and stage setting detracted from the conjuring power of Shakespeare's language. Emphasizing imagination rather than performance, Coleridge delineated the process of engaging an active, willing response to the dramatic poet (ibid., pp. 128–30). In the second lecture (21 November 1811) of his 1811–12 series, Coleridge distinguished between *copy*, as a replica of the real, and *imitation*, as the imaginatively created ideal, in order to demonstrate how imagination operates in artistic representation. The effects of reality are tied to the moment: 'If mere pain for the moment were wanted, could we not go to our hospitals: if we required mere pleasure could we not be present at our public fetes'. Coleridge attributed the aesthetic experience to an aware-ness of difference: 'dramatic exhibition' required a sense of difference in representation. In Coleridge's formulation, drama provides an experience of illusion that gives us pleasure in the power of our own imagination: 'The real pleasure derived from knowing that the scene represented was unreal and merely an imitation' (ibid., pp. 210–11). In the third lecture (25 November 1811), he went on to clarify why only an imitation, not a copy, can produce 'the great total effect'. A copy reflects only the accidents of the moment. An imitation reveals the informing presence of the mind. The word *imitation*, Coleridge explained, 'means always a combination of a certain degree of dissimilitude with a certain degree of similitude'. It is our recognition of the difference that delights us. Even if the poet or artist has selected the 'purest parts' of his material, they must still be blended with the mind. Poetry results from 'blending the nobler mind with the meaner object'. It is 'not the mere copy of things, but the contemplation of mind upon things'. Thus, the effect of art can never be, and should never be, a confusion with reality. Our willing acceptance of the 'truth' of art never lapses into a belief that it is real. Coleridge distinguishes illusion from delusion in terms of the conscious awareness of difference. He amplifies this crucial aspect of imitation by defining various degrees of illusion that result from the exposition of difference. Domestic tragedy and opera provide the two extremes of the scale. In domestic tragedy, the difference is minimal and the effects may be 'too real to be compatible with pleasure'. In opera, the sense of reality is minimal, but the use of music and dance can 'deeply affect and delight an audience'. On this scale of reality and difference, Shakespeare achieves true balance; he 'seems to have taken the due medium, & to gratify our senses from the imitation of reality' (ibid., pp. 224–7). In achieving dramatic illusion, Shake-speare depended on the imagination of the spectator unsupported by the decorations of the stage. To document Shakespeare's own recognition that illusion was addressed to imagination rather than sensation, Coleridge was fond of quoting the Prologue to *Henry V* with its reference to the performance 'Within this wooden O' as 'ciphers' which work on the spectators' own 'imaginary forces'. The disadvantages in present-day theatre Coleridge attributed to dependence on stage machinery and the 'endeavour to make everything appear reality', rather than relying, as Shakespeare would have it, on the imagination of the spectators (CC *Lectures on Literature*, I, 228).

With this advocacy of the imagination over the physical apparatus of the stage, it would follow that the access to Shakespeare's plays might well circumvent the stage altogether. The plays might best be performed in the theatre of the mind. Lamb was even more emphatic in recommending that Shakespeare be read rather than seen on stage. Lamb's *On the Tragedies of Shakespeare, Considered with Reference to their Fitness for the Stage* concludes that 'Shakespeare is *not* fit for the stage'. This conclusion did not result simply from his dissatisfaction with how the plays were performed, with the alterations to Shakespeare's text, with the tendency toward sentimentality and melodrama in contemporary perform-ance. Indeed, the more powerful the acting, the more Lamb would be likely to object that theatrical representation had succeeded only in crudely externalizing the emotional and imaginative vitality of Shakespeare's play. In that very act of externalizing, the spectator's attention is drawn away from the inward qualities and subjectivity which are the source of Shakespeare's great strength: 'The things aimed at in theatrical representation are to arrest the spectator's eye upon the form and the gesture, and so to gain a more favourable hearing to what is spoken: it is not what the character is, but how he looks; not what he says, but how he speaks it'. To restore attention to what is said rather than to external appearances and actions, Shakespeare must be read. Lamb made it clear that the amorphous conjurings of one's own imagination are much to be preferred to the characters and actions physically concretized in performance. On stage, for example, 'Othello's colour' arouses a xenophobic fear by rendering visible that 'a blackamoor in a fit of jealousy kills his innocent white wife'. Lamb raises no objections to Shakespeare's text. The text is safe; the physicality of performance is dangerous. In reading the text one might imagine a Moor of 'shades less unworthy of a white woman's fancy' instead of 'a *coal-black Moor*' as represented on the stage.

> But upon the stage, when the imagination is no longer the ruling faculty, but we are left to our poor unassisted senses, I appeal to every one that has seen Othello played, whether he did not, on the contrary, sink Othello's mind in his colour; whether he did not find something extremely revolting in the courtship and wedded caresses of Othello and Desdemona; and whether the actual sight of the thing did not over-weigh all that beautiful compromise which we make in reading.

Lamb's comments on this particular play reveal most clearly the fears of physicality that prompted him to reject the theatre and to retreat into his safe haven as armchair critic of 'closet drama'. Upon the stage, he says, we must confront the 'body and bodily action', whereas in reading we can enjoy 'exclusively the mind, and its movements'.

In Hazlitt's appraisal of Shakespeare's plays, it is the impassioned expression of the feelings, carrying them 'to the utmost point of sublimity or pathos', that elevates them as the highest examples of dramatic art. As exhibited in the drama, the passions are inseparable from 'the moral and intellectual parts of our nature'. Therefore the tragedy of Shakespeare does not address the emotions alone, but 'stirs our inmost affections; abstracts evil from itself by combining with all the forms of imagination, and with the deepest workings of the heart, and rouses the whole man within us' (Howe, V, 5–6). Hazlitt stressed the universality of Shakespeare's mind, 'its generic quality, its power of communication with all other minds'. Like Coleridge, he discerned a selfless projection of self into the wide array of characters: 'He not only had in himself the germs of every other faculty and feeling, but he could follow them by anticipation, intuitively, into all their conceivable ramifications, through every change of fortune or conflict of passion, or turn of thought'. Once he has conceived a character the passions evolve organically as from the character's own being: 'it is a passion modified by a passion, by all the other feelings to which the individual is liable'. Shakespeare's imagination seems to reside not in the author but to infuse itself into the very objects of its own creation (ibid., pp. 47–53).

Thomas De Quincey opens his essay, *On the Knocking at the Gate in Macbeth*, with the observation that the comic scene which follows the murder of Duncan somehow 'reflected back upon the murderer a peculiar awfulness and a depth of solemnity'. De Quincey asked why Shakespeare's strategy of interrupting the course of tragic action should achieve such an effect. Because a complex array of mental and emotional response may be aroused, the understanding alone cannot be expected to explain the matter. The drunken porter in *Macbeth* (II. iii) presented a case, De Quincey argued, in which the critic must analyse the feelings. Whereas the sympathy in an ordinary murder case is directed toward the murdered person, Shakespeare's task is to redirect the sympathy toward the murderer: 'in the murderer, such a murderer as a poet will condescend to, there must be raging some great storm of passion, – jealousy, ambition, vengeance, hatred, – which will create a hell within him; and into this hell we are to look'. Indeed, it is a double hell: 'in Macbeth the strife of mind is greater than in his wife, the tiger spirit not so awake, and his feelings caught chiefly by contagion from her'. The 'murderous mind' is constituted by both together. He commits the deed; she takes his bloody daggers to 'smear / The sleepy grooms' that they may bear the guilt. She no sooner returns from her horrid act than the knocking is heard. To create the vision of hell, 'the murderers are taken out of the region of human things, human purposes, human desires'. With the knocking at the gate, the vision into the murderous hell is dissolved and 'the goings-on of human life are suddenly resumed'. Shakespeare restores dramatic immediacy through the seemingly contrary device of disruption: 'the human has made its reflux upon the fiendish; the pulses of life are beginning to beat again; and the re-establishment of the goings-on of their world in which we live first makes us profoundly sensible of the awful parenthesis that had suspended them' (Masson, X, 389–94).

After Coleridge had analysed the profound intellectual constituents of Shakespeare's art, the older notion of Shakespeare's untutored 'natural genius' no longer seemed tenable. In his remarks on Shakespeare in 1844, Leigh Hunt began by redressing Milton's reference to 'native wood-notes wild', which he deemed unwarrantedly condescending, 'hastily said by a learned man of an unlearned'. His 'wood-notes wild', Hunt declared, 'surpass Haydn and Bach'. Critics of a previous century had recognized only the 'natural' instincts of 'the uneducated interloper'. For Hunt, Shakespeare was an autodidact given to unrestrained display of his intellectual attainments. An attentive cerebral engagement, Coleridge maintained, was necessary to comprehend Shakespeare's imaginative power. In the aftermath of this criticism, Hunt was prompted to declare, not that Shakespeare was untutored, but rather that he was 'too learned; too over-informed with thought and allusion'. As for their suitability for the stage, the very 'stimulancy to mental activity' renders the language of the plays 'neither always proper to dramatic, still less to narrative poetry'. Failing to provide adequate modulation of voice, Shakespeare 'makes all of his serious characters talk as well as he could himself – with a superabundance of wit and intelligence'. According to Coleridge, Shakespeare 'made himself all characters; he left out parts of himself, and supplied what might have been in himself' (CC *Lectures on Literature* I, 117). Correcting 'what Mr. Coleridge would have us believe', Hunt declared that 'the over-informing intellect which Shakespeare thus carried into all his writings, must have been a personal as well as a literary peculiarity'.

Coleridge may well have been right in claiming that 'those who went to the Theatre in our own day... went to see Mr. Kemble in *Macbeth*, – or Mrs. Siddons's Isabella [*Measure for Measure*]'. It was the era of the virtuoso performer, and the supporting cast, as Coleridge also noted, had served their acting apprenticeship 'snuffing candles' (CC *Lectures on Literature*, I, 254). Coleridge was also right in objecting to the altered versions that were being played. Even after the restoration of accurate texts, John Philip Kemble continued to perform Nahum Tate's version of *King Lear*, and it was not until 1823, with Edmund Kean in the title role, that Shakespeare's play was restored to the stage. But it is also true that Shakespeare was immensely popular throughout the period, with the history plays receiving more attention than they had during any previous period. While the critics wanted to venerate their bard as 'closet' dramatist, Kemble insisted upon treating Shakespeare as playwright of the theatre. A play, by his definition, was written 'for the purpose of being acted'. To Kemble it was irrelevant that the vast auditorium of Drury Lane required a style of acting far different from what Shakespeare might have intended. As actor and manager, his task was to make a performance succeed. Under his management, historical costumes and historical stage designs became the requisite vestments of the 'Kemble religion'. The acting was mannered, with heavy declamation and formal gesture. He pleased the audience with spectacles, processions and elaborate settings.

Although Hazlitt had said of Shakespeare's plays that 'we should never go to see them acted if we could help it', he and Leigh Hunt were the major theatre critics of the period. Hazlitt's description of Kemble playing Hamlet 'like a man in armour' effectively conveys what other commentators have said of Kemble's measured mannerisms. Kemble was best, according to Hunt, 'in characters that are occupied with themselves and with their own importance'. Thus, Coriolanus was one of his most successful roles, but he could also give an effective intensity to 'the indignant jealousy of Othello', or to 'the desperate ambition of King John'. Sarah Siddons, Hunt asserts, so entered into 'the bewildered melancholy of Lady Macbeth walking in her sleep', that it was easy to believe that the actress herself must have been affected 'by the real agitation' of the emotions she performed. In 1814 Edmund Kean brought to the stage a new style of acting which Coleridge described as 'like reading Shakespeare by flashes of lightning' (CC *Table Talk*, II, 41). 'Mr. Kean's acting', Hazlitt reported, 'is like an anarchy of the passions in which each upstart humour, or frenzy of the moment, is struggling to get violent possession of some bit or corner of his "fiery soul" and "pygmy body" – to jostle out and lord it over the rest of the rabble of short-lived and furious purposes'. Kemble's style was defined by formal restraint, Kean's by 'an over-display of the resources of the art' (Howe, V, 174–6, 372).

In 1789, 20 years after Garrick's 'Shakespeare Jubilee', the Shakespeare Gallery opened to the London public at 52 Pall Mall. Newly completed paintings from the dramatic works of Shakespeare were unveiled each spring, so that the Shakespeare Gallery, before it finally closed in 1805, eventually housed 167 canvases by 35 artists – among them Sir Joshua Reynolds, George Romney, James Barry, Thomas Stothard, James Northcote, Benjamin West, Henry Fuseli and Angelika Kauffmann. The paintings exhibited in the gallery were also published by John and Josiah Boydell as engraved prints: large ones to be gathered in an imperial folio album without text; small ones to be incorporated in George Steevens's edition of the text. To avoid duplication of the paintings in these two series, Boydell began in 1794 to commission separate designs for the small engravings. The promised edition of Shakespeare as well as separate volumes of prints appeared between 1791 and 1805.

The very fact that the Shakespeare Gallery lacked uniformity of style has ensured its continued interest among art historians. John Boydell may have claimed it his purpose to 'establish an *English School of History Painting*', but his artists were eclectic both in their styles and in their national heritage. They were Irish (James Barry, Henry Tresham), Scottish (John Graham, Gavin Hamilton, William Hamilton), Sardinian (Jean-François Rigaud), German (Johann Heinrich Ramberg), Swiss (Henry Fuseli, Angelika Kauffmann) and American (Mather Brown, Benjamin West). Most had Italian training, and most had gained membership in the Royal Academy of Arts in London. Although fully neo-classical in style and manner, Angelika Kauffmann's representation of Silvia recoiling in fear of rape, and Cressida pleading to Diomed not to hold her to her oath, both contribute significantly to the debate over the role of women that had gained strength during the final decade of the eighteenth century. The paintings of the Shakespeare Gallery were commissioned during the very years (1789–1805), which witnessed the transition from neo-classic to Romantic. Paintings in contrary styles hung side by side. The predilection for the sentimental, which was to persist throughout most of the nineteenth century, is as much in evidence in George Romney's adherence to allegory, as it is in James Northcote's evocation of melodramatic pathos. The scenes depicted by these artists provide valuable insight into the staging and acting of the plays during the period.

Romantic critics judged the Boydell's Shakespeare Gallery much as they had the staging of Shakespeare's plays. Because of the priority granted to 'reading' over 'seeing', Lamb wanted neither the play as performed by actors nor the play as illustrated by artists. Any performance, any visual representation, is an infringement, a curtailment of the conjuring power. Lamb, to be sure, might close his eyes at the theatre in order to relish the poetic power of the spoken word (presuming it not to have been badly spoken). But a painting could offer him only external appearances: 'the infirmities and corpulence of a Sir John Falstaff' were made as obvious to the eye as 'Othello's colour'. An illustrated edition, Lamb asserted, is to be tolerated only when the plates are 'execrably bad' and may, without intrusion upon the reader's attention to the plays, 'serve as maps or modest remembrancers, to the text'. Because they do not dictate to the imagination by 'pretending to any supposable emulation' of the text, bad illustrations 'are so much better than the Shakespeare gallery engravings', which dared to rival the text.

## WRITINGS

*Shakespeare's Dramatic Works*, with explanatory notes by Revd Samuel Ayscough, London, J. Stockdale, 1790.

*The Plays of William Shakespeare*, accurately printed from the text of Mr. [Edmund] Malone's edition, with select explanatory Notes, 7 vols, London, J. Rivington and Sons, 1786–90.

*The Dramatic Works of Shakespeare*, revised by George Steevens, 9 vols, London, printed by W. Bulmer and Co., for John and Josiah Boydell, G. and W. Nicol, 1802.

*The Dramatic Works of Shakespeare*, with notes by Joseph Rann, 6 vols, Oxford, Clarendon Press, 1786–91.

*The Dramatic Works of Shakespeare*, from the correct edition of Isaac Reed, with copious annotations, 12 vols, London, Walker, 1820.

*The Dramatic Works of Shakespeare*, ed. Revd William Harness, 8 vols, London, 1825.

*The Dramatic Works of Shakespeare*, ed. Charles Henry Wheeler, London, 1825.

*The Family Shakespeare*, 4 vols, ed. Thomas Bowdler, London, J. Hatchard, 1807.

*The Family Shakespeare*, [. . .] *in which nothing is added to the original text; but those words and expressions are omitted which cannot be read aloud in a family*, 10 vols, ed. Thomas Bowdler, London, Longman, Hurst, Rees, Orme, and Brown, 1818.

Addison, Joseph, Steele, Richard and others, *The Spectator*, 5 vols, ed. Donald F. Bond, Oxford, Clarendon Press, 1965.

Bate, Jonathan, *Shakespeare and the English Romantic Imagination*, Oxford, Clarendon Press, 1986.

——*Shakespearean Constitutions: Politics, Theatre, Criticism 1730–1830*, Oxford, Clarendon Press, 1989.

Burwick, Frederick, *Illusion and the Drama: Critical Theory of the Enlightenment and Romantic Era*, University Park, Pennsylvania State University Press, 1991.

Burwick, Frederick and Pape, Walter (eds) *The Boydell Shakespeare Gallery*, Bottrop, Peter Pomp, 1996.

Duff, William, *An Essay on Original Genius* (1767); facsimile reproduction, ed. John L. Mahoney, Gainesville, Scholar's Press, 1964.

Houtchens, Lawrence H. and Houtchens, Carolyn W. (eds) *Leigh Hunt's Dramatic Criticism, 1808–1831*, New York, Columbia University Press, 1949.

——(eds) *Leigh Hunt's Literary Criticism, 1808–1831*, New York, Columbia University Press, 1956.

Hunt, Leigh, *Critical Essays on the Performers of the London Theatres*, London, John Hunt, 1808.

Lamb, Charles and Lamb, Mary, *Tales from Shakespear. Designed for the use of young persons*, plates engraved by William Blake from designs by William Mulready, 2 vols, London, Hodgkins, 1807.

Lucas, E. V. (ed.) *The Works of Charles and Mary Lamb*, 7 vols, London, Methuen, 1903–5.

McKenna, Wayne, *Charles Lamb and the Theatre*, New York, Harper & Row, 1978.

Young, Edward, *Conjectures on Original Composition*, London, A. Milar, 1759; facsimile reprint Leeds, Scholar Press, 1966.

# 52

# Milton and the Romantics

*Nicola Trott*

John Milton (1608–74) is famous for his learning ('after I was 12 years old I rarely retired to bed from my studies till midnight');[1] for advocating divorce and for being three times married; for writing propaganda on behalf of Cromwell and the Commonwealth, and for going blind as a result (he was Secretary for Foreign Tongues, 1649–55); for having copies of his books burned, and being himself briefly imprisoned, at the Restoration of the monarchy; and for rowing with his daughters (on hearing of her father's intention to remarry, Mary is reported to have said that 'if shee could heare of his death that was something').

As a poet, Milton has had an influence second only to Shakespeare. And the early nineteenth century sees a revival of sorts. William Hayley's influential and honorific *Life* (1794, revd 1796) is an answer to Dr Johnson's hostile account, and the first of a string of Romantic biographies culminating in De Quincey's of 1838.[2] A landmark in textual scholarship is Hayley's four-volume edition of *Milton's Life and Poetical Works*, with notes by Cowper (1810). In the visual arts, Milton's poetry is the subject of many powerful works, most prominently and inclusively those of William Blake, who, besides his illuminated prophetic book *Milton*, produces eight sets of illustrations, 76 plates in all (c. 1801–16), though they never appear in the edition for which they are commissioned (again by Hayley). Henry Fuseli, a friend of Blake, opens a 'Milton Gallery' in May 1799, for which he has been painting for the last decade (also originally for the abortive edition). Two published illustrators are John Martin, painter of apocalyptic scenes, who succeeds best at Satan on the burning lake and the devils' city, Pandemonium; and the magnificent French artist Gustave Doré. The favourite subject of Satan's meeting with Sin and Death at the Gates of Hell (in Book II) is well-enough known to make it into the world of the political cartoon, for Gillray's rendering (after an engraving by Hogarth) of the Royal Family Crisis of his day (9 June 1792).

But it is in literature above all that Milton's effect is felt. Many works (and genres) are relevant here – *Comus* and *Lycidas*, *L'Allegro* and *Il Penseroso*, *Samson Agonistes* and *Paradise Regained* – but by far the most important, and a founding text for Romanticism, is *Paradise Lost* (1667). Its theme, according to Coleridge, is 'the origin of evil and the combat of Evil and Good'; its contents, he adds, may be summarized thus:

The Fall of Man is the subject; Satan is the cause; man's blissful state the immediate object of his enmity and attack; man is warned by an angel who gives him an account of all that was requisite to be known, to make the warning at once intelligible and awful, then the temptation ensues, and the Fall; then the immediate sensible consequence; then the consolation, wherein an angel presents a vision of the history of man with the ultimate triumph of the Redeemer. (Lecture, 4 March 1819; see Wittreich, pp. 241, 242–3)

While these bare bones cannot convey the richness and density of the blank verse, they may suggest the vastness of the conception. *Paradise Lost* is a self-consciously epic poem: it has roots in Homer and Virgil; but as *Christian* epic it also repudiates these Classical antecedents, with their themes of war and empire. And this deliberate revision of a genre is of great significance for the kinds of spin that the Romantics, in their turn, are to put on *Paradise Lost*.

A crucial element here is the self-awareness of the response. The Romantic engagement with Milton involves not just single works and innumerable instances of echoic or allusive practice (intertextuality, or the verbal and formal relation one text bears to another), but also a large body of critical material – in essays, prefaces, letters, marginalia and so forth. Joseph Wittreich has helpfully drawn this material together, and notes the originality of Romantic criticism of Milton (p. 26). Many writers of the late eighteenth and early nineteenth centuries make brilliant forays into Milton's text, a few pursuing their quarry so far as to ask some of the fundamental questions that are posed by what we call 'Romanticism'.

If Milton is the daddy of Romantic theorizing, his influence on Romantic poetry has also been richly productive of modern theories of literary influence.[3] As their more startling personal revelations indicate, the poets are themselves aware of a compelling, if not compulsive, relationship. 'Milton is his great idol', Hazlitt records of Wordsworth, 'and he sometimes dares to compare himself with him' (ibid., p. 119). Coleridge desires 'To have a continued Dream, representing visually & audibly all Milton's Paradise Lost'.[4] Blake, too, has a vision, but is by contrast quoted as saying, 'I saw Milton in imagination and he told me to beware of being misled by his *Paradise Lost*'.[5] Keats's situation is different again, and if anything still more odd: 'Life to him would be death to me',[6] he writes of Milton, on giving up his epic project of *Hyperion*, which tells of the fall of the Titans. (Keats's sense of being trapped within the Miltonic corpus is allied to his brilliant imaginings of Satan's 'serpent prison'.)[7] Although in each case the fuller picture is far more complex, several distinct positions emerge here. Wordsworth is plainly the 'wannabe', measuring himself against Milton in order to claim an equivalent status, either as rival interpreter, or as natural heir. Coleridge is the devotee, but his dreamy repetitions have a latent cunning, in that their effect is to interiorize Milton's works as part of his own mentality. Blake is the refusnik, making Milton speak against himself in order that he should be free to testify to his 'true' identity and, it follows, to the efficacy of Blake's revisionary methods. Keats is the defeated adorer,[8] whose near death-by-Milton has nevertheless given him an insight into his own, quite different poetic nature.

Lest this should seem an exclusively male preserve, it should be said that there are many female respondents. The actress Sarah Siddons publishes an abridgement of *Paradise Lost* in 1822, Eliza Bradburn a prose paraphrase eight years later. What is more, Joseph Wittreich argues that, far from being submissive or obedient readers, many women (Mary Wollstone-craft and Mary Shelley among them) choose to subvert the patriarchal applications of *Paradise Lost*: 'A poem that men would often use against women is being turned, by women, to their own advantage'. Indeed, Wittreich contends that, despite his misogynist reputation, Milton himself is an 'early sponsor' of feminists. Eve is an ideal of female capability as well as a model of feminine behaviour; and her example is often used to urge women's education, as well as being cited in 'conduct-books'. In particular, women readers draw attention to the sexual politics of Milton's Eden, and lead the 'interpretation of Books XI and XII during the Romantic period'.[9] And yet the writing of epic remains a daunting and undeniably masculine pursuit.

That the male Romantics tend to mythologize Milton as a figure of singular authority – a Milton made or read in the image of his own God – may signal the exclusion of women. It also reflects trends laid down by the poet himself (in his *Defences*) and continued by his eighteenth-century admirers. Recent discussion has taken these cultural and historical factors into account. His canonical position makes Milton the appropriate point of origin for Bloom's anxiety theory; yet, as Lucy Newlyn has shown, the text of *Paradise Lost* reveals a poet of far greater flexibility than this monolithic image would, on the face of it, accommodate. To her way of reading, Milton's hard authoritarian outside (or supertext) co-exists with a soft ambiguous inside (or subtext). The Romantics, then, may be said to exploit both the (firmly established) idea of Milton, and the (newly glimpsed) twilight zone of his poetry: myth is played off against text. In this sense, the heterodoxies of Romantic reading practice are not so much a denial of influence as a development of potentialities in Milton himself.

It is time to look at some of these readings in greater detail. I shall do so under thematic headings, in each of which a variety of voices may be heard.

## Heroic Argument

As the most lofty of the Classical genres, epic is an arduous and competitive field. Even in rejecting the Homeric subject of war, Milton has the rhetoric of poetic battle to hand: he will present an 'argument / Not less but more heroic than the wrath / Of stern Achilles'. In turning to the 'tragic' narrative of the Fall, Milton claims to undertake a subject that is at once 'Unsung' and 'higher' than what has gone before.[10] This search for an 'argument' or theme is intrinsic to the writing of epic as inherited by Wordsworth.[11] Of all the Romantic poets, it is Wordsworth who most nearly aligns himself with the Miltonic tradition, and with the pursuit of the 'heroic argument': 'Of genius, power, / Creation and divinity itself / I have been speaking', he declares in Book III of his great poem, *The Prelude*,

> for my theme has been
> What passed within me. Not of outward things...
> but of my own heart
> Have I been speaking, and my youthful mind....
> This is in truth heroic argument... (III. 171–82)

Here, Wordsworth takes Milton on by assuming that the forces which *Paradise Lost* has attributed to supernatural agency are already contained within the mind itself. A similar edge is found in the Prospectus Wordsworth writes for *The Recluse*, the epic work to which he plans to dedicate his life. His Prospectus to this project makes a detrimental comparison between Milton's vast invented machineries and the profound simplicity of his own 'shadowy ground':

> The darkest pit
> Of the profoundest hell, night, chaos, death,
> Nor aught of blinder vacancy scooped out
> By help of dreams, can breed such fear and awe
> As fall upon me often when I look
> Into my soul, into the soul of man –
> My haunt and the main region of my song. (23–9)

The Prospectus constitutes the most audacious manifesto of the quest to sustain an epic 'argument' on Romanticism's own terms. Although it may appear limited (Hazlitt notices Wordsworth's 'narrowness'), the choice of the subjective 'soul of man' is a decisive turn for modern poetry. It is also connected to a wider critique of Milton, stemming from Dr Johnson's comment that *Paradise Lost* is 'too remote from human life', and burgeoning in the humanist readings of Wordsworth and Keats. The anti-supernaturalism developed by Wordsworth in the Prospectus, and other writings of 1800, contributes to a larger Romantic analysis of literary history. For Keats, the Prospectus (which he knows from its publication in the Preface to *The Excursion*, a long narrative poem of 1814) shows that Milton had 'less anxiety for Humanity' and 'did not think into the human heart, as Wordsworth has done'.[12] Quoting Milton in the Preface to *Lyrical Ballads*, 1800, Wordsworth assures his readers that 'Poetry sheds no tears "such as Angels weep," but natural and human tears';[13] annotating *Paradise Lost* about the same date, he objects to its description of Heaven by observing 'how much of the real excellence of Imagination consists in the capacity of exploring the world really existing' (Wittreich, *The Romantics*, p. 104; see *PL* III. 543–54)

Nevertheless, it is to Milton that Wordsworth turns for his central self-image. For a time, Coleridge seems to regard Wordsworth as almost a reincarnation of the poet,[14] largely on the assumption (never in fact fulfilled) that, in *The Recluse*, his friend is going to write, not just an epic, but the first truly philosophical poem. Coleridge, it should be said, himself nurses schemes of a similar kind, and is handing on the 'hard task' he set himself in his early attempts at Miltonic epic (Charles Lamb wildly ranked *Religious Musings* higher even than *Paradise Lost*).

The witticism that Wordsworth manages only a 'Prelude' to *The Recluse* and an 'Excursion' from it, holds good. Keats also has epic ambitions; they, too, go unrealized. And yet the Romantic period is surprisingly rich in long poems, two of which at least – the autobiographical *Prelude* and Byron's anti-heroic *Don Juan* – manage to reinaugurate the epic in a way that Milton's eighteenth-century imitators, Thomson, Akenside and Cowper (however impressive), did not.

## Falls, Fortunate and Unfortunate

Milton's account of the Fall is perhaps the site of greatest interpretative energy for the Romantics. In *Paradise Lost*, man's Fall from innocence is both a climactic event (in Book IX) and strangely dispersed throughout, since it is sneakily previewed in the progressive changes of Satan (from angel to devil, to toad and snake), and Eve's dream of flight and transgression (in Book V). This multiplying of the Genesis narrative gives the Romantics a kind of licence, and leads in several different directions.

One point of departure is opened when, in his final Book, Milton extends to the fallen Adam the promise of 'A paradise within thee happier far' than the Eden he has lost (XII: 587). In the Christian tradition, the idea of the 'fortunate Fall' (or *felix culpa*) comes of the special grace we are granted through the Atonement and our Redemption in Christ. In much Romantic thinking, the Fall is fortunate in the sense that only through 'fallenness', or what Coleridge terms the 'under consciousness of a sinful nature', can the full range and potential of humanity be disclosed.

'Imaginative' or mind-centred revisions of Milton's epic, such as *The Prelude* or De Quincey's *Confessions of an English Opium-Eater*, tend to seek a confirmation of this 'fortunate' state of affairs in the 'growth' of the individual consciousness. 'Political' revisions, such as those by William Godwin, Mary and Percy Shelley, and Lord Byron, tend to regard the Fall as a social and ideological phenomenon, and hence to treat it catastrophically (even if the final outcome is Utopian). These politicized 'falls' often take the persecutory or neglectful godhead as a symbol of abusive or tyrannical human power: in Shelley's *Queen Mab*, God is exposed as the 'prototype of human misrule' (VI, 105). Mary Shelley's *Frankenstein*, whose epigraph is drawn from *Paradise Lost* X, assumes a post-lapsarian and sceptical questioning of the deity. Here, the creature talks back: 'I was benevolent and good', the monster tells his creator, the ironically named Victor, 'misery made me a fiend' (chapter ten). In *Frankenstein*, as in *Caleb Williams* (the novel by Mary Shelley's father, William Godwin), rationalist and Enlightenment theories of human benevolence and social justice confront the atavistic guilts and retributions carried over from Milton's myth of the Fall. *Frankenstein* literally incorporates *Paradise Lost*, since in chapter 15 the monster actually discovers and reads the poem. As a result, it becomes the mould into which his own history is cast, and is itself radically altered in the process: 'I ought to be thy Adam; but I am rather the fallen angel, whom thou drivest from joy for no misdeed' (chapter ten). In the mouth of Frankenstein's monster, the Miltonic Fall testifies to an unjust oppression and exclusion, and to the 'Satanizing' of an otherwise humane and innocent 'Adam'.

At the same time, a great many Romantic texts entertain the expansive possibility of 'wandering' or 'error' that is introduced by both diabolic and human agents in *Paradise Lost*. Even the cautionary and moralized setting of an Austen novel includes such calculated 'lapses': in *Mansfield Park*, for instance, the grounds of Sotherton contain a 'wilderness', which, with its 'serpentine' path and forbidding gate, is inevitably the scene of sexual temptation and transgression (chapters nine and ten). High Romanticism is more interested in mental trespass ('I loved to . . . read / Their looks forbidding', says Wordsworth of the Cumbrian cliffs, 'read and disobey': *Home at Grasmere*, 919–20), and in imaginative excess: 'I trod heaven in my thoughts', confesses Frankenstein towards the end of Mary Shelley's novel, still intoxicated with his early vision. There are invitations to interpretative excess and trespass also, if only in the formal terms of digression (a fine art in Coleridge, Byron and De Quincey).

However equivocally, Romanticism prizes experience over innocence. Creativity is allied to fallenness. That said, there is a very important sense in which experience is seen as *anti*-creative: where it denotes the 'habit' or 'custom' of material existence, a familiarization which is seen as the enemy of the 'immaterial' mind. Here – and Wordsworth's 'Immortality' ode would be a supreme example – Milton's myth of the Fall and the Romantic ideology of imagination meet. In these moods, Milton's Paradise may be yearned for, though it tends to be located in the 'world which is world / Of all of us' (*Prelude* X. 725–6), and, especially, in the figure of the child, to whom the experience of life is still new. The great mythologizer of experience is Blake. Though he argues its necessity, and celebrates sexual energy, he also retains a view that the Fall itself 'produced only generation and death' (Wittreich, *The Romantics*, p. 96). In Blake's thinking, however, the Fall is implicit in the Creation (another Genesis narrative much enlarged by Milton, in *Paradise Lost* VII). *The Book of Urizen* parodies the seven days of Creation by recasting them as the process by which 'Urizen' is separated from eternity. Urizen's Fall is from a unified state into a series of divisions that eventually results in the degradation of sexual differentiation and procreation. Put another way, it is a Fall from imagination, the divine humanity, into the divisions of reason (U-rizen) and the finite 'ratios' of mere sense perception.

The potency of Milton's myth is that it provides an essential narrative structure. But one of the main reasons for this is historical rather than literary. The single greatest impetus to the movement we call Romanticism is the sequence of events beginning in France in 1789. All the Romantic poets take on the French Revolution, whether in narrative or myth;[15] and all have to cope with the fact of the Revolution's having disappointed their hopes and expectations. It is here that Milton uncannily returns to the scene. He, too, experienced a revolution, and saw it fail. His *Paradise Lost* is the work of this post-revolutionary defeat; and one of the passages the Romantics most often recur to is Milton's description of himself, at the opening of Book VII, as 'fallen on evil times', 'In darkness, and with dangers compassed round'.

The Romantics could hardly do otherwise than find in Milton's experience of the English Revolution a reflex of their own knowledge of the French. At this point, however, we need to distinguish between a wide range of responses, even within individual writers, and to be aware of the sharp disagreement between the early and later Romantics. Wordsworth, for example, hails Milton as a fellow-republican in 1793, just after the execution of Louis XVI;[16] but by 1802, when Napoleon is already First Consul, and Britain and France have struck an uneasy peace, Milton becomes the representative of lost national virtues, and a rallying point for a new moral order. Inspired by Milton's sonnets to his fellow-parliamentarians, Wordsworth turns to the same verse form, alternately to castigate and to invigorate his nation: one of the greatest of these sonnets calls out explicitly, 'Milton, thou shouldst be living at this hour, / England hath need of thee!' It is not just that the present state of the nation falls short of the heroic past. With Britain on the verge of another decade of war with France, Milton is also being enlisted in the anti-Napoleonic ideology that Wordsworth has come, however reluctantly, to endorse. Looking at it from the other end of the Napoleonic era, the younger Romantics, Shelley and Byron in particular, see a terrible failure of nerve. When, in 1815, Shelley writes his own sonnet *To Wordsworth*, he expresses his disillusionment with the older poet's 'enslavement' in the most telling manner possible: by suggesting, in his metaphor of the 'star', that Wordsworth has fallen from 'Miltonic' grace.

Both then and now, controversy surrounds those who, like Wordsworth, Coleridge and Southey, changed their political minds. What seems clear is that an 'inward turn' followed upon the failure of the Revolution; a turn which, in the influential view of M. H. Abrams, was also the very basis of Romantic poetics, and its claim to the imagination as a revolutionary mode of perception. A redirection of energies certainly features in Coleridge's explanation of how it was that Milton came to write *Paradise Lost*:

> finding it impossible to realize his own aspirations, either in religion or politics, or society, he gave up his heart to the living spirit and light within him, and avenged himself on the world by enriching it with this record of his own transcendent ideal. (Lecture, 4 March 1819: Wittreich, *The Romantics*, p. 245)

Keats, who mixes in the republican and liberal circles of Hazlitt and Leigh Hunt, instead pleads the political effectiveness of the poem, and of what Blake calls 'mental fight', despite the ruin of what Milton himself fought for: 'How noble and collected an indignation against Kings', exclaims a marginal comment to *Paradise Lost* I: 591–9:

> His very wishing should have had power to pull that feeble animal Charles from his bloody throne. 'The evil days' [VII: 25–6] had come to him – he hit the new System of things a mighty mental blow – the exertion must have had or is yet to have some sequences.

Whether the Romantics are seen as turning in or selling out, their thinking about Milton and the myth of the Fall readily lends itself to the story of their own revolutionary dreams and losses.

## Satanism

The notion that Satan is the 'hero' of *Paradise Lost* is first put about by Addison, and taken up by Burns, Hazlitt,[17] and Byron. In the Romantic period, a widespread appreciation of the grandeur of Milton's devil expands into the possibility of a 'diabolic' interpretation of *Paradise Lost* itself. This 'Satanist position', as it has been called, posits a rebellious or ironic reader, who refuses to comply with the moral structure of the poem. The Romantic advocacy of the devil takes three main forms: political, aesthetic and emotive. The last assumes an identification with Satan as the creature most 'like us': having already fallen, he evokes our sympathies as the tragic, and in some sense fully human, centre of the poem. The aesthetic argument, on the other hand, is interested in how questions of artistic merit may be loosened from moral considerations, when (as is pre-eminently the case with Satan) the poetic representation has an overwhelming power.[18]

The political is in many ways the most far-reaching of the Romantic Satanisms: it understands Satan's rebellion against God, and Milton's republican approval of king-killing, in the context of contemporary political debates and, in particular, an ideological contest about the source and legitimacy of power. Between 1790 and 1830, Satan serves as the representative of almost every political position under the Romantic sun – and is a reliable measure of the changing climate. In the 1790s, Satan participates in the Great Debate incited by the French Revolution, which centred on issues of liberty and justice, sovereignty and the state, rights and the constitution. William Godwin's *Enquiry Concerning Political Justice* (1793) uses Satan to question the *in*justice of current systems of government: 'Why did [Satan] rebel against his maker? It was, as he himself informs us, because he saw no sufficient reason for that extreme inequality of rank and power which the creator assumed'.[19]

The early Coleridge also holds radical views, but later seeks to 'demonize' Satan, as it were, by attributing to his character what he now regards as religious and political heresies.[20] Satan becomes the image of the dictator-demagogue which the Revolution, and the wars that followed, have brought to power: 'these are the marks, that have characterized the masters of mischief, the liberticides, and mighty hunters of mankind, from Nimrod to Bonaparte'.[21] And yet, however morally antipathetic, Satan inspires some of the most appreciative and impassioned of Romantic prose.[22]

In their own day, Shelley and Byron were the most notorious Satanists, for their private lives as well as their public views, and for religious and sexual, as well as political, unorthodoxies. The diabolic connection was confirmed when Byron's infamous drama *Cain* (1821) gave Lucifer the very best lines, and was greeted as the work of a 'cool, unconcerned fiend'.[23] In fact, Byron's own position is as usual uncertain, and probably ambivalent. An earlier drama, *Manfred* (1816–17), finds the credo of the liberated mind in Satan's famous lines, 'The mind is its own place, and in itself / Can make a heaven of hell, a hell of heaven' (I, 254–5). In *Cain*, a predictable Satanism – 'Who is the hero of *Paradise Lost*? Why Satan . . .'[24] – merges into a thoroughly 'diabolic' voice, which insinuates doubts about the received version of the murder of Abel so as to undermine various moral and political pieties. And, in *The Vision of Judgment*, Satan passes a damning verdict on the reign of George III.

Shelley offers still more subtle applications. His Preface to *Prometheus Unbound* refuses Satan as a model for uncritical imitation; and his hero is quite as much martyr as rebel:

> Prometheus is, in my judgement, a more poetical character than Satan, because, in addition to courage and majesty, and firm and patient opposition to omnipotent force, he is susceptible of being described as exempt from the taints of ambition, envy, revenge, and a desire for personal aggrandizement – which, in the hero of *Paradise Lost*, interfere with the interest.

Shelley's drama seeks to ethicalize Milton's devil, by showing in Prometheus the transformation of a vengeful into a merciful consciousness. Taking the Greek god as a symbol of universal human potential, *Prometheus Unbound* envisages the psychic liberation that comes of upholding the Christian virtue of charity, even as the Christian idea of God is eradicated. Shelley's drama is a Utopian revision, not just of the rebellion in *Paradise Lost*, but of the history of the Revolution; and central to both is a critique of the character of Satan on moral grounds.

By far the most spectacular example of the rebellious and ironic reader is William Blake – though, since his work was almost unknown outside a small London circle, he did not take part in the public dialogue of the other Romantic poets. Nevertheless, it is to Blake that we owe the purest expression of the voice of 'The Devil': 'The reason Milton wrote in fetters when he wrote of angels and God, and at liberty when of devils and Hell, is because he was a true poet, and of the Devil's party without knowing it'. This famous formulation, from plate five of *The Marriage of Heaven and Hell*, depends upon a widespread recognition that *Paradise Lost* is strongest (or, in Blake's terms, most 'active') in delineating 'evil'. Indeed, 'Milton' is a split identity, in that he is torn between the opposing characters of Satan (where his poetry succeeds) and God (where it does not). But Blake is not exactly signing Milton up to the devil's party.[25] Rather, he is proposing to free Milton from himself (or that part of himself that is the oppressor of Satan and the maker of bad gods, like Blake's 'Nobodaddy' or 'Urizen'). Milton's poetry is inhibited, not because its intentions are moral, but because its morality is false. Blake is seeking a new 'marriage', or an end to the divisions *Paradise Lost* itself has instituted, between 'good' and 'evil', heaven and hell. To become the liberator *of* Milton in this way could also be seen as Blake's triumphant liberation *from* Milton, or the burden of influence.

## Egotism

In a *Notebook* entry of 1810, Coleridge describes two poetic personae, one belonging to Shakespeare, the other to Milton: 'The one darting himself forth & passing into all forms of human character & passion; the other attracting all forms and things to himself, into the unity of his own grand Ideal' (Wittreich, *The Romantics*, p. 194).[26] As the last word in the quotation suggests, Coleridge's division of poetic labour has a philosophical basis: Shakespeare is allied with the 'objective' and a realist aesthetic, Milton with the 'subjective' and idealist. These are, in effect, contrary types of mind, constituting opposed poetic 'worlds'. Behind the Shakespeare–Milton distinction, as indeed at the back of almost all Coleridge's deeper speculations, lies a concern with religion. The poets are exemplary of two, antithetical, conceptions of divinity, between the rival claims of which Coleridge spent much of his intellectual life arbitrating. In the context of the 'universe' of his writings, Shakespeare is an immanent God, self-effacingly immersed in the forms of his creation; Milton, conversely, stands transcendently proud of his work, yet with his identity stamped on every line.

Coleridge's distinction between the two 'gods' of English poetry becomes the common currency of Romantic criticism.[27] Predictably enough, it also becomes a way of trading insults, albeit of a very insightful and influential kind. When Keats coins the key slogan for Wordsworth, as a poet of the 'egotistical sublime',[28] he is mapping his older contemporary onto the 'Miltonic' half of the equation. Keats himself, needless to say, assumes the Shakespearean role.[29] His cue is taken from Coleridge, who has repeatedly lectured on the two poets in London;[30] his prompter is Hazlitt, who has attached the label of egotism to Wordsworth in reviewing *The Excursion*,[31] and has mediated Coleridge's thinking on Milton in his own *Lectures on the English Poets* (1818). Keats's effort is to place himself, and his admiring and wary response to Wordsworth, in terms of his relation to another powerful field of influence: Milton.

Throughout this debate, you will have noticed, the identity of the poet is central: in Coleridge's words, 'Sh[akespeare] becomes all things, yet for ever remaining himself –

while all things & forms become Milton' (*Notebooks*, 1810: Wittreich, p. 194). This 'egotistical' Milton fits into a century-long tradition: in the case of *Paradise Lost*, poet and poem have become almost indivisible.[32] In addition, Milton has been closely allied to the divinity of which he writes and from which he claims inspiration. Either way, the poet becomes the centre of authority and meaning, and this centrality inevitably begs the question of Milton's presence in his work: 'In the Paradise Lost the sublimest parts are the revelations of Milton's own mind, producing itself and evolving its own greatness'.[33] Coleridge here implies the whole history of High Romantic autobiography, and its determination to rewrite the Miltonic epic. In Classical epic, the narrator does not as a rule put in a personal appearance. In Romantic epic, the interrogation of the self, the special 'egotism' of the poet, is on the contrary of paramount importance. Indeed, Coleridge's remarks on the production and evolution of Milton's own mind could be seen as an inspired summary of the finest achievement in this line, Wordsworth's *Prelude, or Growth of a Poet's Mind*.

That Coleridge has his eye on the present is confirmed by the grandiloquent theory which emerges from his thinking about *Paradise Lost* (the opening lines of Book III especially): 'In all modern poetry in Christendom there is an under consciousness of a sinful nature, a fleeting away of external things, the mind or subject greater than the object, the reflective character predominant' (Wittreich, pp. 244–5). Clearly, 'Milton' is being used to express, and to legitimize, claims which 'Romanticism' wishes to make on its own behalf. In isolating its (in fact relatively rare) reflexive moments, Coleridge identifies *Paradise Lost* with subjectivism and self-consciousness, and hence with the concept of imagination that lies at the heart of High Romanticism. Milton's established place in the canon lends authority to a new critical discourse; but this authority is also being deflected and diffused by a 'Romantic' poetics of process and becoming – the mind 'producing itself' in the act of writing.

In Blake, as you might guess, this 'egotistical' line of interpretation is completely reversed. *Milton*, Blake's long poem of 1804–8, takes its epigraph from the 'argument' of *Paradise Lost* Book I ('To Justify the Ways of God to Men'), but perversely dedicates itself to the undoing of Milton and Milton's God. In an ironic version of Christ's Incarnation and Harrowing of Hell, Blake's Milton proceeds, not to self-becoming, but to self-annihilation:

> I will go down to the sepulcher to see if morning breaks:
> I will go down to self annihilation and eternal death,
> Lest the Last Judgment come & find me unannihilate
> And I be seiz'd & giv'n into the hands of my own Selfhood . . .
> I in my Selfhood am that Satan: I am that Evil One!
> He is my Spectre! in my obedience to loose him from my Hells,
> To claim the Hells, my Furnaces, I go to Eternal Death! (Book the First, Plate 14)

Milton renounces the self who wrote the grand mistake of *Paradise Lost*. In deciding to 'fall', he also collapses the structure of the organized religion his work has helped to uphold. Abstract categories of 'good' and 'evil' have been forged, and these divisions have been institutionalized in the concepts of 'Heaven' and 'Hell'. By exiling aspects of the self, as in the beings called 'God' and 'Satan', we have forgotten that 'all deities reside in the human breast'.[34] Once externalized, these forces gain, or are used to gain, oppressive power, a power which is rationalized and enforced in the codes and doctrines of formal religion. Milton, who has been tied to a false divinity, 'falls' in order to regain his humanity – the only divinity Blake recognizes. (His physical fall ends, appropriately enough, when he enters the left foot of Blake himself: Book the First, Plate 14.) In this way, Milton attains to a vision of a general and Blakean redemption, in which 'To bathe in the Waters of Life' is 'to wash off the Not Human', and so enable the restored powers of imagination and inspiration to 'cast off' the enslavements of reason and memory (Book the Second, Plate 43).

## Aesthetics

*Paradise Lost* is the epitome of 'the sublime' – so much so, that Byron's Dedication to *Don Juan* (1818) drily observes that 'the word "Miltonic" mean[s] "*sublime*"'. Byron is in fact distrustful of the grandeurs of Miltonic Romanticism, especially when it acts to suppress the memory of Milton 'the tyrant-hater'; but he accepts the cliché of sublimity. Milton himself, rather surprisingly, referred to poetry as 'simple, sensuous, passionate' (*Of Education*). Romanticism is much given to definitions of poetry, and Milton's doubtless contributes to its restoration of feeling and emotion to the heart of intellectual endeavour. Taken out of its original context (where it had served to distinguish poetry from rhetoric), the phrase becomes a touchstone for Coleridge,[35] and is felt behind Wordsworth's dictum that 'Poetry is passion' (Note to *The Thorn*); though it is Keats who most appreciates the sensuousness of Milton, or what he calls his capacity for the 'poetical Luxury' of 'solacing himself at intervals with cups of old wine'.[36]

Nevertheless, it is the Milton who 'committed himself to the Extreme' (Keats again) that proves irresistible. A vital element of this extremism is linguistic. Coleridge illustrates his thesis 'extremes meet' by reference to the paradoxical fiery cold of Milton's Hell;[37] and is drawn to the controversial idiom that has entered the language in the oxymorons 'darkness visible', 'precious bane', 'bad eminence', 'blind mouths'. Miltonic epic is quite as much about style as 'argument'. One of the key moments in *Paradise Lost*, for Burkean and then Romantic aesthetics, is Milton's extraordinary conjuring of Death in Book II (line 666, 'The other shape, / If shape it might be called that shape had none'). For Coleridge, this passage is the *locus classicus* of the 'sublime feeling' that is generated by creative activity itself:

> The grandest efforts of poetry are where the imagination is called forth, not to produce a distinct form, but a strong working of the mind, still offering what is still repelled, and again creating what is again rejected; the result being what the poet wishes to express, namely, the substitution of a sublime feeling of the unimaginable for a mere image. (Lecture, 9 December 1811: Wittreich, p. 201)

Whether the mind in question is the poet's or the reader's, its continuous 'working' depends upon an aesthetic of process, a work that is unending because it is 'unfixed'. This sense of *non*-definition, non-decidability and non-limitation is one definition of Romantic imagination. Remarkably, then, allusions to Milton's Death are a mark of intense creativity – as is recurrently the case in *The Prelude*.

Another, highly important, definition of imagination also relies on a passage in *Paradise Lost*: the explanation, given in Book V (467–505), of the *scala naturæ*, or ladder of being, on which all creatures are ranged in a hierarchy ordained by God. Coleridge, especially, interprets this as a scale of mental activity, ascending to the highest (godlike) acts of imagination; and (aided by Kant's philosophy) he uses Milton's terms to draw a distinction between the 'discursive' understanding, and the higher 'intuitive' reason or imagination.[38] The most significant of all Coleridge's references to this passage occurs in *Biographia Literaria*, when it becomes the epigraph to chapter 13, 'On the Imagination', and to the famous (and famously problematic) definitions of the faculty's 'primary' and 'second-ary' forms.

As *Biographia* is being written, Wordsworth publishes his own manifesto of the imagination in his Preface of 1815. Here, too, Milton is definitive, though Wordsworth's interest lies chiefly in illustrating, by Miltonic example, the various 'operations' which the faculty performs upon external objects (see Wittreich, *The Romantics*, pp. 128–31).

Although Keats also draws on *Paradise Lost* for his conception of the imagination, he is unusual in placing it, not among the angelic or satanic episodes, but in the feminine-erotic moment in which Adam dreams of the creation of Eve (VIII. 452–90): 'The Imagination may be compared to Adam's dream', writes Keats, 'he awoke and found it truth'.[39] The dream of Beauty, which haunts his own poetry, is realized in the imagination's power to make 'true' – a reconciliation of aesthetic and philosophic principles which for Keats is often in practice fraught with difficulty. Elsewhere, the allusive patterning of Keats's poetry sometimes reveals his distrust of the imagination – as, in their different ways, do Shelley's sceptical echoings of Milton in *Alastor*, say, or *Julian and Maddalo*; and Words-worth and Coleridge's references to Adam's diagnosis of the merely 'fanciful' or arbitrary workings of mind.[40]

The idea that the imagination has a power of realization, or 'making true', is related to another theory, that the artwork is a heterocosm or independent world.[41] At its most daring, this theory conceives the artistic creator as analogous to God the Creator. Here, Milton functions, not just (as I have suggested) by authority, but by example: there is the parallel between his image of the Holy Spirit brooding over Chaos and his own enterprise of *Paradise Lost* in the opening lines; the lengthy account of the Creation in Book VII; and the representation of God's presence in the universe in the Morning Hymn of Adam and Eve in Book V.[42] That the poet is to his work as the Deity is to Creation becomes especially attractive to Coleridge, who writes of the imagination as 'a repetition in the finite mind of the eternal act of creation', who talks of poets as 'gods of love, who tame the chaos', and, in *Kubla Khan* (together with the preface he added in 1816) symbolizes both the embodi-ment, and the loss or destruction, of that idea.

The God-poet analogy is also at work in the climactic episode of Wordsworth's *Prelude*, known as the 'Climbing of Snowdon'. Here, the mind's relation to the objects of its own imagining is conceived as having a 'visible...counterpart' in the power of 'nature' to transform 'the outward face of things' (XIII. 88, 74–8). If the 'Resemblance' of mind and nature secularizes God's presence in the natural world, the link with the divine is maintained for the representation of 'imagination': Wordsworth's Snowdon deliberately alludes to the scenery of Milton's Creation,[43] and enlists as a cognate term the mind's 'sense of God, or whatsoe'er is dim / Or vast in its own being' (XIII. 69, 87, 72–3).

The Romantic adaptation of the idea of the heterocosm ramifies in distinctive views about the status of the text. These include such notions as inviolability, integrity and 'organic' form. Milton lends authority to this textual absolutism, and to its implicit assumption of a kinship between the word and the Word. He is also, by reverse logic, the focus of textual failure or anxiety. In Charles Lamb's *jeu d'esprit* for the *London Magazine*, October 1820, the experience of seeing the manuscript of Milton's early works is couched as a textual 'fall' after the paradigm of *Paradise Lost*:

> I had thought of the Lycidas as of a full-grown beauty – as springing up with all its parts absolute – till, in evil hour, I was shown the original written copy of it . . . How it staggered me to see the fine things in their ore! interlined, corrected! as if their words were mortal, alterable, displaceable at pleasure! as if they might have been otherwise, and just as good! (Wittreich, p. 298)

Lamb's piece demonstrates how Milton serves the needs of a Romantic aesthetic and ideology. It may remind us that, in responding to his work, the Romantics are also pursuing their own ends. In each case, the use to which it is put stems from and reflects upon the distinctive interests and instincts of the speaker concerned. Conversely, as we have seen, Milton is an essential part of a contemporary dialogue, and of the views authors take, on one another as well as themselves, and on society as well as on their own art and its traditions.

## NOTES

1  *Defensio Secunda*.

2  See Wittreich, *The Romantics*, pp. 28–9 n. 30: hereafter Wittreich.

3  Notably Harold Bloom's Freudian model of anxiety and denial: see the Introduction, and, for Satan as 'modern poet', chapter one, of *The Anxiety of Influence*.

4  *Notebooks*, c. 27 February 1800: Wittreich, p. 162.

5  See the spectacularly zany conversation recorded by Henry Crabb Robinson, 17 December 1825: Wittreich, p. 96.

6  Letter of 24 September 1819: Wittreich, p. 562.

7  Satan's entering the sleeping form of the serpent prior to his temptation of Eve (*Paradise Lost* [hereafter *PL*] IX. 179–91) attracts both marginal comment, c. 1818 – 'Whose spirit does not ache at the smothering and confinement . . .? Whose head is not dizzy at the possibly [*sic*] speculations of satan in the serpent prison – no passage of poetry ever can give a greater pain of suffocation' (Wittreich, p. 560) – and poetic re-enactment (see especially *Lamia*). Coleridge understand the serpent's 'mode of motion [at *PL* IX. 498 ff.] exactly to emblem a writer of Genius' (Wittreich, pp. 161–2).

8  Letters of 14 and 24 August 1819 (Wittreich, p. 561): 'the Paradise Lost' is becoming 'every day . . . a greater wonder to me'.

9  Wittreich, *Feminist Milton*, 80, IX, 81.

10  *PL* IX. 13–15, 33, 42.

11  For commentary, see Wilkie, *Romantic Poets and Epic Tradition*, pp. 65–77.

12  Letter, 3 May 1818: Wittreich, pp. 551–2.

13  For Keats, the same line is evidence of Milton's being 'godlike in the sublime pathetic': Wittreich, p. 557.

14  Letter of 21 March 1800 (Wittreich, p. 163): 'I do not hesitate in saying, that since Milton no man has *manifested* himself equal to him.'

15  See for example, Blake's *French Revolution* and *Marriage of Heaven and Hell*; Coleridge and Southey's *Fall of Robespierre*, Southey's *Joan of Arc* and *Wat Tyler*; Wordsworth's *Prelude* IX and X, and *Excursion* II and III; Byron's *Don Juan* VII and VIII; Shelley's *Revolt of Islam* and *Prometheus Unbound*; Keats's *Hyperion*.

16  See *Letter to the Bishop of Llandaff*.

17  For Burns and Hazlitt, see Newlyn, *'Paradise Lost' and the Romantic Reader*, p. 39.

18 Thus Keats: *'the sense of power'* has been *'abstracted from the sense of good'*, 'the enormity of the evil overpowers and makes a convert of the imagination by its very magnitude' (letter of 13 March 1819: Wittreich, p. 564). Cf. De Quincey, who makes *Paradise Lost* the archetype of the 'literature of power', as distinct from the mere 'literature of knowledge'.

19 *Political Justice*, p. 309 (quoted in Newlyn, *'Paradise Lost' and the Romantic Reader*, p. 39).

20 See Wittreich, pp. 207–8: Satan as 'sceptical Socinian'; cf. Lamb: Wittreich, p. 294.

21 *The Statesman's Manual* (1816): Wittreich, p. 229; repeated in 1819 lecture: Wittreich, p. 244 (the idea is implicit by 1809: see Wittreich, p. 191).

22 See, for example, Hazlitt, and Opie: Wittreich, pp. 384–5, 100 n. 18.

23 Sermon by Revd John Styles.

24 Letter of 12 May 1821: Wittreich, p. 521.

25 Viz. Blake to Henry Crabb Robinson (Wittreich, p. 100 n. 18): 'he denied that the natural world is anything. "It is all nothing, and Satan's empire is the empire of nothing."' Note how Blake turns 'mainstream' Romantic thinking – here, about 'nature' – on its head.

26 Repeated verbatim in Coleridge's Lecture of 28 November 1811 (Wittreich, p. 199); his literary criticism is littered with statements of a similar kind.

27 With Hazlitt, in *Lectures on the English Poets* (1818) III, 'The power of his [Milton's] mind is stamped on every line' (Wittreich, p. 381); cf. Coleridge's later *Table Talk*, 12 May 1830 (Wittreich, p. 270): 'Shakespeare is the Spinozistic

deity – an omnipresent creativeness. Milton is the deity of prescience; he stands *ab extra*... Shakespeare's poetry is characterless; that is, it does not reflect the individual Shakespeare; but John Milton himself is in every line of the Paradise Lost'.

28 Letter of 27 October 1818.

29 Ibid.: a Shakespearean intellect has the dramatic power of 'in for[ming] and filling some other Body'.

30 In 1808, 1811–12 and 1818.

31 'The recluse, the pastor, and the pedlar, are three persons in one poet' (Howe, XIX, 11).

32 Viz. Collins's *Ode on the Poetical Character* stanza 3, where Milton appears as though he were the *genius loci*, or presiding deity, of his own Eden.

33 Lecture, 4 March 1819: Wittreich, p. 245; Coleridge ventures the same idea as early as 1796: see Wittreich, p. 159.

34 *The Marriage of Heaven and Hell*.

35 See Wittreich, pp. 205, 209, 183, 268.

36 Wittreich, p. 553, no. 25; see also pp. 547–9, nos 15, 16, 17; p. 559, no. 41.

37 *Notebooks*, 11 December 1803: Wittreich, p. 169.

38 Cf. *Prelude*, XIII. 113.

39 Letter of 22 November 1817: Wittreich, p. 547.

40 See *PL* V: 100–13; and cf. *Prelude*, VI. 305–16; VIII. 599–610.

41 See Abrams *ML*, pp. 272–85.

42 See *PL* V: 153–208 – lines that echo throughout Coleridge's 'Conversation Poems' and *Hymn Before Sunrise*, and Wordsworth's song of the 'one life', *Prelude*, II. 417–34.

43 *Prelude*, XIII. 45; *PL* VII. 285–7.

## WRITINGS

Blake, William, *Milton: A Poem*, London and Princeton, William Blake Trust and Princeton University Press, 1993.

Carey, John (ed.) *John Milton: Complete Shorter Poems*, Harlow, Longman, 1968, reissued, 1971.

Fowler, Alastair (ed.) *John Milton: Paradise Lost*, Harlow, Longman, 1968, reissued, 1971.

Shawcross, John (ed.) *Milton 1732–1801: The Critical Heritage*, London, Routledge and Kegan Paul, 1972.

Wittreich, Joseph Anthony, Jr (ed.) *The Romantics on Milton: Formal Essays and Critical Asides*, Cleveland and London, Case Western Reserve University Press, 1970. Contains all the material on eleven male authors, and bibliographical notes on each referring to further critical discussion.

## REFERENCES AND FURTHER READING

Abrams, M. H., *Natural Supernaturalism: Tradition and Revolution in Romantic Literature*, New York, Norton, 1971.

Bloom, Harold, *The Anxiety of Influence: A Theory of Poetry*, New York, Oxford University Press, 1973.

——*A Map of Misreading*, New York, Oxford University Press, 1975.

Bracher, Mark, *Being Form'd: Thinking through Blake's Milton*, Barrytown, NY, Clinamen Studies, Station Hill Press, 1985.

Brisman, Leslie, *Milton's Poetry of Choice and its Romantic Heirs*, Ithaca and London, Cornell University Press, 1973. Valuable heir to Bloom.

DiSalvo, Jacqueline, *War of Titans: Blake's Critique of Milton and the Politics of Religion*, Pittsburgh, University of Pittsburgh Press, 1983.

Dunbar, Pamela, *William Blake's Illustrations to the Poetry of Milton*, Oxford, Clarendon Press, 1980.

Grierson, Herbert J. C., *Milton and Wordsworth, Poets and Prophets: A Study of Their Reactions to Political Events*, Cambridge, Cambridge University Press, 1937.

Griffin, Dustin, *Regaining Paradise: Milton and the Eighteenth Century*, Cambridge, Cambridge University Press, 1986. Opening chapters on Milton's politics and Milton as literary hero, as well as on genres.

Havens, Raymond Dexter, *The Influence of Milton on English Poetry*, New York, Russell & Russell, 1961.

Jarvis, Robin, *Wordsworth, Milton and the Theory of Poetic Relations*, Basingstoke and London, Macmillan, 1991.

Newlyn, Lucy, *'Paradise Lost' and the Romantic Reader*, Oxford, Clarendon Press, 1993. The best book in the field.

Schulz, Max, *Paradise Preserved: Recreations of Eden in Eighteenth and Nineteenth Century England*, Cambridge, Cambridge University Press, 1985.

Vogler, Thomas, *Preludes to Vision: The Epic Venture in Blake, Wordsworth, Keats and Hart Crane*, Berkeley, University of California Press, 1971.

Webber, J. M., 'The politics of poetry: feminism and *Paradise Lost*', *Milton Studies* 14 (1980) 3–24.

Wilkie, Brian, *Romantic Poets and Epic Tradition*, Madison and Milwaukee, University of Wisconsin Press, 1965.

Williamson, G., 'Milton the anti-Romantic', *Modern Philology* 60 (1962) 13–21.

Wittreich, Joseph Anthony, Jr, 'The "Satanism" of Blake and Shelley reconsidered', *Studies in Philology* 65 (1968) 816–33.

——*Angel of Apocalypse: Blake's Idea of Milton*, Madison, University of Wisconsin Press, 1975.

——*Visionary Poetics: Milton's Tradition and His Legacy*, San Marino, Ca., Huntington Library, 1979.

——*Feminist Milton*, Ithaca, Cornell University Press, 1987.

# Contributors

**John M. Anderson** teaches at Tufts and Boston College. He is the author of an essay about Charlotte Smith in *Seeing into the Life of Things: Essays on Literature and Religious Experience* (forthcoming), and of an article about Anna Laetitia Barbauld in *Studies in English Literature* (1994). He is currently working on a book about epics by Romantic-era women.

**Rosemary Ashton**, Professor of English at University College London, has written books on nineteenth-century literary, cultural and intellectual history, and critical biographies. Works include *The German Idea: Four English Writers and the Reception of German Thought 1800–1860* (1980, 1994); *Little Germany: Exile and Asylum in Victorian England* (1986, 1989); *G. H. Lewes: A Life* (1991); *The Life of Samuel Taylor Coleridge: A Critical Biography* (1996); *George Eliot: A Life* (1996). She has edited several George Eliot novels and her critical writings, and a number of other nineteenth-century works of fiction and criticism.

**John Beer**, Professor Emeritus of English Literature at Cambridge and Emeritus Fellow of Peterhouse, is author of *Coleridge the Visionary, Coleridge's Poetic Intelligence, The Achievement of E. M. Forster, Blake's Humanism, Blake's Visionary Universe, Wordsworth and the Human Heart, Wordsworth in Time, Romantic Influences: Contemporary – Victorian – Modern* and *Love and Providence: Studies in Wordsworth, Channing, F. W. H. Myers, George Eliot, and Ruskin*. Besides editing Coleridge's *Poems* for Everyman, his *Aids to Reflection* for the *Collected Coleridge* and the essay-collections *Coleridge's Variety, E. M. Forster: A Human Exploration* (with G. K. Das), and *Questioning Romanticism*, he is General Editor of the series *Coleridge's Writings*.

**Stephen C. Behrendt** is George Holmes Distinguished Professor of English, University of Nebraska. Recent books include *Shelley and his Audiences* (1989), *Reading William Blake* (1992) and *Royal Mourning and Regency Culture: Elegies and Memorials of Princess Charlotte* (1997), as well as two collections of poetry, *Instruments of the Bones* (1992) and *A Step in the Dark* (1996).

**David Bromwich** is Professor of English, Yale University. He is the author of *Hazlitt: The Mind of a Critic* (1983), *A Choice of Inheritance* (1989) and *Politics by Other Means* (1992), as well as the editor of the historical anthology, *Romantic Critical Essays* (1987). His current work deals with Wordsworth and Burke in the 1790s.

**Miranda J. Burgess** is Assistant Professor of English at the University of New Brunswick. She has published on eighteenth-century and Romantic fiction and cultural theory, and is completing a manuscript on *The Work of Romance: British Novels and Political Discourse 1740–1830*.

**Frederick Burwick**, Professor of English and Comparative Literature at the University of California, Los Angeles, whose recent books include *Illusion and the Drama: Critical Theory of the Enlightenment and Romantic Era* (1992) and *Poetic Madness and the Romantic Imagination* (1996), has also co-edited, with Walter Pape, a collection of essays and visual catalogue on *The Boydell Shakespeare Gallery* (1996), and is currently supervising a series of exhibitions of the Romantic illustrations to Shakespeare.

**James A. Butler** is Professor of English and American Literature, La Salle University, Philadelphia, and one of the supervisory editors of the Cornell Wordsworth Series. In that series, he edited *The Ruined Cottage and The Pedlar* (1979) and co-edited, with Karen Green, *Lyrical Ballads and Other Poems, 1797–1800* (1992). He is now working on a book on the concept of 'home' in the works of William and Dorothy Wordsworth.

**John Creaser** is Hildred Carlile Professor of English Literature, Royal Holloway, University of London, and Executive Secretary of the Malone Society. He writes mainly on Renaissance poetry and drama (notably Milton and Jonson), and has edited works by Jonson and Middleton.

**Damian Walford Davies** is the Andrew Bradley–J. C. Maxwell Junior Research Fellow at Balliol College, Oxford. His publications include a translation of Friedrich Dürrenmatt's *Die Physiker* (1991), *William Wordsworth: Selected Poems* (1994), articles on medieval and eighteenth-century Welsh literature, Wordsworth, Blake, R. S. Thomas, Dylan Thomas, Idris Davies and numerous scholarly notes and reviews. He has also published articles on the poetry of popular music. Forthcoming are an edition of the poetry of Gerard Manley Hopkins, a study of the Welsh reaction to the French Revolution, and the *Collected Prose* of the Welsh poet Waldo Williams.

**David Duff** is Lecturer in English, University of Aberdeen. He is the author of *Romance and Revolution: Shelley and the Politics of a Genre* (1994), and is currently writing a book on Romantic genre theory.

**Angela Esterhammer** is Associate Professor of English and Comparative Literature at the University of Western Ontario. Her published work includes *Creating States: Studies in the Performative Language of John Milton and William Blake* (1994); articles on Blake, Coleridge, Hölderlin, W. von Humboldt, and issues of language and creation in the Bible and in twentieth-century fiction; and translations of German literary and critical works. Her current project is a book on aspects of performative language in English and German philosophy and literature of the Romantic period.

**Elizabeth Fay** is Associate Professor, University of Massachusetts–Boston, and author of *Becoming Wordsworthian: A Performative Aesthetic* (1995), *Eminent Rhetoric* (1994) and of several forthcoming articles on Anna Seward and biography. Websites include 'The Bluestocking Archive' (http://fay.english.umb.edu) and the Features Page (co-edited with Alan Richardson) of the 'Romantic Circles Website'.

**Nelson Hilton**, Professor of English at the University of Georgia, has for many years been review editor for *Blake: An Illustrated Quarterly*. He is the author of *Literal Imagination: Blake's Vision of Words* (1983) and *Lexis Complexes: Literary Interventions* (1995). His web address is http://www.english.uga.edu/nhilton.

**Anne Janowitz** has worked at City Lights Books, San Francisco, and taught at Smith College, Brandeis University, and Rutgers University. She is the author of *England's Ruins: Poetic Purpose and the National Landscape* (1990) and *The Communitarian Lyric in the Tradition of Romanticism* (forthcoming). At present, she is Reader in Romantic Literature, University of Warwick, and serves as Director of the University of Warwick's Humanities Research Centre.

**Peter J. Kitson** is Senior Lecturer in English, University of Wales, Bangor. He is editor of *Romantic Criticism 1800–1825* (with T. N. Corns, 1989), *Coleridge and the Armoury of the Human Mind: Essays* *on his Prose Writings* (1991), *Coleridge, Keats and Shelley: Contemporary Critical Essays* (1996) and *Romanticism and Colonialism: Essays on the Representation of Colonial Otherness in the British Romantic Period* (with Tim Fulford, forthcoming). He edits the annual evaluative bibliography, *The Year's Work in English Studies*.

**Jacqueline M. Labbe** is Lecturer in Romantic Literature at the University of Sheffield. Her publications include articles in *Genre* and *The Wordsworth Circle*, and her book, *Romantic Visualities: Landscape, Gender, and Romanticism 1780–1830*, is forthcoming from Macmillan Press and St Martin's. She is currently researching the connections between the romance, violence and disorder in Romantic-period poetry and visual arts, and is planning a monograph on Charlotte Smith.

**Beth Lau** is Professor of English, California State University, Long Beach. She is the author of *Keats's Reading of the Romantic Poets* (1991) and co-editor of *Approaches to Teaching Brontë's Jane Eyre* (1993). She has also published numerous essays on Keats and other Romantic writers.

**John Lucas** is Research Professor of English, The Nottingham Trent University. Among his many books are *The Melancholy Man: A Study of Dickens's Fiction* (first published in 1970, revised 1980), *Romantic to Modern: Essays and Ideas of Culture* (1982), *England and Englishness: Ideas of Nationhood in English Poetry, 1688–1900* (1990 and 1991), *John Clare* (1994) and *Writing and Radicalism* (1996). His translation of the poems of *Egil's Saga*, first published 1974, is now an Everyman Classic. His latest collection of poems is *One for the Piano* (1997).

**Scott McEathron** is Assistant Professor of English at Southern Illinois University, Carbondale, where he teaches Romantic and Victorian literature. His essays have appeared in the *Keats–Shelley Journal*, *The Charles Lamb Bulletin* and *Victorian Institute Journal*. He is currently working on a study of Wordsworth and peasant poetry.

**David S. Miall** is Associate Professor of English, University of Alberta. His previous work includes studies of Coleridge and Wordsworth, articles on the teaching of literature, empirical and theoretical studies of reading, and discussions of computers in literature. His anthology, *Romanticism: the CD*, edited with Duncan Wu, was published by Blackwell in autumn 1997.

**Michael O'Neill** is Professor of English, University of Durham. His books include *The Human Mind's Imaginings: Conflict and Achievement in Shelley's Poetry* (1989), *The 'Defence of Poetry' Fair Copies* (1994) and *Romanticism and the Self-conscious Poem* (1997).

**Morton D. Paley**, Professor in the Graduate School at the University of California, Berkeley, is the author of a number of studies of William Blake, including *Energy and the Imagination* and *The Continuing City*. He is also editor of the Blake Trust edition of *Jerusalem*, co-editor of *Blake: An Illustrated Quarterly*, member of the advisory boards of *Studies in Romanticism*, the *European Romantic Review* and *Romantic Circles*. He has been a Guggenheim Fellow (twice), Study Fellow of the American Council of Learned Societies, Research Fellow of the National Endowment for the Humanities, and a Senior Fulbright Lecturer at the University of Heidelberg. His most recent book is *Coleridge's Later Poetry* (1996), and he is currently completing two others: a study of the portraits of Samuel Taylor Coleridge and *Apocalypse and Millennium in English Romantic Poetry*.

**Janice Patten** teaches at San Jose University. Her conference work includes papers on Romanticism, nineteenth-century theatre, and children's literature. Having begun work on Joanna Baillie in 1988, she has inspired further research in the field principally through papers delivered at the Wordsworth Summer Conferences in Grasmere, PAMLA, INCS and MLA conferences. She is currently revising her dissertation, *Dark Imagination: Poetic Painting in Romantic Drama* for publication, co-editing a volume of essays on Baillie, and writing a book about children's literature.

**Seamus Perry** is Sir Walter Oakeshott Junior Research Fellow in English Literature at Lincoln College, Oxford. His *Coleridge and the Makings of English Romanticism* is forthcoming from Clarendon Press, and *Coleridge: Interviews and Recollections* from Macmillan.

**Tony Pinkney** is Senior Lecturer in English at Lancaster University. His publications include *Women in the Poetry of T. S. Eliot* (1984), *D. H. Lawrence* (1990) and *Raymond Williams: Novelist* (1991). He is working on a book on William Morris's *News from Nowhere* and the problems of interpreting Utopian fiction.

**Alan Richardson** is Professor of English, Boston College. He is the author of *Literature, Education, and Romanticism: Reading as Social Practice, 1780–1832* (1994) and co-editor of *Romanticism, Race, and Imperial Culture 1780–1834* (1996). He has published numerous essays on Romantic-era literature and culture, particularly in relation to gender, colonialism and the social construction of childhood.

**Adam Roberts** is Lecturer in English, Royal Holloway, University of London. He has published on a number of nineteenth-century topics, including Romantic and Victorian poetry. He is the author of *Robert Browning Revisited* (1997), and has edited Browning for the Oxford Authors series (1997), as well as serving as associate editor on the *Oxford Companion to Dickens* (ed. Paul Schlicke, forthcoming). His *Romantic and Victorian Long Poems: A Guide* will be published by Scolar in 1998, and his study of contemporary Arthurian fantasy, *Silk and Potatoes*, is shortly to appear under the imprint of Rodopi.

**Fiona Robertson** is Reader in English Literature at the University of Durham. She is the author of *Legitimate Histories: Scott, Gothic, and the Authorities of Fiction* (1994) and of the volume on Scott in the series *Lives of the Great Romantics by their Contemporaries* (1997). She has also edited Scott's *The Bride of Lammermoor* (1991) and (with Anthony Mellors) is completing an edition of Stephen Crane, *The Red Badge of Courage and Other Stories*. Forthcoming books include a study of British writers' accounts of America in the Romantic period and a collection of writings by women, 1778–1840.

**Philip Shaw** is Lecturer in English at the University of Leicester. He is co-editor, with Vincent Newey, of *Mortal Pages, Literary Lives: Studies in Nineteenth-Century Autobiography* (1996), and has written widely on Romantic subjects.

**Michael James Sider** is currently writing program administrator at the University of Western Ontario. He recently completed a two-year Social Sciences and Humanities Research Council of Canada postdoctoral Fellowship at the University of Pennsylvania. Publications include '"Isabella" and the Dialogism of Romance' (*Nineteenth-Century Contexts*) and *The Dialogic Keats: Time and History in the Major Poems* (forthcoming).

**David Simpson** is Professor of English at the University of California, Davis. He is the author or editor of various books and essays on Romanticism and literary theory, most recently *Subject to History: Ideology, Class, Gender* (ed., 1991), *Romanticism, Nationalism, and the Revolt against Theory* (1993) and *The Academic Postmodern and the Rule of Literature* (1995).

**Jane Stabler** is Lecturer in English Literature at the University of Dundee. She has just completed a short selection of Byron's poetry for the Everyman Poetry Library and is working on a Byron Critical Reader, a study of transitions in English Literature 1790–1830, and a study of Byron's modernity.

**Graeme Stones** completed a doctoral thesis on Romantic parody at Merton College, Oxford, and subsequently taught at St Edmund Hall. He has written a number of articles on the subject and is co-editor with John Strachan of the forthcoming five-volume collection, *Parodies of the Romantics*, for Pickering and Chatto.

**John Strachan** completed a doctoral thesis on Gothic fiction at Wolfson College, Oxford, in 1992. He has taught at St Edmund Hall, Oxford, and is currently Principal Lecturer in English at the University of Sunderland, where he is also head of the English Department. He is co-editor with Graeme Stones of the forthcoming five-volume collection, *Parodies of the Romantics*, for Pickering and Chatto.

**John Sutherland** is Lord Northcliffe Professor of Modern English Literature, University College London. His recent publications include *The Longman Companion to Victorian Fiction* (1989), *Mrs Humphry Ward* (1990), *The Life of Sir Walter Scott* (1995), *Victorian Fiction: Writers, Publishers, Readers* (1995) and *Is Heathcliff a Murderer?* (1996). He is currently working on the *Oxford Companion to Popular Fiction*.

**Michael J. Tolley** is Associate Professor of English at the University of Adelaide. He has written widely on Romantic authors, especially on Blake. He was co-editor, with John E. Grant and Edward J. Rose, of *William Blake's Designs for Edward Young's Night Thoughts: A Complete Edition* (1980), and he has written on Australian crime fiction and science fiction.

**Nicola Trott** is Lecturer in English Literature, University of Glasgow. She is the editor of the forthcoming *Blackwell Anthology of Gothic Fiction*, and has written on several Romantic writers, including Wordsworth, Coleridge, Lamb, Keats and Mary Wollstonecraft.

**Mary Wedd** was, until retirement, Principal Lecturer in English, Goldsmiths' College, London. She has published short stories, a book, numerous articles and reviews. She had a long and distinguished career as editor of *The Charles Lamb Bulletin*.

**Douglas B. Wilson** is Professor of English at the University of Denver. He is the author of *The Romantic Dream: Wordsworth and the Poetics of the Unconscious* and an essay in *Coleridge, Keats, and the Imagination*. He has published articles in *PMLA*, *Studies in English Literature*, *The Wordsworth Circle*, *English Language Notes* and *Dreaming*.

**Susan J. Wolfson** is Professor of English at Princeton University and the author of *The Questioning Presence: Wordsworth, Keats, and the Interrogative Modes of Romantic Poetry* (1986) and *Formal Charges: The Shaping of Poetry in British Romanticism* (1997). She has written numerous essays on topics in the Romantic period, including several involved with issues of gender, among them: '"The Mouth of Fame": Gender, Transgression, and Romantic Celebrity' (forthcoming, 1998); 'Shakespeare and the Romantic Girl Reader' (forthcoming, 1997); 'Gendering the Soul' (1995); '*Lyrical Ballads* and the Language of (Men) Feeling' (1994); 'The Domestic Affections and Sword of Minerva: Felicia Hemans and the Dilemma of Gender' (1994); 'Editorial Privilege: Mary Shelley and Percy Shelley's Works' (1993); '"A Problem Few Dare Imitate": Sardanapalus and "Effeminate Character"' (1991); 'Feminizing Keats' (1990); '"Explaining to Their Sisters": Mary Lamb's Tales from Shakespear' (1990); '"Their She Condition": Cross-dressing and the Politics of Gender in *Don Juan*' (1989). She is currently completing a book on this subject, *Figures on the Margin: The Problem of Gender in British Romanticism*.

**Bonnie Woodbery** is Honorary Research Fellow, University of Glasgow, where she is working on a project about British grammar books, gender and nationalism. She has published articles in *The Charles Lamb Bulletin*, *Literature and Psychology*, and *Nineteenth-Century Contexts*.

**Pamela Woof** lectures in literature at the Centre for Continuing Education, University of Newcastle upon Tyne, and is a Trustee of the Wordsworth Trust, Dove Cottage, Grasmere. She published an edition of Dorothy Wordsworth's *Grasmere Journals* (1991), freshly read from the manuscripts and annotated. Critical and textual articles on Dorothy Wordsworth's writing appear in *The Wordsworth Circle* for 1989, 1991, 1995, and there are essays in two collections: *Wordsworth in Context*, ed. Pauline Fletcher and John Murphy (1992), and *Romantic Revisions*, ed. Robert Brinkley and Keith

Hanley (1992). A monograph, *Dorothy Wordsworth, Writer*, was published by the Wordsworth Trust, 1988. She is at present working on an edition of *The Shorter Journals and Narratives of Dorothy Wordsworth* for Oxford University Press.

**Jonathan Wordsworth** is Professor in English Literature at St Catherine's College, Oxford. He is descended from the poet's brother, Christopher, and is Chairman of the Wordsworth Trust, Grasmere. He is the author of *The Music of Humanity* (1969), *The Borders of Vision* (1982), *William Wordsworth and the Age of English Romanticism* (1987, with Michael C. Jaye and Robert Woof), *Ancestral Voices* (1991), *Visionary Gleam* (1993), and *The Bright Work Grows* (1997). He edited *Bicentenary Wordsworth Studies* (1970), the Norton *Prelude: 1799, 1805, 1850* (1979, with Stephen Gill and M. H. Abrams), and the new Penguin *Prelude: The Four Texts (1798, 1799, 1805, 1850)* (1995).

**Ian Wylie** is the author of *Young Coleridge and the Philosophers of Nature* (1989) and has written and lectured widely on Romantic science. He works for the King's Fund in London.

# Index